D1336926

HIDDEN TREASURES
of
ENGLAND

HIDDEN TREASURES
of
ENGLAND

A Guide to the Country's
Best-Kept Secrets

MICHAEL McNAY

BOOKS

Published by Random House Books 2009

2 4 6 8 10 9 7 5 3 1

Copyright © Michael McNay 2009

Michael McNay has asserted his right under the Copyright, Designs
and Patents Act, 1988, to be identified as the author of this work

First published in Great Britain in 2009 by
Random House Books
Random House, 20 Vauxhall Bridge Road,
London SW1V 2SA

www.rbooks.co.uk

Addresses for companies within The Random House Group Limited can be found at:
www.randomhouse.co.uk/offices.htm

The Random House Group Limited Reg. No. 954009

A CIP catalogue record for this book
is available from the British Library

ISBN 9781905211838

The Random House Group Limited supports The Forest Stewardship
Council (FSC), the leading international forest certification organisation. All our
titles that are printed on Greenpeace approved FSC certified paper carry the FSC logo.
Our paper procurement policy can be found at www.rbooks.co.uk/environment

Typeset by Palimpsest Book Production Ltd,
Grangemouth, Stirlingshire

Printed and bound in China by
C&C Offset Printing Co., Ltd.

To the women in my life: Sue, Lois, Anna, Morgan, Maisie and little Isla

CONTENTS

PREFACE

The historian A.J.P. Taylor once remarked that the parish churches of England constitute its greatest treasure. So they do, and other writers, principally Nikolaus Pevsner, have explored every aspect of the architectural style of these buildings, ancient and modern. In this book I concentrate on the things to which the others normally devote a sentence or two at most, paintings, sculpture, stained glass, porch carvings, though occasionally a whole interior as well; and not just in churches but in art galleries and country houses too (and parts of the street scene, from mileposts to shop fronts, bridges, bars, market squares, and a seaside promenade). The sculpture in parish churches constitute a massive part of the national artistic heritage, and the sculptors of the 18th century, particularly Michael Rysbrack and Peter Scheemakers, were at least as good in their field as Joshua Reynolds was in his, but did most of their work on church monuments and are not household names.

I had seen a number of the treasures in this book before I started travelling around England, mostly the paintings. It was an excellent excuse for revisiting them. The rest has been a voyage of discovery for me; several voyages, actually. The title of this book, *Hidden Treasures of England*, gave me latitude. Some objects really are in backwaters, almost literally when the River Severn was in flood. One involved searching along the verges of a field, one magnificent sculpture is in a museum where the last visitor had signed in four days earlier (he had of course left by the time I got there), but some are in full view, and some, like the red phone box, in full view all over the place, so I've chosen the examples opposite the Royal Opera House to stand for all of them. The tomb of Henry VII and his queen in Westminster Abbey is in full view and also unique; like most church monuments, it goes unattributed, but it is by Pietro Torrigiano, the Florentine sculptor who sought his living abroad after falling into disfavour when he broke the nose of his fellow apprentice, Michelangelo. His sculpture in the abbey is the first fully realised work of the Renaissance in England, and, intriguingly, is set in an almost contemporary Gothic chapel. Similarly, I have singled out occasional paintings even though they are in famous galleries, because they are not much noticed — see, for instance, the small Delacroix *Odalisque* in the Fitzwilliam Museum in Cambridge, and the landscape painting of the lake of Annecy, painted against the grain by Cézanne and hung in the fabulous Courtauld Institute's Gallery which, despite its location in central London, isn't visited nearly as much as it merits. A general reminder: galleries are subject to rehangs from time to time, so it's worth checking whether specific works are on show before travelling.

Many people have helped with information, not least B&B landladies with pointers to things in their areas. I would particularly like to thank the staff of the Harris Art Gallery in Preston, who arranged for me to see their latest acquisition of paintings by Arthur Devis while the gallery was closed for refurbishment; and the Cecil Higgins Gallery, Bedford, which produced its Alan Davie painting from storage so that I could reacquaint myself with it after a gap of around 45 years. I am grateful to English Heritage and the National Trust for giving me press passes, with a special thank you to the National Trust staff at Tatton Park for giving me a personal tour when I arrived out of opening hours. Also to the man on the stage door at the Grand Theatre, Blackpool, who smuggled me into the theatre during a brief lull between rehearsals. Otherwise I have only written about what was available to see at the time I visited. That means that many churches, especially urban ones, were inaccessible because they were locked and gave no keyholder number. A particular horror, in a village on the outskirts of Darlington, had a well-manned office which refused me the key because the curate had left orders that no one must enter the church unless he was present. I hope the vicar was excepted. And there was the delightful Catch-22 of a Herefordshire church's listed keyholder: when I rang the number it responded with the message, 'This telephone does not take incoming calls.' But by and large churches are open in daylight hours and when they aren't can be seen with a little patience; some are warmly welcoming.

Among people who have helped me with information are David Butters of Swaffham Museum (about the butter cross), Dr Mary Cowling of the Royal Holloway College (an expert on Frith's *Railway Station*), my colleague of many years ago, Fiona MacCarthy (for information about the commissioning of her husband David Mellor's fountain in Cambridge Botanical Garden), and Doug Oldfield, secretary of the Frank Matcham Society, who went out of his way to help me.

I have used many literary sources. Among them was the London Library, which now gives home access to the online *Oxford Dictionary of National Biography*, a huge bonus, as also is its access to specialist journals like the *Burlington Magazine* through the website Jstor. I dipped into Simon Jenkins's *Thousand Best Churches* for his sharp eye for the best places. As I wrote I kept by my side the catalogues for three great exhibitions in the last decades of the 20th century, *English Romanesque Art 1066–1200* at the Hayward Gallery, *The Age of Chivalry: Art in Plantaganet England 1200–1400* at the Royal Academy and *Gothic Art for England 1400–1547* at the Victoria and Albert Museum; also the multi-volume Oxford History of English Art and three Pelican histories in particular, *Sculpture in Britain in the Middle Ages* by Lawrence Stone, *Sculpture in Britain 1530–1830* by Margaret Whinney, and *Painting in Britain 1530–1790* by Ellis Waterhouse. The Buildings of England were my indispensible gazetteer and constant companion. I have in two or three cases cannibalised articles of my own in the *Guardian* and the now defunct *Design* magazine to add to my current observations.

My friend Lisa Darnell, the *Guardian* and *Observer* books publisher, effectively my agent as well, has been completely wonderful in pitching for me tenaciously. When Random House sent in some muscle, he was called Nigel Wilcockson: he has harried me without mercy and whipped me into line. He is also an astute editor. His assistant Emily Rhodes has been constantly on the ball, not least in digging out photographs. The copy editor, Lydia Darbyshire, has introduced lucidity to my most unlovely and overloaded paragraphs.

It's customary to thank wives; I thank Sue (who ducks between McNay and Pilkington) from the bottom of my heart. She also accompanied me on a couple of my journeys. My daughters Lois and Anna McNay gave me their time and company on some journeys. So did Marian McNay. John Pilkington supplied ideas and enthusiasm. Lois and her partner Murray Hunt also put me up for several nights in Oxford; as did my friends Daphne and Euan Duff in Lincolnshire, Rosemary and Arthur Fairhurst in Yorkshire, and Pat and Benny van den Burg – and I'd like to thank Benny's BMW for taking me places: Benny both lent it to me and also drove me to north-western treasures himself when at his suggestion I arrived in Manchester by train.

The West Country

CORNWALL * DEVON * SOMERSET

Atherington

Buckland Filleigh ❖

Blisland
❖

❖ St Neot

❖
Bodmin

CORNWALL

Plympto

St Germans ❖
Plymouth

❖ Pencarrow House

St Ives
❖

Botallack
❖

WALES

BRISTOL

❖ Bristol
Bristol

❖ Bath
Bath

Mells ❖

SOMERSET

❖ Brent Knoll
Burnham-on-Sea

Minehead ❖

❖ Frome
Frome

Wells ❖

Arlington

❖ Dunster

❖ Over Stowey

Shepton
Mallet ❖

Street ❖

❖ Westonzoyland

❖ Butleigh

❖ Burrow Mump

❖ Nynehead

Curry
Rivel

❖ Montacute

DEVON

DORSET

❖ Exeter

❖ Drewsteignton

❖ Doddiscombsleigh

❖ Bovey Tracey

❖ Dartington
Hall

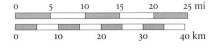

0   5   10   15   20   25 mi

0   10   20   30   40 km

Arlington

DEVON

Blake's world of innocence, at
Arlington Court

Rosalie Chichester was born in 1863 into the gentry when they were the gentry. She loved her ancestral Arlington estate, where she was always known to the agricultural workers as Miss Rosalie, and lived by a piece of doggerel by the 19th-century versifier Felicia Hemans that went:

> *The stately Homes of England,*
> *How beautiful they stand!*
> *Amidst their tall ancestral trees,*
> *O'er all the pleasant land.*

So when Miss Rosalie died without an heir in January 1949 she had arranged two things: that her ashes should be buried at Arlington Court, and that the early 19th-century plain Greek revival house with the 3,500 acre estate and its eighteen villages should pass intact to the National Trust.

When the Trust officials arrived and began combing through seventy-five cabinets full of hundreds of pieces of pewter, seashells, thirty tea caddies, five cases of candle snuffers, five cases of stuffed birds, two cases of African clubs and Maori skirts collected on her travels, 52,000 stamps and forty paperweights among other junk, they found on top of a cupboard in a heap of broken glass a package containing a framed watercolour measuring 16 × 19½ inches. Part of the packaging consisted of a copy of *The Times* for 11 January 1820. The picture was signed 'W. Blake inventor 1821'. It was accompanied by a note in the handwriting of Miss Chichester's great-grandfather, Colonel John Chichester, ascribing the framing to James Linnell, a Bloomsbury framer and father of John Linnell, the closest friend of the visionary artist and poet William Blake

(1757–1827). The date of the newspaper suggests that Colonel Chichester had bought the picture from Blake, had it framed almost immediately, then, when it was delivered in the packaging of old journals, dumped it on top of the cupboard where it was found.

Miss Rosalie's slimmed-down collections still fill the house, the memorabilia of a gentlewoman with time on her hands. Among them in an ante-room to the white drawing room hangs the Blake, duly authenticated. It is now known as *The Circle of the Life of Man*, a strange allegorical theme, though everyday stuff to an artist who, as a child of under ten, saw a tree filled with angels. He trained as an engraver, and the techniques of the craft marked everything he did in other media and partly account for the throbbing intensity and compression of his closely worked imagery. *The Circle* seems to be a mystic representation of the return of the spirit of man from his material existence to the spiritual heights. The man, or rather Man, kneels in a blood red robe on the edge of the ocean by the side of Woman in diaphanous garments, who points down to the earth and up to the heavens. Another being rides four horses through the sea, and men, women and children swim among roots stretching from trees on the bank. The branches link the earth and the heavens, where women perform a slow dance and the Creator with a conductor's baton sits haloed by the sun bursting through a hole in turbulent clouds. It's as strange and gripping as Blake's verse, created under the influence of his lifelong yearning for a return of the world to primal innocence.

The William Blake masterpiece, The Circle of the Life of Man, *found discarded on top of a cupboard at Arlington Court*

Atherington

DEVON

Devon's only surviving rood loft, Church of St Mary

Atherington's apple-dumpling cottages cluster around a green, and on a hill above, the 15th- and 16th-century Church of St Mary commands fine views over Exmoor. In the 1540s nine parishioners clubbed together to raise the money for two carpenters from nearby Chittelhampton, Roger Down and John Hill, to make a rood screen across the width of the church. Rood screens were, of course, about to go seriously out of fashion, with Henry VIII's zealous reformers poised to sweep away these supposed icons of idolatry. The parishioners must have ignored the ominous rumblings from London and paid Down and Hill £10, but the two men billed for £14 7s 7d and went to law about it. There the documentation and the carvers' story ends. What remains is the evidence that they were among the finest artists in England. At the beginning of the 19th century St Mary acquired another quite pretty chancel screen from a defunct church, but the north aisle screen of Down and Hill is not only much superior, but, alone among the many fine screens in Devon, it retains the tall rood loft as well.

Five ribs rise from the screen's wainscot and spread into coved fan vaults to support the loft. The intersections of the subdivided ribs are delicately carved ensembles of leaves, and between the ribs is more carving, vaguely floral, and little putti, evidence of European Renaissance influence. Above that are three exquisitely carved horizontal bands marking the transition from screen to loft, and the loft itself is a sequence of five lacy canopies. In all, a consummate piece of design executed with a thrilling density of detail.

Bath
SOMERSET

The Romans came, saw and built hot baths, a temple and a town. The three thermal springs already had their Celtic house goddess, Sulis, so in their relaxed way with all religions (except troublesome Christianity) the Romans simply named the town Aquae Sulis and identified the goddess with their own Minerva. Her bronze head is in the Roman Baths Museum, a complex that includes the baths, with Nicholas Grimshaw's discreetly brilliant Bath stone-clad New Royal Bath. Minerva's temple lies beneath the Grand Pump Room, partly visible and adjoining the Great Bath, which is still fed by the lead pipes plumbed in by the Romans and thus, alas, out of bounds to bathers for that very modern reason, health and safety. The renaissance of Bath (as we know Aquae Sulis) from Tudor decrepitude came in the 18th century, when Ralph Allen realised its potential and shipped in the stone from his quarries on Combe Down in the hills to the west. The city welcomed John Wood the Elder, John Wood the Younger (who built the pedimented entrance to the baths opposite the Gothic abbey) and, later in the century, Thomas Baldwin, who built the magnificent Bathwick estate, enabled by the new Avon crossing, and Robert Adam, who built Pulteney Bridge, which is Bath's sotto voce response to the shop-lined Rialto Bridge of Venice.

Bath suffered from the Baedeker raids – the Luftwaffe's response to the Allied bombing of Lübeck. It suffered much more at the hands of its own city council, determined in the 1970s to rebuild Bath in the modern fashion. In the benighted post-war decades that meant conserving the famous sights – the Circus, the Royal Crescent, Queen Square, Pulteney Street – and restoring the bombed Assembly Rooms, but tearing apart the everyday Georgian fabric of the city as far out as suburban Twerton, the Lower Bristol Road and Oldfield Park, and as close to the abbey and baths as Walcott Street, where there is a dire Hilton hotel and Waitrose supermarket (no blame accrues to either of those admirable organisations). The conservationist tide swept in and saved Bath from further damage and today, if you didn't know it before, you'd hardly notice the damage.

So the texture is still there, and that's important because apart from Bathwick the city grew up almost at random, Queen Square first, then the other set-pieces and terraces rising up the hill towards the open plain of Lansdown. All of this was speculative, and all of it held together, partly by style, but much more by the use of that famous Bath stone from Ralph Allen's quarries. Fine though the Perpendicular abbey is and the museums are – the Holburne Museum, the Victoria Art Gallery, the Roman Baths Museum, and, in the Assembly Rooms, the Fashion Museum – it is the city itself, so assured, so smart, so all of a piece, that is the star of the show. Minerva maintains a watching brief.

Thomas Gainsborough's calling card, in the Assembly Rooms

Into this boom town shooting up on the banks of the sleepy old Avon after Queen Anne had been to try the waters came Beau

Nash to organise the season and John Wood the Elder and his son John Wood the Younger to build Queen Square, the Circus, the Royal Crescent and the streets linking them. After them came Thomas Gainsborough (1727–88), a struggling provincial artist who decided in 1759 to raise his game by moving to the flourishing spa with its 'very good company' and trawling for aristocratic patronage.

Early in his career, in his East Anglian home town of Sudbury, Gainsborough had painted *Mr and Mrs Andrews*, the rural double portrait that has become just about Britain's best-loved painting. In Bath, Gainsborough quickly realised, his clientele did not wish to be portrayed as doll-like gentry at ease with country pleasures; they wanted to be shown in their aristocratic finery, as Van Dyck had shown their ancestors a century before. They did not want to be seen in the arable settings of farmers. If landscape there must be, then it should be a hint of trees and sky, an indicator of wealth and possessions, something glimpsed beyond a cornice or a fluted pillar. So Gainsborough dutifully rode down to Wilton and drew a copy of the Pembroke family portrait to work out how it was done.

That knowledge gained, when he came in 1767 to paint Beau Nash's successor as master of ceremonies, Captain William Wade, for the proprietors of the new Assembly Rooms being built by John Wood the Younger, he spurned the fee, knowing that though his portrait would be hung disadvantageously high, it would serve as his calling card to high society. Even at this point his impulse to paint landscape asserted itself, and he finished up having to repaint the background with just a hint of countryside beyond a neoclassical balustrade. Since the restoration of the Assembly Rooms after wartime bombing the Gainsborough has returned on loan from the municipal gallery to its rightful spot 20 feet above floor level, where painted detail is inscrutable without binoculars.

For this reason Gainsborough might not have worked at full throttle on the commission and, though fine enough, the portrait is not among his finest pieces. But his head told him where his lifetime's income would be found, so although he railed against the necessity of 'face painting', as he called it, and complained that he could not sell his 'landskips', it is in portraiture that his real genius lies. And the Assembly Rooms after all are a magnificent setting for his gallant Captain Wade, and for us a key to understanding 18th-century Bath and the artist's relationship to Georgian society.

Crocodile Dundee crosses the Styx, Bath Abbey

Tucked away among the clutter of monuments in the south aisle of Bath Abbey is one of John Flaxman's happiest creations, a mildly eccentric little memorial to Dr John Sibthorp, Oxford professor of botany and renowned traveller, showing him in profile on his last journey, having been conveyed across the River Styx into Hades by the ferryman Charon, stepping out on to the far shore. The prospect could be worse. In the background is the agreeable view of an Athenian temple. He is lightly wrapped in a cloak, bare legged and shod in light, flexible footwear, the ancient Greek approximation to trainers. His broad-brimmed hat hangs on his back between his shoulders so that, despite his fine-drawn features and the exquisitely carved posy of flowers that he clutches to his chest as a passport to botany in the hereafter, Dr Sibthorp looks a touch like Crocodile Dundee in the outback.

Flaxman (1755–1826) was just about the most famous of English sculptors, at any rate until the 20th century, and he has one very English quality, a great affinity with linear

JUXTA TUMULATUS EST
JOHANNES SIBTHORP M.D. R.S.S.
BOTANICES
IN ACADEMIA OXONIENSI
PROFESSOR.

RERUM NATURALIUM INVESTIGATIONI
PER VITAM BREVEM DEDITUS
PHYTOLOGIÆ IN PRIMIS AMANTISSIMUS
REGIONES LONGINQUITATE AC METU
PEREGRINANTIBUS TANTUM NON IMPERVIAS
ADVERSA DISSUADENTE VALETUDINE.
OBSTANTIBUS INSUPER EX OMNI PARTE PERICULIS
EXPLORAVIT.
ITINERIS MOLESTIARUM PLENI
QUOD PER GRÆCIAM NUPER CONFECERAT
LABORE OPPRESSUS
OBIIT BATHONIÆ
DIE OCTAVO FEBRUARII
ANNO ÆTATIS SUÆ TRICESIMO OCTAVO

movement, shared with his friend William Blake and developed through studying the lovely 13th-century angels in the spandrels of a triforium above the nave in Westminster Abbey. But almost none of Flaxman's abilities relates to sculpture. He was really at his best working on a small scale, and once he magnified his ideas they tended to look awkward. Fortunately, having failed to win the gold medal at the Royal Academy school and thus been unable to travel to Rome to study grand sculpture, he began to design classical motifs in low relief jasperware for Josiah Wedgwood's pottery and from his mastery of line in this medium developed his draughtsman's skills well enough to make his famous sets of line illustrations for Alexander Pope's translations of the *Odyssey* and *Iliad*. His fashionable reputation as a sculptor was based on major commissions, like his memorial to Nelson in St Paul's Cathedral and the gigantic St Michael overcoming Satan at Petworth's sculpture gallery, both carved after he had finally made it to Rome and seen the Vatican collection of ancient sculpture. It has to be said, though, that the first is a strange miscegenation of classical and contemporary, the second bland, both of them pompous in conception and bloodless in execution. In 1798, when he began work on the Sibthorp memorial, he turned back to what he did best, profile relief on a small scale. It is easily missed in the abbey's south aisle but gives a sense of what Flaxman might have achieved had he not been a slave to the fashionable market. As for that flower posy, tantalizingly it speaks either of Flaxman's craftsman's skills or to those of his stone worker, bringing the flowers and foliage to life with a high order of rich, crisp and delicate carving.

A Crocodile Dundee of academe: Dr John Sibthorp, 18th-century Oxford professor of botany, on his way to the hereafter as Flaxman shows him in a carving in Bath Abbey

The artist 'formed to paint women', at the Holburne Museum of Art

Over shop-lined Pulteney Bridge, along Great Pulteney Street away from the town centre to the quiet backwater where Jane Austen had once taken lodgings in Sydney Place. Swankily closing the vista from Pulteney Bridge is the old Sydney Hotel of 1796, standing tall with its Corinthian portico, pediment and, a later and slightly overweening addition, a balustrade with great stone urns above the pediment. In 1916 it became a museum for the collection of art left by Sir William Holburne, a twelve-year-old volunteer at the Battle of Trafalgar, who succeeded to the baronetcy of Holburne of Menstrie in his mid-twenties and began to collect paintings, silver, majolica, English porcelain and small sculptures. Today, as I visit, the main draw at the Holburne is a display of illustrations of Winnie-the-Pooh – the real fuzzy bear in the drawings by E.H. Shepard, not the hard-edged Disney impostor – though it has to be said that the gallery is not exactly swarming with small schoolchildren, saying 'I think I'll be six now for ever and ever'. Sixty might just about meet the lower end of the scale.

And there are none too many of any age upstairs where Alan Ramsay's portrait of Rosamund Sargent hangs. This is one of a group of three paintings of the Sargent family by Ramsay (1713–84), who was born in Edinburgh but, south of the border, was appointed painter to George III in preference to Reynolds. Rosamund's likeness, taken in 1749, is a companion piece to a portrait of John Sargent that still hangs alongside, and they are presumed to have been wedding portraits. The third, larger, painting is of Sargent's father, also John Sargent, and it doesn't seem to have engaged Ramsay's interest anything like as much. He certainly generally painted women better, and this meltingly beautiful portrait is second only in his work to the portrait of his own wife, now in the National Gallery of Scotland. Walpole said that Ramsay, 'formed to paint women', was better than Reynolds at it.

Gainsborough was the fashionable portraitist in Bath. Ramsay was more familiar with the society of Tunbridge Wells, and as the seat of the younger John Sargent was Halstead Place in Kent (now demolished), it seems likely that it was in London, where Ramsay had a studio in the piazza at Covent Garden, or in Kent that these portraits were made. But a 20th-century descendant of the family, Sir Orme Sargent, retired to Bathwick Hill House close to the Holburne Museum of which he became chairman of the trustees. In 1962 the museum received the portraits in his bequest.

Rosamund Sargent was twenty-seven when Ramsay painted the wedding portraits, a healthy, fresh-faced young woman, not beautiful but with a frank gaze, which to Ramsay denoted a woman happy in her new marriage, as he wrote to his friend and compatriot, the historian David Hume. He painted the features as carefully as porcelain, but he has brushed in her lace cap trimmed with blue ribbon swiftly and with panache. The chiffon cape trimmed with black over a deep pink bodice is clumsier, an indication that Ramsay like many other portrait painters with a flourishing business left this task to an assistant entrusted with painting drapery, a practice Ramsay was to give up later in his career.

The natural world of John Nash, Victoria Art Gallery

Bath's art gallery is an ugly 19th-century baroque duckling next to the Pulteney Bridge over the Avon, but its good collection has an intriguing line in paintings of Bath or Bath people starting, of course, with Gainsborough. Zoffany and Lawrence visited too and, in the 20th century, Walter Sickert. So it might seem a touch eccentric to pick out from these a painting by a half-forgotten artist, John Nash (1893–1970). Unlike his better-known elder brother Paul, John had no training as an artist – no training in anything, in fact, except for a short time in journalism with the *Middlesex and Bucks Reporter*, which fired him almost as quickly as it hired him. But although he lifted little else from life's lucky dip, he did take a school prize in botany, and plants and the landscape of southern England shaped his art, which he took up for want of anything else but with the useful encouragement of Paul (though decades later Paul was confiding to John Rothenstein that he still didn't know whether he had given the right advice).

After going to the front with the Artists' Rifles in 1916, Nash took up a commission from the Imperial War Museum to paint the war, but his first notable canvas came from rediscovering the post-armistice peace of the English countryside in an ecstatically dreamlike evening harvest scene called *The Cornfield*, now in the Tate collection. The Bath painting of about 1927 has a similar but calmer sense of enclosure, a tactile, almost womb-like view of the bridge over the Kennet–Avon canal in Sydney Gardens beyond the far end of Great Pulteney Street from Pulteney Bridge. The flat, receding planes of the picture, the framing trees and the buildings in the background pull the painting together, but then it is hauntingly destabilised by the slightly off-true horseshoe arch of the bridge and the reflections in the canal where the water reciprocates by throwing light reflections across the shadows on the bridge. It's a 20th-century but only peripherally modernist take on pastoral English, a retro mode that would become increasingly popular and nostalgic after the outbreak of

An archetypal view of Bath. To the right of Robert Adam's Pulteney bridge across the Avon is Argyle Street, a scene of sober gaiety with domesticity and commerce closely consorting

the next war, and with it Nash claimed his own niche in history.

Argyle Street scene beyond Pulteney Bridge

East from Pulteney Bridge is the grand, geometrically planned 'new' Bath, known as Bathwick, following on from the Palladian Bath of the Woods, father and son. It was built between the late 1780s and about 1820 to designs by Thomas Baldwin. Even Laura Place, which is a square tipped on to a corner, fails to add a lighter tone to the grandeur of the view from the bridge to the Holburne Museum along the wide vista of Great Pulteney Street, but between the bridge and Laura Place is a short stretch called Argyle Street, a scene of sober gaiety, like the vicar dispensing with his dog collar and letting his hair down at a parish knees-up. Starting at the east end of the street there's an informal grouping of No. 8, A.H. Hale, a chemist's shop since 1826 (which has retained the name though it is now run by B.R. Doshi and R.B. Doshi), and No. 9, the Boater pub. The chemist's is a sprightly example of Greek revival, a window holding the centre of the composition, deep rectangular panes breaking into arches with glazed spandrels in the top row and fluted Ionic columns framing doors on each side. Above the name board sits a wildly inventive coat of arms, seemingly a child's invention, but which was actually the armorial bearings of George III's wife Queen Charlotte. It has a pretty garland of flowers as a surround, is draped with ermine, has a gold-studded crown stuffed with crimson plush and a startled golden lion and a white unicorn as supporters. The queen died in 1818, around the time Argyle Street was completed, so presumably the coat of arms was introduced before Hale took over the shop. The pub is gaily bow-fronted, painted crisp black and white, and with the top row of glazing bars designed in a cobweb pattern. Across the road, No. 6 is McColl's, an off-licence, with four Corinthian columns, this time spaced right across the front. No. 5 is a restaurant, black with a green cloth canopy, the fascia set below a window as deep as the first floor, flanked by flat pilasters supporting a hood carved with festoons of laurel.

Between No. 5 and No. 6, Grove Street runs off Argyle Street at a right angle. The street name is carved into the stone in big, elegant, serif capitals with a lovely flourish to the tail of the R and picked out in black paint. This is the side of No. 5, which was a bookstore and lending library from 1886 to 1916 and has painted below that fading sign a *trompe l'oeil* window with a glimpse of globe ceiling lights inside, bookshelves and a bearded man just inside the window holding a book to catch the light.

Blisland

CORNWALL

Church restoration that works, Church of St Protus and St Hyacinth

Of all that army of Celtic saints lost in the mists of Cornish myth and mystery, St Protus and St Hyacinth surely have two of the prettiest names, though, as saints tended to, they met ugly deaths by beheading and burning. Set on Bodmin Moor and beset by ancient stone crosses and two modern chunks of granite, one to celebrate the golden jubilee in 1810 of mad King George III, the other for Queen Elizabeth II's golden jubilee in 2001, Blisland is nevertheless, untypically for Cornwall, laid out around a big village green, pub one side, church the other. The church itself is typical in being quirky: Norman and medieval, just a south aisle to the nave, but a north one for the chancel, transepts with the tower on the end of the north one. It was not so much this that made the church a favourite of John Betjeman, though it probably helped, but the 1890s work by F.C. Eden (1864–1944). 'As a restoration – even improvement – of a medieval church,' Betjeman said, 'this can hardly be bettered.'

Eden, master of any style as long as it was florid (see North Cerney, West and East Midlands), brought to English church restoration the rare quality of interpretive exuberance. You bend the knee to the genius of his Gothic revival predecessor Pugin; you applaud Eden. His Renaissance-style altar here is good enough, but the Gothic rood screen is totally captivating. It has a filigree delicacy and sparkling detail in the carving and colouring, gold, green, blue and red, that isn't a direct imitation of the great carved screens of neighbouring Devon but does catch their spirit. Eden has reintroduced a rood itself with carved figures from Oberammergau in Bavaria, Christ crucified and flanked by angels, the Virgin Mary and St John. Wood carving has been a major cottage industry in Oberammergau for hundreds of years, and the figures are no more than folk art (for the difference from fine art, compare them to the life-size Madonna and Child in the north wall of the nave, a good copy of a piece by the 16th-century German sculptor Tilman Riemenschneider), but they work well as part of this fine ensemble.

Bodmin
CORNWALL

*Celtic Romanesque font in
the Church of St Petroc*

There is a small group of these almost
barbaric fonts in a belt across the middle
of Cornwall. Bodmin's is the best. It comes
when Romanesque was already giving way to
Gothic in the rest of England, but Cornwall's
links were still at least as strong with the
Celts of Ireland and Wales. The font is a big
bowl on a stubby pillar with four columns
around it attached to the bowl by heads of
tremendous angels, with splendid wings
and powerful heads with solemn, great eyes
and noses like hammerheads. Around the
bowl of the font are bands of foliage, heavily
undercut to throw them into greater relief,
and sinister dragons that seem to have
emerged from beneath the earth.

Botallack
CORNWALL

Industrial landscape

The Tamar marked the division between
England and Cornwall until the 9th century,
and crossing from Devon still feels like
entering, not a foreign land, but somewhere
different. The further west, the more
different. The harsh moors and the treeless
horizon are part of this impression, as are the
dolmens and quoits, the brilliant ocean light,
but mostly it's the prevalence of the kilns
of china clay works and the roofless engine
houses and chimneys of abandoned copper
and lead mines. Though only the unquiet
ghosts of miners and their families live here,
the mines seem as much part of the present
life of the landscape as the fishing villages
and scatter of low, slated rural farm cottages,

humble churches and iron age field patterns.
Botallack has this and the rocky coast as well.
Its bleak engine house clings to the cliffs,
and its galleries drive out under the sea. The
bodies of twenty workers have never been
recovered from West Wheal Owles, one of the
workings, after floodwaters broke into the
mine in 1893. Artists looking for something
primal are fascinated by Botallack. Four
friends in particular found what they needed
here: the maverick artist Roger Hilton lived
nearby until his death in 1975, Peter Lanyon, a
native of Cornwall, explored it on the ground
and from the air, and Bryan Wynter, who
lived in a tiny cottage on the moors above
Zennor, dissected it in paint. When Lanyon
died in a glider crash, the Cornish-domiciled
Scots poet W.S. Graham felt that an
irreplaceable link of friendship and mutual
experience had broken and memorialised
him:

> *I called today, Peter, and you were away.*
> *I look out over Botallack and over Ding*
> *Dong and Levant and over the jasper sea.*
> *Find me a thermal to speak and soar to you*
>   *from.*

Bovey Tracey
DEVON

*Church fittings at St Peter, St Paul and
St Thomas of Canterbury*

Bovey Tracey is an attractive little market
town that climbs up a hill with the 15th-
century parish church highest of all. The
church's eleven-bay rood screen of 1427 had
the colours restored in 1887 and forms a
joyful ensemble with the stone. The vault of
the screen dates from the restoration work
but sits well with the lovely cornice carved
with big leaves of gold, winding tendrils in
purple and green bunches of grapes. The
stone pulpit, also 15th century and coloured

with similar exuberance, has funny little carved figures in niches under canopies of oriental exoticism set in rows of lush, almost crusted, foliage, more folk art than high art but highly enjoyable.

Devon escaped the worst of ravages of the Reformation. Perhaps because of the remoteness from London the commissioners were satisfied so long as the rood itself was destroyed, and more than a hundred of these wonderful wooden screens survive in the county. Painted panels on the screen aren't as common as in East Anglia, nor as fine or richly rendered, but Bovey Tracey's 16th-century prophets and Apostles, though restored, are in the original colours against a white background and very fine.

Brent Knoll
SOMERSET

Medieval satire at the Church of St Michael

Usually misericords and bench ends are incidental enjoyments in church furnishing, more or less crudely carved folk art and, where it can be guessed at, social history. Not all churches with misericords encourage visitors to look for them, even to the point of roping off the choir stalls. Some, like Christchurch Priory in Dorset (see South) and St Mary in Nantwich, Cheshire (see Northwest), have particularly fine sets and display them proudly. At Brent Knoll, along with the masterly carved wooden roof embellished with angels and big flower and leaf bosses with ninety-six panels, each with a different and lovely ornament, the extraordinary 15th-century bench ends are

The tremendous Romanesque angels of Bodmin, a powerful reminder of Cornwall's ancient links with the Celts of Wales and Ireland

the main reason for seeking out this church, which is tucked on the lower slopes above the village on one of those tors and mumps and knolls whose only function seems to be to accentuate the levelness of the Somerset Levels. Brent Knoll rises sharply from around sea level to a peak at 450 feet. Like other eminences in the Levels, Glastonbury Tor and Burrow Mump, the knoll's church is dedicated to St Michael, no doubt so that the archangel would discourage Satan from resting there when he had finished his devil's work in the marshes.

Brent Knoll's benches show the Christian symbols of the lamb of God, the pelican (emblematic of sacrifice) and the symbols of the evangelists, but the three remarkable ones tell the medieval fable of a fox preaching to the birds, feasting with a monkey, being put into the stocks and being hanged by geese. The story originates in French folklore as the satirical *Le Roman de Reinart*, and the author of the pamphlet on the wood carvings speculates that because the Brent Knoll fox preaches in an abbot's robe and mitre and carries a crosier, the sequence is a satire on a grasping abbot of Glastonbury. First, however, there is no evidence that any abbot cast envious eyes on Brent Knole's tithes, which belonged to the bishop of Wells; and second, the British Library has a 14th-century illustrated volume called the *Smithfield Decretals*, which also shows the preaching fox in abbot's kit. But it is true that after the Black Death country folk fought to shake off the feudal labour dues that they saw as shackles, and there's no doubting the glee and panache with which the woodcarver has depicted the scenes of the preacher with his congregation of birds and three fat pigs in monks' cowls, the fox's discomfiture after his arrest and the determination of the goose hanging on to the end of the rope as the fox swings in the noose at the other end. The bench ends' survival for all to see suggests that the parish, too, enjoyed a parable rooted in more than a popular folk tale.

Bristol

King Edward III took Bristol out of Gloucestershire and Somerset in 1373 and made it a county in its own right, almost, at times, a city-state. Its rich history of trade and exploration made it intermittently England's second city. From here the Italian John Cabot and his (possibly) Bristol-born son Sebastian set sail in 1497 in the 100 ton *Matthew* for Newfoundland. This venture opened up the North Atlantic fishery to Bristol and added cotton and tobacco to the old European trade of wines and sherry. The modern counterpart to the exuberantly ugly 105 foot Cabot tower on Brandon Hill is the slavery trail, devised to guide schoolchildren around the 18th-century houses of the merchants who profited from the half million Africans transported to slavery by Bristol shipping between 1698 and the early 19th century – education rather than expiation, though expiation has been tried and found wanting. The black population of Bristol still feels exploited and persuaded Nelson Mandela not to attend the city's bicentennial celebration of the abolition of slavery.

It's extraordinary that so much of Bristol's history in stones should have survived the Second World War bombing that rent apart the city's fabric. The visitor's best approaches do not include the quickest, the M32 spur from the M4. Instead, take the A4 from Avonmouth past Brunel's magnificent single-span Clifton Bridge across the Avon gorge to his SS *Great Britain* in the floating harbour where she was launched in 1843, or, from the south, the A38 or A370 linking with Brunel Way and its spectacular vistas across the harbour. Everywhere there is evidence of the city's prosperity in the Middle Ages and beyond: the churches, especially the cathedral and the even more splendid St Mary Redcliffe; the docks and their converted warehouses, one of them, the Arnolfini, among the best four or five modern art galleries in England; Spike Island, sandwiched between the floating harbour and the New Cut for the Avon, with old quays and new marinas, sculpture on Baltic Quay and views across the harbour to the cathedral; the grandly spacious 18th-century Queen Square with its Rysbrack equestrian statue of William III; and the oldest playhouse in England, the Theatre Royal of 1766, though its Georgian origins have been pretty well obliterated under Victorianisation and later updates. The theatre is in the finest street in Bristol, King Street, north of Queen Square, with mid-17th century St Nicholas's almshouses and end-of-the-century Merchant Venturers' almshouses, houses built for merchants, handsome warehouses and the three-gabled, four-storey, timber-framed Llandoger Trow inn of 1664.

There are little secret places: historic pubs down alleys; the lord mayor's chapel, St Mark, on Clifton Green; the old town and fine suburbs like Hotwells, a spa that failed during the Napoleonic Wars; and Clifton. But everywhere too there is the sudden fracturing emergence into dual carriageway traffic, sewers and big, empty lots turned into car parks that seem to be where they are because that's where the bombs fell. But get hold of a good town map and walk.

A Bristol dignitary in a Venetian Renaissance altarpiece, Bristol City Museum and Art Gallery

Up on Exmoor, so high I drove to it in summer with fog lights on, there is a village forgotten by time called Withypool: pub, shop, B&B and tearoom. The population is about 230, hardly increased on the 15th and 16th centuries when the Withypool family lived here. They were Bristol merchants and among their number was Paul Withypool, who carried out at least part of his trade from a London base – in the 1540s he acquired property in Walthamstow. He is remembered because Bristol art gallery has an extreme rarity for England, an altarpiece known as *Virgin and Child with St Joseph and Donor* (1514), that includes a portrait of Withypool. It stands clear of the walls in a gallery with a fine collection, ranging from local topography to an outright Northern Renaissance masterpiece, Lucas Cranach's portrait of Martin Luther, and a wonderful range of 19th-century English and French painting. The Withypool altarpiece survived the Reformation and slumbered for many years with the dukes of St Albans, a title created for a bastard son of Charles II and Nell Gwynn. It was the work of a Venetian called Antonio da Solario (active 1502–18), like Withypool, a man almost forgotten until 1905 when Roger Fry disentangled his identity from a Lombard called Andrea Solario. Guessing by his dates and judging by his style and distinction, Antonio da Solario could have worked in the studio of the great Giovanni Bellini. He signs this painting 'Antonius Desolario Venetus 1514'.

It is a triptych, and the central panel shows the patron, Paul Withypool, kneeling in prayer before the infant Christ and the Virgin. Two Bellini-esque landscapes seen through openings behind the Virgin let light on to the scene. The two wings show St Catherine and St Ursula, and when they fold over as shutters the reverse side shows St Paul, Withypool's name saint, St John the Baptist, the patron of the Merchant Taylor's company of London, and crucially, the Withypool arms. Solario may have painted it when Withypool was in Italy on business – the Englishman was known as Vedipolo

and kept a bank account in Genoa. In those pre-slavery days, Bristol trade had grown fat on exporting wool from the Cotswolds and Somerset, the Gascon and Spanish wine trade was flourishing, the Cabots, John and Sebastian, were exploring the Americas, and Henry VII was encouraging Bristol merchants to challenge Venice. Withypool may have traded from both Bristol and London, and he was well known in Italy. Equally, Solario may have painted it in England where, like a few other peripatetic Italians, he worked for a period; other paintings by him have been recorded in collections of the time. The two evidently met, because the likeness of Withypool shows a real personality, one of the new class of entrepreneur in the acquisitive society of the Tudors. This is a living portrait, in no way idealised like the Virgin and Child.

The triptych must have survived the Reformation because it was for private use and remained with the family during the years of destruction. At any rate, the two wings became separated and found a home at the National Gallery. The main panel turned up in the St Albans collection, disclosed in an article in the *Burlington Magazine* in 1936. Bristol acquired it from the duke in 1937, and the National Gallery enabled the triptych to be reassembled by placing the wings on long loan. The duke's line, incidentally, has survived the loss of this rare and beautiful painting with a lively sense of its own privileges: at the abolition of the voting rights of hereditary peers in the House of Lords in 1999 the current heir to the title, Lord Burford, cried 'Treason!' and was ejected.

The Arnolfini Gallery's café-bar in Bristol, designed by the artist Bruce McLean, and the finest bar in art since Manet painted his Bar at the Folies-Bergères

Bruce McLean's walk-in artwork and café-bar in real time, the Arnolfini Gallery

Bruce McLean (b.1944) studied from the age of eighteen at St Martin's School of Art in London when the big-name teacher was Anthony Caro, who made steel sculpture that inhabited wide areas of floor space. McLean thought, if a creation has no plinth, why does it need a gallery to house it? Why not place it out in the gutter between parked cars? Or floating on a pond ('floataway sculpture')? Situations where, perhaps, no passer-by even recognises the works as art. Situations like walking into a café for a drink and a sandwich. Or perhaps you take the installation out of the gallery, introduce a coffee machine, just add water, and bingo.

In the Arnolfini, which is a gallery, McLean designed the café-bar and it instantly became the best bar in art since Manet painted

the one in the Folies Bergère. It is in blue, green, deep red, a touch of orange and a twist of lemon, a stripe painting for living in. The bottles of exotic liqueurs behind the bar, catching the light (like Manet's), the pumping gear, the tall bar stools, the glass screen guiding visitors to the gallery towards the café, the long bench tables are all part of it. Walk in and buy a pink wine and a sandwich of roasted peppers and the visitor too becomes a participant.

McLean is sculptor, painter, ceramicist, performance artist, film maker, stage designer, a bit of an architect and a satirist. There are hints of Dadaism, Secessionism, Cūbism and upyouism. When he produced some sketched diagrams as designs for a performance in the 1980s, someone pointed out that they were art in their own right, and McLean thought, 'why not?' and saved them to exhibit. He has spun work off that approach ever since, calligraphically sketching on impermeable surfaces. At the Arnolfini it's the shiny screen blocking the draught from the street door, decorated with a swift semi-abstract doodle that reminds me of *The Picasso Mystery*, the film by Georges Clouzot in which Picasso faces the audience through a large sheet of glass on which he draws with a torch, improvising, constantly transforming the image. The McLean work, too, seems improvisatory, provisional, liable to change at any moment, yet instinctively and arrestingly structured.

Twenty years or so before, McLean had also designed this bar's predecessor as part of the Arnolfini's refit by David Chipperfield. In 2001 a lottery grant of £7.5 million enabled the Arnolfini to buy the whole of the former tea warehouse of 1830 after having subsisted as a tenant of only two floors. This time the architect responsible for opening out the sequence of galleries and performance spaces was Robin Snell, working with Susanna Heron as design team artist. McLean must have seemed to them and their clients the inescapable choice to redo the café-bar.

A king for Queen Square

Queen Square in Bristol was the first of the West Country's town squares, started thirty years before Queen Square in Bath. But Bath's square is a masterpiece of grand unity, with the north side of the square grouped like a palace under a single great pediment. Queen's Square, Bristol, is too big, and the buildings were added hotchpotch. Even so, Michael Rysbrack's flamboyant equestrian statue to William III pulls together the buildings, plane trees and paths crossing diagonally into a loosely knotted composition, an urban space for strolling in, and out of, to the docks a minute's walk away.

Rysbrack (1694–1770) won the commission for the statue in competition with Peter Scheemakers and was paid £1,800. Scheemakers impressed the Bristol city fathers enough for them to give him compensation of £50 (and he then sold his William III to Hull; see Northwest), but they made the right choice in Rysbrack. Both versions show the king as a Roman general, but Rysbrack's is the nobler Roman, relaxed in the saddle, the muscles of his arms and legs hardened in campaigns, his face sternly alert, his horse, too, prancing as though with the noise of battle in its ears.

Medieval sculpture at the Church of St Mary Redcliffe

Like Bath Abbey, Beverley Minster, Pershore and Tewkesbury, St Mary Redcliffe is one of the few and very beautiful stone-vaulted parish churches in England, 'the fairest and goodliest in England', as Elizabeth I observed, grander even than the city's cathedral. But more astonishing even than the church vaulting is the north porch. It is remarkable for its oriental look, an influence that might have reached the great trading port of Bristol via North Africa, Spain and Portugal. Its form, a hexagon with an exotically cusped entrance framed by three wide bands of foliage, is an extravagant kick against the traces, since the date is 1300 – a time when unfussy Early English forms predominated. The porch is two storeys high and inside has the proportions of a great chapel. The external sculpture in the niches is all replacement, except for the extraordinary little pieces in among the sculpted doorway foliage.

From beyond the broad flight of stone steps that leads up to the entrance the three bands look no more than an intricate web of carving, but close up the little biblical figures almost nesting in the foliage and the birds literally nesting are tiny masterpieces. There are, for instance, a couple of panels of angels kneeling, or rather, sitting back on their haunches to pray among the fleshy acanthus leaves, fully realised, their bodyweight palpably pressing down on their lower limbs, gowns tucked under them but the ends escaping to fill the triangular space of the panel beneath them. There are prophets too, each sitting as though in a grotto, and Samson doing battle with a lion, more crudely carved though expressive and spot on architecturally.

The old port reinvigorated at Baltic Wharf

The old harbour of Bristol had a major problem: at low tide the docked ships were left lying on their sides when the water level of the River Avon dropped 30 feet at ebb tide, so the city elders called in the ever-ingenious Isambard Kingdom Brunel (1806–59) to devise a solution. He introduced lock gates, to produce a steady water level, and cut a fresh narrow course for the Avon just south of the new lock-bound floating harbour. After the war port activities emigrated to Avonmouth and the city centre floating harbour has become a focus of pubs, restaurants, the brilliant Arnolfini Gallery in a 19th-century warehouse, the 21st-century science centre and planetarium Explore-at-Bristol, and vivid waterside markets.

Baltic Wharf is away from the popular activity at the Cumberland basin end of the floating harbour, redesigned with apartment blocks for the rich and its inevitable adjunct, a marina. In 1986 the developers commissioned three pieces of sculpture to be sited on the edge of the harbour, and the most notable of these is by the internationally known Bristol sculptor Stephen Cox (b.1946). His piece, *Atyeo*, carved from red Verona marble, looks like an enlargement of some sort of sea life, with waving fronds rising from a globular base. In fact, it's the response of an abstract sculptor

who was asked for some figurative content and intended the globular part to represent the globe and the wavy section the river. It hardly matters. The piece is in effect an abstract in a calm melding of its exotic stone (chosen partly because, unlike Carrara, it is not porous). Cox carves against the trend of modern art, grounding his work on ancient Western and Indian cultures, even older than Bristol's, though in this context the title is a mildly skittish reference to a boyhood sporting hero, John Atyeo, a free-scoring Bristol City centre forward.

East, through a forest of yacht masts, the view discloses the cathedral with its thickets of pinnacles. North across the harbour are terraces of houses painted blue, pink, yellow and dun. It's such a pity that the developers didn't show the same imagination when they were hiring an architect for the Baltic Wharf blocks of flats as they did for the sculpture.

An 18th-century way-sign near Temple Meads

It is an iron fluted Doric column, with the addition of a base, and it has a scrolly top and two direction pointers, just horizontal frames really, with pointing hands at the end and giving the names of Bath and Wells in cut-out letters. On top of the column is a pretty, scrolly plant form, which supports an electric light globe, and there is another pair of globes above the pointing hands. The style of the lettering suggests early 19th century. It's delightful, but as it stands at the point near Temple Meads where the A4 (Bath) merges with the A37 (Wells), anyone stopping to look would risk infuriating other motorists. Just grab the chance if the lights turn red. The signpost was designed in calmer days. Now it's almost lost in a competing clutter of no U-turn signs, bus stop signs, signs pointing the way to local amenities and then, ultimate irony, a sign with the message: 'However you disguise it, it's still litter … bin it! Or risk a fine of £75.'

Buckland Filleigh
DEVON

Flaxman monument in the Church of St Mary and Holy Trinity

Somehow or other the 2001 census found 170 souls willing to admit to living in Buckland Filleigh. They can't all have been sheep, but among the narrow winding lanes between Sheepwash and Shebbear there is no sign of a village at Buckland Filleigh, only big Buckland House and little St Mary's in close embrace in a green swath of parkland. In the church I finally came upon a neighbouring inhabitant, the sister of the former Tory defence secretary, John Nott, who told me as though it had happened last year that the house had burned down and been rebuilt Greek classical. I nodded sagely and observed that it didn't look quite the pukka thing. When I looked it up later, I found that the fire was in 1798 and the house was rebuilt in 1810.

Maybe the last big event round here was the death of Ann Fortescue in 1815. The Fortescue family held the manor from the mid-15th century. Ann was the wife of John Inglett Fortescue, the man responsible for the rebuilding, and he commissioned John Flaxman (1755–1826) to carve a memorial tablet in the church, which has been much mucked about without benefit of fire.

Flaxman was ideal. He was Britain's pre-eminent sculptor, revered by both William Blake, who made engravings from Flaxman's drawings, and Jean-Auguste-Dominique Ingres, France's greatest neoclassicist after Jacques-Louis David, who kept a volume of Flaxman's engravings at his elbow. At Buckland Filleigh the tablet simply shows in deep relief the husband, standing with one elbow resting on an obelisk and his bowed head resting on his hand, the son on one knee with his elbow on the other and his head, too, supported by his hand. It's a simple statement of Roman grief elegantly and compactly composed. The father wears what might be a toga falling in classical folds; the son wears contemporary dress.

It has to be said that there is some scholarly debate as to whether Flaxman really was the sculptor here, but it certainly has his stamp of quality. For a genuine, no-questions-asked Flaxman memorial, you should visit Bath Abbey (see above).

Burnham-on-Sea
SOMERSET

Seaside angels by Grinling Gibbons's grey eminence, Church of St Andrew

A westerly breeze whips off the Bristol Channel, so insistently that it's difficult to imagine it different. No wonder the church council closes St Andrew to visitors in winter. It isn't even the weather for walking a dog on the beach. The blue cross of St Andrew snaps to the horizontal on the flagmast at the top of the tower as I join the huddle of townspeople sheltering in the south porch while they wait to pick up relatives after Sunday morning service. When the doors open I slip in to see the angels under the west tower. It's well worth it.

They have a curious history. They are what are left of the principal achievement of Arnold Quellin (1653–86), a Fleming who came to London with a brother and carved many of the marble figures adorning monuments designed by Grinling Gibbons. The great Gibbons, unparalleled as a decorative carver in pearwood, as his work at St Paul's Cathedral shows, was lumpen in his large marble figures. Quellin, as the angels of Burnham demonstrate, was not.

He made them as part of an altarpiece designed by Christopher Wren for James II's private chapel at Whitehall. After the king's hurried departure from the realm in 1688, the altarpiece was dismantled and stored at Hampton Court until 1706, when Queen Anne presented it to Westminster Abbey. In 1820 the abbey replaced it with another altar and gave the old one to Walter King, bishop of Rochester, who simultaneously held the living of Burnham on Sea, where he installed it. But it blocked the east window, and Victorian parishioners once again dismantled it, disposed of most of it and installed two angels under the tower and two groups of cherubs in the aisle windows. The cherubs are cherubic, and one of the angels is as handsome as a young Apollo, the other faintly worldly – the sort who, had he checked in his wings, Samuel Pepys would undoubtedly have recognised gracing the court of King James. Both of them are carved with utter assurance, freedom and Italianate flair.

Burrow Mump
SOMERSET

The shell of a church in the Somerset Levels

The road forks at Othery, a name that gives a feel of the mildly disengaged nature of this landscape, below sea level, poised always between winter flooding and rich alluvial farmland in summer. Roads run like dykes through the Somerset Levels, flanked by low, pollarded willows and reeds and the irrigation ditches known as rhines. The left fork at Othery, towards Taunton, becomes Burrow Wall and there to the left is one place that never floods, Burrow Mump, a lovely conical hill crowned by the remains of a 17th-century church. After Glastonbury Tor it isn't mysterious, but it's very lovely in its isolation,

with the little village of Burrowbridge at its foot (population at last count, 526), on the banks of the River Parrett and at the edge of the Isle of Athelney, slightly higher than the surrounding wetlands, where King Alfred the Great built an abbey and where the Alfred jewel (Ashmolean Museum, Oxford) was found in 1693. The church on the Mump is actually a sketch for a Gothic church, a shell, not a ruin, because it was never completed. It's called St Michael, as churches on a height usually are.

Butleigh
SOMERSET

Monument to Admiral Hood

This tale wouldn't exist had I gone equipped with the Ordnance Survey Landranger map to the area, on which my quarry is clearly marked. It is the monument to Sir Samuel Hood, a column raised to the heroic admiral by popular subscription after the Napoleonic Wars and placed on a hill high above Butleigh, the village where he was born in 1724, the son of the vicar. The glory has passed, and when I asked at the Rose and Portcullis how to find the monument, the villager scratched his head, then brightened up when I described it. 'Ah, the Butleigh monument,' he said. Even stranger was to be unable to find the tall column despite pretty good advice. I caught a few swift glimpses of it through the trees, but then kept losing it again. It's worth persisting, though. From the summit up a muddy, churned-up track there is a glorious view from the monument across the vale to Glastonbury Tor.

Hood (1724–1816) was a veteran when

When the Glorious Revolution of 1688 unseated James II, his Whitehall chapel was dismantled. This is one of the angels that found its way to Burnham-on-Sea. It is by the Flemish sculptor Arnold Quellin

young Horatio Nelson was making his way, but he promoted the promising young sailor vigorously. He lost his own right arm just before Trafalgar and couldn't join his protégé in battle. His own fame was earned defeating the French roundly in the Caribbean, and he later captured Toulon, sank thirteen ships of the line and razed the arsenal. Fittingly, the carving on top of the great Tuscan column shows, not the man, but ships under sail and engaged in combat. He died as commander-in-chief on the India station, a post that, the inscription on the plinth declares, was 'of the highest distinction among the illustrious men who rendered their own age the brightest period in the naval history of their country'.

While I stood with my back to the monument taking in the view to the tor, woodsmen were planting saplings. Soon the memorial will be invisible from near and far.

Curry Rivel
SOMERSET

Capability Brown's Burton Pynsent column

High on a hill above Curry Rivel stands the 160 foot Burton Pynsent column, a landmark wrapped in obscurity. The Wellington monument is not far off, equally off the beaten track, but everyone knows what it marks. The Hood memorial is close by, and though the admiral has dropped out of the popular memory, it marks a glorious moment in national maritime history. As for Burton Pynsent, it was not, as I imagined, a person. It is a house. The column was erected by William Pitt the Elder to celebrate

Ships were life itself for Admiral Hood, who made his name in the Napoleonic Wars. Fittingly, the carving at the crown of this monument above his native village of Butleigh celebrates his naval command

the gift of Burton Pynsent to him from Sir William Pynsent in exchange for a political favour, but although it might seem that sleaze was not, after all, the recent invention of a select group of MPs on the take, the Burton Pynsent story is at once stranger and more interesting than that.

The prime minister in 1763 was Lord Bute. The national debt was big and getting bigger. Beer was already taxed, so Bute thought it reasonable to introduce a tax on cider of 4 shillings a hogshead. But beer was made in breweries, while cider-making was practically a cottage industry, so advocating a tax on it was to invite the excise men into every home that had an apple tree. From the City of London, therefore, where they were always looking for a brave radical cause to support, to the towns and apple-rich villages of Herefordshire and Somersetshire, the citizens poured on to the streets and burned images of Bute, and in Westminster they hurled stones through his windows. Pynsent was a gentleman, so he didn't do that, but his daughter, who was in line to inherit the estate, was engaged to be married to the future prime minister Lord North, who was in favour of the tax. Pitt opposed it. So Pysent disinherited his daughter and presented the house to Pitt. The column is the great statesman's thank-you letter.

He called in Capability Brown to design it, as well as other amenities of the estate. Brown gave him a Tuscan column with a cupola above, and on top of that an urn with a ball finial, and a prospect of the Levels with more than thirty churches: classical good manners with a view. The big pediment is inscribed, doubtless with deep sincerity, 'Sacred to the memory of Sir William Pynsent'. On 6 August 1770 Pitt wrote to his wife, 'dairy enchanting, pillar superb, terrace ravishing'. But that was before Geoff, Stan, Budge and the lads had carved their names with pride on the pediment.

Dartington Hall
DEVON

Henry Moore's Mexican makeover

As with the Great Hall itself, falling apart
after 600 years and given a 20th-century
facial by the new American owners of
Dartington, Leonard and Dorothy Elmhirst,
Henry Moore (1898–1986) did a makeover
on Mexican blood sacrifice sculpture in
his reclining figure so perfectly sited in the
grounds. The Elmhirsts commissioned the
piece from Moore in 1945 as a memorial to
the head of Dartington's arts department
who had died the year before. All Moore's
reclining figures come from his admiration
for pre-Columbian chak-mools, harsh
statues with a receptacle held on their bellies
to receive the blood of human sacrifices, yet
Moore's figure is nothing more than a serene
offering from his native Yorkshire heath to
the earth goddess of Dartington's gardens.

In fact, it seems timeless in the slow pulse
of its landscape-like flow from the head set
on a trunk-like neck to great thighs held
apart with folds in the garment like rifts in a
valley. Actually, however, the piece is already
dated with its resemblance to the romantic
surrealism of Paul Nash and even to art
deco. This doesn't necessarily detract much
from its success, and it will be decreasingly
noticeable as the mid-20th century recedes
beyond living memory. As it is, its measured
intervals and Yorkshire imperturbability
mediate nicely between garden landscape
and hall, and between hall and the high and
shiny white modernism of the best of the
outbuildings put up in the 1930s.

Its South American roots seem quite in
harmony with the ethos of Dartington. In
1935 the Elmhirsts set up a trust to manage
the hall and the 1,300 acre estate with all
its outbuildings and activities, from an art
school to conferences, innovative approaches
to land use and a famous progressive co-ed
school, which ran out of time and support
in 1987 after its headmaster and his wife were
discovered being altogether too progressive
in their private lives.

Doddiscombsleigh
DEVON

Five 15th-century stained glass windows, Church of St Michael

Exeter Cathedral has four full windows of
medieval glass, yet this little village with
the big name has five in St Michael, a little
Perpendicular church (much rebuilt in the
19th century) hidden among the wooded
eastern hills of Dartmoor. They are clearly
not by a local craftsman – glass was too
expensive and the call for it too rare for a
small community or group of communities
to support a stained glass workshop. At
any rate, although Devon produced many
painters, from the artists who painted the
screens to Joshua Reynolds, there is no record
that there was ever a stained glass workshop
in Devon. Additionally, the glass is of very
high quality.

The finest narrative sequence of the five is
the east window of three lights in the north
aisle, which illustrates the seven sacraments
running, top to bottom and left to right,
Eucharist, Marriage, Confirmation, Penance,
Ordination, Baptism and Extreme Unction:
a brief lifecycle from birth to death in vivid
action and colour. The central light above
Penance has a large Christ in Majesty made
in 1879 by Clayton and Bell fully in the pre-
Reformation groove and much better than
the normal run of Victorian glass.

One of the windows in the north wall,
again of three lights, shows two saints
flanking the Virgin Mary. Beneath all three
are the coats of arms of the donors. She wears
a red gown and blue mantle and stands,

Henry Moore's Memorial Figure (1945–6), *reclining on the terrace above the grass amphitheatre at Dartington Hall*

hands clasped before her, in the serpentine pose favoured in Gothic stained glass, her hips swaying gently to her left, her shoulders to the right, and her head inclined to the left. She wears a white sash, and the deep cuffs and hem of the mantle are trimmed with gold. The bearded, careworn saint on the right (Paul?) holds a sword, point resting on the ground to make the shape of a cross. The saint on the left has a quill pen in one hand and a chalice with a snake in the other (an attribute of John the Evangelist). He is rendered with the face of a sensitive

intellectual, a philosopher monk, perhaps. He wears a blue gown with a white cloak patterned with gold and falling in a complex and visually satisfying rhythm of folds. The rich colour in the window is reserved for the figures, the coats of arms, and a border to each light with bars of glowing red, blue, leaf green and a dark green with such a kick that artists on canvas hardly used it in large passages of paint until Matisse came on the scene. Otherwise the glass is white, lightly decorated with star and leaf patterns, good white glass and yellow stain (for gold)

Even the humble kitchen table becomes a mighty artefact beneath the circular dome at Lutyens's Castle Drogo, Drewsteignton

being 14th-century inventions, lessening the vibrant colour pitch of the great glass of, let's say, Canterbury, but letting in more light and introducing an appealing note of naturalism.

Drewsteignton
DEVON

A Lutyens castle 900 years late, Castle Drogo

Nine hundred years ago Drogo, or Dru, a Norman lord, bought land a 1,000 feet above sea level and perched on an inaccessible Dartmoor plateau over the gorge of the River Teign. Although he became known by the territorial appellation of Baron Drogo de Teign, somehow he neglected to build a castle on his stretch of blasted heath. That was left to his 20th-century descendant, a shopkeeper called Julius Drewe. Living in Sussex in prosperous retirement founded on the success of his Home and Colonial Stores chain, Drewe conceived the romantic idea that he would buy back the parcel of land on the edge of the 200 foot gorge and rewrite history by building the missing castle in his spiritual homeland. His architect, Edwin Lutyens (1869–1944), gave Drewe his castle, but in spirit it was as much a massive block of 20th-century sculpture as a medieval citadel, a dramatic play of thunderous masses and cavernous spaces hacked out of Dartmoor granite.

Lutyens was an inspired pasticheur, though the pastiche runs to solidly crafted details in the tradition of English vernacular building. He loved wooden dowelling and blacksmith-made hinges and handles turned by carpenters and even built whole Tudor cottages that looked like the real thing. He enjoyed nothing more than to build light-hearted but convincing neo-Georgian houses, like Salutation at Sandwich. In New Delhi the domes on his Viceroy's House look like school-issue solar topis. In 1910, when Drewe asked him to build Castle Drogo, Lutyens wrote to his wife: 'I do wish he didn't want a castle – but just a delicious loveable house with plenty of good large rooms in it.'

Internally Drogo is a house fit for Citizen Kane but without the grossness, a modern statement of ancient values. They laid the foundation stone in 1911, and the castle was ten years in the building. At full throttle the workforce was about a hundred local men, masons, stonecutters, carpenters and labourers, on something over £3 a week. Of course, no ideal home should need 6 foot thick walls or raw granite fireplaces or great wells apparently scooped out of granite to contain stone staircases and lit by gigantic mullioned windows in bays as big as barns. It's the materials Lutyens used and his reputation as an amiable magpie that prevent him from being recognised as the modern master he sometimes was.

The vaulted corridors of Drogo's two ranges, hinged on a circular lobby, suddenly give on to rooms that belong to 'a delicious loveable house': the dining room, the library with a coffered oak ceiling, and the drawing room with an exquisitely moulded plaster ceiling, walls wood panelled or hung with tapestry and family portraits from Drewe's previous house at Wadhurst. But the truest statement of Lutyens's intent, the stomach of

the building, is below stairs, in the servants' quarters. This is cook's domain, her kitchen, pantry and scullery with its thick, barbaric piers. Here are a massive Lutyens-designed chopping block and a gargantuan pestle and mortar, glass-fronted crockery cupboards, and in the kitchen, picking up the circular motif, directly beneath a central glass roof dome, is a monumental, circular, wooden-pegged table of beech, the daylight shining on to it as though it were an altar. Drewe wanted a castle, and he got the lot, including the wooden kitchen sink.

Dunster
SOMERSET

A monument to medieval industry, the Yarn Market, High Street

Dunster is the last plateau in a series of ascents and descents up the Exe valley, a fine street scene at the wild Exmoor extremity of Somerset on the edge of the Brendon Hills. From here it is one more short descent to the sea. At one end of Dunster's winding main street, flanked by ancient buildings, the castle sits on a hill above. At the other is the Yarn Market, an octagonal market cross. The fabled landowning medieval Luttrell family, remembered especially for commissioning the magnificent illustrated psalter now in the British Library, lived in the castle and built the market cross though not, probably, the Luttrell Arms, though they took the building over from the abbots of Cleeve after the dissolution. It became an inn in the 17th century.

George Luttrell built the Yarn Market in 1609. Not grand, like the great market crosses of Ludlow or Bury St Edmunds, it is an edifice of rough-hewn magnificence, with a massive stone central pier rising to a little cupola. The grey-slated roof, splayed at the bottom, is supported by wooden posts set

Edward Burra made his name with paintings of the clip joints and speakeasies of New York, but this big watercolour of Dartmoor painted a year before his death in 1976 is his masterpiece. It hangs in Exeter's Royal Albert Memorial Museum and Art Gallery

into a low stone wall, and the upper part of the roof has triangular gables with dormer windows. It fixes the street handsomely, though as in so many places parked cars spoil the scene. (I notice from my photograph that my own car is parked on a space painted 'keep clear'. Tut.)

Exeter
DEVON

A celebration of Devon by Edward Burra, Royal Albert Memorial Museum and Art Gallery

The gallery doesn't seem proud of Exeter's native genius, Benjamin Robert Haydon, the 19th-century romantic. At any rate, when I visited nothing of his was on show, and I can't say I blame Exeter. The trouble is that nothing much of a good collection was on show either. One measly room is given over to the permanent collection, two are for temporary shows, and the rest to the museum. You don't have to question the

notion of 'world culture' to wonder whether British art couldn't have a bit more space. That said, there is one wonderful piece by Edward Burra (1905–76), an artist for the one-off if ever there was. As a child he had little formal education after developing rheumatic fever and anaemia – illness dogged him all his life – and after an art education at Chelsea Polytechnic and the Royal College of Art he adopted watercolour as his medium so that he could sit down to paint instead of standing at an easel. But if he was feeble physically, there was nothing weak about his painting. He lived in Rye most of his life ('Tinker Bell Towne'), but visits to New York in the 1930s provided his most typical paintings of Harlem streets, bars, strip joints and clip joints, the speakeasies, the stars and the down-and-outs, very like the famous exposés of decadent Berlin after the First World War by German Expressionists like Max Beckmann and Otto Dix, but metamorphosed by Burra into a camp *Guys and Dolls*. Late in life this sardonic observer took up landscape, and *Dartmoor*, a very big watercolour of 1975, is a masterpiece: white boulders on a promontory in the foreground, grey hills like blankets slung over boxes, a silver ribbon of river running from deep space towards the picture plane between coppices of trees, clouds rising behind the hills like volcanic blasts of smoke and a huge grey streak of light. You look at all this waiting for the hand of God to appear from behind a cloud. Before the war Burra exhibited with the Surrealists; this landscape is super-real. (The museum is closed for refurbishment and will re-open in 2010.)

Frome
SOMERSET

Memorials to early deaths in the Church of St John

The successive earls of Cork and of Orrery propagated a formidable lineage. They spawned viscounts and barons, a lord lieutenant of Ireland and Members of Parliament in Ireland and England; they fought in the Napoleonic Wars, the Boer Wars, the First World War, and with the Chindits through Burma in the Second World War. Lord Burlington fits in somewhere, but he merely revolutionised 18th-century taste. There was a vice admiral, a rear admiral and the admiral of the fleet who coordinated the attack on Narvik in 1940. There was a colonel in the Coldstreams who sat as MP for Frome, a governor of Newfoundland, a master of horse and master of the buckhounds. But nobody knows anything much about two young women of the family, the sisters Lucy and Louisa Boyle, daughters of the 8th earl and his wife Isabella. Lucy was born in 1804 and died in 1827; Louisa was born in 1806 and died in 1826. We do surmise that they were much loved, for there could be no other reason in those days for two such young women – children,

almost – to be commemorated in marble sculpted by the eminent royal academician Richard Westmacott (1775–1856).

First impressions of this low, wide parish church are best. Close to it is a mélange of styles from the 12th century to the 16th, which Victorian 'improvements' did nothing to pull together. The best thing in it is Westmacott's carving. His memorial to the young woman embellishes the north transept of St John. He was at his best as a young man, but even past his best he was usually better than anyone else in England. He had already sculpted an effigy of Louisa when she died and was buried in the parish church of the family seat of Marston Bigott near Frome. Now for the tomb of Lucy in St John he carved a large deep relief of the two sisters standing in each others arms. They wear long, classical gowns falling in loose folds, and their hair too is tied back loosely. They peer down into the church as though they're looking for someone they know. Such a composition executed a few years later would probably have been unbearably sugary. As it is, it's a fine, relaxed and touching elegy to blighted youth.

Mells
SOMERSET

Edwin Lutyens war memorial

Little Jack Horner sat in a corner eating his pudding and pie; that's certain. What we didn't know is that the plum he pulled out was the manor of Mells. His descendants, Sir John and Lady Horner (who denied the truth of the nursery rhyme on the grounds that it implied corruption), brought in Edwin Lutyens in 1905 to help with designs for the manor park, a loggia and a music room. In 1907 the Horner's daughter, Katharine, married Raymond Asquith, son of the man who would be prime minister during the war in which Raymond died, and Lutyens was there again to design Raymond's memorial in the church. This is a plinth similar to his Cenotaph, but pompous where the Cenotaph is sublime, with an equestrian sculpture by the horse painter Alfred Munnings.

Finer by far is the small column built into a park wall at Mells. There is no hard evidence that this too was by Lutyens, but Pevsner attributes it to him, and since he did so much other work at Mells the probability is that Pevsner is right. The name of Raymond Asquith appears again, but this time among the other dead from the village, including a Horner. The memorial with its little St George on top of the slender column slaying the dragon should have been smaller or bigger. As it is, it is a little bit lost against an unruly background of trees, but it is a subtle and elegant design.

Minehead
SOMERSET

Francis Bird's other Queen Anne statue, marketplace

The stone saints that can be seen gesticulating from the south front pediment of Wren's St Paul's Cathedral from the Millennium footbridge are the work of Francis Bird (1667–1731). His, too, is the carving of St Paul falling from his horse at the shock of the vision on the road to Damascus that fills the west pediment. His Queen Anne, imperious at the foot of the western steps to the cathedral, is no longer to be seen: it had deteriorated so badly over the next couple of centuries that it was replaced by a copy. It was his most famous work, and his least famous work is another statue of Queen Anne.

Jacob Bancks or Banks, born a Dane, married into the distinguished Luttrells of Dunster Castle, was knighted in 1698

Among the work Edwin Lutyens carried out for his friends, lords of the manor at Mells and descendants of little Jack Horner, is this elegant First World War memorial

as an Englishman and elected Member of Parliament for Minehead. He presented this Queen Anne statue to the parish church in 1719, and it remained there until it was moved to Wellington Square in 1893, when the town was relying wholly on tourism instead of its trade from its fine harbour with the Caribbean. It brings distinction to this little space. Bird's baroque fell out of favour in 1720 – along with Christopher Wren's – when the cognoscenti went mad for Palladian classicism, and Minehead's Anne is a baroque statue featuring a strong naturalistic head above a hieratic rendering of costume in every stitch. Bird shows Anne, on the plump side, undoubtedly plain as she might well be after bearing seventeen children, but with sensitively modulated hands emerging from wide lace cuffs and lightly holding the orb and sceptre. The ringlets of hair, the bows and pearls and the embossed stuff of the queen's gown are finely rendered. A sculptor can't, like a painter, get away with a few swift touches, though he might use an assistant. Since the statue moved to this spot it has inhabited a round, temple-like canopy with its back against the churchyard wall of St Andrew. A low baluster supports four pink Doric columns, and above those a drum supports the dome.

Montacute
SOMERSET

The court of the virgin queen, Montacute House

No safari parks here, no funfairs or kidzone, no adventure castle nor even a pets' corner.

Montacute House stands on the dignity of its Ham Hill stone and venerable retirement years in a quiet corner of Somerset. Building began here in 1588. It was to be the overweeningly splendid house of the Phelps family, whose coat of arms is silver with a chevron between three roses gules with a quartering of gold with a chevron vert charged with three birds' heads silver razed. It was the year of the Armada, and the house was finished in 1601, the year that Shakespeare wrote *Twelfth Night*. Here today, in an occasionally changing display, may be seen Drake in a portrait by an anonymous hand and Shakespeare in the famous Droeshout engraving of a balding clerk that has adorned a thousand collected works. These works belong to the National Portrait Gallery because in the 20th century, deserted by Lord Curzon and his lover Elinor Glyn and standing empty, Montacute was in danger of destruction. The National Trust saved it in 1932, and in 1975 the National Portrait Gallery weighed in with a display of Tudor portraits in the long gallery and adjoining rooms that could hardly be better placed.

Here too is the child who survived being the son of Mary Queen of Scots to become the sixth James of Scotland and the first of England: shrewd grey eyes peer out of his white, eight-year-old face above its white ruff. He was one of nature's politicians like the toad-featured Nicholas Bacon, the lawyer who kept his place in the politburo of Elizabethan England and father of Francis, essayist, philosopher and Lord Chancellor. And, of course, Queen Elizabeth, in daunting finery, bodice blazoned with rubies and pearls, an expressionless mask, a red wig laced with more jewels. In 1975 the National Portrait Gallery firmly believed that it was the work of her house artist George Gower (d.1596), but the more art historians discover, the less they know, and today the portrait is merely 'attributed'. Gower doubtless set down the face, which became the template for later faces of Elizabeth, a template that would make her ageless, both queen and goddess, 'married to England', in the words spoken by Cate Blanchett in her movie role as Elizabeth. It is one of many Armada portraits. It has been cut down at the sides, but there is still a glimpse to the left of ships engaged in the battle. Only Marcus Gheeraerts the Younger painted the queen as an old woman near death.

Montacute is the perfect setting for this and an assembly of these ferret-faced Cecils and Sidneys and Howards, the grit in the oyster that fostered the pearls of Shakespeare and Fletcher and Ben Jonson and Raleigh and Elizabeth herself. For Montacute, like England at the time, is both modest and magnificent. There is an east door wide enough, it is true, to have taken Elizabeth's father and two more besides. Views from east and west fronts command the pavilions, turrets, sculpted façades, English Renaissance regularity, Flemish gables, balustrades, urns and a conservatory. Built 50 yards to the east there is a ha-ha beyond which the cowpats start. A broadside away to the west, the village of Montacute huddles under the folly-crowned sharp hill that the village and the house were named for.

Nynehead
SOMERSET

The Renaissance in ceramic, Church of All Saints

At first sight the grouping of All Saints with Nynehead Court and its garden is one of the prettiest sights in Somerset, and then, inside the church, are two of the most unlikely treasures, ceramic reliefs by the Florentine Renaissance sculptors Luca and Andrea della Robbia.

The church is built of local red sandstone and sits on a mound in friendly conjunction with the house. The churchyard wall to the west overlooks a lovely area of lawn and topiary. The Sanford family, who lived at Nynehead Court in the vale of Taunton Deane from the 16th century to the early 20th, kept a paternal eye on the church, as was the English way, and the ugly 19th-century wheel window with which the family replaced a Perpendicular window in the north chapel when they converted it for use as their own memorial chapel is only one of the many changes they wrought to All Saints, not necessarily beneficial. But they did supply the Rev. Arthur Sanford as vicar in the early 19th century. His privileged standing enabled him to indulge himself with a tour of Italy, and in 1833 he brought back to the church from Florence the della Robbia works, fine Madonna and Child tabernacles, one by Luca (1399–1482), the other by his nephew Andrea (1435–1523).

Luca is a great master on the basis of one work, the *Singing Gallery* of the cathedral in Florence, which now hangs from a wall in the cathedral's museum opposite its companion piece of a couple of years later by Donatello. Donatello is at another level, but Luca's cheerfully singing boys and girls and angels on the front of the gallery were an early sighting of a human and natural approach to religious imagery. Soon afterwards, he discovered a process for glazing terracotta models and placed them everywhere in Florence, even outdoors on the façade of the church of Orsanmichele on the main drag between the duomo and the Pitti Palace. But he also invented the notion of the Madonna with Child glazed in white on a blue background, and because of their sweetness and simplicity these reliefs have never lost their popularity. Nynehead's version shows the Madonna kneeling beside her baby with her hands closed in prayer. She has stretched out her cloak to cover the ground where the child lies, and the blue background is embellished with two lilies, symbols of purity. The della Robbia family joined in to run a Virgin and Child production line. The best of the others was Andrea, and his Madonna and Child in All Saints, if not as inventive as Luca's, is not inferior in lightness of touch, with the mother holding the boy upright and leaning her head against his: a lovely portrait of the girl as mother. Luca della Robbia has a lot to answer for in opening the gates to sugar and spice and all things nice, but though the family's own production did become predictable it never descended to kitsch.

Over Stowey
SOMERSET

Mary Magdalene at the tomb, at St Peter and St Paul

Much-visited Nether Stowey is where Coleridge lived, and the Wordsworths nearby at Alfoxden. Over Stowey lies more secretly on its slope of the Quantocks. St Peter and St Paul's medieval origins have been obliterated by insensitive 19th-century restoration, but in the north aisle Morris installed really good stained glass designed by Edward Burne-Jones (1833–98) of the encounter of Mary Magdalene and the angel at the tomb in 1870, early in the life of William Morris's firm (see Bexleyheath, Southeast). The angel and Mary inhabit one light each of the two-light window, the angel sitting on the edge of the sepulchre, right hand raised in greeting, left hand holding a palm branch, Mary standing, slightly stiff with alarm, holding the casket of spices she has brought to anoint Christ's body. This is the sole drama. There is nothing of the electricity of St Matthew's account of the angel, 'his countenance was like lightning, and his raiment white as snow'. Nothing, in fact, of the snowy whiteness. Burne-Jones's angel is apparelled in gold, his golden locks crowned with a wreath of golden laurel, binding this left-hand panel with Mary on the right, who is golden haired and in a golden gown.

Incidentally, the other glass in the north and south aisles is from the Morris workshop as well, but all of it made after the deaths of Morris himself (1896) and Burne-Jones (1898) from a cache of Burne-Jones designs held in the workshop and used far into the 1920s, when the company finally closed.

Pencarrow House
CORNWALL

The four Misses Molesworth: dolls in a landscape

On the mile-long drive to the house through beech forest, hydrangeas and rhododendrons is a notice advising, 'You are now entering an iron age fort', and sure enough, there are all the deep indentations and turf mounds. Later: 'Slow please, peacocks crossing.' There is a Celtic cross in the grounds, another on the Bodmin road outside. The house itself is merely mid-18th century, plain Palladian, built by Sir John Molesworth, the 4th baronet, and still inhabited by the 16th baronet, Sir William Molesworth-St Aubyn, and his family, but discreetly in quarters around the back. It's a lovely, welcoming house strewn with the toys of childhood in centuries past, but you have to take a guided tour and that means making a nuisance of yourself if you want to linger over the paintings.

Since this is close to Joshua Reynolds heartland, the best of the family portraits is an impressive group by Reynolds, a very fine intact sequence in the dining room, but almost everybody's favourite, from staff to visitors, is the little conversation piece in

the ante-room where the tour ends. It's by Reynolds's inferior in fame, social standing and talent, the Preston painter Arthur Devis (1712–87). Like the young Thomas Gainsborough, he used lay figures to model clothes for the portraits of his sitters, which accounts for the doll-like appearance of his subjects (the Harris Art Gallery in Preston (see Northwest) owns a selection of costumes for the manikins from Devis's kit-box). The Pencarrow painting shows the four Misses Molesworth in a garden overlooking St Michael's Mount. The garden may be fictitious, like many of Devis's settings, or at least transposed. St Michael's Mount only looks fictitious, but at least Devis could paint a convincing sky, with stately clouds sailing by, and trees, and a patchy lawn, something Reynolds couldn't cope with and never tried. The sheen of the silken dresses, of course, is the most important thing in these portraits of four plain girls, one bright blue dress, one steely blue, one silver, one gold, all impeccably rendered. A niece of these four married a cousin and brought the families together in the surviving Pencarrow alliance, Molesworth-St Aubyn.

Plymouth and Plympton
DEVON

Plympton has been swallowed by Plymouth, but Mount Edgcumbe, even though the estate overlooks Plymouth Sound, has not. It's in Cornwall, but is managed by both the Plymouth and the Cornwall councils. All this area though was Joshua Reynolds's stamping ground. Today Plymouth Art Gallery has a fine collection of his work that includes portraits of his father, the headmaster of Plympton grammar school, and his sister Fanny. He was born in Plympton and was often to be found at Saltram House visiting his best friend in boyhood, John Parker, the future Lord Boringdon. His other schoolroom friend was Dick Edgcumbe, later the 2nd Baron Edgcumbe. And the first family to commission family portraits were the Eliots of Port Eliot, St Germans. Lord Eliot would later be a pall-bearer alongside the Duke of Dorset at Reynolds's funeral in St Paul's. Reynolds obviously loved the area, otherwise he would hardly have taken the risk of bringing the acerbic Samuel Johnson to visit, and he returned frequently himself to fulfil commissions from Boringdon and Edgcumbe. So in this one instance I have taken a leaf from the Local Government Act of 1974 and invented an area to cover Reynolds's heartland.

Of course, Francis Drake is Plymouth's most romantic historical figure, although not much remains of Drake, Raleigh or Grenville in this city except streets named after them and the legend of Drake's game of bowls on Plymouth Hoe, which, it is said, he nonchalantly insisted on finishing when news of the approach of the Armada was brought to him. The Plymouth he knew was burned to the ground under bombing attacks by the Luftwaffe, and although a few narrow Elizabethan streets survive near the harbour, the rebuilt city is an urban disaster area. Plympton, though, retains its character, and Saltram House, with its great views east to west over the Sound, has very fine Robert Adam interiors as well as the Reynolds's Parker family portraits.

Early Reynolds portraits of his own family, City Art Gallery

Joshua Reynolds's portrait of Charles Rogers, a customs officer born in Soho, hangs at the entrance to the first-floor gallery. Rogers had befriended Reynolds and many of Reynolds's friends, and became a Fellow of the Royal Society and a collector specialising mostly in drawings and engravings. Reynolds (1723–92) painted him in 1777, a prosperous Londoner in a fur-faced, velvety red jacket and a striped yellow waistcoat. Rogers died in 1784 and left his collection to his brother-in-law, William Cotton. Two generations down the line, William Cotton III moved to Ivybridge having added many pieces of Reynoldsiana to the collection, which he donated in 1850 to Plymouth Proprietary Library, which in turn gave it to Plymouth Museum and Art Gallery in 1916.

Among the collection was a portrait by Reynolds of his father, the Rev. Samuel Reynolds, which looks like an act of filial piety and is believed to be posthumous, which would account for its oddly insubstantial look. Samuel and his wife Theophila had eleven children, so he was probably relieved when Joshua went off to London at the age of seventeen to be apprenticed to the (boring) portrait painter Thomas Hudson. Samuel was also notoriously absent minded, so perhaps he just didn't notice. Joshua fell out with the boring Hudson after a couple of years and returned to Plympton, where he painted both the portrait of his father and of his sister Frances (Fanny), both of them, probably, in 1746. Fanny is not a beauty, but she is beautiful, her dark, round-necked dress and dark hair in a light fringe merging with the darkness of the background and framing the unadorned pallor of her face and throat as her brown eyes gaze dreamily at a point beyond her brother's easel. She never married, though Samuel Johnson, who came to know her when she moved to Leicester Fields (now Square) to keep house for her brother, loved her dearly and she returned his affection. Joshua, though, was unable to sustain love for any individual woman, and that included Fanny, because in about 1779 he ejected her from his house, though he sustained her in a house in Dover Street.

Joshua Reynolds, born on the outskirts of Plymouth to a parson, the Rev. Samuel Reynolds, painted members of his family in 1746 after he had fallen out with his tutor in London and returned home. This is his portrait of his father, in Plymouth City Art Gallery

Reynolds's lifelong friend, at
Saltram House, Plympton

It all began in Plymptom for Joshua
Reynolds. He was born here and went to
Plympton Grammar School where his father
was headmaster, and his main patronage as
he embarked on his career as a professional
artist came from the Parker family of Saltram
House over the road. To Reynolds, John
Parker of Saltram House was the boy-next-
door. It was Parker who, when he inherited
Saltram and was created Lord Boringdon,
commissioned the fine Robert Adam interior,
and it was Boringdon and his wife Theresa
who serially commissioned family portraits
from Reynolds. There are eleven in Saltram
House, including those of Boringdon and
Theresa.

The painting of John Parker is quite clearly
the portrait of a friend. Reynolds painted
the portrait, which hangs in the morning
room (not Adam, but charming), some time
in the 1760s after Parker had been elevated
to the peerage, but its informality makes it
seem more akin to early Gainsborough than
standard Reynolds. Boringdon leans casually
against a five-barred gate with a gun in the
crook of his arm, his rustic features haloed by
a patch of sky showing through a gap in the
trees.

St Germans
CORNWALL

Monument to Edward Eliot,
by Michael Rysbrack

The parish church of St Germans was the
cathedral of Cornwall. It was not named,
as was usual in the far west, for a local saint
but instead for Germanus, a 5th-century
Christian bishop of Auxerre who came to
Britain to combat Pelagianism, the argument
that held that man could be saved by good

works and that was thus condemned by the
Church as foul heresy. In 1040 the see passed
on, eventually, to Exeter, and St Germans
became an Augustinian priory. Church and
village both belonged to God until Henry
VIII broke with Rome, passed the priory
church to the village and secularised the rest.
The Eliot family, local gentry, bought the
estate in 1564, renamed it Port Eliot and have
been there ever since. The rambling house in
its landscape shaped by Humphrey Repton
now belongs to Peregrine Eliot, 10th Earl of
St Germans, is private, is not a port but is on
an estuary off Plymouth Sound.

What mainly remains of the Romanesque
priory church is a mighty west doorway
with seven orders of arches carved with
abstract designs and flanked by two towers.
Just inside, beneath the north tower, is the
monument of 1722 by Michael Rysbrack
(1694–1770), a complete break in the culture,
though in the way of these things, the rough
granite of the builders enhances the riotously
carved marble. It is the grandest exposition
of baroque statuary in the region, with
light from a tower window above spilling
dramatically over the tempestuous marble
sarcophagus on which the figure of Edward
Eliot, the rich and indolent owner of Port
Eliot, the house built in St Germans on the
site of the Augustinian priory, reclines in
the costume of a Roman general against
the background of a polychrome marble
pyramid, and a woman sits holding an
open book, a cloak thrown over her head.
She turns towards him in mourning,
revealing a noble Greek profile, as a group
of putti disport themselves at the top of the
monument.

It is the absurd, mannered and vividly
composed and carved work of a sculptor
born and trained in Antwerp and newly
arrived in England (1720), possibly because
after the first frenzy of the Counter-
Reformation had burned itself out the

This bronze version of Barbara Hepworth's Epidauros *on the Malakoff at St Ives is surely one of the finest-sited, and its visual impact belies its relatively small size*

demand for great sculptural projects had declined. He found a ready market and a home in England where, in the words of Horace Walpole, 'Gothic tombs owed their chief grandeur to rich canopies, fretwork, and abundance of small niches and trifling figures'. The Catholic sumptuousness of Rysbrack's work quickly established ready appreciation among Protestants and his co-religionists alike in a nation where 'statuaries' were more highly rated than 'face painters'.

St Ives
CORNWALL

Two Hepworth sculptures from one death, on the Malakoff and in St Ia

Barbara Hepworth visited Epidauros in 1954 to recover from the death of her son Paul, an RAF pilot whose jet crashed in 1953. The purity of the landscape appealed to her, just as she was attracted to the ruggedness of her native West Riding moors and the Penwith peninsula with its scattered menhirs and iron age field patterns. She carved the first *Pierced Form (Epidauros)*, to give it its full title, in 1960, from a block of guarea, a tropical hardwood, polished it deep brown outside and painted it in sensuous contrast white inside.

So when she adapted the piece for casting in bronze some of her admirers were dismayed by the loss of subtlety and human sensitivity that she herself valued. But in bronze on the Malakoff, a small terrace at the top of Tregenna Hill with a panoramic view of the harbour and St Ia, the parish church, and over the sea to Godrevy lighthouse, *Epidauros* takes on a different quality. Hepworth had drilled through the wood carving in a spiral movement – it is more enclosed, more womblike than the bronze – but because of the tensile strength of the metal she has opened up the hole further and, though it is quite a small piece, on its tall plinth the changing light on its dark surface and the view through the sculpture give it a magnetically dominating quality, and it becomes an outdoor piece, a town piece, a form that suggests the shape of the harbour and the curve of the bay.

St Ia contains her immediate response to Paul's death, a *Madonna and Child* of 1954. She had made wonderful figurative pieces as a young woman before the war, but she came to St Ives in 1939, and through her then husband, Ben Nicholson, and their friend the Russian émigré sculptor Naum Gabo (1890–1977), she had refined her work into abstraction. She no longer needed to make human figures to express her humanity. Instead, abstraction enabled her to expand beyond that into something more timeless, so the late and sole return to a little figurative group is a failure. (See also Liverpool, Northwest, and Wakefield, Northeast.)

St Neot

CORNWALL

15th- and 16th-century stained glass in fifteen windows, Church of St Neot

By the River Loveney in St Neot is a holy spring, doubtless created in the normal fashion by the patron saint of church and village striking the ground with his staff. St Neot, though, did exist. He was a 9th-century monk of Glastonbury, who, according to the *Anglo-Saxon Chronicle*, a collection of more or less contemporary documents, came as a hermit to this place 'ten milestones from St Petroc's monastery [Bodmin]'. His other claim to fame is that King Alfred visited him here, and Neot chastised him for his godless ways, although before the decisive Battle of Edington in 878 Neot appeared to Alfred in a dream to assure him of victory. His sainthood could hardly be denied after that, and Christianity, which had been clinging

on in the face of pagan Danes, has never wavered in the hallowed spot of St Neot where the ground remains thick with ancient granite crosses, one of them right outside the church's south porch.

Tradition here isn't a PR gimmick; it lasts. The current patron of the church, Richard Grylls, who commissioned fine engraved glass by Arthur Bradley to close off the belfry in the west tower from the nave, is a descendant of the 15th-century Colway and Tubbes families, who donated some of the fifteen windows full of stained glass that, remarkably, remain. There was a thorough but careful restoration in 1830, but around half of the glass is original.

There is a lovely window in the south wall (the top lights are original) detailing the story of Noah, one light showing him in a red tunic and jolly green hat aboard a ship such as a man like Caxton might have taken sail on for Bruges. In the north wall is the story of St Neot himself, up to the time of his temporary departure from Bodmin on a pilgrimage to Rome, where an angelic-looking, golden-crowned pontiff receives him graciously. The donors of this window were the young men of the parish, another window was given by the young women, and a third by the wives, something that takes on a deeper significance since the publication of Eamonn Duffy's study of a north Devon parish, *Morebath*, showing how deeply rooted pre-Reformation communities were in the life of the church, splitting up into separate clubs of maidens and youths collecting money for anything from plate to vestments for the priest to celebrate requiem mass. Filling windows with stained and painted glass by master craftsmen must have been a huge tax on St Neot, and one that required a faith almost unimaginable to us.

Shepton Mallet
SOMERSET

A magnificent timber roof, at the Church
of St Peter and St Paul in the town centre

Across the lane from St Peter and St Paul
is an art school and cultural centre. Many
people apparently don't like its stark
modernism, but I think it sets the church
off well. I asked nicely and was given willing
permission to climb to the first floor, where
large plate glass windows give on to a fine
close view of the church's 14th-century
west tower. But the real reason for visiting
Shepton is to look at one of the great
timber roofs of England. Nikolaus Pevsner
was clearly a great fan of English timber
construction, and he revels in it where it is at
its best, in East Anglia and Somerset. It may
be that this is the key to his admiration for
the pure undecorated modernist architecture
of the 20th century. Anyway, he wrote in the
North Somerset volume of the *Buildings of*
England about the roof of St Peter and St
Paul in his workmanlike prose better than
anyone had before or is likely to do ever
again. I won't make the attempt. Here is
Pevsner:

And then the roof, the most glorious of all the
wagon-roofs of England, solid and trustwor-
thy, the back of a strong and nimble animal
and yet extremely richly wrought. There are
350 panels and over 300 bosses, every one of
them of a design not repeated in any other.
The motifs of the panels are not in themselves
eminently imaginative – quatrefoils of all
kinds, wheels of three mouchettes or of four

mouchettes [curving motifs], and so on, but in
their totality they appear as close and dense as
the foliage of an arbour. The principal beams,
not otherwise recognisable in a wagon-roof, are
given angel figures at their springing points.

Street
SOMERSET

Phillip King's moment of
truth, Clarks village

This is not the most propitious site for a past
president of the Royal Academy to show his
work, a patch of tree-shaded grass on public
land outside the car park for Clarks Shoes
industrial and shopping estate. It's off the
A39 just as a motorist has negotiated the
last roundabout in Street and put his foot
down for Glastonbury. The past president in
question is Phillip King (b.1934), who until
2005 reigned in a turbulent period over an
academy split into pitched camps of war.
Born in Tunisia, King came to England in
1945, and his parents had him educated at
Millfield School in Street, which may have
some bearing on the placing of these two
sculptures.

King's two pieces here descend from
his work after he saw the international
exhibition Documenta 2 at Kassel in 1960.
He had obtained an MA in modern
languages at Cambridge University before
studying at St Martin's School of Art under
Anthony Caro for a year in 1957–8, but
Kassel was his moment of truth. For King,
the scale and fearlessness of Americans like
Jackson Pollock and Mark Rothko wiped out
Britain's tortured, inward-looking post-war
sculpture. He threw away his own tortured
clay and began to work with coloured plastic,
painted sheet metal, glass fibre, ceramics
and laminates, producing large, declamatory
abstractions with highly unsculptural titles
like *Tra-La-La* (pale blue, pink and mauve)

All aboard: in this fine 15th-century glass in the church
at St Neot, Noah indicates the dove flying back with
an olive leaf, showing that the flood waters have
'abated from the face of the earth' (Genesis)

or *And the Birds Began to Sing* (red and black) and lately *A Swell Day for Dolphins* (uncoloured bronze). The titles in all his work are little unexploded bombs of implicit meaning. All his work yields layers within visual layers, but primarily they are gravity-defying lyrical abstractions.

Of the two pieces at Street, both steel, one is called *Steps*, and despite its great jauntily tipped wedges of steel and bendy linking steel ribbons is sad to look at now, disgracefully neglected and rusting. The other work, *Diamond* (1972), is still in reasonable condition. It is a 21 feet high silvery structure, contained within a rigid, diamond-shaped framework of steel bars, and within that eight rectangular plates are each tipped on to a corner, irregular diamonds poised in fearful asymmetry like acrobats, in two rows, one above another, with thin flanges of steel curving dynamically upwards towards the apex so that even this apparently static sculpture suggests exhilarating movement and reveals a still more vivid complexity as you move around it. Ask not 'What the hell is that?' but 'What can it do for me?'

Wells
SOMERSET

Wells, which sits at the foot of the Mendips, is a town with a population of only around 10,000, yet with a cathedral with the finest west front in the land, covered with about 400 13th-century sculptures and a clock with its original Decorated face of 1390, pre-Copernicus, showing the earth at the centre of the universe. As well as this, it has a parish church with one of the showpiece Somerset towers. Near the cathedral, Vicar's Close is a practically unaltered 14th-century street of stone sets lined by stone-built houses. The bishop's palace is 13th century, the little marketplace, presumably, older, though its finest buildings are the 18th-century town hall, the 19th-century market hall, now the post office, and Bishop Bekynton's Pennyless Porch, a modest name for the monumental 15th-century gateway leading from marketplace to the great cathedral green. At the high street end of the marketplace is an 18th-century conduit, and halfway along the north pavement is the plaque commemorating Mary Rand's Olympic long jump gold medal of 1966.

Two Caroline coats of arms, Church of St Cuthbert

Royal coats of arms in churches tend to go unseen, as boring as they are big, lent a touch of celebrity only by age. Henry VIII introduced them as a subtle reminder that his royal reach extended to the church as well. Mary I, of course, got rid of them, and they never reappeared in numbers until the Stuarts. The three Georges have lots, there is the occasional one for Victoria, and even Elizabeth II is occasionally modestly celebrated.

Most of the best are Caroline, and of these St Cuthbert has one for each Charles. They are equally florid, use the same range of colours – gold and silver and primary colours of red, blue, green and black – and each is a glorious ornament. It is recorded on the Charles I arms, which must have been concealed by the congregation during the supremacy of Cromwell, that they were presented 'at the cost of Robert Thomas and William Mills, Churchwardens, 1631'. The inscription on Charles II's reads, 'This armes set up when King Charles the Second was proclaimd in the 12 yeare of hs raine 1660,' which, if this wasn't politics, would be a mealy-mouthed way of brushing the rule of Cromwell out of history (1648/9 was, of course, the year of Charles I's execution). Both sets of arms are full-bloodedly regal though quite small, each of them with the arms contained within a circular scroll surmounted by a visored helmet and crown and supported by the lion and unicorn, all within a richly carved tabernacle. They sit especially well in this church, so full of light and under an angel roof not especially wonderful in detail but as clamorously painted as a joyful organ peal.

Sculpture from the cathedral west front, Wells and Mendip Museum

The west front of Wells Cathedral was designed as an architectural and sculptural spectacular, like Peterborough and Lincoln. Peterborough is wider, Lincoln is later, Wells is more poetic, set before a greensward in a little market town. At 147 feet, it is much wider than the body of the church, effectively a stone screen like a massive reredos, and it displays around 176 full-length standing figures, forty-nine Bible narrative scenes, thirty half-length angels in quatrefoil niches, the Virgin and Child in the tympanum above the central door, a frieze of the resurrection of the dead across the top of the screen and, higher still, Christ in Majesty in the gable. Someone has bothered to count up to nearly 400 figures still extant. It constitutes an immense feat of production, involving an incalculable number of specialist masons working over a period of about twenty years from 1220.

The originals of several pieces are now in the Wells and Mendip Museum, too fragile to go back on to the west front. There are two angels, one of them holding a crown in each hand, a famous scene depicting Christ among the doctors and carved in two blocks, one half to sit on the face of the cathedral, the other at right angles on one of the six giant buttresses. And there is the bottom half of the Christ in Majesty (the top was too badly mutilated to do anything with

and the restorers have had to invent a new top half for the reproduction in the gable). They are not imaginatively presented. A graphic mapping the sculptures on the west front would help comprehension of the full scheme, as would photographs of the sculptures remaining on the west front. But then the cathedral is there a few paces across the lawn for checking, and the pieces in the museum yield the geekish satisfaction of being able to spot the difference in the kind of stone the masons used and make a shot at guessing why – again, more informative placard information would be a reasonable idea. As it is, a booklet on sale in the museum discloses that the Christ was carved in limestone quarried in Doulting, a village just to the east of nearby Shepton Mallet, and downhill all the way to Wells – the cathedral building itself is extensively built with Doulting stone (which is still being quarried after 800 years). The angels were carved in Dundry, a creamy limestone from a village further away, in the northern Mendips close to Bristol. Close to, it is obvious that the Christ is carved in the coarser textured stone and that the stone for the angels is smoother.

Either way, it is clear that the sculpture is better seen as an ensemble. The bottom half of the Christ shows that its broad folds of drapery were nicely judged to be seen from something like a hundred feet below. The rest – kings and bishops, sinners and saints, knights and ladies – constitutes a rich display of sculpture and architecture in communion, incomparably the best of its sort in England, a testament to the will and ability of those forgotten craftsmen.

Wells's modern heroine, Mary Rand, won the long jump gold medal at the Tokyo Olympics of 1964. This brass memorial set in the pavement of Wells market square measures out the length of her winning leap

Mary Rand's gold marked out in brass, Wells Market Square

People constantly walk over the brass plaque set in the pavement. Occasionally a couple will stop and pause to read and discover that it has been set there to celebrate the accomplishment of Mary Rand, born Mary Denise Bignal in Wells in 1940, at the Tokyo 1964 Olympiad. Running into a headwind of 1.6 metres a second she leapt 6.76 metres, or 22 feet 2.25 inches, to win the gold medal and, incidentally, to break the world record. As a schoolgirl from a council house she was said to run and swim faster and jump further than any of the boys of her age in Wells. At the age of sixteen she was invited for the experience to the Olympics training camp in Brighton and beat the British high jump aspirants at their own discipline. She never looked back, and having won the Tokyo gold, she went on to win silver in the pentathlon and bronze as one of the quartet in the 4 × 100 metres relay.

Wells took Mary Rand to its heart. Assuming the brass plaque as a symbol for the long jump take-off board, there follows a sequence of Olympic rings interspersed alternately with the cross of St Andrew (the cathedral's saint) and the Tudor rose of England measuring out 22 feet 2.25 inches. The plaque itself spells out her golden achievement in forty-two words, economically arranged in seven rows clamped between what typesetters would call rules, long thick lines. The lettering is in unostentatious capitals without serifs, but with enough quirkiness between letters to make them lively to the eye – a slight tapering here and there, some letters marginally taller than others, a low slung bar in each letter A, the hint of a wobble in the Ss. When Mary left her husband, Sid Rand, to live with the American decathlete Bill Toomey in the US, her mother wrote to her: 'They have put your jump in the Market Square. It's all drawn out on the pavement, outside the shops so that people always see it. It's got the cathedral emblems on it and it's beautiful how they've done it.'

Westonzoyland
SOMERSET

A death trap with an angelic roof, St Mary

On 5 July 1685 the Duke of Monmouth climbed the tower of St Mary, Bridgwater, and looked out across the Somerset Levels.

Six miles away he could see the even finer tower of St Mary in the obscure little marsh village of Westonzoyland. In this village lay Lord Feversham and the cavalry of James II's army, waiting for Monmouth's next move at the head of his rebel force. Early the following morning, under cover of mist and darkness, 'King' Monmouth moved across the watery terrain and attacked, but his army of farm labourers and miners from the Mendips was quickly routed and Monmouth himself was executed. This was the last time a battle was fought on English soil, and it is celebrated in pictures on the pub sign of the Sedgemoor inn adjacent to the church. Five hundred rebels were imprisoned in the church overnight. The next day, writes Macaulay, 'the bells of Weston Zoyland and Chedzoy rang joyously, while the soldiers sang and rioted on the moor amidst the corpses'. He does not say whether the imprisoned 500, in the knowledge of their certain death, took comfort from the angels roosting in the roof of St Mary. It seems unlikely; they were Puritans.

Westonzoyland is one of the community of villages that grew up on little islands in the watery marshes. As the marshes were reclaimed and turned into alluvial farmland, the villages prospered and most built church towers, which, as a group with the other great towers of Somerset, are the most glorious in England with bell openings carved in intricate similarity to the Mughal marble screens of the Taj Mahal. But Westonzoyland has a timbered roof that, if not as good as the great roof of Wymondham in Norfolk (see East Anglia), is at least as good as most of the great East Anglian roofs and is one of the two or three noblest in Somerset. It is a medium-pitched, tie-beam roof with glorious bosses beneath the main beams and kingposts above, with more bosses like stars among the rafters. Between each side of each kingpost is an intricately carved tracery screen. Angels appear to support the kingposts, and there are more angels between the kingposts running west to east along the nave.

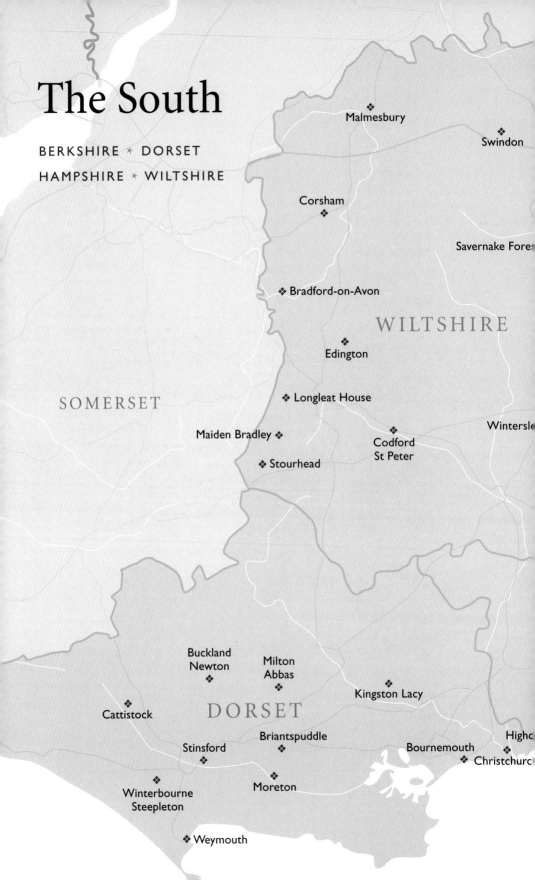

The South

BERKSHIRE * DORSET
HAMPSHIRE * WILTSHIRE

Malmesbury

Swindon

Corsham

Savernake Fores:

Bradford-on-Avon

WILTSHIRE

Edington

SOMERSET

Longleat House

Maiden Bradley

Wintersl

Codford
St Peter

Stourhead

Buckland
Newton

Milton
Abbas

Kingston Lacy

Cattistock

DORSET

Briantspuddle

Highc

Stinsford

Bournemouth

Christchurc

Winterbourne
Steepleton

Moreton

Weymouth

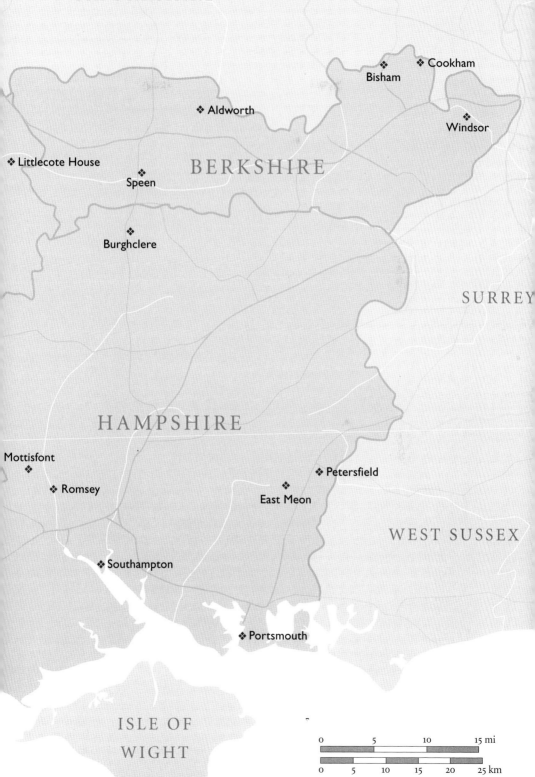

OXFORDSHIRE

Cookham

Bisham

Aldworth

Windsor

BERKSHIRE

Littlecote House

Speen

Burghclere

SURREY

HAMPSHIRE

Mottisfont

Petersfield

Romsey

East Meon

WEST SUSSEX

Southampton

Portsmouth

ISLE OF
WIGHT

0   5   10   15 mi

0   5   10   15   20   25 km

Aldworth

BERKSHIRE

Nine medieval stone giants, Church of St Mary

There seems scarcely room for a congregation. The giants under their canopies in this famous but still out-of-the-way village dominate the church. The nine effigies lie in rows down the north wall, in the nave arcade, and along the south wall of the aisle. The De la Beche family were lords of the manor, and they weren't going to let anyone forget it. One of the nine, Sir Philip de la Beche, the third of three Sir Philips, was reputed to have been 7 feet tall. His pose is innovatory; necessity, perhaps, was the mother of invention. He has his crossed legs drawn up to fit into his canopy, and he half turns into the church as he raises himself with the weight of his body supported on an elbow – at least, it would be if the arm hadn't been broken off. All of these monuments are badly defaced. The nine statues were carved between 1300 and 1350. Philip, one of the latest, died in 1336, by which time the yew tree in the churchyard, which to this day survives, just, was already around 300 years old.

From Sir Robert de la Beche, knighted by Edward I in 1278, to Sir Philip and his brother Sir John, who died in 1337, the affairs of the men of the family are practically a social and political history of the period: landowners in and around Aldworth, sheriffs of Berkshire and Oxfordshire, Members of Parliament as knights of the shire, soldiers on campaigns in France and against the Scots, collecting expenses for guarding prisoners, and one of them constable of the Tower of London. Sir Philip's father and possibly all three brothers fought for the rebel Duke of Lancaster against Edward II and were defeated at the Battle of Boroughbridge in 1322. All of them

were imprisoned, but all were pardoned in 1327 and restored to full honours. They were fortunate; Lancaster was beheaded.

Aldworth sits high up and remote on the chalk Downs near the prehistoric Ridgeway, so high up that the villagers had to dig the well more than 370 feet deep to reach water. Abingdon, where there was an important statuaries' workshop, lies about 10 miles to the north. Its most famous mason, Alexander of Abingdon, was one of that select band of craftsmen who, during the reign of Edward I, was decreed to possess such high and necessary skill that in 1291 he was designated *le imagour* or *le imagineur*. It seems likely from the quality of the two earliest Aldworth figures that Alexander designed them. Lady Joan de la Zouche, wife of the first Sir Philip, has the drape of her dress carved with the full elegance of this age of chivalry in a style quite close to Alexander's figure of Queen Eleanor, once part of Waltham Cross and now in the Victoria & Albert Museum, London. Both she and her daughter-in-law, Lady Isabella de Elmridge, turn slightly inwards to the aisle with a touch of warm naturalism. So too does Lady Joan's son, the second Philip, lying softly at the east of the south aisle as though asleep, his head on a thick pillow and rolling slightly to the side, visor raised, hand on sword. This ruined figure is my favourite, but I suspect I was seduced by the ancient sunlight falling on the old stone in its cobwebbed niche.

Bisham

BERKSHIRE

Hoby chapel with a memorial to Elizabeth I's cousin, All Saints

All Saints is beautifully set on the Thames, and there are prominent notices warning anglers not to fish from the churchyard, which, of course, immediately excludes

Christ and the disciples, but then, this is the Church of England, not some peasant outfit. Anyway, it's a good place to sit and read the paper while the key-holder finishes breakfast. The tower is old and handsome, the rest of the church mostly 19th-century restoration, but the Hoby chapel is special.

It illustrates another recurring and uncomfortable fact of life bequeathed to the church down the ages: the class system persisted all the way to heaven. The rich could buy their way in rather more easily than the biblical camel passing through the eye of a needle. Henry VIII granted Sir Philip Hoby the Bisham estate after he had abolished the abbey. Sir Philip began to build a mansion (a Sport England training centre now) almost immediately, and when he died in 1558 his half-brother, Sir Thomas, finished it. They lie together in effigy on a tomb chest of alabaster. This is the first example in England of the effigies each shown propped on an elbow, fist supporting head as though in life, an educated reference to the ancient Etruscan tomb sculpture that English merchants and travellers in Italy had seen and that developed into a convention. For as Bosola says in Webster's *The Duchess of Malfi* (1614):

> My trade is to flatter the dead, not the
>   living;
> I am a tomb-maker ...
> ... Princes' images on their tombs
> Do not lie, as they were wont, seeming to
>   pray
> Up to heaven; but with their hands under
>   their cheeks,
> As if they died of the tooth-ache.

The several other Hoby monuments are not exactly beautiful either, but splendid in that rich, rigid Tudor fashion. The astonishing centrepiece is Jacobean, a tall marble obelisk crowned by a red heart and resting on a cube of alabaster with decorative friezes above and below, and at the very bottom a stand, a little like a large, elaborate footstool. Sir Edward Hoby, constable of Queenborough Castle, erected this in 1605 in memory of his wife Margaret Carey, cousin of Queen Elizabeth I (who visited them at Bisham Abbey in 1592). It has, around the base of the obelisk, the Carey symbol, four swans carved with a high degree of realism in plaster. The mysterious combination of Tudor richness in the plinth, poetry in the red-beaked swans, ancient austerity in the obelisk and touching sentimentality in the heart lift this piece quite out of the ordinary.

Bournemouth
DORSET

A window on Victorian taste, the Russell-Cotes Museum, East Cliff

When Sir Merton Russell-Cotes, former mayor of Bournemouth, died in 1921 he left the shrine of his collections, East Cliff House, to the town as the Russell-Cotes Museum. Now even the museum itself feels like a museum piece. Although his shopping expeditions took Russell-Cotes and his wife all over the world to buy items for his collection, a unifying film of Victorianism lies like gauze over the furniture, bric-a-brac and paintings by such luminaries as Alma Tadema, Lord Leighton, Albert Moore and Evelyn de Morgan, with their milk-and-water Pre-Raphaelitism. The collections offer a snapshot view of entrepreneurial middle-class values of the late 19th century – a memorial to Victorian energy, confidence, enthusiasm, cash and awesomely bad taste. Since I first saw it in 1972 someone has had the bright idea of clearing a space for a school room, and there's a café and a shop, so the closeted intensity of the place has been dissipated, but room by packed room it is still good.

You feel that Russell-Cotes bought the pictures because they were there, but that his real enthusiasm was for travel. He visited the orient, then rapidly being demystified, and there toured China, Japan and Ceylon. He sailed to Australia and the Americas, and in Europe he delved into Finland, France and Italy. He bought voraciously and without any sense of pattern and shipped home armour and metalwork, Noh masks, porcelain, a Buddhist shrine, *ukiyo-e* woodblock prints, carved ivories and a set of Sèvres to put with his Bristol Delft, Royal Crown Derby, Swansea and Worcester pottery, and Doulton.

He dispatched from foreign parts Moorish door arches and Florentine doors to hang in East Cliff House. He made collections of stamps, shells, stuffed animals, bits of rock and butterflies. He was a friend of the actor-manager Henry Irving, who visited him to admire the collections, and he added a little Irving collection: the great man's make-up box, his black costume for Hamlet and the skull prop for lamenting Yorick, a lock of Ellen Terry's hair, cameos of Irving and Terry, and the prescient Bradford bill announcing Irving's farewell performance – he died in Bradford that week after a tear-jerking performance of Becket, which he himself had adapted from Tennyson.

Russell-Cotes built the house in 1894 to celebrate his year as mayor, and he built it beside the Royal Bath Hotel from which he had made his fortune. The front high above the beach has a nondescript seaside exoticism, with salt and pepperpot turrets sitting on the first-floor verandah canopy. The roof is set with a coffin-shaped glass dome, which illuminates a deep atrium, and at the bottom of this well is a little fountain in a mosaic inlay that shows the sun rising and setting, a motif that had taken his fancy in Japan and adapted to make it eternally Bournemouth.

Bradford-on-Avon

WILTSHIRE

10th-century Saxon angels, Church of St Laurence

Gustave Courbet, the realist's realist, remarked once: 'I cannot paint an angel because I've never seen one.' He spoke for the times, his and ours. Pier-Paolo Pasolini came close in the Annunciation scene in his film of St Matthew's Gospel, with a fantastic angel, blonde hair streaming like a pennant on a hot windless day while Mary sits in her hovel with sweat beading her upper lip. But Pasolini was a Marxist making movie magic. The masons who carved the angels at Bradford-on-Avon had seen the real thing.

That, anyway, is how it seems looking at them from a distance of a thousand years, though we know these craftsmen worked to orders, following an iconographic scheme. Probably these two 5 foot long angels were originally part of a big rood, not necessarily in this tiny church. In its deep valley plunging to the River Bradford is a palimpsest of England, starting by the river with the 10th-century Saxon Church of St Laurence, then the mostly 14th-century parish church, Holy Trinity (and possibly, the remains of an 8th-century church beneath that), a 14th-century tithe barn as big as a church, from the 17th century a pub and a Baptist chapel, each serving the needs of a working class alienated from the ways and religion of their masters, a scatter of medieval houses near the marketplace, terraces of Georgian houses and a big handsome cloth mill of the 19th century. Among all this St Laurence was lost for centuries until the vicar of Holy Trinity discerned in the schoolhouse opposite the signs of a former church. Restorers removed the extension of the schoolhouse that abutted on the south nave wall and door and re-converted the one-up one-down cottage that had been the chancel.

It is, like so many of these remains of ancient faith, moving. It is very small, plain, understated and powerful, with a nave almost twice as high as it is wide and a tiny round-arched doorway leading to the chancel, where recently the church raised an altar built from carved Saxon remains. And then there are the two angels high up on the wall separating nave from chancel, having lost detail through the passing years but carved with the authority of belief and still showing the evidence of Byzantine influence transmuted through the scriptoriums of Winchester.

Briantspuddle
DORSET

War memorial by Eric Gill, ¼ mile west of the crossroads

In this patch of thatch and whitened Dorset mud beside the River Piddle a lot of original Briantspuddle survives, but 400 yards to the west of the crossroads in the hamlet of Bladen Valley is a cosily amusing 1920s reinterpretation of Dorset vernacular, pink-and yellow-washed cottages with thatches like pie coverings. Macdonald (Max) Gill built some of them, grouped around a green below a wooded slope and obviously inspired by the old woman who lived in a shoe. On the green at the focal point of the composition is a war memorial by Max's better known elder brother, Eric.

Eric Gill (1882–1940) had served the last few months of the First World War as a driver at an RAF transport camp near Blandford, but his true war service was post-war: carving memorials to the fallen. This is one of the best, a tall, lichen-covered cross of Portland stone with a figure of Christ on the north face and a Madonna and Child in a niche somewhat suggestive of the stable in Bethlehem on the south. Christ stands rigid as a guardsman and presses a downward pointed sword to his body with one hand while the other is raised in blessing; both show the deeply incised stigmata. On the other side the infant Christ is a nicely observed baby, half-asleep in his mother's lap with his mouth to her nursing breast, though the sculpture is flawed because breast and baby don't meet: it looks like a problem with the shape of the block of stone that Gill failed to resolve. Gill's finest works were his elegant and shocking erotic woodcuts, his best abstraction the wonderful letter carving, but this Briantspuddle cross puts almost all rural First World War memorials to shame.

Buckland Newton
DORSET

An early carving of Christ, in the Church of the Holy Rood

Above the vale of the Cerne giant, 180 feet long and 1,800 years old, is a sculpture much smaller, tantalisingly mysterious and incomparably more splendid, an uncompromisingly savage ideograph readable as Christ in Majesty. It's tucked away inside Holy Rood, moved from the exterior, like so many carvings in Dorset, to save it from erosion. Experts say it is Merovingian, which means 7th or 8th century; others speculate that it is German. Either way, it fits. Benedict Biscop brought Merovingian stonemasons from France in the 8th century to build and decorate the stone churches of Jarrow and Monkwearmouth (see Jarrow, Northeast). The Merovingian dynasty was Frankish, and Franks and Germans crossed each others' paths frequently and bloodily and no doubt the cultures cross-fertilised.

The Buckland Newton Christ is 'primitive' in the usage that we now tend to define edgily with the quotation marks – that is, the forms

This dynamic carving of Christ the King in the church at Buckland Newton is probably 8th century, and possibly Merovingian, a western European dynasty some of whose masons came to England to work on the abbeys at Monkwearmouth and Jarrow

are even more brutally abstracted than in the Romanesque that succeeded. No doubt it was equally subject to fitting in closely with architectural forms. The most remarkable reduction of form in this Christ is the head, of which the bottom half is a semi-sphere, like a toy boat, with huge, oval eyes extending beyond the upward-curving line of the jaw and arrowing into a jug-handle ear on the right; on the left the ear has broken off. The nose is long, broad and flat, narrowing from top to bottom, and the mouth is a cartoon line, upturned at the corners, not conceivably in a smile but to follow the line of the jaw. A broad rectangular block serves for the torso, scored by two diagonal lines for drapery as taut as ship's rigging, and the arms bend at the elbow in a V-shape with forearms and hands extended in rough benediction. Beneath are two bold, inverted U-shapes for

the drapery over his thighs. His legs show from below the knee, built of little abstract elements. This is a northern Christ of awful aspect and irresistible power.

Burghclere
HAMPSHIRE

The Giotto of the home counties, in the Sandham Memorial Chapel

Soon after the outbreak of the First World War Stanley Spencer enlisted in the Royal Army Medical Corps. He took his notebooks and pencils to war with him, and between kit inspections and scrubbing floors and the duties of a military hospital orderly in Bristol he sketched his fellow enlisted men. His reputation as a village mystic painting visionary religious pieces set in the boatyard and churchyard and streets and fields of his native village of Cookham (see below), by the Thames in Berkshire, didn't prevent his selection as an official war artist, but the War Office intervened and prevented him from taking up this role by posting him as a private soldier to Macedonia. There, this tiny, frail, sensitive man volunteered for action with the Royal Berkshires, came under fire, contracted malaria, bungled many of his duties but shirked none and, after the end of the war, was swiftly demobbed when his war artist commission belatedly became effective. Despite his vicissitudes he filled notebooks with sketches. These were lost in Macedonia, but he immediately painted from memory maybe his finest single work, the great *Travoys with Wounded Soldiers Arriving at the Dressing Station in Smol, Macedonia, September 1916* now in the Imperial War Museum (see Greater London, London).

His military experiences continued to haunt him, and he drew up a plan for a sequence of paintings to do with the redemption of man. Out of the blue in 1923 a couple of rich acquaintances, Louis and Mary Behrend, commissioned him to paint them for a memorial chapel they proposed to build to Mrs Behrend's brother, Lieutenant Henry Sandham, who had died of malaria in Macedonia. The couple had the chapel built beside a quiet country road near their home in Hampshire. Spencer wanted a large box to paint in, and he got just that, a high brick box with wings, which, behind a neat lawn, make it look like a soulless crematorium chapel. But when the box was finished in 1926 Spencer began to transform the material filed away in the pigeonholes of memory since the war and translate them into a paean to the obduracy and comradeship of men in the implacable face of an unwanted destiny.

'What ho, Giotto!' Spencer exclaimed when he knew the commission was clinched, and though he wasn't able, as he had hoped, to work like Giotto in fresco, he did follow the old master's scheme of tiers of narrative. He worked, mostly in the chapel itself, in oils on bolts of canvas, which he unrolled as he needed, and in a colour scheme in which nothing sings louder than khaki except the white of the resurrection. The side walls are filled, four paintings each side, with episodes of army life: bedmaking, painting wounds with iodine, filling tea urns, getting dressed at reveille under mosquito nets, map reading, standing to in a dugout. Above each set of four panels on the north and south walls are paintings of men in camp on a hillside and in a dry riverbed stretching the full length of the wall. The whole of the east wall is *The Resurrection of the Soldiers*. Each of the three paintings is a vast Macedonian landscape painted from the viewpoint of a low-flying aircraft, or an angel. So there is no horizon, and visitors reconnoitre a flattened terrain under intense military activity, including even the resurrection scene in which dead tommies clamber from their graves and check in their regulation issue War

Commission crosses to a figure in the mid-distance looking in his white surplice more like an army padre than Christ, the divine quartermaster sergeant. The only weapon in use is in the hands of the little man in person, self-portrayed bayoneting discarded newspaper like a council worker with a spike by the river in Cookham.

Cattistock
DORSET

A shrine for gorgeous Morris stained glass, in St Peter and St Paul

The A37 between Dorchester and Sherborne runs quite high above the valley of the Frome, and in the valley below the lovely tower of St Peter and St Paul signifies the moment when the architect son, George Gilbert Scott Jr, broke away from the architect father, George Gilbert Scott. In 1857 Scott senior rebuilt it as a church of his favourite period, 14th century with a pretty octagonal apse, but in 1874 the young George took over and imposed his own favourite style, the Perpendicular, and thus built a tower to hold its own with the finest in the county (later, George Gilbert's own son, Giles Gilbert, would outdo both father and grandfather with a great Gothic cathedral for Liverpool in the 20th century). For lovers of stained glass, St Peter and St Paul is a shrine for a gorgeous two-light window from Morris & Co. inserted into one of G.G. Scott Sr's 14th-century windows in the north aisle.

Two of the figures for this installation of 1882 are by Edward Burne-Jones in the years of his pomp, any time from about 1870, the other four by William Morris himself. Although they were companions from Oxford until death, the differences in their art are marked, and it was Morris, the driving force of their lifetime project, who gave their work unity. None of these six panels was

specifically designed for Cattistock – they came from the firm's pattern book – but Morris gave all six splendid angel figures a dark blue background scattered with wonky white stars spinning like catherine wheels. Each angel treads a plush velvety blue carpet of vegetation known only in heaven. The two Burne-Jones angels, St Michael in sumptuous orange and red with long locks in a white headband with sword held high and elongated trumpet reaching from his mouth almost to his feet, and a guardian angel with huge, folded, red wings, wearing a flowing white gown and holding a man child by the hand, are typically languid, although this signifies not torpor but easy command. Morris's figures are, again as always, more modest, without the lovely sinuous line of Burne-Jones, but sweetly disposed, one a censing angel, another carrying a small organ, the third a stringed instrument, and the fourth merely standing with head bowed in adoration. This one is as white as a star with flowing locks like those of his wife, Jane (though hers were coal dark). One of the others is garbed in flower-flecked pink, another in fiery red, and the third in white figured with golden blossoms and a coronet of goldish-white leaves and flowers.

Christchurch
DORSET

14th-century stone screen, in Christchurch Priory

Confronted with the choir screen of Christchurch, we have to close our eyes and think of England. Think hard and shut out thoughts of France, for there is nothing

This angel, part of a two-light window in Cattistock church, is by William Morris. Burne-Jones did two typically sumptuous panels, Morris four in his habitually quieter manner.

here to rival Gothic sculpture across the Channel. Not just in Christchurch, where the main figures are joyously clumsy, but anywhere in this island, even the famous west front of Wells Cathedral. All the same, as an ensemble, the screen is glorious. It is the full, ripe fruit of the decorated Gothic, an English development as fresh as the spring day I looked at it, with the sun slanting across the screen from a window high in the south wall.

The wall is covered with a series of niches as far up as the springing point of the ribs of the roof vault, large to carry the sculpted genealogy of Christ's ancestor Jesse, tiny to carry a small host of incidental figures arranged in two rows across the top, medium sized, of the well-to-do, looking like nothing so much as parliamentarians, but alert, and in the interstices between niches, soldiers, seers, a king, nobles, a cleric, a woman in an off-the-shoulder dress, right off the shoulder. What's she doing in here? And is that an apple in her hand or a mirror? Columns with a stippled decoration separate the niches and break out into extraordinarily fine-drawn ogee arches and pinnacles, as though they'd been spun out of icing sugar.

In the lee of castle and priory, at the confluence of the Rivers Avon and Moors, Christchurch provided the nucleus for precisely the kind of growing urban community where this naturalistic, life-enhancing art would flourish. After the rigours of Norman society and its Romanesque art, based on serfdom and arranged around self-sufficient manors, this was the age of the crusade, merchants moving by sea between England and the Levant and to Russia and Germany. England developed a prototype market economy with consumers who valued the rich and rare, wines and spices and silks and beautifully dyed woollens, even furs. They can be seen disporting themselves on the church brasses of parishes all over the country, fashionably elegant, determined that they will have their paradise now, and later.

The secular mingled with the religious, in life and on the stone screen at Christchurch. The tiny figures are like the marginal scenes on the Bayeux Tapestry, a breeze of common life freshening the important scenes of politics and war, though the Christchurch artist has treated even the great central theme as a bucolic tale. Jesse, flanked in adjoining niches by his son David and grandson Solomon, reclines in a garden where the genealogical tree grows from the earth behind him instead of from his loins. The picture cuts immediately to the birth of Christ in the panel above, a scene crammed with the Virgin and Child, Joseph hovering warily, one king already on his knees proffering his gift, the other two huddled in waiting, and then, in a sardine-can byre, an ox, an ass, the shepherds and, with a neat suggestion of perspective, their flock of sheep grazing on a hill behind.

Codford St Peter

WILTSHIRE

9th-century carving from the reign of Alfred the Great, in the Church of St Peter

The man reaching up and grasping a branch of a fruit tree on the stone shaft in Codford is unlike anything else in sculpture, not just in England, but anywhere. It's usually supposed to be a work of the second half of the 9th century, which would make it a product of the artistic Renaissance that took place during Alfred the Great's reign. It has survived in prime condition, presumably because it could never be construed as idolatrous and has always been indoors, so neither state-licensed vandals nor weather got at it. Its bold simplification of form and clarity of exposition make it look almost modern. The extreme angle of the man's

head as he looks upward at the fruit has prompted some experts to compare it to the so-called Winchester School of illuminated manuscripts. Work from the Winchester scriptorium doesn't on the whole impinge much on the general consciousness today, but in its time its whirligig style, which freely mingled figurative subject with decorative border, was influential in all the visual arts across Europe. Codford man came earlier.

Codford stretches along a wooded road parallel to the A36 between Bath and Salisbury. The southern half is called Codford St Mary after its church, in the northern half, Codford St Peter has remnants of Norman zigzag patterning from the original church, a Norman font, a Perpendicular tower and a lot of Victorian work, none of which is anything near as interesting as the 9th-century carving. We can only guess that this fine work of art is in the church of St Peter for the usual reason, lost in time, that the lord of the manor was a great force in the land. The carver seems to have treated his subject with all the innocent morning freshness of William Langland's Piers Plowman setting out 'In a somur sesoun whan softe was the sonne', though in fact the design is one of high sophistication. The man throws his weight on to one firmly planted foot; the toes of the other foot point downwards like a dancer. A dagger-like brooch pins his mantle around his shoulders over a crisply pleated tunic. A fillet ties his beaded hair in the style of King Alfred shown on coins of the time, and his smooth oval face is as young and as ancient as a Buddhist sculpture. His left hand clasps what could be a mallet but has been read as a rattle, because this doesn't seem to be a workman but one of the carefree rich. The branch loaded with fruit looks like a chiming mobile caught in a breeze, and the right hand clasping the branch is a nice combination of schematic and realistic, bent

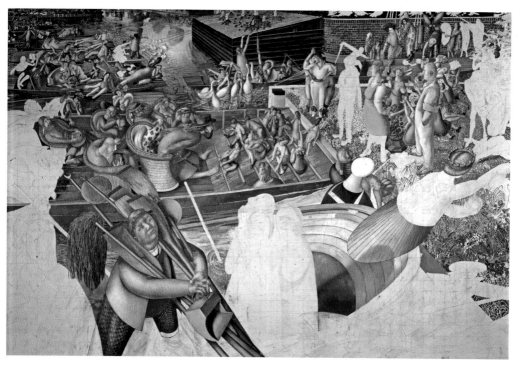

The unfinished state of Christ Preaching at Cookham Regatta *(detail here) reveals Stanley Spencer's inch-by-painstaking-inch approach. He began the painting in 1953 and was still at work on it when he died in 1959*

at an angle to set off the dancing rhythm of the drapery folds beneath.

Cookham
BERKSHIRE

Christ Preaching at Cookham Regatta, in the Stanley Spencer Gallery

Christ would never make it through the traffic along Ferry Lane these days for his personal appearance at Cookham regatta, but otherwise the village looks much as it must have done when Stanley Spencer (1891–1959) was born here, though the church and churchyard are quieter since the busy judgement day when the graves yawned open for the resurrection in 1924. Mildly bemused local faces fill that Tate painting of the risen dead, including Spencer's own, and his first wife Hilda Carline's – she sniffs a flower, Spencer said, to see whether it still smelled the same. From then on most of

his best work was done in Cookham. Today's celebrity-stuffed Cookham includes Ulrika Jonsson, Clive Woodward and Jim Rosenthal as residents. Had Spencer lived in their time, no doubt they would have figured in the regatta paintings.

Mrs Spencer took the young Stanley and his eight siblings to worship at the Wesleyan chapel on the corner of High Street. In 1962 the chapel became the Stanley Spencer Gallery, but the paintings were hung as though they were on park railings. Now a national Lottery grant has produced a smart new glass entrance and a staircase and cantilevered mezzanine floor neatly devised to provide clear views under bright new modern lighting, a transformation not to be regretted because, although it is a constricted space, it has been possible to hang the big loan canvas *Christ Preaching at Cookham Regatta*, all 7 feet by 17 feet 9 inches of it. This painting, unfinished when

Spencer died in 1959 after six years' work on it, is a focus for the mixture of loans and bequests, including beautiful pencil studies for details of the figure groups in the regatta painting. Because he was a student at the Slade School of Art when Roger Fry mounted the groundbreaking first and second Post-Impressionist exhibitions in London in 1910 and 1912, it is often assumed that his early paintings, with their shallow perspective and flat passages of colour, were influenced by Gauguin. It is just as likely that it was the 15th-century frescos of Masaccio and Fra Angelico that Spencer had in mind.

Spencer was a singular character, coming on like a holy idiot pushing his decrepit pram around the village loaded with portable easel, charcoal, paints and brushes, a palette and a beautifully lettered, framed notice asking the public to let him get on with his work in the churchyard without interruption (the pram and all this paraphernalia is in the gallery). *Christ Preaching at Cookham Regatta* shows that, as a modernist, Spencer did everything 'wrong'. After Cézanne it seemed inconceivable not to work up all areas of the canvas at once so that the image gradually appeared from the mesh of brushstrokes, but Spencer painted in minute detail, like a Pre-Raphaelite, squaring up the canvas, transferring his final study to it as a drawing and filling in the outlines one at a time so that now the canvas looks like a gigantic unfinished jigsaw puzzle.

Christ is in it, tubby as the village butcher, in a flat-bottomed ferry with a row of crowded punts moored alongside. He has on a long grey garment buttoned up the front and a grey boater, and he leans forward energetically in a basketwork tub chair, fixing the holiday crowd with a fierce eye. Some listen, some don't, as the children in his line of vision fidget, the ferryman, Mr Brooks, walks off shouldering oars and a mop and pan, and a sailor nurses a baby. It

seems impossible that a slumbering southern English village could produce such work. A humble heart and a mighty talent must be the answer. (See also Burghclere, above.)

Corsham
WILTSHIRE

An Italian masterpiece, at Corsham Court

'Poor brother Lippo,' was the Browning version of Fra Filippo Lippi (*c*.1406–69), a libertine monk in verse and in fact. Robert Browning has him telling his life story to the night watchmen of Florence, who have caught him emerging from a brothel one night soon before dawn. Fra Filippo argues: 'You should not take a fellow eight years old/ And make him swear never to kiss the girls.' The poet isn't far from his source in Giorgio Vasari's life of the artist, written a hundred or so years after the monk's death. Fra Filippo's own letters show him as a thorough professional and a businessman skilled at eliciting payment for work done and advances on materials for the job. In Britain, but for Browning, he would remain a more or less unknown quantity because here there are only about ten works by him. One of the best is *The Annunciation* in Corsham Court.

After the Second World War this house was home to a famous art school, now morphed into the art department of Bath Spa University. Now it is wholly occupied once more by the Methuen family, whose ancestor Paul Methuen hired Capability Brown in 1761 to rebuild it with a picture gallery to take the collection Methuen was about to inherit from a cousin. And such a rare collection. It includes one of the finest Van Dyck religious paintings, *The Betrayal of Christ* (now on loan from Bristol Art Gallery), a group portrait of some of her siblings by the long-lived 16th- to 17th-century artist from Cremona, Sofonisba

Anguissola, and a St Jerome in the Desert by another of Browning's subjects for verse, the Renaissance master Andrea del Sarto; these, with Filippo Lippi's painting, are the cream of a grand tour.

Filippo was orphaned early and sent to be a novitiate in the Carmine monastery in Florence where his potential in art was quickly recognised. He was in his mid-teens when Masaccio painted the frescos on the life of St Peter in the Brancacci chapel at the monastery, so great that it was compulsory even for Michelangelo to mine this work. If Filippo wasn't actually apprenticed to Masaccio, he certainly saw the work in progress, and it would have been normal for him to prepare colours and brushes, and perhaps help to lay in the *intonaco*, the fresh lime plaster on which the pigment was laid. At any rate, the earliest known works by Fra Filippo show Masaccio's influence, and this persisted in the revolutionary perspective and antique solemnity of the heads of his figures. Fittingly, the fruit of the womb of a nun Fra Filippo seduced, Lucrezia Buti, was named Filipino and followed his father as an artist, and he completed the unfinished frescos in the Brancacci chapel.

The Corsham Annunciation is a work of Fra Filippo's last decade. The drama of the subject was always a huge challenge to painters. Filippo's painting is bathed in calm daylight, though the holy spirit descends in a narrow, fiery tracer of heavenly light. It is one of a handful of surviving Annunciations by Filippo, and the last. The Madonna, eyes lowered in humility, reaches out to accept the lily from the angel; behind Gabriel the room opens on to a landscape stretching into the far distance, a daring feat of accurate perspective, which Lippi was the first artist to accomplish fully and which, of course, he developed from his first acquaintance with Masaccio's work.

East Meon

HAMPSHIRE

Adam and Eve on a medieval marble font, Church of All Saints

East Meon is a small village that must have been big in its day. Its day was about 900 years ago when the new lords of the land built All Saints, big for a Norman parish church, handsome, sitting on an eminence above the village hard against the upward slope of the Downs, as much castle in its bullying statement as church. It's easy to sympathise with the parishioner who died in 1659 and had a wall plaque inscribed:

Here lieth the body of Richard Smyther,
Who departed this life in hope of a better.

The church is relatively unaltered, but an addition was a businesslike broach spire on the dominating central tower, which the Normans would surely have enjoyed. It looks more like a broad-bladed dagger than a rapier.

The prime treasure is the font, of black marble, probably made in 1130–40 in Tournai, home of one of the great Romanesque cathedrals, and possibly given to East Meon by Henry of Blois, Bishop of Winchester and half-brother of King Stephen. At any rate, there were two more Tournai marble fonts like East Meon's in Hampshire parish churches in Henry's diocese. This is the best, though it isn't as good as Winchester Cathedral's, which is a masterpiece of powerfully organised rhythmic carving. The type is the same though: square, wide and shallow, tapering away at the bottom to meet a barrel-like central pillar with four slender pillars at the corners. The carving is carried throughout with a sense of rustic pleasure. On one side the mason has sculpted a band of dragons moving below the rim in arabesques – creatures you could make pets of; below that a band of almost loose, almost impressionist carved abstract patterning, and then a stretch of blind arcade on stubby pillars with leaf-like chevron patterns instead of the normal geometrical severity of Romanesque carving. More blind arcading on the far side, with plump birds interspersed with the dragons, and on the remaining, narrative, sides, the story of Adam and Eve: the creation of Adam, the creation of Eve from Adam's rib, and the temptation on one side, the expulsion from paradise on the other and the angel demonstrating digging techniques to Adam. In the only recorded case of a man giving birth, Adam seems to be having an easy time of it. In the temptation, the serpent is simply another dragon, crossed perhaps with the wolf in Red Riding Hood and with teeth that would fool nobody except Adam and Eve, seen charmingly concealing their nakedness with massive flowers. Eve has her hands full, of course, since she also raises to her mouth an oversized apple.

Edington
WILTSHIRE

All human life in 14th-century sculptures,
St Mary, St Katherine and All Saints

Edington lies high up in folds of the Downs between the Warminster plain and the Vale of Pewsey, perfect country for choosing your ground and winning a battle, as King Alfred did in his crucial victory over the Vikings in May 878 that determined the furthest advance of the borders of the Danelaw. Perfect, too, for a monastery. This was the native hearth of the mid-14th-century Bishop of Winchester, William of Edington. He duly founded a chantry chapel here, and then, under the persuasion of the Black Prince, converted it into a foundation for the rare order of Bonhommes. Here in the

1350s he built a priory church, and though the priory survived for less than 200 years before succumbing to the Reformation, the sculpture in the chancel is some of the finest of its period in the country, mostly small scale but charming and telling.

It can't strictly be appreciated separately from the chancel itself because the whole thing is an ensemble. At intervals along the walls tall, cusped, fan-vaulted niches supported by carved corbels contained full-length statues until Henry VIII's hatchet men smashed them up; but somehow two female figures survive, lacking only their heads and hands, which would have held their identifying saintly attributes. They are exquisitely carved, giving a sense as only the best naturalist artists can that under the drapery is a sinuous female body. The dresses, close fitting down to the hips, spill out in broad folds, falling to the ground except where one hand gracefully holds the hem clear of the ground in a gesture familiar through the centuries. Both these inhabited niches are effortlessly supported by tiny female angels, their heads wrapped in wimples, their wings spread so that they double up as wings and abstract decoration to the base of the corbel.

The figures beneath the other corbels find the task anything but effortless. There is a seated woman with ringlets, perhaps of the yeoman class, one arm akimbo with hand flat on her thigh helping to support the weight as she tries to keep her back straight. A young man in a cap supports a corner niche, one foot planted on one ledge, the other on the ledge at right angles, the swirl of drapery carved with wonderfully rhythmic artistry. There is a bearded old man with wild hair, feet splayed, knees being forced together, one raised hand grasping the edge of the corbel platform, the other groping for support, his open mouth gasping for breath, his eyes staring. We may be wrong if we assume

The intricately carved late Gothic oriel window over the doorway at Highcliffe Castle is from the Grand Maison Andelys in Normandy, part of Lord Stuart de Rothsay's plunder from his period as ambassador to France from 1828 to 1831

that these are the usual good-humoured portraits of villagers. The mason, I can't help feeling, is saying something else, something perhaps about what today we might call the human condition but that here may simply be something much closer to the life of the sculptor, the condition of labouring folk.

Highcliffe

DORSET

Relics of France in an English setting, Highcliffe Castle

Appointed as British ambassador to France in 1815, Charles Stuart went native. He stayed in the post until 1824, was created a baron in 1828 when he returned to Paris and chose the title Lord Stuart de Rothsay. Before finally departing from France in 1831 he bought an extensive collection of furniture and works of art, which he used to furnish Highcliffe Castle, the stately home he built to replace the humbler villa High Cliff, that his grandfather, the prime minister Lord Bute, had built in 1771. Stuart kept Bute's semi-formal parkland landscape, heavily planted with trees carved through with avenues opening up on to the sea, and employed one of the founding members of the Royal Institute of British Architects, William Donthorn (1799–1859), to build a big mansion in the fashionable Picturesque style of the period.

More than that, Stuart bought the Grande Maison Andelys in Normandy, cannibalised its finest stonework, added an arch and chimneypieces from Jumièges Abbey and from one of the many churches in Normandy dedicated to St Vigor, and passed them to Donthorn as montage material for Highcliffe. After the Second World War the family sold the house. The furnishings and pictures went to the sale room and are dispersed between

This wonderful Judgement of Solomon *at Kingston Lacy is by Venice's lost genius, Sebastiano del Piombo, a contemporary of Titian and Giorgione. He left the picture incomplete when he departed for Rome in 1511*

Los Angeles, New York and the British embassy in Paris, but after a period when the house was a religious seminary, Christchurch borough council bought it in the 1990s and saved it from dereliction with help from English Heritage and the Heritage Lottery. The principal attraction is what never went away: the looted stonework from France built into Donthorn's romantic Gothicism, which he's had the sense to treat as a relatively subdued setting to French magnificence: the Romanesque arch from Jumièges set into the north porch with little French decorative carvings and roundels and, finest of all, the gorgeous, detailed late Gothic oriel window from les Andelys above the south porch, carved so delicately that it's as fine as a piece of French lace. From the interior it gives on to a knockout view down one of Lord Bute's avenues to the lighthouse on the Needles rocks off the Isle of Wight.

Kingston Lacy

DORSET

The Judgement of Solomon, by the missing genius of the Venetian Renaissance

Kingston Lacy is the house the Bankes family built after they had fought the Civil War in the royalist cause in Corfe Castle and for their pains saw the castle turned by Cromwell into a romantic National Trust ruin. The house that resulted couldn't be more different, an emparked 17th- and 18th-century Palladian house with lovely interiors full of great paintings by Titian, Rubens and Velázquez – so great, that it might seem eccentric to dwell on an unfinished work by an artist who faded from the mainstream of art history early in his career and was reduced to borrowing drawings from Michelangelo as the basis for new compositions.

Sebastiano del Piombo (*c.*1485–1547) is a mystery, the unacclaimed genius of the

Venetian Renaissance who sharpened his skills alongside Titian and Giorgione as apprentices in Giovanni Bellini's studio during the first decade of the 16th century, then went missing and spent most of his working life in Rome, where, after Pope Clement VII gave him the honorary post of keeper of the pope's seals (made of lead, hence the name Piombo), he sank into a half-mad old age obsessed by alchemy. Skip a little over 300 years to 1820 when William Bankes bought Sebastiano's *The Judgement of Solomon* under the impression that it was by Giorgione and brought it home to Kingston Lacy. Until quite recently guidebooks still held the painting to be Giorgione's, not just because of its glorious Venetian colouring but also because the severity of the painting's architecture resembles an undisputed Giorgione work, the Castelfranco Madonna. As always when a painting has been reassessed, the new attribution looks inevitable. Sebastiano's architecture has taken over, and its vast solemnity looks unmistakably like other paintings we know are by the artist (there are a handful in the National Gallery, including the great Salome of 1510 when he was still in Venice).

Sebastiano failed to complete the Solomon before leaving for Rome in 1511. In fact, as the current Kingston Lacy guidebook aptly remarks, it was 'neither finished nor resolved'. The marks of irresolution are everywhere to be seen, in the overpainted landscape (in favour of a colonnaded marble hall), in the changed positions of some of the ten figures in the painting, in the missing baby (the painting is based on the passage from 1 Kings 3:16–28, in which two women each claim that a baby is hers. Solomon orders his executioner to cut the baby in two, at which point one woman yields to the other so that the baby shall live, thus revealing that she is the true mother). And yet for all its evident changes of direction this canvas is not just an interesting historical document but a sublime work with its austere classical interior as magnificent in its way as Raphael's in the great *Disputa* in the Vatican, and in its colours, the ice blue toga of Solomon as he half-turns on his throne to gaze at the real mother as she yields to the aggressive pretender, the olive greens, the pale blue of the mother's tunic, the gold, the pink, and the yellow tiles of the floor's dramatically foreshortened perspective. What pressures was Sebastiano under to have left for Rome in 1511 without finishing this great work?

Littlecote House
WILTSHIRE

Cromwellian chapel

Littlecote spreads itself comfortably in its gardens somewhere just over the Wiltshire border near the banks of the River Kennett among the winding lanes between the Berkshire towns of Hungerford and Lambourn, or, to put it unromantically, sandwiched between the A4 and M4. The lovely gardens don't look authentic to my untutored eye, more a hybrid of a formal Tudor and an open modern English garden to laze in, but then gardens more than buildings should have the licence to roam through periods. There is a Roman villa to the west of the house within the grounds where the restorers have cheated a little by having the damaged Apollo mosaic repaired so that the joins don't show, but it looks brilliant.

So this has always been a site for a des res, but the oldest parts of Littlecote House are pre-Tudor, the bulk of it Tudor (and yes, Henry VIII, they swear, visited Jane Seymour here – he must have done because she was a distant relative of the owners), and the most fascinating is 17th century. Less happily, Warner Holidays, the owners, have placed sandwich boards all over the place advertising a coffee bar. But fair's fair, they rescued Littlecote in 1996 and are relaxed and welcoming to non-resident visitors; just check at the reception desk.

The route to the chapel lies past a 17th-century parlour comprehensively and entertainingly decorated in the following century (1712) by prisoners of the long-running Dutch wars over trade routes. There is a wall of panels entertainingly painted with Dutch versions of scenes from *Don Quixote*, and, even better, on the fireplace wall and on and around the door into the room are real rural and ribald Dutch genre scenes, painted in pretend frames with pretend bits of ribbon attaching them by pretend nails to the real walls. There seems to have been one accomplished artist in charge of his comrades, but they all reach a decent level, the best of them in the tradition of Pieter Bruegel the Elder.

The Cromwell chapel is rare if not unique. Edward Popham, of the family who owned Littlecote from the Tudor period, was a colonel of horse in the Civil War – he adapted his great hall to be effectively Cromwell's west country armoury (the armour was rescued from receivership by Leeds Armoury but would ideally return to the empty brackets at Littlecote) – and he adapted an older chapel (medieval piscina still in evidence) as a Puritan place of worship. It is rigorously organised around the handsome pulpit with sounding board in the middle of the east wall instead of an altar. The pulpit rises above a parapet with linenfold panelling. The marble floor before the pulpit look vaguely modern, but that may only be because its black and white star pattern looks quite similar in style to Abram Games's famous logo for the 1951 Festival of Britain. There are original stalls and a three-sided gallery carried on pillars as plain as a Cromwellian pikestaff.

Longleat House

The poetry of Titian

The drive to Longleat House is through the banks of rhododendrons, among some of the thousands of trees planted by Capability Brown. Suddenly the land drops away to the right and there below is the great Elizabethan house, anchored in history and the sheep pastures, the best sight the West Country has to offer. Many more people choose to visit Longleat for its funfair than for the prodigious Elizabethan house of the late 1560s or early 1570s, the first of its sort, all windows and turrets, domes and ornate chimneys. Even fewer people make their way to *The Rest on the Way into Egypt* by Titian (*c.*1488–1576), though among the visitors were thieves who stole it in 1995. Police recovered it in 2002 in west London, without its frame but otherwise in good health.

Like many early Titians the melting poetry of this painting of around 1511–12 has caused it in the past to be ascribed to Giorgione, Titian's short-lived contemporary of equally sublime gifts. In fact, most of the loveliest of Giorgione's works turn out to have been by Titian. It hangs in the state drawing room at the end of an enfilade of state rooms with ceilings beautifully copied from Venetian palaces, tables groaning with Sèvres and Meissen, the walls of one clad with hand-tooled leather from Cordoba. The Titian is the outstanding painting at Longleat. The problem now is that it is difficult to see properly, beside a window and behind both a rope and glass. Titian was the first artist, even in the early works, to create paintings in which the immaculate conception of the paint surface gives way in the finished work to the visible passage of the brush through pigment and of one colour showing through another laid on above with a dry, dragging brush. These are an integral part of the thrill of the finished work. Here it is still easy to appreciate the deep yellow of Joseph's cloak against the red of Mary's dress, the delicate, feathery leaves of a tree standing dark against a bright sky, the idealised landscape and Mary's expression, sad and loving. But this is where the painting has hung in its almost 200 years at Longleat, and I was told that the management is considering lighting it artificially.

Maiden Bradley
WILTSHIRE

Memorial to Sir Edward Seymour by Rysbrack in the Church of All Saints

Sir Edward is at his ease. If I can't take it with me, he seems to be thinking as he reclines, leaning casually on one elbow on his tomb chest, then I'm not going. He lived in Bradley House next door to All Saints in the days of its glory when Colen Campbell (1676–1729), architect of the first villa, Mereworth Castle in Kent, in the English Palladian revival of the 18th century, included it in his *Vitruvius Britannicus* (1715), the bible for other classicists like Lord Burlington, who designed Chiswick House (see Greater London, London). The family cruelly amputated the wings of the house in the 19th century, but the park is not ignoble, even in the same corner of Wiltshire as Stourhead (see below). Sir Edward was a descendant of Henry VIII's third wife Jane Seymour and cousin to the Duke of Somerset. He was, the encomium on his memorial table reads, 'the fairest pattern to posterity … A friend to his prince, a servant to his country … His manhood saw the church and monarchy restored and he lived in dutiful obedience to both.'

Who was this paragon? In October 1665 Samuel Pepys thwarted him in a plan to seize prize money due to Pepys's employer Lord

Sandwich. In November he met Seymour socially and pronounced him 'a most conceited fellow, and not over-much in him'. In truth, the compliments on the memorial plaque wrap in perfumed verbiage the reality of a seasoned and wily politician, speaker of the house, privy councillor, leader of the faction of west of England landed magnates, but also a libertine and turncoat, dancing nimbly to new tunes from new masters, a supporter of James II who, as soon as Prince William landed with his armed force at Torbay, effortlessly switched to the cause of the house of Orange before James had shaken the dust of England from his feet.

When Seymour died in 1707 Rysbrack (1694–1770) was a youngster growing up in Antwerp, so twenty years later when he worked on the monument his reference material was most likely an existing portrait. Perhaps too, by meeting Seymour's grandson, who gave him the commission, he took some measure of the family and of his subject, a descendant of the family of Jane Seymour who was arrogant even by the standards of his class. At any rate, the memorial is a convincingly vivid portrait of a Tory aristocrat confident of his powers. It's all there, the haughty stare down the imperial nose, the down-turned mouth, the full-bottomed wig, stock at the throat and senator's cloak thrown lightly over the shoulders and wrapped around the legs. His attitude catches something of the hauteur of Michelangelo's famous reclining tomb figure of Lorenzo the Magnificent but also proclaims that life's a picnic, and it closely prefigures Manet's casually grazing bourgeois gentleman of a century and a half later in *Le Déjeuner sur l'herbe*.

Above Seymour the veined marble plaque bearing the ripely sycophantic epitaph is crowned by a splendid classical pediment with two reclining putti on each side. There isn't much that a figure on a pediment can do but recline, but surely there is about these urchin angels on this sumptuously realised baroque monument just a touch of pointed wit at the values of the departed gentleman below.

Malmesbury
WILTSHIRE

Porch sculptures of the twelve Apostles, Malmesbury Abbey

The wave of energy that swept the Normans in diverse channels across Europe, to the conquest of Sicily in 1066 and, in the same year, to the throne of England, only increased after William I took the crown. His commissioners carried through the enormous enterprise of the Domesday survey of the new English lands, his barons built castles, and his bishops and his successors' bishops appointed masons to rebuild churches. The power and solemnity of Durham Cathedral and the naves of Gloucester and Winchester mark the Anglo-Norman Romanesque as something quite different from the finer drawn version of Lombardy and Burgundy, though all of them took their inspiration from the basilicas of Rome and the Byzantine empire. At Malmesbury, only the nave of the abbey survived the dissolution of the monasteries under Henry VIII, but its commanding bulk dominates the little town from a hill where it stands behind a square with a grand 16th-century market cross. Even so, when visitors arrive on the hilltop it is not the church itself that draws attention but the carvings of the twelve Apostles within the south porch.

The building is rich in decoration, most of it decaying, but within the porch there is a tympanum above the door containing the image of Christ. It is the centrepiece in physical fact but not in impact. The thing to see here, the work that can hardly be missed, is the Apostles lining the walls of the porch, six to a side, but on a much bigger scale than the central figure of Christ in Glory. Here are two more tympanums, and each group of six figures crowds into the shallow area of a tympanum, carved out of the great blocks of the wall's masonry, and on each wall the central Apostle ducks his head to allow the passage of an angel blasting horizontally through the space above them. There's no Renaissance elegance about these two angels, none of the sweetly androgynous beauty of Raphael's angels or Botticelli's. These are hard-bodied warrior angels, their raiment closely wrapped, their tapered wings trimmed and streamlined for flight.

Beneath, the Apostles sit, Christ's envoys on earth, fishermen and, we must suppose, peasants. Side by side the loose drapery of their mantles falls between their knees and sets up a zigzag rhythm in a hugely magnified form of the vigorous chevron patterning common to almost all Anglo-Norman buildings – there is some on the shallow arches of the blind arcade beneath the Apostles. Their faces have never been touched by razors and their bare feet, square and broad toed, are shaped to walk through burning deserts and to climb rugged hills.

There is no complete sculpture like it in England, certainly of the period, probably at any time. This, too, is Byzantine in feeling, a rugged version for the West Country of the solemn and splendidly hieratic mosaics of Ravenna. Romanesque was generally regarded as backward and ignorant in the early 19th century, but William Cobbett, who had the advantage of knowing little of art but reacting to what he saw with simplicity of heart and massive intelligence, when he came to Malmesbury in the early 19th century reported: 'It was once a most magnificent building; and there is now a doorway, which is the most beautiful thing I ever saw, and which was nevertheless, built in Saxon times,

This panel of six peasant apostles and a warrior angel in the porch of Malmesbury Abbey (the remaining six apostles and another angel are on the opposite wall) was, wrote William Cobbett in the early 19th century, 'the most beautiful thing I ever saw'

in "the dark ages," and was built by men, who were not begotten by Pitt nor by Jubilee-George. What fools, as well as ungrateful creatures, we have been and are!'

Milton Abbas
DORSET

Little-known sculptor teamed with Robert Adam, in Milton Abbey

It is often held that Milton Abbas was the first planned village in England. It's certainly true that the genesis of the plan was to flatten the village of Middleton so that it wouldn't offend the eyes of Baron Milton of Milton Abbey as he gazed over his estate. The land thus liberated, Lord Milton brought in Capability Brown to landscape the wooded hills and valley, with a lake where the village had been, and William Chambers, architect

of Somerset House in London, to turn the monastic buildings into a house. Today the house is a small public school gathered to the north of the abbey church just as the conventual buildings were in the Middle Ages, with the addition of the splashes of yellow and red and tangerine and black jerseys on the playing fields as little boys knock bits out of each other at rugby. In 1780 Chambers (1723–96) moved on to build the new village of Milton Abbas on the other side of a hill, two rows of thatched houses flanking lawns either side of a broad street, totally lacking in imagination but unexpectedly attractive.

This great benefactor Lord Milton, later the 1st Earl of Dorchester, had married Lady Caroline Sackville, sister of the 1st Duke of Dorset, and when she died in 1775 he ordered a memorial for Milton Abbey, with effigies of wife and bereaved husband by Agostino

Agostino Carlini arrived in London from Genoa to became one of the original Royal Academicians, although his output was small. These effigies of Lord and Lady Milton in Milton Abbey are his most sensitive work, enhanced by Robert Adam's tomb chest

Carlini (*c.*1718–90) on a tomb chest by Robert Adam. The Benedictine abbey was founded in the 10th century but was rebuilt after burning down in the 14th century. It is 136 feet long, compact but massive, yet what survives today as the school chapel is only the choir, the crossing under its fine tower with balustrade and pinnacles, and transepts, all of it quite richly endowed with sculpture, painting and stained glass. Lady Milton's tomb is in the south transept. Carlini was born in Genoa but came to England at some indeterminate period. He was one of the original Royal Academicians and keeper of the Royal Academy until his death, yet not much is known about him, and his output was small. Milton Abbey's carving is his best. Lady Milton is recumbent in a long gown on

a sofa, her head, hair, arms and hands carved with great sensitivity. Her husband lies beside her, propped on an elbow, head resting on his hand in an attitude suggesting Christian resignation. It's a very fine if unexciting sculpture, but what lifts it out of the ordinary is that it sits so well with Robert Adam's chaste design. A chest is supported at each end by slightly projecting plinths carved with the Milton arms in roundels. Between them the slightly recessed surface is carved with shallow niches under three slightly pointed round arches and separated by two triangular arches, like a sequence of tiny sedlilia under a decorated entablature.

Moreton

DORSET

Laurence Whistler's light fantastic, in the Church of St Nicholas

A lone German bomber unloaded over Moreton in 1940, blew out windows all over the village, demolished the north wall of the little Georgian Gothick church and destroyed all the stained glass. It might have been the answer to a prayer, because when the restoration was complete the church was encircled by fourteen windows of clear glass engraved by Laurence Whistler (1912–2000). There was no particular plan: from 1955 Whistler executed the windows as donors came along over a thirty-year period. Most of the fourteen Whistler windows are utterly uncontroversial. Some get by on their technical efficiency and contribute to the general lightness of being, but three or four of them are outstandingly good, and they are all late ones.

Whistler had, like his brother, the painter Rex Whistler, a springtime but faintly melancholy feeling for the English scene. He had set out to be a poet, but after Rex was killed in action in Normandy in 1944 and his own much loved wife died a few weeks later he turned to glass engraving, perhaps because exercising a craft shut out the grief more completely. His tableware engraved with sylvan scenes is much prized and better, in fact, than the first five windows at Moreton in the west of the church, with their straightforward symbolism and nostalgic English landscapes in a circular format like those snowstorm scenes in a glass globe that can be bought at Christmas markets. He engraved no more windows until 1975, and then started again with a darkened outlook, clear references to life and death, candles burning, candles snuffed out gaining depth and lyricism from a darkening view of life.

More importantly, he had learned to work convincingly on a larger scale, and in 1982, when he engraved the three-light window of the Trinity chapel in memory of an RAF fighter pilot shot down in the battle of France, he commanded a wide variety of brilliant stippled and linear effects to render cloud, rain and sunshine. The fighter aircraft appears in the bottom of the right-hand light as the remnant of a smashed wingtip with the RAF roundel poking up out of the soft earth. The vapour trail emblazoning the sign of omega in the sky indicates that the plane has looped diagonally across the three lights out of the eye of the sun, doubling at the top of the left-hand light as a gigantic sunflower above a field of tulips and butterflies. In the centre light three doves fly free above the low horizon.

The final window, the four-light west window of 1984, is simply a joyful explosion of energy, a gaseous spiral galaxy spangled with closer planets and flower/stars, a symbol of eternal life and the mystery of creation, not least by the artist himself.

Mottisfont

HAMPSHIRE

Modern meets ancient at Mottisfont Abbey

Mottisfont Abbey lies in gardens full of ancient trees and watered by the River Test, which runs a few feet from the abbey's east front. It is a house of many periods, and the secret of its oddity is that it is wrapped around the original abbey, founded in 1201 by William Briwere for the Austin friars. Signs of it are everywhere apparent in the surviving fabric. Gilbert and Maud Russell bought this house of many periods in 1934, and after the purchase Gilbert Russell discovered that he was descended through twenty-six generations from Briwere. But Russell was

Like a snowstorm in a little glass globe, this is one of the earlier clear-glass windows Laurence Whistler engraved for the Church of St Nicholas, Moreton, which had lost its stained glass to a German bomb. He engraved all fourteen windows between 1955 and 1984

also a great-grandson of the 6th Duke of Bedford, and for ancient grand families networking across a millennium is as simple as joining Brook's or Pratt's.

Maud Russell was a patron and friend of artists, one of them Derek Hill, who left his own collection of art to the National Trust with a request that it should be displayed at Mottisfont. The work is mostly by his contemporaries and pupils, the abstractionist Victor Pasmore, here in an earlier phase of delicate impressionism, Derrick Greaves and John Bratby of the so-called Kitchen Sink school, the painter of louche Soho (among much other work), Michael Andrews, with interventions such as a landscape oil sketch by the great 19th-century landscape painter Camille Corot, so it is worth visiting Mottisfont for them alone. But the Trust has infiltrated a handful of works by Rex Whistler (1905–44), plans for a *trompe l'oeil* neo-Gothic room, bequeathed to them by his younger brother, the glass engraver Laurence Whistler (see Moreton, above), and they hang in the hall outside the very drawing room that Rex Whistler created in 1938–9.

The plans, which are actually fully worked out views of the proposed decor, show that he initially intended painting a series of illusionistic niches containing romantic landscapes with picturesque ruins, but Maud Russell rejected that idea, so instead he filled the pink niches in the pink walls with grey mock trophies, military, sporting, ecclesiastical, musical. He designed the rococo mirror over the mantelpiece, painted the chimneypiece to look like marble and added pretend rococo plastering. The real green velvet curtains have trompe l'oeil

pelmets. One weekend he arrived while Mrs Russell was away and added colour to a niche with a smoking urn draped with ermine, a lute and a stack of books, like an outbreak of Technicolor in a black and white movie. Whistler's was a slender talent, a beguiling licence to amuse, but beneath his front of suave wit he was a committed professional.

Whistler was trained by Henry Tonks, the magisterial head of painting at the Slade School of Art, and was barely out of art school, aged twenty-two, when Tonks recommended him for his first job and still his most famous, the decorations for the Tate Britain restaurant, a sequence of fantasy hunting scenes called *In Pursuit of Rare Meats*. He expanded into book and magazine illustration and poster design, but devised a few more amusing rooms – Plas Newydd in Anglesey, Edwina Mountbatten's London house in Brook Square and Port Lympne in Kent (open to paying visitors to John Aspinall's zoo). Mottisfont was the last. Whistler completed his final session while he was on wartime leave from the army, and in a corner of the room on the outside wall above the (mock) cornice planted another little joke: a pot of paint, some brushes and a box of matches – his way of saying he'd be back to wrap up the commission. He never did come back. He died in Normandy in July 1944, a few weeks after D-Day and in his first few hours in action with the guards armoured division.

Petersfield
HAMPSHIRE

A garden sculptor takes on William III, statue in the market square

There is something touching about William III on horseback in this market square. Partly this is because it was cast in lead, for cheapness. Originally it was gilded, but its naturally leaden state sits well in an English climate. Partly it's because William, though clutching a field marshal's baton and grandly got out in the toga of a Roman, sits his sturdy mount with becoming ease and unusual modesty. It only needs comparison with the grander braggadocio gilded equestrian statues of the same king in Bristol (by Rysbrack; see Southwest) and Hull (by Scheemakers; see Northeast) to point up the difference.

One thing is common to them: their distant sire, a horse with three hooves on the pediment and one pawing the air, is the steed bearing Marcus Aurelius on his back in the 1st century AD statue that Michelangelo re-sited in the middle of the Capitol piazza in Rome. The Petersfield sculpture doesn't attempt competition and is the better for it. The sculptor realised that since lead is not conducive to subtle modelling, he might as well settle for broad effects. He was used to working in lead – many of the garden sculptures at Stourhead are outstanding examples (see below). Here, too, he has succeeded splendidly. A few years ago, like many equestrian statues, the imbalance on this heavy object with only three legs on the ground was stabilised by a rod. There's no shame in that: Donatello's horse in Padua has a cannonball supporting its supposedly unmoored hoof. Now, however, the Petersfield charger is once more serenely unaided.

The king on his horse looks well, set among the 18th-century buildings of the square of this market town that became affluent on the wool trade and maintained it at a modest level as a coaching stop between London and Portsmouth. But the sole reason the regal rider is here is that the owner of Petersfield House commissioned it in 1753 for his garden. The house was demolished in 1793; the town got the statue. The name and practice of John Cheere (1709–87) seems

to fit it best. Had there been 18th-century garden centres, that's where Cheere would have been making a living. He bought most of his moulds as a job lot from Antony Nost, the sculptor who had previously owned the yard near Hyde Park: classical gods and goddesses, wood nymphs, satyrs and athletes. He learned sculpting from his more famous brother Henry, and completed many other similar commissions. Rysbrack wouldn't have feared the competition, but if he ever saw it before it left the London yard for Hampshire, he would surely have admired the Petersfield William.

Portsmouth
HAMPSHIRE

Coins of Henry VIII's realm, in the Mary Rose Museum

The plan is that in 2012 the timbers of Henry VIII's stricken flagship the *Mary Rose* will have dried, and the boat and the artefacts discovered aboard will be united in a single museum. This will be a great centre of Tudor studies and a crowd puller. Meanwhile, most visitors come to see the ship, and some of those also wander across the Royal Navy yard to take a look at the artefacts in their temporary shelter. In truth, this collection of equipment and possessions gives a better sense of life at the time of Henry VIII than the battle-tried vessel itself, which capsized off Southsea in 1545. There are long bows and arrows, leather jerkins and shoes and leather book covers, mittens, dice in leather pouches and a backgammon set, bottles, flasks, chests, carpenters' tools, cut throat razors, a chest with a complete medical kit, quill pens, inkwells, letters, fishing equipment and a portable sundial. There are cannons fashioned with realistic sculptured lions' heads and men with Francis Bacon screaming heads, their backs arched so that they could be used as handles to drag the gun into position. And there are twenty-seven gold coins, not many it is true, but only higher ranking officers would have had them. The silver coinage for the groats and pennies that paid the men solidified into a mass underwater and can't be identified.

English mints around the country produced the coins in the reigns of Henry VI, Edward IV, Henry VII and Henry VIII, and they have a symbolical significance in history beyond their quantity. The quality of design is high, especially the ship on the reverse side of many coins, built up of parallel elliptical lines following the curve of the coin's shape with, typically, a crowned coat of arms instead of a mast. Apart, possibly, from the 20th-century farthing with a wren on the reverse side, nothing in English coinage has been as good. There are eighteen gold angels (ship one side, St Michael overcoming the devil on the other), one of them from Henry VIII's first coinage of 1509–26 and valued at 7s 6d; two of them from his third coinage, same value, but nobody believed it. For Henry had taken over his father's impeccable coinage and under the pressure of his costly wars debased it from his second coinage in 1526 under his chancellor, Wolsey, and again in his third coinage of 1544, but at the same time increased the supposed face value. Wolsey's first tentative step was to reduce the gold from 23 to 22 carat, and then to 20. The new alloys made the gold go further, the number of coins increased, and people hoarded the good coinage (Gresham's law: bad money drives out good). Henry had defrauded his people. There were sharp price rises, galloping inflation and widespread financial ruin. Even the design of the token coinage suffered: the portraits of Henry are abysmal.

Romsey

HAMPSHIRE

Two roods marking a political connection with Germany, at Romsey Abbey

The big story at Romsey Abbey is the pre-Conquest 11th-century rood, a crucifixion carving on the exterior west wall of the south transept of this massive Norman church. It has a figure well over 6 feet tall and the hand of God above emerging from a cloud. It was clearly a very powerful carving in its time, but its worn condition has rendered it as negligible aesthetically as most medieval wall paintings. Inside the church there is a much more affecting rood. It is of the late 10th to early 11th century, when the abbey was being built, and is placed today above an altar in the chancel south aisle. Although it is very small, someone has had the excellent idea of insetting it into part of a Perpendicular screen reused as a reredos, placing two large sculptural candlesticks on either side of the altar and playing a soft spotlight on to the rood.

Athelstan, the 10th-century king of Wessex and Mercia, had employed his sisters in setting up political alliances by marrying them to rulers in France and Germany. One of the sisters was wife to the German Emperor Otto I, and the Ottonian style of art adapted from the Byzantine empire came to mark the English art of the 10th and pre-Conquest 11th centuries. Both Romsey roods fit the pattern. The cross is tall, and the figure of Christ upon it hieratically rigid, his head held upright, a symbol, intended or not, of the church invincible. Two angels with swords appear above the crossbar. Beneath are the Virgin on the left and St John on the right, and beneath them again Longinus, the Roman soldier who pierced Christ's side with his spear and the soldier with the sponge of vinegar offered as a drink to torture Christ

Lady Ailesbury, whose family still own Savernake Forest, founded the church of St Katharine in 1861. The monument installed to her memory when she died in 1892 is by Alfred Gilbert, creator of Eros in Piccadilly Circus. Head in a cowl, she peers through a grill formed by a tree symbolising the forest that she loved

further. It cannot be said that there is in much sense a composition here – the figures are slotted in and fill the available space on the stone slab – but the vigorous linearity of the figures and the remnants of the acanthus leaf decoration give the carving a sense of movement that is similar to Saxon illustrated manuscripts and is quite foreign to the Romanesque architectural grandeur of the sculpture the Normans would introduce to England.

Savernake Forest
WILTSHIRE

The sculptor of Eros in a Wiltshire forest, at the Church of St Katharine

Alfred Gilbert (1854–1934) gave nothing to modern art, but towards the gaiety of the nation he bequeathed his greatest gift, the memorial to Lord Shaftesbury, better known as Eros, which stands in Piccadilly Circus. He worked in Italy for several years from 1878 and developed a love of the sculpture of Donatello, though that is visible in his own output only because his typically epicene heroes of mythology are a languid Victorian translation of Donatello's pubescent and electrifyingly sexy David. Like many Royal Academicians, Gilbert professed to despise the frivolity of art nouveau, but his monument in St Katharine to Lady Ailesbury, who founded the church in 1861 in a favourite spot and was entombed there in 1892 aged 78, shows that the sinuous charms of the style drew him in.

Lady Ailesbury, born Mary Caroline Herbert, married George William Frederick Brudenell-Bruce, Marquess of Ailesbury and later Earl of Cardigan. The family still owns Savernake Forest, the only privately owned forest in the kingdom, 4,500 acres of oak and beech between Marlborough and Hungerford. In the marchioness's enchanted plot today the distant rumble of artillery and rattle of automatic fire from Salisbury Plain are another kind of memorial, to the marquess's predecessor Lord Cardigan, the colonel infamous for the charge of the light brigade at Balaclava in 1854. Within the fence and ha-ha surrounding St Katharine the yews closely clasp the east end of the church, and in spring primulas, dandelions, violets and wild strawberries are scattered among the gravestones. The church itself is no more than a stage backdrop for this semi-wild garden, though the stonemason, George Howitt of Devizes, obviously looked closely at foliage engraving of the rich late period of Decorated Gothic and has produced his own beautifully crafted version, deeply undercut to catch the light and shadow within the church that became the Marchioness's resting place.

Gilbert's memorial to her is a stone tablet, quite small, set into the wall and containing a standing effigy of the marchioness as a young woman. It is cast in polychromed bronze, the face and hands flesh coloured, her head and body covered in a white cowl and ankle-length cloak with gold floriate patterning. She folds her arms across her chest and clasps a tree, which is to say a slender bronze shaft bursting into an ornately abstract pattern of branches through which her composed face appears, eyes closed in death.

Southampton

HAMPSHIRE

A war veteran's satire on jingoism, in Southampton Art Gallery

Patiently, throughout the first four decades of the 20th century, Southampton accumulated an art collection. Finally, it incorporated an art gallery into its grand new Civic Centre, along with a library, council offices, a concert hall, an art school and the town lock-up. But no sooner was the art collection installed than the Second World War broke out and everything had to be taken down and moved to a safe place among the code-breakers of Bletchley. Soon after, the Luftwaffe set to work, and though the Civic Centre survived a hit, a lot of the town was erased, so now the way in to Southampton along broad, tree-lined boulevards through parkland is towards a grand town centre that no longer exists. Still, Southampton has its points: one of them is that it is easy to get in and out of, and the other is that it is worth getting into

to see the art gallery. Like all the best regional galleries it continues to show the in-names of yesteryear who are the unknown warriors of today, work that has shed nothing but its fashionable reputation. The sculpture by George Fullard (1923–73) stands up easily to that kind of attrition.

Fullard trained at Sheffield College of Art before being conscripted in 1942 and being wounded at Monte Cassino, one of the fiercest battles of the Second World War, an experience that marked his art. After the war he studied at the Royal College of Art and, working in bronze, quickly developed a quirky, highly personal style based on Cubism. In 1959 he began to work in assemblage, a kind of sculptural collage of odds and sods of found objects. *The Patriot* was one of the first.

Fullard intended it, apparently, as a satire on jingoism, but it doesn't really make it in those terms, even though throughout his work lies an unease about the human impulse to kill and maim. It doesn't make it as satire because the vivid invention outweighs the serious intention: the sheer pleasure in throwing together discarded bits of furniture surmounted by rudely planed blocks of timber for the heads of a child waving a union jack and his mother, seated in a rocker that imparts its curved dynamic to the whole ensemble. The deft wit in its assembly make this a lovably Picasso-esque piece. In the late 1960s he lost the obvious influence and created a highly original sequence of sculptured marine pictures, toylike and playful again and apt for Southampton, but one called *Forever* has a toy ship nose diving to the bottom of the ocean: a bit close to the mark, perhaps, because it was from Southampton that the *Titanic* left on its fateful maiden voyage.

Put together from odds and ends of house fittings and discarded bits of furniture, George Fullard created this Cubist-inspired sculptural collage, now in Southampton Art Gallery, as a satire on wartime jingoism. He himself had been involved in some of the bloodiest fighting of the Second World War

Speen

BERKSHIRE

Monument to the Margrave of Anspach, Church of St Mary

In his day Antonio Canova (1757–1822) was the most famous sculptor in Europe, ranked alongside the painter Jacques-Louis David as a leader of the neoclassicists. The Margravine of Brandenburg-Anspach-Bayreuth would have turned to no lesser artist to commemorate her husband, the margrave, on his death. Born Elizabeth Berkeley and married at the age of sixteen to Lord Craven,

'the beautiful, gay, and fascinating Lady Craven', as Boswell describes her in his life of Dr Johnson, became a playwright and traveller, the scandal of London but adored by all who knew her, not least those to whom she distributed her promiscuous favours. Discarded with an allowance by her husband, she met and captured the Margrave, married him when Lord Craven died and brought him back to England. He bought the Craven family home, Benham Park, a mile to the west of Speen, subsidised the margravine's theatre productions in Berkshire and London, died at Benham in 1806 and left her a wealthy widow.

Canova's monument, one of only two in English parish churches (the other is at Belton, see North Midlands), is a triumph of stripped-down power that graces an unworthy Victorian church in the seclusion of a wooded glade quite close to Newbury and the M4. It's a relief sculpture of a mourning female on a marble stele. Bowed down in heavy drapery, she kneels with her arms around an urn, one leg stretched elegantly behind her towards a slender pole supporting a Roman oil lamp. There is a similar lamp in David's Louvre portrait of Mme Recamier reclining on a chaise longue, so perhaps it was a fashionable item of furniture on the continent. In its few years of prominence neoclassicism swept everything before it, not only in architecture and town planning, but in furnishings too, and ceramics and interior design, from Berlin and Rome to Paris and London, from Wedgwood and Worcester to Meissen and Sèvres, Adam ceilings, commodes, vases, tables, chairs. Even the master of rococo, Chippendale, chipped in. If it didn't influence the 20th-century modern movement in art and architecture, its economy of means makes it look like a blood relation.

Canova first began his career as a virtuoso naturalist, and he discovered neoclassicism in Rome with the force of a conversion. The Speen stele is one of several adaptations from a monument he devised five years earlier for the civic hospital in Padua to commemorate its founder. Like the other favourites of monumental sculpture, the obelisk and pyramid, the stele is as old as Egypt. It becomes a convention that Canova animates with the power and economy of his sculpture, so although everything about this mourning woman represents ideal beauty and Canova disposes her limbs and drapery with the lucid formality of a philosophical proposition, his roots in naturalism save her from chill formality. Her face, her hands,

her feet are all we can see of her, but the cold white marble remembers the warmth of flesh and bone under her cloak at shoulder, hip and thigh.

Stinsford
DORSET

The Saxon angel of Mellstock, in the Church of St Michael

This is the Mellstock of Thomas Hardy's poetry and his novel *Under the Greenwood Tree*, and that is why people visit it. His heart is buried in the churchyard, literally and metaphorically, close by the River Frome. The ashes of his body are interred in Poets' Corner in Westminster Abbey, but in a simultaneous service in 1928 under an ancient yew in this southern Dorset chalk country, his heart was laid to rest with his first wife between the graves of his father and mother, his siblings and his distant forebears. In St Michael he played the violin in the church orchestra in the west gallery, and in the 1850s he fell in love with a girl in the box pews below:

She turned again, and in her pride's despite
One strenuous viol's inspirer seemed to throw
A message from his string to her below,
Which said: 'I claim thee as my own forthright!'

But a new high church vicar in low church Dorset ripped out the pews and earned Hardy's abiding detestation. Later the gallery went too, and on the west wall today, brought inside from the wall of the west tower to prevent further deterioration, is the much eroded Anglo Saxon carving of an angel, a ghost of an angel almost, but bearing the marks of a former magnificence.

Vandals seem to have been at it as well.

The head has been almost entirely sliced away, leaving only the halo, yet the piece has an almost festive air, the wing feathers architecturally precise and articulated like organ pipes, the fluttering cloak, the feet placed one before the other beneath the folds of a long gown, everything suggesting movement and purpose. It is just possible that he is striding over a fallen dragon and that what looks like a torch in his hand, repeating the diagonal of the forward thrust right leg, might be the remains of a spear, on which slender evidence this carving might be St Michael, thus fitting the church's dedication.

Stourhead

WILTSHIRE

A garden for Hercules

The 18th century is littered with the bankruptcies of great magnates who overstretched themselves fashioning houses and parks for their country seats. Even the great Lord Burlington was stretched. But Henry Hoare never was. He owned the family bank in Fleet Street at the sign of the golden bottle, Messrs Hoare, and as the grandees borrowed and spent he raked in the interest, and with that interest he shaped the park around his house at Stourhead. It precedes the career of Capability Brown and is said to have inspired him, but unlike Brown's landscaping, Hoare's park at Stourhead is natural only as the paintings of Claude Lorraine are natural. Half-close your eyes as you gaze across the Palladian bridge and the lake towards the trees banked up around the Pantheon, and you could almost be in a Claude scene. Nowhere has a nature been so cunningly wrought. And at the heart of all this, within the Pantheon, is the marble figure of Hercules by Michael Rysbrack (1694–1770).

In the 1740s Rysbrack's career had stalled in the face of fresh competition from two rivals, Roubiliac and Scheemakers. It was not that they were necessarily better than him (Scheemakers certainly wasn't), but rather, as Horace Walpole explained it, 'no merit can chain the fickleness of fashion'. Eschewing expensive marble he made a few pieces in terracotta, and one of them, a 2 foot figure of Hercules, was really an advertisement for his practice. Henry Hoare saw it and immediately caught on. He was at this precise moment reshaping the park lying below the twenty-year-old Palladian house built for his father by Colen Campbell (1676–1729). Hercules had been a deity of gardens in ancient Greece and Rome, and Hoare already owned Poussin's painting *Hercules Choosing Between Pleasure and Virtue*. Here was Hercules to perfection. He commissioned a large marble version from Rysbrack and meanwhile adapted his plans to focus the sylvan scene on a temple of Hercules to be built by his favoured architect, Henry Flitcroft (1697–1769).

The temple is known as the Pantheon since it is a miniature version of that most admired and complete of Roman buildings. It stands upon a little hillock above the lake, dome, colonnade, pediment, exterior niches with female divinities, and Hercules, beneath the dome, standing centrally in a niche at the rear. Rysbrack took the conception of the figure from the 3rd- or 4th-century BC Farnese Hercules (now in Naples) but modelled the musculature on the best limbs of seven or eight of 'the bruisers and boxers of the then flourishing amphitheatre for boxing' in London (Walpole again). Hercules cuts a fine figure, a prototype for all those oiled torsos and biceps in the body builders' Mr Universe competitions, and thought of at the time as the summit of Rysbrack's art. That may be for the same reasons that 'history painting' was thought to be a higher art than portraiture not least by the century's most famous portrait painter, Joshua Reynolds. Personally, for all that Rysbrack's Hercules is indispensable to the full effect of Henry the Magnificent's great garden, I prefer his portrait sculpture of Edward Seymour in a village a little further north, Maiden Bradley (see above).

Swindon
WILTSHIRE

England's finest modern landscape painter at the Museum and Art Gallery

Swindon's collection of English 20th-century art started as the brainwave of a wartime librarian and was made concrete by a businessman called Jimmy Bomford, who first loaned his collection to the library and then, when Swindon opened an arts centre in 1946, donated it. In 1966 Richard Morphet of the Tate Gallery agreed to advise Swindon on purchases. Operating on a budget of £1,000 a year, Morphet put together an eclectic assembly of paintings and drawings that is the major part of what Swindon owns today. It hangs in the museum and art gallery, a mildly down-at-heel 19th-century Greek revival building in the centre of the old town (old in Swindon means marginally older than the Great Western railway boom) with an extension, now far too small, to show the art.

When I visited, the display was devoted to paintings of the 1940s, which today includes a varied selection of work (to pick at random) by Ben Nicholson, and by one of the founders of Pop Art, Richard Hamilton, through to younger artists like the land artist Richard Long, and pre-dating all of them, the neglected figure of England's finest landscape painter of the 20th century, Ivon Hitchens (1893–1979).

Hitchens was a student when Picasso, Braque and Matisse irreversibly changed the direction of art in the first decade of the 20th century. He had his own first solo show at the Mayor Gallery in London in 1925, and Swindon's *Spring in Eden* dates from that year and, indeed, was in that first show. It contains the germ of everything that followed for the rest of his life. Its elements are a bowl of fruit, a bunch of daffodils, a cast of a sculpture of a woman's torso shown twice, once as a reflection in a mirror, and a landscape, which is actually a canvas propped against a wall. In sum, it's a wittily contrived comment on the nature of reality and illusion with a warm, suffusing glow of colour, pink, lemon and peachy yellows, magenta, greens, blues, a touch of mauve, in broad, easy brushwork, the sensually echoing shapes of the sculptured torso and the rhythm of the subtly varied diagonal accents across the surface of the painting creating pockets of shallow space between. It is an assured performance from a painter only just entering his kingdom, and one that quite matches his later work.

Weymouth
DORSET

Weymouth sits close to the western horn of the crescent of Weymouth Bay. At its back is Lyme Bay, with Chesil Bank, that great natural rampart of pebbles, guarding Dorset's soft shore from the battering of the Channel seas. Portland is a comma dangling from the shoreline between, punctuating two of the finest bays in England, the raw Jurassic of incomprehensible age from the elegant curve of Georgian Weymouth, where James Thornhill, the man universally known as Hogarth's father-in-law, was born and returned to bestow upon the Church of St Mary in the old town (see below) his painting of the Last Supper in thanks for

George III's patronage turned Weymouth into one of the most attractive south coast seaside towns. The local architect of much of the new resort, James Hamilton, created this sculptural tribute to the king on the Esplanade

granting him the freedom of the borough.

In truth, Thornhill was actually born in Melcombe Regis to the north of the little land-locked harbour that separated the two rival towns of Weymouth and Melcombe, but this was already ancient history by then because the two boroughs were merged by royal decree in 1581, and Melcombe's identity was swamped by Weymouth's. In any case, Weymouth's greater fame consists in its being the first place to use bathing machines, and George III was a happy patron, using one daily as a conveyance to reach the sea in privacy. Weymouth grew in prosperity on the basis of the king's pleasure in holidaying in the town, and its great charm remains in the contrast between the huddle of old shops and pubs on the rudimentary grid of streets beside the harbour and the suave 18th-century town houses on the seafront.

A bucolic George III by Weymouth's principal architect, on the Esplanade

He stands hand on hip, weight on his left foot, right knee casually bent, right arm extended: Farmer George about to order a pint at the local, except that, though bareheaded, he is clad in the imperial regalia, ermine-lined robe, gold-edged blue coat and gold waistcoat, cream trousers and white leggings. Beside him, on a table supported by an old Assyrian lion, is a small stack of impressively large books, no doubt on the governance of his islands, and on another table, the imperial crown. The union jack, a crimson pennant that is embroidered with his monogram, GR, and other royal accoutrements complete this naive and simple statue, which is as jolly as a coronation mug.

This was James Hamilton, an architect who built swaths of Georgian Weymouth, bursting out enjoyably into sculpture or, at any rate, model making. He made the statue of Coade stone, which isn't stone at all but a ceramic composite resistant to weather that had been invented by Mrs Eleanor Coade and marketed with great success until 1840. As it happens, King George bestowed his royal patent upon Mrs Coade's firm, though for unrelated reasons. He stands at the west of Weymouth esplanade on its perfect horseshoe bay with its sweep of largely Georgian terraces almost completely surviving wartime bombing, a bathing machine before him, at the very least similar to the one in which he himself used to be hauled by horse power down to the sea, with the old town behind. Hamilton placed him on a high plinth of Portland stone, which really is stone, engraved: 'The grateful Inhabitants To George the Third On His entering the 50th Year of his Reign.' As well it might be. George's patronage made its fortune, and in one of his sane periods he graciously chose it to receive the suffix Regis.

Thornhill's Last Supper for his birthplace, in the Church of St Mary, Melcombe Regis

Weymouth had its melancholy post-war period but now combines one of the grandest of esplanades with a quaint old town, sporting styles from cottagey to free-wheeling Renaissance and seaside baroque, dotted with good pubs, from the Black Dog to the Milton Arms in St Albans Street, which has old stonework that was or was not part of a former priory. In St Mary's Street there are tantalising glimpses of a pretty cupola with clock, which, when the visitor reaches it, turns out to be the crown of the Georgian Church of St Mary, built by the local favourite, James Hamilton. Inside, the tunnel-vaulted nave points you straight to the reredos, a Last Supper

painted by James Thornhill (1675/6–1734), who was born in Melcombe Regis the eighth son of Walter Thornhull of Thornhill in Dorset. Baptised in the pre-Hamilton St Mary, Thornhill was eventually elected MP for Weymouth and Melcombe Regis and remained so until his death. By 1722, when he painted the Last Supper, he was already rich and famous enough to buy back the ancestral Dorset manor in Thornhill and built a grand house there (extant), and he was the first native English artist to be knighted (the year before). In 1722 he was granted the freedom of Weymouth and Melcombe and the painting was his grateful acknowledgment.

Thornhill was still working on his painted hall at Greenwich (see Greater London, London) when he undertook the Last Supper, which is a more restrained baroque in a grand Corinthian architectural setting. He seems overawed by his God in a way that he wasn't by the monarch of his Greenwich decorations, and the figures suffer from too much *politesse*. The colour covers a broad spectrum, but it too is over-restrained. Despite this, it is an impressive painting in a genre that Hogarth, the much greater genius, could never emulate. The best passages of the painting are still life: Chardin would have acknowledged the white lace-edged tablecloth over a red covering, the loaf in Christ's hand, the metal wine pitchers. Tellingly, Sir James finishes with a flourish – a florid cartouche outlining the freshest credentials of Jacobus de Thornehill, 'Historice Pictor Regius', for he had been appointed sergeant painter to the king in 1720.

Windsor
BERKSHIRE

Inconveniently, William the Conqueror built Windsor Castle under the flight-path into Heathrow. It is the biggest castle in England and has been in continual royal occupation throughout the reigns of the thirty-nine monarchs since the Conqueror, forty if one counts the nine-day reign of poor, abused Lady Jane Grey. In the state apartments are works by Rembrandt, Rubens and Canaletto, and the famous triple portrait of Charles I by Van Dyck, both profiles and full face on a single canvas painted as a model for an even more famous portrait carved in marble by the Roman sculptor Bernini in 1638. The English sculptor Nicholas Stone was working in Bernini's studio in Rome at the time and recorded Bernini telling him: 'I conclude that itt is the impossiblest thinge in the world to make a picture in stone, naturally to resemble any person.' The marble portrait disappears from history after the Whitehall fire of 4 January 1697–8 but the Van Dyck template returned from Rome and hangs at Windsor.

Royal history from the time of the Tudors is told in portraits, and of all the portraits in all the palaces, the Holbein studies in the drawings gallery are, I think, the greatest single treasure from England's past. Hans Holbein (c.1497–1543) came to England with an introduction from the philosopher Erasmus to the future chancellor, Thomas More, for his first visit in 1526 and returned for good in 1532. Henry VIII valued Holbein first as a 'painter of Physiognomies', as a courtier wrote. Fine as the paintings are, the drawings are more immediate, in their speed and certainty, which seems to embody the thought processes of the sitters. These men and women could be alive today, the ill-shaven toughs, even a murderer (Robert Southwell, the hardened accomplice of

More's arch enemy Thomas Cromwell) are here, a record of life in the leading circles of a nation beginning clamorously but edgily to build its independence from pope and foreign Catholic power.

A Holbein portrait in Windsor Castle's drawings gallery

To the south of Windsor Castle is Great Park, a hunting chase in the time of the Norman kings. From Norman times too the town grew up the hill with its historic Pizza Huts, Big Macs and Starbucks. The castle itself, despite its passages of ancient masonry, shows a highly romantic profile of purely 19th-century fantasy (Jan Griffier's 17th-century engraving from about where the future M4 would be shows merely an enormous run-of-the-mill palace). In the state apartments – apart from the king's dining room with its opulent limewood carvings of fruit and game by Grinling Gibbons and his predecessor as Windsor Castle's 'master sculptor and carver in wood', Henry Phillips – the contents are the great treasure: porcelain, of course, beautifully conserved Gobelins tapestries, furniture, the cream of Van Dyck, Hans Holbein – ah, Holbein.

Hans Holbein the Younger (see above) painted Thomas More and his family and some friends at court, returned after a few months to Basle and then left his wife and family again in 1532 to work as king's painter for the rest of his life, though he remained a citizen of Basle. When he died Henry VIII was left with what an inventory called 'a great booke of Pictures done by Haunce Holbyn of certyne Lordes, Ladyes, gentlemen and gentlewomen in King Henry the 8: his tyme' – the greatest single body of portraiture by any one artist in history, since unbound and framed separately. There are eighty-five drawings at Windsor, no more than a few

M Souch.

This exquisite Holbein chalk and ink portrait in the Royal Collection at Windsor Castle is probably of Mary Zouch, a young woman in the service of Ann Boleyn. A scribbled reference to black velvet on the bodice and the merely indicative detail of costume shows that it was a preliminary study for a painting that does not survive inches in height or depth, shown just a few at a time in the little drawings gallery off the route between Queen Mary's dolls' house and the state rooms.

The two drawings on exhibition when I went were portraits of Sir Nicholas Poyntz, whose grandfather had fought with Henry Tudor against Richard III at Bosworth at the end of the Wars of the Roses, after which the Poyntz family remained in favour. The second shows, probably, a young woman called Mary Zouch, who was in the service of Ann Boleyn. They were both drawn in the 1530s on Holbein's last visit. The Poyntz study is wonderful, but the portrait of Mary Zouch is a work of outright genius. It is in black chalk with some colour and some ink contours on one of the sheets of pink paper from Zurich that Holbein stockpiled. He suggests mass and volume with the minutest touches. The razor-edge certainty of his line achieves an utter accuracy of delineation that is confirmed by the testimony of those contemporaries who knew his sitters. Mary Zouch is full of face, blue eyes slightly averted, beautifully delineated nostrils, exquisite line describing a slight smile, elusive pink smudge of lips, auburn hair tied tightly back from a central parting: you know this woman as well as someone you might see commuting daily – better, because you can gaze at Mary Zouch. Holbein finishes with a scribbled tube of a bodice on which he has made an ink note in transition from the German he once used to the English he would use: 'black felbet' (black velvet). So it was the study for a painting that, if it was ever done, is now lost. Never mind; this is enough.

Winterbourne Steepleton
DORSET

Anglo-Saxon angel, in the Church of St Michael

There are more than a dozen Winterbornes and Winterbournes in Dorset, split between two streams called the Winterborne, north and south. Tucked away on the southern Winterborne, the main road of Winterbourne Steepleton borders the river, which in reality is no more than a stream in a culvert. The first thing that takes the attention, given the name of the village, is the steeple. It is not a disappointment, a lovely 14th-century spire with spirelets around its base. But you have to look for the 10th-century angel that was until recently built in to the outside south wall because it has recently been taken indoors to save it from the weather. Rightly so, because it is a national treasure, ruthlessly composed, like other sculpture of the Saxon and Norman Romanesque, to meet the imperatives of architecture. The church building contains many remnants of its Saxon origin, as the quoins in the nave show conclusively, so the angel is not totally torn from context, though the rest of the sculpture (thought to have been an Annunciation) is missing, and this single remaining figure can only be admired for the intense internal rationality of its form. The angel's body thrusts horizontally in flight, and the head bends at a right angle and leans into the curve of the wing's root where it grows out of the shoulder. Further up, the wing bends into the horizontal as well, its feathers scored with long, deep, horizontal speedmark incisions picked up by the gaps between the toes on feet kicked up into the legs, which are bent at a right angle at the knees. The two angels in Bradford-on-Avon (see above) are 10th century as well, but more linear and elegant, lacking the power and massing of the Winterbourne angel.

Winterslow

(NEAR SALISBURY) WILTSHIRE

Uncompromising modern sculpture at the New Art Centre Sculpture Park, Roche Court

Roche Court is that happy invention, a sculpture park, the rural manifestation of the New Art Centre, which started life in Sloane Street in London in 1958 and moved to Wiltshire in 1994. It's based on a small, plain house with a big garden, and there are changing displays of sculpture featuring leading British modern artists. There's usually a big Anthony Caro piece on show. When I visited it was *Trunk Flats*.

Caro (b.1924) had his first big success with *Early One Morning*, a piece that still shocks as it did when he made it in 1962. It's an assembly of steel rods, I-beams and a large steel plate painted bright red (another 1960s sculpture, *Sun Feast*, was a flamboyant yellow). It covers quite a lot of the ground on which it stands, without the dignity of a plinth, representing nothing but itself and looking like nothing on earth had looked before. Not only does it not look like anything in life, it then didn't look like

sculpture either. I still have to take a deep breath each time and reorientate myself when I see it. In 1972 Caro visited a rolling mill in Italy and began to work with the freshly manufactured, curling, ragged-edged sheets of steel. It opened fresh prospects, and he began to haunt steel works on both sides of the Atlantic, the Consett mills in County Durham, the York Steel Company plant in Toronto, where he was given the use of heavy mobile cranes to help in shifting and assembling big sheets of steel. In the mid-1970s, with his lifting gear and the assistants who had now become a constant necessity, he made over a two-year span thirty-seven sculptures at York Steel, composing what he called the Flats series. *Trunk Flats* is one of them, rusted and varnished as an equivalent to the patina on bronze.

The series was called Flats because I-beams were still in the equation. The sculpture is predominantly composed of flat sheets balanced vertically, leaning against each other. At Roche Court the piece is in a field beyond the garden, barred to visitors so that sheep may safely graze, so you regard it from a distance. Stonehenge is a few miles north, and a henge is what springs to mind with Caro's piece. There are trees, but well beyond and to the sides so that *Trunk Flats* dominates and modifies the whole of the wide space around it.

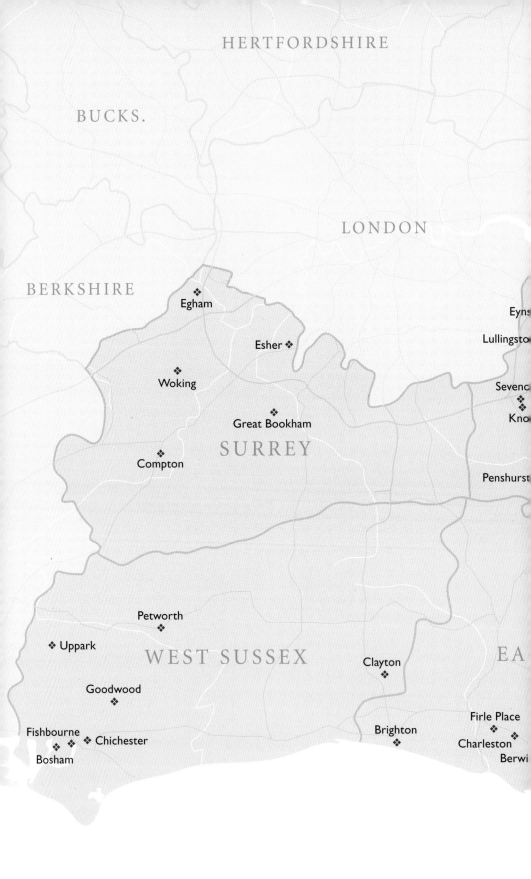

The Southeast

EAST SUSSEX * KENT
SURREY * WEST SUSSEX

ESSEX

KENT

SSEX

Upnor
Castle

Cobham
Rochester
Birchington-on-Sea

Lynsted
Wickhambreaux

Richborough Fort

ham

West Malling
Maidstone
Canterbury

xtol

Teston
Bridge
Lenham
Deal

Barfreston

Tudeley
Dover

Brenchley
Staplehurst

bridge
ells

Wadhurst

Brookland

Burwash

Dungeness

Bexhill

Eastbourne

0   5   10   15 mi

0   5   10   15   20   25 km

Barfreston

KENT

A possible carving of St Thomas a Becket, Church of St Nicholas

Old popular accounts of Barfreston assert that the carved half-figure of a churchman inserted at the apex of the archway of the south door is the martyred Archbishop of Canterbury, Thomas Becket. Art historians, aware of the total lack of documentary evidence, more cautiously refer to it as a bishop. But circumstantial evidence suggests that the old popular accounts have it right. St Nicholas was built in the last quarter of the 12th century. Henry II's knights murdered the archbishop in Canterbury Cathedral in 1170. Becket was canonised in 1173. In 1174 Henry paid public penance at Becket's tomb. These events appalled Christendom. Barfreston is barely 10 miles from Canterbury, and nothing would have been more natural than for a new church to include a homage to a popular churchman perceived as a bulwark against the oppressor. In fact, the clerical figure (let's call it Thomas) shows every sign of being the response to late breaking news: it has been clumsily spatchcocked into the arch to displace two or three smaller carvings of the multitude adorning the building.

What no one can know for sure is why a church less than 48 feet long, near, but not on, the pilgrim route from Winchester to Dover by way of Canterbury, should have been chosen for such singular treatment. Why would it be worth levelling a plateau out of the steep hillside rising from a dark secluded valley? Why use the local material, flint, up to halfway but find it worthwhile to float Caen stone across the Channel to complete St Nicholas, with its simple chancel and nave (and no bellcope at all; the single bell hangs in a yew tree)? The answer may be, as in Herefordshire (see Kilpeck, West

and East Midlands), that a rich patron of the church had walked one of the several pilgrimage routes to Santiago de Compostela and brought back ideas from the sculpted façades of pilgrimage churches, if not actual masons.

Dozens of leering gargoyle heads enrich the corbel table running around the church. The east wall is pierced by one of the few extant Romanesque wheel windows, and on each side of it is a niche, one now empty, one with a headless rider on a horse. There are a priest's door and a north door, both blocked, carved like the chancel arch with zigzag and chevron patterning. And there is the south door on which Becket is only a minor incident. The arch is carved with fantastical scenes – a hare playing pipes while a woman dances, a bear and a wolf feasting, a monkey riding a goat and with a dead hare speared on a stick over its shoulder – and everyday cameos of two coursing hounds, a woman riding a horse side saddle, armed soldiers, an archer, a man drawing drink from a cask into a skin, a musician with a viol, a stonebreaker and a peasant wielding a spade (Adam delving?). Among all this is Samson (you'd know him anywhere by his long hair) wrestling a lion, but the climax comes just at the top of the door, in the tympanum, that surface between the squared-off door top and the lower arch. Here is Christ in Majesty, hair swept back and braided, left hand supporting the gospel balanced on his knee, right hand raised in a blessing that might equally be a judgement. This central image is adapted from Byzantine art, but the Christ figure is surrounded by little carvings linked by winding foliage: two crowned heads (Henry II and Eleanor of Aquitaine?), angels, mermaids and the fabulous griffin. None of this is superfluous. It speaks across the centuries of Christianity and of the varied and invigorating life of the times, but the massive unity of carving and architecture speaks as much about the power of the new Norman elite as of the majesty of Christ.

In the early 1930s a promising sculptor called Henry Moore lived in Barfreston. There is no record of what he thought of the Christ seated in the arch of the church's south doorway, but a look at Moore's seated, draped *King and Queen* or his *Madonna and Child* suggests that he had looked at it closely.

Berwick

EAST SUSSEX

Murals by Duncan Grant and Vanessa Bell, Church of St Michael and All Angels

In December 1941 Vanessa Bell (1879–1961) wrote to Angelica, the daughter of her union with Duncan Grant (1885–1978): 'The house is chaotic and all a dither with Christianity.' The house was Charleston, and Christianity was very much on the agenda. Bishop George Bell of Chichester, a great patron of the arts, who, among other projects had commissioned T.S. Eliot's *Murder in the Cathedral*, had invited Grant to paint wall decorations for Berwick church. The bishop hoped to revive the medieval practice, of which there was as much evidence in Sussex as anywhere, of decorating church interiors with religious murals. Grant suggested that as he lived with Vanessa, she and her son with Clive Bell, Quentin, might help as well. Bishop Bell (no relation) agreed.

Berwick is only a couple of miles from Charleston. Today, even though the hectic A27 between Brighton and Eastbourne bisects the parish, the peace in the tiny churchyard looking out over the South Downs is as it must have been in the 1940s, given the odd stray bomb. At that time the church served the agricultural workers of the Firle House estate, but the protesters who took up arms against Bishop Bell's project were the usual group of the well-bred middle classes led, in this case, by the chief flower arranger. They apparently believed that art stopped in the Middle Ages and that Quentin Bell (1910–96) was a conscientious objector. He wasn't, and the church consistory court dismissed the objections, to the relief of the great and the good, including Kenneth Clark, then director of the National Gallery, who declared that if the objectors won the day it would be a massive blow to British art. Well, it would certainly have left All Saints a gloomier place, but it scarcely shows Duncan Grant and Vanessa Bell in the vanguard of their art. Their work here is a retreat from the vivid if mildly slapdash Post-Impressionism of their early work into quiet English pastoralism. But fun.

Quentin Bell's altar screen, *The Supper at Emmaus*, is journeyman stuff. Grant was basically a happy pagan, and Christ in Majesty on the chancel west wall was beyond him. His Christ is clad in a robe freely adapted from Gothic sculpture, but he looks like a benevolent off-duty parson. The angels in a circle around him wear dresses of apple-fresh red and green and might be girls dancing around a maypole. Grant was more at home with his bucolic illustrations of the seasons in roundels on the chancel screen.

Vanessa Bell has the best of it here. She posed Angelica for the Virgin in the nativity scene with shepherds and sheep borrowed from Firle to fill the spaces. The Nazareth stable opens out on to a green hill as far away as the Sussex Downs. The Virgin wears a pink dress and blue mantle, and the glow from a lantern in a shepherd's hand illuminates her and the baby reclining in her lap. In her Annunciation daylight floods the room from a door behind the Angel Gabriel and Mary as she drops gracefully to one knee and bows her head submissively. It might be a herb garden or vegetable plot outside the window, and in any case it is

The spectacular staircase and lighting fixture form part of the sensitively restored De La Warr Pavilion in Bexhill. The plaque set in the floor celebrates the architects, Mendelsohn and Chermayeff, and the socialist mayor, Lord de la Warr, who funded the building

a very English scene, lacking the tension of the great Annunciations of the past but suffused in calm acceptance, which may reflect something of Vanessa Bell's own state of mind. She had suffered traumatically at the loss of her son Julian in the Spanish Civil War four years before and from the suicide of her sister Virginia Woolf early in 1941, so despite her cheerfully professed agnosticism her two paintings movingly suggest her own acceptance of how the divine dice had fallen.

Vanessa Bell painted this Annunciation in Berwick church, setting it in a rudimentary house and a Sussex garden. She and her partner Duncan Grant lived nearby and, helped by the rest of their family, filled the church with murals

Bexhill

EAST SUSSEX

Hitler's gift to the south coast, the De La Warr Pavilion

By some political sleight of hand in 1932, the 9th Earl de la Warr, a minister in Ramsay MacDonald's Labour and National governments, became a visionary mayor of resolutely Tory Bexhill-on-Sea. Against a background murmur of public vituperation he pushed his reluctant town council into going along with his plan to build a modernist entertainment hall on the seafront. De la Warr pulled strings, among his friends, in government, with the good and the great in the architectural world, and set up a competition for the new building. This was duly won by the newly arrived émigré architects, Erich Mendelsohn (1887–1953), from Hitler's Germany, and his business partner, the Russian Serge Chermayeff (1900–96). In December 1935 the hall was opened to international acclaim and disgruntled mutterings from the *Bexhill Observer*, and named the De La Warr Pavilion.

By the 1960s this astringently 1930s purist landmark of concrete and glass, elegantly asymmetric, painted white with decks and railings above the sea like an ocean liner's, had become a drag on Bexhill's finances and a target of the council's combined inertia and vandalism. The original Alvar Aalto furniture was consigned to the attic, flock wallpaper was put on the walls, plastic chairs and an atrocious bar were installed in the restaurant, red patterned carpets were fitted, metal doorframes were replaced with wood. In the 1980s a group of pavilion supporters infiltrated the town council and began to organise and agitate. They formed a trust, fixed the pavilion's elevation to a grade I listing, raised money locally, publicised their case in the architectural press and attracted big Arts Council and national lottery funding. Now it houses terrific art exhibitions from modern to contemporary, Ben Nicholson to the Turner prize-winning ceramicist Grayson Perry; there are jazz, pop and classical concerts, mostly by young artists on their way up; ballet and cabaret are performed; there's a circus workshop; and there's a restaurant.

The best act of the lot though is still the south entrance, gleamingly restored, with three floors of curving glass intersected by balconies and within a sculpted spiral staircase with a spectacular light fitting suspended from the ceiling through the three floors. This is the modernism of hope in the teeth of a low, dishonest decade, as Malcolm Muggeridge named the 1930s. And the Alvar Aalto furniture is back. Hidden treasure? Maybe; it is Bexhill, and no one I know has visited it.

Birchington-on-Sea
KENT

Tower Bungalows, the first in England

The ailing Dante Gabriel Rossetti came to genteel Birchington-on-Sea in the environs of raffish Margate in 1882. He arrived at the invitation of an old friend, an architect and one of the original Pre-Raphaelites, John Pollard Seddon, to stay in a bungalow Seddon had just built on spec as one of a group. Rossetti found the bungalow commodious and didn't outstay his welcome because he died there within a few weeks. He lies in the churchyard of All Saints, Birchington, under a well-meant but drab Celtic cross designed by another old friend, Ford Madox Brown. Alive or dead, it was an odd place for the farouche Rossetti to be, but his association with them helped to give bungalows the reputation of being dwellings for bohemians.

Seddon (1827–1906) imported the concept from India, and his Birchington bungalows were the first in Britain. They helped to make the Margate environs of Birchington and Westcliffe and Cliftonville fashionable enough to attract John Betjeman, laureate of the suburbs, to hymn its praises in 1940 and suggest elegiacally that it was the heart of civilization

> *Now dark is the terrace, a storm-battered stretch;*
> *And I think, as the fairy-lit sights I recall,*
> *It is those we are fighting for, foremost of all.*

The word bungalow, like the associated verandah, is from the Hindi (*bangla, varanda*). In India they were single-storey, often single-roomed houses but, adapted to the desires of empire-building British families, they caught on and sprang up in every military cantonment and on the fringes of all British-occupied cities from Sind to Bengal, New Delhi to Simla. In Britain they lost their cachet between the wars when the unplanned itch of Peacehaven spread as a rash along the south coast. But a number of Seddon's Birchington houses survive, most notably the group in Spencer Road called Tower Bungalows. One of these, the Old Coach House (and apparently, even in 1882, intended as just that), is decorated with George Frampton's grey and white sgraffito friezes, a rare technique of laying one colour over another on a stucco surface then engraving so that the bottom colour shows through. On them jolly children ride in procession in a chariot drawn by lion cubs in pastiche of a Roman triumph, or gaily play at being workers on a farm, or perform on pan pipes. One drinks from a leather bottle like a young Bacchus, and another, naked but for a large straw hat, stands painting at an easel. These slight, amusing and almost unknown works have arrived into their third century as fresh as the sea breezes and were a precursor of the statue for which, whether he liked it or not, the rich and fashionable Frampton became best known, Peter Pan in Kensington Gardens.

community. It lies low down on the west of one of the little peninsulas jutting into Chichester harbour. Seen from across a creek the tiled nave roof and the little broach spire stand up above the flint, brick, tile-hung and whitewashed houses, a row of trees and the masts of small sailing craft with only the low South Downs and the sky as backdrop. The unmarked road leading from Bosham along the coastline is submerged at high tide. The churchyard stands on the very edge of the sea.

Of course, the church arch in the tapestry isn't a literal copy of the Saxon chancel arch in Holy Trinity. It looks closely similar because that's how the Saxons built their arches, faintly horseshoe shaped. If the seamstresses had seen Bosham, they would have included the tower, because that too is Saxon, with its arch and a triangular-headed window inside looking over the nave. The chancel arch is the thing though, a tall, commanding structure carried on moulded columns and revealing a five-lancet Early English window in the chancel beyond. It is not just the sense of history that we bring to this place that holds us in thrall, it's the living presence of history in this lovely interior that imposes itself.

Bosham
WEST SUSSEX

Where Harold embarked on his fateful voyage to Normandy, Holy Trinity Church

There is a copy in the nave of Bosham parish church of the third frame of the Bayeux Tapestry showing Harold arriving at the church in 1064 to pray for a fair crossing to Normandy with the news from Edward the Confessor that Duke William is to succeed to the throne of England. Of all the places on the southeastern coast associated with the events of the Conquest, Bosham most nearly maintains the remoteness of a pre-Conquest

Brenchley
KENT

No smoke without a fireplace, Marle Place

Built in 1619 and still deep in the Weald on the road to nowhere, timber-framed and tile-hung Marle Place sprawls above its lawn to the south, with gables, hipped roofs and chimney stacks indicating additions, but at the north-facing front of the house it is expressively compact. It has two gables above two-storey canted bays either side of a two-storey porch with an overhang. Climbing from the hearth and heart of the house a

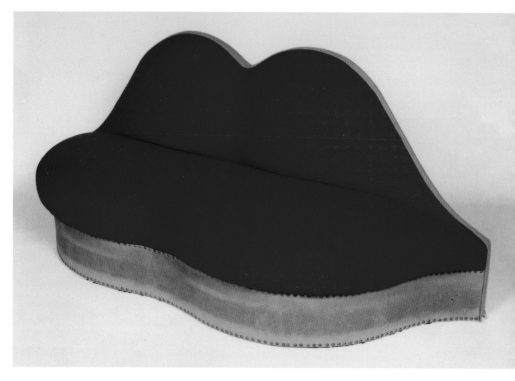

Mae West couldn't have every man she ever wanted, but Salvador Dali certainly made her more widely available with this sofa simulation of her lips designed for his friend, the art collector Edward James, now in the Brighton Museum

great chimney stack thrusts through the roof ridge as four linked octagonal chimneys of mellow brick, moulded at the bottom and with oversailing courses of brick in a star pattern at the top.

Marle Place is one of the finest expressions of the day-to-day Wealden building style with its mellow tones of brick and tile, and the central chimney stack is not just a funnel for escaping smoke, it's a statement of social status. Pre-16th-century hall houses had halls rising to the ridge beam with an open hearth in the middle from which the smoke curled up to an escape vent in the roof. Most of the halls had a second floor inserted later, but in Battle there is an example of a medieval hall (now a café) that has been restored to its original condition, though without the central fire (at grand Penshurst a central fire is still laid, but never lit). The importation of Newcastle coals prompted the practical device of built-in fireplaces with chimney stacks. In the grander houses chimneys became status symbols, a touch of swanky style, not many finer than at Marle Place.

Brighton
EAST SUSSEX

Mae West's Lips, by Salvador Dali, Brighton Museum and Art Gallery

The art gallery was part of the holiday fantasy of the Prince Regent, later George IV, who first ordered Henry Holland to build him a villa off the Steyn in Brighton, then commanded John Nash, builder or inspirer of most of the seafront crescents and terraces, to do it up in 'Hindoostan' style. Nash draped the outside of the building with his Regency take on Indian architecture and left the interiors alone, so the Pavilion is chinoiserie inside, mock Mughal outside, an early 19th-century monument in meringue to royal frivolity.

The art gallery exists alongside the Dome in the Pavilion grounds, built as the prince's tennis court, converted to a gallery after the prince became bored with the place, and reopened in 2002 after a spectacular refurbishment. The collection relied from the beginning on bequests, so it never had a particular shape, though there are frequent gems like the portrait of a woman that the much-travelled Swiss artist Angelica Kauffmann, friend of Joshua Reynolds and one of the original Royal Academicians, painted with no sense of forcing herself to finish a commission, and so with a freshness not often seen from her except in the ceiling cartouches she worked on for interiors by Robert Adam.

The modern work is the best of the collection. It's a mixed bag, but the cheeriest of the exhibits is a piece of furniture: a sofa shaped into a likeness of Mae West's lips, brilliantly magenta, oversize, promiscuous-looking, funny, like Mae West herself. It's by Salvador Dali. 'When I'm good I'm very good, but when I'm bad I'm better' (Mae West, attrib.), might have been Dali's motto, but not quite. He was bad a lot of the time, and when he was bad he was very very bad, pretentious, self-publicising and making paintings with surfaces like lacquer worked up for shock effect and maximum publicity. George Orwell got Dali's work bang to rights in remarking on 'the old-fashioned, over-ornate, Edwardian style of drawing to which Dali tends to revert when he is not being Surrealist'.

As a matter of fact, that is a perfect description of Dali when he was being Surrealist. When he was making applied art, on the contrary, he was good. As a jeweller, he was sensational – all those glowing colours,

all those rubies (lips), all those pearls (teeth), all those emeralds (eyes). And the same for *Mae West's Lips*. The idea started life in 1934 as a painting, but in 1938 Dali's friend Edward James, the rich, dotty, exotic art fancier who was popularly and maybe rightly believed to be an illegitimate son of Edward VII, persuaded him to make it as a sofa for him. Dali delivered, so for the rest of his life James could relax on the lower lip and lean back against the top lip. The idea was padded beyond what it would sustain, but it's fun and sits perfectly in its fantasy Mughal home, if in slightly faded glory.

It seems that Mae West's lips remained sealed about this usurpation of her intellectual property.

Brookland
KENT

Labours of the months on a Romanesque lead font, Church of St Augustine

In the Middle Ages a lot of the 24,000 acres of Romney Marsh was owned by the see of Canterbury, and Thomas Becket followed the example of the Romans and Saxons by putting work in hand to make sure that congregations could worship with dry feet. Until 1930 inhabitants of the marsh paid a levy called 'wall scot' towards keeping the sea at bay.

The church at Brookland is one of a marsh full of oddball, unrestored, lovely churches – Ivychurch, once stuffed full of smuggled 'brandy and baccy', St Rumwold, Bonnington, 'like a plump grey hen' (John Newman in the *Buildings of England*), Burmarsh, behind a moat of dykes, water-locked Fairfield, where frogs are said to form the congregation more frequently than people and sheep graze at the door – but of all these Brookland has the dizziest feature, a free-standing, 60 foot, shingled wooden belfry built in three stages like an oversized ornamental Christmas tree for a parlour mantelpiece. The church is largely 13th century and has the luck to have preserved part of a wall painting of the murder in the cathedral. But the font is the thing. England was the major source of lead in Europe, and there would be no reason to suppose that Brookland's font was French except that it bears no resemblance to any other font in England but does bear close resemblance to a northern French psalter now in the Royal Library in The Hague. Given that the sparse population of this hundred square miles of wetland has always turned its back on the rest of Kent to face the sea and its problems, perhaps a French origin is not surprising.

The round font is encircled by scenes of the labours of the months with, above each, a sign of the zodiac; so, for instance, beneath Pisces (February) an old man warms himself by the fire, beneath Taurus (April) a woman prepares to plant two seedlings, beneath Gemini (May) a horseman rides abroad with a hawk on his wrist, beneath Scorpio (October) a man three-quarters hidden in a deep tub treads grapes, and beneath Capricorn (December) a peasant swings an axe above his head to slay a pig gripped between his legs.

There is nothing extraordinary about the subject matter, a staple of medieval year books, except that each single scene repeats precisely the disposition of the separate illustration in the French psalter. It isn't conclusive proof that the font is French, since the churches on both sides of the English Channel were so intimately bonded, but for historians of the Middle Ages, searching for documents that do not exist, for precedents without apparent linkage, for names gone absent without leave, it is enough to seize upon the clearly apparent resemblances with a glee equal to the pleasure the rest of us feel at the charm of Brookland's unique font.

Burwash

EAST SUSSEX

Kipling and the empire at Bateman's

Rudyard Kipling (1865–1936) was thirty-six when he bought Bateman's in a wooded tract of the Weald with the little River Dudwell at the bottom of the garden and the hill on which he would set *Puck of Pook's Hill* within view to the southwest. He was born in Bombay, came to England to be schooled, returned to India when he was fifteen to be a reporter on the *Civil and Military Gazette* in Lahore and left India never to return in 1889, though he nurtured the imperial idea of the white man's burden throughout his life.

He already had a reputation in England for the satirical *Departmental Ditties* (1886) and his brilliant short stories, *Plain Tales from the Hills* (1888). The big India books, *Barrack-Room Ballads*, *The Jungle Book* and *Kim*, were written in England and published by the time he and his American wife Carrie came to Bateman's in 1901; *The Just So Stories* in 1902. They lived the rest of their lives here, years of worldly success (he spent the Nobel Prize money of 1907 on the garden) and, after their son John died in the First World War, years of inconsolable sorrow.

Bateman's is a big stone house of an irregular shape, built, according to the date above the porch, in 1634. As old India wallahs did, Kipling and Carrie filled it with Indian furniture, brass objects, a terracotta Ganesh, the elephant-headed god of good fortune, plaster reliefs by his father, the artist John Lockwood Kipling, illustrating *The Jungle Book*, oriental rugs and minor Victorian pictures. The best single work of art in the house is the hand-coloured woodcut profile portrait of Kipling by his friend William Nicholson (1872–1949), the father of one of the best of modern English painters, Ben Nicholson. Nicholson Sr had enrolled as a student at the Académie Julian in Paris, and his painting and printmaking were markedly different from the work of his English contemporaries, their uncluttered clarity influenced by Manet, Whistler and Japanese prints. The Kipling woodcut is as powerful an image as a poster, a profile portrait of the writer as he stands, hands behind his back, wearing wire-framed spectacles and his big Kaiser Bill walrus moustache with a loose collar and soft jacket. Nicholson made the portrait in 1897 and published it in a well-received album of twelve eminent Victorians, including the old Queen. It hangs on the landing outside Kipling's study.

Like the rest of the house, the study is maintained by the National Trust as it was in Kipling's lifetime (they used old *Country Life* photographs to put it together again). It is the heart of the house, with its 10 foot walnut desk across the window. Kipling had a typewriter but didn't use it much, complaining that it couldn't spell, and for preference he used a pen instead. The typewriter stands there on the edge of the desk. It is, of course, an Imperial.

Canterbury
KENT

Earliest Christianity at the Church of St Martin, St Martin's Hill

Everybody from the time of the Venerable Bede of Jarrow (see Northeast) in the 8th century until now wants to believe that St Martin is the church that survived in Canterbury from the time that the Emperor Constantine made Christianity the official religion of the Roman Empire throughout the early Middle Ages when the pagan Saxons and Danes ruled. When the Benedictine monk Augustine landed on Thanet in 597 and converted King Aethelbert of Kent, Aethelbert's queen,

Bertha, was already a Christian, and St Martin is where she worshiped. The little church on St Martin's Hill on the road to Sandwich has courses of Roman brick between the stone and flint. That alone makes the 7th century possible, but extensive passages of the walling are purely in courses of Roman brick, which suggests construction during the Roman occupation. The clincher, though this too is only circumstantial, is what Bede wrote:

On the east side of the city stood an old church, built in honour of St Martin during the Roman occupation of Britain, where the Christian queen of whom I have spoken [Bertha] went to pray. Here they first assembled to sing the psalms, to pray, to say Mass, to preach, and to baptize, until the king's own conversion to the Faith gave them greater freedom to preach and to build and restore churches everywhere.

After that, one might almost expect the mosaics and carvings of St Martin's 5th- and 6th-century contemporaries, the basilicas of Ravenna. No such thing, of course, but there is evidence of early Saxon work in some of the windows and a satisfyingly solid Norman tub font decorated with relief blind arches at the top and rows of interlocking rings below. The church stands in a small graveyard among trees in breezes that don't blow in the centre of the city with a fine view of Bell Harry, the cathedral's fabulous Perpendicular central tower built by the mason John Wastell in the reign of Henry VII, more than a thousand years after the building of St Martin, maybe.

Charleston
EAST SUSSEX

Bloomsbury in the country, Charleston farmhouse

Charleston was Bloomsbury in exile. Vanessa Bell (1879–1961) first rented it in 1916 as a house where she and her lover, Duncan Grant (1885–1978), could get away from London and share a studio to paint in. There was the bonus that here they could live on and off with his other lover, David Garnett, and her two children, Julian and Quentin, by her husband Clive Bell. There were frequent visits from others in the Bloomsbury group, John Maynard Keynes, Lytton Strachey, Roger Fry, E.M. Forster and even Vanessa's sister, Virginia Woolf, though she too had a country cottage at Rodmell only 4 miles away with her husband Leonard. Keynes married the ballerina Lydia Lopokova. Whether she frightened the horses when she danced naked through the lanes and woods is not known, but certainly the postman is reported to have taken exception.

In 1939 Clive Bell moved in and after the Second World War they never resumed London residence and lived here as one big happy family. The Charleston guidebook's great entertainment is its 'Bloomsbury relationship tree'. It has grey lines for married couples, red lines for offspring, yellow lines for heterosexual affairs, blue lines for homosexual affairs and mauve lines – the rarest – for close non-sexual friendships (it applies solely to Forster and the Woolfs). Among a complex of sexual relationships, the tree shows the highly active Grant producing a child with Vanessa Bell and having homosexual affairs with Keynes, Strachey and Adrian Stephen (Vanessa's brother). The child of Vanessa and Grant grew up as Angelica Bell, believing until the age of seventeen that her mother's husband was

her father, and when she reached maturity she married her actual father's male lover, Garnett. Despite an age gap of nearly forty years they produced a brood of four.

What has all this to do with art? Search me, but the painting was almost as promiscuous as the sex. Grant and Vanessa Bell painted just about everything that didn't move at Charleston: bed ends, walls, fireplaces and fire screens, bookcases, tables and window embrasures. Doors were decorated with caryatids, nymphs, still lifes, portraits, landscapes and nudes. There is a plaque behind the Aga by Grant in honour of the cook. Chairs were covered with Omega prints (joint props, Fry, V. Bell, Grant) or made in the Omega workshops, like the ceramics and curtains. Grant, Bell, Quentin and Angelica painted the wallpaper. Their painting was always milk and water modernism to suit the taste of the Heals market – not so much significant form (in Clive Bell's resonant phrase) as insignificant form – but the farmhouse is good to visit and must have been wonderful to live in, with its walled garden and ponds, certainly when the heating had been fixed. And in between the painting and sex at Charleston Maynard Keynes, who had his own bedroom here, managed to write the left-wing economics text that predicted the Second World War and changed the face of capitalism, *The Economic Consequences of the Peace* (1919).

Chichester
WEST SUSSEX

It isn't easy to lose your way in Chichester. Four roads radiate from the famous 15th-century octagonal market cross, North Street, South Street, East Street and West Street, just as the Romans laid them down in the place they knew as Noviomagus, and between the four gates at the end of these roads a ring

road encloses the city, following the line of
the defensive walls (still quite extensive)
and creating a shape like the circled cross on
a bishop's crosier. The cathedral lies close
to the market cross, homely rather than
majestic, a shepherd to his sheep, and home
to two of the finest Romanesque carvings
existing. The Georgian city as we know it
grew up around the cathedral. Pallant House,
one of its finest buildings in the district,
called the Pallants, is now the impressive art
gallery with its modern extension by St John
Wilson and the collection of British Pop Art
he donated to add to the modern collection
already in existence.

Early carvings, Chichester Cathedral

The cathedral, remarkably for a Norman
building, is as cosy as the city itself, with
piers lining the nave and supporting a
shallow-arched arcade that could have been
assembled from Lego, and walls with homely
fish-scale decoration, just like the patterning
so common in the much later tile-hanging on
Sussex half-timbered houses. So the drama
of the two Romanesque relief sculptures
– of Christ outside the house of Mary and
Martha and the raising of Lazarus from the
dead – come as a change of pace. They are
the best of the period in England except for
the sculptures in the porch of Malmesbury
Abbey (see South), but though they have the
vigour of Malmesbury, they have none of its
architectural stateliness. Instead, they have
a rude, narrative vigour, a little chaotic but
dramatic, early signs of a new humanity, a
new expression of the individual. Indeed, the
historian of Romanesque sculpture George
Zarnecki has suggested that the carver
may have been inspired by the religious
mystery plays. That would explain the
drama expressed in the faces of the figures
(assuming medieval players 'acted' in that
sense instead of wearing masks, so to speak).

Christ gazes into space beyond the kneeling,
beseeching figures of Mary and Martha,
perhaps seeking strength from his father,
as he arrives at the exotic house with barley
sugar columns under a round arch and
many turrets. His disciples follow him with
troubled faces. In the second panel Christ
makes a sign of blessing above the head of
the awakening Lazarus, but the faces of the
two women are still etched with grief, though
one of them registers dawning awareness.

The unease of the compositions is nothing
compared to the chaos surrounding the
history of the carvings. They were recovered
in 1829 from behind the choir stalls where
they had been chopped into blocks and
re-used as building stones. The best guess
is that they were originally part of a stone
screen. For many years afterwards they were
considered to have been carved in about
1000. Current betting, based on stylistic
resemblances to certain Romanesque ivories
and illustrated psalters, is on 1125–50. The
date is likely to remain vague because,
although the architectural role of the
Malmesbury sculptures in the abbey porch
is there for all to see, it's not clear how the
Chichester panels fitted in to any scheme.
What remains is their abiding power. A pity
about the glass screens that now protect
them.

Richard Hamilton's swinging sixties, Pallant House

Pallant House was the stateliest of mansions
in the warren of Georgian streets off the
city centre. In due course after the Second
World War it became an art gallery, and
when it needed an extension it appointed
the architect of the British Library, Colin
St John Wilson, and his architect wife, M.J.
Long, in a neat deal that involved the St John
Wilson collection passing to the Pallant
House Gallery. Richard Hamilton, Eduardo

Paolozzi, R.B. Kitaj, Peter Blake (see Carlisle, Northwest), Colin Self, Patrick Caulfield and others arrived in the very modern, very fitting extension, a grouping so strong it tends to take centre stage among a fine set of British paintings of the century already at Pallant House.

In 1965 Hamilton (b.1922) had acquired one of the pads of front page dummies that *Time* magazine supplies to its cover artists with the logo and contents already there and a space left for the artist's work. In this space he made a short sequence of portraits of himself as a *Time* celebrity. *Time* never took the bait, possibly because Americans regard Pop Art as an exclusively American concern, so in their view Hamilton was a hanger-on from old Europe. They were wrong. Hamilton was among the first Pop artists and the one who articulated the approach, ahead of the Americans. He produced the statement that, in a nutshell, announced that art based on mass-produced items, from toasters and automobiles to magazine covers and comic strips, was the art most appropriate to the admass society.

Hamilton and like-minded friends held a show at the ICA in London in 1956 called This Is Tomorrow, which featured Hamilton's *Just What is it that Makes Today's Homes so Different, so Appealing?* It was a collage done up like a nightmarish ad, bundling in all the consumer items necessary for instant domestic bliss. Each item of the collage was a bit of yesterday that amounted to a glimpse of the bland tomorrow. The critic Laurence Alloway applied the label Pop Art, and away they went. The Pallant House Hamiltons mostly step straight from his Pop manifesto. *Hers is a Lush Situation*, for instance, is an abstraction of a Buick airbrushed like a glossy magazine advertisement, and the title is from a phrase from an advertising campaign for the automobile. But *Swingeing London* is a silkscreen print with highlights

in oil paint on a *Daily Mail* photograph showing Mick Jagger and Hamilton's gallery agent, Robert Fraser, handcuffed together in the back of a car in Chichester on their way to a court remand hearing. They were charged along with Keith Richards with using cannabis and amphetamines (the police took away Chinese joss sticks too). Jagger and Richards were each sentenced to three months but won their appeals; Fraser pleaded guilty and served his six months. As a political comment on social hypocrisy this print was outside Hamilton's norm, but it stands as one of the symbolic images of the faraway 1960s.

Clayton
WEST SUSSEX

Ghostly 12th-century murals at the Church of St John the Baptist

Clayton is sandwiched by expanding well-heeled suburbia to the north and Brighton to the south, in a narrow strip of the proposed South Downs national park, which would protect it should it ever happen. It has a railway tunnel of 1840 on the London to Brighton line with a sham castle marking the entrance, and on the hill above it are two windmills. It has a pub named after the windmills, Jack and Jill. The parish church, dedicated to John the Baptist, is tiny: low chancel, higher nave and a small bell turret clad in wooden shingles. Inside the Norman north doorway to the right the west window is a piece of finely engraved clear glass for the millennium by Tony Gilliam. To the left, even more unexpectedly, around the 10th-century Saxon chancel arch and on the nave walls, are decorations painted not much later than the last millennium, in 1080 or 1140 according to whose verdict you accept. Pevsner goes unequivocally for c.1140.

They are true frescos, what Italy knows as

buon fresco, brushed swiftly on to wet plaster laid a stretch at a time, enough to be covered in a day, so, as it dried, the pigment soaked in and was incorporated into the plaster. Like all church paintings in England these survived tenuously and are badly faded. The best of our experience of them is the first impact, but there they are, legible in long passages, the earth colours of brown and white alone surviving, ghostly but grave visions of past glory. Henry VIII's placemen ordered the parish to destroy the paintings. It covered them in whitewash, and Charles Kempe, the Victorian ecclesiastical glassmaker and restorer, found them in 1895 and coaxed them back to life.

Plumb centre above the chancel arch in a Last Judgement is Christ in Majesty in a vesica, that almond-shaped space that stands for infinite space. There are supporting angels flanked by Apostles, tall, willowy figures with tiny heads. It is a standard Romanesque/Byzantine arrangement. The influences come from all over – from Sicily, from Normandy, maybe from the great abbey of Cluny in Burgundy, since Clayton's mother church, Lewes Priory (now long gone), was a Cluniac foundation.

Above the painting is a wide Greek key pattern border, the sort of repeating square shape that once upon a time would have been seen on the hems of togas. The border below the painting is a pattern of scroll and leaves. Christ overlaps them both just like a cut-out photograph overlaid on the masthead of a newspaper. Some good old design tricks never die. Beneath the second border is a second tier of biblical stories ruined beyond easy reading. But the upper tier on the chancel wall shows Christ delivering the keys to Peter and the book to Paul. On the nave north wall good folk approach the heavenly kingdom heralded by an angel with a trumpet. On the south wall another angel blows the last trump as the damned head off to hell accompanied by a single surviving horseman of the apocalypse, more angels and the instruments of Christ's Passion. Stern stuff for your average Jack and Jill.

Cobham
KENT

Family brasses, Cobham College

Cobham College and Cobham church, St Mary Magdalene, are locked in close embrace, the college hidden from the village street by the bulk of the church and separated from it only by a processional path. There is no doubt who the patron was: there in the centre of the chancel, built with Cobham family money, stands the 15th-century tomb chest with effigies of Sir George Brooke, 9th Lord Cobham, and Lady Cobham, blocking with its overweening arrogance the view of the altar. It reminds me of the 1962 *Private Eye* cover caption to a photograph of the great and the good assembled for the dedication of the new Coventry Cathedral: 'All right God, you can come in now.' Except that at Cobham he had better keep clear with the rest of us of the roped-off Cobham brasses. Spread almost the full width of the chancel at the foot of the tomb, this is the greatest display of church brasses in England, some say the world. There are fifteen of them in two rows. All but one are Cobhams or husbands of Cobhams. The one that is not is John Sprotte, the master of Cobham College, which, of course, was founded by a Cobham, the 3rd baron, a great soldier, man of affairs and JP (he served alongside Geoffrey Chaucer). His brass is down there among the others (fourth from left in the first row looking towards the west), showing him in armour under a canopy holding the collegiate church in his hands.

Lord Cobham founded the college for priests to say prayers daily for him and his wife and for their souls after death, and similarly for King Edward III and Queen Philippa, and for their ancestors and heirs. Eventually this onerous task demanded the services of a master, a sub-master, seven chaplains, a deacon, three clerks and a retinue of servants. No doubt they had their hands full. The physical relationship of church to college is similar to the relationship between Merton College chapel and Mob Quad, Oxford's oldest, built in the same period as Cobham. Like Mob Quad, Cobham College is a small quadrangle, about 50 feet square, and like it, it is two storeyed, with little pointed doors and square-head mullioned windows. After the dissolution in Henry VIII's reign it was converted into almshouses. The hall remains of the original building, but a separate quad and kitchens are ruined, and the other three sides of the almshouse quad were rebuilt in the 16th century to serve their new purpose, but to the same design and using the original Kentish ragstone. They remain as almshouses, but today the number of dwellings has been reduced and converted into modern flats. One feels that not many of the current tenants has said a prayer for the soul of the 3rd baron for some time.

Compton
SURREY

'England's Michelangelo' at the Watts Gallery

The Compton Gallery was set up by Mary, second wife of the popular Victorian painter George Frederick Watts (1817–1904), across the road from the house they had moved to from London for the sake of his health, beside the Portsmouth road near Guildford, but hidden in a little wooded decline. He died here, and Mary designed his intensely mawkish memorial chapel close by. Watts's first marriage, in 1864, was to Ellen Terry.

He was forty-six, she was an ingénue of sixteen, and he hoped to save her from a fate worse than death, the stage. Instead, he inflicted on her a fate much, much worse than death: being married to a pompous old bore. She left him within a year to became Edward VII's mistress and a pretty good actor too. The next time Watts married it was to someone who would nurse him through old age. But before Ellen left him, he painted her in *Love and Life*, the sort of woeful title he was all too prone to give his paintings. This one, though, was different: it was bad, but interesting because it featured a male and a female, Ellen Terry, embracing naked on some very sharp and uncomfortable looking rocks.

It's a total mystery that this man could have been known as 'England's Michelangelo'. He had more natural talent as a painter than any of his younger contemporaries, the Pre-Raphaelites, and was famous as a portrait painter to eminent Victorians, but even when he attacks the canvas directly the texture is dry, as though his sitters all had dandruff. His work, though representative of Victorian taste, really comes alive only when it involves a woman he loves. So in the swooning *Paolo and Francesca*, Francesca was modelled by the definitely un-nude girl-next-door with whom Watts was infatuated; but instead of accepting his offer of marriage, she chose to become Virginia, Countess Somers.

Watts had an exhibition in Paris in 1883 and hated the Impressionists and Post-Impressionists, which he perceived as mediocrity. For himself, he declared that he painted because he 'wished to stimulate the mind and awaken large thoughts'. Queen Victoria made him a member of the Order of Merit.

In this Victorian version of the characters in Dante's Divine Comedy *(Compton Gallery), G.F. Watts based Francesca on the girl next door, who turned him down when he proposed marriage*

Deal

KENT

This is where Julius Caesar landed in 55 BC, although, as always, there are contrary theories. The beach then was probably closer to the hill where Upper Deal has grown into a fine 18th-century hilltop village above the seaside town, with a church, Norman at core, but with a big 17th-century brick tower and a neat white cupola. After Sandwich silted up in the 16th century, 'new' Deal became an important commercial harbour. Its secret, of course, was the Goodwin Sands four miles out at sea which protects the waters off Deal. Protecting shipping from attack was the reason for the Tudor castles of Sandown, Deal and Walmer on this stretch of coastline – a practical military design that heralded the Martello towers of the Napoleonic Wars and the machine gun pillboxes of the Second World War.

Somehow, the sheltered waters failed to attract Victorian tourists and the seafront remains a quaint, largely 18th-century street of shops and houses with wooden fishing boats drawn up on the shingle beach. There's a brick-built town hall and, almost opposite the utilitarian concrete post-war pier, a tower with a time ball which was once electrically connected with the one at Greenwich Observatory to signal 1 o'clock; the tower is now an information centre. Towards Walmer there was a handsome Georgian Royal Marine barracks. The IRA bombed it in 1989 and killed ten marines. The barracks has since been converted into flats.

Turner on his travels, in Deal town hall

J.M.W. Turner was an omnivorous traveller. At the age of sixteen, when he was a student at the Royal Academy Schools, he went on his first sketching trip, to the west of England. The following year he was in Wales. Soon after it was the Midlands, the first of his expeditions to make watercolours the basis for engravings that would then be disseminated to a growing middle-class public avid for affordable art. After that came Scotland and the Lakes, the north of England, France, Switzerland and through to Italy, where he found one of his enduring subjects, Venice. In 1823 he travelled along the southeast coast of England, and in 1824 he travelled more generally in the south and southeast, filling sketchbooks as he went and producing some of his most magnificent watercolours. On one of these journeys he painted a view of Deal from offshore where the end of the pier now is (in truth more jetty than pier). At the time, he probably hired a fisherman to take him out, though presumably not in the stormy weather of the watercolour. In the town hall today a container, like the boxes pubs use to contain dartboards, hangs on a wall protecting the Turner watercolour inside from the light. The council doesn't advertise it but will show the watercolour on request.

The purely topographical interest of the watercolour is that Deal still looks much as Turner painted it: a simple high street along the seafront with a row of 18th-century houses strung out along the town side of the street and a large building, now a hotel, above the pebble beach. Turner shows it during a thunderstorm. A jagged streak of lighting flashes across a storm-tossed sky, the storm flags snap horizontal at their masts, and the sea rages as only Turner could paint it, the spray as the waves break almost palpable. Fishermen on the beach attend to their boats, and scattered couples

Walmer Castle, on the outskirts of Deal: one of the 'Tudor rose' designs for Henry VIII's coastal fortifications, adapted as the home of the wardens of the Cinque Ports. The Duke of Wellington died here in a room furnished with his old Napoleonic wars camp bed

gaze at the storm, at a safe distance. These couples, possibly, are from those very leisured classes at whom the Turner enterprise was aimed. William Radclyffe, a celebrated Birmingham craftsman, engraved the Deal storm. Turner had notoriously difficult working relationships with printmakers, but this engraving was one of a successful run of prints he did with Radclyffe and, ironically, the hand-coloured versions capture the original scene better than the now slightly faded watercolour.

The Iron Duke's last resort, Walmer Castle

The least of the Duke of Wellington's appointments was as Warden of the Cinque Ports. It was a once-exalted position that had become a sinecure after the ports themselves, initially Hastings, Romney, Hythe, Dover and Sandwich, dwindled in importance; but for Wellington it was the most enjoyable perk of a lifetime in war and politics because it bestowed on him a residence in Walmer Castle. It was here on 14 September 1852 that the old soldier chose to fade away, in the room he called home, dropping off in his old armchair that had been built straight-backed as a guardsman.

Henry VIII built Sandown, Deal and Walmer along a couple of miles of seafront to give landwards protection to the anchorage of the Downs, a stretch of the Channel protected from the direct incursion over the open sea by the Goodwin Sands. The potential enemy was François I of France and his ally the Emperor Charles V, nephew of Henry's divorced first wife, Catherine of Aragon. But the attack never came. Today Sandown is a small, dwindling remnant on the beach north of Deal. Deal Castle is still impressively solid and worth visiting, and Walmer on the southern outskirts of town has become a country mansion. Like the other castles, Walmer is low-lying and

centred on a circular keep surrounded by four semicircles: a Tudor rose, romantics say, but devised to deal death towards all possible approaches. The moat (now part of the gardens) is crossed by a bridge to the main entrance on the landward side. William Pitt the Younger, appointed warden by George III, laid out the first gardens, and they improved over the years. Finally Janet Hobhouse redesigned the walled garden under the lee of the castle as a ninety-fifth birthday present to the then warden, the Queen Mother.

Of all the illustrious wardens, Wellington was the most glorious bar one, Winston Churchill, but Churchill never stayed at Walmer. Wellington, the old soldier, the formidable old Tory, loved it, loved the sea bathing and his new friends of the neighbourhood, loved entertaining, doubtless loved living in a former military bulwark. Today his room remains much the same, spartan, picking up the theme of the armchair and his army camp bed, which had been good enough in the Peninsular Wars and was more than good enough in his declining years. Most of the few possessions he kept beside him remain here, principally, of course, the boots.

Dover
KENT

A Roman lighthouse, at Dover Castle

Claudius, emperor because he was the last man standing after the purges of Caligula, initiated his reign with the invasion of Britain of AD 43. This time the Romans had come to stay, and one of their first acts was to establish the port of Dubris, or Dover, Probably in AD 46, once the port had been consolidated and a closely built populous

This is the fifth Dungeness lighthouse since James I licensed the first in 1615, and, with a lantern of 1,920,000 candlepower, easily the most powerful

town was in construction, the Roman garrison built an octagonal, 80 foot high pharos, or lighthouse, on each of the cliffs flanking the port to guide ships crossing the Channel from Boulogne safely into harbour: one pharos on the eastern cliffs within iron age earthworks, now the medieval castle, and one on the western cliffs, which has disintegrated. Around the year 1000 the Saxons built St Mary in Castro and built it so close to the pharos that it seems they must have had designs on it, though as far as is known the pharos wasn't adapted for use as St Mary's belltower until the 13th century, and then in the 15th the top 19 of its current 62 feet were rebuilt to take rehung bells.

It is the nearest thing to a complete Roman building in England, unique also in its sibling relationship to the church in the embrace of the mother castle. St Mary in Castro has been the garrison church for most of its existence, certainly since Henry II built the first stone castle in 1168, but in the gung-ho fashion of the military mind it became a fives court in the 18th century and then a coalhouse during the Napoleonic Wars. After that, it might be thought, any restoration would be good, but William Butterfield's gross chancel mosaic and tiles of 1882 make that touch and go.

Dungeness

KENT

Lighthouse by Ward & Co.

The fame of this terminal beach of shingle rests on its sheer size, extending 8 miles by 4 miles, another 4 miles below the surface, and spreading at 4 metres a year. The bleak headland has two nuclear power stations, Dungeness A, closed but simmering on into the 22nd century if the rising sea doesn't reverse the onward progress of shingle and get there first, and Dungeness B. There are

a lifeboat station; Lydd's tiny airport and the westernmost station of the Romney, Hythe & Dymchurch miniature railway; gaily painted beach huts for all the world as though this was another genteel Southwold; a fish and chip caff; gigantic, three-armed pylons marching in double file northwards across Romney Marsh like an invading army; and wires strung between telegraph poles, as rickety as backgarden washing lines, serving a collection of huts mocked-up as cottages from old railway carriages, wood and corrugated tin, of which the most celebrated, Prospect Cottage, belonged to the film director Derek Jarman. And then there are the lighthouses.

There have been five of them since King James I licensed the first in 1615. It was no more than 35 feet high and involved hauling buckets of coal by pulley to the brazier at the top of the structure. Number two followed in 1635 and was higher but technologically no further advanced. James Wyatt, the fashionable society architect, built number three in 1792. It was 116 feet tall and lasted until the fourth came along in 1904, lit by vaporising paraffin and the use of glass prisms, which increased the light to 164,000 candlepower. But even this was dimmed by the proximity of the nuclear power station, so Ronald Ward & Co. built number five closer to the sea, and it opened in 1961. The legacy of the third Eddystone lighthouse on a rock off Plymouth was the archetype of a tall building tapering towards the top, built by Smeaton to succeed a sweet polygonal structure with a flag flying from a bracket and a lantern with leaded windows and a weathervane. Wyatt followed Smeaton's plan, and so did Patrick and Co., architects of the fourth (which still stands, open to visitors). But Ward & Co., constructing the latest version, used pre-stressed concrete rings, so the column rises smooth and straight as an amaryllis from

War artist meets man o' war in this painting by Eric Ravilious of an RN submarine in the Atlantic tracking a Luftwaffe spotter plane. The painting is part of a collection of his work in his home town gallery at Eastbourne. Ravilious died when a plane he was flying in to Iceland vanished

the unfurling spiral ramp at its base, then opens into a funnel shape at the top, poised to burst into blossom. It is banded black and white, and the ring below the funnel shape is nicely pierced all round with ten rows of holes six-deep to allow the sixty-speaker foghorn to sound over the sea. A little lantern at the top throws out a big light: 1,920,000 candlepower projecting a beam 27 marine miles, a lamp of life to those in peril on the sea.

Eastbourne
EAST SUSSEX

An Eastbourne artist at the Towner Art Gallery

No matter how wonderful the art may be that the newly housed Towner Art Gallery acquires with the £1 million it has been awarded by Art Fund International, it will certainly find added room for the art of Eastbourne's native son, Eric Ravilious (1903–42), one of its few sons, in fact, to die young in this old folks' haven, killed while commissioned as an official Second World

War artist working in the front line at sea. The Towner moves in 2009 from the 18th-century flint and brick manor house in the old town to Rick Mather's new lottery-funded gallery, a rock 'n' roll update of the Mendelsohn–Chermayeff 1930s De la Warr Pavilion in Bexhill (see above). The new building, a few months from completion as I write, is adjacent to the Congress Theatre and Winter Gardens just behind the stuccoed fleshpots of Grand Parade. It turns its back on the original gallery founded by Alderman John Towner in 1923 with his collection of Victorian art. The building he bequeathed simply became too small for a growing modern collection.

Apart from its own holdings, the Towner benefited from a bequest from Ravilious's family. There was plenty to choose from, for Ravilious was an illustrator, graphic artist, watercolourist and designer for Wedgwood. His watercolours of the 1920s and 1930s of the South Downs are atmospheric, gentle Georgian pastorals. Ravilious himself recognised that his wartime lithographs were the best of his work – war lent him a sharper focus, a journalistic focus one might say.

He was on the official war artist scheme and made several series of prints of aircraft and submarines that play heavily on the sense of enclosure, the armed tube with men inside relaxing as best they could, the printed colours thinly scraped, scratchy steely blues and yellow ochre and burnt umber, the submarine compositions always turning into the enclosure of a circle, even the patch of blue light thrown on to the commander's face as he peers through the periscope. And Ravilious neatly insets the skipper's circular view of a high winged spotter plane flying above the ocean outside.

He had finished the submarine series when he set off in a plane bound for Iceland and was never seen again. He left behind the sense that he would not have developed much further, that his paintings of war and peace together constituted his elegy to an England that was already fading away and leaving so many artists of his generation stranded.

Egham
SURREY

Frith's The Railway Station, Royal Holloway College

'A more characteristic illustration of the age could not have been selected,' commented the *Illustrated London News* when William Francis Frith's *The Railway Station* went on exhibition for several months in 1862 at the Haymarket Gallery. Like praising like. But in fact most of the press similarly saw the canvas as painted social history, something perfectly encapsulating the appearance of the uneminent Victorian, the man on platform 1 in the brave new world of railway travel as it broke out of the Puffing Billy era into trains that could travel at 60 miles an hour, the grandeur of the new engineered architecture of the terminals (this railway station shed is Paddington). The *Illustrated London News* again: 'The railway … is the grandest exponent of the enterprise, the wealth, and the intelligence of our race. The iron rails are welded into every life-history, and sometimes interwoven with our very heartstrings. The steam-engine is the incarnate spirit of the age – a good genius to many, an evil demon to some.' (And both simultaneously; the art critic John Ruskin excoriated railways but learned to travel by them and treated the porter at Coniston civilly.)

Frith (1819–1909) had already experienced huge successes with his *Derby Day* and *Ramsgate Sands*, minutely detailed panoramas of the railway age British at play, but *The Railway Station* is his masterpiece. Thomas Holloway bought it for £2,000 in 1883 from its previous owner, who had made £40,000 from it by buying up the rights to have an engraved copy made and printed in its thousands. Holloway made his own money by selling quack patent pills and potions. He built Holloway College, a huge and astonishing orange brick edifice, originally housing only twenty young women students and Holloway's art collection. Frith's painting is the star, even though the medicine man did buy better paintings, supremely a Constable sketch for *View of the Stour, Near Dedham* (1822).

Frith doesn't compete in that territory of rendering natural appearances naturally and with virtuoso technique; nor, though his approach might be called photographic, is he in the field with photography. Photography shows detail as well, but Frith's canvas, almost 4 feet high by over 8 feet wide, is a series of chapters in Dickens, something to be read detail by detail, each group of travellers physically overlapping with another, but each sealed in its own hermetic world of social class and Frith's narrative: two top-hatted Scotland Yard peelers feeling the collar of a villain; a redcoat sergeant hoisting his child in the air; parents seeing their two boys off to boarding school (a portrait of the Frith family); a posh bridal party sending off the bride and groom on honeymoon; porters loading luggage on to the carriage roofs; an aggressive cab driver negotiating a fare. Not a moment in time, but a timeline, a social document.

Esher
SURREY

The temple of costly experience at The Homewood

The house that the architect Patrick Gwynne built in a leafy glade on the A307 southwest of Esher became a lifetime's love affair. He completed The Homewood in 1939 when he was twenty-six and lived in it, wartime RAF service apart, until he died aged ninety in 2003. In his last years, penniless, he worked with the National Trust on restoring it to its pristine white modernist perfection. It was his first solo architectural job. He had done a couple of years training in a traditionalist architect's office, then worked for the pioneer English modernist Wells Coates, had toured Germany and France and been bowled over by Le Corbusier's Villa Savoye in Poissy, Paris's Esher. Then he launched out on his own by persuading his parents to knock down their cranky old Victorian house in the stockbroker belt and allow him to build a new family home instead. The Homewood is Gwynne's homage to Le Corbusier and gift of love to his parents and, since they both died in 1942, to himself.

It is built on stilts, or pilotis, like the Villa Savoye, and not beside the road like the original house but on a small hill. The entrance hall, office and garaging for four family cars (pre-war!) are on the ground floor and the living spaces on the first floor, wide shallow windows along the front, again following Le Corbusier, with wall-to-ceiling windows at the rear giving on extensive views across the garden, which Gwynne Sr had already planted, and thickly wooded Esher Common. Bedrooms, two of them, for Gwynne and his long-term companion, the pianist Harry Rand, are identical and simple if not exactly spartan. The entrance has a solid glass-block wall to allow daylight in and glass-block walls appear at strategic points on the first floor too.

Gywnne oversaw the creation of perfection aided by a contractor supplied by Wells Coates who was skilled in reinforced concrete construction. Gwynne's fixtures fit flush and impeccable, doors slot into walls like shells into gun barrels, cupboards set flush with the walls, a desk light that, switched off, sinks silently out of sight beneath the desk top, Gwynne-designed settees and armchairs with others by the architect Eero Saarinen and by Charles and Ray Eames (this last a gift from the widow of Gywnne's friend and client, the actor Laurence Harvey). Walls are variously clad, one in Swedish fabric, another in Indian wood, and in the living room a slab of black Levanto marble veined red, white and green.

Gywnne preferred to work alone, building posh modernist houses for clients who wanted absolute quality – his father resignedly dubbed The Homewood 'the temple of costly experience'. There were a few other jobs, like the 1951 Festival of Britain Crescent Restaurant in Battersea Park and two on the Serpentine in Hyde Park, one of which survives. But Gwynne's heart was in The Homewood, so that, 1930s monument though it is, it took on aspects of the decades after the war, a house with a history, which feels lived in because it is. The National Trust brought in a young couple to live there (so the public can visit only six months a year on Fridays); it's rent free, but entails looking after the garden, and that, like Gwynne in his house, looks like a job for life.

Eynsford
KENT

A champion's jousting helmet, at Lullingstone Castle

The story of Lullingstone starts as a romance. It was built in 1497 on the River Darenth a few hundred yards south of Lullingstone roman villa (see below) by Sir John Peche, Henry VII's champion jouster, who triumphed at the royal tournament in Westminster in 1494 and received in token of this a golden ring set with a ruby from the king's daughter, Princess Margaret. Fast forward 500 hundred years, and the romance

takes a twist. Guy Hart Dyke (the family descended from the Peches by marriage) and his wife Sarah are struggling to keep the estate afloat with an income barely sufficient to cope. Their twenty-year-old son Tom, a horticulturist, sets out on a plant hunt of the world, but while he is looking for a rare orchid in Panama close to the Colombian border, he is taken hostage by armed guerrillas and held hostage under threat of death for nine months. In captivity he draws a plan for a 'world garden' at Lullingstone within the ancient walls of an old orchard. When he is released he writes a bestseller about his experiences, then sets about creating the garden he had planned with seeds he collected around the world, some of them never planted in Britain before. The bestseller and the garden bring in more visitors than Lullingstone Castle has ever seen, and the future suddenly looks sunny.

The brick turreted Tudor gatehouse remains of the Peche building, and there's a little 14th-century church dedicated to St Botolph opposite a lake through which the Darenth flows. Across a big lawn the house gained a new west front and grand staircase when Queen Anne was a frequent guest. Through the centuries the owners accumulated the fashionable possessions of their time, and the rooms spell out a modest history: family portraits, oak chests, a set of kettledrums that one of the Hart Dyke ladies played in a local band, a venerable oak-panelled library with thousands of ancient volumes and manuscripts, and above a door a little scene of a hunting party gathered outside the gatehouse, a portrait of Queen Anne and rooms furnished for her occupation. And, rightly in pride of place in the great hall, a stately triptych of full-length portraits painted in 1575: the bulky figure of Sir Percyvall Hart at the age of eighty in the central panel flanked by portraits of his sons.

The most improbable survival is in the

state dining room: the tilting helm that the original Sir John took with him when he accompanied Henry VIII to the meeting in 1520 with François I at the Field of the Cloth of Gold outside Calais, a gorgeously decked camp where the French and English courts met in amity. It was so successful that two years later English troops invaded France. The helm is practically as good as new, burnished metal designed to cover the head entirely with just a wide slit for the eyes and with three ostrich plumes, one red, one white, one yellow, the colours Henry's royal father had chosen for the jousting tournament at which Sir John became champion.

Firle Place
EAST SUSSEX

John, Count of Nassau-Siegen, and his family, by Anthony Van Dyck

The Gage family moved to Firle in the 16th century and is still there by continuous succession through the male line. Maybe they came to the remote Downs to escape persecution as Catholics. Anyway, after two centuries of groaning under the yoke, Sir William Gage, 7th baronet, pragmatically if a little late, decided on behalf of the family to embrace Anglicanism and thus transformed their fortunes. His successors became viscounts, and luck has smiled upon them ever since. Earlier, General Sir Henry Gage negligently lost the nascent American empire by leading his troops to the defeat at Bunker Hill. This was considered a less serious defect than being a Catholic, and, in the English way, he was promoted to general and took a leisurely retirement. He was a second son, but his son, Henry, became the 3rd viscount. The fifth Henry is the current, 8th viscount. The house itself is Tudor, encased in Georgian.

Henry the fifth's grandfather's marriage to the Hon. Imogen Grenfell brought three collections of art to Firle to add to the Gage collection. Chief among them was Imogen's share of the Cowper collection, which had been founded by her ancestor Henry Nassau d'Auverquerque, Lord Grantham. This includes Reynoldses and Gainsboroughs, Zoffanys and, in the dining room, a great landscape by Philips de Koninck, but the *chef d'oeuvre* is the group portrait of Lord Grantham's kinsman, *Count John of Nassau-Siegen and his Family*, which Anthony Van Dyck (1599–1641) painted in Brussels in 1634 on a visit home from the English court while he was waiting for the new Spanish prince regent of the Netherlands to turn up to have his portrait painted.

In a way, Firle Place is the wrong place for it. The canvas is one of Van Dyck's largest, not as big as the Pembroke portrait at Wilton House, but too big to turn into a billiard table for Firle's billiard room. Consequently, it hangs in the entrance hall off the courtyard – the old great hall, and the only chamber able to accommodate it comfortably.

This work is what used to be called a 'grand machine', and Van Dyck doesn't seem to have been altogether comfortable with it. The count and countess have none of the opulent ease of the Pembrokes but seem slightly frozen into pompous convention in the operatic setting of a dais, big classical columns and heavy curtains draped to reveal a stage-set landscape. Certainly it is beautifully composed, with the family arranged in a semicircle running counter to the semicircle of the dais, but it is only with the son and three daughters that Van Dyck is finally at ease. The older daughter, Ernestine, is aged about fourteen and thus ready for marriage. Her dress is of white silk, and she stands in a pose mirroring the pose of Lady Mary Villiers, the bride in white silk of the Pembroke family portrait. The little boy in red silk and lace collar, who ought to be outside playing conkers, stands superciliously conscious of his status as heir to the count. The two younger daughters stand obediently out of the limelight. The room attendant told me that she believed these two girls were a later addition, and indeed there does appear to be a vertical seam between the two girls and the rest of the family; raise your hand to block out that part of the painting and it works perfectly well. The attendant preferred the two fine 15th-century Umbrian coffer lids, *cassone*, in the billiard room, charmingly painted with wedding procession scenes. I don't, but I would give them house room.

Fishbourne
WEST SUSSEX

A palace for King Cogidubnus

Of all the finds of Roman art in Britain, it is the thin, wooden, leaf letters found dumped at the fort of Vindolanda on Hadrian's Wall, postcards from abroad (they are the right size), that most stir the imagination since they are the first hard evidence in writing we have outside the pages of the Roman historian Tacitus of the life of Roman garrisons in Britain.

Like the postcards, the remnant of the building at Fishbourne is a post-war discovery, the biggest Roman palace in northern Europe with more than twenty surviving mosaics. Archaeologists found evidence that the Romans had a military presence at the vanished harbour of Fishbourne even before the Claudian invasion of AD 43, but the palace itself was begun in the invasion year, possibly by the post-invasion client king Cogidubnus who was, Tacitus wrote tartly, 'an example of the long-established Roman custom of employing even kings to make others slaves'. Cogidubnus's palace grew over the centuries into the extensive and ornate splendour of

which we see the vestiges. It had four wings, about 500 feet square, around a large open garden courtyard. Fire destroyed it in 270, and the remains are sandwiched between the A27 trunk road from Portsmouth to Chichester and the A259 meandering along the coast. Some of the palace lies under the houses and gardens lining the A259.

For the historian, Fishbourne is an incomparable resource and palimpsest, with the pattern of planting trenches in the garden exposed, pieces of surviving moulded plaster from friezes, later mosaics laid over earlier, a total of about twenty. Although most of the mosaics are relatively complete, they are mostly patterned abstracts that would have worked as part of a decorative scheme but don't amount to much in isolation.

The exception is an extraordinary 3rd-century mosaic, 17 feet square, with a circular central panel showing Cupid riding a dolphin. Inside a wide decorative frieze a happy arrangement of frisky seahorses and winged lions, decorative shell shapes and urns surround the main motif. The cupid and dolphin in a decorative roundel are outstanding. It looks as though the craftsman has worked from a cartoon, something between the old sense of a model for the finished work and the modern sense of a swiftly drawn scene. The Fishbourne mosaic takes what must have been a freely brushed calligraphic style and translates them in the static medium of little coloured stone tesserae, pieces of pottery, and, for the black portions, shale from Sussex beaches, into an astonishing impression of speed – speed of execution and speed in the pictorial action. Cupid leans back insouciantly, like a horserider easy in the saddle, his liquidly outlined wings, the swishing tail of the dolphin and the highlights of white tesserae like wet speedmarks joining Cupid and leaping sea mammal in a harmony of freedom.

Goodwood

WEST SUSSEX

The Goodwood estate is about horses. Oh yes, the Duke of Richmond's country house is there as well, but even here paintings of horses by George Stubbs are dominant (see below), and way above the house, 600 feet above sea level, is the racecourse, Goodwood, glorious Goodwood, commanding wonderful views across the Downs inland and holding race meetings since 1802. Amid lamentations, the Goodwood Estate Company knocked down the much-loved old grandstand, but in 1980 replaced it with something better by the Festival of Britain architect Howard Lobb, a raked stand beneath ten elongated, cantilevered ribbed shells, which everyone except the most obdurate haters of glass and concrete loves at least as much as the rickety old stand. Since then Michael Hopkins has built his own interpretation of festive: a cluster of airy tented pavilions around the stand. The great house below, never completed, might almost have been built as an afterthought. The estate itself, all 12,000 acres of some of the finest downland in Sussex, has room at an eastern corner for the far-sighted enterprise of the Cass Foundation's sculpture park (see below), showing some of the best of contemporary sculpture by rising young artists as well as established names.

George Stubbs, the master of horse painting, at Goodwood House

'Now, gods stand up for bastards!' cries Edmund in *King Lear*, a cry from the dispossessed, although, even without divine intervention, king's bastards seem to have done well enough for themselves. King Charles II produced fourteen with the cooperation of his seraglio and at their birth created them either countesses or dukes. The Goodwood line, the Lennoxes, dukes of Richmond, sprang from the womb of Louise de Kéroualle, a new mistress pimped for the king in 1671 by the Duke of Buckingham. When the Lennoxes' London home, Richmond House, burned down in 1791 the 3rd duke hired Wyatt to add to the small existing house at Goodwood a big new range. Here he installed his art collection. More recently a room in the house was devoted to memorabilia of the Battle of Waterloo. The 4th duke commanded a reserve battalion with the brief to defend Brussels should Napoleon break through, and the night before the battle his wife threw the ball (immortalised in Thackeray's *Vanity Fair*) at which Wellington confessed to Richmond: 'Napoleon has humbugged me, by God, he has gained twenty-four hours march on me.' Like all such collections the Goodwood collection has the whiff of mothballs. Not so the greatest of the house's art, the horse paintings ordered by the 3rd duke from George Stubbs (1724–1806). This was Stubbs's first important commission, and he stayed at Goodwood for nine months to produce the three pictures that hang today in the front hall, *The Charlton Hunt*, *Henry Fox and the Earl of Albemarle Shooting at Goodwood* and *The Duchess of Richmond and Lady Louisa Lennox Watching the Duke's Racehorses at Exercise*.

The Charlton Hunt is really a conversation piece on horseback with the 3rd duke and his brother Lord George in the blue livery of the hunt. Like most conversation pieces, nobody actually converses. The duke had a consuming interest in breeding hounds, and Stubbs was the man to paint them in all their individuality. The shooting picture is stolen by a black groom in the gold and scarlet Goodwood livery holding the reins of a black horse; likewise, in the racehorses picture there is a lovely cameo of one groom holding a horse by the head while another rubs it down and a couple of lads fetch straw. In each of the three paintings the Downs landscapes of Goodwood are identifiable today. They do their job pictorially in holding together disparate groups of men, horses and hounds, a disparateness and slight stiffness that Stubbs would overcome later in his career as his confidence in handling major compositions increased.

There's one more Stubbs painting to look out for, a small one in the long hall of the old part of the house, and this shows him at his best, not anxious to please but simply painting a lioness snarling at a lion, both of them tawny gold against velvety darkness in which a third lion is dimly discernible.

Modern sculpture, Goodwood gardens

A walk in the glades among a big selection of sculpture under the tall trees in a copse carved from the Goodwood estate on lease at a peppercorn rent from the Duke of Richmond – what could be finer? It is called Sculpture at Goodwood and is run by the Cass Foundation, a public-spirited initiative by Wilfred and Jeannette Cass to promote British sculpture, partly by supporting ventures like the sculptures to fill the fourth, empty, plinth in Trafalgar Square, and by commissioning sculpture and enabling sculptors to cast ambitious work in bronze, a material that they would mostly be unable to afford without financial backing. It's not strictly a collection, because the foundation sells the work, retains the costs and passes on the profit to the artist, but sculpture moves off the grass slowly and there is a sense of continuity and a constant education in how wide the variety of sculpture is today in Britain.

For Lynn Chadwick (1914–2003) it was a godsend. He had shown at the '52 Venice Biennale with, among others, Reg Butler,

Bernard Meadows, Eduardo Paolozzi and William Turnbull, but the post-war flush of his and Butler's fame as expressionist sculptors had long faded. Herbert Read called their work 'the geometry of fear', though given their straining allusiveness he might have called it the fear of geometry, but his phrase does imply that the work was made in the shadow of Hiroshima. In 1956 Chadwick was back at the biennale and won the International Prize for Sculpture. After that it was all downhill.

First came Anthony Caro's completely abstract sculpture of rods and sheets of painted steel, and then another generation, mostly taught by Caro, the New Generation of Bryan Robertson's famous 1965 Whitechapel exhibition, making polychrome sculptures that could almost have been three-dimensional paintings. Of the older generation, Paolozzi and Turnbull in particular survived the competition, but history binned Chadwick's reputation. He plugged on, changing, but not much, becoming more mannered if anything. Then the Cass Foundation took him up in the 1990s and started showing his work at Goodwood. Very old now, he began to approach abstraction in his works. He made a model for the large abstract sculpture called *Ace of Diamonds*. The form of this maquette, the diamond shape, looked like an abstract finesse of the shapes peculiar to him, the attenuated bronze bat-winged figures straining against an imaginary gale. He may have made it as a way of telling his younger contemporaries, in the words of gun totin' Annie Oakley's song, 'Anything you can do I can do better', but it evidently grows naturally out of his earlier work, and in 2004 the foundation had it constructed in stainless steel, though Chadwick died before he saw it. The diamond shape slots into the triangular jaws of a great rectangular flange, which swings in the breeze on a central spindle.

This impressive piece is roped off behind a warning notice, because anyone who stepped in the way would find the geometry of fear translated into an almighty clout behind the ear.

Great Bookham
SURREY

A Wren church meets a country house, at Polesden Lacey

As the illegitimate, much-loved daughter of William McEwan, the patriarch of the Edinburgh brewery McEwan's, Margaret Greville inherited his fine collection of Dutch 17th-century and early Italian art. She added it to her own collection at Polesden Lacey, which she and her husband Ronald had bought in 1906, two years after the architect Ambrose Poynter, a cousin of Rudyard Kipling, had rebuilt the house around a small quadrangle. Richard Brinsley Sheridan, author of *The School for Scandal*, had owned the estate and previous house at the beginning of the 19th century and remarked that it was the nicest place in England, qualified by 'within a prudent distance of town'. It arguably has the best view in Surrey, over a lush valley in the North Downs.

Ronald Greville died in 1908, but Margaret Greville became a celebrated society hostess, entertaining Edward VII in 1909, lending the house to the future George VI and Elizabeth for their honeymoon in 1923, and welcoming Hitler's crony Joachim von Ribbentrop to Polesden – she was no different in her taste in people from many of her class. But first the Grevilles called in the architects of the Paris and London Ritz Hotels, Charles Mewès and Arthur Joseph Davis, to design interiors fit for a king. They put in the saloon lifted almost entirely from an Italian palazzo, decorated with so much gold that sunglasses are a help, and the tunnel-vaulted corridors copied lock stock and barrel vaulted ceiling from the Jacobean long gallery at Chastleton (see West and East Midlands). At least as decisively, they brought in the decorators White, Allom & Co. This firm were past-masters at picking up etceteras from demolished buildings. In very short order Polesden was alive with Italian painted ceilings, French rococo and sculptured 18th-century English fireplaces, wooden panelling from who knows where, Venetian wellheads in the garden and on the terraces, and maybe even the books furnishing the library shelves, for a well-stocked library was a necessary embellishment even for a hostess with no time to read.

Margaret Greville herself supplied the extraordinary Japanese 17th-century and Chinese 18th-century porcelain and, at the end of a corridor vista, her own full-length portrait by the Parisian society artist Carolus-Duran. White, Allom however, with bravura effrontery, produced and installed as a firemantel in the central hall the reredos Edward Pierce had carved for Wren's City church, St Matthew, Friday Street. The church had been demolished in 1883, and White, Allom picked up the reredos at a sale and refitted it expertly to cover a complete wall with the fireplace slotted in where the altar had once stood. Pierce (*c*.1635–95) had worked with Wren after the fire of London and made the superlative bust of him now in the Ashmolean Museum, Oxford. He carved this reredos with a directness and clarity that can in no way be confused with the finesse of Grinling Gibbons but that stakes out its own distinct claim. Between fluted Corinthian columns is a wide, curved pediment, and between that and the veined marble fireplace is the head of a cherubim flanked by rich swags of flowers. Immediately above the fireplace are two panels, blank where once the Ten Commandments were inscribed in gold on black. Outside the columns are doors fitted under pediments in place of the panels that carried the Lord's Prayer and the Creed. Sheridan would certainly have applauded this *coup de théatre*.

Ightham

KENT

A humble chapel for a royal dynasty, Ightham Mote

'Mote' has nothing to do with the impressive moat that surrounds the house. It means meeting place. Who met there is moot, for standing in a thickly wooded valley, Ightham Mote was always one of Kent's most secluded places. Visitors on the one day a week the house was open to the public in post-war years had to park with two wheels in the road and two high up on a grassy bank, so narrow was the lane passing by. But then Charles Robinson, the American who had bought it in the 1950s, cherished it and saved it from falling down, decided it was time to pass on the baton. In February 1985 I was at the press conference in the great hall of Ightham Mote for the announcement that Mr Robinson had donated the house to the National Trust. When I left the meeting I knew that things would never be the same again.

They aren't. Despite the necessary car park, the necessary restaurant, the necessary shop, they are better. Over the years the Trust has rescued the Mote from death by beetle, dry rot, damp rot and the general decrepitude of old age. Today the house is in better condition than at any time since, probably, the 14th century. The Mote is, in fact, a compendium of the centuries, four ranges built around a courtyard by a variety of owners, starting with the great hall and the old chapel in the south wing, both *c.* 1330. None of the owners was outstandingly wealthy, so changes were merely minor concessions to current taste throughout the house's history. Thus Selby family portraits, accumulated in the almost 300 years of their ownership (1592–1889), still hang in the great hall and domestic suites. When the owners needed space for servants, they built a range of cottages beyond the moat.

The old chapel fell out of use during the reign of Henry VIII and Sir Richard Clements, the lord of the manor, ordered the conversion of a tunnel-vaulted room in the east wing into a new chapel to celebrate the marriage of Henry VIII and Catherine of Aragon. It is the most remarkable room in the house. The linenfold panelling, the stalls and pulpit with its sounding board, the screens and pews, the candlesticks and Spanish processional cross were scavenged or bought, like almost everything else at the Mote, from other houses and churches, ending with the font, which a milkman rescued from a bonfire in 1951. The jewel is the faded but declamatory splendour of the oak-plank vault, which is decorated with the roses of Lancaster, York and the Tudors, the portcullis of the king's mother's family, the Beauforts, the pomegranate and the arrows of Aragon and the castles of Castile, the fleur-de-lis of France, to whose throne Henry laid claim. It's the faded work of a local craftsman, crude as Tudor art often is but a definitive homage that survived the death of its political relevance. Clearly, the king never visited the house after the divorce but the owners must have kept the old faith because in the reign of Elizabeth I the church authorities denounced Ightham Mote as 'a vile and papistical house' and ordered the closure of the chapel.

The Tudor chapel in Ightham: the decorations of the tunnel vault celebrate the marriage of Henry VIII and Catherine of Aragon and survived the divorce

Knole

KENT

*Joshua Reynolds off duty with Dr
Johnson's literary club*

Archbishop Thomas Bourchier built Knole
as a palace in about 1460. It has remained a
famous palace ever since, set in a 1,000 acre
deer park and with a fabulous collection
of silver furniture added by the Sackvilles
after they had bought the house in the
16th century. In its time it matched the
Versailles silver and is now unique, because
the Jacobins melted down the French royal
pieces. But when Horace Walpole visited
Knole, on the same terms as any modern
tourist, he remarked waspishly: 'The first
little room you enter has sundry portraits
of the times; but they seem to have been
bespoke by the yard, and drawn all by
the same painter' – which is still the first
impression today. But the 3rd Duke of
Dorset, John Frederick Sackville, who had,
it was generally thought, more money than
sense and was a sportsman, gambler and
womaniser, began to buy art by the great
painters of his time, and not just family
portraits. Vita Sackville-West, a watered-
down descendant, believed that among the
duke's mistresses was Marie Antoinette.
Certainly Giovanna Baccelli was. She was a
dancer who modelled in the buff for a full-
size plaster reclining figure, which graces the
well beneath the great staircase. Her lover, the
convivial, over-moneyed aristocrat, was also
the friend of writers and artists.

The Reynolds room best commemorates
the duke's gift for enlightened patronage.
There are a couple of Sir Joshua's show-
pieces, one of the duke, one of the little
Chinese servant, Wang y Tong, but the real
interest is the lesser group, the subfusc
portraits of Dr Johnson, Oliver Goldsmith
and David Garrick. The painting of Johnson,

largely because of Reynolds's habit of using
bitumen, an experimental glazing medium,
has lost some of its colour to fissured, tarry
blackness, but, stripped of the pomp of
baroque portraiture, it remains of great
intrinsic interest, because it shows both artist
and sitter unbuttoned. The duke bought it
wet from the easel. It catches Johnson making
what Reynolds called the 'strange antic
gesticulations' to which he was prone when
he was thinking in the presence of friends,
and Reynolds himself, Johnson once wrote to
him, was 'almost the only man whom I call a
friend'. The artist shows him with hands half-
clenched, eyes half-closed, thunderous brow
– 'a mind feeding upon itself.'

Reynolds painted the Knole portrait in
1769. Dorset next bought a companion
piece, the portrait of Goldsmith, who was
co-founder with Johnson and Reynolds
of the Literary Club. Both portraits were
shown in the Royal Academy exhibition of
1770, and they appear to have been painted
to celebrate each writer's election (at
Reynolds's behest) to professorships at the
academy. Later, the duke completed the set of
portraits of his friends with the purchase of
Reynolds's Garrick, the boy who had arrived
from Lichfield on the same horse as Samuel
Johnson (because the writer was unable to
afford a second horse) and found his own
way to fame.

Lenham

KENT

A village mortuary and lock-up

Lenham looks at its best on one Sunday a
month, when the farmer's market pushes
the parked cars off the little market square
with its mixture of Wealden timber-framed
halls and Georgian architecture, roof lines
a matter of whim. The church has its own
square southeast of the market square, and

behind the church is an enormous aisled tithe barn and a green pond with ducks. A few yards north an innocent terrace of 18th-century brick cottages at right angles to the Faversham road terminates with an impressive little ragstone edifice. It's not much more than a single cell, but the façade, though rough hewn, has pretensions: it is an arch with a pediment surmounted by a clumsy cross, just two stones spatchcocked together at right angles. The arch itself is heavily rusticated with a long keystone overlapping the bottom of the pediment. It's like the nightmare vision of baroque architecture translated by a village mason into this one-night stand for corpses.

For that's the purpose it first served, the last repose from the mid-18th century of the passing vagabond or village wastrel who had sullied the village with his untimely death before being whisked off for burial in an unmarked grave. By the late 19th century it became the parish gaol with a similar clientele, usually drunk or just a destitute nuisance. In the Second World War it saw service as an air-raid shelter, reinforced with concrete (since removed). Concrete or not, this would have been death's little dominion once again had a V-bomb from Hitler scored a direct hit.

Lullingstone
KENT

A British Roman villa with the trappings of enslavement

It's only a rich man's farmhouse, not especially big, although rooms were added as the business of supplying produce to the legionaries in their northern outposts flourished, but it is one of the key sites of Roman Britain. It lies at the foot of a hill down a winding lane beside the little River Darent, and it is a palimpsest of the years of occupation from around twenty years after the death of Claudius in AD 54 until after Constantine made Christianity the official religion in 324. It was built, originally of wattle and daub and then, in the 2nd century, of stone, and its origins lay in the years of about AD 75 to 100, a period covered by Agricola's pacification of the island, which, as his son-in-law Tacitus pointed out, ushered in a class of Briton who spoke Latin, wore the toga and abandoned the circular dwelling for the luxurious advantages of the Roman villa. 'And so the population was gradually led into the demoralising temptations of arcades, baths and sumptuous banquets,' Tacitus wrote. 'The unsuspecting suspects spoke of such novelties as "civilisation", when in fact they were only a feature of their enslavement.'

The Romans are often despised as the bourgeois to the aristocrats of ancient art, the Greeks; but Roman intellectual energy and engineering imagination also produced the soaring aqueducts at Pont du Garde and Segovia, the great stadiums, the dome of the Pantheon, inimitable for another millennium and a half, and as much works of civilisation as the Parthenon is. Given their belief in the possibilities of individual genius, it is hardly surprising that the figurative art form the Romans excelled at was portrait sculpture. They invented this form of realism and have never been surpassed. The archaeologists found two such pieces when they excavated Lullingstone. Though they are carved in Greek marble, they may have been portraits of the owners, or, more likely according to current thinking, of great Roman rulers, acquired for similar reasons to courtiers of Charles I displaying copies of Van Dyck royal portraits in their homes as a sign of allegiance and preferment. The original busts are in the British Museum, and Lullingstone displays only plaster copies, good enough to make a point, particularly in the splendidly refurbished display with soft spotlighting

Europa and the Bull, a Mediterranean myth transposed into a gentle Kentish river valley in this mosaic in the Romano-British villa at Lullingstone

picking out the sculptures, the mosaics, the paintings and the displays of grave goods, including the 4th-century pieces for a predecessor of backgammon called *duodecim scripta*, one of them carved with a gorgon's head.

The loveliest of the remains, partly obliterated and very faint, is a graceful fresco of water nymphs in an alcove in the cult room, apparently in obeisance to a deity of the little River Darent, which runs by a few yards away. The most spectacular is the mosaic floor in the apsidal dining room and adjoining audience chamber. It is provincial work, unlike the portrait busts, but decoratively satisfying and almost complete. One scene shows Europa being abducted by the god Jupiter in the guise of a bull, and the other shows Bellerophon slaying the chimera, a pagan parallel to St George and the dragon. The floor was laid in the

mid-4th century and may have some coded Christian significance. What is indisputable is that the cult room's last manifestation was as a Christian chapel, because when the cellar beneath the chapel's floor was examined after the excavation, painted fragments of plaster from the chapel's ante-room were reconstructed to show that they had constituted a painting of the Christian monogram the *Chi-Rho*.

Roman hegemony in Britain collapsed at the beginning of the 5th century. The villa was destroyed by fire and then covered by a landslip from the hill behind the house. With its works of art, it lay under the earth by the River Darent until after the Second World War.

Lynsted

KENT

Monument to Lord Teynham by
Epiphanius Evesham, Church of St Peter
and St Paul

Not much of the work of Epiphanius
Evesham (*c.*1570–*c.*1633) has survived and
not much of his reputation except among
connoisseurs. None of his work from his
fifteen years in Paris from 1600 survives
at all, even though he received illustrious
commissions there, including one for a
memorial to the bishop of Sens in Notre
Dame. No wonder, then, that despite his
wonderfully euphonious name, it doesn't
come readily to many lips. When he returned
to work in London in 1615 he received
plentiful commissions, but the best of
what does survive has to be tracked down
under the big skies of the North Downs of
Kent along obscure lanes winding between
pretty villages between Sittingbourne and
Faversham – Boughton-on-Blean, Lynsted
and Otterden, which has disappeared off
many road maps because all that survives
out of sight is a decommissioned bare barn
of an 18th-century church in the great park
of Otterden Place. ('Turn right at the big oak
and go straight on to the white gate on the
right,' a neighbouring farmer directed me,
directions his predecessor might have given in
the same terms three centuries ago.) Of these,
the finest is the monument to Lord Teynham
(died 1622) in St Peter and St Paul, Lynsted.

Evesham actually came of Herefordshire
stock, and he was Epiphanius because
he was born on the feast of epiphany (6
January). Henry VII had brought the Italian
Renaissance to London in the person of
Michelangelo's colleague Torrigiano, but
his magnificent tombs of Henry VII and
Elizabeth of York in Westminster Abbey had
few imitators, and what followed for the

rest of the 16th century were great tombs of
alabaster and even greater boredom. In the
second decade of the 17th century, however,
as Inigo Jones was introducing the nation
to Renaissance architecture and Van Dyck
was doing the same for the best European
painting, Evesham helped to breath life into
sculpture once more.

In Paris Evesham had worked for a while
with the sculptor Pierre Jacquet, whose
renown rests on the remains of a huge relief
sculpture in Fontainebleau with a life-size
equestrian portrait of Henry IV at its centre.
Nothing of this ambition would ever be
asked of Evesham, but what he brought
back to England was a complete working
knowledge of the northern post-Renaissance
style, Mannerism, with its heightened
physical expressiveness and evocation of
emotions that was the forerunner to the
drama of baroque. Each one of Evesham's
sculptures in the North Downs churches
have these characteristics, but Lynsted's
monument is quite magnificent. It shows
Lord Teynham, modelled in painted plaster,
flat on his back, eyes open and stunned. His
widow kneels beside him in a brilliantly
modelled black cloak with a great black
hood over her head. The canopy and plinth
are of alabaster with achievements at the
crest (stags supporting a shield and a helm
with flamboyant plumes either side) flanked
by two beautifully carved classical female
figures. On the plinth are two panels, one
with the mourning daughters, the other
with the mourning sons, both under rolling
clouds through which cherubim swim. Both
sets of figures, the young women praying
and weeping, the young men piously
kneeling with their hawks and hounds out
of mind behind them, are composed with
an assurance and lively naturalism that had
not been seen in England since the high days
of medieval cathedral sculpture. (See also
Knaresborough, Northeast.)

When the essayist William Hazlitt wrote, 'From the moment that you take up the pencil, and look Nature in the face, you are at peace with your own heart,' he was writing from experience: he painted this self-portrait, now in Maidstone Museum, as a young man before turning to writing to make a living

Maidstone

KENT

Local boy made good: William Hazlitt's
self-portrait at the Maidstone Museum
and Bentlif Art Gallery

William Hazlitt (1778–1830) was born in
Maidstone, the son of the Unitarian minister,
and in 1909 William Carew Hazlitt, his
grandson and keeper of the flame, donated
family paintings to William's native town.
William became famous as one of England's
great essayists, but he had originally set
out to be a painter, and it is from this early
period (1802, in fact) that the self-portrait
in the museum comes. It is a strong piece,
but you have to search for it – it is hung on a
staircase and no argument can shift the local
authority into hanging it in a better position
in this cluttered museum (I've tried). Three
years after he painted it he realised that he
didn't have what it took to be a great artist
and gave it up. But although he became a
critic and journalist, painting was always in
his mind. He wrote on Poussin, on Van Dyck
and Hogarth; he took an adversarial position
on Reynolds's *Discourses* about the principles
of art. He wrote about his first experience
of great art, in Paris, with open-hearted
emotion that would be impossible to us, the
easyJet tourists of the 21st century, and was
probably a bit barmy even then, addressing
the Louvre itself as a deity with his own
kind of flight: 'How often, thou tenantless
mansion of godlike magnificence – how
often has my heart since gone a pilgrimage
to thee!'

This paean comes from one of the great
English essays, 'On The Pleasure of Painting',
which is devoted mainly to his own painting
and what it felt like to be an artist. 'In
writing,' he wrote, 'you have to contend with
the world; in painting … No angry passions
rise to disturb the silent progress of the
work, to shake the hand, or dim the brow;
no irritable humours are set afloat: you have
no absurd opinions to combat, no point
to strain, no adversary to crush, no fool to
annoy – you are actuated by fear or favour
to no man.' When he undertook a portrait
of his father, Hazlitt wrote: 'I thought my
fortune made; or rather it was already more
than made, in my fancying that I might one
day be able to say with Correggio, "I also am
a painter!" It was an idle thought, a boy's
conceit; but it did not make me less happy at
the time.'

Hazlitt's father made himself unpopular
in the town by using his pulpit to argue the
American case in the War of Independence
and departed. His son's self-portrait shows
the romantically sombre face of the poet,
a white stock at his neck and gazing out of
a dark background. He probably studied
painting under his older brother, John,
a professional who had himself studied
under Joshua Reynolds and made a steady
living, mainly as a miniaturist. On the
evidence of William's self-portrait and one
of William Lamb (1804, now in the National
Portrait Gallery), the younger Hazlitt was
as proficient as his professional brother and
a lot more spirited. You could check it out,
but you would have to ask. Not much of the
Hazlitt holding in Maidstone is shown at any
one time, although the walls are covered with
nonentities.

Penshurst

KENT

A great family portrait by Sir Peter Lely,
Penshurst Place

Penshurst Place still displays the funeral
helm of the Elizabethan poet-warrior Sir
Philip Sidney, 'the god-like Sidney', as his
contemporary Ben Jonson called him. In the
great hall is a painting of the latest Sidney

J.M.W. Turner probably painted Brighton from the Sea *because his host at Petworth, Lord Egremont, had invested in the chain pier. The picture still hangs at Petworth*

warrior, the 1st Viscount de L'Isle, who won a Victoria Cross in the Second World War, mingling in a gathering in the hall of surviving fellow holders of the VC. Penshurst has been the ancestral home of the Sidney family since 1552, and it was the Sidneys who built the 280 foot long west wing of the 16th and 19th centuries. But from the south the view is of a perfect 14th-century house, built in 1341 by Sir John de Pulteney, four times mayor of London, with the steep pitched roof of the hall dominating the roof line. This is the best surviving 14th-century hall in England, with a massive roof of chestnut, the screens passage that led from the kitchen and the original arrangement of an open hearth in the centre of the hall. Ben Jonson wrote the best known lines on Penshurst, its apples and nuts, its famous gardens, and the welcome to its table, 'whose liberall boord doth flow,/With all, that hospitalitie doth knowe!'

Like most rich post-Restoration families, the Sidneys employed Peter Lely (1618–80) to supply portraits. Lely painted the child Henry Sidney in the 1650s, like many other of his portraits in the long gallery, before his production line of assistants was fully automated, so the touch is his rather than the firm's, and the quality higher. The portrait of Henry is a total artifice, its conceit almost beatific, with the boy like a young Apollo in a belted toga and open-toed sandals, a hound at his heels and in a sylvan landscape with the same russet tones as his costume. Later Henry Sidney became a reliable confidant of William of Orange and accompanied him to Torbay with the invasion force of 1688 that removed James II from the throne. Even so, he has had a mixed reception from history. Macaulay sums it up in his history of England when he described Sidney as having 'a sweet temper and winning manners' and that his 'face and form were eminently handsome' but the 'he was the terror of husbands', was 'deficient in capacity and knowledge' and 'sunk in voluptuousness and indolence'. All of which, somehow, might have been predicted from the appearance of the beautiful boy in Lely's painting.

Petworth

WEST SUSSEX

Turner at Petworth House

The 3rd Earl of Egremont collected artists as well as art, J.M.W. Turner (1775–1851) especially. Turner visited Petworth from early in the century and was more often there than not for the ten years before the earl died in 1837, after which he never came again. Petworth is a huge 17th-century mansion sitting in 3,000 acres of parkland but with close ties to the little town outside its walls. Another artist, Benjamin Robert Haydon (1786–1846), wrote of Lord Egremont's establishment: 'The dogs, the horses, the cows, the deer & pigs, the Peasantry & the Servants, the guests & the family, the children & the Parents, all share alike his bounty & opulence & luxuries.' In those years, Turner used the old library as a studio. Nobody would interrupt him except Egremont, and even he knocked at the door first. Egremont threw fêtes for his estate workers and encouraged townspeople to play cricket in the park, and there they are in the background of Turner's painting of fighting bucks, tiny figures in white playing a match in the Capability Brown landscape. Today Petworth is run by the National Trust, so it's no longer the pigsty of Egremont's liberty hall. The earl's descendant lives in the south wing, and his mother, the dowager Lady Egremont, lives in Cockermouth Castle in Cumbria. Sure enough, as well as paintings of Petworth by Turner in the carved room, there is one of the castle.

The oddity among the paintings is *Chichester Canal*, because Turner painted it after the failure of the canal, part of a grand scheme to link London to the south coast, and the enterprise was Lord Egremont's. It seems curious that he should not mind being reminded of this failure, but he was as unreadably odd as Turner himself, and anyway, the painting is one of Turner's great successes. Even handedly, the main feature of *Brighton from the Sea* is the iron chain pier, another enterprise with Egremont money invested, this time successfully. It was built in 1823 as a terminal for the Brighton to Dieppe ferry service, which made Brighton the busiest Channel port on this stretch of coast until the railway came to Newhaven.

These four key Turners are displayed in the carved room for which they were executed between 1827 and 1829, set in four wide, shallow recesses in the panelling made to take the canvases amid the profusion of Grinling Gibbons limewood fruit and birds, but low down in the wall so that they could be seen at eye level by seated diners. Look at the two paintings of the park now, turn around, and there is the same view outside the windows. At Petworth Turner had seen *Landscape with Jacob and Laban* by Claude Lorrain, the first painting by the 17th-century French master probably that Turner could have examined closely, and in 1815 he painted *Dido Building Carthage* in emulation. The later Petworth paintings are like liquefied vistas by Claude, the lake coalescing with the sun, melting as it drops over the horizon, casting a stream of light on the surface of the water, the tall-masted ship in *Chichester Canal* dominating the twilight spire of the distant cathedral, the elegant iron pier and fishing boats under the huge vault of sky arguing man's dominion over the elements (though in fact chunks of the pier kept collapsing into the sea before it was demolished at the century's end). Egremont's patronage produced some of Turner's best work, the grand manner without grandiosity, the sublime bending the knee to keen judgement.

Plaxtol
KENT

A rare 13th-century survival, Old Soar Manor

A solar room with a massive hearth, a chapel, an earth closet or garderobe and a newel staircase spiralling down within the thickness of a stone wall to a pointed undercroft beneath the solar: that's it, a complete survival of the domestic quarters of a rich family in 1290. Not much in the vicinity is different today. The maze of narrow lanes (take an Ordnance Survey map) are surfaced and the fields, famous for wheat in the 13th century, are famed for fruit now. In the solar, most of the original kingpost roof remains and the rest of it is restored. The earth closet is above a pit, which was cleaned out through a pointed arch at ground level. The ancient Aylesford family of Colepepper, still extant, built the manor with defensive cross-loops to allow light in and arrows out, a defensive measure against the marauding bands of robbers who bedevilled the Weald in the days of Edward I. In the 14th century the Colepeppers knocked two big holes into the solar, east and west, to allow pointed windows. The chapel has a window of the same period, as well as an elaborate restored piscina and a pretty corbel beside the window.

At the beginning of the 17th century the Colepeppers had departed and Old Soar was a farmhouse, no doubt already lacking modern comforts, and in the 18th century the farmer demolished the great hall where the manor court was held and built an up-to-date Georgian brick farmhouse added to the solar wing, which became a barn. Entry is free, so there is no ticket office. Coaches can't get near, so nobody much comes, and the light filtering through a slit window in the ancient whitewashed undercroft is magical. You don't have to believe the ghost stories to understand why they arose.

Richborough Fort
KENT

Where the Emperor Claudius dug his heels in

Richborough is as resonant in history as Hadrian's Wall and more central to the story of the Roman expansion into Britain. Julius Caesar had landed at Deal in 55 BC and pulled his boats up on the shingle shore for a quick getaway. But this desolate stretch of landscape at Richborough, reached along a narrow lane, with the Stour below it at the west, a mothballed power station on the northern horizon towards Ramsgate, and the sea now 2 miles off, was the place where Claudius's invasion force landed in AD 43. Here they built their first depot, dug in behind a fortification of triple ditches (still visible). There followed a walled castle (the ruined walls stand to a height of around 20 feet), quarters for a garrison and an 80 foot high triumphal gate faced in Italian granite, long gone except for the foundations. To step through it meant to cross into Britain and set out along Watling Street towards Londinium and points north. Richborough is the place the Romans called Rutupiae, so important to them that the 'Rutupine shore' became synonymous with Britain and even with the coast of Gaul.

Through the years Rutupiae became a town, and the discovery of a font suggests that towards the end of the Western Empire in the 5th century there was a little Christian church within the walls.

At its height, Richborough was the heart

of the Saxon Shore defensive lines, stretching in Britannia from Brancaster in Norfolk to Portchester in Hampshire, with one fort in Gaul, unidentified but thought to be near Calais. Kent itself was always hellfire corner, and later came Saxon fortifications, Dover Castle, Henry VIII's clover-leaf castles of Sandling (almost vanished in the sands), Deal, Walmer and, around the coast to Southsea near Portsmouth, and finally (perhaps) the fighter aerodromes of the Second World War.

Rochester

KENT

Rochester lies in the twisted gut of the Medway before the river emerges past the pretty but historically useless castle of Upnor into what effectively is an inland sea before it narrows to a short strait between the Grain and Sheerness to flow into the Thames estuary. The bridge is three bridges now, for east- and west-bound traffic and the railway. The old bridge chapel, almost entirely rebuilt, stands on the esplanade between High Street and Castle Hill at the point where the medieval bridge once emerged a few feet to the south of the present crossing. The castle keep, the tallest in England, stands on its eminence above the cathedral, the two of them a heart-catching sight from the Downs above Strood. The fine High Street runs seamlessly into Chatham, Chatham merges with Gillingham, which merges with Rainham, and all that separates these four from the fifth Medway town, Strood, is the river. The history is ships and shipping. *Victory* was built here, and Nelson started his naval career at the age of twelve in Chatham, where the magnificent naval dockyards, the most complete in the world and backbone of the navy from the time of the Armada, were shut down in 1984 and are now open to the

public, largely unaltered since the days of sail with its rope shop, timber seasoning sheds, sail lofts, joiners' shop, dry docks, covered slips, commandant's house of 1702 and the cashiers' house where Charles Dickens's father worked. The small residential centre of Rochester holds its head high and handsome and around the centre, the city still has the post-Industrial Revolution feel of a down and dirty working town: that is part of its charm, much more so than the ersatz Dickens industry, whose latest manifestation is a 4 acre Dickens theme park in Chatham.

A glorious 14th-century carved doorway, Rochester Cathedral

Although Rochester is the second oldest diocese in England, behind only Canterbury, its cathedral is one of the least known. It hides behind the massive castle keep, it has an ignoble spire, a modest Romanesque west door with, as Churchill said of Attlee, much to be modest about, and it has been mauled by 19th-century restorers and has boring 19th-century glass besides. Yet as part of an ensemble with the castle and the pretty little 15th-century St Nicholas in the precincts it is highly enjoyable. Inside, the Norman nave with a fine arcade and the Early English choir survive handsomely. But the most extraordinary item is the glorious Decorated doorway to the chapter room to the east of the south choir aisle. The timber door itself is 19th century, and so quite obviously are the heads of the two female figures, Ecclesia, the holy church, and Synagogue (blindfolded because she doesn't accept the divinity of Christ) – an example of the best reason I know for not replacing missing sculpture or missing bits of sculpture. The ogee arch is set against a rectangular, diapered frame with the point of the arch breaking through into space above. Within the ogee arch is a simpler pointed arch containing a band of

Rochester Cathedral from the castle. Both buildings are basically Norman, although Rochester's great treasure is the 14th-century carved doorway to the chapter room

sculpture. Ecclesia and Synagogue are at the foot each side, then prophets and angels rise to the apex where a very fine naked boy, who can only be the young Christ, stands with his hands held, palms together, in prayer beneath an elaborate and very tall canopy. Inside this again is a narrower foliate band of carving and worn but spirited little heads of working men.

A munificent gift from a celebrated admiral, Rochester Corn Exchange

In Rochester's mixture of fact and Dickensian fiction the illustrious name of Cloudsley Shovell must appear to be fictional. It isn't. It adorns a cartouche on the façade of the corn exchange in the High Street, a building that, the inscription proclaims, was erected at the 'sole charge and expence [sic]' of 'Sir Cloudsley Shovel, Knight'. Sir Cloudsley was an admiral in the heroic age of great

English mariners. It is well testified that he was popular among his men for his exploits in the Caribbean, the Mediterranean and the English Channel, although his actions verged occasionally on the intemperate. In an early exercise of gunship diplomacy, in 1694 he ordered one of his ships of the line to open fire on a Danish warship for failing to salute the queen's flag in English territorial waters. As he was promoted the following year this act clearly found favour at the Admiralty. In 1698 he became commander-in-chief of vessels in the Thames and Medway and was elected MP for Rochester. In 1706, celebrated and richly rewarded, he presented the corn exchange to his adopted city and the following year he drowned with 1,315 of his men as three ships were wrecked on rocks of the Scillies and was interred, much lamented, in Westminster Abbey.

Sir Cloudsley's corn exchange (now a public library) is as exotic as the man and his name. His contribution was only ever a façade to an older building – but what a façade! It is glimpsed first from the river end of the street, a gigantic clock suspended from it over the highway on a long bracket with a scrolly plinth. The clock face is quite plain, as it needs to be under curly volutes supporting the Shovell coat of arms. The façade is tall and narrow with tall, narrow windows and a splendid wide doorcase with a florid swan neck pediment and more scrolls. All this white wood, plaster and metalwork is set into deep red-orange local brick, with moulded brick brackets either side of the door and heavily accented quoins, alternately long and short, adorning both edges all the way up to a fine, deep pediment capped by an open cupola with a bell. This street looks from the end the prettiest in England and might be so in truth if it weren't for the criminal post-war insertion of some very bad buildings.

Mile marker, High Street

Everywhere in England distances from London are marked from Charing Cross. Everywhere, that is, except Rochester, where an oval mile marker on an 18th-century building (now a furniture shop) on the north side of the High Street reads: 'XXIX miles from London Bridge.' Rochester bridge trust once owned property on the north side of the street, but not this building. So I can only guess that the bridge was so important to the life of Rochester that the citizens thought naturally of distances in terms of miles between one river crossing and another. It is likely that Rochester has had a bridge longer than London, since the Romans put up the first bridge to carry Watling Street over the Medway, and Watling Street itself (today the A2) linked Rochester bridge and London bridge. Another possibility is that, since Watling Street was turnpiked by 1850, this High Street building may have

housed a tollbooth. The mile sign, like the building, looks 18th century, a metal plaque nicely refurbished with gold lettering on black. In fact, everything 18th-century craftsmen touched was on the gold standard. It has a sense of distinction even when the workmanship is quite humble. This mile marker is part of the culture; it fits the street scene in a way no modern street furniture gets near to doing.

Early Victorian pillar box, High Street

Rowland Hill's introduction of the penny post in 1840 produced an avalanche of letter writing, and in 1850 Anthony Trollope, novelist and surveyor with the post office, recommended street pillar boxes instead of carriers collecting from door to door. The first post boxes were installed in St Helier in Jersey in 1852, a decent interval for bureaucracy to make up its corporate mind. The first on the mainland was at Botchergate in Carlisle a year later. Different places ordered different pillar boxes. They came cylindrical and oval and square and hexagonal; some had mushroom tops; some had a floral pattern; some had vertical slots; there was even an 8 foot tall Doric column pillar box with a crown on top. A House of Lords committee debated the matter and designed a very fine pillar box, but forgot to include a slot to post letters through. Another version failed to incorporate Queen Victoria's monogram. It didn't last very long. And then there was the Penfold.

It was hexagonal in shape and came in three sizes and nine types but all had an acorn finial, and it derived its name from its designer, an architect named J.W. Penfold.

This Penfold pillar box of 1866 in Rochester High Street is one of the few originals in Britain, and and one of yet fewer that still wear the original livery of green-bronze and gold

The post office introduced it in 1866. Eventually it had its day, and most examples of it were replaced, but a few hung about, in places like India and New Zealand, as well as in England, including several in Oxford and in London, lots in Cheltenham, and one beautifully placed on Great Pulteney Street in Bath. The Penfold outside the Guildhall in Rochester is painted the original green bronze, but they have turned it into a museum piece by blocking the slot with wood. A shame, really – they do similar things to churches when they fall out of use. But at least this one is original. The one at the southern approach to Tower Bridge in London is a replica, as are the many that are to be found in Scotland, which has no original Penfolds at all.

Sevenoaks
KENT

A classical cricket pavilion at the Vine

John Frederick Sackville, 3rd duke of Dorset, granted part of the Knole estate, the Vine cricket ground, to the town of Sevenoaks in 1773 on payment of an annual rent of one cricket ball a year. In turn, the town charged Sevenoaks cricket club one peppercorn a year. It is rumoured that the duke's Sackville-West descendants no longer claim the ball, but over the years, inflation has driven the annual rent for the cricket club up to two peppercorns. Despite this, Sevenoaks Vine Cricket Club still finds the wherewithal to play there, though there is no Sackville-West descendant to take first knock as, noblesse oblige, the 1st and 3rd dukes were wont to do. Nor, as far as we know, are there still fifty guinea sidestakes placed on the outcome of matches.

Cricket was well established at the Vine by 1734, but it has been some time since the first class game was played here. The last

such match, in point of fact, was in August 1828, when Kent beat Sussex inside two days. By this time the ground already had its cricket pavilion at the southern boundary, facing out across the wicket to a red brick 18th-century mansion house embowered in great beech and chestnut trees – six of the fabled seven oaks blew down in the hurricane of 1987. The pavilion is a low, wide, white, weatherboarded structure with a clubhouse in the middle and team changing rooms on either wing. There are classical clasping columns on the façade and a little pediment with a clock and a weathervane sporting a batsman at the crease. The town council added a later 19th-century bandstand beside the pavilion, which is still well used. Its conical roof is supported on tall, narrow iron columns rising from a rustic stone base and blossoming at the top into scrolly decoration supporting the conical roof. Painted yellow and black, the bandstand adds a festive note to an archetypal scene.

Staplehurst
KENT

12th-century door, Church of All Saints

What a turbulent Nordic imagination created the beaten ironwork of the south door. The church stands at the top of a steep Wealden hill in the middle of Staplehurst. The main entrance is the west door; the south door is small and hidden from passers-by but is still used for weddings and christenings. Of all the surviving doors with decorative ironwork in England, and there are a lot, this is the wildest, the surreal doodlings with hammer, anvil and molten metal of a 12th-century blacksmith with an artist's urgent need to create. Between the iron strap hinges are a flying fish with saw-edged piranha teeth and a rivet as an eye, and inside the bowl of the big C-shape, a common decorative element of Norman ironwork, is a decidedly uncommon little shoal of four fishes with, if the iron strap above can be read as the surface, a Viking boat on the sea above. It is obvious that the door was made to fit a space with a round arch and was altered, possibly within a hundred years, to fit a pointed door arch. So the decoration may have been replaced in random order, is unreadable for meaning, and although some of it is missing or broken, the surface of these rude and roughly planed planks remains crowded with alarming incident.

Teston Bridge
KENT

The medieval bridges of the Medway

The Medway rises on a height somewhere between Gatwick Airport and East Grinstead, and from these unpromising beginnings becomes navigable at Tonbridge. It meanders eastwards through rural Kent, and at the confluence with the Rivers Beult and Teise floods Yalding at appropriate seasons. It takes a U-turn through Maidstone and at Allington lock, adjacent to the home of the Tudor poet and rebel Sir Thomas Wyatt, it becomes tidal, turns north through the Medway Gap in the North Downs and debouches into the Thames estuary between the notional Isle of Grain and the actual Isle of Sheppey. The Elizabethan poet Edmund Spenser celebrates the meeting as a marriage between the bridegroom Thames and his bride, the Medway:

Her lovely lockes adowne her back did flow
Unto her waist, with flowers bescattered,
The which ambrosiall odours forth did
*   throw*

but the point is lost where a motorway and the Eurostar railway violate the bride

with a crossing of the wide valley on three separate but parallel soaring concrete viaducts. Originally, the norm was for great landowners to build the bridges and keep them in repair. This usually meant monastic institutions – in Kent the biggest were the dioceses of Canterbury and Rochester – and they operated with a 'grant of pontage' from the king – that is, the right to collect tolls for a limited period to cover repairs. Enough to say that the Medway has been important in the local economy and in national history. Now it is important chiefly to a variety of flora and fauna, including weekend people who like to mess about in boats. In the distance of just above 40 miles from the estuary to Tonbridge there is a collection of the five finest medieval bridges on any one stretch of river in England: Twyford bridge in Yalding parish and the crossing to Yalding itself (actually over the Beult close to the confluence with the Teise and the Medway), Teston bridge, East Farleigh bridge and Aylesford bridge.

All of them are fine bridges with dramatic cutwaters and some with pedestrian refuges. Of them all, Teston (pronounced Teeson) is the best, set in the valley with a view to the north of the pretty little hillside village of Teston with a little church, a little cricket ground and a big, plain 18th-century stuccoed manor house; and to the south woods and orchards. The bridge has been close to submersion by the floods of recent years and was regularly impassable in the time of Edward Hasted, the 18th-century historian of Kent. Between the cutwaters are slightly pointed arches, two of the five totally rebuilt, but well. Drive, if you must, from bridge to bridge; if you can, walk. There's a new riverside path all the way from Rochester to Tonbridge, but East Farleigh to Yalding is a good compromise.

Tudeley

KENT

Magnificent modern stained glass, Church of All Saints

Tucked behind farm buildings along a Wealden road, the unremarkable little brick and stone All Saints with its short tower and stunted spire just happened to be the parish church where the owner of the great house, Sir Henry d'Avigdor Goldsmid, was a Jew. His wife, Rosemary, was Christian. The couple agreed that any sons would be brought up as Jews, daughters as Christians. There were no sons, and of the two daughters, Sarah drowned aged twenty-one in a sailing accident in the Channel off the Rye coast in 1963. The parents commissioned Marc Chagall to create a memorial window for the parish church, a Jewish artist for a Christian community. He had no deep problems of conflicting faiths – for Chagall, work was prayer.

He came to Tudeley for the first time in 1975 for the unveiling of the big east window and spontaneously offered to fill the other eleven. The east window is specifically about Sarah, the others a lustrous setting. We see her drowned with a toy-sized yacht floating beside her; a mourning woman embracing two infants, possibly Sarah's mother; a red horse bearing Sarah to a ladder, which she climbs to a heaven where Christ waits, arms open in welcome as well as crucifixion. The predominant colour is blue, bleeding from azure to pale turquoise, but mingled with small passages of intense indigo and crimson, sapphire and lemon yellow.

The great 20th-century artist Marc Chagall was commissioned to design this window in Tudeley in memory of a young woman of the parish who had drowned. When he saw it in situ, he offered to fill the remaining windows and now all twelve contain Chagall's stained glass

Chagall started making glass in France only after the war, to replace windows destroyed in conflict, but you wonder what kept him from it so long. Born in Vitebsk in 1887, he had worked from a boyhood full of Jewish folk art and tales. From the beginning, his humans and land-bound creatures flew as freely as birds, fiddlers on the roof, animals on the hoof in a generalised pantheistic hymn. His palette needed only natural daylight filtering through stained and painted glass for completion.

Broadly, the technicalities were that Chagall produced the coloured designs and handed them on to Charles and Brigitte Marq, who worked for a stained glass firm that had perfected its techniques conserving the glass of Reims. The Marqs used coloured glass thickly blown to produce the happy accident of bubbles characteristic of the Middle Ages, then etched it with acid to interpret Chagall's washes of colour. Finally, Chagall added, not just the outlines of angels and fishes and birds, but also the splashes and rivulets of paint that are the modern equivalent to the bubbled glass, touches suggesting the soft dawn whisper of life.

The first window in the west wall of the north aisle shows Adam and Eve with a bright red apple. Between that and the east window's figure of Christ there is no biblical programme. Everything depends on the light: the yellow glass in the south adding sunshine to the light of an overcast day; the cool northern light glowing through the woodland and waterland blues of the north aisle.

In 1985, soon after Chagall's death on the final day of his great exhibition at the Royal Academy, the four exquisite single-light chancel windows, one with a separate quatrefoil filled with an angel's head, arrived from Burlington House and completed the plan of a church filled entirely with the finest post-Reformation glass in England.

The church of King Charles the Martyr was built at Tunbridge Wells in a hotbed of 17th-century Dissenters. It survived them, however, and has a fine ceiling by Wren's plasterers, John Wetherell and Henry Doogood

Tunbridge Wells

KENT

Ceiling by Sir Christopher Wren's great plasterers, Church of King Charles the Martyr

The chapel of King Charles the Martyr was the first building of any note in this area of rocky hills, woodland and, crucially, bubbling springs north of Tonbridge. At the time Tunbridge Wells didn't exist. Its springs had taken the fancy of the nobility for its supposed health-giving properties and were surrounded by temporary structures during the season. The traveller Celia Fiennes credits the springs in her journal for 1697 with the property of retrieving 'lost limbs that are benumbed', though she adds that she herself 'cannot tell, only tasteing half a glass which I did not like'.

Today the chapel seems a plain, not to say cack-handed, brick box squeezed into an awkward space beyond the springs end of the Pantiles, crowded in by a bank, a bookshop, a busy alley at the rear and the busy road to the Sussex coast towns to the front. That said, in the last years of the 17th century enough money was washing around for its subscribers not just to hire chaplains by the season but to turn to two of the best available plasterers to beautify the interior.

All the same, the founders went ahead cautiously, probably because the chapel was built in 1676 on inhospitable ground among Puritans. They had already given the hills the names they bear today, Mount Ephraim, Mount Sion, Mount Pleasant. But when fashionable society started building for permanence they brought in first, John Wetherell, and then Henry Doogood, both of whom had worked with Wren in the City of London and at Greenwich. Wetherill produced the masterly design of 1679–80 with eight ceiling domes, or inverted wells, which Doogood reproduced when the chapel was extended to the west ten years later – the date 1690 is moulded on a plaque among the roses and daisies, nuts, apples, pears and cherubs. The ceiling is Grinling Gibbons fashion though not quite Grinling Gibbons, but then plaster is not susceptible to the sharpness that carving bestows on Gibbons's preferred medium, limewood. Nevertheless, it gloriously transforms a chapel that would be decidedly makeshift without the ceiling, and, more than that, especially since the Luftwaffe destroyed most of the City of London ceilings, it is among the finest in England.

There is incidentally an intriguing theory that Samuel Pepys was responsible for the dedication of the chapel to which he was a subscriber and visitor. It goes like this. Catherine of Braganza brought the possession of Tangier with her as part of her dowry when she married Charles II. The government developed it for a few years as a base from which to combat Barbary pirates. Pepys was a high official of the Tangier commission and had seen the Church of King Charles the Martyr in the north African port before the English scuttled. Queen Catherine became a frequent visitor to Tunbridge Wells. The rest follows; except that there is no documentary evidence.

Upnor Castle
ISLE OF GRAIN, KENT

The castle that failed to keep out the Dutch

In 1559 Queen Elizabeth I ordered the building of a fortification on the west bank of the Medway opposite Chatham to defend shipping against enemy attack. For a hundred years Upnor dozed on its sleepy hillside and never had to fire a shot in anger. So on 10 June 1667, when the brilliant Dutch naval commander Michiel Andriaanszoon de Ruyter led his fleet up the River Medway, the fort was completely unprepared. The gallantry of its defenders was not in doubt, nor was the indolence of the men in the navy office in Mincing Lane in the City of London. Powder and shot were insufficient, and de Ruyter sailed as far as Chatham, burned several English vessels, and the following day carried off the flagship, the *Royal Charles*, whose small caretaking crew, possibly unpaid, had deserted in the face of this daring action. It was the biggest naval disaster in English history, a rout that caused as much panic in London as the plague of 1665 and the Great Fire of 1666.

The first action of Samuel Pepys on hearing the news was to write his will. Later, he entered in his diary that the Dutch men o' war had 'made no more of Upner castle's shooting than of a fly', and that 'Upner played hard with their guns at first, but slowly afterward, either from the men being beat off or their powder spent'. What he doesn't whisper even to his diary is that he was one of the navy office staff responsible for the shortage of gunpowder. Ten years later Upnor was regarded as obsolete, and the bastion facing the river was converted into a powder magazine.

Today it remains very much as it was in the late 17th century. The castle and the high street of brick and weatherboarded houses leading downhill to the river are a loveable sight. The castle looks quite domesticated with a gold figured black clock set into a buttressed gateway tower of ragstone completed by an upper section of red brick. On top is a bell cope. A turkey oak in the courtyard is thought to have been grown from acorns brought back from the Crimean War. The bastion fronting the river is flanked by a tower at each end, two round turrets and, at the centre, a polygonal bay the height of the building. The views from the top of the bastion take in an outstanding panorama of river, little boats for messing around in, wooded hills and light industry on the eastern shore. In the river below is a palisade of wooden stakes sharpened into points (parts of the original Elizabethan palisade are still visible at low tide). Cannons raised from the sunken English ships are on display in the castle and the little grass park surrounding it, but two of them are from the two ships the Dutch lost. They were manufactured in England, probably in the Weald of Kent, and exported for the use of de Ruyter's fleet.

Uppark
WEST SUSSEX

Paintings of the prodigal son, bought on the grand tour

Hidden in its uplands woods, Uppark is something over twelve years old, going on three hundred. Which is to say William Talman, great Wren's only less great contemporary, built it Dutch style in brick trimmed with stone for the 1st Earl of Tankerville in 1695, but in 1989 it was consumed by a ferocious blaze. Uppark stands high on the wooded west Sussex Downs where the fire could be seen in the valleys below and from the Solent estuary beyond. Looking at it in newspaper pictures

and on television it seemed a lost cause, and among the chorus of voices raised about the future of the ruin, one buffoonish MP was heard demanding that it should be razed because nowadays it would never have been given planning permission anyway. As it happens, enough of the ground floor survived with help from the fire services above and beyond the call of duty for the house to be rebuilt and its partly destroyed decor to be reconstituted. It reopened in 1995 after an unprecedented feat of swift and thorough conservation, of plasterwork, paint, fittings and some of the fabric.

The carved chimneypieces survived, doors survived, four of the eight Canaletto views of Venice survived and most of the other paintings. They had been collected by Sir Matthew Fetherstonhaugh during his grand tour of Italy for three years from 1749. He was already forty-five and married (his wife toured with him), and had bought Uppark from the 2nd Earl of Tankerville two years earlier. Pompeo Battoni, face painter to the English gentry, much over-praised in his own day (except by his rival Reynolds), much under appreciated now, was at his best when he painted separate portraits of Sir Matthew, his wife, Lady Sarah, and their son and heir Harry.

Among the paintings that it is presumed Sir Harry bought in Rome were the four-episode cycle of the wanderings of the prodigal son by Luca Giordano (1634–1705), of which two hang in the red drawing room and two next door in the little drawing room. Giordano was born in Naples and apprenticed to the Spaniard, Ribera. Naples was ruled by Spanish viceroys, and Giordano spent time in Spain painting ceilings for Charles II in the Buon Retiro and the Escorial as well as the baptistery of Toledo Cathedral. Not for nothing was he known as Luca Fà Presto ('Luca go fast'), though the speed came with an unshakeable technique. He went through styles fast as well, starting his career with Ribera, moving on to Venice to the study of Titian and Veronese, and ending as an old man painting magnificent, swiftly brushed frescos prefiguring the sublime Tiepolo. The Uppark oils must be of the Ribera period, sombre hued, thunderous night scenes, yapping dogs, chiaroscuro *à la* Caravaggio, as Luca's brush picks up the biblical drama at the point where the prodigal is reduced to herding pigs, then is driven off by his employers, returns home penitent and receives the blessing of his father and the celebration of a feast on the fatted calf.

Wadhurst
EAST SUSSEX

Last resting place of the ironmasters, Church of St Peter and St Paul

There are still Furnace Lanes scattered around the borderland of Kent and Sussex, distant memories of the days when the iron industry of the Weald was the most important in the land. They are at Lamberhurst in Kent, one of the biggest producers, and at Brenchley and Horsemonden. In Sussex they are in Horam, Beckley and Broad Oak. And everywhere is a scattering of Furnace ponds. At one point in the late 16th century, when cannon for the navy was in high demand, there were fifty-one wood-fired furnaces in the Weald but only seven elsewhere in the Midlands and Wales. Even at that time people were complaining of deforestation, but with a little exaggeration, it might be said that the iron industry of the Weald determined the victory over the Spanish Armada.

The invention of smelting coal to produce coke and the impossibility of moving heavy ordnance over boggy Wealden winter roads combined in shifting the industry to the north and Wales. It staggered on in Kent and Sussex until the 18th century, producing items like firebacks and railings for St Paul's Cathedral, but the glory days when Wealden fortunes could be made from armaments were gone. In the little village of Cowden in Kent there are iron gravestones in the churchyard, but at Wadhurst, one of the biggest iron manufacturing communities, there is something grander: the church itself is practically paved in parts with iron memorial slabs, the richer ones for the richer parishioners in the chancel, the plainer ones below the salt in the nave and aisles. At least ten of them are inscribed to members of the Barham family, three of them from nearby Scragoak, which is still there as an organic farm. William Barham, who died on 'November ye 6 1701 aged 80', has a slab emblazoned with a florid coat of arms, possibly illegitimate, featuring what look like three handsome wild hogs. Some of the slabs in the nave have heavily underscored inscriptions, the way the *Daily Express* and *Daily Mail* at one time in the 1960s and 1970s dramatically underscored headlines, a practice also picked up by the designer of the monument in a pavement at Wells to Mary Rand's Tokyo Olympiad gold medal leap (see South West). Is it far-fetched to suppose that these all have their origins in the disciplined lines of type in post-Caxton printshops? What certainly is far-fetched is the lovely wall monument in the Wadhurst porch inscribed, 'Beneath this iron plate lies the body of Mrs Ann Luck' – but the monument is carved in stone.

West Malling
KENT

The abbey and parish church are at opposite ends of West Malling, both of them dedicated to St Mary the Virgin. The church stands just

HEER·LYETH·THE
BODYE·OF·IOHN·
BARHAM·OF·SHE
OOSMITHE·×·GE·
NT·WHO·DIED
THE·FIFT·DAY·OF
DECEMBAR·1648
T G

off the southern end of the High Street, lined with Georgian-fronted buildings, though the core of many are several hundred years old. The street widens towards the north into a space large enough to take a market, a custom that has had a vestigial revival in the farmers' market held monthly. Swan Street leads east from this market space and is named for the former coaching inn, now a Michelin-recommended brasserie. Further down is the abbey (see below) and then the finest house in a town of good houses, a wonderfully modulated brick building with a beautiful wrought iron gate and a big garden. The manor house, now flats, lies above the road and opposite a lovely country park, which was once the manor's grounds. Further south is King's Hill, which once had a spike where George Orwell put his head down while hop picking in nearby Wateringbury (and collecting material for *Down and Out in London and Paris*). Later King's Hill was a Battle of Britain aerodrome; now it is a business centre and housing estate, a massive imposition on what was once a beautiful area of mid-Kent.

All Muggleton vs. Dingley Dell

West Malling's most enduring fame is pure supposition: the cricket ground along Norman Road is said to be the setting for the illustration by Phiz (H.K. Browne) for All Muggleton versus Dingley Dell, the cricket match witnessed by Mr Pickwick. *Pickwick Papers* was the start of a long partnership between Dickens and Phiz, and the illustration featured on the Bank of England £10 note first issued in 1992. The church in

When the Kent and Sussex weald supplied the king's navy with cannon, the ironmasters grew rich and left their mark in the iron tombstones of Kent and Sussex. Among them, the yeoman craftsmanship of this one in St Peter and St Paul, Wadhurst, is one of the best

the drawing, with an insufficient spire rising from a sturdy tower, certainly looks like St Mary, and the ground is renowned in cricket history, with a match first recorded in the press in 1705.

The old order restored, at St Mary's Abbey, Swan Street

In 1097 Gundulf, Bishop of Rochester, founded a sister community of nuns to the monks of Rochester Cathedral and chose West Malling as the site of the abbey. He bestowed on it the right to fairs and markets, and later in the 12th century Henry I granted it the right to all whales found in the bishopric. It endured the usual trials by fire (which consumed most of the town and convent in 1190) and pestilence (there were three abbesses in the Black Death year of 1348, two of whom perished), then fell in the second wave of Henry VIII's dissolutions in 1538. The nuns retired and lived unhappily ever after with pensions of between £2 13s 14d and £3 a year each, and private owners developed the garden with a stream emerging prettily as a cascade into Swan Street. The abbey is the highlight of a lovely village (once known as Town Malling), but what makes it special is that the last private owner prepared the way for an Anglican community of Benedictine nuns to return to the abbey.

It's a closed order, so normally all that is visible of the abbey is from the street. The cascade, boundary wall and rock solid Romanesque tower with fine arcaded turrets were good enough for J.M.W. Turner, passing by as a seventeen-year-old prodigy in 1792–3; his watercolour is in Tate Britain. The abbey opens to the public on one of the architectural heritage days each year, and the nuns (more than twenty of them of all ages) show small parties around, totally at ease with their exposure to the profane world.

Alongside the gatehouse there is an old

pilgrims' chapel with 14th-century windows, reconverted from a period as a carpenter's shop in a natural transition, as a nun pointed out, since Christ was a carpenter. East of the tower there's an old Norman wall with herringbone pattern masonry east of the tower, which must have been the south wall of the nave, and a terrific church of 1966 by the architects Robert Maguire and Keith Murray, externally fortress-like with its great windowless flanks, internally an inverted ark, and altogether a nicely judged accompaniment to the 900-year-old tower. Maguire and Murray designed new cloisters too, eliding with the single surviving 13th-century cloister arcade with exquisite trefoil arches. These are closed to the public even on open day, but a glimpse is possible for the nosy from a church doorway and with the tolerant connivance of the nuns.

Wickhambreaux

KENT

Tiffany-style glass, St Andrew's Church

Wickhambreaux is an archetypal Kentish village, in denial of the 21st century, apart from the odd 4×4 parked adjacent to the Rose. Tucked away up a lane not half a dozen miles from Canterbury on the Sandwich road, it clusters around a triangular green. Mellow brick and dewdrop bright white stucco, there is a tall white weatherboarded watermill, now flats, beside the Little Stour, and a 14th-century church with a tower and a dotty tiled porch. A visit to the church shatters the cosy stereotype. For there behind the altar is the big east window, opalescent and gleaming with colour, dealing with one of the great religious subjects, but more Tiffany than Canterbury, more Burne-Jones than Burne-Jones.

Indeed it was made in New York for St Andrew's in 1896, after a time when craftsmen had jostled on the sidewalks of Manhattan as they rushed to take out patents for new ways with stained glass. The manufacturing methods were similar, and so was the new translucency of the colours. The market was out there in the grand mansions and the elite colleges serving the New York dollar aristocracy, and, yes, in churches, in synagogues and cemeteries and hotels: windows, glass domes and, from 1899, Tiffany Studio table lamps. Of the new patent holders, John la Farge was the greatest innovator. Louis Comfort Tiffany's genius was to domesticate it, and his dubious reward was that Tiffany became the generic description for all glass of this kind.

The artist Arild Rosenkrantz (1870–1960) was a Dane who, in career terms, was really only passing through New York, but in that brief space he met Count James de Gallatin, scion of a Swiss-American family, and received from him the commission for the Wickhambreaux project. For reasons history has mislaid, Gallatin's mother is buried in Wickhambreaux's churchyard and he wished to commemorate her with a window. Rosenkrantz designed it, and the Decorative Stained Glass Company of New York made it in the Washington Square building it productively shared with La Farge. Rosenkrantz came to England to oversee the installation, married a Scot, stayed and made more glass, but none as good.

In one sense the Annunciation is a failure. For Renaissance artists the challenge of the subject was the space, the momentous silence, between Gabriel and the Virgin in the moment after he has told her she is to be the

The east window in St Andrew's, Wickhambreaux, was designed in New York by a Danish artist in memory of a Swiss American woman buried in the Kentish village. The glowing colours are created by a process popularised by Tiffany but used in a greater range by La Farge, the manufacturer of this glass

mother of God. Rosenkrantz won't allow this silence. His scene is heaving with archangels, Raphael, Anael, Adoniel, Saluthiel, Uriel and Michael, with a supporting cast of baby angels. Gabriel bears in his right hand the lily, symbol of purity, but Rosencrantz piles in a whole field of lilies. The Virgin stands among them, head bowed and hands folded, like an actor before the cameras pretending that she is alone with her prayers. It takes a great artist to suggest the drama of the Annunciation. Rosenkrantz is not a great artist. Yet this is an inspired design and a triumph of art nouveau.

First of all the colours: white, greens, golds, blues, reds, indigo and turquoise, terracotta, orange and purple, tiny splashes of ruby blood at the foot of a glowing cross (Mary's premonition; you see that from her tightly closed eyes). And then the drawing: at first, the lead holding the glass panels together is unnoticeable, because it constitutes the drawing, following the flow of drapery and the sway of flowers, flowing splendidly from the opened wings of the angels in the four main lights of the window into the spaciously coiling abstract ribbons of colour suggesting turbulent heavens in the panels of tracery, lit, of course, by the actual light of the heavens.

Woking

SURREY

The Shah Jehan Mosque, England's first

When Edwin Lutyens arrived in India in the 1920s to build New Delhi, among his baggage was a bulldog imperialist contempt for Indian architecture. The viceroy, Lord Hardinge, insisted that the Viceroy's House must nonetheless contain Indian decorative elements. Lutyens acceded. 'Within reason,' he grumbled. None of this grudging attitude is evident in the mosque that stands in

Oriental Road, Woking. Commissioned by Gottlieb Wilhelm Leitner – a multilingual Hungarian scholar, educated in Istanbul, who was the son of Jewish converts to Christianity – it was designed by an architect, W.I. Chambers, who never went nearer to India than the India Office library in London. Leitner chose Woking because a failed actor's retirement home was up for sale and offered a good site for an Islamic institute with a mosque to serve it. The institute has vanished; the mosque flourishes.

Careful from the start, Leitner and Chambers engaged a ship's captain from the Pacific and Orient line to take the bearings for the alignment of the mosque on Mecca. On this orientation Chambers raised a small, lovely place of worship that easily could be picked up and put down in Lahore, where it would raise no eyebrows. It was opened in 1889 and was named, not for the Mughal emperor who built the Taj Mahal as a memorial to his dead young wife, but for the Begum Shah Jehan, a woman ruler of Bhopal who was the mosque's main benefactor. It was also the first purpose-built mosque in England. In 1887 William Quilliam, a Scouse solicitor and convert known thereafter as Sheikh Abdullah Quilliam, had established a prayer room in Liverpool, but this was incorporated within a terraced Georgian house, while the famous Jamia Mosque in Brick Lane, London, began life in 1753 as the Neuve Eglise serving Huguenot asylum seekers.

The Shah Jehan Mosque is something different. It is classically square in plan and has a central onion dome with a tall finial supporting the crescent moon of Islam. Its surrounding lotus domes supported on little pavilions show clearly its Indian Islamic inspiration. They are a riff on domes adapted by the incoming 16th-century Mughal architects from Buddhist and

The Shah Jehan mosque in Woking opened in 1889 and was the first purpose-built mosque in England. Its easterly alignment on Mecca was supplied by a Pacific and Orient ship's captain and it was built in full-hearted Islamic style by an architect who had been no nearer India than the India Office in London

Hindu architecture – that is, onion domes tapering inwards at the base and resting on the decorative forms of lotus leaves. In Woking they are prettily painted deep green and gold with a ring of gold stars around the main dome. The entrance arch is white with a brilliant red line tracing the ogee form. The big chamber beneath the central dome is decorated with calligraphy, and the inside of the dome is scattered with gold stars, picking up the exterior motif. The mihrab in the east wall is a little like a priest's sedilia in a Christian church, but more important because it indicates the direction worshippers should face to pray.

As I departed, a white-bearded patriarch in round white cap and jacket over shalwar kameez sat reading a newspaper on a bench in the pretty rose garden surrounding the mosque. It might in fact have been Lahore.

London

CITY OF LONDON · GREATER LONDON

WEST END

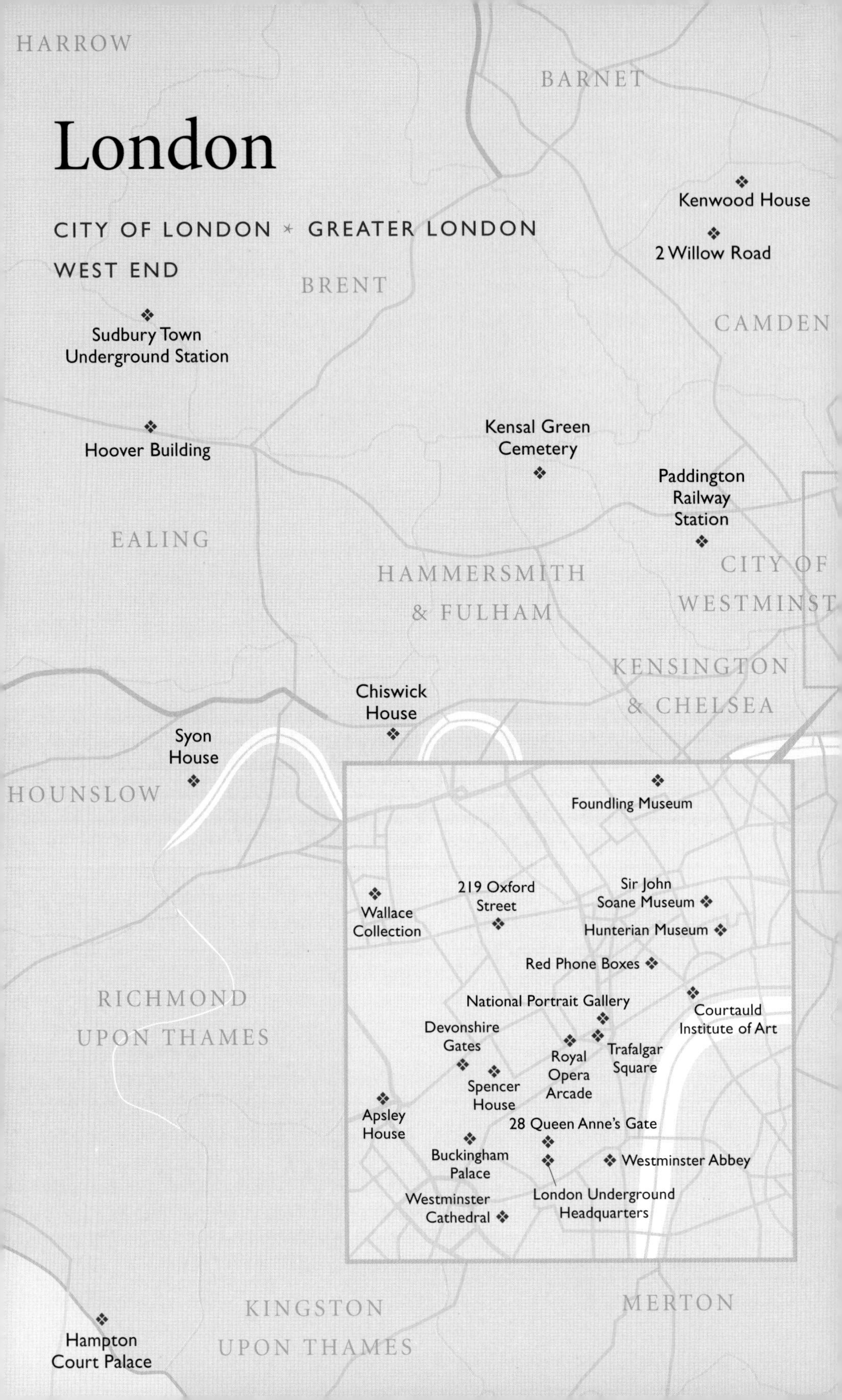

HARROW

BARNET

Kenwood House

2 Willow Road

CAMDEN

BRENT

Sudbury Town
Underground Station

Hoover Building

Kensal Green
Cemetery

Paddington
Railway
Station

EALING

HAMMERSMITH
& FULHAM

CITY OF
WESTMINST

KENSINGTON
& CHELSEA

Chiswick
House

Syon
House

HOUNSLOW

Foundling Museum

219 Oxford
Street

Wallace
Collection

Sir John
Soane Museum

Hunterian Museum

Red Phone Boxes

RICHMOND
UPON THAMES

National Portrait Gallery

Courtauld
Institute of Art

Devonshire
Gates

Apsley
House

Spencer
House

Royal
Opera
Arcade

Trafalgar
Square

28 Queen Anne's Gate

Buckingham
Palace

Westminster Abbey

Westminster
Cathedral

London Underground
Headquarters

KINGSTON
UPON THAMES

MERTON

Hampton
Court Palace

ARINGEY

REDBRIDGE

Water House

WALTHAM
FOREST

HACKNEY

LINGTON

Church of St Bartholomew
the Great

Broadgate

Liverpool
Street Railway
Station

Fleet Place

Guildhall
Art Gallery

Bevis Marks
Synagogue

Estorick Collection

Daily
Express Building

Temple
Bar

Monument

Leadenhall
Market

Church
of St Benet
Paul's Wharf

Church of
St Stephen
Walbrook

TOWER
HAMLETS

NEWHAM

CITY

Bishop of Winchester's
Palace

Blackwall
Tunnel

St George's
Circus

Butler's Wharf

Borough
High Street

Canada Water
Underground
Station

Imperial
War
Museum

Greenwich
Royal Hospital

Queen's House

GREENWICH

Goldsmiths

Ranger's
House

SOUTHWARK

LEWISHAM

Dulwich
Picture Gallery

Eltham
Palace

MBETH

CROYDON

Bethlem
Royal Hospital

BROMLEY

0   0.5   1   1.5   2   2.5   3 mi

0   1   2   3   4   5 km

The West End

Eight million people live in London. It is dwarfed by Mexico City and Calcutta and Tokyo, but it is still the biggest city by far in Europe, and every day millions more travel in and out again. For visitors, London is the West End: the cross-currents of thousands of shoppers in Oxford Street, the Household Cavalry at William Kent's admirable Horseguards, and the changing of the guard, the theatres of Shaftesbury Avenue and the vibrant pubs, restaurants, shops, stalls, buskers, and hucksters around the Royal Opera House in Covent Garden, the National Gallery and the National Portrait Gallery and Tate Britain, Green Park, St James's Park, and Hyde Park, Piccadilly Circus with the Shaftesbury Monument, known only as Eros. Westminster is the centre of government and Buckingham Palace the key symbol of royalty, a mystique losing its grip and opening its secrets to the public, if only for a couple of months in summer. Secrets, yes, London has those, too; how could it not with so many hiding places? Spencer House, down a quiet side street a minute's walk from Piccadilly; the great Wallace Collection, tucked in a square north of Selfridges; and some of the greatest Impressionist paintings in the world in an entrance off a gateway between the Strand and the courtyard of Somerset House (the Courtauld Collection). Downing Street has become a secret, locked behind guarded barriers, but on the other side of Whitehall, the Banqueting House hasn't, one of the earliest of Inigo Jones's Palladian buildings in England, the only part of the old royal palace that didn't burn down in the seventeenth century, and with an immense ceiling painting by Rubens celebrating the accession of James I to the throne of England; a glorious chapter but in its own way a secret too, because it is hugged close by the buildings of government, most visitors pass it by. It is the most cosmopolitan of cities and no ruder than New York, but it is the most cockily parochial: I once heard a London bus conductor as he was fumbling for coins in his leather pouch warn an American tourist off decimilisation: 'Don't touch it with a bargepole guv, it's a nightmare.'

The selection that follows is arranged west to east.

A jewel among jewels at the Wallace Collection, Manchester Square W1

It took four Marquesses of Hertford and the illegitimate son of the 4th, Sir Richard Wallace, the whole of the 19th century to put the Wallace Collection together. The most interesting of the marquesses was the 3rd, Francis Charles Seymour-Conway (1777–1842), if only because he was Thackeray's model for the cultivated, vicious and dissipated Lord Steyne in *Vanity Fair*. He bought Hertford House in Manchester Square, and Sir Richard, who took his mother's maiden name as his own, rebuilt the house as an undistinguished but functional showcase for the collection and left instructions for everything to be left to the nation on the death of his wife. Strictly speaking, we should talk about 'collections' because here, quite apart from paintings and sculpture, is one of the greatest European and oriental armouries in the world, a wonderful collection of French furniture and an assembly of Sèvres porcelain second in size only to the royal collection and the equal in quality of the smaller Rothschild collection at Waddesdon. But these are specialist interests. It was 'Lord Steyne' and his son who gave the central art collection its French accent, and the 4th marquess who bought Hals's *The Laughing Cavalier*, Poussin's *A Dance to the Music of Time* (which gave a title and theme to Anthony

Powell), the big holding of paintings by Boucher, master of the pink nude, and *The Swing*, by Boucher's fellow rococo artist of the *ancien régime*, Fragonard.

The great thing about this collection is that in this wonderful setting the rococo style holds its own. Despite current revisionist art history, rococo is still arraigned on the charge of sheer frivolity. To this Jean-Honoré Fragonard (1732–1806) would probably have pleaded guilty but incomparable. The subject of *The Swing*, a dalliance between a couple of the young filthy rich, was par for the course. The workmanship is sheer genius. In the foreground of the painting, the face of the idling man lying on the ground propped on one elbow says most of it; the blush on the face of the young woman on the swing says the rest. She kicks one stockinged leg high into the air and he has a clear view up inside the froth of pink dress as one little pink shoe flies off. This is more than a sweet disorder in the dress, and the old man in the shadows, pulling the swing with a rope in each hand, smiles slyly, knowing what is to follow.

A common fallacy is that great art must have a great theme, which, manifestly, would commit Mozart's *Così fan tutte* as a failure. *The Swing* is positively Mozartian, sublime in its masterly handling of the artificiality of the park. The two bewigged men in the scene are dressed in greyish-green, tonally in harmony with the wooded landscape; only the girl commands attention in her vivacity and anticipated pleasure, glowing in her pink finery in one of the best renderings in all art of a pool of green sunlight filtered through trees and swinging in a magically rendered pocket of space between the trees. Fragonard had travelled in Italy and Flanders and had carefully studied Jacob van Ruisdael's 17th-century landscapes and Giovanni Battista Tiepolo's *coups des théâtre* on the ceilings of Venetian palaces. Ruisdael fortified his understanding of landscape and distance;

Tiepolo's gods and princes in implausible flight showed him how to handle animated figures with vivacity and total plausibility. The girl flies too, but on a swing and as part of the game of life.

The Festival of Britain lives, at 219 Oxford Street, Westminster W1

It's a fair bet that anyone too young to remember George VI won't have a clue what the reliefs on the façade of 219 Oxford Street in the West End of London signify, and, since the whole world shops in this crowded and unlovely thoroughfare, no foreigners at all. The corner building itself has a tall, narrow frontage on Oxford Street east of Oxford Circus, but its four stories of alternate bands of stone facing and windows wrap in an elegant curve into a longer façade on Hills Place. The curve and the metal fenestration suggest the 1930s, but actually this was one of the first buildings of the Festival of Britain year, 1951. And the reliefs alongside the window strips on the top three stories above Oxford Street represent the Dome of Discovery and the Skylon, the festival logo designed by Abram Games, and the Royal Festival Hall.

In 1951 London was still a bombed ruin, full of rank weeds and gaily decorated if fading wallpaper peeling from indecently exposed inside partition walls. The festival was a nationwide manifestation aimed at suggesting a bright new dawn after a bruising night, but the focus was on the South Bank near Waterloo. Because the Labour government was underwriting it, Lord Beaverbrook's *Daily Express* attacked it. But, as Michael Frayn commented later: 'It quickly became clear that the South Bank, conceived in austerity and shaped by expediency, was a knockout.' The crowds flocked in. Domestic design took off into a decade of funny furniture with knobs

One of the relief plaques on the façade of 219 Oxford Street shows two Festival of Britain buildings on the South Bank, the Dome of Discovery and the Skylon. The trend-setting Oxford street shop was built in the year of the festival, 1951

wherever they could be screwed on, but at least it didn't look like wartime utility style. The elegant cigar-shaped Skylon has gone, as well as the Dome of Discovery (granddad to the Millennium Dome) and the Lion and Unicorn Pavilion; so have all the murals and mosaics and sculptures. Just the Festival Hall remains, some curling pages of Women's Institute scrapbooks, maybe a few park benches around the country, and the Oxford Street shop that in its small way set a benchmark for commercial architecture to follow.

A king's bounty at Apsley House (the Wellington Museum), Piccadilly w1

Arthur Wellesley, Duke of Wellington, was many men to the same public. After the Battle of Waterloo in 1815 he veered from being people's hero to diehard Tory opposed to parliamentary reform, and on his retirement he was once again the laurel-wreathed Iron Duke who had defeated the best marshals Napoleon could send against him in Spain and then the emperor himself. His London quarters, Apsley House, known in his pomp as Number 1 London, was a Robert Adam building of 1771–8 commissioned by Lord Apsley, the Lord Chancellor. Today it stands isolated in possibly London's heaviest traffic on an island at Hyde Park Corner, to be sought out via pedestrian underpasses. It's worth it. Wellington turned it into a shrine to his Napoleonic campaign. Gifts were poured upon him by the future king of Portugal, by the king of Spain, by the tsar of all the Russias, by King George IV of England: Sèvres dinner sets, paintings, statues, vast collections of silver and a mind-boggling 11 foot Carrara marble sculpture of a lean and naked Napoleon by Antonio Canova, commissioned in 1801 by the emperor himself, who was then sufficiently embarrassed to banish it to a cellar of the Louvre. But the pick of the collection is *The Water Seller of Seville* by Diego Velázquez (1599–1660). It was one of the paintings seized by French troops from the king of Spain's collection and liberated by Wellington at the decisive battle of the Peninsular campaign, the Battle of Vittoria. There were 165 pictures, and King Ferdinand VII granted them to Wellington with the royally worded message: 'His majesty, touched by your delicacy, does not wish to deprive you of that which has come into your possession by means as just as they are honourable.'

Velázquez has always been the painter's painter. Luca Giordano, the 18th-century Italian artist, in Spain at the behest of the Spanish king, examined Velázquez's unquestioned masterpiece *Las Meninas* in the royal collection and concluded: 'That contains the whole theology of painting.' In our own time Velázquez's countryman Picasso, too, became fascinated by *Las Meninas* and based on it a long sequence of variations on a theme. *The Water Seller* was one of a class of paintings called *bodegone*, tavern paintings. The dispassionate eye of Velázquez takes in the great clay jug beaded with water and the glass with drops running down the outside and a fig at the bottom to keep the water fresh, and gives them the same emphasis as the leathery skin and rough garments of the old water seller, a Corsican well known in Seville. When his obvious genius led him to service in the royal palaces of Madrid and the Escorial and he had the chance to study the great canvases Titian had painted in the previous century for the Habsburg emperor Charles V and for Philip II of Spain, he felt empowered to embark on some of the grandest paintings in Western art.

The Water Seller hangs in the Waterloo Gallery that Wellington added to Apsley House for the annual dinner celebrating the defeat of Napoleon. Here the veterans ate from the best of the silver and porcelain under the rows of paintings from Spain, perhaps in ignorance of the duke's personal favourite tucked away in a corner, a tiny Italian masterpiece, Correggio's *Agony in the Garden*.

Ducal gates that never open, at Green Park on Piccadilly W1

The Devonshire Gates at the Piccadilly end of the broad walk through Green Park never open and shut, as gates are supposed to do. This 17th-century gold and blue wrought iron portal between 19th-century piers as stately as a cenotaph, each with a sphinx on top, remain shut, apparently, for ever. That may be why they are taken for granted as simply another part of the urban scene, street furniture like the tall lamp post on the other side of the pavement obscuring a clear view of the gates. The hanging flower basket only compounds the offence. Commuters and tourists hurry by, heads down, anticipating the steps a few feet away into the depths of Green Park underground station, and on Sundays the hawkers of bright pictures along the railings of Green Park tie their screens to the gates and obscure the bottom two-thirds.

It's a shame because these gates are the very lovely sole survival of a lost gem, Devonshire House, which was built by William Kent (*c*.1685–1748) in 1734 as the London mansion of the Cavendishes of Chatsworth, Dukes of Devonshire, destroyed in 1921 to make way for a motorcar showroom and a block of flats above. The gates are probably by the skilled Huguenot craftsman in ironwork, Jean Montigny, who had certainly worked at the Duke of Chandos's famous and short-lived country seat in Edgware, Cannons (glass and paintings from Cannons in the same pretty

The elaborate gates separating Piccadilly from Green Park came from Devonshire House, the demolished London home of the Cavendish family, Dukes of Devonshire. This detail shows the Devonshire coat of arms

rococo taste beautify the Church of St Michael's at Great Witley, (see West and East Midlands). Although the Devonshire Gates were made in 1735, the commission was for a house in Turnham Green, and the gates didn't arrive at Devonshire House until 1897, when the Devonshire arms supported by two deer with golden antlers were added to adorn the centre of the arch above the double gates. There is a fine view through the gates along Broad Walk to the Queen Victoria Memorial in front of Buckingham Palace.

Athenian splendour at Spencer House, St James's Place SW1

The 1st Lord Spencer was a member of the Society of Dilettanti, which in the 18th century might have been described as a drinking club with discrimination and which lived by the motto, 'Roman Taste and Greek Gusto'. When he built Spencer House in St James's he opted for Rome downstairs and Greece upstairs. The family departed this palace overlooking Green Park in 1927, since when wartime bombing and several years serving as offices left Spencer House not remotely like a stately home. In 1985 Lord Rothschild bought the lease on behalf of RIT Capital Carpenters plc and set afoot the training of a group of craftsman to replicate what had been lost and carry though a total restoration with a few offices remaining out of sight. Today, open to the public on Sundays, the state rooms are once again in good order, just as they were when the house was ready in 1766.

Lord Spencer's first hiring was John Vardy (1718–65), a friend and associate of William Kent, who had seen through the completion of the Horseguards in Whitehall after Kent's death. In 1758 he built the exterior of Spencer House with its majestic eight-column first-floor pediment overlooking Green Park – at the time there was only grass and fresh air between Spencer House and Buckingham House (the predecessor to the palace). Vardy had completed the designs for the ground-floor rooms with its themes of love, hospitality and the arts, drawing richly on the apses, coffered ceilings and friezes of the ruined temples of Rome, when Spencer fired him in favour of the new darling, James Stuart. Stuart had just returned from Athens with notebooks stuffed with drawings and measurements of the Erechtheion and a head full of winning enthusiasm. Very soon he would be known as Athenian Stuart, a nickname that has stuck, although when Lord Spencer commissioned him to design the state rooms on the first floor he slyly filled in the gaps in his Greek invention with Roman details.

Between them, Vardy and Stuart created two magnificent suites of rooms, Vardy's Palladian (Rome), Stuart's neoclassical (Athens). Each has one climactic room. Vardy's much photographed palm room is his show-stopper, built in the belief that ancient architecture had its origins in organic growth. It has carved columns wreathed in gilded palm leaves spreading wide into fronds across the spandrels of arches leading into a glorious alcove with a coffered dome. Stuart's masterpiece is the painted room, a celebration of the loving marriage of the Spencers, completed in 1765 and thus the earliest room of the neoclassical revival in the world. This is near perfection in the delicacy and discrimination of the decor, the friezes, the painted roundels, the flower-decked pilasters, the grandeur of the fireplace carved by Scheemakers (the original; many of the others have been faithfully copied from the originals now at Althorp), and the chimneypiece painted with a copy of the famous ancient Roman *Aldobrandini Wedding*, the candelabra on the chimneypiece, and the small forest of gilded Corinthian columns articulating the bowed, apse-like alcove to the south. The splendour is not dimmed from the day when the 18th-century travel writer (and agriculturist) Arthur Young wrote: 'All is richness, elegance and taste, superior to any house I have seen.'

A royal collection at Buckingham Palace
sw1

The royal collection is one of the greatest in the world and an incomparable private collection (though unlike, say, the Duke of Northumberland, the Queen cannot offload objects, because she holds them in trust for the nation). Had it not been for the intervention of Cromwell, it would have been greater still because Charles I's collection was already pre-eminent. Some of the best work, like the Mantegna sequence at Hampton Court (see Greater London, below) and the Raphael Cartoons in the Victoria & Albert Museum remained, and Charles II managed to re-gather some of his father's collection. George III, dull old 'Farmer George', bought and commissioned far better than he directed his family firm, the nation, and managed as well to claw back more of what Cromwell had dispersed. Something over 3,000 works are on long loan to museums all over the world, and there are constant loans to temporary exhibitions: in the Holbein show at the Mauritshuis in The Hague in 2003, there were three paintings, fifteen drawings and one miniature from the British royal collection, and at Tate Britain three years later there were four paintings by Holbein and one copy, twenty-five drawings and four miniatures.

All the palaces are open some of the time; the state rooms in Buckingham Palace itself have opened in August and September to help to pay for the restoration at Windsor Castle after the fire of 1992, and it is worth the admission money to see paintings in the context of decor, ornaments and furniture. But the Queen's Gallery behind a small modern pastiche of a classical portico in Buckingham Palace Road beside the royal mews is always open. Over the years the gallery has shown the cream of the collection in a run of magnificent and little publicised shows drawn from the palaces and accompanied by expert and well-illustrated catalogues. It continues to do so in a setting much expanded and improved this century, with galleries that feel like state rooms, as well they might since they were adapted from palace rooms. Windsor and Hampton Court are the other major places, magnificent in themselves and with magnificent paintings. Apart from the state rooms at Windsor there is the drawings gallery with its unparalleled holdings of Leonardo and Holbein, as well as Michelangelo and Raphael. Inigo Jones's Banqueting House, from which Charles I walked to the scaffold in Whitehall, has no collection but does have the great Rubens ceiling, *The Apotheosis of James I*, as political a painting as Holbein's defining image of Henry VIII if not as effective. The Queen's House at Greenwich (see Greater London, below), that other Jones masterpiece, is no longer a royal palace but is annexed to the maritime museum and contains another stupendous collection of top-of-the-heap English portrait painting.

One word of caution: what's on show in the royal collection is not dictated, like other private collections, by private whim, but because of loans, conservation and, especially, the fragility of drawings if they are constantly exposed to light, objects are often given a rest; so if you want to see anything specific it's worth checking before visiting that it is on display.

Portraits of the Windsors are a staple of the Queen's Gallery, from the delightful portrait by Johann Zoffany, master of the conversation piece, of Queen Charlotte and some of her brood in a room with a view on to the palace gardens, which, apparently, still exists, to portraits of today's royals, with the Hanoverian features repeating themselves faithfully through the generations.

Queen Charlotte, by Thomas Gainsborough (1727–88), is the best English 18th-century portrait I know, and I think it may be a palace favourite too, because it has returned two or three times in recent years in different contexts. Reynolds remarked on Gainsborough's ability to work on all parts of the painting together, a talent that unifies the canvas with its appearance of an ambient atmosphere, an early spotting in art history. And Reynolds's pupil James Northcote remarked on the queen's apparent movement: ''Tis actual motion and done with such airy facility.' Gainsborough and his nephew Gainsborough Dupont worked through the night by lamplight to paint the queen's white silk, gold-spangled dress. It is sheer magic.

For other parts of the royal collection see Windsor (South) and Hampton Court (Greater London, below).

The Renaissance feminist, in Buckingham Palace sw1

In August and September the Queen opens the state rooms of Buckingham Palace to the paying public. The best of them are those John Nash created when George IV came to the throne in 1820. Nash (1750–1835) built and decorated the throne room, drawing rooms and state dining room, ballroom, picture gallery and music room, borrowing whatever he fancied, ancient or modern, inventing from scratch. Neither George IV nor William IV, nor, for that matter, Nash, lived to see it

Artemesia Gentileschi's self portrait in the Royal Collection is also an allegory of painting, but its immediacy, passion, daring composition and technique lift it above the genre

completed, but within it finally Victoria disposed hundreds of thousands of old master prints, Sèvres porcelain ordered especially to match the decor of each room, tapestries, red hangings, gilt trim, glorious chandeliers and a part of her collection of 7,000 paintings.

So although the best way of gaining an overview of the collections is to visit the shows at the Queen's Gallery on Buckingham Palace Road (see above), nothing can take the place of seeing in opulent context whatever happens to be displayed in Nash's rooms in any one year. ('They move around a bit,' as an attendant remarked to me.) The base of the collection is the royal portraits, and nobody later matched Van Dyck's depictions of Charles I and his family. But Charles in person, his representatives and his successors scoured the continent for works of art other than portraiture, like the *Mantgena Triumphs of Caesar at Hampton Court* (see Greater London, below) and the Raphael cartoons for tapestries on permanent loan to the Victoria & Albert Museum. Among smaller easel paintings, he acquired surpassing work by Vermeer, Rembrandt and Rubens. Orazio Gentileschi was already in England working for the royal court, and the king invited his daughter Artemesia Gentileschi (1593–1651/3) to join him. From this working visit of about three years he acquired her great self-portrait, seen also as an allegory of painting. Its distinction is its graphic power and intensity, the female as dynamic mistress of her art. Artemesia learned to paint in her father's studio and at the age of eighteen or nineteen was raped by a collaborating artist of Orazio's, Agostino Tassi. Orazio pursued him through the courts and secured a conviction. There seems no reason to doubt that the horror of Artemesia's three gory depictions (in Rome, Florence and Naples) of the Jewish Judith's slaughter of the enemy Assyrian general Holofernes show the marks of her

trauma. It is incomparably more expressive than the contemporary treatment of the subject by Caravaggio. But then, Gentileschi was a woman of powerful emotions. She followed her father to England at the invitation of Charles I, and this self-portrait is of an uncourtly, uncourted working woman with tousled blue-black hair, as muckily unkempt as a fishwife, the locket from a golden chain around her neck hanging in space as she leans outwards towards the viewer and forwards to work pigment on to the primed canvas, very like a 'snapshot' portrait by Degas, but three centuries earlier. She could have produced this unusual and dynamic viewpoint only by deploying a carefully positioned combination of mirrors. It serves as an allegory of painting as well as a portrait: the locket hanging from her neck among other attributes were the prescriptions in a text of the time for the figure of Painting. But primarily this is a freely brushed work of breathtaking immediacy that surpasses the history of its making.

A fine Queen Anne doorway at 28 Queen Anne's Gate sw1

The terraces of dark red brick houses of 1704–5 with sumptuous doorcases make Queen Anne's Gate one of the grandest streets of its kind anywhere. It was once divided into two: Queen Square, where the best houses are, and, after a sudden narrowing, Old Queen Street. At the join halfway down, where the narrowing provides a corner, stands a weathered statue of Anna Regina, as the plinth is inscribed, installed by

At No. 28 Queen Anne's Gate, across Bird Cage Walk from St James's Park, is the finest of the doorcases in a fine street. Actually, it is a reproduction: the original was moved to the Victoria and Albert Museum to save it from the elements

1708, six years after her accession to the throne. Opposite it is No. 28 Queen Anne's Gate, which has the best doorcase and history.

Between the two world wars the owner of the house was Ronald Tree, a bisexual Conservative MP who also owned Ditchley Park in Oxfordshire, which he lent to Winston Churchill as a wartime hideaway. At No. 28, following the resignation of Anthony Eden in the run-up to the Munich Agreement, Tree entertained the members of a supposedly secret grouping of MPs opposing prime minister Neville Chamberlain, including Harold Macmillan, the socialist and diarist Harold Nicolson, Duff Cooper, who resigned as minister of war after Munich, Eden himself and Leo Amery, who would later make the key speech from the floor of the Commons demanding Chamberlain's resignation ('in the name of God, go!'). The group had no name until it was contemptuously dubbed 'the glamour boys' by a former MI5 operative and Chamberlain groupie who succeeded in bugging No. 28. It probably wasn't worth doing, because the group seems to have been merely a glamour boys' talking shop.

Like the other houses in the old Queen's Square, grotesque heads are carved on the keystones above the windows. But what's so good about the door is that, where the detail of the others in the street (apart from No. 1, which is a grandiose modern invention) is clogged by white paint, No. 28's has been left, or brought back, to natural wood, possibly anti-historically, with lacy pilasters as doorposts and on the doorhood a double arch with opulent foliage and a beautiful hermaphrodite head in the centre. Actually, in the necessary modern way, the original doorway is preserved in the Victoria & Albert Museum and an exact replica is installed on the house.

A suitably modern sculpture for the London Underground headquarters, St James's sw1

Charles Holden was an austere architect and an austere man, but he loved the sculpture of Jacob Epstein with a passion. So although Epstein (1880–1959) had been execrated by the gutter press for his naked figures on the British Medical Association building in the Strand (triumphantly mutilated after the building became Rhodesia House), Holden once again invited the sculptor to provide carvings over the two main entrances of the new stepped-back pile at 44 Broadway, St James's, designed as the headquarters of London Underground. Once again the press ran amok, a public-spirited company director kindly offered to pay the costs of having the two carvings removed, and Frank Pick, the brilliant and enlightened managing director of the London Electric Railway Company as it was then known, offered his resignation (it was refused). Only one figure on the two groups, Day and Night, was naked, and that was a little boy stretching upwards to wrap his arms around his father's neck. Epstein chipped a bit off the lad's penis and the row subsided.

The real problem was always about placing sculpture on a building that relies for its effect on its broad undecorated surfaces. Some of it is invisible anyway, and some of it might just as well be. Judging by photographs, Eric Gill has a nice-looking East Wind, though as always he funks the modernist challenge thrown down by Epstein in favour of linear grace. Gill was the senior sculptor in charge of a team that included Henry Moore, but the younger man's North Wind is infinitely more effective, an archaic female figure throwing her massive limbs horizontally across the face of the building like a runaway tube train, though the idea is actually clearly based on a Romanesque angel, like those at Malmesbury (see South).

Epstein is best placed to be seen. Day is the father and son; Night is a mother and dead child, a primitive pietà, carved in situ, using primitive tools, dispensing with accuracy in favour of vitality, a powerful sculptural authority that he only occasionally equalled in his long life.

Our Lady of Westminster at Westminster Cathedral sw1

The cathedral in Westminster, tucked away near the railway terminus at the wrong end of Victoria Street, is the poor but proud relation of the abbey. Built at the end of the 19th century of red brick with cream stripes, like the surrounding blocks of flats, it might almost be a railway station itself, but for the absence of buses in its piazza and its slender 284 feet campanile. Unworthy thoughts must be checked in at the entrance, because the sooty, light-swallowing darkness of the domes above the nave seems a solemn metaphor for life and death, and here are more worshippers on their knees seeking salvation or at least forgiveness than there are among the hordes of us tourists and the vainglorious monuments of the abbey at the other end of Victoria Street.

I came to see the fourteen relief carvings of the Stations of the Cross, a famous early work by Eric Gill (1882–1940), always said to be the most valuable of the cathedral's works of art; but I left humbled by a small statue known as Our Lady of Westminster, lately so called because it is a medieval Virgin and Child presented to the cathedral only in 1955. It is probably of the late 14th or the 15th century, since that's when the workshops of the city were geared up to full production and export mode. Some of it was the work of monks responding to market demand, most by professional masons. These small sculptures, from stone quarried in the north

Midlands, were sold all over Europe; those that stayed in England suffered destruction like most other religious imagery when Henry VIII sent his unsparing commissioners into the regions to root out papist idolatry.

The Westminster piece was saved because it was one of the exports. It is a stock Virgin and Child of the period, she crowned and the child rendered as a little manikin standing on her knee. It's not that sculptors of the time were incapable of carving a realistic child – the figure of the mother gives the lie to that in its tenderness of face and pose. It is more likely that the sculptor was encapsulating the adult Christ in the child, foreshadowing his fate as saviour of mankind. The Virgin's crown and mantle are brown, tinged gold, her face is glowing cream alabaster, her eyes downcast in love and sorrow. It is a Christian image like many other Christian images, alike in iconography, idealisation and pose, and yet it is uniquely beautiful. Whatever the harsh realities of life in Nottingham in the Middle Ages, the artists who made these objects knew a peace that passes the understanding of our own age.

The Renaissance arrives in England at Westminster Abbey sw1

One of the early frames of the world's biggest comic strip, the Bayeux Tapestry, shows Harold being crowned king of the English in 1066 in Westminster Abbey, the event that precipitated the invasion by William of Normandy. Today the abbey's appearance is dominated by Henry III's rebuilding in pointed Gothic. There is the tall, clean-limbed nave by Henry Yevele, the master mason who also built Canterbury's nave; a glorious and intricate jewel box of a Gothic choir screen of 1833–4 by Edward Blore and George Gilbert Scott's glittering reredos, which is the façade on a 15th-century stone screen separating Edward the Confessor's

When the Florentine sculptor Pietro Torrigiano fell out with his sponsors, the Medici banking family, for breaking Michelangelo's nose, he accepted a commission from Henry VII to design the tomb for his queen, Elizabeth, and himself in his chapel in Westminster Abbey. The chapel is pure Gothic; the tomb, ready in 1510, the first wholehearted Renaissance art in England

chapel, and the sanctuary and probably the greatest medieval sculpture in England adorning the interior of the church. Not to mention, of course, Poets' Corner, the burial place of poets from Geoffrey Chaucer to T.S. Eliot. For all this, the function hasn't changed: ever since Harold, the abbey has been the place of coronation for English monarchs. For centuries it was their mausoleum as well with its glorious culmination the lady chapel, now named for

Henry VII, first of the Tudors, who rebuilt it and is buried there with his queen, Elizabeth of York, under an astonishingly intricate fan vault with its hanging pendants, a last fling of Perpendicular Gothic before the Reformation and the culmination of a glorious building in which it is easy to lose sight of the detail, not least in Henry's chapel.

It was finished in 1510, a year after the king's death, and work on the tomb started in 1512. Henry had chosen the Florentine Pietro

Torrigiano (1472–1528) as sculptor and designer of the effigies of Elizabeth and himself and of the plinth-like sarcophagus with medallions containing lovely relief sculptures. As in most churches, where the work of man is placed in subservience to the exaltation of God, there is no labelling in the chapel to identify Torrigiano as the author of this tomb, medieval England's first fully Renaissance work of art, even though the format, effigies lying side by side, pays respect to the Gothic. Torrigiano had studied side by side with Michelangelo, learning painting and drawing in the workshop of Ghirlandaio and sculpture under the patronage of Lorenzo the Magnificent. In the first decade of the 16th century nothing in this turbulent offshore island had previously been seen to compare with such sculpture and nothing as modern as Torrigiano's work would be seen again before Hans Holbein arrived at the riverside home of Thomas More twenty years later (and even so England never fully took to the Renaissance until Inigo Jones, Peter Paul Rubens and Anthony Van Dyck began to work for the first Stuart kings a hundred years later).

Torrigiano is infamous as the fellow who broke Michelangelo's nose in an argument in the Brancacci Chapel, Florence, where both were making studies of the Masaccio fresco cycle. He was, in the words of the 16th-century art historian Vasari, motivated by envy, and Condivi, Michelangelo's other biographer, simply wrote him off as bestial. Does any of this matter 500 years later? Well yes, because Michelangelo's bad break was England's good fortune: Torrigiano fell out of favour with the Medici rulers of Florence and left Italy to pursue a peripatetic living in the rest of Europe.

Henry VII's mother, Lady Margaret Beaufort, died, like her son, in 1509, and Torrigiano began her separate tomb in the south aisle of the chapel in 1511. The gilt bronze figure of Lady Margaret lies on a lower sarcophagus than those of her son and daughter-in-law, so it is easier to see the moving humanity of the portrait. The lines of age and suffering marking her exquisitely modelled face and the long, easy curves of the gown cloaking her body are a new world of Renaissance art compared to the severe angularity of the later Gothic memorials in the abbey. The gilded sculptures of Henry VII and his queen lie side by side above eye level upon a sumptuous marble tomb like a great sculptural plinth contained within an open Gothic screen of brass. Torrigiano has treated their heads like the emblematic royal portraits on coins, though they may have been actual portraits made on the basis of death masks. All the warmth here is lavished on the winning angels at the corners of the tombs, and the lions at the couple's feet combine an architectural formality with a flowing line of contained energy. The enterprise suggests quite a different Torrigiano from the one described by the friends of Michelangelo.

Charles I at Trafalgar Square sw1

Richard Weston, lord treasurer to Charles I, commissioned an equestrian statue of the king for his garden in Mortlake Park, as great courtiers did, but it became a dangerous political symbol in the war-torn years of the mid-17th century. Lord Weston died before he could take delivery, and it lay in store in the crypt of St Paul, Covent Garden. But in 1650, acting on orders from the Cromwellian parliament, agents tracked it down and sold it as scrap metal to a brazier of Holborn, one John Rivet, ordering him to break it up and melt it. Instead, he hid it. When Cromwell fell, Weston's family reclaimed it, and the widow sold it to King Charles II for £1,600. For precisely the reasons Cromwell had wished it destroyed, Charles erected it on a pedestal by

Christopher Wren at Charing Cross (now Trafalgar Square) on the spot where the last of Edward I's Eleanor crosses (see Geddington and Hardingstone, West and East Midlands) had stood until Cromwell destroyed it. Ostensibly, it was a homage to his father; at least as much, it was a covert indication that normal service had been resumed.

The sculptor was Hubert Le Sueur (c.1580–after 1658). He was king's sculptor in Paris at the court of Louis XIII, but in 1626 he came to London from Paris, at the instigation, it seems, of the Duke of Buckingham, King Charles's principal lieutenant in artistic as well as most other matters, including his marriage to Louis XIII's sister, Henrietta Maria. He was a man of supreme vanity, who submitted invoices to the king signed 'Praxiteles Le Sueur', Praxiteles being, of course, the most famous sculptor of ancient Greece, and got away with it until Charles received the bust of him by Bernini (from the triple-view template in oils by Van Dyck now at Windsor Castle) and realised that Le Sueur was a comparative duffer; worse, a duffer who overcharged. Critics have pointed out that his work looks as though it had been pumped up rather than modelled. But approaching Trafalgar Square along Whitehall on the top deck of a number 11 bus it might look majestic if it weren't overwhelmed by Nelson on his column. Close to, it is high in artificial decorative content but formulaic, as though Le Sueur had designed it as a small table-piece. Indeed, though this was the hub of London and is

This sculpture of King Charles I by Hubert le Sueur was the first bronze equestrian statue made in England. Le Sueur undertook it as a private commission when Charles was still secure on the throne in the 1630s, and it was placed at this point between Whitehall and what is now Trafalgar Square on the orders of Charles II

still the point from which distances to the capital are measured, Charles and his horse, the first equestrian bronze in England, are stranded on a traffic island. Could it be that the look on the bronze face expresses wistfulness as it gazes towards the spot of the actual Charles I's execution? No such luck; it's a blank.

The coffee house virtuosi, at the National Portrait Gallery WC2

The National Portrait Gallery has always been as much historical archive of the nation's great and good as art collection, though its possession of works with the weight of Holbein's defining life-size image of Henry VIII, feet spread, arms akimbo, make it unmissable for art buffs. The Tudor gallery is its greatest strength, but there are good unsung areas, such as the collection of 18th-century portraits, a visual equivalent to the picture of the period in the letters, diaries and memoirs of the time, Horace Walpole, Elizabeth Montagu ('Queen of the Blues'), James Boswell, Edward Gibbon and all. Among these were the virtuosi, clubbable men of accomplishment and taste, in their own eyes certainly, gentlemen like the sober, not to say pompous-looking, group in the team picture by Gawen Hamilton (c.1697–1737), *A Gathering of Virtuosi*, untypical in that all but one of them are celebrated artists of their day. Here Hamilton portrays them in 1735 at their regular meeting place, the King's Head in New Bond Street. It was the age of coffee house assemblies and the nascent clubs of St James's, some devoted to politics, some claiming to be devoted to cultural pursuits but actually dedicated to debauchery. Hamilton's conversation piece hangs in an area of the second floor where, small and under regarded, the *Virtuosi* is nevertheless the document that pulls it all together, a portrait of men too involved in the vulgar reality of making a living to take up the higher debauchery.

The odd-man-out is the elegant fellow on the scarlet chair in the centre with a pencil between his fingers. This is Matthew Robinson, coffee house wit and father of an even greater wit, the acknowledged 'Queen of the Bluestockings', Mrs Montagu (her name surfaces in dictionary definitions of the word). He is the sole amateur artist among the virtuosi, rich and fawned upon. Robinson and the dozing dog are the only ones here who have it made. He looks particularly contented because he is in town instead of at his normal residence on his daughter's country estate – living in the country, he told her, was like being asleep with one's eyes open.

Those hanging on his words here include the busy portrait painter Michael Dahl, sitting opposite him, and the architect of St Martin-in-the-Fields, James Gibbs, standing behind the centre of the table. Then there are two artists who were soon too be overtaken by other talents: the sculptor Michael Rysbrack (see Bristol, Southwest), showing off an antique bust, and, leaning chummily over Rysbrack's shoulder, the painter of sporting pictures, John Wootton, who suffered later when the great horse painter George Stubbs usurped him. On the right, putting his best foot forward, is William Kent, interior designer of genius and Lord Burlington's architect at Chiswick (see Greater London, below) and Burlington House, who went on to build Thomas Coke's Holkham Hall with its grand Roman sculpture gallery (see Holkham, East Anglia). Hamilton himself is at work behind him, remembered today for this picture. He is the only one with his painting hat on rather than a wig (a self-portrait of Hogarth at work wearing similar headgear is in the same room). At the far left is George Vertue, well known as an engraver but remembered today as the forefather of English art history. Horace Walpole bought Vertue's bulging

notebooks about the artists of his time and based his own *Anecdotes of Painting* upon them.

Like other clubs, the virtuosi contributed towards artistic causes, and to help to raise funds Hamilton agreed to raffle the painting on 15 April 1735. Joseph Goupy, a miniaturist and portrait painter, who stands behind Robinson in the picture, won it with the highest throw of the dice. He died in 1747, and at the auction of his goods Robinson (who else?) bought *A Gathering of Virtuosi*.

Red phone boxes opposite the Royal Opera House, Covent Garden WC2

Giles Gilbert Scott, the 20th-century Scott (1880–1960) of the architectural dynasty, is more famous than either his famous Gothicising grandfather or his father in the same line, first, for the stupendous and stupendously late-Gothic Anglican Liverpool Cathedral (completed in 1978), then for the power station that now houses Tate Modern, and third for what's popularly known as the red telephone box, even though almost all types of telephone boxes are red except in Hull, where they are privately owned and grey. Scott's red telephone box is the thatched cottage of modern design, even more popular, if possible, than the old half-timbered Morris Minor, still to be spotted by keen watchers of the street scene and not totally dissimilar from Scott's sturdily mullioned and transomed phone boxes.

Since the introduction of mobiles they are on borrowed time, even though they are listed as protected grade II buildings. At their best they stand smartly to attention in their guardsman-fresh red livery like the six in Broad Street on sentry duty opposite the Royal Opera House, but among the other 2,000 or so listed booths some are dilapidated, some working, some not, some ankle-deep in urine, some vandalised –

because, of course, their protected status doesn't stop the happy work of vandals, among whom the phone box is even more popular than with the general public.

The finest moment in art for the red box (all right, its proper name is K2) must be the few moments of total anarchy in Alexander Mackendrick's film comedy *The Ladykillers* (1955) when Alec Guinness, Peter Sellers, Herbert Lom and Danny Green all pile struggling into a red phone box somewhere near King's Cross, a reprise of the Marx Brothers' mad moment in *A Night at the Opera*, though of course Groucho, Chico and Harpo had to make do with some inferior American call box.

London's best shopping arcade, the Royal Opera Arcade, Haymarket SW1

The English font of all those egregious modern shopping malls is the Royal Opera Arcade, nowhere near the Royal Opera House but running between Charles II Street and Pall Mall. It is the earliest and best of the group of four West End arcades, Burlington, Princes, the Royal Arcade and the Royal Opera Arcade. Everyone knows the Burlington Arcade (1819), the toffs' Woolworths, with its beadles in top hats and tailcoats, full of little jewellery shops, art dealers and boutiques for the fashion-conscious hunting set leaving the summer show at Burlington House next door. The Royal Arcade of 1879–80, off Old Bond Street, has an entrance that wouldn't disgrace an East End music-hall and an interior that is a cross between the Burlington Arcade and a miniaturised Leadenhall Market. The Edwardian and passably soigné Piccadilly Arcade and the 1930s Princes Arcade both link Piccadilly to Jermyn Street, so shirt-makers join the lists. The Royal Opera Arcade, though the shops are nothing like as flash, is the gem, its window casings, hanging

lamps and flowerpots painted dark as sapphire against the cream of the walls and vault.

John Nash (1752–1835) and his chief assistant, G.R. Repton (1786–1858), the son of Humphry Repton, the landscape gardener and former partner of Nash, built the Royal Opera Arcade in 1816–18 as part of their recasing of the Haymarket Opera House. This was then rebuilt in 1896 as Her Majesty's Theatre, whose superior back alley the arcade now is, with a backdoor too into the fifteen-story New Zealand House. North and south, the entrances are crisply carved stone archways. The arcade has Doric pilasters and is groin vaulted with small glass domes. There are 19th-century iron-cased lanterns suspended in the centre from brackets curving out from the walls between every second bow-fronted shop and lunettes set into arches above the display windows. It is effortlessly elegant Regency architecture, a last kiss bestowed by the 18th century on the early years of the brasher 19th.

Charity at the Foundling Museum, Brunswick Square, Bloomsbury WC1

Captain Thomas Coram RN, born in Lyme Regis in 1668, sent to sea at the age of eleven, now retired and shocked by the sight of babies abandoned in the streets of London, sets out to create an asylum for foundlings. It takes him seventeen years, tramping the streets of London collecting signatures to a petition, soliciting contributions, at the age of seventy covering 15 to 20 miles a day. The money is raised, land in the countryside north of Gray's Inn bought, the Foundling Hospital is built and the children flood in. The new board of governors finds the blunt sea dog an embarrassment and cast him off. For the rest of his life he is the ghost at the feast, visiting daily, sitting in the colonnade (still there in Coram Fields north of Guilford

William Hogarth was a governor of the Foundling Hospital founded in 1739 by the sturdy old sea dog, Captain Thomas Coram. He bestowed some of his best paintings on the hospital and added this fine, affectionate portrait of Coram. Although the hospital was blitzed during the Second World War, most of its interiors and paintings survive

Street in Bloomsbury), distributing gingerbread to the foundlings.

William Hogarth (1697–1764) paints him seated with a globe at his feet, a bluff, white-haired old man, and donates the painting to the hospital. George Frederick Handel 'Generously and Charitably offered a Performance of Vocal and Instrumental Musick' to raise funds to complete the chapel, and he composes the *Foundling Hospital* anthem for the occasion. Hogarth and Handel each become governors, and Hogarth encourages other artists to contribute paintings. They do, Reynolds and Ramsay, Francis Hayman, Joseph Highmore, Richard Wilson, Thomas Gainsborough, the marine painter Samuel Scott, Hogarth's roistering companion on a well-recorded weekend's boozing voyage up the Thames to Rochester, and others.

But Hogarth is the top of the bill in his own show. He was a popular though uneven painter, still often thought of as the first truly English artist. He was born in the shadow of St Bartholomew's Priory and studied with the history painter Sir James Thornhill, but his own history painting is a rite of passage and doesn't suit his rough nature. London in the here-and-now was his project, its abject down-and-outs, its hopeless drunks, its dissolute rich and its licentious soldiery crowd his canvases (in the Foundling Museum too is his famous response painted in 1749–50 of the government reaction to the Jacobite rebellion of 1745, *The March of the Guards to Finchley*, which might be called *The March of the Guards and Their Whores*). He was attracted by Coram's plans, and what they built together lasted until 1954, though after the blitz it moved out to Berkhamsted. Here in Bloomsbury, in interiors rescued from the bombing, hangs Hogarth's portrait of the founder. It is one of his best. Alan Ramsay painted the hospital's physician, Dr Richard Mead, as a pendant portrait. It hangs alongside, and the two paintings take up a whole wall. Hogarth's painting wipes Ramsay's out. Everything – the strong, heavily veined hands, the big red coat with huge cuffs and collar, the big red face under a wild white thatch – is in your face, utterly vital, unpolished, utterly unacademic, a living presence.

Soane, the star of his own show, at the Sir John Soane Museum, Lincoln's Inn Fields WC2

Hogarth is everywhere in London; in his time he *was* London. But though Number 13 Lincoln's Inn Fields contains two of his great series of paintings, *The Rake's Progress* and *The Election*, it is primarily the house and museum that John Soane (1753–1837) built in 1792–4 for himself and his huge, eccentric, eclectic, jumble of collections, his pictures, sculptures, plaster casts, an ancient Egyptian royal sarcophagus and an invaluable cache of extraordinary drawings and plans by many of the great architects of the century and earlier. They inundated the house to such a degree that he bought and rebuilt numbers 12 and 14 on either side, and in his house, unchanged except that it is now known precisely as the John Soane Museum, Soane himself is the star to navigate by through the shifting spaces of his genius. When he died in 1837 Soane left his house to the nation. It is, as the museum's curator Margaret Richardson writes, 'a museum piece among museums'.

The brick-built house announces itself from the outside as quirkily quasi-classical, with a Portland stone projection of three bays (the full width of number 13) narrowing to one bay at the second floor. At the first-floor angles of the projection stand two caryatids freely adapted from originals at the Erechtheion in Athens (there's a large fragment of the real thing inside, if you can find it), but on the face of the projection are four Gothic brackets lifted from Westminster Hall.

Like all Soane's buildings, it is subliminally disturbing, as though the architect had come by the design in a dream. But if the outside is disconcerting, that's nothing compared to the interior. Although it is stuffed with classical artefacts, the spaces themselves are mysteriously Gothic, reaching a climax in the lurid monk's parlour in the basement, where the main feature is the sepulchral chamber, a deep rectangular space as deep as the house. And then there are the apparently solid walls of the picture gallery, which fold back once to reveal more pictures and fold back again on to a vertiginous view of the floors below.

From the ground floor the visitor looks down on an area lit by a large dome in the roof. Here is the translucent sarcophagus of Pharaoh Seti I, who reigned from 1294 BC until 1271 BC and whose tomb was uncovered during the excavations of the necropolis at Thebes. In 1824 the British Museum refused to pay £2,000 for it, so Soane stepped smartly in. It is wonderfully, though now very faintly, incised with tiny tomb figures, inside and out, which well repay a close look from a wooden step at each end of the sarcophagus. Soane, of course, showed this prize acquisition to visitors by lamplight.

Off the entrance hall are two rooms merging into one, the dining room and library, and they make a perfectly useable living space, even homely with its deep red walls and little canopies composed of semicircular arches (another feature throughout the house). Soane's portrait by Thomas Lawrence hangs in the dining room and shows him apparently sane and civilised. Always bear in mind that the answer he supplied to questions about the monk's parlour was a quotation from Horace: *Dulce est desipere in loco* ('It is pleasant to be nonsensical in due place').

An exotic rhino at the Hunterian Museum, Royal College of Surgeons, Lincoln's Inn Fields WC2

John Hunter was one of those 18th-century Scotsmen like James Boswell who came to London and made a great name for himself, in his case as a surgeon. He arrived from East Kilbride in 1748 at the age of twenty to stay with his brother William and work with him at his anatomy school in Covent Garden. In 1761 he became an army surgeon and worked on treatment for venereal disease and gunshot wounds, the biggest threat, probably in that order, to the health of the rude soldiery. Empirical research became the basis of his approach to surgery, and by the time of his death in 1793 he was famous for his teaching, his salon where artists and scientists met to exchange ideas and his breadth of interest. His medical collection was interspersed with works of art, and after his death the government bought it and gave it to the Royal College of Surgeons. As the Hunterian Collection, it is open free to the public in the grandiose home of the college directly opposite the John Soane Museum across Lincoln's Inn Fields. From the birds and tiny mammals bottled in formaldehyde to the human nervous system flat against a board and nearly as complex looking as the circuitry of a computer, this museum is the ultimate natural scientist's play room.

The art interspersed through Hunter's collection is always there for its interest to scientists, mostly portrait busts of eminent surgeons, including one of Hunter himself by the 18th-century sculptor John Flaxman, but even the pictures in the small gallery

This scene of controlled chaos in a basement room of the phantasmagoric house and museum John Soane built for himself at 13 Lincoln's Inn Fields helps to explain why he found it necessary to buy the houses at 12 and 14 on either side to take the overflow

devoted to them are there for reasons other than their quality as paintings: dwarfs, Siamese twins, the nation's fattest man. The Indian rhino, *Rhinoceros (rhinoceros unicornis)* by George Stubbs (1724–1806), was only the third sighting of one of these beasts in England; the previous one had been almost sixty years before. It arrived from the subcontinent aboard an East Indiaman in 1790 and went on exhibition at the Lyceum in the Strand where, the *Morning Herald* reported, 'a greater living curiosity has never appeared in this country'. One visitor remarked that its temperament was similar to 'a tolerably tractable pig', and despite the fierce samurai-style armour plating of its hide, Stubbs shows it manifesting every sign of boredom with its mild brown eyes and down-turned mouth. After three years of touring the country the poor creature lay down and died.

Hunter probably commissioned Stubbs to paint the rhinoceros, since it was in his collection before he died in the same year as the rhino. Nobody could have been better qualified for the commission. He had spent years making impeccable anatomical studies of men and beasts and was easily the best painter of horses this country has ever seen. He shows the rhinoceros on a stony plateau with a louring sky behind, a stage set really for a close portrait of an animal the artist regards with utter objectivity. Hunter, certainly, was pleased: in 1791 he bought at sale a painting by Stubbs of a yak (Tartar ox), an animal that the first governor general of India, Warren Hastings, brought back to Daylesford, his ancestral home in Gloucestershire. Like pendant portraits. the two exotic rarities hang, still curious to us where they hadn't been to Stubbs.

A French vacation at the Courtauld Institute of Art, the Strand WC2

The Courtauld collection moved to Somerset House from a drab block in Bloomsbury, where a few desultory members of the public would ride to the first-floor galleries in a rickety lift ('like a short prison sentence,' wrote the art historian and curator David Piper, himself once a Japanese prisoner of war). Finally, the collection arrived in the galleries of the Royal Academy's original home in Somerset House, and still a few desultory members of the public ride to the first-floor galleries in a rickety lift (or climb a steep staircase), while the rest of the world passes by in the Strand and attends to its business in Starbucks. It's a mystery, because these paintings, mostly Impressionist, put together in the early half of the century by the chairman of the family textile company, form one of the great 'small' collections of the world, or rather, several collections, because to the original one several more have been added, of Renaissance art and pre- and post-Renaissance works.

Tell a Frenchman that Samuel Courtauld's buys include Renoir's *The Theatre Box* and Manet's *Bar at the Folies Bergères*, and like as not he will refuse to believe it. Tell him about *Lake of Annecy* by Paul Cézanne (1839–1906), and he will struggle to place it. As it happens, Annecy didn't suit Cézanne as a location. In July 1896 he went from Provence to Talloires on the edge of the lake for a change of scene and colour. But Annecy was too picture-postcard gorgeous. Provence was Cézanne's country, especially Mont St Victoire viewed from his stone cabin at the Bibémus quarry. He returned day after day, year after year to this motif with its harsh geometry and sun-baked colours. Despite his unease, Cézanne returned from his expedition to Annecy with this most sumptuously beautiful blue landscape, painted with care and passion, discipline and warmth and the final, unanalysable, sense Cézanne always imparts of natural appearances reinvented through emotion. Cézanne's classicism revealed itself gradually as he worked through an accumulation of marks evenly applied across the canvas, none of them apparently signifying anything until the coherence of the ensemble at last revealed the subject, emerging like rocks from beneath the sea at low tide. What is it about Cézanne? Renoir once asked; he couldn't put two strokes of colour on a canvas without already having something good. In the painting of Annecy, the 'two strokes of colour' are blue and green, the deepest blues for the depths of the lake, the greens for the trees and mountains and reflections in momentous harmony. The broad diagonal brushstrokes build a massively serene work of pictorial architecture. Other painters saw in Cézanne's canvases the grand sobriety of the wall paintings of Pompeii.

It is characteristic that the last letter he wrote was on 17 October 1906 to his paint dealer complaining about the non-delivery of ten tubes of burnt lake number 7. 'I am determined to die painting,' he had said, and on 22 October he died working in his garden on a portrait of the gardener, Vallier, leaving behind a body of the greatest art of the 19th century and probably the 20th as well. 'He is the father of all of us,' Picasso once remarked.

The City

In living memory the Wren churches were the skyline of the City of London. Now, the best public view of them is from south of the river, on one of the terraces of Tate Modern. Yet the Wren churches remain the City's great treasure, along with a handful either done under his direction or by other architects, like St Benet St Paul's Wharf by Robert Hooke and St Mary Woolnoth by Nicholas Hawksmoor. In one of the City's many courtyards half hidden among offices is another Wren-like building that turns out to be England's oldest synagogue, Bevis Marks, a reminder of one of the communities which continues to enrich London culturally.

Among all this there are enough so-called trophy buildings, designed without the context in mind but adhering in impressive asymmetry and adding excitement to the medieval plan of narrow winding streets and alleys and courtyards to which they adhere closely — Richard Rogers's Lloyds, Norman Foster's 10 St Mary Axe, and 13 Fleet Place with its steel frame on the outside by the Chicago skyscraper specialists Skidmore Owings and Merrill (SOM).

The newspapers have decamped from Fleet Street though the *Express* and the *Telegraph* have left their exotic mark. The wharves are silent after centuries of trading and the river banks are inhabited by offices; Billingsgate fish market has moved off downriver, but the the centuries-old meat market remains to the north of the historic open space of Smithfield; and, south and east of Smithfield, are the two 12th-century institutions St Bartholomew's Hospital and St Bartholomew's Priory, both founded by the monk Rahere after a pilgrimage to Rome.

Once the Tower was the heart of London and the symbol of authority. Now it's the financial institutions that perform these roles. In artistic terms, the shift in power has had its benefits. Broadgate, which a few years ago was a rundown railway station, is now a City equivalent to New York's Rockefeller Plaza,with, incidentally, the best collection of public modern sculpture in England outside the Tate, from the Cubist Jacques Lipchitz to a huge steel abstract by the American Richard Serra. When Westminster was still a marshy island this very walkable square mile underpinned by the old Roman town *was*

London, and some say that as the financial capital it still is.

The selection that follows is arranged west to east.

The glory days of newspapers at the former Daily Express building, 120 Fleet Street EC4

Fleet Street was the street of ink and had been ever since Wynkyn de Worde set up his print shop here in 1500. The *Daily Telegraph* was here in a monumentally oppressive Greco-Egyptian headquarters, Reuters was here and the Press Association; the *Evening Standard* was along Shoe Lane; the *Daily Mail* was in Tudor Street, and at 120 Fleet Street, outrageously, completely off-the-wall architecturally, was Lord Beaverbrook's *Daily Express*. The architect Owen Williams (1890–1969) built it for Beaverbrook in 1930–2, and followed with a near replica for the *Express*'s Manchester office in 1939. It is a curved black sheath of glass, the first curtain wall in England, rising four floors as a sheer cliff and then stepped back a further three, and it encompassed the machine room, composing room, editorial floors, the business offices and what *Express* hacks called the bank in the sky – the accounts office where they picked up their expenses after weaving an unsteady route back from the nearest pub. By the end of the century only real banks could afford to remain in Fleet Street.

Most of all what caught the eye of any passer-by was the entrance hall, more exotic than any other art deco office or factory, cinema or theatre interior in England. This is what Evelyn Waugh had in his mind's eye when he wrote his classic Fleet Street novel *Scoop* (1938), when his timid hero William Boot attends for an interview with Lord Copper, proprietor of the *Daily Beast* (based by Waugh on Lord Beaverbrook and the *Express*) and is 'rudely shocked by the

Byzantine vestibule and Sassanian lounge of Copper House'. This golden hall is the decorative masterpiece of the architect Robert Atkinson (1883–1952). Everything shines or reflects or glitters: the floor in wavy bands of blue, green and black reflects the central hanging pendant lamp with roots that spread like a sunburst across the ceiling, and a studded metallic arch spans the width of the hall, giving on to the smaller archway entrance to the staircase that spirals upwards like the cream topping on a sundae. One wall is filled by a climactic moulded plaster mural, gilded and silvered, showing a great goddess of plenty surrounded by industrious troglodytes, natives and settlers of many climes and cultures, one charming cobras, a couple drilling roads, another shearing sheep, others bearing baskets of fruit from the palms, a vision of empire to glorify the proprietor's politics sculpted by Eric Aumonier (1899–1974), a native himself, of northwest London, creator of the sculptures of the great dead on the escalator to heaven in the Powell and Pressburger film *A Matter of Life and Death* (1946) and of the stylised archer on East Finchley underground station, the invisible arrow doubtless symbolising the speed and dispatch of Northern line services.

Bankers, unlike newspapermen, are shy creatures, and curtains now hanging at 120 Fleet Street draw a veil over their activities. It's possible to enter and take a peek while claiming an appointment with Lord Copper or to wait for the annual London open day when Goldman Sachs throws wide the doors to this splendidly restored Xanadu.

Writing in the air at Fleet Place EC4

It wasn't until I sat down on a bench and made a rough sketch of Bruce McLean's calligraphic sculpture that I realised that it was based on a man smoking a pipe. I checked with the label, and sure enough it's called *Man with Pipe*. It's as mischievously creative as most of McLean's work, in the spirit of Picasso's wittily innovative little sculpture *Glass of Absinthe* of 1914, which has a spoon and lump of sugar precariously balanced on a cubist glass. McLean (b.1945) studied at St Martin's School of Art under Anthony Caro when the Caro who brought sculpture down from its plinth was already on his way to becoming a sacred cow like the sacred cow before him, Henry Moore. So McLean's piece mildly sends up pipe-smoking Caro with his acolytes standing around him, like reverential junior doctors with a surgeon, as he dissected the work of students.

McLean constructed *Man with Pipe* from ribbons of metal, red, yellow and subdued orange, and bent into shapes that can be read as a head, a couple of eyes, a mouth, a pipe and a curl of smoke. Alternatively, all of it could be a curl of smoke. But primarily it's a happily poised unity of abstract writing in air riffing on a leisurely subject among ten-storey monuments to capital built by Skidmore, Owens & Merrill in a place that used to be Holborn Viaduct railway station platforms.

The return of Temple Bar, at the entrance to Paternoster Square EC4

Temple Bar, the elaborate stone arch at the point where Fleet Street meets the Strand, once marked the spot where the king's authority ended and where he needed the permission of the Lord Mayor of London to enter the City. Or so the polite charade went, though, of course, the king's need to keep the City onside was never a fiction. Never mind the monarch, in 1878, whether or not the original design was Christopher Wren's, it was deemed to be a traffic nuisance and was taken down stone by stone. The brewer Sir Henry Meux bought the stones and re-erected Temple Bar as the entrance to his estate of Theobald's Park, Hertfordshire. There it quietly mouldered away, like Sir Henry himself and even 'Meux's Celebrated Ales', though they had a malty afterlife as Friary Meux.

The modern Temple Bar replaced a 16th-century arch in 1672 (and an earlier one is known to have been there in the 14th century). In 1984 a City organisation called the Temple Bar Trust bought Temple Bar, spruced it up and placed it on the pavement to the northwest of St Paul's Cathedral at the entrance to (the pallidly redeveloped) Paternoster Square. It is a grand structure of one large arch flanked by two narrow pedestrian gates (though, of course, all three are now for walkers). Above the main arch is a second pedimented story with central windows on the north and south façades flanked by niches on each side with statues by John Bushnell, also refurbished, of James I, his queen, Anne of Denmark, Charles I, and Charles II. Bushnell (d.1701) was a celebrated sculptor, Italian trained, who, the connoisseur William Vertue reported, thought 'that this nation was not worthy of him, nor his works'. Nevertheless, the City paid him for his work, and they look good restored to their niches. Perhaps one day Fleet Street will become a pedestrian way and Temple Bar will be restored to its rightful place. Meanwhile, this is just fine.

Tomb of the monk who founded Bart's hospital, in the Church of St Bartholomew the Great, Smithfield EC4

On a pilgrimage to Rome in about 1120 the Augustinian monk Rahere fell ill with malarial fever picked up at a holy but insanitary fountain. He took an oath that if he lived he would build a hospital for the poor. He recovered, and in 1123 Henry I granted him land in Smithfield. Rahere

dedicated the hospital to St Bartholomew and went on to build the priory of St Bartholomew hard by. With the exception of the grandly elemental Romanesque chapel of St John in the Tower of London, it is the finest church of its age in the capital. The nave was lost in the Reformation but the east end of the church was left for the parish. It stands to the east of Smithfield, with the great meat market to the north, pubs and shops opposite, and Bart's hospital and the 15th-century Church of St Bartholomew the Less to the south. The Luftwaffe bombed the warren of alleys that hugs St Bartholomew the Great, but the maze would still be recognisable to William Hogarth, who was born in St Bartholomew's Close, baptised in St Bartholomew's Priory and played marbles in the church precincts.

Despite restoration in the late 19th and early 20th centuries, the nave, choir and ambulatory with part of the remaining section of the cloisters are still basically Rahere's. He died in 1144, and his remains were translated to this tomb on the northern side of the sanctuary (between choir and apse) in 1405. It is a classic of the period and stands opposite another 15th-century classic, Bolton's window, so called, a lovely oriel from which the prior might observe the monks at prayer. Rahere's effigy on a tomb chest shows him in the black habit of the Augustinian canons, his head on a tasselled cushion. A crowned angel kneels at his feet holding a shield bearing the arms of the priory, two lions, gilded, on a scarlet background with two ducal coronets. There are two tiny monks at each foot reading from Bibles. It's all contained in a tabernacle with a vaulted

Temple Bar, the gate deemed a traffic obstruction in Fleet Street in 1878 and taken away, but now back in the City, beautifully refurbished. Erected in 1672, it is said without proof to be by Christopher Wren; the sculptures are by John Bushnell

ceiling within an elaborate arched and crocketed canopy with quatrefoil windows cut into the rear wall overlooking the ambulatory, a fine and private place across the square from the bustle of Smithfield meat market.

A painting to restore the confidence of a nation at the Guildhall Art Gallery, off Gresham Street EC2

The single most famous painting by John Singleton Copley (1738–1815) is not quite the size of the pitch at the new Wembley, but it had some of the same teething problems. He won the commission for *The Defeat of the Floating Batteries, September 1782* partly on the promise that he could deliver within two years, but it took eight. Then the army officers complained that he made the Gibraltar action it portrays look more like a naval victory, so he had to repaint, and he had to travel to Germany to make sketch portraits of the officers he needed for the canvas. When he finished this time the City discovered that it was on a flat stretcher, whereas the wall where it was to be hung was a curved apse. It was simpler and quicker to knock down the wall and build a new one than to set Copley to painting once again. When he finally delivered in 1791 it was itself a victory of sorts, but the artist was left emotionally ragged.

Copley's painting celebrates the defeat of a Spanish attempt to recapture Gibraltar while Britain's attention was engaged by the little affair across the Atlantic triggered by the Boston tea party. It shows General George Augustus Eliott mounted on a white horse insouciantly directing the rescue of Spanish sailors in peril in the sea. It was removed to safe keeping in the Second World War three weeks before the Luftwaffe flattened the old art gallery. Today it looks tremendous on its new, huge gallery wall either from ground level or from the first floor, with smoke pouring from billowing and blazing Spanish sails. It was a painting to restore the confidence of a nation that had comparatively recently been humiliated by the American colonies from which, by a poignant little irony, Copley hailed.

A Wren church not built by Wren, St Benet Paul's Wharf, Queen Victoria Street EC4

Swaggering brick-built St Benet, standing above a steep slope, is, externally, the prettiest church in London, even though it is now almost hemmed in between major traffic arteries, a worse destroyer of urban environment even than aggressive, tightly budgeted office blocks. It has swags of fruit and leaves above the round-headed windows, white stone dressings against the red brick, a tall tower with a circular window in the west face second stage and white-shuttered rectangular windows on all sides of the third stage capped by an entablature bearing a lead cupola with bull's-eye windows and an open lantern with a weathervane.

That reads as practically a prescription for a Wren church, and indeed to Wren it has always been assigned, but research, that destroyer of romance, has thrown up architectural drawings by Robert Hooke (1635–1703), which are powerful if not conclusive evidence that he designed St Benet. Never mind, he has his own romance as an unsung hero of the rebuilding in brick in only six or seven years of the houses destroyed by the Great Fire of 1666. St Benet was one of the sixteen City churches that escaped heavy damage from Second World War bombing, and internally, regilded and repainted, it is excellent as well, with its neat, early 19th-century organ, galleries with fronts carved with fruit and 18th-century slate monuments in the floor. The old church destroyed by the fire was the burial place of the great precursor

of the Wren generation, Inigo Jones, whose tomb went with the church, though the inscription has been copied and set into the floor to mark the old vault.

St Benet is the place to hear services in Welsh: since an Act of Parliament of 1879 it has been the City's Welsh church.

Henry Moore meets Sir Christopher Wren in the Church of St Stephen Walbrook EC4

Wren's finest church of all, including St Paul's, hides (the apt word) behind the Mansion House and hugger-mugger office buildings by the old Walbrook stream, now underground. St Stephen Walbrook (built 1672–80) has an unassuming exterior, though its tower (post-Wren) has an attractive dome, cupola and lantern of which some viewpoints give glimpses. It is Wren's interior that is so spectacular – a mathematician's solution to the problem of worshipping God in a curious and confined space. That may sound forbidding, but the result is simply astonishing in its complex clarity.

The floor space is rectangular west to east with a notional nave, chancel and north and south transepts: notional because the separate spaces of the church are defined, not by walls, but by groups of Corinthian columns. These carry a continuous entablature that follows the shape of a cross, so in effect the church's interior plan is drawn in the air, an idea of immensely subtle yet lucid ingenuity. The entablature itself carries a series of round arches, and resting on those is a coffered dome of Roman grandeur. In other words, this big dome rests ultimately on the slender Corinthian

The grandeur of the interior of St Stephen Walbrook make it in many people's eyes Wren's greatest building. In more recent times, the installation of a Henry Moore altar of rough travertine on a polished circular plinth proved controversial

columns. You don't have to understand the engineering (I don't) to recognise that this is abstract art in a high stage of evolution.

So where does that leave Henry Moore's famous altar? The rector, Chad Varah, had founded the Samaritans in 1953 to operate a hotline from the vestry under the tower to offer aid and comfort to potential suicides. By the 1970s he and the congregation wanted a church to reflect a ministry that took into account the City's secular activities – in short, a peoples' church. The property developer, art collector and former chairman of the Arts Council, Peter Palumbo, who had already put huge amounts of money into restoring the church, commissioned Henry Moore (1893–1976) to fashion an altar to stand centrally under the dome and fit in with the new liturgy, which drew the congregation around the priest. Every Tom, Dick and Harriet attacked it, at first on the grounds that it looked, allegedly, like a large camembert, then because it was liturgically unsound. Finally, an ecclesiastical court ruled in favour of the altar. Moore carved it from a block of rough-textured travertine marble 8 feet across and many tons in weight. It is a noble piece, informally accenting the circle of the dome above, but there's no question that it runs counter to Wren's obvious aim to stress the basic rectangle in which the people enter through a carved wooden screen at the west and look towards a reredos at the east, behind an altar and a priest. The reredos is now isolated, and the altar and the circular benches around it devised by Varah are the focus beneath the sublime dome.

London's greatest disaster commemorated, the Monument, Fish Street Hill EC3

In 1666 the fire of London destroyed well over 13,000 houses, fifty-two company halls, St Paul's and eighty-four parish churches. There was plenty of work in the years following for architects, builders and sculptors, and among them was Caius Gabriel Cibber (1630–1700), a Dane who had managed to gain admission to the Leatherworkers' Company, which entitled him to work in the city instead of joining the great unwashed enclave of foreign sculptors in Southwark. He won the commission for the huge narrative panel on the Fish Street Hill façade of Wren's Monument, that 202 feet high Doric column set up exactly 202 feet from where the fire started and crowned by a flaming urn. In the fashion of the time, he carved a baroque allegorical scene showing Charles II succouring the City, urging the figures of architecture and science to the rescue, while a female representing the City is supported by the figure of time. On the right the new City rises behind scaffolding even as the stones burn in the old City on the right. This is not one of Cibber's fancies, for on the morning of 2 September when the fire was at its height Samuel Pepys took a boat at the Tower and was rowed upriver under London Bridge where, he observed, 'everything, after so long a drought, [was] proving combustible, even the very stones of the churches'. Cibber's work doesn't show him at his best: he is uncomfortably tidy with the perspective view behind the baroque surface activity of the main figure group, but it launches Wren's 202 foot monument into space with élan.

Designed by the architect of Tower Bridge, Leadenhall Market, Gracechurch Street EC3

Horace Jones (1819–87) was born at 15 Size Lane, Bucklesbury, just south of Cheapside, and although he visited the buildings of ancient Greece and Italy as part of his training for architecture, it was the Cockney in him that won through decisively. At first he felt his way with the shop in Oxford Street for

Leadenhall Market was founded in the 14th century, and this rebuilding took place some 500 years later. Designed by Horace Jones, it is a cheerful mix of styles in wood, glass, and cast-iron Cockney Corinthian

Marshall & Snelgrove (now Debenhams) and the British and Irish Magnetic Telegraph Company in Threadneedle Street (company and building, sadly, both gone). But his making was his appointment in 1864 as architect to the City of London. It brought about the triumph of this Falstaffian, bearded and knighted servant of the City with the rebuilding of the three great markets, Smithfield, Billingsgate and Leadenhall.

Leadenhall, tucked away off Gracechurch Street, stands where a market has been since at least 1321. Beneath that lies the remains of the 2nd-century basilica of the Roman forum. The modern Leadenhall is the smallest of the three Horace Jones markets, the latest (1882–3), and the prettiest, outrageous in detail like his gross Tower Bridge, but unlike the bridge, entertaining. The central concourse at the crossing of the two main lanes within the market, paved with stone sets, is a big, unequal octagon with an octagonal glass dome. The entablature supporting the dome ought to be carried in turn on the capitals of Corinthian columns, but between capitals and the entablature are sandwiched fire-breathing dragons gone walkabout from the City of London's arms. Big lamps hang from the wooden trusses of the tunnel-vaulted louvred glass roofs of the lanes, and a recent gorgeous restoration has coloured the interior in the dusky reds, pinks and greens of Pompeii, with details picked out in gold and little painted friezes of Greek urns. And among all the iron grills and heavy embossed ornament stylised floral patterns have been painted as delicately as an Adam interior. The top two-thirds of the fluted columns of the crossing are striped red and gold, the bottom all white, like jester's tights, and the City arms are everywhere, in the unlikely event that anyone should forget where they are.

The bronze fat lady above a refurbished Liverpool Street railway station EC2

Liverpool Street was always the prettiest of the London railway stations, when its interior could be seen through the smoke and stygian gloom. Today the Victorian Gothic buildings have been replaced by modern imitations or outright modern buildings, but the station is better than it ever was. In 1995–2001, under the guidance of Nick Derbyshire, the now defunct Network Rail architecture and design department refurbished the great iron and glass naves and installed a new paved concourse, which sweeps broadside across the platforms and has brought clarity and easy access to the underground in place of labyrinthine confusion. The ironwork pillars and arches shine in blue and red livery, and Derbyshire returned the iron acanthus leaves that had, for obscure reasons, been stripped off to the capitals between pillars and arches.

All this happened as part of the Broadgate development, and absolutely the best thing to come out of it is at the unknown northern end off Primrose Street. A raft floated on massive parabolic arches across the railway tracks bears the whole of Exchange Square, its office tower, its lunchtime city workers with their packets of sandwiches lazing on the great steps to the north of the square and a 5 ton fat bronze female nude of awesome aspect by the Colombian sculptor Fernando Botero lying as though she has just fallen there above a wide cascade. With a shiny new office block by the famous American architects of skyscrapers, Skidmore, Owings & Merrill, towering above, it would all be more Chicago than City of London except that at the southern edge of the platform, past the naked lady and cascade, is an old railway carriage converted to dispense food and drink, and beyond that is a magical view towards what railwaymen charmingly call the country end of the station, with the pretty replaced decorative wooden valence at the end of the train shed precisely like a rural station, and beneath, the tracks emerging from between the platforms – a wave of the wand to rescue a great square from a hint of megalomania.

The best monumental sculpture in London, Broadgate EC2

Intensely imaginative and sculpturally inventive, *Bellerophon Taming Pegasus*, by one of the grand old men of 20th-century art, Jacques Lipchitz (1891–1973), is surely the finest monumental sculpture in London by an artist of his generation, and it stands in Broadgate, the City's Xanadu, where few venture except on business. It's about 12 feet high, a barely controlled explosion of violence, with two wrestling figures standing as a symbol of man's struggle with unbridled nature. Pegasus is all flying hooves and tail, with a wing raised like a huge open hand about to smash down his adversary, the wooer of Zeus's daughter setting out to perform the impossible task the god has set him as the price of winning her hand. Bellerophon, a barrel of stocky strength, feet solidly planted on earth, has a rope around the neck of Pegasus. The winged animal bares its teeth and rolls its eyes like the horse in *Guernica*. The resemblance to Picasso is unsurprising – Lipchitz and Picasso shadowed each other intermittently through the century.

Lipchitz was Lithuanian and travelled to Paris at the age of eighteen. He returned to Russia briefly to sort out a passport problem, and the interlocking forms of the pre-Christian art of Near Eastern nomads he then saw in the Hermitage planted a seed that germinated when he saw the Cubist collages of Picasso and Braque in 1913–14. Lipchitz's early work in sculpture was influenced by the Cubist painters' way of designing everything

More than a touch of a Wren City church, but this handsome interior is at Bevis Marks, the oldest surviving synagogue in England. It was built by Joseph Avis, one of Wren's carpenters in the rebuilding after the great fire of 1666. Avis was a Quaker who refused to take a profit out of the job

within the picture frame as part of the picture, so that there is none of the 'left-over space' of, for instance, traditional portraiture. Lipchitz took over this close organisation of mass and space for his sculpture. And as Picasso moved off into other ways of painting, Lipchitz developed a curvilinear approach, which came to full fruition when the United States offered him shelter after the Nazis invaded France.

The Broadgate Lipchitz is a version of an even bigger piece commissioned in 1964 for the University of Columbia law school, but though Lipchitz had burst the bounds of Cubism, the essential dynamic is still Cubist, the ferociously battling figures controlled by a taut spatial intelligence. Other sculptors in

the 1960s were bringing sculpture democratically down to earth from its plinth, but Lipchitz places this lurid struggle on a slender column and holds it there in startling equipoise.

England's oldest synagogue, Bevis Marks, off Heneage Lane EC3

Edward I expelled the Jews from England in 1290. Oliver Cromwell welcomed them back in 1656 after negotiations with Rabbi Menasseh Ben Israel and his community of Spanish and Portuguese Sephardic Jews conducting international trade in Amsterdam. Cromwell wanted them in with their lucrative links to the Spanish main, but without a public display of their religion, so he allowed them to build synagogues, but not on high streets. This is why the oldest synagogue in England, Bevis Marks, stands in a little court off Heneage Lane. (An earlier synagogue off Creechurch Street became an 18th-century doss house and was later demolished.)

A Quaker carpenter, Joseph Avis, was contracted in February 1699 to deliver the Spanish and Portuguese Synagogue, to use its official name, 'in a good and workmanlike manner … one large building with a gallery round the same'. He delivered just such a building in time for the dedication on 12 September 1701. It remains effectively unchanged today. There is more than a touch of a typical Wren City church about it, which is hardly surprising since in the building bonanza that followed the Great Fire of 1666, Avis and his carpenters and joiners had been involved in many of the new churches built by Wren or to his commission. Bevis Marks is a plain rectangle, 50 feet by 80 feet and top to bottom red brick with white stone dressings, the west façade three bays with round-headed windows and its sole display, a handsome doorcase with moulded hood and long brackets from either side of the door clasping an iron-bound glass lamp (there is a nice 19th-century street lamp at the northwest corner of the church).

The interior is divided into a nave with two aisles by columns carrying galleries to north, south and west. The furniture is a mixture of stern Cromwellian and mildly relaxed Queen Anne. Avis's handsome marbled green ark at the east, which contains the Torah, the holy writings delivered by God to Moses, looks a lot like the screen in the Merchant Taylor's Hall, where Avis was a member and had been working when the architect craftsman Robert Hooke (see St Benet, City of London, above) was building the screen. The ark has attached Corinthian columns framing the three doors,

and there are urns either side of the gilded entablature and great, gilded baroque scrolls supporting tablets inscribed with the Hebrew text of the Ten Commandments. In the body of the church there are ten big candlesticks, standing for the ten commandments, and seven joyously spectacular chandeliers, one for each day of the week, hanging low and used for candlelit services.

Benjamin Disraeli was born into the congregation of Bevis Marks, and on the 350th anniversary of the Jewish resettlement Disraeli's prime ministerial successor, Tony Blair, spoke in the synagogue of the benefits the Jewish community had brought to England since 1656 in 'arts, sciences, commerce, politics, the world of learning and thought, philanthropy and many more areas'. To Cromwell and Menasseh Ben Israel go the credit and, in this little City courtyard, the Quaker carpenter who refused to take a profit out of the building of Bevis Marks.

Greater London

Greater London began to the south of London Bridge, along Borough High Street, and to the north, in Clerkenwell. The Borough was Southwark, a starting point for pilgrimages to Canterbury, Rome and Jerusalem and a bolthole for the riffraff of London, the actors and playwrights, the whores and the owners of cockpits and the bull and bear baiting arenas, the boozers, the tinkers, and the foreign sculptors who, barred from the City of London by the guilds, founded workshops on Bankside.

By the 19th century London's emergence as the capital of a vast empire attracted more millions, though Constable was in the country when he painted on Hampstead Heath in the 1820s, and in the early 1870s, when the Impressionist painter Camille Pissarro took refuge in London from war-torn France, the paintings he left of the area around Norwood show it as a rural community. By the 1890s, with the introduction of the Metropolitan line, followed in the early years of the twentieth century by the Underground, London pushed the boundaries wider. Soon it was 30 miles across and had gulped down towns and villages that had once belonged to the outlying counties and swallowed Middlesex whole.

Yet the villages of London retain their separate identities and adapt. Islington is a medieval parish distinguished by its handsome squares and terraces of the 18th and 19th centuries. In Canonbury Square, still residential, is now one of the most remarkable museums in London, the Estorick collection of modern Italian art, mostly Futurist. True, William Morris would hardly recognise the Walthamstow where he grew up in the house which has become a museum to his enterprise, nor possibly Bexleyheath, but the lanes around his Red House would stir memories. Wartime bombing and the loss of the royal shipyard obliterated most of the old Deptford, yet the Greenwich the Stuarts built survived, with the old Royal Naval Hospital, the Queen's House, and Wren's Royal Observatory on the hill in the park, Hawksmoor's church down by the market, Vanbrugh's house on the hill poised between Greenwich and Blackheath, and the close-knit texture of the streets and pubs down by the Thames.

Eltham, one of the places where Henry VIII left his mark on a great house, is a dormitory with nothing much to offer otherwise except the palace, given new life in the 1930s by a scion of the Courtauld family, its art deco interiors refurbished beautifully in recent years by English Heritage. The Bethlem hospital traced a path from the City to Beckenham, where its tiny museum of art commemorates the days when lunatics (sic)

were whipping boys in two powerful sculptures by Caius Gabriel Cibber: if they look Hogarthian, that's because Hogarth took from it for his *Rake's Progress*. In that south London conglomerate of old villages like Norwood and Sydenham, Dulwich maintains its well-heeled middle-class charm, a school founded by Shakespeare's associate Edward Alleyn, and an unparalleled public collection of great paintings. In west London the string of country houses along the Thames from Chiswick to Osterley are caught in the urban web promoted by the Underground though Syon and its suite of great Adam rooms escape it, just – in Sudbury, incidentally, the Piccadilly line tube station is a little beacon of early modernism in England, built in 1903. Hampstead, the grand dame of London villages, has survived least perturbed of all, absorbing the modernism of Ernö Goldfinger and accepting the public amenity of another grand Adam house and its great collection of art and furniture, Kenwood, as of right.

The selection that follows is arranged clockwise from North London.

Italian art at the Estorick Collection, 39a Canonbury Square, Islington N1

Eric Estorick (1913–93) was criss-crossing the Atlantic after the Second World War from his native Brooklyn to London, where he was collecting material for a biography of Clement Attlee's chancellor Stafford Cripps. On one of his London sojourns he began to collect drawings of the modern French school. On one of the voyages he picked up a wife, Salome Desau, the daughter of a Nottingham textile manufacturer. And on honeymoon in Switzerland he discovered the work of the Italian Futurists and began what is now certainly the finest collection of its sort in Britain. A few months before his death Estorick placed all his pictures in a foundation set up in his wife's name and his own, and the foundation bought and converted a detached Georgian house in a quiet corner of Islington to display the collection.

The Futurists were a group of Italian artists who formed in 1909. Superficially their work was quite like Cubism, but where the archetypal Cubist picture would be a still life, the Futurists exalted speed and power, even though they were limited to the static materials of pencil and paper, paint and canvas. The face of the fascist leader Benito Mussolini, Il Duce, scowls behind their bombastic exhortations, their exultation in war and speed, the glorying in machines, their denunciations of past cultures. What they prefigured came to pass: the movements of masses across the world, the slaughter of great wars, the triumph of art by diktat, the conquest of the world by capital, the new weightless architecture to go with space-eating flying machines. The Futurist manifesto proclaimed, sinisterly yet quaintly as it now seems, the art of the 'racing motorcar, its frame adorned with great pipes, like snakes with explosive breath', 'the nocturnal vibrations of arsenals and workshops beneath their violent electric moons' and the aeroplane, 'the sound of whose propeller is like the flapping of flags and the applause of an enthusiastic crowd'. What about the work? Beautiful paintings and drawings of tautly organised abstract shapes, splendid visions of the Citta Nuova, the new city, by the architect Antonio Sant'Elia, who fell in the war before he could build a single thing, a fine quasi-Cubist sculpture by Umberto Boccione called *Development of a Bottle in Space*, and a more nearly Futurist one called *Unique Forms of Continuity in Space*, which tries to fly but stays rooted. That's what.

Among them is *Dancer: Ballerina and the Sea* by Gino Severini (1883–1966), a wholly successful abstraction of the energy of a dancer's movements, like a sequence of the photographs by Eadweard Muybridge of a woman in motion, but here gathered into a single image. Severini worked with oils, gouache and black wash for different surface effects, and the brown tonality interrupted by thin patches of blue is the work of an artist with a real feeling for paint. He was one of the lucky Futurists who had a future. He survived the war, turned to Cubism and naturalism but then, towards the end of his life, took up the project of repainting some of his early Futurist paintings that had been destroyed.

William Morris in Walthamstow E17

William Morris (1834–1896) was born at Elm House in Walthamstow and the family moved to Water House in Forest Road, now the Morris Gallery, when he was fourteen. Walthamstow was changing from a village even while he lived there, and the population has since gone through the six-figure mark – many of the humble cottages built for workmen when the railway came during Morris's time are doing a turn as sex shops or cheap caffs. There is even an arts and crafts shop still selling Letraset, which almost takes it back to Morris's time. Across the road, beside Water House, is a Hindu temple gaily decked with images of avatars and attendants of the gods with the elephant-headed god of good fortune, Ganesh, centrally placed over the door.

Is all this what Morris meant when he complained bitterly about a decline of the arts? His own faith was rooted in the Middle Ages, where crafts and arts united in an elysium where creative work was not the preserve of genius or posturing would-be genius, and the gallery even has an iron sword and helmet, which he constructed beautifully as a prop for his models in the ridiculous enterprise of the murals for the Oxford Union, painted with his friends Burne-Jones and Rossetti when he and Burne-Jones were scarcely beyond the stage of taking brass rubbings and immersing themselves in the Arthurian legends, and Rossetti was probably simply susceptible to the attentive hero worship of the two young acolytes who had thrust themselves upon him. The original romantic dreaminess lay at the root of everything that was to follow – the socialism, the application of hand-crafted art to socialism, the research into stained glass, the hard-learned skills of tapestry weaving and stitching – and the reason, too, why his holy grail proved in the end an illusion, because only the rich could afford his kind of art.

It's here in Water House in abundance: acanthus wallpaper, St James's wallpaper in different colourways, a rug with a tree pattern and another with a paired birds pattern, his pretty chintz Strawberry Thieves, and African Marigold and Wandle, both chintzes. There is stained glass, from the loveable but coarse early shots for private houses at subjects like the labours of the months (also produced as tiles) to the consummate sophistication of the later church glass. There is furniture, like the painted settle originally designed for his own use with his wife Jane at the Red House at Bexleyheath and then put into production when he set up in business, and a hefty tub-shaped chair also for his own use. 'If you want to be comfortable,' he would say, 'go to bed.'

The new London Underground: Canada Water station on the Jubilee line E14

After the Second World War the Victoria line opened and the Fleet line was planned, finally to come to fruition as the Jubilee line with brand-new stations bolted on in 1999 to an older section wrested from the Bakerloo line, basically to service the new empire of capital at Canary Wharf. It was achieved by commissioning designs from the high-tech masters Will Alsop at North Greenwich, Norman Foster at Canary Wharf itself, Ian Ritchie at Bermondsey, with Michael Hopkins creating a brand-new superstructure at Westminster around the established Circle and District lines. At subterranean Canada Water an in-house London Underground architectural team created a glass and concrete drum above the surface in clear homage to Charles Holden, the great underground innovator, and his brick drum at Arnos Grove. But the most exotic is Southwark tube station by Richard McCormack, clean, elegant and fantastic, with its signature flourish the glowing blue glass wall by McCormack and Alexander Belschenko based, McCormack has said, on Karl Friedrich Schinkel's famous 19th-century starlit stage setting for the Queen of the Night scene in Mozart's *The Magic Flute*. And, for all the fantasy, the work ethic of Holden's 1930s carries through into the new millennium in the classic house style sans serif letterface for signposting, tube maps, posters and all the paperwork bureaucracy is heir to. The calligrapher and typefounder Edward Johnston (1872–1944) created it for the underground in 1916, Holden tweaked it, and it still stands proud in the high-tech wonderland.

Ventilation and sculpture at the Blackwall Tunnel E14; SE10

From South Kensington underground station to Seoul and Singapore, Paramatta and Lisbon, Terry Farrell (b.1939) has projects worldwide. But when he was an employee of London county council in the early 1960s he was already looking for inspiration across continents, to Brazil. In 1961 the council was

building a second Blackwall Tunnel to add to the original one bored in the 1890s. Farrell was given the job of designing the new tunnel's lungs, the ventilation shafts, two on the north bank of the Thames, which are best to see because the two on the south are wrapped now inside the O2 arena, the former Millennium Dome. His solution produced some of the first free-form architectural shapes in Britain, based on a use of reinforced concrete extensively pioneered in 1960 in the buildings of Brasilia, the new capital of Brazil, where the cathedral, national congress and national library were built in a wonderful interplay of curved and straight forms, though, consciously or not, Farrell's shafts look a bit like ship's funnels.

They drew too on the dawning awareness that in architecture, especially architecture for mass-habitation or mass-transit, the service aspects need not be hidden away. They are built of sprayed concrete, known as gunite, which had previously been used for patching up but is cheap and flexible, and anchored here by stressed cables fixed in reinforced concrete slabs. So the two shafts, a short, 40 foot, one to expel fumes from the tunnel, and a tall, 90 foot, one to draw in fresh air, curve almost sensuously above ground, in an evolving cityscape already displaying the work of succeeding generations, from the once again fashionable Balfron tower block by Ernö Goldfinger (1902–87), to Richard Rogers (b.1933), with plans sitting in the computers of Terry Farrell & Partners for a regenerated north Greenwich.

These coolly elegant structures are lungs for the Blackwall Tunnel. The architect Terry Farrell was a London County Council employee in 1961 when he designed this ventilation

Liberty and Tyranny on a ceiling at the Greenwich Royal Hospital SE10

There are painted cartouches in the vestibule of James Thornhill's painted hall that bear the names of donors to the building fund. These include the name 'John Evelyn Esqre' and list his gift of £1,000. Evelyn lived a mile or two upriver in Deptford (the John Evelyn pub in Evelyn Street marks the corner of his vanished estate). He had been treasurer of the project from the beginning, laid the first stone for Wren's building in 1696 and nine years later notes in the journal by which he is remembered today: 'I went to Greenwich Hospital, where they now began to take in wounded and worn-out seamen, who are exceeding well provided for. The buildings now going on are very magnificent.' Rather too magnificent for the wounded and worn out, it soon became clear. Thornhill (1675/6–1734) started work on decorating the hall in 1708, and the old seamen were dispatched pronto to dine in the undercroft, leaving the hall fit for tourists.

Thornhill took third place in country house commissions to Verrio and Laguerre, his contemporaries from abroad, but rightly believed his own talents superior and lobbied successfully for the commissions to decorate the dome of St Paul's Cathedral and the great hall at Greenwich. In time-honoured fashion, his subject, *Peace and Liberty Triumphing over Tyranny*, shows the monarchs William and Mary sitting in pavilioned glory in the heavens. While Apollo, shedding light, thunders above the scene in his chariot drawn by white horses, William III receives in his right hand an olive branch from Peace, a lightly clad young woman, and with his left, he passes the cap of liberty to Europe, another semi-nude female, and places his right foot firmly on the head of Tyranny, represented by the fully clad but supine Louis XIV. On the ceiling above the high table in the upper hall Queen Anne and her consort survey the five continents, and on the walls, the landings in England of William III and George I – the painter expeditiously updated the subject as he laboured for nineteen years.

For his services to the cause of the higher sycophancy Thornhill was knighted, like Rubens before him for similar if much greater work in Whitehall. Naturally, there was a political agenda too. Catholic James II had been forced to abdicate in favour of William of Orange, but William was the son of Charles I's daughter Mary, so Stuart blood ran in his veins, and Mary, the daughter of James II, is by his side in the painting as well as in life to assert continuity.

As for the banished seamen, one remained in the hall. Thornhill chose John Worley, insubordinate and drunken at the age of ninety-six as he had been as a young sailor, to sit among the seasons in the William and Mary ceiling, anointed in dignity, white bearded and representing winter.

Pepys's apotheosis, the Queen's House, Greenwich SE10

Inigo Jones built the Queen's House at Greenwich astride the old Dover Road on the divinely ordained spot where Sir Walter Raleigh laid down his cloak so that Queen Elizabeth would keep her feet dry as she crossed to Greenwich Palace. The road survives as a cobbled passageway beneath the house. The building, with its famous 40 × 40 foot cube hall, is one of the most beautiful houses in Britain, and was the first fully classical one. James I commissioned it in 1616 for his queen, Anne of Denmark, but she died before the house was finished, so Charles I's queen, Henrietta Maria, succeeded to it. Today it is run as part of the National Maritime Museum and contains a rousing collection of paintings of the naval hierarchy

of the 17th and 18th centuries by the great portrait painters of the day.

By one of those strange quirks of history, the queen's dressing room is known today as the Pepys Room, thus signalling a triumph of genius and industry over social class. His diaries and his work in helping to turn the navy into a fully professional fighting force have made him more pertinent in this place than Henrietta Maria and more famous than any of the thirteen so-called Flagmen, the English admirals who fought with the Duke of York (later James II) in the Battle of Lowestoft in 1665 and who are celebrated by a first eleven of portraits by Peter Lely (1618– 80) in this room, including Pepys's kinsman and patron, Edward Montague, 1st Earl of Sandwich. The other two are in the royal collection. On 18 April 1666 Pepys visited Lely's studio 'and there saw the heads, some finished and all begun, of the Flaggmen in the late great fight with the Duke of Yorke against the Dutch. The Duke of York hath them done to hang in his chamber, and very finely they are done endeed.' Indeed. The thirteen portraits are some of the best of Lely's work. The royal family retained the paintings after James's exile until George IV gave the eleven to the old Royal Naval Hospital at Greenwich.

As Pepys's star rose through the 1660s, he commissioned John Hayls (1600–79) to paint portraits of himself, now in the National Portrait Gallery, and his wife Elizabeth, destroyed in the 19th century. But by 1689, after he had retired, he had an ample fortune and could afford to commission portraits of himself and his former clerk and faithful friend, Will Hewer, from the much more fashionable and grander court artist, Sir Godfrey Kneller (1646–1723). This portrait, with the adjacent likeness of Hewer, now takes precedence in the Pepys Room over Lely's admirals. It is a half-length inside a painted oval and shows a handsome man running to plumpness with a sensually curved mouth and a level gaze and with a finely painted white stock at his throat and a handsome wig of brown hair. It is every inch the portrait of a successful man, though in fact Pepys had been forced out of office after the revolution of 1688, tarnished by his association with the papist James II.

A mini-masterpiece at the Ranger's House, Crouch Hill, Greenwich SE10

Julius Wernher trained his eye choosing diamonds in the days when he operated out of a corrugated tin shack in Johannesburg. By 1903 he had a town house in Mayfair and Luton Hoo, a country house in Hertfordshire, which he filled with a diverse collection of objets d'art, beautiful, curious, bizarre and historic. After his death Luton Hoo became 'an exciting development in the leisure industry' (a hotel with an eighteen-hole golf course), and the collection is now in the fine 17th-century red brick balustraded Ranger's House at Blackheath, outside the western wall of Greenwich Park. (The Ranger's House is so called because it was the grace and favour residence in the 19th century of Greenwich Park's ranger.) The house is ideal for the Wernher collection, because in the 18th century the Earl of Chesterfield added a big Palladian gallery to the house's amenities.

No doubt Wernher bought one item of the collection, a tiny bronze plaque, no more than about 4 inches square, with a low relief Madonna and Child, as a work by Donatello c.1386–1466), Michelangelo's greatest Florentine predecessor as a sculptor, and no doubt at the time it was accepted as such. It is an outstanding work. I'd like to call it a masterpiece, but I am not sure that 'workshop of Donatello' qualifies. Experts have narrowed down the Donatello oeuvre, and the Wernher Donatello missed the cut. It

is almost identical, except more 'finished', to another little Madonna and Child on a plaque in the Schnütgen Museum in Cologne, which is accepted as by Donatello himself. In each the Madonna has a classical profile that does nothing to dilute the tenderness of her expression. Her hair is indicated by schematic wavy horizontal lines, a rhythm picked up by the sweeping arc of her sleeve and the Christ child's clothes, and again more gently in the curve of her arm as she lays her hand on the child's. Though tiny, the definition of the broad planes and the lucidity of the space in and around the two figures are monumental. The Cologne and Wernher plaques are equally beautiful, which is not a surprise since 'workshop' usually implies the master's supervision. All this makes the point that the cash value of an autograph work is often justified by nothing more than its aura as a piece of extreme rarity with a name attached.

The 'scribble sculpture', at Goldsmiths, New Cross SE14

When Will Alsop was sixteen his father died. Alsop (b.1947) took himself out of school, went to work for an architect, studied for his A levels at evening class and did a foundation year at Northampton College of Art. It was an unconventional start to a maverick career, and in his design for Goldsmiths' Ben Pimlott Building in New Cross he has paid his dues on that foundation year. The Pimlott building is named for the political biographer who was warden of the college until his death in 2004, a few months before the building's opening. It contains Goldsmiths' art studios, and is a seven-column slab, a sheer glass curtain to the north. It is very purist Mies van der Rohe, aluminium with punched window spaces on the other three sides, though the glass wraps

round to the west above the terrace. On the south front are abstract sculptures (or features, in the bloodless terminology), clipped on to the raised seams of the aluminium panels like gigantic brooches. But what the passer-by sees from New Cross Road (the A2) is the gigantic scribble sculpture on the terrace like a loose skein of wool, two storeys high to range with the top of the building, a piece of freehand gestural art that enlivens the street scene like nothing else in London. Alsop has taken a lift in this piece on the bandwagon of his close friend Bruce McLean (see Fleet Place, City of London, above).

He has done more interesting buildings, like the fantastic Blizard building for Queen Mary's College and maybe Peckham Library, where much more goes on inside – Goldsmiths is basically a shell for flexible studio space – but nothing quite rivals it for instant impact, which, in a drab, traffic-heavy area of south London, is a very good deed. One critic has described the sculpture as gratuitous. Free-spirited, it is; gratuitous it isn't. The story is that Alsop starts all his buildings with a sketch in oils or charcoal, but that's about as far as the improvisation has gone here. A close look shows that the so-called scribble sculpture has been carefully perfected, possibly on a computer, for maximum clarity of linear form and its effect in space. It doesn't fill the terrace, as it appears to do from the street, but instead forms a 9 metre high open screen, leaving an uncluttered area as working and display space for other sculptors.

The spectacular metal scribble on the terrace of the Pimlott Building at Goldsmiths is a landmark sculpture, quite literally, by the maverick architect himself, Will Alsop. It stands over the art school's studios

An art deco palace, Eltham Palace SE9

Everybody knows what art deco is but nobody has yet defined it very clearly. The dictionary gets no closer than 'the style of decorative art characteristic of the 1920s and 1930s'. It was there (still is, where it's been saved) in cinemas and tube stations, hotels and bars, theatres and even street furniture. It featured bent wood, Lalique glass, Susie Cooper ceramics and a broadcasting headquarters in Portland Place that looked like a bakelite wireless set. It had circular mirrors and square chairs, kitsch table lamps dressed up as exotic dancers, low relief sculptures like jolly Egyptian tombs. It came in flat, bright primary colours in bright South Seas flower patterning. It was vividly modern, but not modernist. And when two socialites called Stephen and Virginia Courtauld, he a war hero and son of the founder of the textile business, she the former Marchesa Peirano, bought the crumbling great hall of the crumbled medieval royal palace of Eltham and stuck a squash court and orangery on one end and a house by the fashionable firm Seely and Paget on the other, they created the jazziest art deco home east of the Atlantic (that ocean that would be crossed by the Cunard liner *Queen Mary*, with its ostentatious luxury so like Eltham's down to some quite small details). And under Edward IV's hall, with its great hammerbeam roof, the Courtaulds threw the ritziest parties as well.

Stephen and Ginie, as she was known, built a circular entrance hall lined with Australian blackbean veneer inset with marquetry and lit from above through a circular glass and concrete domed roof, and for the space below Marion Dorn designed a circular rug. Ginie liked the circular concept so much that she had a circular bedroom too, this time in maplewood, with a curved sliding door and an en-suite bathroom with gold-plated taps,

The circular entrance hall of Eltham Palace, lined with Australian blackbean veneer inset with marquetry and with a circular rug designed by Marion Dorn. Stephen Courtauld and his wife Virginia, socialite members of the textile family, commissioned the house to append to the great hall of the medieval palace of Eltham

and, in an apse lined with gold mosaic, she placed a big bath with a golden lion's head spouting water.

Does this all seem inexpressibly vulgar? Curiously enough, it isn't. It is zestful, good humoured and stylish, well this side of tackiness. It shows an almost naïve faith, certainly from a viewpoint in the 21st century, in progress, perfectibility, science and technology. There are touching examples everywhere of their faith in the new and the functional. In Ginie's boudoir there is built-in furniture with a huge couch, bookshelves, tables and ledges for their g and ts all locked in one immovable embrace against the wood-panelled wall. Opposite, the wall is hung with leather cladding inscribed with a

map of the district. Into the leather map a clock is inset absolutely flush and correct to the second because it and all the other clocks in the house worked on a pulse fed directly from the newly instituted national grid. Siemens fitted up an internal Eltham Palace telephone exchange. The vacuum cleaners had pipes that siphoned dust through handsome bronze fixtures in the skirting boards to the basement below. Sad to say, there are also coal- and log-lookalike electric heaters.

Towards the end of the war the Courtaulds realised that the brave new world would be a boring old world without servants. They moved out, leaving the building to pass ultimately (1995) to English Heritage, which has lovingly brought the house back to life. Stephen and Ginie moved to Southern Rhodesia, where he founded what is now the Zimbabwe National Gallery and, no doubt, solved the servant problem.

At the gates of Bedlam, Bethlem Royal Hospital, Beckenham BR3

When the governors of the Bethlem lunatic asylum asked Caius Gabriel Cibber (1630–1700) to produce statues to crown the entrance gateposts, they got what they asked for: statues of a couple of lunatics, one called Melancholy Madness, the other Raving Madness. The asylum had been founded as the priory of St Mary of Bethlehem in Bishopsgate in the City of London in 1247, and through the centuries the name mutated, from Bethlehem to Bedlam to Bethlem. A document of 1329 refers to it as a hospital. Another of 1403 mentions that it has six insane patients. One of the fashionable treatments was to chain lunatics to the wall and whip them. And still in 1680, when Bedlam reopened at Moorfields, Cibber's carvings showed Raving Madness as a howling, naked, manacled man.

Bethlem moved a third time into a building that now commemorates global madness as the Imperial War Museum, and in 1930, with the recognition that patients were suffering treatable mental illness still relatively fresh, it fetched up in Beckenham. There, in a little outbuilding, is a small room that constitutes its own wonderful museum. You press a bell push, you are shown in, and you sign in; the previous visitor was four days before me. One showcase has a nasty assembly of manacles and chains and leather 'restraints' that were utilised during the Age of Enlightenment, but the collection is mostly art, sombre paintings of children bereft of company and studies of compulsive handwashing by a couple of late 20th-century manic depressives, and some preternaturally calm and routine portraiture by Richard Dadd, the 19th-century artist committed to Bethlem for slitting his father's throat in the belief that he was the devil incarnate. His most famous work, painted in Bethlem but now in Tate Britain, was The Fairy Fellers' Master Stroke. Then there is a gaggle of bishops carousing in the foreground of a big apocalyptic 19th-century drawing by Jonathan Martin called London Overthrown. He was committed to Bethlem after trying to burn down York Minster. It was the bishops he was after.

Caius Gabriel Cibber was assuredly sane, but his two sculptures of madness are his best work, exhibited recently in an exhibition in Paris and Berlin, though transporting them must have been a challenge. They look as though they are carved from hard limestone, intransigent yet pockmarked by exposure to London, and London's patina has added depth to them. The two men lie propped on their elbows, bald, vacant-eyed, their muscularity contorting to some internal imperative. The figure of Melancholy is closely similar to the final episode in Hogarth's The Rake's Progress, in which Tom Rakewell is reduced to naked lunacy by his life of profligacy. Moorfields was only a few minutes' walk from Hogarth's manor, the alleys of St Bartholomews, and the Cibber sculptures were there for all to see on the gateposts of Bedlam. The debt by Hogarth to Cibber was repaid when Cibber's grandson Theophilus translated Hogarth's The Harlot's Progress to the London stage.

Caius Gabriel Cibber was born in Schleswig-Holstein. He arrived in England after touring Italy, and the two Madness carvings seem to be the godless progeny of Michelangelo's Night and Day in the Medici chapel. They are deeply expressive and tell more of man's inhumanity to man than any other sculpture of the age.

An iceberg in the history of art at Dulwich Picture Gallery SE21

When the gallery John Soane designed opened in the village of Dulwich in 1813 it was the first public picture gallery in England. It remains, with the mausoleum for its founders, the Frenchman Noël Desenfans and the Swiss Louis Bourgeois, an architectural masterpiece, embellished by Rick Mather's fine extension of 1999. Its remarkable collection in an essentially local gallery with the intimate feel of a church coffee morning includes *Girl at a Window*, which the Berlin Gemäldegalerie borrowed for its great Rembrandt exhibition in 2006 and used as the poster image. There is a Watteau of which John Constable wrote, 'this inscrutable and exquisite thing would vulgarise even Rubens and Paul Veronese', and there are several canvases by Rubens and Veronese for that matter, as well as Van Dycks, magnificent Gainsborough portraits of the Linley family, and other great paintings from France, Holland, Spain and England: Claude, Cuyp, Murillo and Hogarth.

The collection is based on paintings bought by the dealer Desenfans for the king of Poland. But in one of its regular cycles of history, Poland's neighbours dismembered the country, the king abdicated, and Desenfans and his business partner Bourgeois were stuck with a homeless royal collection. Desenfans died in 1807, and Bourgeois settled on Dulwich for no better reason than that the British Museum didn't want the collection and Dulwich College provided a captive audience educated by its own small gallery, originally designed to show the collection of Edward Alleyn, the actor and friend of Shakespeare who had founded the school in 1619.

Among the core collection in Soane's new gallery *The Triumph of David* by Nicholas Poussin (1594–1665) looms like an iceberg in the history of art, between Hellenic and Roman carved friezes of triumphs and bacchanals and the 18th- and 19th-century classicism of David, Ingres and Cézanne. The generally accepted date of completion for the *Triumph* is 1635, when Poussin was moving away from the poetry of paintings like the *Rinaldo and Armida* (also at Dulwich), which was influenced by the warmth of the great Titian. The *Triumph* is Titian with ice and lemon, his yellows sharply acid, his blues as cold as outer space, and the turban and blouse worn by a woman in the foreground are the white of an Alpine snowcap. All the colours are Titian's – the cinnamon, gold, russet, vermilion, absinthe green – but instead of Titian's soft broken touch Poussin introduces cool lucidity. He arranges his figures in little whirlpools before the podium of a great colonnaded building, a group of women on the left, reverend grave seigneurs to the right, and more groups upon the podium. David himself, preceded by blaring trumpet and horn (the horn itself describing a vortex), his hair a deeper red than his scant tunic, moves barefoot through a clear space carrying Goliath's head impaled on a pole. All these participants in the triumph are classical figures removed, as it were, from the face of the podium and given individual life and colour. It's a bold staging too: the only central figure is a seated woman in the foreground with her back to us, her vertical accent continued in the central column on the podium. She forms part of a stabilising triangle with the mother in the white turban and blouse, her two children and an old woman, and then the whole composition of figures is both triangle and vortex.

This gigantic scalped head on Butler's Wharf outside the Design Museum has become known as Invention *because the most prominent of the words hammered as wedges into the gaps is 'invenzione'. The sculptor, Eduardo Paolozzi, lifted the words ad hoc from a Leonardo da Vinci passage, and reassembled them in English at the back of the head: they have to do with nature being more wonderful than art*

A dream of grotesque genius, Butler's Wharf SE1

The colossal bronze head by the Scottish artist Eduardo Paolozzi (1924–2005) lying on its side outside the Design Museum might easily be called *Portrait of Boris Karloff as Frankenstein's Monster*. The head is split vertically and horizontally, with wedges embossed with Italian words driven into the gaps, the back of the head apparently sheared off and stuffed with junk machinery, the neck end embossed with big capital letters bringing together all the words in a quotation from Leonardo (in translation): 'Though human genius in its various inventions with its various instruments may answer the same end, it will never find an art more simple or more direct than nature because in her inventions nothing is lacking and nothing superfluous.' So now we know that this is one of Paolozzi's grown-up works, not his 1940s blueprint for Pop Art. The piece is popularly known as *Invention*, because *invenzione* is the most prominent of the embossed words. Paolozzi's own title is *Newton After James Watt*, as if the great engineer had reduced the great scientist to a matter of constructed parts, a work of grotesque genius and a usurpation of nature: a monster for the age of computers. It is, in any case, a fine and disturbing piece of work that arrived at the edge of the Thames because when Paolozzi taught Terence Conran design at the Central School of Arts and Crafts, they became lifelong friends, and when Conran cast his spell over Butler's Wharf he commissioned Paolozzi to produce a sculpture. It was Conran, incidentally, who taught Paolozzi welding.

A remnant of the hop trade, in Borough High Street, Southwark SE1

Borough High Street is the ancient heart of Southwark, to all intents a bustling 19th-century city carrying the vivid imprint of its medieval past. The quarter mile between St Thomas's Street opposite Borough Market and the 18th-century Church of St George the Martyr is lined by tall, narrow-fronted business premises that are the mark of medieval burgage plots, awarded to citizens in return for some form of service. They have survived the 19th-century building boom, although a few buildings have amalgamated and have a frontage double the medieval norm.

The street was the sole route into London from the south since London Bridge was the only crossing, hence the famous pubs like the King's Head in King's Yard, Chaucer's Tabard Inn (long gone) and the George Inn, of which part still survives with its ancient gallery. This, too, was the destination and market for Kentish hops, to be sold in the great hop exchange where hop factors bought and sold on commission and which was built when 19th-century Southwark Street was cut to link the area with Blackfriars. On the eastern side of Borough High Street, looking down Southwark Street, there is a remarkable survival: a single-burgage plot in terracotta-coloured stone of a late 19th-century business with the name, W.H. & H. LeMay Hop Factors, picked out in fanciful lettering above the arched entrance against a surround of green hop bines. The keystone of the arch bears the well-cut street number, 67. The first floor has three tall, round-arched windows separated by little attached columns, and

above that, beneath a balustrade, is a full-storey exotic art nouveau relief frieze that seems to have been modelled in terracotta. It looks like the magnified freehand decoration of the title page of some Victorian book of romantic verse, with the business name in a curly letter face with the bottom bar of the L in LeMay underscoring the E. Around the name curlicues of hop bines twine around tall poles, and the man and woman who effortlessly pull down the hops look more like faery figures from *A Midsummer Night's Dream* than the east Londoners who every harvest piled out of London to spend their fortnight's holiday earning beer money by stripping the bines, sleeping at night in small, very basic brick huts.

A rose window among the ruins, the Bishop of Winchester's palace, Clink Street, Bankside SE1

The Bishop of Winchester's palace on Bankside sat like an exotic bloom on a bed of dung. Through the centuries, until the time of Shakespeare, Londoners came to Bankside to take their pleasures and indulge their carnal desires. It's even possible that some still do, though they hardly run the same risks as when the bishop also ran the Clink, the prison that gave the world the generic slang for a lock-up. Here were the playhouses, cockpits, bearpits, alehouses and bawdy houses, and the bishop sat at the middle of it, licensing the brothels. Wencelaus Hollar, the 17th-century artist from Prague whose engravings of London before the Great Fire provide us with our best record, showed the palace, an accumulation of interlocked buildings beside the Thames, sitting within walled orchards. The main courtyard has become modern Winchester Square; everything else is gone, except for a stretch of the great hall's southern wall to the north of the square and

Beneath this rose window guests gathered in 1424 at the wedding reception of Joan Beaufort, niece of the Bishop of Winchester, and King James I of Scotland. It forms part of the former great hall of Winchester Palace which, with the hall's southern wall, is all that remains of the bishop's palace on Bankside

the whole of the west wall with its three linked doorways, one to the buttery, one to the pantry and one to the kitchen. The floor has gone, so the undercroft is open to the sky. Above the doorways, in the gable, is a 13 foot rose window. Its survival seems a miracle. The palace was a royalist prison in the Civil War, started to fall down in the years afterwards, and its remains were lost to view among new buildings. Today, among great 19th-century warehouses, this astonishing remnant stands in clear view: the hall where Henry IV's half-brother, Cardinal Beaufort, Bishop of Winchester, held the reception in 1424 for the wedding of his niece, Joan Beaufort, to James I of Scotland. With glass, the rose window must have been glorious; as a ruin it is impressive but stark. It is built on straight lines. Inside the main roundel a big hexagon is just about discernible, and there is a small hexagon at

its heart, with the rest of the stone frame built up of triangles, a rose with thorns.

A milestone of liberty, in St George's Circus, Southwark SE1

The obelisk at the centre of St George's Circus was erected in 1771, the eleventh year of King George III's reign (see the inscription on the obelisk), as a milestone at the confluence of five major roads. In 1905 it was removed to a site opposite the Imperial War Museum in favour of an unimpressive clock tower. With the growth of motor traffic in the 1930s, the clock tower was demolished. A mere sixty years later, the obelisk returned to its rightful spot. May it never be removed. It performs two functions: in a circus that was once surrounded by fine 18th-century buildings but that now is distinctly unbeautiful, it is the finest structure in view.

And as it is a milestone, the almost pedantic accuracy of the distances, awry when it stood outside the war museum, has presumably been reasserted: 1 mile 40 feet from London Bridge, 1 mile 350 feet from Fleet Street, and 1 mile precisely from Palace Hall, Westminster.

As a milestone its height might be thought over-demonstrative, but it also serves as a monument to Brass Crosby, lord mayor of the City of London when it was erected. Earlier the same year he stood up against a House of Commons command that three printers should be arrested for breach of privilege in reporting parliamentary debates. From the bench, Brass Crosby (sitting with the great libertarian John Wilkes and Richard Oliver) delivered the ringing declaration that as lord mayor he was a guardian of the liberties of his fellow citizens, and no other power, not even the Commons, had a right to seize a citizen of London without an authority from him or some other magistrate. For this he himself was committed to the Tower, but he was released at the end of the parliamentary session and returned to Mansion House in a triumphant procession.

War from the captive's viewpoint at the Imperial War Museum, Lambeth Road SE1

It's a children's paradise, 'boys' toys,' as a woman friend remarked. Friendly looking Spitfires and Messerschmitts hang from the ceiling, de-natured tanks from both wars stand on the floor, a captured V2 rocket points towards the sky (it has had a cladding panel removed so visitors can see the works, just like Damien Hirst's shark). The paintings are upstairs, mostly by official war artists, some unofficial. The finest is Stanley Spencer's masterpiece, *Travoys Arriving with Wounded at a Dressing Station at Smol, Macedonia, September 1916*, and he said that was a painting of peace, not war (see Burghclere, South). Mostly, they are very much museum pieces. They meant so much in the making to Paul Nash and William Roberts, to name two of the better artists who were so affected by the sight of those potholed, shattered battlefields, and although the paintings solicit shame and awe for the horror, the medium isn't right, too literal or too remote. 'My subject is War, and the pity of War,' wrote Wilfred Owen, and it remained a subject best handled by poets – and reporters.

In his own fashion, Ronald Searle (b.1920) was a reporter. Even as the Japanese marched into Singapore in the war after Stanley Spencer's, Searle, a twenty-one-year-old sapper with the Royal Engineers recently removed from a cushy billet packing cardboard boxes for the Co-op by day and studying at Cambridge School of Art in the evening, sat by the road sketching the conquerors. As a captive he was first confined to Changi prisoner of war camp, then laboured on the Burma railway as far as the Thai River and Siam. Constantly threatened by discovery, he continued making these remarkable sketches. He was close to death on several occasions. His fellow PoW Russell Braddon (author of *The Naked Island*) later observed: 'We would only have known he was dead if he had stopped drawing.' Far from stopping, he recorded the daily round of horror as an ill and underfed prisoner and the terrible hardships and the deaths from cholera of his comrades, and he continued to draw his captors, from the relatively amiable to the smirkingly cruel (and later he would bestow the goggle-eyed look of some of them on his St Trinian's girls). This is not the horror of Goya; nor does it have the pungency of a Daumier; instead it is the astonishingly objective record turning the witty pen line of a lightweight newspaper cartoonist into an instrument tough and

The final panel of one of the greatest but least seen 15th-century Renaissance paintings: a frieze by Andrea Mantegna, The Triumphs of Caesar, *commissioned by the house of Gonzaga, rulers of Mantua. Charles I bought them in 1629 and they have been at Hampton Court ever since*

slender as bamboo, compiling in sweat and fear 'the graffiti of a condemned man', as he put it. We look at these drawings and shudder, but since the revolting images of Abu Ghraib, no longer with the comforting sense that it couldn't happen here.

A Caesar of the 15th century at Hampton Court Palace KT8

Cardinal Wolsey bought the old manor of Hampton Court in 1514 and turned it into the grandest Gothic palace in all England. Henry VIII confiscated and expanded it.

William and Mary brought in Christopher Wren to build Fountain Court, with the king's and queen's state apartments on either side, and the great south and east fronts. William and Mary wanted to rebuild the whole palace. Had it been finished it would have been a splendid creation, but what we have is a happy mix of Tudor and baroque, park, river and town, a setting for one of the greatest but least seen masterpieces of Renaissance painting, *The Triumphs of Caesar*, by Andrea Mantegna (1430/1–1506), bountifully hung in a hall to itself, the Lower Orangery in the palace gardens, which was never easy to find, although at last, in 2007, the keepers of the palace made an easier approach out of the house and into the garden.

In the ante-room to the Mantegna display there is a fragment of a sculptured frieze from a Roman sarcophagus of the 2nd century AD. Mantegna had a famous personal collection of just such archaeological finds, and his painting was based on them throughout his career, most spectacularly in these nine canvases. They gleam in the half-light of the Lower Orangery, each one 9 feet square, separated by pilasters along the length of the building, great ruins like their source.

Mantegna painted them for the Gonzagas, rulers of Mantua, during about ten years towards the end of his life. The Gonzagas started unpromisingly for the future of the paintings by using them as scenery in an outdoor masque. Charles I bought them at the Gonzaga sale in 1629, when they were still the most famous paintings of the 15th century, and they have remained in Hampton Court ever since, accelerating towards oblivion and their reputation fading along with the painted surfaces. Mantegna seems to have worked in distemper, but all the restorations from the 17th century, until the latest one (1962–74), did them little service. Finally, John Brealey, the pre-eminent conservator of his day, worked on them from 1962 to 1974, saved them, reversed some of the damage and revealed what remained of Mantegna's own brushwork, which, especially in the passages like white tunics, looks like broadly applied pastel (no doubt partly because the surface is abraded). Anyway, the restoration is a triumph to add to the *Triumph*.

The sequence adds up to a frieze like a Roman sarcophagus, a procession, preceded by trumpeters and followed by standard-bearers, holding up paintings of Julius Caesar's victories: bulls prepared for sacrificial slaughter; elephants; trophies of captured armour carried aloft on poles; prisoners (on the one canvas that cannot be restored because none of Mantegna's paintwork survives beneath the repainting, only the design); and, bringing up the rear, Caesar in his triumphal chariot, a vehicle that seems carved from stone and is drawn by a sculptured horse from a stone plinth. I like to think of Mantegna plotting the sequence, working on the balance between living art and ancient history, working out the continuity of design and colour like a magazine art editor shuffling small dummy pages. Who knows.

What is certain is that Mantegna drew on both his own knowledge of antiquity and that of his academic friends in Padua, his native city, and the literary sources, principally Petrarch. But he never slips into pedantry. The triumphal arch in the final painting bears no exact relation to any in Rome, and where Mantegna paints buildings, as likely as not he paints them as the ruins he saw in the couple of years he spent there, which, of course, is not what they were in Caesar's time. The Gonzaga who commissioned the sequence was himself a leader of mercenaries, a *condottiere*, so Mantegna's paintings were a tribute to a general of his own time in the form of a tribute to the noblest Roman of them all.

Roman grandeur at Syon House, Isleworth TW8

Syon House is where the Scottish architect Robert Adam (1728–92) proved himself the finest interior designer of his time. The 1st Duke of Northumberland would not allow him to rebuild the Tudor original, so the only bravura touch to a dull exterior is the Northumberland lion above the east range, moved from the demolished

Northumberland House in the Strand in the 19th century, which gives the old pile the cheery look of a riverside brewery. The 18th-century aristocracy liked to think of themselves as Romans, and here Adam has indulged by creating a suite of state rooms with an elegant opulence that would have made Nero envious.

Adam's early experience had been working in the early 1750s with his father, William, and his brother, John, in their native Scotland. By the time he received the Percy commission in 1761 he had been on the grand tour. Grand tourists came in two kinds: the rich, who returned to Britain with shiploads of booty, and the artists, who returned with nothing but minds enriched and notebooks filled. At Syon the interests of client and designer dovetailed, for in the glorious setting of the ante-room of the entrance hall with its polychrome scagliola floor, its mahogany doors, its gilded statuary on the entablature and gilded military trophies on the walls, and sumptuous white and gold moulded plaster ceiling, the verde antique columns were, in the words of Sacheverell Sitwell, 'dredged, appropriately, from the bed of the Tiber, and ransomed by Sir Hugh Smithson, first Duke of Northumberland of the new creation, for a thousand pounds apiece'.

In truth, except for William Kent's grand staircase entrance at Holkham, the fanfare of Syon's almost double-cube basilican entrance hall is the finest in England, or at any rate, now that I think of Vanbrugh's Blenheim and Grimsthorpe, my favourite in England. It has an apsidal end, floor paved in black and white marble, walls and ceiling whitish with decorative details in grey (a new colour scheme since Sitwell's time), slender Roman Doric columns, antique busts, medallions painted with details from the Arch of Constantine, and apses with copies of the Apollo Belvedere in marble and the Dying Gaul in bronze. Horace Walpole waspishly disparaged Adam in comparison to Kent ('From Kent's mahogany we are dwindled to Adam's filigree'), and it is true that Adam's decor has a feminine delicacy undreamed of in Rome or in Palladian England. But the excitement manifest in Adam's work at Syon shows that the heady mixture of the power and wealth of Hotspur's descendants with his recent experience of the imperial and republican heart of ancient Rome gave him the impetus to leave behind the severe Palladianism of Burlington's Chiswick.

There follows the white and gold apsidal dining room, with niches for sculpture and a coved ceiling with arcadian figures painted in medallions by the peripatetic Giovanni Battista Cipriani, which Adam's rival William Chambers likened to skied dinner plates. He should be allowed his little envy. Then there is the red drawing room of equivalent splendour, hung with crimson Spitalfields silk and with an Adam carpet echoing the ceiling design. Finally comes a mauve, green and gold long gallery, exquisitely divided by the horizontal thrust of pilasters separating the bookcases and with painted medallions above: one of them is Harry Hotspur as interpreted by the gilded nonchalance of the 18th century. Rome? Up to a point, m'lud.

The birth of the English villa and informal garden at Chiswick House W4

After the pure classicism of the first full-throated Renaissance buildings in England, Inigo Jones's Queen's House in Greenwich (see above), the muscular forms of Wren's St Paul's Cathedral and Vanbrugh's Blenheim Palace became the new architecture, baroque. What goes round comes around: baroque in turn fell from fashion and in the 1720s, on the banks of the soft-running Thames from Chiswick House to Marble Hill and Ham House, Georgian grandees set about creating their own revolution – in the image of Inigo Jones.

The most celebrated of the new buildings was Chiswick House of 1727–9, 'too small to live in and too big to hang to a watch', as the foppish wit Lord Hervey quipped, but Lord Burlington (1694–1753) designed it for his own family and preferred it to any of his other homes, including Burlington House. This domed house on a podium, like a villa in the Veneto, has decor by Burlington's acolyte William Kent (1685–1748), who was not much of an artist when he took to canvas but possessed a sense of colour and form that served him well in the blue and gold brackets, picture frames, doorways and porticoes in Burlington's study, the white and gold coffered ceiling of the red velvet room, and the richly coffered apses in the gallery. These rooms in a suite are contained within strict mathematical parameters, but each one is different – square, octagonal, circular – the first marker of the style of Burlington and Kent throughout their collaborations.

Kent also created the garden. He concluded that smaller Palladian villas like Chiswick did not need to dominate the landscape like a Chatsworth or a Castle Howard and that the natural setting for Chiswick should be within a park of artfully distributed groves of trees, long vistas towards tiny classical follies, an exedra lined with sculpture, a composition with echoes of paintings by Claude or Poussin. It was at Chiswick that the Palladian villa within an informal garden was born, and although it needs restoration it can still be seen as the prototype of those artfully natural gardens, the *jardin anglaise* and the *Englishcher Garten*, which became popular all over Europe.

Hoover's hymn to commerce, of the A40 at Perivale UB6

Is it a bird? Is it a plane? No, it's the Hoover building. It's a factory of such joyous vulgarity, a hymn to trade, industry and the profit motive, that it was not until our own vulgar, commercial and nostalgic decades that it became generally appreciated. The contrast is best illustrated by the gulf that exists between the description given by Pevsner in the 1951 Middlesex volume of his *Buildings of England* series and that offered by his successors. The grand old man himself describes the Hoover factory as 'perhaps the most offensive of the modernistic atrocities along this road'. The new all-embracing northwest London volume of 1991 with the added by-line of Bridget Cherry, quotes the prophet of modernism with measured respect but adds: 'Forty years on we can enjoy the brash confidence of the façade with more detachment.'

The American manufacturer of vacuum cleaners so popular that the trade name became generic commanded it, and an English firm, Wallis, Gilbert & Partners, designed it in 1931 with stars and stripes in their eyes, the kind of romantic attachment to an idea of America as land of the free 'n' easy that marked post-war British Pop Art and that came with enjoyment of Bogart, Cagney and Mary Pickford, of Chrysler automobiles and the Chrysler skyscraper, Marvel comics, Joe Louis and the lights of Broadway. That's a big billing to live up to, and the Hoover building doesn't really attempt it. Apart from the US, it is, like all art deco buildings, a child of the Egyptian revival of the 1920s – not always a thing of explicit Egyptian imagery, like the sphinx-like black cats outside the old Carreras cigarette headquarters in Camden Town, but of flattened-out architectural decoration, streamlined wrap-around windows, flowing

Modernism in 1931, and the first of Charles Holden's run of variations on a theme on the expanding Northern and Piccadilly lines of the London Underground: clean lines, nice balance, lots of light

lines, emphatic bands of colour and interchangeability. In art deco a building's decoration might translate to a scarab ring, and an ashtray could bulk up to a swimming pool. All these are characteristic of the Hoover building's astonishing totemic entrance, its zigzag paving, its astringent reds and greens and yellows, mirrored lift doors engraved with motifs that are picked up in window lights arranged like a hand of poker. Round the back is the former canteen of 1939. It might be an airport control tower or it might be a cinema, but today it's a Tesco supermarket. Hoover abandoned Perivale in 1982, English Heritage listed it to prevent it being demolished like the lurid Firestone building nearby by the same firm, and Tesco picked it up, restored it with immense care,

rented out the main building as offices, and built possibly the only art deco supermarket trolley park in existence.

London Underground at its finest, Sudbury Town underground station HAO

It's the classic English double cube, the space whose most famous exposition is the 17th-century room by Inigo Jones at Wilton House, a cube times two beside a simple cube room. But Sudbury Town underground station (which, as it happens, is above ground) was absolutely on the nail, a piece of modernism as advanced as anything in the world in 1931, concrete, brick, steel and glass in tall clerestory windows between entrance lintel and roof, the façade staring austerely

One of the elegiac vistas of Kensal Green Cemetery, opened in 1833 – a fit setting for the minor royalty and East India company army officers buried here, some with splendid ostentation, like the tomb memorial to Major-General Sir William Casement

down Station Way, two broad bands of brick either side of the building, one down the centre, separating into two four broad bands of glass, each pair in turn divided by a narrow pillar of brick. It is still modern, still almost raw in its spartan lack of ornament, a bracing morning dose of puritanism for commuters emerging from behind their privet hedges at the start of the daily journey into London.

Charles Holden (1875–1960) built it when its section of the District line between Park Royal and South Harrow was handed over to the expanding Piccadilly line, and it was the first of a run of variations on a theme on the Northern and Piccadilly lines that culminated in 1935 with Arnos Grove's drum surmounting a rectangular box shape. The original Sudbury building, which replaced a shack in 1903 to coincide with the introduction of electrification, was part of a plan to push out beyond the suburbs. A poster of 1909 shows passengers in a train passing through open countryside, and the message is: 'Right into the heart of the country. Book to Harrow, Sudbury or Perivale.' Sure enough, the bricks and mortar followed the train lines further into Surrey, Middlesex, Hertfordshire and Essex, destroying as it went the rural idyll shown on the poster and creating in its place subtopia, in the architectural critic Ian Nairn's disparaging word.

The Victorian way of death at Kensal Green Cemetery, Harrow Road NW10

Napoleon established the Père Lachaise cemetery in Paris in 1805, although he himself is entombed in lonely splendour under a pile of red porphyry in Les Invalides. Père Lachaise inspired the creation of Kensal

Green, London's oldest and classiest city of the dead, 72 acres of mournful vistas, sombre draped urns, symbolically broken columns, crucified Christs, grand tombs as big as modest houses, crumbling walls and fallen headstones, all sandwiched between the halal groceries of Harrow Road and two rusting gasholders on the Grand Union Canal. There's an Orthodox Christian sector, another for Catholics, and an Anglican church, All Souls, got up as a Greek temple with colonnades either side and enclosing an open square behind.

The General Cemetery Company opened Kensal Green Cemetery of All Souls for trading in January 1833 in a bull market for death as a cholera epidemic took hold in London. Business remains healthy today, and the very same company retains control. The early boom years peaked with the burials on the central avenue of two royals, the Duke of Sussex (d.1843), sixth son of George III, buried under a massive stone slab, and Princess Sophia, the king's fifth daughter (d.1849), interred in an elaborate Carrara marble sarcophagus on a high, dignified pedestal. There followed scores of writers, Thackeray and Trollope among them; engineers, including Rennie (see Lancaster, Northwest) and Brunel; an Archbishop of York; the first man to cross Niagara Falls on a tightrope, Emile Blondin; lawyers, architects and artists, including Frith (see Egham, Southeast) and Bonington (see Nottingham, North Midlands). There are no doubt fornicators, thieves, drunks, wife beaters, journalists and worshipers before foreign idols as well. The modern world has edged in, too. Feet from the princess's tomb a modern black marble headstone commemorates 'Kevin and Ted – Together in peace'.

There are, too, an alarming number of bellicose tomb carvings representing military ordnance; soldiers to the left of us, soldiers to the right of us, many of them old Indian

Army wallahs, the grandest of them the Hon. Sir William Casement (1780–1844), Knight Companion of the Bath, major-general in the Bengal Army and member of the Supreme Council of India. His ordnance is real enough: old cannon have been adapted as bollards around the tomb. His death from cholera came thirteen years before the Indian Mutiny caused the British government to withdraw its commission to the East India Company and itself assume power. So the young Casement's battles in 1803 and 1804 against the Marathas and, incidentally, Napoleon's French lieutenants, was a fight for company and lucre rather than king and country, fine drawn though the distinction was. He died neither celebrated for corruption nor for singular military prowess; but he was buried with full military honours in Calcutta, so his tomb in Kensal Green is presumably a memorial only. On a plinth four caryatids, proud Bengal warriors, stand wrapped against the English weather, arms crossed over their chests, light turbans (known as pugrees) tied on their heads. These stoics bear the weight of a big coffered entablature sheltering a draped tomb chest on which is placed the plumed pith helmet of Casement sahib, a last symbol of the raj in a west London sepulchre.

A poignant reminder of the First World War at Paddington railway station w2

Having a body scarred with shrapnel, having suffered the hell of gas burning the lungs, having lain in no man's land among the dead listening for the enemy: these things mark a man and they are what made the war memorials by Charles Sargent Jagger (1885–1934) different. His Tommy on the Great Western Railway war memorial tucked away up the side of platform 1 at Paddington isn't a muted, neutered soldier remembered from some corner of a foreign field, standing with head solemnly lowered and rifle upended, bayonet point to the ground. Jagger's soldier is off duty and obviously dog tired, his helmet shoved back clear of his forehead, his greatcoat slung over his shoulders, his long, heavy-knit scarf knotted loosely and hanging below waist level, gaitered legs and boots wide apart and planted firmly on the earth. His head is lowered, certainly, but that's because he is reading a letter from home.

Jagger has read that letter, worn this half-inch thick greatcoat and turned its collar up against the biting wind. He had been due to take up the Royal College of Art's Prix de Rome in 1914 as war broke out, and instead he enlisted. Four years later he had served with the Worcesters in Gallipoli and on the Western Front, been wounded, gassed and won the Military Cross. When he came back to civvy street and a South Kensington studio financed by the British School in Rome with a year's funding in lieu of the Rome scholarship and a recommendation from a member of the British School in Rome to a war memorial committee in the Wirral, he was interested only in creating something out of his savage experience. Many memorials followed, and the GWR bronze soldier is among the two or three best. Close up, you can see that Jagger modelled it in clay; his thumb and finger marks are there where he pressed lumps of clay to the armature, sticking to the earth he knew best; 'was it for this the clay grew tall?'

By this time sculpture had moved towards abstraction, or the semi-abstraction of Epstein and Gill, and Jagger was ignored, a craftsman among journeymen turning out soldiers for monuments, his evident superiority forgotten. Yet the figure of the dead soldier covered by his cape and helmet on one façade of Jagger's famous Royal Artillery memorial at Hyde Park Corner (though few know who created it) shows he could harness the sublime to the reality of violent death. And the soldier on platform 1 is a first; as he lingers for eternity over his letter he makes the connection with the hearth at home. This was the first war that affected everyone in the country, and Jagger's monument says so.

Goldfinger's utopian machine for living, 2 Willow Road, Hampstead NW3

The architect Ernö Goldfinger (1902–87) once sued his near neighbour in Hampstead, Ian Fleming, over the publication of his seventh 007 thriller, which borrowed Goldfinger's name for its title and its villain, who was billed succinctly on the paperback cover as 'James Bond's most devilish adversary – an evil genius with a lust for gold'. A colleague of Goldfinger told him the only difference he could spot between the two Goldfingers was that one was called Ernö and the other Auric. Ernö sued anyway and settled for his costs and six copies of the book. Fleming had to be talked out of renaming his character Goldprick.

In point of fact, Ernö Goldfinger was a utopian Marxist, comfortably reconciling this with a wife, Ursula Blackwell, who was a canned soup heiress. After the war he built Trellick Tower in Ladbroke Grove, an apartment block with its services packed into a slimmer adjoining tower, semi-attached like a jet refuelling a monster transport plane in midair. Once popularly dubbed the tower of terror, it has been listed, and when flats come on the market, utopianism comes at around a quarter of a million.

He had already, in 1937, built 1, 2 and 3 Willow Road, with glass windows the width of the house, the structure concrete, but brick clad, subtly detailed and inspired by his admiration for the continuity in design of Georgian terraces. He sold numbers 1 and 3; No. 2 was for himself and his family. Ernö died in 1987, Ursula a little later, and the

The house Ernö Goldfinger built for himself at 2 Willow Road, Hampstead, in 1937, one of a short terrace, is a concrete example of a turning point in English culture. It is stuffed with art, has walls which retract, and neat devices like the desk in the photograph with drawers that swivel open instead of pulling out

National Trust acquired 2 Willow Road in 1994, its first modernist house with a large part of the original furnishings and works of art. Goldfinger had made a wide circle of friends both in the artistic community of Paris, where he went from Budapest to study in 1920 and where he met Ursula, and in Hampstead, where Henry Moore, Ben Nicholson and Barbara Hepworth lived and which became home to artist refugees from the gathering clouds of war in Europe. Two framed photographs by Man Ray of Ursula are in the living room along with a portrait drawing of Goldfinger by the English surrealist Eileen Agar (1899–1991). There are drawings by Amadée Ozenfant (1886–1966), the French founder with Le Corbusier of Purism, in the dining room, with paintings by Prunella Clough and Bridget Riley, a drawn version of Robert Delaunay's refracted prism paintings of the Eiffel Tower, a surrealist collage by Roland Penrose featuring the nude torso of his wife, Lee Miller, and a tiny sculpture by Henry Moore.

Some of the furniture that Goldfinger made has aged and dated, but other pieces are still wonderful, like the desk in his study with its drawers that swivel open instead of pulling out. Walls fold back between rooms so that intimate spaces become a great party

arena (and there were plenty of parties). The spiral staircase, toplit and ultra modern, is a take on the medieval practice of installing space-saving newel stairs. My personal benchmark for the beautiful ingenuity of modernist domestic architecture is the Marseilles flats in Le Corbusier's Unité d'habitation, one of which I was lucky enough to be shown round by its owners. Goldfinger isn't Corbusier, but seventy years after its conception, 2 Willow Road stands as a concrete example of a turning point in the cultural history of England.

A domestic masterpiece at Kenwood House, Hampstead NW3

If you could leg it from Kenwood with one painting, how would you choose between a Rembrandt self-portrait and a Vermeer?

Vermeer's stunning painting of a woman playing a guitar is one of the highlights of Kenwood House. The guitar, the pearl necklace, the ermine-trimmed, pale yellow jacket (Vermeer yellow) may have all come out of the artist's costume box, but the painting itself has a lucid yet mysterious and enduring timelessness

Rembrandt's self-portraits are a book in which you can read his history and some of the history of art in the technical majesty of the artist's technique. It's all there. Vermeer's paintings of women in neat Dutch interiors are almost unreadable. Sometimes the woman has a man in attendance, usually not, daylight streams through a window, illuminating a picture hanging on a wall, a silken dress, a head, a shoulder, a hand. Faced with this dilemma you can only choose what you love, and I love Vermeer's inscrutable painting above Rembrandt's scrutable human document.

Kenwood, up there on a corner of the heath, is the national gallery of Hampstead with a collection of paintings, the Iveagh Bequest, bestowed upon the house in 1927 by one of the Guinness family, the former owner Lord Iveagh. The self-portrait is one of Rembrandt's finest, the Vermeer one of only thirty-five or so extant. There is a great Reynolds painting of the actress and courtesan Kitty Fisher and a couple of delicious Bouchers, all in a building remodelled by Robert Adam with a library that is among the best rooms he created.

Like the other women by Jan Vermeer (1632–73), we don't know who the woman with a guitar is: she has no history, she is simply there, smiling at someone outside the frame, caught in the act of playing her instrument with the most beautiful hands in painting. She sits with her body square to the picture plane catching full light, but tilts her head and looks to the left so that the light falls on the right side of her perfectly oval head. She wears a beautiful yellow jacket,

Vermeer yellow, trimmed with fur, over a white silk dress that falls in rich folds over her thighs and the knee supporting the guitar. The pearl necklace on her throat is like the ring around the planet Saturn and each separate pearl a planet (actually, looked at close to, they are merely brilliant white highlights dabbed on to an off-white band), and the head itself is a larger planet in light and dark, while her hands are positioned in a different orbit. Her ringlets swing in corkscrew arabesques against the wall behind her and the painting on it, speeding the pictorial rhythm in this one important part of the canvas.

As I write this, I wonder whether I am imagining it, so I pick up the catalogue of the big Vermeer exhibition in The Hague in 1996 and see that in the very different Vermeer of the kitchen maid pouring milk he does the same things: the head a strongly lit orb, the mouth of the jug tilted at an angle from the head, the folds of the blue skirt falling in a broad rhythm, the tabletop with the angle towards the viewer completing a diamond shape with the corner of the room.

Incidentally, Vermeer was the friend in Delft of a famous optical instrument maker, Anthony van Leeuwenhoek, and it was probably van Leeuwenhoek who modelled for Vermeer's paintings *The Astronomer* and *The Geographer*. In both of these is a globe of the Earth, and in *The Astronomer* the globe and the astronomer's head lie one behind the other while the arms are spread to mark out the far points of a wider sphere. It seems sure that Vermeer was fascinated by the new disciplines made possible by advances in optics and that the harmony of the spheres was very much in his mind as he worked on these compositions. No wonder he produced so few pictures. No wonder he left his wife poor when he died.

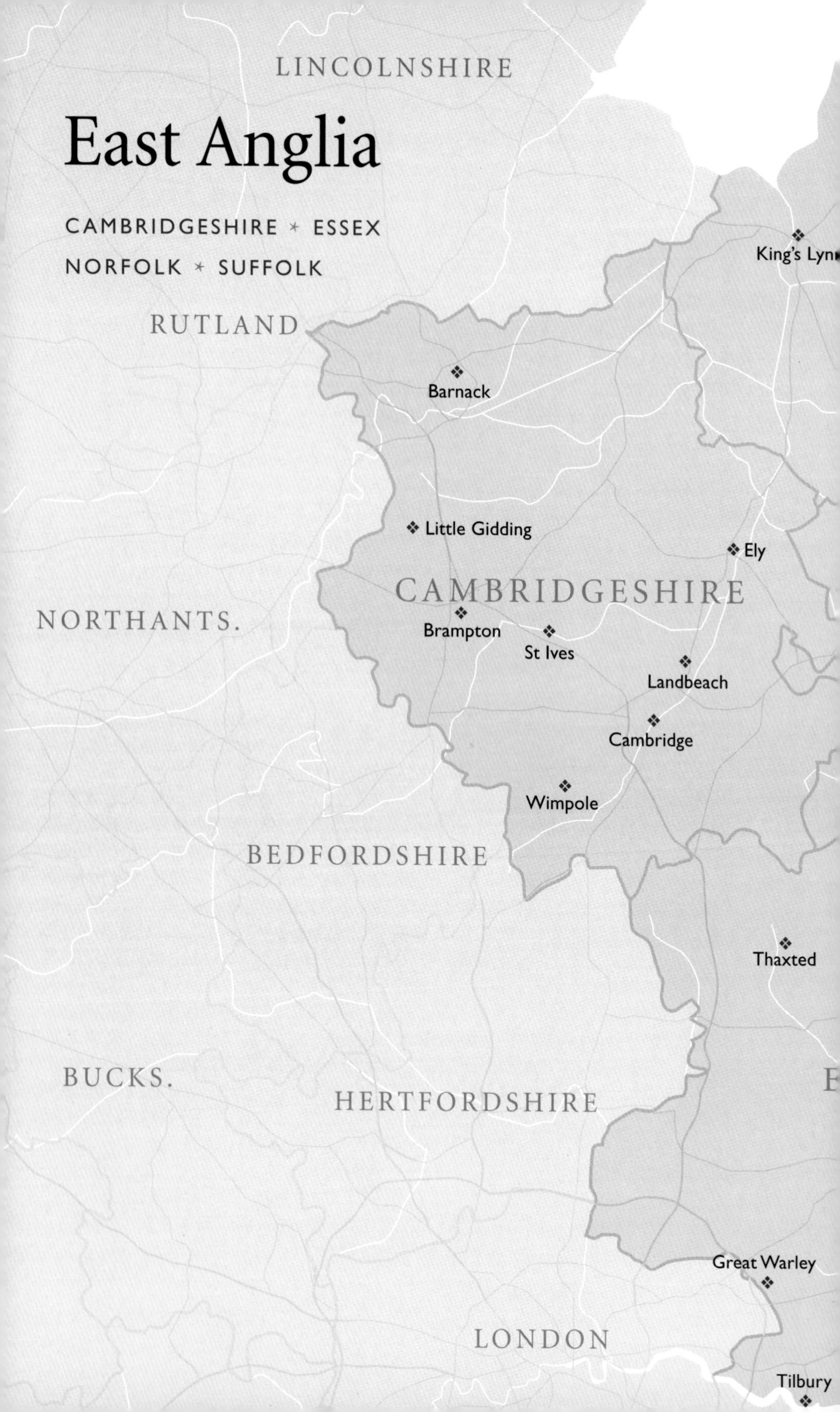

East Anglia

CAMBRIDGESHIRE ✳ ESSEX
NORFOLK ✳ SUFFOLK

LINCOLNSHIRE

RUTLAND

NORTHANTS.

King's Lyn

❖ Barnack

❖ Little Gidding

❖ Ely

CAMBRIDGESHIRE

❖ Brampton   ❖
St Ives

❖ Landbeach

❖ Cambridge

❖ Wimpole

BEDFORDSHIRE

❖ Thaxted

BUCKS.

HERTFORDSHIRE

E

Great Warley
❖

LONDON

Tilbury

Holkham

Barton Turf

Ranworth

NORFOLK

fham

Norwich

Wymondham

Bungay

Southwold

Thornham Parva

Blythburgh

Saxtead Green

Woolpit

Framlingham

SUFFOLK

Snape

Needham Market

Lavenham

Milden

g

ord

Acton

Ipswich

Sudbury

Nayland

Harwich

Colchester

ting

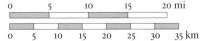

Canvey Island

0   5   10   15   20 mi

0   5   10   15   20   25   30   35 km

Acton
SUFFOLK

A yeoman's brass in All Saints church

Acton is an untidily straggling, largely 20th-century village on the edge of a suburb of light industry in Sudbury; but it has a village sign that is a throwback to the 14th century. It's a copy of a memorial brass in the parish church showing Sir Robert de Bures, then lord of the manor. The church was built in Sir Robert's lifetime and, standing at the end of a fine avenue of tall lime trees, is the parish's redeeming feature

De Bures was of typical yeoman stock. He was probably born in the 1260s in the village of Bures a few miles south, and he grew up as a soldier in the service of Edward III, gaining lands as a reward for successful stewardships. Brasses were an affordable way for all classes below royalty to commemorate the dead and the De Bures brass set into a Purbeck marble slab in the chancel is one of the earliest and finest in the country. The date always given for this brass was 1302, but 1331, the year of Sir Robert's death, is now generally accepted.

His 6 foot 6 inch effigy is shown, head, hands, feet and all, in a suit of mail with a gown trimmed at the edges with a border of trefoils, held at the waist by a cord with a sword belt slung lower across the hips bearing what must be a 3 foot scabbarded sword. The gown is split at the front revealing embroidered textile thigh pieces, called cuisses, and knee protectors called poleyns. His feet rest on a splendid little lion. He bears a shield emblazoned with the arms of De Bures, two rampant lions at the top, ermine beneath (in the exotic language of heraldry, ermine, on a chief indented sable, two lioncels or). The coat of arms was more important than the individual face, and this shield has been incised on a different sheet

of metal from the rest of the piece, which suggests that the main part of the brass might have been made for a different client and picked up as a second by De Bures. In any case, it was probably produced by Adam de Corfe, a London dealer in Purbeck marble who seized on the new craft of setting brass plaques into stone and clearly, in the case of De Bures, or person unknown, employed an artist of exquisite skill.

Barnack
CAMBRIDGESHIRE

Timeless Christ in Majesty at the Church of St John the Baptist

Barnack Hills and Holes is a national nature reserve that supports hundreds of wild plants, including eight species of orchid. It has lain undisturbed since the end of the 15th century, by which time builders had exhausted the limestone quarries and left the pocked and potted surface that gives the area its name and butterflies their habitat. Before that, Peterborough Cathedral was built of Barnack stone; so too were Bury St Edmunds, Crowland, Ely and Ramsay. And, of course, Barnack, where the Anglo-Saxons got in first. At the centre of the community of fewer than a thousand people lie a pub and post office and the old rectory, renamed Kingsley House after the author of *Westward Ho!* and *The Water-Babies*. The core of this is the Church of St John the Baptist, and the heartbeat of the church is the early 11th-century Christ in Majesty, possibly the finest surviving piece of Saxon sculpture in England.

It is a relief set into the wall of the north aisle in what is now largely a Decorated

The Church of St John the Baptist in Barnack is visibly Saxon in origin, nowhere more so than in this magnificent early 11th-century relief carving of Christ in Majesty

church with lots of pretty detail, but where the really striking elements are still Saxon, especially the tower, with carved slabs like sections of free-standing cross-shafts set into the outside wall and, inside, the big tower arch with all the heft of Norman architecture, a touch of insouciance in the way it has been thrown together. The Christ in Majesty has the heft as well, but its contained sublimity is the work of a master mason. Christ sits with one hand before him raised in blessing, humanity and majesty combined in his expression; the figure is animated by the slow rhythm of garments draped from the shoulder, falling as wide sleeves from the wrists, draped over the knees and falling to the ankle. It has the transcendent and timeless solemnity of the Byzantine art from which the Romanesque developed, and traces of pigment on the sculpture argue that this Christ might once also have displayed the polychrome splendour of Byzantium; that, too, could explain the curiously unmodelled legs, which appear as flat panels tapering from knee to ankle, perhaps because the illusion of modelling was created by paint. Barnack's Christ speaks not of the hard authority of an expanding Norman empire but of a pre-Conquest community living in full acceptance of Christian values and settling into an agrarian civilisation after the upheavals of previous centuries.

Barton Turf

NORFOLK

15th-century painted rood screen in the Church of St Michael and All Angels

The exoticism of the rood screen at Barton Turf is quite similar to another exceptional Norfolk broads screen, at Ranworth, and though Barton Turf's isn't up to that level, it is the most magical of the mid-15th-century painted screens of East Anglia. These screens once supported a loft upon which was set the crucified likeness of Christ known as the rood. Like Ranworth too, the Barton Turf paintings are of saints and the pecking order among seraphim, cherubim, angels, archangels – the heavenly hierarchies. Perhaps because of its morning-dew freshness, the tender pinks and vermilions, the bluebird feathers of an angel, the golden armour of St Raphael and the faintly roseate pallor of the female saints Apollonia, Cytha and Barbara it seems essentially English, but it might just as well be Flemish. In fact, the monster laid low by St Raphael has the old punch-drunk, gap-toothed, flat-nosed, glaring-eyed look of the monster at the mouth of hell in the Flemish-made stained glass at Fairford in Gloucestershire (see West and East Midlands), and the facial types of the women saints and the angels are quite close to the contemporary and highly popular Flemish artist Hans Memlinc, though in this comparison the difference is between genius and the journeyman ability of peripatetic artists. But in this place, a little 14th-century church among fields in a quiet lane a few hundred yards from Barton Broad, these village Memlincs are something to treasure.

Blythburgh

SUFFOLK

15th-century angel roof at the Church of the Holy Trinity

'Shot down from its enskied formation,' Peter Porter wrote in his poem 'An Angel in Blythburgh Church':

The only agent of change in Holy Trinity, Blythburgh, has been time, plus a little cautious restoration to the glorious angel roof which has left the huge parish church looking more nearly as it was originally intended than any other in East Anglia

*This stern-faced plummet rests against the
wall;*
*Cromwell's soldiers peppered it and now the
death-watch beetle has its thrall.*

That was in 1977, the very year when the
Suffolk Institute of Archaeology made and
painted a replica of one of Blythburgh's roof
angels, scarlet, silver, black and gold, and
presented it to Holy Trinity, where it adorns
the wall above the south door. In point of
fact, the leaden touch of history overrides
Porter's greater poetic truth: Cromwell's men
intended removing 'twenty cherubim', as
their orders described the angels, but they
were too far out of reach; the buckshot found
in the angels actually found its way there in
the 18th century, when men were hired to
shoot at the jackdaws infesting the church.

Blythburgh's past is a history of benign
neglect. The Black Death of 1349 decimated
the population, and unlike other places the
village never recovered. But about 1120 Henry
I had granted the church to the Priory of St
Osyth in Essex, and in the 15th century the
priory and a few rich patrons who were
founding chantries towards their everlasting
salvation together rebuilt the church on the
hill where it stands like a great barque poised
for the launch but stranded because the sea
walls of whatever sort of harbour Blythburgh
ever had have long since collapsed and left
marshes hospitable to mud-seeking birds
alongside the River Blyth.

Benign neglect of the village becomes
benign splendour inside the church. Unlike
nearby Southwold, Victorian restorers never
reached Blythburgh in force, the plans of the
arch restorer G.E. Street frustrated in a stand-
off with the anti-scrape movement (William
Morris's Society for the Protection of Ancient
Buildings). Instead, throughout the 20th
century conservation moved ahead
cautiously and bequeathed a church with no
alterations in its appearance, so it seems,

since the Wars of the Roses, except the
intervention of time. The interior looks vast,
both because it actually is big and because
the benches of the west end have been cleared
away, revealing the fine brick floor. The
remaining benches have excellent carved
ends, but the great magnificence in a region
of angels is the shallow, arched, tie-beam roof
with a dozen angels along the centre, wide
wing spans, two by two each side of a large
boss set on a white cross-beam (there were
maybe twenty angels originally, but some
were destroyed when the spire fell through
the roof in 1577; the round dozen will do just
fine).

The colours are faded, but bona fide 15th
century. Each large boss has a gorgeous
abstract floral pattern, the beams are
organised in groups painted in series with the
sacred monogram, IHS, the first three letters
transliterated from the Greek of Jesus's name,
in red, and alternate series with a lovely
heart-shaped abstract decoration in black,
which with a little imagination might be seen
as a symbol for the holy trinity, both symbols
prettily interspersed with little red and white
flower shapes. The colours are conspicuous
on all the rafters and in the interstices, on the
hair and wings of the angels, and on the
heraldic shields, both those the angels display
against their chests and others that are free
standing. Like a faded family photograph
from a couple of generations ago this interior
carries a tantalising emotional charge, a sense
of a history laid out before us but
withholding some vital ingredient, the lived-
in moment, the faith or simply the hope that
doesn't quite match our own yearnings.

Brampton
CAMBRIDGESHIRE

Somehow Brampton just about clings to its Domesday Book description of a rural community with a church and a priest, many acres of woodland and a couple of mills on the River Ouse (one remaining, now a pub). In the village itself the green survives, and there are charming ancient pubs and thatched cottages. But the village is host to a large RAF station, a racecourse and a lot of new houses, indistinguishable in style and materials from those in a thousand other ancient villages all over the southern half of England. It's impossible now to look at a photograph of 1905 showing cattle watering in the village pond without a sense of melancholy. The main interest here today is the association with Pepys, for this is where the diarist spent some of his boyhood in his uncle's home walking to Huntingdon grammar school a mile along the road, and where, in his years as an ambitious servant to Lord Sandwich, he was a frequent visitor with his wife to the Sandwich seat of Hinchingbroke, a fine house and park, now a school, but visible from the road and open to the public every Sunday afternoon in summer.

Where Pepys stashed his fortune in gold pieces

The Pepys of Brampton were humble relations of the aristocratic Mountagus of Hinchingbrooke, a mile or so down the road to Huntingdon, and in due course Samuel Pepys inherited the yeoman's house at Brampton from his uncle Robert. It was Edward Mountagu, the Earl of Sandwich, who had told Pepys in the hectic days of jostling for position after the Restoration: 'We must have a little patience and we will

rise together. In the meantime I will do you all the good Jobbs I can.' He was as good as his word, and the acquisition of Brampton made Pepys and Mountagu country cousins.

Even though Brampton has greatly expanded, Pepys's Tudor bolt-hole from London remains at the Huntingdon edge of the village, owned by the Pepys Society (which has fixed on the gatepost a little brass plate recalling its history), but close enough to other properties to bring to life the passage in the diaries when, having sent his gold out of London with his wife and a friend in the panic after the Dutch invaded the Medway in 1687, he later took carriage to Brampton to recover the treasure and realised that his wife and father had buried it in full view of the neighbours. He and his close companion Will Hewer waited until after dark to dig:

I was out of my wits almost … I did perceive the earth was got among the gold and wet, so that the bags were all rotten … which, all put together did make me mad … and as many of the scattered pieces as I could with the dirt discern by the candlelight, and carry them up into my brother's chamber and there lock them up till I had eat a little supper.

By two in the morning they were finished, and Pepys was content that most of the gold was safe. It is one of the choicest comic passages, not just in Pepys but in English literature, and to anyone who has read it, it comes vividly to mind at the gates of this handsome old house.

How different down the road at civilised Hinchingbrooke. Here, behind the double row of bay windows through two storeys with fretted balustrades and emblazoned with the Cromwell arms (Oliver sold it to Lord Sandwich's father), Pepys would walk with 'the excellent, good, discreet' Lady Sandwich and measure how far he had come in life:

But the house is most excellently furnished,
and brave rooms and good pictures, so that it
doth please me infinitely, beyond Audly-End.
Here we stayed till night, walking and talking
and drinking, and with mighty satisfaction.

He dreamed of retiring one day to Brampton,
but this quintessential Londoner could not
bring himself to die anywhere further from
London than the little country house he had
bought himself at Clapham.

By the way, a sculptural three-way signpost

Milestones have become a part of the
heritage industry, a sure sign that satnav has
finally displaced them from functionality.
The death agonies began during the Second
World War when the government ordered
local authorities to remove them to confuse
passing Nazis. Many milestones were buried.
Some were dug up after the war and restored
to the grassy banks of the roadside, but many
more were lost. Mostly they are 19th century,
iron or stone, triangular in section. Quite a
lot are mid-18th century and stone, from the
initial period of turnpikes (when tollhouses
became common and can often still be easily
recognised: ordinary cottages at a corner of
the road but with a couple of projecting
windows so that the toll collector could
watch for approaching traffic).
      Cambridgeshire and Suffolk are quite rich
in milestones. But the quirkiest are the best,
and one of these is a few yards from the
Pepys house in Brampton on the corner of
the road leading from Thrapston to
Huntingdon. It's 18th century and not exactly
a milestone since no distances are marked,

Close to Samuel Pepys's house in Brampton is this
18th-century waymarker, a survivor of the Second
World War clearance for security reasons of English
milestones and roadside indicators

but a rough hewn triangular obelisk tapering
to the top and ending in a ball finial. It is
charmingly carved on one side in upper and
lower case letters picked out in black paint,
including the long s, 'To Thrapfton' and 'To
Huntingdon' underneath with a finger
pointing in the opposite direction. On
another side 'To LONDON' is emblazoned in
declamatory capital letters. Above each
legend a finger extends from a podgy
Georgian hand to point the direction,
knuckles up one way, palm up the other,
warm and human helping hands held out in
aid to strangers, passing Wehrmacht not in
mind.

Bungay
SUFFOLK

The statue of justice in the marketplace

Bungay town centre burned down in 1688,
but since then it has been singularly lucky. It
was big enough to have a priory, of which the
present parish church was probably the nave,
and there are two large gatehouse towers and
the remains of a keep of a 12th-century castle.
The population still hovers at under 4,000.
The old fabric of the marketplace remains
along with the necessary tradesmen around a
little triangular space with a big octagonal
butter cross of 1689, the year after the fire. It
stands on a central space paved with big
stone slabs and is supported on eight Doric
columns with a deep entablature crowned by
a lead dome and a square plinth for a fine
figure of Justice with sword and scales.
      The cross, like the marketplace, is smaller
than Swaffham's (see below), but Justice cuts
a finer dash than the Norfolk goddess of
plenty. Justice was a late addition, of 1759,
and is thought to have been by Henry Cheere
(1709–87), a jobbing statuary who could
produce to order casts of Homer or Virgil,
Shakespeare or Milton, Mercury, Pluto,

Apollo, Samson or the Four Seasons. Perhaps because of his versatility, he has never been given due credit (since his lifetime, that is: he was knighted by his contemporaries), but his well-placed workshop near St Margaret's, Westminster, doubtless helped to bring many fruitful commissions, particularly at the Queen's College and the Sheldonian in Oxford.

The Bungay Justice is a vivid stone carving, beautifully poised with her weight on one foot, the other trailing, her delicately shaped left hand holding the scales, her right hand grasping the sword hilt and pointing the blade upwards. She is not blindfold in the usual way and directs her gaze into the market square, suggesting compassion as well as justice.

Cambridge
CAMBRIDGESHIRE

For many visitors Cambridge consists of one building and a series of vistas. The building is King's College Chapel, a ship's length of soaring stone, exquisite fan vaulting and jewel-like stained glass. The vistas are the colleges strung out along the two roughly parallel roads that run through the city centre. They were designed, of course, to be seen from the front, but Cambridge's great glory is that those that lie along Trumpington Street, King's Parade and Trinity Street (all one road, rather bewilderingly) look as good, if not better, from the back, with their gardens stretching down to the winding River Cam.

It's because of the overall impression that Cambridge makes that, King's College Chapel apart, it's easy to miss individual highlights. Yet most of the colleges have something remarkable to offer, whether it's Wren's earliest architecture (the chapel at Pembroke), the great set-piece of Trinity's

front court or the late medieval brickwork of Magdalene (Cambridge discovered the beauty of bricks long before its Oxford rival did). Confronted with so many choices I've opted for three that reflect different aspects of college life: a gateway, a chapel and a library.

Town is inevitably overshadowed by gown in Cambridge, and in many ways that's fair enough. With the exception of the very grand Fitzwilliam Museum, there aren't really any notable public or private buildings – rather as with the colleges, one is left with overall impressions: some attractive shopping streets, a few gracious 18th- and early 19th-century houses, particularly those that surround Parker's Piece, and a reminder of how rural Cambridge once was in the humble cottages that now form the Kettle's Yard art gallery. Similarly with Cambridge's churches. Those that are of historical importance (St Benet's with its Anglo-Saxon tower; the so-called Round Church, built after the First Crusade with eight massive piers defining the circular nave, but vandalised by 19th-century 'restoration') are perhaps easier to admire than to like. Others have their individual charms, but it is often their setting rather than their architecture that makes them what they are.

The canvas Delacroix kept for himself, in the Fitzwilliam Museum

The range and quality of the Fitzwilliam's collections are undisputed, the antiquities, the Renaissance art, including one of Titian's greatest canvases, *The Rape of Lucretia*, the decorative arts, the coins, the oriental sculpture and porcelain, the illuminated manuscripts. Tucked away among them on a small section of wall hangs a painting, *The Odalisque*, no more than about 15 inches by 18, which Eugène Delacroix (1798–1863) painted towards the end of the 1820s, sold, bought back almost immediately, and kept by him for the rest of his life. Today, faced with Delacroix's great machines in the Louvre (*Liberty Leading the People*, *The Massacre of Chios*) or in the left bank Church of San Sulpice (*Jacob Wrestling with the Angel*) we pay lip service; respect, not love.

The Odalisque explains in an instant why his reputation was so high among the men who were young artists as Delacroix was growing old or long gone – Baudelaire, Renoir, Signac, Degas and both Picasso and Matisse. He painted it before his first visit to Morocco, about the time that he was working on another of those huge Cecil B. De Mille canvases, *The Death of Sardanapalus*, and it has the same qualities of utterly free yet totally controlled brushwork, wonderful passages of colour and sensuous delineation of a wholly realised female nude in an abandoned pose on a bed. But in the big canvas the nudes are incidents in a historical drama. *The Odalisque* is closer to our own taste, certainly men's, doubtless women's too: a lone figure on whose erotic reverie we intrude. She sprawls in sensuous post-coital abandon on a dishevelled bed covered with a white mattress and a rich red sheet, crumpled, a hookah beside her suggesting that a man was here but, as we read from the distance in her eyes, has departed. Delacroix is accounted a Romantic, but in this small canvas are concentrated the qualities of all great painting: wonderful skills, magnificent colour, distilled emotion.

A founder's gift, the Gate of Honour, Gonville and Caius College

Squeezed between the University's Senate House and the Great Court of Trinity College, Caius is quite easy to miss, and it's even easier to miss the college's Gate of Honour – not much more than a setting for a side gate on to Senate House Lane and built on a diminutive scale. Yet the Gate represents one of the earliest intrusions of the European Renaissance into the still largely medieval atmosphere of 16th-century Cambridge.

Dr John Caius, who was responsible for the gate, was the college's second founder; multiple founders are a common feature of Cambridge history. He had studied ancient languages at Gonville Hall (founded by the Rev. Edmund Gonville in 1348), then went to Padua in 1539 to study medicine and to travel. In Italy Brunelleschi had long before built the dome for the cathedral of Florence; Michelozzo, basing his architecture on the square and the circle, had built the Medici Palace; and in Rome Bramante had designed a new St Peter's. All made their mark on John Caius.

He returned to Cambridge already rich from his medical practice and determined to use his new wealth in re-founding impoverished Gonville in 1557 as Gonville and Caius, of which he became master. He rebuilt in the unexceptional medieval style seen in the palaces and great houses of England at this time, but nagging away at the back of his mind was the new architecture he had seen abroad. Within his college he built three gates: the Gates of Humility, Virtue and Honour.

The first of these was Humility, through which new students entered the college from Trinity Street in a fit state of mind. This is a more or less unadorned arch. The next gate leads from Gonville Court into a second quad: this is the Gate of Virtue, indicating dedication to study, and it is avowedly classical but also awkwardly provincial, with its structure articulated by Ionic columns, a round arch supported on Corinthian capitals, a couple of scrawny female figures of victory and the word *Virtutis* carved and gilded in stately Roman capitals above the arch. This is what students of architectural history generally come to see, but it is the

The Gate of Honour at Gonville and Caius College, an early sighting of Renaissance architecture in England. Undergraduates pass through on their way to graduate at the Old Schools

third, the Gate of Honour, through which students passed on their way to the Old Schools to graduate, that catches the eye.

It is not set into a building but stands against a wall, framed by shrubs and small trees. There are Ionic columns again, but this time on either side of a slightly pointed medieval arch; there are classical medallions, but they are decorated with the Tudor rose. A second storey looks like a model for the façade of a Greek temple. The design was probably part derived from the contemporary and influential Roman architect Sebastiano Serlio, whose treatise, *General Rules of Architecture*, had been published in England. But this is Serlio in Wonderland, Serlio anglicised by the coniferous shrubs against the wall, the manicured lawns, the trees filtering softly dappled light, the ranges of homely stone buildings and by a third storey, which is a quaintly unclassical hexagon with sundials and a little dome crowning it.

Victorian Gothic at its best, the chapel, Jesus College

In 1497 Bishop Alcock of Ely persuaded Henry VII to grant him a charter to dissolve the nunnery dedicated to the 'glorious virgin St Radegund', as the charter described her. It was a 12th-century Benedictine foundation outside Cambridge, but when the bishop made his application only two nuns remained, one of them infamous. The details of the charge are left vague, but it seems as though the unfortunate nun failed to live up to the standards of 'the glorious virgin'. Bishop Alcock took the lands and money to found Jesus College. All that was left standing

of St Radegund was the church, and that, with the nave truncated and the aisles torn down, became the chapel of the new college in the redeeming embrace of Bishop Alcock's new buildings. The bishop knocked out the 13th-century east window lancets and put in a big Perpendicular window, but in the 19th century the great gothicist Augustus Pugin rebuilt the five tall lancets using some of the original masonry and gave back this abruptly attenuated building its splendidly austere chancel. It was up to the artistry of William Morris, Ford Maddox Brown and Edward Burne-Jones to add colour to Pugin's scholarship.

This shows clearly in a comparison of the stained glass by different hands. Pugin professed himself happy to follow precedent, and his stained glass figures for the tall slender lancets in the north of the chancel in clear crimson, green, blue and white, set in roundels and lozenges against clear glass with a colourful patterned border, are convincingly in the spirit of medieval craftsmen (similarly his organ case decorated with angels that might have come from an illuminated missal). Pugin was working on the chancel in 1846–9; Morris, Burne-Jones and Brown arrived more than a quarter of a century later. They installed one window with good Burne-Jones designs in the south wall of the chancel and then turned their attention to the ante-chapel, as the shortened nave had become. Morris's clamorous ceiling of heraldic panels set about with stylised foliage is an inescapably Victorian fanfare. Burne-Jones, who could be as insipid on canvas as any Victorian artist, was set free by glass, and here he is at his best, especially in the big south window of the ante-chapel, and his angels, less Pre-Raphaelite than art nouveau (years before the fact), have great scimitar wings scything from shoulders to feet, an elongated trumpet like a golden lily and a white broadsword; both saints and angels sinuous in sapphire and ruby and gold. More believably real people, the four left-hand saintly bishops in the bottom row are by Brown; less satisfactorily, because they don't fill the space adequately, the figures of St Augustine and St Catherine are by Morris. Morris's too is the row of small angels in white in the simple 16th-century tracery at the top of the window – modest but a fine foil for the others.

A Wren masterpiece, the library, Trinity College

College libraries tend to remain relatively unvisited – and not always just by tourists – but both Oxford and Cambridge contain stunning buildings. Oxford has the upper library of Merton College, with its medieval fittings and chained books. Cambridge has its Wren library.

In any library the books are the main subject of contemplation, and this is true even in this building, which is one of Wren's finest – baroque with the calmness of classicism, a 150 foot first-floor saloon above an arcaded loggia open to Neville Quad. When I visited the books displayed in the eight public showcases included Shakespeare's First Folio but, with due deference to the Bard, I have to say the crowning glory was a copy of Hartmann Schedel's *Nürnberg Chronicle* of 1493, open at a double-page spread of a woodcut of Venice in dew-drenched colours.

With such treasures, Wren had to create a treasurable casket, and he didn't have to look far for an answer: Grinling Gibbons, the foremost wood carver of Europe, was his ready collaborator. At each end of the library Gibbons provided elaborately carved screens; Wren himself designed bookcases running along the walls but with every second one at right angles, pushing into the library's central space and forming cubicles down each side –

a commonplace today, but Wren at Trinity was the first to adopt this approach. On the ends of the bookcases Gibbons carved coats of arms decked with exquisitely delicate fruit and flowers and ears of corn, each one slightly different from the next.

The college, meanwhile, had been collecting marble busts by Louis-François Roubiliac (*c.*1705–62) of famous alumni and fellows of the college: Newton, Francis Bacon, the famous classicist and master of the college, Richard Bentley and Edward Coke, great jurist and ancestor of the Leicesters of Holkham Hall. In time the decision was made to collect the various busts, which had been freely distributed around the college, and display them together in the library. Roubiliac was a French Huguenot who came to England in his mid-twenties and stayed, producing some of the greatest art and certainly the greatest sculptures of his time on either side of the Channel. At Trinity they stand on plinths below the Gibbons carvings: sensitive, brilliantly characterised, virtuoso portraits.

Rejected by the Tate, Gaudier-Brzeska at Kettle's Yard

The Fitzwilliam may be Cambridge's most famous museum and art gallery, but Kettle's Yard, hidden away near Castle Hill, is its most inviting. It was founded by H.S. Ede, who had been a curator at the Tate Gallery but who moved to Cambridge and with his wife Helen renovated Kettle's Yard, a group of four crumbling cottages, and installed their collection of paintings and sculpture. They opened it in the afternoons to undergraduates who were welcome to come and look at the art or just take a book off the shelves and sit and read. The university has built a lovely, light extension, which houses part of the permanent collection and a gallery for temporary shows, but the house is as it was.

The Red Stone Dancer by the avant garde sculptor Henri Gaudier-Brzeska. He died in action in the First World War, aged 23, when his brilliant career had reached a climax of modernist invention. This cast (the original is in the Tate Britain) is set in the modernist extension to the house at Kettle's Yard, designed by Leslie Martin

Visitors still have to knock on the door to be admitted; and as always, they can park themselves in the armchairs ('but please do so gently and without moving them, as some are over 300 years old') or simply wander among the works of art: a Ben Nicholson painting at ankle height between washbasin and toilet bowl, a small, abstract Prometheus, cast in cement, by Brancusi on the lid of Helen's Bechstein grand, ethereal watercolours by the 20th-century poet and artist David Jones, a little oil by Miró, a row of seascapes by Alfred Wallis – one of more than a hundred, many of which dropped through the letterbox in the post from St Ives.

While at the Tate Jim Ede (as he was always known) had found himself with work which came to the nation from the English-domiciled French sculptor Henri Gaudier-Brzeska, who had been killed during the First World War. The nation, however, didn't want it, and Ede was able to acquire for a mere £60 nineteen sculptures, a few oils and pastels, more than 1,500 drawings and an archive of letters gathering dust. Among them is *The Red Stone Dancer*, the piece that was the start of the brilliant sequence of modern sculptures that Gaudier-Brzeska created towards the end of his short life (he died when he was only twenty-three). It is actually a bronze cast of the red Mansfield stone carving picked up initially by the Contemporary Arts Society. Gaudier was at the vanguard of a revival in carving and a cement cast of a stone carving ought not to work, but it does. Various influences are at work here, but Gaudier-Brzeska successfully brings them all together in a dynamic nude that bears a relief triangle on its head, an incised circle for one nipple and a square for the other.

Cambridge's contribution to the English language, Hobson's conduit, Trumpington Road

Two deep runnels on either side of Trumpington Street have been a feature of life in Cambridge since 1614; or, for cyclists and drivers who have fetched up in one of these open stone channels, an unnecessary and embarrassing encumbrance to their lawful progress. Things could be worse, because until about 1794 the conduit had run down the middle of the road. This was the means by which Cambridge was supplied with fresh water from the spring in Great Shelford known as Nine Wells.

A print of 1840 shows a pretty hexagonal structure on Market Hill. It was a drinking fountain at the terminus of the conduit that at the beginning of the 17th century was spanking new and up to date, as much classical as Jacobean, with a shallow, shell-topped niche on each façade, an entablature with fretted ornament and the royal arms, added at a cost of £7 in 1660 at the Restoration of Charles II, and a faintly onion-shaped cupola capped with a golden pineapple. Stall holders probably already regarded it as a quaint encumbrance; at any rate, five years later it was moved a mile from the town centre to the verge of Trumpington Road opposite Scroope Terrace, where it stands as an ornament and advertisement for charms to come. As for Thomas Hobson, he had grown physically and in fortune on his business of carrying letters between Cambridge and London, gave generously to the town and probably contributed cash for the conduit's construction. When they were not needed for his business, he rented out his horses on a rota basis so that the best ones would not be over used. Dons and students had to take whatever horse was next in line, hence the phrase, apparently coined by John Milton, 'Hobson's choice'. One thing is sure:

perhaps because of his wealth and girth, Hobson was not altogether popular with Milton, who, after the carrier's death, jeered at him in verse:

> Here lies old Hobson. Death hath broke his
> girt,
> And here, alas! hath laid him in the dirt;
> Or else, the ways being foul, twenty to one
> He's here stuck in a slough, and overthrown.

David Mellor's well of living waters, Cambridge University Botanic Garden, Trumpington Road

At the centre of a small pond deep inside the Botanic Garden is 'a well of living waters', in the biblical phrase, a fountain designed by David Mellor (b.1930), purveyor of cutlery to British embassies abroad. It has been there more or less unremarked except by lunchtime picnickers since 1968, the year after he had delivered a new square pillar box to the post office and the year before he designed disposable white plastic cutlery to be stamped out by the million. He designed the traffic lights in use now, a hacksaw frame, bus shelters (we have 140,000 of them), litter bins and, in 1953 when he was still a student, his range of Pride cutlery, still in production and a modern design classic. So this son of a Sheffield toolmaker is certainly versatile, but no matter how useful the objects he makes, most of them just happen to be beautiful as well.

The Botanic Garden job followed his completion of a set of silver candlesticks for the fellows' dining table at Darwin College. The garden needed a fountain, so Jack Goodison, the college fellow who commissioned Mellor, recommended him to the governing body of the garden. Mellor made the maquette for it in plywood and left it standing in the garden of his house in Sheffield for a season while he contemplated it. Satisfied, he had the fountain cast in metal, seven stems opening out into seven circular dishes like lotus pads. It stands in a round pond, four of the lotus-pads at the lowest level, then two, then one set high at the centre. I saw it when the garden was wrapped in freezing fog and small ice floes covered the pond, but the short foaming jets of water continued to play, falling back on themselves, spilling out of the lotus pads in a veil; a magically misty scene.

Canvey Island
ESSEX

A modernist café, on the Western Esplanade

Canvey Island is separated from the mainland merely by a narrow tidal mudflat creek, but it might as well be an ocean. At first glance, and not only if the glance happens to take in the seaside funfair down at the Western Esplanade, Canvey Island seems stuck in the 1940s. But it is different in other ways, too, different in its population's unerring attraction to 'independent' politics, so it elects a majority of 'independent' councillors and has a UKIP Member of Parliament. Above all, it is different for the local commitment to all things Canvey, from the unremarkable football club to the Canvey Island pub rock band Dr Feelgood, which local fans insist is better than the Stones. There's even a hit song called *Canvey Island* by British Sea Power, a rock band that's not from the island:

> *On Canvey Island, 1953,*
> *Many lives were lost*
> *With the records of the football team*

(a laconic reference to the flood that killed fifty-nine islanders that doesn't seem quite the same without music).

Almost alongside the funfair is the most modern thing about the island, Dr Feelgood notwithstanding: the Labworth café. It is the only architectural work of the engineer Ove Arup (1895–1988; see Kingsgate Bridge, Durham City, Northeast). He built it in 1932–3 when he was a young man working for a firm not his own. These were the optimistic days when architects believed that the purity of the modern movement could save the world and when Canvey islanders believed they could make it as a seaside resort. The café sits upon a massive sea wall, a two-storey, circular, concrete and glass drum with two single-storey wings supporting a terrace on top and a shelter within, all painted white. Sadly, the ground floor was shuttered with steel on my visit. It must have been the weather. But the restaurant and beach bistro (as it is now known) is esteemed by the locals. It's an ideal building for an imperfect world, though Arup had the last word as well as the first, deploring the cheap materials used in its construction.

Colchester
ESSEX

Colchester is both the oldest and the newest of towns, one good and the other, oh dear, not so good. The invading Romans knew it as Camulodunum, the ancient capital where the British kings surrendered to Claudius in AD 43, and, not twenty years later, in AD 61, where the ferocious Boudicca, queen of the Iceni tribe, who had been flogged and seen the Romans rape her two daughters, led the disaffected and overtaxed British to a bloody siege and sacking of Colchester. To this day the signs of devastating fire mark the foundations of the last redoubt of the Romans, the Temple of Claudius, which lie beneath the Norman keep (now Colchester Museum). Afterwards Rome rebuilt

Colchester, and there are still stretches of the Roman wall and the ruined arch of the Balkerne Gateway on Balkerne Lane, the exit for the main road to the upstart city of Londinium. Boudicca never went away: she's there today as a statue ensconced among others on the 162 feet tall tower of the showy Edwardian town hall in the High Street.

After the wilderness years of the Nordic invasions Colchester became a great Norman citadel, but the Civil War of 1642–51 tore the heart out of the town, and today all signposts lead to shopping centre car parks. It takes an effort of will for the stranger to drive out of these traffic sewers and into the town's byways. The effort is worth it.

On the perimeters of, roughly, a square around the old centre now so heavily devoted to mass-market retail the massive Norman castle keep lies north of the High Street and a few paces further to the east (as always, the town is better explored on foot) is the Minories, a good 18th-century house, now an art gallery. Down Queen Street and into Botolph Street are the Roman brick ruins of England's first Augustinian priory, St Botolph's, and over the road off Southway is the last remaining building of St John's Abbey, the intact 15th-century northern gateway. But Colchester is not a town of fragments. The texture of the centuries is there in whole streets of buildings of different periods and, in the southern outskirts on a stream that feeds the River Colne, the remarkable Bourne Mill in Bourne Road, a 16th-century fishing lodge that was converted at some point into a watermill.

The remnants of a parliamentary siege, St John's Gate

When Sir Charles Lucas marched into the walled town of Colchester in 1648 as one of the commanders of 3,000 royalist troops,

with General Fairfax and a parliamentary force in pursuit, he probably saw it as a great opportunity for revenge. He had grown up in Colchester, at the family home of St John's Abbey on a green hillside above the town centre. The Lucas family had owned the abbey since Henry VIII disposed of it after the dissolution of monasteries, but in 1642 the townspeople had turned on his older brother, Sir John Lucas, a royalist and high churchman, who fled into town and was jailed by the mayor for his own protection while the Puritan mob ransacked St John's. Now, six years later, a Lucas was back, but soon found himself besieged. Ten weeks later, in a harrowing ten-week siege of Colchester, instead of tasting revenge, Sir Charles saw the abbey destroyed and himself before Fairfax, who ordered his execution by firing squad.

All that remains of the green hill is a large triangle of grass, St John's Green, among a maze of suburban streets. Remarkably, the 15th-century abbey gatehouse survives pretty well intact to the south of the green – Royal Engineers repaired the siege damage in the 19th century and it is now the entrance to a club for army officers of the Colchester garrison. The gatehouse with tall, showy crocketed pinnacles is at the top of an incline above the green. There is a single arch with a pretty canopied niche above, empty, and Gothic decoration picked out in freestone outlines on the showy knapped flint flushwork glittering in the daylight. Inside the gateway is a lierne vault, star shaped, with excellent grotesque corbels badly in need of a clean. The floor, too, is littered with drinks cans and discarded wrappers. As any sergeant-major would observe, someone needs to get a grip.

This monument in Colchester Castle Museum to Marcus Favonius Facilis shows the lightweight fighting dress of a centurion with the crack XXth Legion which came to Britain with Claudius in AD 43. Marcus was alive in about the year 100 and is presumed to have died in Camulodunum (modern Colchester)

Monument to a centurion installed by his freedmen, Castle Museum

To most people Colchester is a direction sign on the A12, not the first place for a long weekend or even a wet away-day. And yet its town centre, though raddled, is still handsome: there are extensive remains from the time when the Romans captured it from the Britons and set it up as one of the most important cities of the empire, and it has a huge castle keep, bigger than the White Tower, the biggest, in fact, in Europe, built by William the Conqueror. This bastion is now the Castle Museum, and it contains a

larger collection of objects from a single Roman site than even the British Museum. Among them is the remarkable sculptured monument to Marcus Favonius Facilis, a centurion of the crack XXth Legion.

Marcus Favonius protects his chest with a cuirass with wide shoulder straps meeting a broad, finely figured band just above the waist, and his dagger belt slung below that. His lower legs are covered by greaves, and he carries his sword on the left from a strap hung from his right shoulder with a toga slung over the left. In his right hand he carries a vine branch, the *vitis*, like a modern British officer's swagger stick, a mark of his office. His hair is styled in a pudding-basin cut. He is standing easy, his weight carried on his right leg, his left slightly bent at the knee, the very type of the naturalism of the Gothic and Renaissance periods. The sculptor probably came with the legions from Gaul; certainly if he also carved the legend beneath telling us the centurion's name, his parentage and that the stele was set up by his freedmen, Verecundus and Novicius, since letter carving of this disciplined fluidity can have been executed only by a craftsman deeply immersed in the culture of the empire: the first impression is of spaciousness, and then of letters full and commanding, serifs just a light flick, a swaggering R with a curl to the tail, letters occasionally intersecting, a small letter u (v in Roman practice) tucked inside a C. This is complete maturity of expression and lovely to behold.

Ely
CAMBRIDGESHIRE

The hole in the heart of history, Ely Stained Glass Museum

Ely Cathedral is a momentous vision across the fens and utterly singular in Gothic architecture for the huge, central octagon with a lantern rising through it surrounded by pinnacles. The Norman nave, too, is a stirring sight, and beyond that to the north of the church is the biggest lady chapel with the widest vault (45 feet) in England. What the cathedral does not have is any half-decent stained glass, so it has made up for this by opening the only stained glass museum in the country, high up in the southern triforium. It doesn't get much better than the opening first exhibits, two stupendous, 13th-century, deep dyed blue and red roundels of the martyrdom of St Vincent, bought privately from France when church glass was going cheap during the Revolution. There is even medieval secular glass, like the lovely 15th-century roundel of Reynard the Fox, painted on cheap white glass, which could be manufactured in England, and, from Ely Cathedral itself, a peasant of the 1340s, the time of the Black Death, so possibly unique (peasants rarely appeared in art of the period). Two of the most beautiful windows constitute a 14th-century Annunciation of infinite grace; but the annunciatory figure of Gabriel is actually a complete 19th-century replacement by Hardman & Co, the firm Pugin persuaded to take up the manufacture of stained glass. What a triumph of sensitivity; how rare in Victorian ecclesiastical interventions.

The hole in the heart of the museum is precisely the hole in the heart of the craft in England, from the Reformation for 300 years until a few 19th-century pioneers like Hardman rediscovered the secrets of the medieval glassmakers. The gap was filled not by stained glass but by enamelled glass, which can be good (as at Northill, see West and East Midlands). There's a token showing of 20th-century stained glass, but that's because the best is still in the buildings for which it was commissioned, and it is our good luck that so much good medieval glass survives in the churches where it belongs, even though, under Henry VIII's malign policies, slash and burn was the order of the day.

Framlingham
SUFFOLK

The soldier poet who introduced the sonnet to England, in the Church of St Michael

Henry Howard, Earl of Surrey, carved in alabaster, lies here in the little town below the great family castle of Framlingham. He is wrapped in a scarlet gown trimmed with ermine, his head on a blue cushion trimmed with gold and with big gold tassels, at his feet is a little golden lion. Commander of Henry VIII's armed forces, intemperately proud courtier, duellist, hell-raiser and poet, he introduced the sonnet form to England and fell foul of the king for applying to quarter the arms of Edward the Confessor with his own. (He was entitled to do so, but to Henry it implied a greater claim to the throne of England than his own.) At his trial for treason his father testified against him and so did his sister, and on 17 January 1547 he fell to the headsman's axe at the Tower of London. He was twenty-nine or thirty and was only the latest of his ill-fated family in this dangerous reign to die at the block. His grandfather Edward Stafford was executed for treason in 1521; in 1536 Howard had attended the trial of his cousin Ann Boleyn and had witnessed the execution of another royal cousin, Katherine Howard, in 1542.

He was buried at All Hallows, Barking, and lay there until 1614, when his son brought his remains home to the 14th-century parish church at Framlingham with its fine timber coved ceiling devised to disguise the hammerbeams. Here, quite unusually, aisles had been added to the chancel to take the

Henry Howard, Earl of Surrey, commander of Henry VIII's armed forces, and poet who introduced the sonnet to England, fell from favour and was beheaded in 1547. He is shown here in painted alabaster effigy in the church of St Michael, Framlingham, where his son had him reburied in 1614

Howard tombs. Henry Howard was laid to rest alongside his wife Frances de Vere, in their glorious Jacobean tomb, a throwback to his own century. There are better tombs in this church – one by the great 18th-century master Roubiliac, another by the Suffolk sculptor Francis Grigs – but nothing quite as triumphantly garish, nothing, in fact, as Tudor. Though the family arms on the tomb chest are not crossed with the Confessor's, in his pomp Howard had been appointed Knight of the Garter, and his armorial bearings are encircled with the Garter motto, *Honi soit qui mal y pense* ('Evil be to him who evil thinks').

Great Warley
ESSEX

The man who hated art nouveau, in St Mary the Virgin

Not just the sober establishment but also the cautiously avant-garde among British artists who straddled the 19th and 20th centuries, men like the architect Charles Voysey, condemned art nouveau for its perceived excesses. And none execrated it more than William Reynolds-Stephens (1862–1943), who regarded himself, like Voysey, as a proud practitioner of the Arts and Crafts movement. He even yoked 'Reynolds hyphen'

William Reynolds-Stephens embellished the interior of St Mary the Virgin, Great Warley, with bronze, green Cipollino marble, shell, walnut, silver and pewter, cornelian and gold and copper. Behind the silver Christ is an apse faced in bands of aluminium leaf

to his plain Stephens in honour of the great Sir Joshua; all he then needed to embellish the name was a knighthood, which in due course he received. Today, the joke is on him: his greatest work, the interior of the new Church of St Mary the Virgin (new in 1904), is regarded as a prime example of art nouveau.

Reynolds-Stephens was a painter who could design furniture, picture frames, fireplaces, dishes, exotic electroliers for light bulbs, statues and statuettes, and, when called upon, the whole panoply of church fittings. He could do it all, and at Great Warley he did. He restricted painting to a few small items: why bother with paint when he could use bronze and brass, several kinds of marble, shell, walnut, coloured glass, silver,

marquetry, pewter, cornelian, copper and gold? Silver bands of aluminium leaf bind the barrel vaulted ceiling and clad the apse roof, which is embossed with vines bearing bunches of deep pink grapes above the walls of green Cipollino marble and a silver Christ at the centre of the reredos raising his hand in blessing.

The church's architect was Charles Harrison Townsend, who started on the plans just as he finished the Whitechapel Art Gallery and the Horniman Museum, both of 1902, both masterpieces whose achievement he never got near again. But St Mary is a sweet little church on a sweet little hill in a sweet little garden, caught in the angle between the M25 and the A127 Southend arterial road, somehow surviving the twin assaults from traffic and creating, behind Townsend's lich-gate carved by Eric Gill, a sense of peace that Reynolds-Stephens within exuberantly dispels. It's not a question of good or bad taste. The sheer proliferation of ornament defies taste to do its worst: the beaten and embossed copper organ casing, the chancel screen supported on elegant rose trees crowned with a heart-shaped arrangement of blooms, the crowns of thorns surrounding more roses, the angels with wings like arched bows inclining their heads before a crucifix inscribed with the word 'Love' and rising from a heart. Who could resist it, or having tried and failed to resist, who could fail to give it best?

Harwich
ESSEX

Cinema's dawning age at the Electric Palace, King's Quay Street

The year 1911 saw Hollywood open its first motion picture studio, and in that year a travelling showman in East Anglia called Charles Thurston opened the Electric Palace Cinema in Harwich. It was among the first cinemas in England and is one of the few still showing films. It may also be the truest to its original design and decor, including the original ticket kiosk and projection room, though not the original projector. Thurston began by screening short films in marquees on village greens or in village halls, mixed up with vaudeville. Harwich's lucky citizens saw their first movie in a Salvation Army citadel in 1906. In 1910 the government passed the cinematograph act, banning the highly inflammable nitrate-based film in marquees, so Thurston paid a twenty-six-year-old Ipswich architect, Harold Ridley Hooper, to build the Electric Palace in Harwich. It cost £1,500, was eighteen weeks in the building and opened on 29 November 1911 with a new

American release called *The Battle of Trafalgar and the Death of Nelson*, directed by one J. Searle Dorley with Willis Secord as Nelson.

The ornamental façade, painted white with 'Electric Palace' picked out in gold, looks like a fairground booth, with carved swags of fruit either side of a laurel wreath over the wide entrance and a decorated semicircular pediment above that. Low wings each side of the entrance have wooden art nouveau balustrades. The medium-sized auditorium is barrel vaulted and nicely restrained with rectangular wall panels in decorative plaster frames.

Today, the Electric is run with a small, reinvested profit by volunteers as a community cinema showing newish releases from Thursday to Sunday. But a photograph of 1912 shows the doorman, projectionist, pageboy, cashier and engineer outside the cinema with the manager, Frederick Benton, who also played the violin, and Mrs Benton, the pianist. I don't think that happens now.

Holkham
NORFOLK

A voice from the past, at Holkham House

Sitting on an estate of 25,000 acres at high water and 26,000 at low tide, as the present Lord Leicester puts it, Holkham's is 'perhaps the most dramatic entrance hall in all England'. 'Perhaps' suggests an unnecessary intrusion of modesty into the earl's handsome new guidebook. It is clad in pink-veined Derbyshire alabaster, although it is called the marble hall, perhaps for the ancient sculpture set in niches that forms a prelude to the sculpture in the gallery above, stuff that not many people pause over because the paintings in the state rooms are rightly famous, particularly those by Rubens, Van Dyck and Gainsborough. Anyway, why should we respond to rows of ancient marbles of doubtful or frankly unknown provenance, mostly copies of even older carvings now lost, some restored with the head of one sculpture spatchcocked on to the torso of another? It's not easy, but it's worth the effort.

Thomas Coke, 1st Earl of Leicester, was responsible for Holkham with the architect William Kent, whom Coke met on the grand tour of Italy, which he undertook in 1712 at the age of fifteen. He returned to Norfolk six years later determined to build a palace fit for the crate-loads of art he had acquired on the continent: the authorised and dubiously authorised pillage even swept up sections of the marble pavements from Hadrian's villa at Tivoli, which have been installed at Holkham as table tops. And despite the elegance of the rooms and the old master paintings, the keynote is the sculpture: a collection of mostly 1st- to 3rd-century Roman marbles. After the marble hall, busts and full figures appear throughout the house in wall niches and alcoves, on pedestals, in the gaps of broken pediments above the doors and, supremely, in the statue gallery and its two apses, known here as tribunes.

Among these voices is the marmoreal stillness of the bust of the historian Thucydides, a Roman version of a Greek original. The pursed lips, the frown, the lined brow, the level gaze, the strong nose, the head set on the powerful column of a neck and broad chest make this one of the most remarkable antique portraits, a representation of the powerful intellect of the historian of the Peloponnesian Wars between Sparta and Athens. Not much in modern sculpture matches the concentrated power of observation in this ancient work.

Ipswich
SUFFOLK

Constable in his father's house, in Christchurch Mansion and Art Gallery

'I fancy I see Gainsborough in every hedge and hollow tree,' said John Constable (1776–1837) of his native patch of Suffolk. The two were born within 10 miles of each other, though Gainsborough was nearly fifty and working in London when Constable was born. Gainsborough had worked in Ipswich before deciding he was ready to take on high society, and it was his naturalistic landscapes of the Sudbury and Ipswich period that Constable naturally preferred. Constable himself knew Ipswich through his friendship with the Cobbold brewing family, so it is just that the Ipswich gallery, housed in a 16th-century mansion built on the site of an Augustinian priory, owns fine collections of the work of both men (for Gainsborough see also, especially, Sudbury, below, and Bath, Southwest).

These two neat little scenes, *Golding Constable's Flower Garden* and *Golding Constable's Kitchen Garden*, painted from an upstairs window in Constable's father's home in East Bergholt, hardly look revolutionary. But they are. The art collector Sir George Beaumont, whose mother lived in Dedham, met Constable in 1795 and gave him all sorts of support and encouragement, but he never bought a single Constable painting because Constable's paintings of nature were so disruptively dissimilar to Beaumont's favourite possession, Claude Lorraine's suavely classical 18th-century sylvan scene *Landscape with Hagar and the Angel* (now in the National Gallery). Even so, Constable studied the painting and from his knowledge of its structure composed one of his early, fresh English views of Dedham Vale (now in the Victoria & Albert Museum, London).

The shadows falling over Golding Constable's flower garden, painted by John Constable from an upstairs room of the family house in East Bergholt, owe something to the scene, but probably also to circumstance: it was summer 1815 and his mother had just died; his father, Golding, was mortally ill. The painting is in the Constable collection at Christchurch Mansion and Art Gallery in Ipswich

There was nothing of the ideal about Constable, who said he saw painting as a branch of natural science.

His father owned Flatford Mill on the River Stour below East Bergholt and built the grand new family house in the village. Constable painted the garden scenes as maps of a contented middle-class boyhood, and beyond the gardens were the fields among which he grew up. He had written about them to Maria Bicknell, his wife to be: 'I can hardly tell you what I feel at the sight from the windows where I am now writing of the fields in which we have so often walked.' Maria's father was threatening to disinherit Maria if she married this young painter with no prospects who was living off his father and pursuing the lowest form of art, landscape painting.

When Constable sat down to paint the flower garden, in July 1815, his mother, who had laid it out, had recently died. That autumn, when he painted the kitchen garden with long evening shadows falling over it, his father was unwell and within months of his death. And Maria and John were planning to marry without her father's consent. Some commentators see in these paintings a poignant sense of one blissful phase of rural life ending and another of struggle in London beginning. No doubt they are right. The evidence of his own words is that he loved these two scenes, but the evidence of our eyes is that the paintings of them were studies of the matter-of-factness of the manmade rural scene raised to the level of genius.

What makes them so unusual for Constable is their quietness. In the same gallery is a sketch he made a few months later, smaller than a painter's palette, of Willy Lott's house with the flashing stream of the Stour reflecting the thick cumulus overhead, vividly sketched with all the controlled excitement of a painter drunk on his skill and

perception and the tightrope act of balancing his emotional impression with his retinal response.

King's Lynn
NORFOLK

The King John Cup in the Trinity Guild

It was Bishop's Lynn until Henry VIII gave it a charter; but bishop's or king's, it was a town of great and growing prosperity from the Middle Ages until the 18th century. If you skirt the tacky High Street, the evidence is there in the two squares, Tuesday Market and Saturday Market, in the Hanseatic warehouse, the famous and beautiful Customs House of 1683 on the quay, the noble town houses of rich merchants and the chequered stone and flint Trinity Guild of 1421, which is also the town hall. Incorporated into this is the gaol of 1784. The town charges visitors to see the cells at the rear but allows them to look at the King's Lynn regalia in a front room free; perhaps on the basis that anything free can't be worth the price, nobody was looking at the regalia while I was there but parties of visitors streamed in to see the cells. What they were missing among the fine pieces in the free show was a priceless and beautiful loving cup, the earliest of its kind in England (*c.*1340) and one of only two in the world (the other is in Milan).

The cup is of silver gilt with more than two dozen panels enamelled in purple, green and blue with courtly scenes of elegant lords and ladies, mostly ladies, hunting and hawking. A 16th-century town hall document calls it

King John's Cup of silver gilt with enamelled panels was made in about 1340, so it isn't old enough to have been, as legend claims, the king's. It is, though, the oldest cup of its sort in England, in impeccable condition, and is part of King's Lynn's regalia

King John's Cup, and the myth grew up that it was the only item of treasure rescued when King John's baggage train was lost in the Wash after a royal visit to the town. Intriguingly, the king was one of the founders of the Trinity Guild, but the unromantic truth is that the costume historian Stella Newton has shown conclusively that the hairstyles and dress of the women on the cup were haute couture in about 1340, more than 120 years after the king's death.

It is extraordinary that the cup should have survived at all, let alone in pristine condition (though the enamelling has been renovated several times through the centuries). It stands on a five-cusped base with a long stem and rises to a tall gold spike on the lid embellished and filled out with oak leaves; on the bowl two rows of figures move against a green field splashed with gold stars representing flowers; moulded gold ribs and sparkling gold cresting around the lid catch and throw back the light. The cup may be Flemish, though expert opinion is tending towards supporting an English origin; either way it is a dream of the life of chivalry created in the years before the Black Death, after which nothing of its sort would be possible until the morning of a new century.

Landbeach
CAMBRIDGESHIRE

A lovely Dutch angel lectern with a lost pedigree, Church of All Saints

The angel looks as though it has just flown down from the rafters and alighted on a pedestal; a renegade angel absconding from his shield-bearing duties with the host of angels among the tie-beams. It's a backpacking Puck of an angel with a mop of tousled hair, dancing legs, a robe tied lightly at the waist, V-necked, sleeves rolled above the elbow, arms held wide apart with palms

upwards, accepting applause and as though about to declaim from *The Tempest*:

Over park, over pale,
Through flood, through fire,
I do wander everywhere,
Swifter than the moon's sphere.

Flying would have been the only way to keep feet dry in this one-street village with its 14th-century church and not much more in the wide, flat wetlands a few miles north of Cambridge off the road to Ely.

The fustian fact is that Landbeach's angel is carved from limewood and is supported on a pretty limewood pedestal. The backpack is a book rest. It is presumed to be Dutch of the first half of the 17th century, and it is very much in the style of Netherlands ecclesiastical furnishing; quite like Arnold Quellin's marble angels at Burnham-on-Sea (see Southwest), though different enough not to be by him. Landbeach's angel arrived from an antique shop in York in 1882. That is all we know of its history.

Lavenham
SUFFOLK

The infinite variety of the Spring parclose screen, in the Church of St Peter and St Paul

Suffolk grew wealthy on wool, and even after the trade declined its towns survived largely unscathed to become points of pilgrimage for modern tourists. Visitors to Lavenham pour in for the quaint buildings in fine streets. Fewer make their way to the church,

This lively, backpacking limewood angel is most likely by a 17th-century Dutch artist, though the only history we know of it is that Landbeach parish church acquired it from a York antique shop in 1882. The backpack, of course, is the book rest of a lectern

though town and church grew up together in the 15th century, and the church is the finest in the county, not for any one thing, not for the tremendous tower, nor for the glorious nave arcades by John Wastell (architect of the great central tower, Bell Harry, at Canterbury Cathedral), nor for the soaring tower arch or great south porch contributed by John de Vere, 13th Earl of Oxford and lord of the manor, but for all these together. I don't know who first applied the tag 'businessman's Gothic' to the Perpendicular style of church architecture, but it's easy to see what is meant: not just that the successful manufacturers and entrepreneurs of the 15th century paid for it, but also because of the style: clear, sharp outlines, no-nonsense window tracery and churches as full of light as Kew Garden's palm house. True, it can appear hard, but that is usually because the religious extremists stripped out and destroyed the fittings. Suffolk, for example, was the favourite stamping ground of William Dowsing, the most notorious of the licensed thugs of the Reformation. Yet somehow in St Peter and St Paul there remains not just the rood screen but two chantry chapels enclosed within carved wooden screens to remind us that no matter how businesslike these businessmen were, they spent lavishly on the cure of their souls, paying for a priest to pray for them daily for eternity. They rendered unto themselves the comfortable big houses of Lavenham, and they rendered unto God all the beauty they could command.

The east end of the south aisle contains the first of the wooden screens, or parcloses, intended for the repose of the souls of Thomas Spourne, manufacturer of blue broadcloth, and his wife, but the Reformation caught up with them and they seem never to have been buried here. Instead, since 1908 it has contained the tomb of their contemporary John Ponder (d.1520), moved from the churchyard to prevent further deterioration, though the shields on the parclose are carved with dolphins, the Spourne device. Much more exotic is the parclose in the north aisle opposite, enclosing the tombs of Thomas Spring and his wife, from the most prominent of Lavenham families apart from the De Veres. Dowsing ripped out the brass effigies, but the screen survived, so it can only be that the church hid it. The intricately carved detail springing from slender clasping columns spreads across the top of the dado like a garden arbour; above that are two light round arches with, doing the duty of tracery, more intricately delicate plant-like forms harbouring birds and beasts beneath a parapet; altogether an earthly imitation of the holy city. So much does the church love it now that it is filled with the rubble of builders and electricians.

Little Gidding

CAMBRIDGESHIRE

An inspiration to T.S. Eliot, the Church of St John

It's a scatter of three or four houses and the tiny church at the dead end of a narrow lane, 'you leave the rough road/And turn behind the pigsty to the dull façade', as T.S. Eliot puts it in 'Little Gidding', the final poem of *Four Quartets*.

> *There are other places*
> *Which also are a world's end …*
> *But this is the nearest, in place and time,*
> *Now and in England.*

In the tiny settlement of Little Gidding today they put Eliot almost on a footing with the founder of their first Christian community, Nicholas Ferrar (1593–1637). Ferrar was a merchant, a privy councillor and an MP, whose business in Virginian tobacco

foundered and who gave up politics and business to found the community of around forty souls: his mother, his brother, his sister and her extended family, himself as newly ordained chaplain.

On the lintel of the 'dull façade' is carved: 'This is none other but the house of God & the gate of heaven.' It is easy to see why Eliot, whose ancestor, the Calvinist Andrew Eliot, left East Coker in Somerset in the 17th century as one of the Pilgrim Fathers, should be drawn by Ferrar, descendant of a Protestant martyr. Ferrar was High Church, and so was Eliot, but the style of life of Ferrar's people was humble, devoted to prayer and readings several times a day and through the night, and to simple labour, bookbinding, embroidery and husbandry. Even the style of the little church, just nave and chancel, seems Puritan, Quakerish almost, with wooden panelling and sturdy, broad-backed, handsome seating facing inwards along the length of the nave and chancel, a tunnel vaulted ceiling (actually polygonal; easier to fashion), and a brass reredos of about 1625, when the original church was built, inscribed with the Lord's Prayer, the Apostles' Creed and the Ten Commandments. When Eliot turned his back to the inscription over the west door all he would have seen would have been rolling fields and meadows. Apart from occasional cars on the road below the horizon, the view is much the same today – and it can't be very different from the prospect that would have greeted Ferrar.

Some of this is guesswork because the Cromwellians came to the church in 1646 and knocked it about a bit. They abhorred it for the fact that Ferrar's followers preferred prayer and readings to sermons and, no doubt, because they placed the altar between nave and chancel instead of at the east end of the church. Ferrar was dead by this time, but in 1714 the community restored the ruinous

The words on the lintel of the unpretentious Little Gidding church say, 'This is none other but the house of God & the gate of heaven'. It is the place that inspired the culminating poem of T.S. Eliot's Four Quartets

old church, rebuilding it with its own rubble in brick with a baroque stone façade. Now it has a lovely brass chandelier, a brass eagle lectern of a pattern manufactured in Norwich in the 18th century and to be seen as far abroad as Italy, and six brass sconces, three on each side of the chancel, each holding five candles at the end of looping tendrils positioned as though in a slow, stately dance. The sconces, the loveliest things in the church, are not 17th but early 20th century, the work of W.A. Lee: the Arts and Crafts movement perfectly dovetailed with the quiet pietism of the church.

Long Melford
SUFFOLK

14th-century alabaster Adoration of the Magi, in the Church of the Holy Trinity

One of the great churches of England, built in the 1480s with a big nave and a sumptuous lady chapel on the proceeds of the wool trade, Holy Trinity, Long Melford, had more to lose at the Reformation than most, and sure enough lost it. It had at least two painted altarpieces, possibly Flemish, tabernacles holding statues of Christ, the Virgin and saints, chalices, reliquaries, a monstrance, crosses, candlesticks, censers and rich vestments. All of this went, a story repeated across the country, parish by parish. Somehow, the famous north aisle wall of glass that is practically a portrait gallery of the wealthy local families who built Holy Trinity escaped destruction because it was originally in the clerestory, too high up to bother with and as much secular as religious.

Many churches hid their treasures. Carvings, typically, would be buried in the floors of churches, sometimes flat side up and exposed as a step or a paving slab. In the 18th century a mid-14th-century alabaster carving of the Adoration of the Magi that could have been part of an altarpiece turned up buried under the chancel floor of Long Melford. This beautiful piece has been reset in the north aisle wall. Mary, a much bigger figure than the others, reclines, her legs stretched out along a couch, her body propped up against cushions held by a female attendant unknown to the gospels. The infant Christ stands magisterially in her lap, prefiguring both the future boy preacher in the temple and a king meeting kings. The three Magi queue on the right, proffering their gifts of frankincense, gold and myrrh. The first in line doffs his crown to the boy, who lays his arm, as of right, across the chalice of incense. Joseph is on the right, perching on a bench and leaning wearily on a stick. A sweet pair of oxen poke their heads out from beneath Mary's couch. The rhythmic pulse of the heads spaced across the surface of this slab of stone and the flow of the garments is more linear than sculptural, a recurring characteristic of English art that

William Blake described as 'the bounding line and its infinite inflections and movements'.

Milden
SUFFOLK

A 17th-century English gentleman commemorated in the church of St Peter

The parish above the Brett valley has not much more than a hundred inhabitants and the state of the church suggests that no one who has ever lived there had riches. Already in 1852 *The British Gazetteer, Political, Commercial, Ecclesiastical, and Historical* was reporting: 'The church is a Norman structure, in a very dilapidated condition.' It is simply a nave and chancel; no aisles, no tower (that was knocked down in 1827 because no one could afford to repair it), paint and plaster peeling from the walls, 17th-century pulpit, and an air of rustic sanctity. Its most splendid single object is the recumbent effigy of Sir James Allington, a parishioner who died in 1626.

Little is known of Sir James, there is no name for the sculptor, and the inscription is indecipherable to the naked eye (but it is beautifully framed by fruit, acorns and leaves). The effigy has lost both feet, and one arm has been smashed at the elbow to allow it to be shoved unceremoniously as close to the wall as possible; closer, in fact. And it lies on a crude, later stone plinth. Yet this is a work of high sensitivity. As always, when status is top of the list to be celebrated, the artist has treated the dead man's costume in detail. Sir James is armoured lightly in the 17th-century manner. Armour would be phased out altogether during the Civil War, but even here in the 1620s the main emphasis is on protecting not much more than the chest, the shoulders and the arms. He wears trousers with deep cuffs above the knee and his legs are otherwise bare, apart from calf-length boots. The ruff was in its last days, but Van Dyck shows that it was still worn in court circles in the mid-1620s, and Sir John wears one as well. He lies with his head on a pillow supported by two hefty tomes. The conventions of memorial sculpture alone advertise a strong talent; but the head and hands proclaim real accomplishment. Allington has a short fringe revealing a good brow. He is full bearded and and has strong cheekbones and a firm mouth. His fine-boned strong hands alone, one by his side, the other on his breast, suggest a gentleman, and though this was a status that could be achieved by men of humble status, these hands clearly never performed manual work. Simon Knott, the popular website connoisseur of East Anglian churches, reports that when he visited Milden someone had placed a posy of laurel in the effigy's hand. There must be something about the peace of this church and the sense of a life quietly extinguished – there was a Peruvian lily (the supermarket shopper's friend *Alstromoeria*) between thumb and fingers of the same hand when I visited.

Nayland
SUFFOLK

Four miles north of Colchester lies Nayland, though on the Suffolk bank of the Stour. It was one of the big villages of the Middle Ages that grew wealthy on the wool trade, and St James was built in the 15th century on wool money. But in the 18th century the village and its industry lay becalmed, so the character of Nayland remains Tudor and Jacobean. Stoke Nayland is a little further on, its fine tower visible from East Bergholt. John Constable (1776–1837) painted it from there and up close.

John Constable, religious painter, in the Church of St James

Constable never painted Nayland, but an aunt lived there, and in 1809 she commissioned him to paint the biblical scene of Christ blessing the bread and wine at the Last Supper. He was already a mature painter, but he was not truly independent until 1828, when his father-in-law left him a fortune. However, his wife also died in that year, and the success that followed was ashes in his mouth.

Back in 1809 he was grateful for handouts and duly applied himself to his aunt's commission. In the painting Christ's hands are spread wide to the bottom corners of the canvas, palms upwards, so that the composition is built on a stable pyramid. His head is supported on a strong neck. He has a full beard, and dark hair falls to his shoulders. He is simply dressed in a brown garment and with a russet stole over the shoulders. He looks upwards in submission, but not meekly. It's nicely done, though it has to be said that while his weekday best was good enough to shake the world of art, this is polite Constable in his Sunday best. Thieves took the Nayland painting in 1985, and although it was soon recovered it has now been reinstalled – presumably for security reasons – in such a way that it is not that easy to look at properly.

18th-century milestone in the High Street

On first sight Nayland's 18th-century milestone could almost be a market cross. It is a rectangular shaft in the High Street, standing opposite the old staging inn, the White Hart, slightly tapering towards the top, a good plinth with simple moulding top and bottom and a ball finial. It is much the finest in a county where more than 100 milestones have survived from the original 200 when

Suffolk was turnpiked. Mostly these are workaday; true, there is another Suffolk obelisk milestone, at Hadleigh, but it is much plainer than Nayland's and its lettering – of very lightly serifed upper case – is strictly business. The most functional lettering is attractive and easy on the eye, and Nayland's inscriptions could hardly be better. The place-names and mileages to London (55), Colchester, Chelmsford, Hadleigh and Bury St Edmunds on three sides of the obelisk are carved in characters with generous variations in the width of the elegant strokes, lots of space within the letter forms and almost lilting numerals: the two figures in '22 MILES to BURY' look like a couple of lissom dancers taking a curtain call.

Needham Market
SUFFOLK

The most extravagant roof in England, in
St John the Baptist

Needham Market, another of Suffolk's attractive towns, suffered because its church was merely a chapel of ease for its neighbouring village, Barking. It was thrown up at the end of the 15th century without tower and without much space, hemmed in by the dull main street and by lanes on the other three sides, so there is no churchyard. It is famous for one thing, but that one thing is quite something: the hammerbeam roof. The point of hammerbeams is to convert horizontal stress into vertical stress to help stop walls falling down. Needham Market has taken that piece of engineering and converted it into an extravagant display of midair wizardry. And the unknown carpenters have had an extravagantly good press ever since. It's true, it does look like a complete church floating in midair – nave, aisles, and clerestory. The hammerbeams project an extraordinary 6 feet 6 inches from

the walls, but they are partly hidden behind coving, which also hides the curved beams bracing the hammers. The two vertical beams climbing from each hammer carry tie-beams running the width of the aisle-less church. The hammerbeams have angels at the ends, not the originals but good replacements, and the coving is decorated with alternating little angels and fleurons, but it is the flamboyant daring of the engineering that seizes the attention, not the decoration.

The clerestory, incidentally, is real enough: good on the inside, but from the street it looks like a row of jerry-built dormer windows in a loft extension. In a 19th-century restoration the architect added a porch with a ludicrous little spire above it. 'Christ IHS have merci on us' an inscription inside reads. Exactly.

Norwich
NORFOLK

Wool was the staple industry in medieval England, and in Norwich it was king. In the 15th century, with a population hovering around 10,000, it was, after London, the biggest city in England with Bristol and York. It had always been important, as various early medieval trappings show: a brutal castle keep of 1160 on a hill above St Peter Mancroft, a marketplace to the west and to the northeast the great Norman cathedral. But in the 15th century the streets were again alive with masons and carpenters and glaziers, adding a dominating spire to the cathedral and erecting churches to the greater glory of God and mammon. Even where there had previously been a church, it was knocked down or reduced so that work could begin afresh. Practically every one of the surviving thirty-two medieval parish churches within the line of the old city walls of Norwich comes from this period.

The cathedral cloisters are the biggest in England and a splendid confection of styles from the 13th to the 15th centuries. Within the cathedral precincts just inside the proud 15th-century Erpingham Gate is the former Carnary College, which was founded for priests in the 14th century and is now Norwich School, where Horatio Nelson was educated. The notional Norwich School, of 19th-century watercolourists, is housed in the Castle Museum, which has a big holding of paintings and drawings by its great master, John Sell Cotman. Among modern work there is a 7 feet square painted and silk-screened image on canvas (1966–9) by the most celebrated modern painter from the region, Michael Andrews (1928–95), of the Lord Mayor's Reception in Norwich Castle Keep on the Eve of the Installation of the first Chancellor of the University of East Anglia – a long-winded title that accords with the sort of occasion but not at all with this cryptic, vivid panorama. The university, on the western fringes of Norwich, was founded in 1963 a year after Denys Lasdun, architect of the National Theatre, devised the overall plan and built the spine of the university with its ziggurat terraces of rooms and raised walkways. Norman Foster followed with his remarkable Sainsbury Centre for the Arts, which houses Lord Sainsbury's big, eclectic, worldwide collection encompassing many periods.

The New Testament in glorious colour, in the church of St Peter Mancroft, Market Place

Norfolk Records Office holds biographical details of at least fourteen glaziers' firms working in stained glass in 15th-century Norwich. There were fifty-one parishes in the city, all building churches through the century, some building more than one, so their order books were full. There is no record of which one worked for the biggest parish and the biggest parish church of St Peter Mancroft, but the glass there is the church's chief and much-loved treasure. The unusual dedication appears to be a combination of St Peter and the name of the man who owned the plot where the church was built. The building, complete in 1455, is 180 feet long (which is long), with transepts, the style Perpendicular, well lit, with an impressive clerestory of big windows, and a steeple 146 feet tall, though above the mighty tower the spire is puny.

During the Civil War an explosion outside shattered the windows, and not until after the Second World War were the surviving panels reset in the chancel east window in a brave display. Of the forty-two panels, seven are Victorian, five of them down the spine of the window, three horizontally in the middle of the bottom row, the other four up along the spine of the window; they look fine from a distance but close to, as usual with jobbing Victorian glass, the bland sentimentality of the faces is an immediate giveaway. The figures across the bottom are mostly donors; the action begins above that.

Whatever the original dispositions of the glass, the reassembly has turned it into an abbreviated New Testament. So the second row from the bottom consists of incidents from the life of Mary, starting with the Annunciation, then the visit to Elizabeth, who was pregnant with John the Baptist, the Adoration of the Shepherds and the Adoration of the Magi, and the Massacre of the Innocents by Herod. The storyline then cuts to the life and death of Christ and the foundation of the early Christian church in the two rows above with saints at the top. The first impression is of the intensity of the work: a couple of brilliant splashes of yellow among the donors, otherwise reds and blues predominating with white, beautifully judged, to clarify, accentuate and lighten

The Marl Pit *in Norwich Castle Museum is one of those paintings that mark John Cotman out as among the greatest watercolourists, not just of the great Norwich school, but in history*

form and colour. The special effects man has been at work in incidents like the big golden compass-like star hovering above the birthplace of Jesus to which it has guided the shepherds, and in the dove and the cherubim slaloming down a burst of sunbeams through a cloud as the Angel Gabriel announces himself to the Virgin.

A giant among watercolourists in Norwich Castle Museum

Norwich Castle is a colossal and timeless Romanesque monument, built around 1160, and, after serving as a prison in the 19th century, it was adapted as a museum in 1894. It houses the most fugitive of the fine arts, a great collection of watercolours by the Norwich School, a large group of 19th-century regional artists, among whom John Crome and John Sell Cotman attained national stature.

The life of Cotman (1782–1842) is a history of troubled genius, a depressive and turbulent personality, unable to get along with most of his colleagues, unable to promote himself, living from hand to mouth, finding peace only in his work, those majestic, serene, structured landscapes in which great planes of rock and water, cloud and banks of trees, so often find a focus in a manmade element – the cliff face of Durham Cathedral, for example, and the arches of Greta Bridge (see Northeast). He made those watercolours during trips to the northeast in 1803, 1804 and 1805. These, and a few more until 1810, constitute the best of his output, after which he devoted most of his time for the best part of a decade to etching in a vain effort to make money. He suffered depressive illness for the rest of his life, but despite this moved to London in 1834 and was a great success as drawing master at King's College School until his death in 1842.

Even before his death Cotman became regarded as a follower of another fine Norwich artist, John Crome (1768–1821). In 1902 the British Museum acquired the Cotman collection of James Reeves (ironically, the first curator at Norwich Castle, which couldn't afford the collection). Norwich came into its heritage in 1946 when R.J. Colman bequeathed thousands of watercolours of the Norwich School to the art gallery, including a lot of the best of Cotman and Crome. The world rediscovered the Norwich painter, and by mid-century his reputation as a watercolourist had overtaken even J.M.W. Turner's. Cotman has that grasp of space and form, mass and disposition of pictorial elements that characterises the greatest artists. The grandeur of *The Marl Pit*, painted about 1810–11, lies in the balance of freedom and organisation of apparently unorganisable elements: the architectural severity of that tawny quarry cliffside lying behind the dark mass of the foreground promontory, and the hillside climbing up to the massy copse of trees on the right under a summer sky punctuated by a soft white mass of cloud breaking away into a diagonal streamer. Written quickly like that as one sentence it seems easy. Since it's watercolour it certainly had to be quick, but because the transparent fluidity of the medium makes it unforgiving it demands a high degree of application. Most watercolourists develop a series of visual tricks to avoid calamity. With Cotman there is none of this: just concentrated analytical intelligence to sort out the data before him, utter objectivity, sensitivity to colour and tone, and a high level of technical skill. That's all there is to it.

A pioneering sculptor, at Sainsbury Centre for Visual Arts, East Anglia University

When he wasn't selling sausages, sliced ham and tinned soup to the British public after the war, Robert Sainsbury was buying art.

He ranged across time and trawled the continents. His collection includes a Cycladian head around 4,500 years old and an abstract sculpture by the modernist Jean Arp; at a glance, the two might be confused. There's pre-Columbian art, tribal art from North America, art from Africa, Oceania and Asia, and modern art – Bacon, Rouault, Modigliani, Epstein, Moore, a Giacometti bronze, *Standing Woman* (1959), a Picasso gouache study, fabulous in its own right, for his great breakthrough painting, *Les Demoiselles d'Avignon*. This is what we now know as the Robert and Lisa Sainsbury Collection, displayed and user-friendly at East Anglia University in the first of Norman Foster's great top-lit sheds in the region (Stansted Airport and Duxford American Air Museum are others), recently extended with a transparent umbilical tunnel at first-floor level linking academic buildings to the arts centre and much more exhibition space running underground beneath the park.

It's clear that though the centre lays out its aim as being to display 'a history which linked art and machine aesthetics, mass production, science and mathematics', the core of the various collections remains Lord Sainsbury's apparent original motivation; that is, the 20th-century rediscovery of pre-Renaissance pre-classical cultures for which Picasso's *Les Demoiselles d'Avignon* is the iconic image. But Alberto Giacometti (1901–66), whose work in the Sainsbury Centre includes drawings and paintings as well as sculpture, is most emblematic here of the early modern artist's struggle towards personal integrity. Like the other pioneers, he looked closely at African art; for a brief period after his first well-known sculpture, *The Palace at 4 a.m.*, he joined the surrealists; but with a body of modernist work behind him that impressed everybody except himself he became the most intense and the

most remote of 20th-century artists, paring down his human figures, like his 4 foot 6 inch *Standing Woman*, which is placed so centrally here. Sometimes he reduced them to the size of string beans, sometimes to invisibility, roughly pressing clay on to the armature in an agitated search for a core that would be the essence of life as well as of sculpture.

For Giacometti, everything was provisional. When his New York dealer Pierre Matisse wrote asking him for a signature to be reproduced in a catalogue, Giacometti replied that he didn't like to sign his name: 'In fact, my relationship to my name is not at all clear. My name is something of a stranger to me.' Obviously this work appealed to Jean-Paul Sartre – being and nothingness – these figures, he wrote, 'pass, hopelessly alone and yet together'.

In this enterprise Diego Giacometti, himself an artist, became his brother's amanuensis as well as his model, looking after his studio affairs, most importantly casting his bronzes. He knew every one of Alberto's fingerprints in clay and reproduced the look in the bronze furniture he made, sometimes with Alberto's collaboration. Design critics greeted it respectfully and collectors buy it, so there is a display of it in the new basement here. It is spiky and hostile, and no one could conceivably sit in these chairs, which are clearly for his brother's army of bronze loners.

Ranworth
NORFOLK

St Helen

Even the best-surviving examples of medieval murals in English churches are hardly ever much more than historically interesting with their colours faded, usually great portions missing, and workmanship usually provincial to downright yokel or so restored that it looks like a pastiche. So it is especially good to have the group of painted wooden screens in Norfolk and Suffolk to show what vernacular painting could be like in this country. The two best are in the Norfolk Broads at Barton Turf and Ranworth.

St Michael, Barton Turf (see above), is one of the loveliest with its orders of angels, but Ranworth's is pre-eminent, the finest pictorial rood screen in England with the best of its panels an attempt to match the exalted prose of the Book of Revelations with a painted vision of a heaven, where God is wrapped in a rainbow and accompanied by elders in white raiment and golden crowns. The Ranworth artist shows heaven at war when the Archangel Michael and his host of angels fight the devil and his army. St Michael is golden crowned with gold feathered body and mauve, pink and white wings; he battles before a field of golden flowers scattered like stars on blue, the blue sombrely oxidised now, but its original splendour discernible in patches.

St Helen's Church sits on a hillock above Ranworth Broad, remote seeming in winter and in the Middle Ages remote in fact. As in other villages of its sort, the painters who worked there were not necessarily members of the big town craft guilds; quite often itinerant masters from Europe were free to fulfil one-off commissions. In Ranworth, Barton Turf and Southwold it is quite easy to pick out the panels painted by masters, sponsored, probably, by the great patrons of the district, from those done by local artisans, paid for by tradesmen. The St Michael painted by an anonymous wandering artist at Ranworth, possibly Flemish, is protected, not by armour but by a sense of serene invincibility as he goes forth to fight in a simple gown emblazoned with a golden cross and a gold-edged ermine cope, and he treads

with naked, long-toed feet, like a wonderfully graceful primate.

St Ives
CAMBRIDGESHIRE

15th-century chapel on a bridge

There is so much water at St Ives that the place seems hemmed in by causeways. Once it can't have been more than an island in the fens with one long bridge to cross the River Great Ouse. Before the bridge, this is the last point at which the river could be forded, which explains the position of the town. In the 12th century the monastery at nearby Ramsay used the flint of the ford as a foundation for the new bridge, rebuilt in the early 15th century in its present form: six arches, big cutaways and a chapel in the middle of the bridge for the succour of travellers. The bridge chapel was once one of many, including one on old London Bridge, another at Rochester (which survives, heavily restored and isolated from the modern iron bridge in a block of houses and offices by the castle) and, in Yorkshire, at Wakefield and Rotherham (like Rochester, heavily restored – Wakefield's was horribly vandalised by George Gilbert Scott in a restoration that he came to regret bitterly). St Ives is Oliver Cromwell country; in fact, there's a statue of him in the marketplace, so you would think the omens could not have been good. Yet the chapel survived with a couple of storeys added when it came successively to serve as an inn and then lodgings. Earlier in the 20th century the additions were lopped off. Inside it has been put together as a chapel again, though nothing of its original fittings survives. The bridge, long and narrow, is closed to traffic and survives for pedestrians between the wharf and the Bridge Street link to one of the oldest markets in the country on one

The bridge and its chapel at St Ives have been there since the town was an island in the Fens. There is still enough water, almost, to launch a battleship. The bridge is now confined to pedestrians

bank and the tall, old mill, now flats with a small marina, on the other. Meanwhile, not quite a museum piece, the bridge and chapel remain as one of the loveliest sights in England.

Saxtead Green
SUFFOLK

Working 18th-century technology in a post mill

Windmills were a beacon of prosperity across East Anglia from at least the 13th century until after the Second World War. By the 18th century they had reached a high degree of functional perfection – and, incidentally, of beauty, sitting gleaming white in the green farmland against the low skies. A group of several windmills survives on the flat

hinterland of Great Yarmouth; and there is a spectacularly sited cornmill of 1760 at Framsden not far from Saxtead Green set at the top of a hill and hugged close enough by a bend in the road for a close-up view (it is privately owned). As for Saxtead Green itself, there has been a windmill on this site, on the high ground north of Framlingham, since 1287, servicing the farming community and building the prosperity of Framlingham. What stands there now is similar to the Framsden mill but of unknown date, though the miller built himself a house within the same compound in 1810. It was a cornmill until the Second World War, when it was conscripted to grind animal feeds. The last miller died in 1947, and operations ceased, but the miller's son-in-law handed it over to English Heritage's predecessor, the Ministry of Works, in 1951.

Saxtead windmill is classified as a post mill: its body, or buck, constitutes half the height of 46 feet, and it stands above its other half, a brick drum called the roundhouse, upon which it swivels on a cylindrical post as the wind changes direction so that the sails always pick up a favourable breeze. The ladder leading up to the door in the back has wheels attached that run on a circular track surrounding the mill, an elegant solution to save the miller the bother of wondering which way the wind blows. That's not the half of it. The sack hoist, spindle beam, windshaft, runner stone, brake wheel and the rest of the machinery, plus grinding stone casings and great spur wheel, sit in the buck as snug as a bug in a sack of meal and work smoothly to feed the spouts and bins in the roundhouse. It's a time capsule in working order.

Snape
SUFFOLK

Barbara Hepworth late masterpiece, at the Maltings

Tucked away behind the Snape concert hall in a clearing among the reeds on the edge of the Alde estuary is a trio of figures from *Family of Man* by Barbara Hepworth (1903–75). The full group of nine, created in 1970, is shown at the Yorkshire Sculpture Park, but three work well enough in this separate casting; better, I thought, when I last saw them on a freezing day of mist. They huddle together, these slightly totem-like objects, their proportions wonkily suggesting human figures each assembled from four abstract shapes that could stand by themselves: slabs, some with Hepworth holes, one solid but with a ridged surface like a washboard, some long, some fat, some solid as ingots. Together they could be a group of the kind of megaliths scattered around Cornwall where

Hepworth lived and worked and which, she acknowledged, gave her inspiration. Her sculpture was shaped on the twin poles of her friendships with, on the one hand, Henry Moore with the sense of rolling Yorkshire wolds in his work and, on the other, the purist asceticism of modernist heroes she came to know, Mondrian, Naum Gabo and her second husband, Ben Nicholson.

But there was a third strand. Technically, Hepworth carved holes through her sculptures to introduce space as part of the equation, but making sculpture is a physical business, and she obviously felt each of these sculptures physically, as part of herself; her body, her mind. A lot of her early figurative sculptures were to do with mother and child, and another function of the holes in her abstracts, even some of the most polished and geometrical, is to allow the inside to show as well as the outside. This dual function of opening and enclosing seems to trail the visceral memory of motherhood. The three pieces from *Family of Man* among the reeds at Snape are very much in that line, earthy and indomitable.

Southwold
SUFFOLK

15th-century painted rood screen, in the Church of St Edmund

Visually Southwold cannot have changed much since Philip Wilson Steer (see Birkenhead, Northwest) used to paint here in the last years of the 19th century. Same beach, same brewery, same pubs, same gaily painted beach huts, though the huts change hands now for thousands of pounds. The genteel little middle-class resort has become a celebrity bolt-hole. The little greens and open spaces have a slightly unplanned look, and that's because they were: fire destroyed the town in 1659, and the greens are the parts

that were never rebuilt. St Edmund, too, was destroyed and rebuilt, knapped flint, flushwork decoration, green copper roof and south porch of some splendour, outside and in with its rib-vaulted ceiling. Best of all, like so many churches in these parts, is the painted rood screen across the width of the church.

This, though, is older than the Perpendicular church that shelters it, and may have been saved from the old church or saved from another parish; one of the lost churches of Dunwich beneath the North Sea is a popular theory. The style of the painted figures and decoration puts it at about 1480, the same as the screens in the Norfolk broads. A few decades later, like all churches in England, St Edmund was issued with the instruction that Christ's rood and the rood loft must be destroyed. Fortunately, the screen and open fretwork support for the loft survived, angels in the north aisle, prophets in the south aisle, and Apostles in the nave. All of the figures are defaced, though George Richmond, once the friend of William Blake, but later a fashionable Victorian portrait painter, repainted the faces of the Apostles. The screen is uneven in quality between its different sections and can never have been as fine as the Ranworth screen; but the best section, running across the chancel, has its own special beauty: the wonderful moulded and red and gold painted gesso background to the Apostles, diaper patterned and embossed with flowers and grape vines in fruit, the golden niches in which they stand under cusped and crocketed arches, luxuriant here, delicate in the open arches of the superstructure and the chancel entrance.

This pristine, early 19th-century post mill in the vast Suffolk landscape is successor to a sequence of windmills, the first of which was built in 1287. The last miller at Saxtead Green died in 1947 but English Heritage have restored it to working order

Sudbury
SUFFOLK

The friends of Gainsborough's youth, in Gainsborough's House

Thomas Gainsborough's brick Georgian house in the little Suffolk town of Sudbury is where he was born in 1727; it is part of the texture of the town, lying in Gainsborough Street just below Market Hill in the relatively uncorrupted heart of the little town fringed by light industry. Gainsborough's House, as of course it is known, became a museum in 1961 and has since built up a collection of his work of all periods, starting with the cut-up double portrait of a boy and a girl, which now consists of two paintings, the head of the girl and the full figure of the boy, and which he painted around 1744. It is astonishingly mature work for a lad of seventeen and tends to support the view that Gainsborough was an untaught native genius, until we remember that when his father's clothing business went bust his uncle subbed young Thomas to go to London and be an apprentice to Hubert Gravelot, the French artist and engraver who had learned his art in the studio of the great popular artist François Boucher.

From Gravelot Gainsborough learned about the contemporary French scene, the paintings of Watteau, Boucher, Fragonard and Gravelot himself. It didn't leave any immediate impression on his native instincts, but the rococo style in eventual improbable combination with the high court art of Van Dyck was the basis of Gainsborough's dazzling freehand art of the later years, of which Joshua Reynolds wrote in puzzled admiration: 'If Gainsborough did not look at nature with a poet's eye, it must be acknowledged that he saw her with the eye of a painter.'

Gainsborough's father died in 1748, and the

artist moved back to Sudbury the following year with his young wife. There the two daughters who would appear as young women in some of his rural scenes were born. In Sudbury Gainsborough produced the wonderful and popular *Mr and Mrs Andrews*, now in the National Gallery, and the rare and sprightly triple portrait of Crockatt, Keable and Muilman disporting themselves under a tree in the Suffolk countryside, which Gainsborough's House and the Tate acquired jointly in 1993 and share on a biennial rota. Crockatt and Muilman were the sons of rich merchants; Keable, seated and playing the flute, was an artist and musician who, it is thought, taught the other two a little about the civilised arts. Gainsborough himself had lifelong friendships with musicians and was adept on the viol de gamba, a form of cello, and music played a part in many of his paintings. This conversation piece looks a thoroughgoing early Gainsborough, but there was always a suggestion, now given some credence by scientific analysis of the paintwork, that he cooperated with Keable on the work. Their interests in common were not just music and painting. Both enjoyed drinking and whoring, though Gainsborough had a gentle disposition, loved his wife and produced an annual birthday portrait of her – there's one in Sudbury of Mrs Gainsborough as an old lady but still with bright green eyes that suggest she could hold her own.

Swaffham

NORFOLK

The 3rd Earl of Orford's cut-price butter cross, Marketplace

It might be tempting to say that nothing much has happened in this town beside a bypass since the days of the Domesday Book when it had a population of around sixty

freemen, bordars, villeins and slaves. As it happens, however, it was a swanky place in the 18th century, mostly thanks to George, the 3rd Earl of Orford (prime minister Robert Walpole's grandson and Horace Walpole's nephew). The earl owned the racecourse, and for a time it was as notable as Newmarket's, but it was his invention of coursing that brought the Norfolk gentry into town and prompted the building of the Assembly Rooms on the marketplace. In 1775 Swaffham had its own great fire, the centre of the town was rebuilt, and the 3rd earl selected the cheapest option for a butter cross from a number of designs (still at the former Walpole home, Houghton Hall).

Still, the bargain-price classical structure, a remote descendant of the Tivoli temple, cuts quite a dash in the middle of the roughly triangular marketplace. It stands on a circular podium with three steps, its lead dome supported on Tuscan columns. On top of the dome a fine big baroque statue of Ceres, goddess of plenty, pauses to distribute largesse, her flowing garments, outflung arm and general demeanour indicating generosity and fulfilment. The local belief is that she was a garden ornament at Houghton. She is probably French and certainly an exotic addition to the Georgian houses and random mix of pubs and shops pleasantly defining the market space.

Thaxted

ESSEX

A medieval Guildhall in Town Street

The composer Gustav Holst (1874–1934) lived in and near Thaxted when he composed *The Planets*. At the top end of this wide market street of good old houses is the 15th-century double-jettied, double-hipped Guildhall, and on the hill above that the immense Perpendicular parish Church of St John the

This major work of 14th-century European art, an English altar painting, was discovered in a loft in Thornham Hall in 1927. Its owner, Lord Henneker, then placed it above the altar in the remote parish church of Thornham Parva, where it remains

Baptist, for which Holst wrote music and ran a festival with the vicar, Conrad le Dispenser Noel. Noel arrived in 1910, and until his death in 1942 passionately embraced the notion of the church militant, ran up the red flag in St John before his bemused parishioners and spoke to them of the church at large as the red army and of Christ as the divine outlaw.

From the Great Dunmow road outside the town, the church and windmill dominate, but in town it is the Guildhall that is the focus of all eyes, a rock around which the traffic eddies, up Fishmarket Lane on one side, up pretty Stony Lane to the church and along the main road to Saffron Walden on the other. For a long time it was thought to be 14th century, but tree ring analysis has shown that it was built in the second half of the 15th. The ground floor is an open arcade, once a market hall, with a single massive central post supporting the building. The whole structure is limewashed, beams and all, as though being cleansed after the plague.

Thornham Parva
SUFFOLK

A thatched church housing a medieval masterpiece, St Mary

What is now known as the Thornham Parva retable (a painting fixed to an altar) surfaced to the public gaze for the first time in 400 years in an exhibition at Ipswich church congress in 1927. After that its owner, Lord Henneker, placed it in the small, thatched, Norman Church of St Mary, in lovely woodland and pasture at Thornham Parva, where it has remained, the subject of occasional exploratory articles in learned journals puzzling out its provenance, its place in English art and the oddity of its having spent most of its time, first, in a small attic chapel at Rookery farmhouse in Stradbroke, to the east of Eye, and then, after Lord Henneker's ancestor had bought it at an auction of the farm's contents, in the loft of Thornham Hall. Only one thing was clear: it was a major work of English and European art, painted some time at the beginning of the 14th century, and ancestor of the fine church screen paintings of the 15th century at churches such as Ranworth, Barton Turf and Southwold.

The low, wide panel takes the form of nine separate carved niches separated by slender columns bearing foiled canopies and containing painted figures on decorative backgrounds of stamped, gilded and painted gesso. The outside figures, St Dominic and St Peter Martyr, show that the retable was made for a Dominican house, which new evidence suggests was probably Thetford Priory, and that it relates to the altar frontal painting now in the Musée de Cluny in Paris. The retable is an East Anglian work, probably by a school of painters in Norwich where script illumination in a similar style was flourishing, and tree-ring dating places the timber as having been felled in 1322, which, allowing time for seasoning, leaves the date for the painting somewhere between 1330 and 1340. The artist or artists were aware of court painting in Westminster and of their great Florentine contemporary, Giotto.

As for the quality, the panel has recently been restored, and its full glory is now revealed: the swaying figures of the female saints and St Edmund, the angular aggression of the Baptist, the beautiful greens and plum colours and silkily rendered folds of the garments, some lined with squirrel fur, the diapered background in four of the niches and the tin stamped gilded decorations of the others, the pathos of the crucifixion, together make this a surpassingly lovely and moving work of art in this most unexpected of rural settings.

Tilbury
ESSEX

A magnificent watergate from the time of Charles II at Tilbury fort

Somewhere in the vicinity of the Henry VIII's West Tilbury blockhouse, later reincarnated as Tilbury Fort, Queen Elizabeth is supposed to have delivered her Shakespearian exhortation to the raggle-taggle troops mustered to repel the Spanish invasion of 1588, 'I know I have the body but of a weak and feeble woman; but I have the heart and stomach of a king, and of a king of England too.' As we know, she was not required to deliver on her promise to lay down her honour and her blood in the dust. Drake and the weather repelled the Armada, and no Spaniard came ashore alive except in chains.

Charles II's chief engineer Sir Bernard de Gomme, a native of Lille and a specialist in forts, depots, naval bases and anchorages, designed the new Tilbury Fort as a response to the Dutch raid up the Medway in 1667. It was almost complete in 1685 when troops moved in, a massive bastioned fortification, as aggressive and spiky in plan as a poisonous scorpion, with extensive low-lying outworks of brick, ragstone, earth and turf, a double moat fed through sluices by the Thames, and the sea wall itself, designated on plans as the west and east gun lines. Its history is symbolised in the generations of artillery mounted within the walls, from the great unwieldy cannon of the 17th century to the QF (quick fire) artillery covering the period from 1892 to the Second World War, 6- and 12-pounders designed to strafe an enemy approaching up the Thames.

The fort, which the army finally abandoned in 1950, is reached along the A276, skirting the great container port and, beyond the London International Ferry Terminal, emerging on the marshes just short of an incongruous little weatherboarded pub that is called, with some justice, the World's End. The road does an S-bend around the pub and leads into the fenced-off area of the fort. Here behind the watergate is a parade square, massive and functional enough to make the heart of any ex-serviceman sink on sight. The fine, plain officers' quarters remain, but only the foundations of the razed men's barracks, covering a similar area but much more heavily occupied. Inside the watergate is a guardhouse with a functionally bare chapel above.

Alone in its decorative riches among all this stripped-down militarism the watergate stands, a great civic entrance in two stages: the arched gateway between four Ionic columns and beneath an entablature with a carved plaque commemorating the thirty-fourth year of the reign of 'Carolus II Rex' (promoting the polite pretence that the republican years between the execution of the king's father in 1649 and the Restoration in 1660 never happened). The gate was thus presumably complete in 1683. Its top stage has the royal arms deeply carved and standing free of the segmental pediment behind it. There is a tall niche beneath. Someone, presumably Charles II, has vacated it, and there are relief carvings of military trophies, cannon, armour, kettle drums and bagpipes. It is an opulent and splendid façade to the grim business of warlike preparations within.

Ulting
ESSEX

The architect of the Pompidou Centre builds a house, off Crouchman's Farm Road

Before Richard Rogers (b.1933) and his lifelong friend Renzo Piano (b.1937) built the Pompidou Centre with its entrails hanging on the outside, all Rogers had built were two or three houses and a factory. He had, of course, talked the talk about an architecture drawing on the pop art, plug-in, shunt about, candy-coloured notions propagated by a ginger group of his peers called Archigram, which published popular broadsheets promoting the ideas of forward-looking

young architects and theorists.

For all its faults, the Pompidou Centre has been a huge success, and it rescued modern architecture from the slough of despond that it had fallen into with the post-war failure of its ferro-concrete social idealism. There had been a hint of what was to come in a little-discussed and less seen house by Rogers and his first wife, Su Brumwell, tucked in a garden down an obscure country lane in Essex.

They built it in 1968–9 to a commission from the typographer and designer Humphrey Spender (brother also of the poet Stephen Spender), who had bought the 19th-century vicarage in the village of Ulting near Maldon and wanted a studio-house in the back garden. What the Rogers team produced was a studio and a separate house, two single-storey structures with a single name, the Studio, constructed of prefabricated parts, the studio top-lit, the house glazed down the whole of one side – effectively a glass skin – the end walls of both buildings blank, the structural steel girders painted bright yellow. It's an end-of-century take on pure modernism, as lucid as a pavilion by the great pioneer Mies van der Rohe but utterly frank about its construction: everything shows. It's just possible to catch a tantalising glimpse of it at the end of a short track, comfortably naturalised in a mature garden.

Wimpole
CAMBRIDGESHIRE

What everyone thinks of as Wimpole is the big estate on wooded chalkland with the hall at the end of a mile-long avenue north of the Biggleswade to Cambridge road. Once, the little village clustered around the Church of St Andrew with the hall on the other side, but one of the improving owners of the estate, who successively employed Capability Brown

NEAR THE REMAINS OF HIS BELOVED WIFE, ARE DEPOSITED THOSE
NORABLE JOHN YORKE, FOURTH SON OF PHILIP, FIRST EARL OF HA
WAS BORN ON THE 27TH OF AUGUST, 1728, AND DIED ON THE 4T OF SEPTEMB
ELECTED IN 1753, BY THE BOROUGH OF HIGHAM-FERRERS,
AND IN 1768, BY THAT OF REIGATE, AS ONE OF ITS REPRESENTATIVE
E FILLED THE OFFICE OF A LORD OF TRADE, AND ONCE THAT OF A LORD OF T
CONTINUED A MEMBER OF THE HOUSE OF COMMONS, TILL THE YEAR 178
ING THE QUIET OF PRIVATE, TO THE TUMULT OF PUBLICK LIFE, HE RETIRED FR
BLEST WITH A LIVELY AND PLAYFUL IMAGINATION, REGULATED AND ENER

and Humphrey Repton to lay out the park, knocked down the village and rehoused the inhabitants in little 19th-century Gothic houses strung along the main road. In the park, the gentleman architect of ready-made ruins for early 19th-century Picturesque landscapes, Sanderson Miller, provided one of his best conceits, a castle with four towers (he was subject to bouts of lunacy, which may not have affected his work). Today with the big park and the home farm the estate attracts more visitors than the hall and church possibly could.

A 'foster-child of silence and slow time', in the Church of St Andrew

Like so many English parish churches, St Andrew sits conveniently close to the local mansion house, and even though Wimpole Hall had its own chapel, the owners annexed the north chapel of the parish church as the charnel house of their dead. The discreet neoclassical memorial to the Hon. John Yorke faces a cascade of marble from ceiling to floor erected to contain the sarcophagus of his father, Philip Yorke, 1st Earl of Hardwicke and Lord Chancellor in Robert Walpole's Whig government of 1721–42. The Hon. John was a mere fourth son, so his memorial is fittingly by the social standards of his time and class one of the smallest in the room; it is also much the finest, and maybe the best work of its begetter, Richard Westmacott (1775–1856).

Neo-classicism was the style of the moment. It came to the fore during the French Revolution in contrast to the frivolity of *ancien régime* rococo. English patrons and English artists and architects took to the style

John Yorke was only a fourth son, but the monument to him by Richard Westmacott at Wimpole is one of the finest neo-classical works of the early 19th century, close in spirit to Keat's 'Ode on a Grecian Urn'

easily, even before the fall of Bonaparte. Westmacott learned it in Rome as a star pupil of the great progenitor of neoclassical sculpture, Canova. He was the son of a sculptor, his brothers were sculptors, and so was his son, all of them successful, but despite his big public commissions, like the Hyde Park Achilles honouring the Duke of Wellington, the early neoclassical sculpture of Westmacott himself worked best in relief, when its shallow space related more closely to its source, not so much ancient sculpture as ancient vase decoration, 'foster-child of Silence and slow Time', in a line from Keats's 'Ode to a Grecian Urn' that perfectly encapsulates the mood of the Yorke memorial and that was composed, like the monument, in the first decade of the 19th century.

John Yorke was seventy-three when he died in 1801, but Westmacott's carving shows a young man and his wife clad as Greeks, with their small daughter sitting at their feet. From the inclination of their heads with melancholy, downcast eyes and pure Greek profiles, and the thick locks of their hair to the cleanly articulated folds of drapery, the couple are in harmony. She rests her left arm upon an urn; her husband's left hand is on her shoulder, and he reaches out with his right hand and tenderly enfolds hers. The simplicity, unity and utter clarity of the figure ensemble admit tenderness untinged by the sentimentality that later 19th-century art so often queasily indulged, and the familial tenderness mitigates the chill of neoclassicism and of the mausoleum.

The greatest room in the greatest house in the county, Wimpole Hall

Wimpole is the greatest house of Cambridgeshire. In its day it was one of the greatest in the nation, a Tory redoubt in the Whig England of the 18th century, home to successive collections of great paintings and an unrivalled private library. The architect James Gibb was employed upon it, then Henry Flitcroft. Humphrey Repton worked on designs for the park. Successive owners spent fortunes on it and went bust. The estate slipped into decline, buildings were demolished, and its collections were sold and broken up. Its library of 50,000 printed books and hundreds of thousands of manuscripts, prints and albums of drawings was as celebrated in its day and smaller circle as the great library of antiquity in Alexandria had been. When it was sold Dr Johnson wrote that it 'excels any library that was ever yet offered to publick sale, in the value, as well as number, of the volumes, which it contains'. In the 1930s the unremarkable couple Captain George Bambridge and his wife Elsie, Rudyard Kipling's difficult daughter, pooled their resources, his from the diplomatic service, hers from Kim, Mowgli and *Puck of Pook's Hill*, bought Wimpole and patiently nursed it back to life, reassembled paintings and furnishings close to Wimpole's history and handed the estate on to the National Trust.

Like so many English houses it is a palimpsest, one house built on top of and around others, and the last and most extraordinary addition was the yellow drawing room created in 1793 by John Soane (1753–1837), as the commanding centre of the house. Soane had met Wimpole's owner, Philip Yorke, later 3rd Earl of Hardwicke, when they were both on the grand tour, Yorke looking, and Soane doggedly measuring buildings. Even allowing that the owners of large country houses tend to have large drawing rooms, Wimpole's is huge; not surprisingly, it was deployed as the great ballroom that the house had lacked.

Soane knocked two big apartments into one and then removed several rooms on the floor above and opened the new drawing room to the roof, which, being Soane, he capped with a glass dome and glass lantern, a grand version of the domes he later supplied in his own house and museum in Lincoln's Inn Fields (see West End, London) and also in Dulwich Art Gallery (see Greater London, London). Soane may have based Wimpole's pagan room hung with yellow silk on a chapel in S. Giovanni Laterano in Rome, which he and Yorke both admired; at any rate, there are two apses flanking the interior half of the drawing room and, above the fireplace and big mirror, the tympanum decorated with a painting of cavorting putti. On either side of the fireplace hang two Romney portraits: on one side is Lady Elizabeth Lindsay, Countess of Hardwicke, Philip Yorke's wife; opposite is the young Philip. Elsie Bambridge first bought the countess portrait and had it restored, removing a black dress that had been painted over the original when her sons died; she added Yorke, scooped up at a sale in 1946.

Looking at the yellow drawing room from the floor above is off-limits, which is a pity, but it is permitted to peer from a little mezzanine floor in the east part of the house into Soane's plunge bath, down a short flight of steps to the little white-tiled pool. Soane's singularity causes constant speculation about his sources; here it becomes clear that his creative cards had been marked during those months in Rome with his measuring rods.

Woolpit
SUFFOLK

Poetic porch to a high and mighty church, St Mary

Woolpit is small, so small that it is almost swallowed by the unlovely chaos of industry between the village and the A14 Bury to Ipswich road, but the intimate charm of its basically medieval centre survives the assault, and St Mary is one of the special churches of East Anglia. The steeple is visible for miles around, the nave is high and mighty, the hammerbeam roof, although largely a 19th-century restoration, is one of the finest. Best of all is the south porch, with its balance of festiveness and lovely proportions. Losing the sculptures that once adorned the stone façade doesn't seem to have done much damage and may even have improved it by turning the niches into a kind of blank arcade with delicate canopies and little platforms for the figures opening like flowers from slender, moulded pillars. More niches climb the east and west buttresses. The pair of shields each carved with the three crowns of East Anglia neatly reverse the shape of the entrance arch beneath, and the crocketed, pinnacled parapet pierced with quatrefoils on all three sides tops it off with a touch of sweet poetry.

Wymondham
NORFOLK

A perfect medieval hammerbeam roof at the Abbey

Ninian Comper, the Victorian ecclesiastical architect (though he lived until he was ninety-six in 1960), did his best to steal the glory with his huge gilded reredos against the east wall of Wymondham Abbey, but in the end it's the hammerbeam roof that takes the eye and the palm. Just as Perpendicular was the ultimate in English Gothic, its contemporary, the hammerbeam roof, was the acme of English church carpentry, not for the carpentry and engineering alone but for the carving. There are great carved roofs in the west country, but East Anglia is pre-eminent in numbers and quality, in Blythburgh, where some of the original colour still clings to the carved angels, and

Woolpit in Suffolk, in the great barn of a church at Cawston in Norfolk and at March in Cambridgeshire, among many others.

The lovely church of Weston Zoyland in Somerset (see Southwest) has angels decorating a tie-beam roof; that is, a roof braced by horizontal beams stretching right across the church from the top of the north wall to the top of the south, supporting the rafters running down the pitch of the roof. It came to seem in the 15th century that if the carpenters could dispense with the tie-beams the roof would be as open as a stone vault. The solution was to chop the central sections out of the tie-beams, leaving short projecting beams, the so-called hammerbeams, which could be decoratively carved. The decoration was almost always an angel. The ultimate sophistication was in churches like St Wendreda in March, where angels seemed such a good idea that carpenters introduced a second hammerbeam further up the roof pitch, not to help hold the church up but purely to accommodate more angels; in March there is another row of angels on the corbels and a fourth along the roof ridge, so that in the end it's all a bit like an infestation of great birds. To my eye, the finest is Wymondham's.

It is a huge church, lording it over one of the prettiest market towns in England, but from the outside it looks wounded, with, oddly, a tower at each end. And it is: until Henry VIII tore down the chancel, the east tower was a central crossing tower, dividing the people's nave from the Benedictine abbot's chancel. Town and black gown were bound in open acrimony, and the glory of the nave's roof was at least partly a work of one-upmanship by the townsfolk. As remains, the abbey is still very big, even by Norfolk parish church standards, but the carved hammerbeam roof has been planned with great restraint and spatial awareness.

Each hammerbeam has been entirely carved as an angel, and though there are child angels on the cornice between the hammerbeams, the carvers deemed the single row of angels on each side of the church sufficient, and in the ridge and on the rafters the decoration consists solely of big stars delicately carved with foliage and looking uncannily as though they had been modelled on the crystalline structure of snowflakes.

The gilded reredos by the Edwardian ecclesiastical architect Ninian Comper is the first thing to take the eye in Wymondham Abbey, but the church's greatest glory is the 15th-century angel hammerbeam roof

The West and East Midlands

BEDFORDSHIRE * BUCKINGHAMSHIRE
GLOUCESTERSHIRE * HEREFORDSHIRE
HERTFORDSHIRE * NORTHAMPTONSHIRE
OXFORDSHIRE * WARWICKSHIRE
WEST MIDLANDS
WORCESTERSHIRE

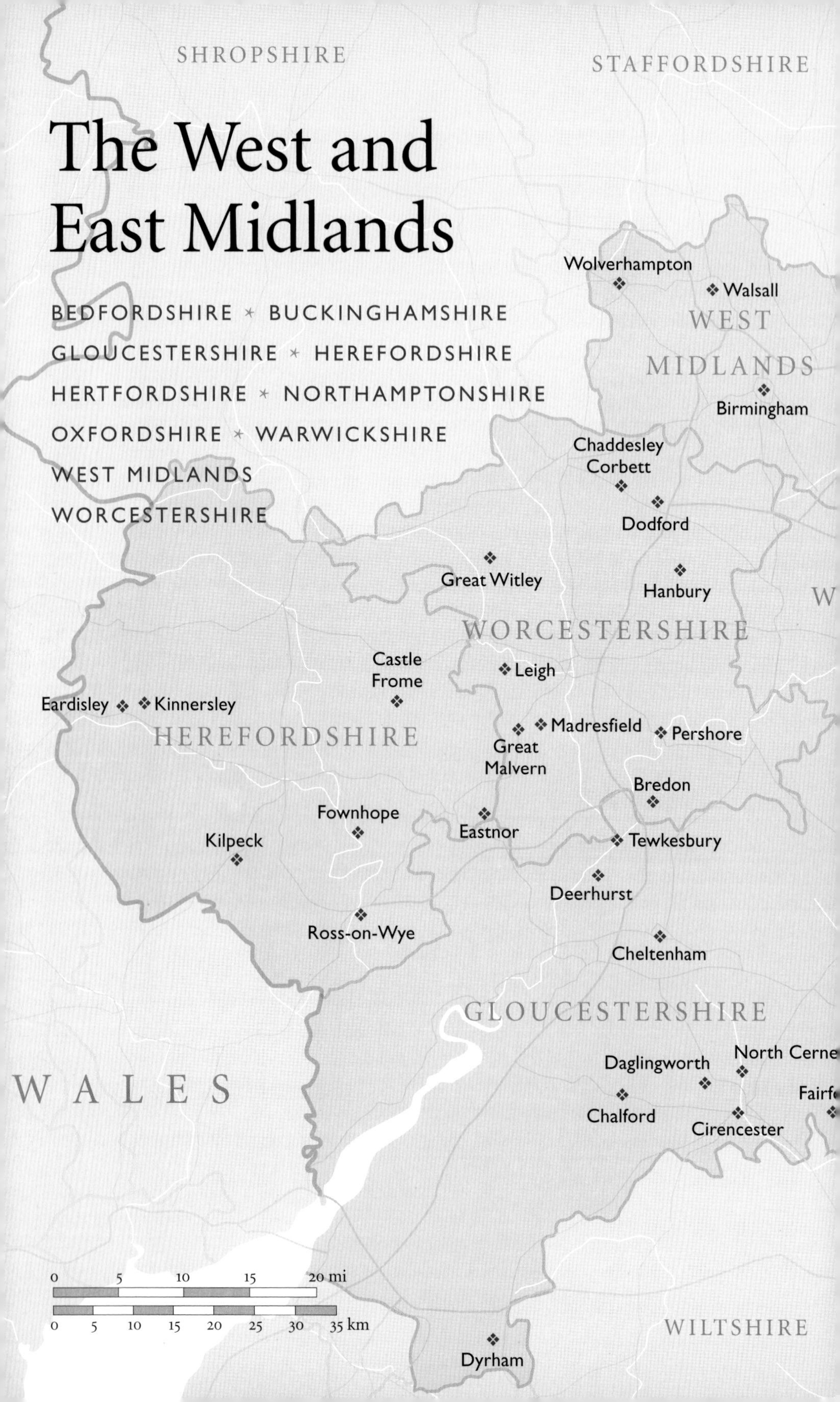

SHROPSHIRE

STAFFORDSHIRE

Wolverhampton

Walsall

WEST

MIDLANDS

Birmingham

Chaddesley
Corbett

Dodford

Great Witley

Hanbury

WORCESTERSHIRE

Castle
Frome

Leigh

Madresfield

Pershore

Great
Malvern

Bredon

Eardisley Kinnersley

HEREFORDSHIRE

Fownhope

Eastnor

Tewkesbury

Kilpeck

Deerhurst

Ross-on-Wye

Cheltenham

WALES

GLOUCESTERSHIRE

Daglingworth

North Cerne

Chalford

Fairfo

Cirencester

Dyrham

WILTSHIRE

0	5	10	15	20 mi

0	5	10	15	20	25	30	35 km

Alan Davie's gouache, First Movement in Pink*, caused a storm of protest when the Cecil Higgins Art Gallery in Bedford acquired it in 1959*

Adlestrop

GLOUCESTERSHIRE

A bus stop invested with nostalgia, 3 miles west of Stow-on-the-Wold

Yes, I remember Adlestrop, the poem, because the subject of the verse was obliterated in the 1960s like 7,000 other railway stations by the so-called Beeching axe (after the name of the perpetrator). Where the station stood is now an iron gate with a half-faded notice explaining that the 'buildings, platforms and infrastructure' were demolished and removed, and please don't disturb the occupants of the remaining station cottage with inquiries.

Nothing beyond this enamelled tin sign suggests 'the willows, willow-herb and grass,/ And meadowsweet and haycocks dry' that the poet Edward Thomas saw when his train from Worcester to Oxford made an unscheduled stop ('drew up there unwontedly') on 23 June 1914:

> *It was late June.*
> *The steam hissed. Someone cleared his*
>   *throat.*
> *No one left and no one came*
> *On the bare platform. What I saw*
> *Was Adlestrop – only the name.*

Yet Adlestrop itself, its cottages and farms,

fields and woods, and the stream by the station where the willows grow, remains, untouched, you would say, though maybe the stableboys on a string of rearing horses crossing the tarmac road between the stables and their gallop are an innovation. And there, in the centre of what passes for a village, is the station sign, re-erected at the bus stop with British Rail's big, decisive Gill sans letterface spelling out Adlestrop. Below it is a bench also rescued from the demolished platform, with a recent brass plate inscribed with Thomas's poem, the rural quiet before the storm of the war in which he died, couched in a line of easy vernacular, a pre-Philip Larkin informality of

delivery that has made his Adlestrop (and its sky and its countryside and all the birds of Oxfordshire and Gloucestershire) the most popular verse in 20th-century English literature on a still half-lost scene.

Bedford
BEDFORDSHIRE

An abstract painting that became a news story, at the Cecil Higgins Art Gallery

Cecil Higgins was the heir to a Bedford brewing family, and he bequeathed his house in a little park beside the River Ouse to the town. It opened as a gallery in 1949, with collections of decorative arts, English watercolours, international prints and small sculptures. In 1979 the local authority added an extension that became the gallery, and the shell of the old house was reconstructed in the form of a Victorian family home, though the Burges room is way beyond what even a Bedford brewer might have been able to afford. It contains artefacts by the talented eccentric fringe Pre-Raphaelite architect William Burges (1827–81), including the washstand that John Betjeman presented to Evelyn Waugh and that Waugh liked so much that he put it into his novel *The Ordeal of Gilbert Pinfold*, in which he fictionalised Burges as 'an English architect of the 1860s, a man not universally honoured but of magisterial status to Mr Pinfold and his friends'.

What I remember most fondly about the Cecil Higgins though is the uproar surrounding the purchase of a fine gouache by Alan Davie (b.1920) called *First Movement in Pink*. Davie was a Scottish painter ahead of his time in Britain, abreast with the continental avant-garde but a loner, as he remains today. I hadn't seen the gouache for around forty-five years until recently, and it is bigger than I recalled. Nor had I remembered its abstract beauty, its resonant colour and design as lucid as stained glass. In 1959 I was in my first year as a reporter on the *Bedfordshire Times*, and when the gallery's board accepted the advice of Ronald Alley, their adviser from the Tate, and bought the painting for its collection, all hell broke loose and *First Movement in Pink* became a news story rather than a work of art.

Professor Sir Albert Richardson, past president of the Royal Academy, architect, founder of the Georgian Society and outvoted board member, told the *Daily Express* in messianic tones, 'The barbarians are at the gates', or if he didn't, the *Express* borrowed it from his letter to *The Times*. The function of RA presidents in the 1950s was to be crusty old fogies, a role the professor filled with gusto. From his gas-lit Georgian house in Ampthill he carried on a second avocation, which was to pronounce judgement on all artistic matters in Bedfordshire. The *Bedfordshire Times*, my employer, ran columns of letters for and against the Davie painting, and Ronald Alley weighed in with a nicely judged defence against Sir Albert's broadside. The keeper, Margaret Greenshield, remained steadfast, and the affair blew over. The gallery, which will be closed until early 2010, has added other Davie paintings, and the artist has donated more than thirty of his prints.

Birmingham

A Parisienne at the Barber Institute, Birmingham University

The Barber Institute was founded in 1932 by Lady Martha Constance Hattie Barber, the wife of a property developer, with the simple instruction that the trustees should fill it with art. The gallery opened at Birmingham University in 1939, and the trustees have met their brief with a small, world-class collection of old masters and 19th-century art, French and English. Among them is a portrait of Countess Golovine by Elisabeth Vigée-Lebrun (1755–1842), hardly among the elite of old masters even within the confines of the Barber collection, but this painting is one of the freshest and most winning in history before Impressionism.

Elisabeth Vigée was born in Paris, and her father, a fan painter and portraitist, taught her the art. Along the way she picked up the hyphen Lebrun from her marriage at the age of twenty-one to a painter and picture dealer, Jean-Baptiste-Pierre Lebrun. Her career spanned the pre-Revolution *ancien régime*, the Revolution and the years of Napoleon, the second revolution of July 1830 and the succeeding liberal rule of Louis-Philippe, known as the July Monarchy, though it lasted until 1848. Vigée-Lebrun sailed serenely through all this. Before the first French Revolution she was Marie Antoinette's favourite painter. That didn't seem to her a point in her favour after the Revolution, and she fled the country. She became a celebrated portrait painter in Russia, Austria and Italy, and in England at the beginning of the 19th century she painted the exquisite likeness of the Duke of Dorset's wife that hangs at Knole in Kent. She painted Emma Hamilton too, better than any of the male artists buzzing around the honeypot, certainly better than Romney, who was besotted by Hamilton. It was not that Vigée-Lebrun's paintings were artless, but that they looked artless.

The alluring personality of Countess Golovine comes across limpid and untrammelled as she turns her head and looks straight out of the canvas as though pleasantly surprised, one hand clutching her red gown with a gold-embroidered border close to her. A headband almost as broad as a turban partly confines her long, flowing hair and enhances its coppery brown colour. Vigée-Lebrun painted the countess in Moscow in the last two or three years of the 18th century and remembered her in her memoirs of 1835 as 'a charming woman, whose wit and talent were enough to keep her visitors amused', which encapsulates what we see in the portrait.

Boughton House
NORTHAMPTONSHIRE

The Duke of Buccleuch's (second) greatest treasure

The Duke of Buccleuch bills Boughton House, the family home in Northamptonshire, as 'the English Versailles'.

It is better than that. It is much smaller but also, to use the duke's own word, much more atmospheric. At Versailles everything is given over to magnificence. Louis XIV lived there on display. His subjects filed through day by day to stare at him, even as he ate his meals. Despite its canals and lakes and thousands of oaks and great vistas, Boughton is a home, and the duke opens it to the public only in the month of August. It looks like a great château, but on the ground floor below the enfilade of state apartments decorated in the French taste with ceilings by Louis Chéron, a group of elegant family rooms look out unexpectedly at sweet little courtyard gardens, as though the palace had originally been a small manor house, which indeed it had.

Of course, the duke has his Scottish homes too – Drumlanrig Castle, Bowhill and Dalkeith – a surfeit of homes, perhaps, for any one man, even if this duke does incorporate in his single person many glorious incarnations as Duke of Buccleuch and Queensberry, Baron Scott of Buccleuch, Earl of Buccleuch, Baron Scott of Whitchester and Eskdaille, Earl of Doncaster and Baron Tynedale, Earl of Dalkeith, Marquis of Dumfriesshire, Earl of Drumlanrig and Sanquhar, Viscount of Nith, Torthorworld and Ross, and Baron Douglas. His wife probably just calls him John, since he owns up to that name too.

In 2003 the last duke's finest painting, Leonardo da Vinci's *Madonna of the Yarnwinder*, which hung at Drumlanrig, began a four-year sabbatical with thieves. It was recovered intact in 2007, but taking this as our cue, we might play the game of choosing an item in Boughton House that we would take if we could. The splendid Annibale Carracci *Portrait of a Young Man*, perhaps; the 18th-century Persian safavid carpet, so lovely it would make the stoniest heart melt, would be difficult to remove unnoticed; maybe the Van Dyck of one of those rich bourgeois Flemish families posing as the holy family; but best of all, with a regretful backward glance at the carpet, is *The Adoration of the Shepherds* by El Greco (1541–1614).

Although this is an early work, El Greco was already about thirty when he painted it. It has been attributed through the centuries to a number of painters, among them the Venetians Leandro Bassano, another Bassano who never actually existed and Tintoretto; there are resemblances to Bassano's night scenes and to Tintoretto's great religious paintings, but, as often happens, now that its attribution to El Greco has been generally accepted it is difficult to see it as anything else. In the early 1570s he had not yet settled in Spain, and his style suggests that he had studied under Tintoretto, but the agitation of the surface, the vitality of the forms, the colour range of reds, blues, yellows and strong greens, and the dramatically fitful lighting, which unifies the surface but eats away the clarity of form and space that the Renaissance had held supreme – all these were qualities El Greco had attained through his contact with Venice, and to them he would later add that intense personal expressionism by which his work is principally recognised. But the Buccleuch *Adoration*, despite having been lopped at the top and having had a couple of angels painted out, is already a masterpiece.

Bredon
WORCESTERSHIRE

Medieval glass showing repentant sinners, Church of St Giles

Apart from the 125 feet long, medieval aisled tithe barn in a really lovely village, here is one of the most rewarding parish churches in the Midlands. Fine and large in itself, basically 12th to 14th centuries, it contains a

modestly beautiful tomb from the 14th century and a richly exotic alabaster tomb (1611) with well-sculpted effigies of Sir Giles and Lady Reed, an Easter sepulchre, windows in the south aisle with detached, slender Purbeck marble shafts and medieval stained glass.

The best of this is in one window to the north of the chancel, grey, early 14th-century glass decorated with trailing vines and with two quite small coloured panels inset, one of them portraying Mary Magdalene, the other Mary of Egypt, both saints, both repentant sinners. Mary Magdalene is one of the favourite figures of Christian art. Mary of Egypt is more obscure, but was a prostitute from Alexandria who reached Jerusalem looking for trade, had a vision at the door of a church, repented of her life and went to live alone in the desert for forty-seven years. The glass is magnificent, darkly glowing with relatively large quarries of stained glass between the lead structure beautifully painted with the details of faces, hair and drapery. Each saint stands in a Decorated church, which might be called diagrammatic were it not for the beauty of the oranges and browns. Mary Magdalene has a blue halo and wears a wonderfully white cowl over her head and a white gown stretching in copious folds to the ground and just showing in parts beneath a black-hemmed yellow mantle. Mary of Egypt wears white over green. The survival of these precious things is an incalculable addition to our heritage.

Burford
OXFORDSHIRE

16th-century monument with American Indians, Church of St John the Baptist

Burford remains the archetypal English country town, teeming with 4×4s, restaurants and boutiques and home, in

Sheep Street, of the *Countryman* magazine. It also has one of England's most famously beautiful churches, which is touched by a celebrated incident in history, marked annually by a visit from Tony Benn: the skirmish between those prototype democrats the Levellers, who had mutinied against what they saw as a new tyranny, and Fairfax's troops who led a night attack and executed three of the ringleaders in the churchyard. Across the church from the entrance in the south porch, set on a quirkily classical architectural structure with Corinthian columns supporting a pediment, is a large relief carving that looks distinctly modern, But it was sculpted in the 16th century. Closer inspection shows that the flattened forms are Amazonian Indians climbing and clinging to an elaborate decoration. Perhaps, like *National Geographic* magazine today, the race of one of the females set the sculptor free to show her sex with uncommon frankness. Below this large panel, suddenly reverting recognisably to period, is a stone chest delightfully carved with two panels in niches, one showing nine cherubic boys, the other seven sweet-faced girls, all kneeling in respect for the departed. The boys wear ruffs, the girls have on long dresses with short, bunched sleeves and each with a bracelet.

The eminence who commissioned this oddity was Edmund Harman, barber to Henry VIII, keeper of the wardrobe and a common packer of the Port of London – an important position despite the unimpressive job description, because it gave him a measure of control over imports and exports, including trade with South America, hence the wonderful exoticism of the monument.

He is buried in Taynton church a mile away but describes himself in his will as a Burford resident, having moved here after the king's death. At the dissolution of the monasteries the king had granted him Burford priory, now a fragmentary ruin. The oddity is that the architectural elements of the Burford monument look as though they were constructed by someone with a verbal report before him but no drawings. Yet the American elements are entirely acceptable, made familiar by the uncanny resemblance to modern art.

Buscot Park
OXFORDSHIRE

Sleeping Beauty at Buscot Park

The owner of Buscot Park in the late 19th century was Alexander Henderson, a successful city financier and art collector, later Lord Faringdon. He joined his collection to the late 18th-century, two-storeyed, nine-bay house he had inherited, including in his Dutch room a portrait painted by the young Rubens during a visit to Genoa in the first decade of the 17th century, presumed to be of the Marchesa Veronica Spinola Doria (sister piece to an even greater portrait at Kingston Lacy), and by Rembrandt a richly melancholy and corporeal portrait of a golden-haired, black-clad young man, now supposed to be Pieter Six, elder brother of the artist's great patron, Jan Six. By coincidence, the owner of Kelmscott Manor a few fields away was the artist William Morris, host at Kelmscott of the Pre-Raphaelites and collaborator since their student days at Oxford with Edward Burne-Jones (1833–98). Henderson must already have heard of Burne-Jones if only because the Grosvenor Gallery in London, where Burne-Jones had scored a hit with an exhibition, became the talk of the town in 1881 when the Gilbert and Sullivan light opera *Patience* opened in London with W.S. Gilbert's lines:

A greenery-yallery, Grosvenor Gallery,
Foot in the grave young man!

which fitted Burne-Jones and the work he produced to a t. When Henderson met him he was painting his epic cycle *The Legend of the Briar Rose*. It took him from 1871 until 1890, but Henderson was determined to buy it.

The fixed star in the occasional ups and despondent downs of Burne-Jones's career was the languor and melancholy pallor of his protagonists. *The Legend of the Briar Rose* has it in full. It is a retelling in four big horizontal paintings of the Sleeping Princess. As is typical of Burne-Jones, his characters are discovered in deeply enervated slumber, expressed in a harmony of twilight blues, greens and mauves of a very high quality. In the first tale the prince is forcing his way without much apparent will or success through the encroaching rose bines; in the second and third paintings bodies strew the ground in the grip of the briars; in the last we see the uncorrupted body of the princess sleeping still. The prince does not kiss her, and there is no resolution. 'I mean by a picture something that never was, never will be,' Burne-Jones once wrote, 'in a light better than any light that ever shone – in a land no one can define or remember, only desire.' As usual, his composition is linear and spatially quite shallow. He saw with a designer's eyes, which is what made stained glass and tapestries from his designs so good and why this sequence sits so well in the saloon.

Some time later, in 1894, Burne-Jones was staying at Kelmscott Manor when Henderson hung the paintings. He walked across the meadows to take a look, went home and painted the little panels of nothing but briars to fill gaps in the wall space.

Castle Frome
HEREFORDSHIRE

A powerfully carved Romanesque font, in the Church of St Michael

The church is utterly rural with its panoramic view eastwards towards Worcestershire, the catslide extension to its tile roof and the little 19th-century half-timbered turret with a short tiled spire. The period is early Norman, like the ruined castle a few hundred yards away, so the magnificent, circular, tub-like Romanesque font of 1140–50 doesn't come as a complete surprise. Its main subject is the baptism of Christ, which is carved crudely but with an overarching design of huge panache and conviction. It packs in every symbol that can be managed. St John stands to the left with cloak thrown over his shoulder like an angel's wing, hands held up in blessing as though he was Christianity's first priest. A miniature Christ sits half-immersed in a series of concentric circles standing as shorthand both for a pool and for the folds of Christ's loin cloth. Four large fish swim either side of him. The mighty hand of God reaches out of the triple layers of interlace patterning below the rim, doubling here as clouds, and the Holy Spirit, a dove, hovers to one side.

Moving around the font, there are, all of them powerfully and cleanly articulated, the almost archetypally bovine bull of St Luke, the lion of St Mark, the eagle of St John and the angel of St Matthew, kin to all those other fiery angels in English ecclesiastical buildings to which these Norman carvers felt so close, stern faced, moustachioed, streamlined, sweeping across the firmament with the winds of heaven.

Chaddesley Corbett
WORCESTERSHIRE

Romanesque font, in the Church of St Cassian

St Cassian is set, unpromisingly at first glance, immediately off the A448 in the hinterland between the M5 and Kidderminster, but the red sandstone church is at the south end of a very fine street lined with half-timbered houses and a good Tudor period pub opposite the lich-gate. Despite the lyrical beauty of its Decorated chancel and the flower-like delicacy of the east window, Chaddesley Corbett was a Norman church. The zigzag arched doorway shows it, as, inside, do the Norman arcades. And then there is the great Herefordshire school Romanesque font, for Herefordshire, like Worcestershire and Shropshire, had been merely an administrative unit of the great kingdom of Mercia, so it isn't surprising that the areas of patronage were not restricted to the county boundaries.

The Chaddesley Corbett font has all the crisp clarity of Herefordshire sculpture, but none of the heavyweight symbolism of the Herefordshire fonts. Instead, this magnificent, chalice-shaped object has a broad band of tight-knit interlace around the rim, thick plaiting on the roll-moulded stem and angular interlace around the short, thick, tapering base. Between the rim and the stem are four dragons, as unfussy as they might be on a Chinese new year pennant, with horseshoe-shaped grins, teeth, like the doorway zigzag, with which each grips the tail of the dragon ahead, and ribbon-like bodies looped into loose hitch knots. This is art as an architectural entity, free, easy, but tautly planned. The dragons must stand for the evil without from which the child will be saved by baptism. But if it's evil, it looks a lot like fun.

Chalford
GLOUCESTERSHIRE

Arts and Crafts interior, in Christchurch

The scarp slope of the Cotswolds looks like an offcut from the West Riding of Yorkshire. The communities in this valley prospered in the broadcloth boom of the 18th and early 19th centuries. But this history is still clearest in the Golden Valley at Chalford, a steep and narrow defile through which the River Frome runs alongside the Thames and Severn Canal, the road to Stroud and Brunel's former Great Western Railway, side by side like production lines. Chalford is still punctuated by sombre mill buildings, some now forming inchoate trading estates and builders' yards, terraces of mill cottages, grand houses for millowners higher up, a Baptist tabernacle and other dissenting chapels. Further down the Church of England clings on behind locked doors with a notice in the porch warning off burglars.

Even if you aren't a burglar it is worth collecting the key from number 3 in the row of cottages opposite. The church is basically a Georgian building with an interior restyled by Cotswold Arts and Crafts workers, an odd mixture of middle-class architects who had seen the light when they read Pugin and Ruskin and Morris, and village workmen, blacksmiths and chippies banded together in a quasi-religious dedication to hand work, returning to the medieval unity of art, architecture and craft. The lingering irony was that, as always, hand-made meant expensive, and most of their work was carried out for the filthy rich. Vintage pieces of their furniture can still be found, at a price, at Liberty.

Chalford was their chance to work in the public domain. The moving spirit was Peter Waals, a Dutch cabinet-maker who had already set up a workshop in Chalford and supplied some of the craftsmen. Norman Jewson (1884–1975), who did most of the designs, was educated at Gonville and Caius and articled to London architects. One of the idealists who had rejected London, he set out in 1907 for the Cotswolds in a donkey and trap, a youngster who outlived the turn-of-the-century pioneers, was in his prime working here in the 1930s and died a very old man in 1975, lamenting the modernist world.

He designed the stone font, with a low relief band of fishes around the bowl, the chancel screen and the organ loft, modest and well mannered, easy on the eye and lovable. He also designed, unexpectedly, a truly remarkable lectern, constructed for Jewson by Waals, chamfered and dovetailed, with the Latin inscription *In principio erat verbum* ('In the beginning was the word') inset in ivory surrounded by a triangle of mother-of-pearl, and on the support a Byzantine cross of ivory with an ancient, nacreous gleam of mother-of-pearl inset between the arms, turquoise, mauve, silver and green.

Charlecote

WARWICKSHIRE

A Stuart monument in the Church of St Leonard

Charlecote Park is where the young William Shakespeare is legendarily said to have been caught poaching in 1584 and arraigned before its owner, Sir Thomas Lucy, justice of the peace sitting in his own case, whom Shakespeare subsequently burlesqued in *The Merry Wives of Windsor* as Justice Shallow. The Lucys had the park in the 12th century from Richard the Lionheart, and in the 19th century remodelled the ancient family mansion and knocked down and rebuilt the church in a harsh Decorated style, though they reinstalled three of the family tombs,

including Shallow's (Sir Thomas died in 1600), but the quaintest and at the same time most interesting is the tomb of another Sir Thomas, who died in 1640, and his wife, by the eminent English sculptor Nicholas Stone (c. 1587–1647).

As English sculpture, like English architecture and English painting, began slowly to leave behind the decorative rigidity of Tudor art, Stone emerged as one of the most inventive of the new generation of sculptor masons. His best known piece is the spectacular memorial sculpture of John Donne in St Paul's Cathedral, both poetry and sculpture, because it was Donne's idea to show him with only a small area of his face showing through his shroud as he stands upright, wraith-like, rising on judgement day. There are others, too, that reveal great originality (see Hatfield, below) and a couple in Westminster Abbey, the accomplished monuments to the brothers Frances and George Holles, which show that Stone had at least seen engravings of Michelangelo's Medici tombs in Florence.

But Stone took on building as well as sculptural contracts and ran a big workshop. The work was uneven, and the monument to Sir Thomas Lucy and his wife is a mild aberration, but at the same time a wonderful illustration of the difficulties artists faced in the craftsman's world beyond Michelangelo's Florence. At 1640 this is quite a late work by Stone, but as a work of art everything is wrong. Four black marble pillars support a very handsome structure of three round arches and a canopy crowned by a flourish of the Lucy arms slipped in above a broken pediment, but the pillars get in the way of the figures. At the back of the monument, behind the three arches, are three shallow arched bays into which Stone attempts to pack in, very nearly, a biography of Sir Thomas, and biography is intractable material for sculpture. The left-hand bay has a relief sculpture of Sir Thomas riding in the countryside with a thatched cottage behind, presumably in the flat lands around Charlecote Park, the early Elizabethan house his grandfather had built. The central bay carries a long encomium in Latin. The right-hand bay shows a section of his library. A representative set of titles and authors' names appear in black on the book spines, Homer, Virgil, Cato, Horace, Winters Ayres and the fattest volume of all simply initialled TL. He was a well-read man and he meant the world to know it.

Stone was paid for the monument, but the figures of the Lucy couple were made by Schoerman, about whom nothing is known, though his name suggests he was one of the army of Flemish carvers who assisted in Southwark workshops.

Chastleton

OXFORDSHIRE

The first time I saw Chastleton I was half-lost and looking for the road to Adlestrop, a village living in equal seclusion (see above). Chastleton arrested me. The house was almost tangibly wrapped in privacy, and the little group of medieval church and Jacobean house seemed perfect, each in lichen-blotched yellow ochre-ish stone, reddish in shadow, with a dovecote in the field opposite. I promised myself I'd return.

I did, and found that the National Trust, which, for all its abundant virtues, has tended to lay the dead hand of good taste upon its houses, has succeeded here in preserving as near as possible what they took over. And when it opens the house, parishioners appear from who knows where to sell coffee in the churchyard if it's fine, in the nave if not.

17th-century arras at Chastleton House

The tapestries have hung in Chastleton probably since four or five years after the night that Hamlet first slew the 'wretched, rash, intruding fool' Polonius as he hid behind an arras. Probably Shakespeare had seen arrases, the Flemish tapestries of the kind that hang at Chastleton, when his company had played country houses around southern England. Walter Jones, a lawyer from a line of Welsh wool merchants in Witney, bought the Chastleton estate in 1602 and soon after built the house within spitting distance of the church. There are a brewhouse and bakery, a pedimented stone gateway before the courtyard and through that a view over the lane to a dovecote built in the field opposite by an 18th-century descendant.

The house was a resounding declaration that Walter Jones had arrived, but, especially after taking the wrong side in the Civil War, these Joneses were so poor they could hardly even keep up with themselves. They and their descendants lived here, accumulating little, leaking a few items in the 20th century until the National Trust acquired it in 1991.

From the beginning Walter Jones wanted the house to look ancient, so he had it built in an outmoded Tudor style with five tall gables facing the courtyard. Old fashioned or not, there was a stairway tower on each side too, like the service tower of a modern block of flats, thus almost fulfilling le Corbusier's definition of a machine for living in (the architect was probably Robert Smythson, who also built Bess of Hardwick's Hardwick Hall). By the time Jones's descendants, the art critic Arthur Clutton-Brock and his family, died or moved out, even the cobwebs were ancient.

The National Trust doesn't deny having taken a vacuum cleaner to the house, but that's about all. One room processes after

another: the screens passage, the hall, the great parlour, the inner hall, the Fettiplace room, the Sheldon room, the elaborately decorated great chamber stuffed with family portraits by forgotten third-rate artists and solid pieces of Jacobean furniture, oak panelling (painted white in the white parlour). Then up the west stairs past a charming still life by Clutton-Brock and, suddenly through a doorway, instead of an attic, the long gallery bursts upon you, barrel vaulted, its original plaster decorated with roses, daisies and fleur-de-lis in Flemish profusion, sculpted in the taste of the contemporary tapestries in the rooms below.

In these circles portraits were merely a respectable gesture towards establishing a family's lineage; tapestries were the valued art objects. The Jones's arrases are in the Sheldon and Fettiplace rooms (named for the gentry families into which offspring had made good marriages). They are older than the house by a few years but were first recorded here in an inventory of 1633. Three are in the Sheldon room ('three peeces of arras hangings') and three in the Fettiplace room. They were woven at the in-places for Flemish tapestry before Brussels took over, Oudenarde (the Sheldon room) and probably Enghiens. Both were best known for verdures (small tapestries of plant life), but Chastleton's subjects are from the Bible and myth. The Fettiplace room tapestries show the story of Jacob and Esau from Genesis, and the more exotic arras in the Sheldon room shows the planetary gods, including Mars, looking like the ghost of Hamlet's father in a plumed helmet. They appear in landscapes framed by classical arches not very different from Chastleton's lichen-covered Cotswolds gateway.

Keeping up with the Joneses, family memorials in the Church of St Mary the Virgin

Inside the church a plain old font under the simple Norman arcade, when I visited, was filled with wildflowers and grasses with fruit and vegetables piled up at the base of the font for harvest festival, a happy marriage of architecture and use. The church tower was built in 1602, you would assume by the Joneses who built and inhabited the house. In this church some of Walter Jones's descendants are buried, with two lovely little commemorative wall plaques marking the burial place beneath a group of them.

The plaques pass as baroque, but they were crafted locally and plonkingly. One has two cherubs on top flanking an elaborate but wonky cartouche of the Jones coat of arms. On the other the cherubs stand on either side of the plaque, above a skull with great hollow eyes crowned with flowers and leaves. On both plaques one of the cherubs weeps into a hanky held to his eyes; on the second one alone he also holds a symbolic torch upside down to extinguish the flame. Among the several names on this plaque are Elizabeth and Henry Jones. He was the son of Arthur Jones, the man who lost the family its fortune by his choice of sides in the Civil War. His successors chose no better than he had, since when James II abdicated they chose the losing side to the point of imbecility well into the 18th century. The arms above this plaque, rather than those Walter Jones so proudly obtained, display the lion rampant of Scotland.

One of the tapestries which has hung at Chastleton House since about the time early in the 17th century when Hamlet slew Polonius behind an arras

Cheltenham
GLOUCESTERSHIRE

A great but forgotten English modernist, in the town art gallery

The Cheltenham Gallery opened in 1907 but was rebuilt by the borough architect, David Ross, with an art deco façade as late as 1987–9 and 'Art Gallery and Museum' lettered in cursive turquoise neon strip lighting. Inside is a group of unexpected classics, like the 17th-century Italian master Guido Reni and a drawing by Michelangelo's friend and biographer, Giorgio Vasari. But the body is British. There's a low-key group of 20th-century English artists, some well known – the magus of Cookham, Stanley Spencer, and the St Ives abstractionist Terry Frost – and lots of others who never made it or did but have been forgotten. One of the forgotten is David Bomberg (1890–1957).

He had been a Vorticist, that outburst of energetic British abstract or semi-abstract modernism that was another of the victims of the First World War. 'I look upon nature, while I live in a steel city,' Bomberg declared before the war. 'I reject everything in painting that is not Pure Form. I hate the colours of the East, the Modern Medievalist, and the Fat Man of the Renaissance.' Afterwards he painted landscape and was binned by art history. His wife pulled him out of a deep depression at his neglect by persuading him in the 1940s to embark on a series of flower pieces, of which *Summer Flowers* is one, a swirlingly brushed cascade of colour as much about the paint surface as about the subject, but getting down not so much the look of the flowers (hollyhock, lupin, foxglove at a guess) but the memory of the look. The Paul Nash *Flower in a Window* hanging adacent to Bomberg's canvas shows by contrast how utterly modern Bomberg was, how much better he was in truth than most of the celebrated English artists of the century. But he had moved from pure form to 'the quest for spirit in the mass', the phrase sticking in the memories of his post-war students when he eked a living with evening classes at Borough Road Polytechnic.

Among these students were Frank Auerbach (b.1931) and Leon Kossoff (b.1926), moonlighting from full-time courses at St Martin's School of Art. Kossoff found Bomberg's teaching a liberation from the daytime job. Bomberg, living under the perpetual sense of failure in the eyes of the world, found it in him to give his students the courage to succeed. Neither Auerbach nor Kossoff ever deviated from their chosen approach, and one of Kossoff's paintings hanging nearby, *Portrait of George Thompson* (1975), shows the debt unequivocally. It emerges from a surface so encrusted with pigment that it distorts the rectangular shape of the canvas with its overlaps. The face is pink, the shirt blue, the chair red, and the background green: fluid yet inflexible statements of painterly fact, an accretion of observation that amounts finally not so much to a portrait as to a testament to the living essence of worked paint.

Cirencester
GLOUCESTERSHIRE

The Boleyn Cup, in the Church of St John the Baptist

Of all the Cotswolds wool towns in the 16th century, Cirencester was the most prosperous. It had a massive abbey until – familiar story – Henry VIII razed it, but in the 1520s the citizens had rebuilt the parish church as one of the biggest in England, with an extraordinary fan-vaulted, three-storey south porch invading the marketplace, a noble Perpendicular tower, nave, aisles, chancel and five chapels.

In 1564 Richard Masters came to Cirencester. He had been Queen Elizabeth's surgeon since 1559. He must quickly have won her confidence and affection because about 1563 she gave him the cup that Henry VIII had presented to her mother Anne Boleyn. In 1565 the queen granted the former abbey lands to Dr Masters and his heirs, and in turn Masters presented the cup to the church of the town in which he now had a home. Cathedrals have treasuries, parish churches don't and tend to keep their precious items in a bank vault. Until 1963 Cirencester, too, kept its treasure under lock and key, but then descendants of Dr Masters paid for a glass-fronted, illuminated safe to be let into the short stretch of wall dividing nave from chancel. Here the Boleyn Cup is on permanent display, celebrated as much because it is unique as for its beauty.

Maybe Henry VIII made a practice of presenting a silver gilt cup to his wives as a love token. Certainly he is known to have given one to Jane Seymour on their marriage. It was melted down by Charles I, and joined all the other royal gold and silver plate, including a piece designed by Hans Holbein in 1534 for Anne Boleyn to give to Henry, none of it now in existence except as designs. The Boleyn Cup's heavily embossed base and bowl and the engraved pattern around the rim are features of the work of another German, Hans Brosamer (c.1500–52). He fashioned the cup of silver gilt in 1535. It is more than 12 inches in height, and surmounting the lid is Anne Boleyn's falcon emblem. The bowl spreads out like an open lily, but as we know, 'lilies that fester smell far worse than weeds', and two years after receiving her gift from the king she had failed to produce a son and heir, was out of royal favour and was executed on charges of adultery and treason rigged up by the king's creature, Thomas Cromwell.

Cockayne Hatley

BEDFORDSHIRE

Flemish Catholic panelling in an Anglican chancel, Church of St John the Baptist

As Napoleon's forces fanned out on their conquering march through the continent they had armies of antique dealers at their heels stripping out the contents of churches and abbeys. These selfless saviours of civilisation prised loose art treasures that had seemed as immovable as the rock of the church itself and sold them off. England was the principal beneficiary, its aristocracy not yet in decline, its commercial classes increasing in wealth. Among them were the leading gentry of Cockayne Hatley, the Cockayne family. They populated the manor house and the vicarage. When Henry Cust, a son of Lord Brownlow of the Hatley estate across the border in Cambridgeshire, became lord of the manor he simply harnessed Hatley to the village name of Cockayne, and Cockayne to the family name. Tricked out now as the Rev. Henry Cockayne Cust, he installed in the chancel windows glass with the armorial bearings of the Cockayne and Cust families, and in the 1820s he bought the Flemish choir stalls of 1689, which had been liberated from the abbey of Aulne near Charleroi. In little St John the Baptist they filled the north and south walls of both nave and chancel with, presumably, pews down the centre for the humble. To these Henry Cust added a screen from Louvain and communion rails from Malines. So Cockayne Hatley, scarcely more than a church tower appearing on the skyline in almost unpopulated landscape where the big night out is in Potton, is fitted today with a collection of sumptuous church furnishings stripped from the richest of Low Country Catholic abbeys.

Even a son of Lord Brownlow, even in

This panelling originally joined a Flemish screen and Flemish communion rails. It was carted off by Napoleon's army and bought by the Rev. Henry Cockayne Cust for his Anglican church in Cockayne Hatley

sleepy Cockayne Hatley, could hardly have got away with this when, a few years later, the Oxford Movement awoke dormant fears in a very Protestant England that Rome – and Roman Catholic practices – were on the march. But for now the established church slumbered peacefully, and Cockayne Hatley gained its luxurious carvings in high relief of saints and sages, popes and cardinals of the Catholic church on the stall backs separated by chubby putti carrying instruments of Christ's Passion: the crown of thorns, the whip with which he was scourged, the pole with the sponge soaked in vinegar, the sword that a soldier thrust into his side, the cloth with which he mopped his brow. The stall seats and headrests have a black pattern inlay, and the saints' busts are surrounded by garlands of foliage with leafy festoons beneath them, not carved with the airy naturalism of Grinling Gibbons but compacted and disciplined, a different art for

a different mindset, but happily bedded down and indicating, perhaps, regained religious tolerance – or merely utter indifference to religious ideology.

Compton Verney
WARWICKSHIRE

A saint by a German master of limewood carving

Lord Willoughby de Broke's name has the ring of a pantomime character, but he was the George Verney who built Compton Verney, a big stone 18th-century house a few miles east of Stratford-upon-Avon. Peter Moores is the son of John, philanthropist and art collector, who bought Compton Verney when it was falling down and lavished £40 million on renovating and converting it into a wonderful gallery of art in a park with a classical bridge crossing a lake and cedars of

Lebanon as old as the house. He has made a point of buying where there are areas of weakness in British collections, so here the star rooms contain his collection of paintings from Naples and from 15th- and 16th-century Germany.

In 2001 the foundation paid the record sum at Sotheby's in New York for a piece of medieval sculpture of £2 million plus: a female saint carved in limewood by Tilman Riemenschneider (c.1460–1531), with her clear brow, slanting eyes, deeply etched tresses and big headdress with a ribbon band floating free. And by a nice irony the saint had to be shipped from Würzburg, where Riemenschneider had carved it in his workshop some time between 1515 and 1520 and to which it had returned on loan after a spell on show at the Met in New York.

Riemenschneider, with Veit Stoss, Dürer's Nuremburg contemporary, was the greatest of the limewood sculptors, the artists and craftsmen (craftsmen in their time, artists to us) whose workshops created a vast trade in objects from small candleholders to huge altar screens. There is something Teutonic about the ambition to make sculptural versions of paintings by their contemporary Italian artists of great biblical subjects, the Annunciation, the adoration of the shepherds, the Last Supper and so on, something faintly absurd, yet though I have not seen Riemenschneider's greatest works in Cracow, I have been to Bamberg and Nuremberg and, so to speak, bowed the head in admiration for his vast achievement. These are some of the greatest works of late Gothic art. Riemenschneider was the first German sculptor to reject a painted finish on his work, opting for varnish, an approach that allowed more variety in the carving, because polychrome sculptures had a layer of gesso beneath the pigment that flattened out subtleties in the sculpted surface.

Compton Verney's rare and beautiful female saint has one hand missing, and it's the hand that held an attribute that would have identified her. The other hand holds a book, which might mean that she is St Barbara, a pagan maiden of Heliopoulos whose reading led her to Christianity, upon which her father quite naturally beheaded her. Compton Verney's 3 feet tall saint, sculpted from a single piece of limewood, has had her back hollowed out in the making, not necessarily because the statue was slotted into a relief ensemble, but certainly because limewood has the quality of drying at a very different speed at the core than at the surface and then cracking. In this case, the sinuous inclination of the saint's figure to her right suggests that she stood to the right of the central figure in a composition.

Daglingworth
GLOUCESTERSHIRE

Anglo-Saxon survivors at the Church of the Holy Rood

The 4×4s and impeccable stone houses show that Daglingworth is at least as commuter rich as farmer friendly, which in a sense returns it to its pre-Conquest condition, when the currents of trade flowed from the Middle East through Europe and spilled into this clearing lost in lush folds of woodland a brisk walk from Cirencester. Restorers worked assiduously to improve the little Saxon/medieval church here and bring it into line with Victorian expectations. Luckily for us, they retained three Anglo-Saxon relief carvings set into the north and south walls of the nave. These show signs of the style of early Christian art of Syria, a contemporary influence that journeyed west with merchants and pilgrims, if only in their memories, some time between the late 8th century and the 11th; the current best guess is around 1020–30.

It was once customary to describe the Daglingworth sculptures as primitive, carved by local masons untrained in the higher skills, but from Gauguin onwards artists worked against the grain to re-create the untrammelled majesty of the 'primitive' in their own work, so it's easier in retrospect for us to admire the grandeur of such simplicity. The calm and ample Daglingworth figures possess not so much majesty, as massive human dignity, a stylisation of suffering. The Christ in Glory of one carving and the crucified Christ of the other have been worked by the same sculptor. In both panels the thick strands of his hair lie close against the head, the sweeping tips of a long moustache overlap the beard, and the almond-shaped eyes are open, even on the cross – the very outline that Picasso borrowed for the eyes of the tarts in *Les Demoiselles d'Avignon*, the painting in which he tore aside the veil of the previous 700 years of Western art. The Daglingworth sculptor has worked with his chisel at the untroubled fullness of form to chip tiny light- and shadow-catching indentations in the white Cotswold limestone.

Incidentally, pre-Conquest art often reached these shores through the filter of the Carolignian courts of Germany, but the clue to the direct Eastern influence on the Daglingworth mason is that the Christ in Glory is wearing a long gown tied with a four-stranded knotted girdle. St Peter is similarly garbed in another carving, in which he grasps a massive key. Long gowns were a Middle Eastern feature very uncommon in England. The second giveaway is that the

The book in the remaining hand of this wonderfully carved saint at Compton Verney may identify her as St Barbara, whose reading brought her to Christianity. What we know for certain is that the sculptor was one of the greatest of German 15th-16th-century limewood sculptors

crucified Christ is accompanied on either side by Stephaton, the bystander who taunted him with a vinegar-soaked sponge when his throat was parched, and Longinus, the Roman soldier who thrust his spear into Christ's side, a pair rarely shown in art west of Constantinople.

Deerhurst
GLOUCESTERSHIRE

Anglo-Saxon west wall, Church of St Mary

January, and the flood waters of the Severn nuzzle up against the churchyard wall. The river is swollen to ½ mile in width, eddying around little islands and with trees poking up through the surface. It's easy to believe that in the Middle Ages the Severn was navigable from the Bristol Channel as far as Tewkesbury, 5 miles northeast of Deerhurst. The 13th-century monk William of Malmesbury reported that in the 10th century Deerhurst was 'a small monastery and now [is] just an empty shell of the past', almost as it appears a thousand years later, although once again it has a congregation.

An arrow at the west front points the way around the ruined apse towards the southwest corner, where, with succinct wit almost, another arrow points towards heaven, because high up on the wall is the carving of an angel, probably of the mid-10th century. Unfortunately, it's really not possible to appreciate it much from ground level. Not even the photograph in the church leaflet is altogether satisfactory since it was taken at an odd angle from, it seems, a first-floor window in the church's Siamese twin, Priory Farm, built where the cloister used to be. It is an almost invariable rule that when an account of Anglo-Saxon art describes an object as important, it means important as evidence in indicating when particular styles were prevalent, if, in fact, a date can be fixed at all. Take a look, but the real stuff is inside.

Let's say straight away that the most 'important' object is the font, 10th century with spiral ornament and vine scrolls (and indeed very handsome), and the most beautiful is a 14th-century stained glass window of a sinuous St Catherine under a filigree canopy and wearing a rich green gown under a glowing brown mantle against a brilliant, heavily leaded red ground. The glass is inserted in one of several Decorated Gothic windows, so that it seems that soon after William of Malmesbury was writing the church moved into better times. But enough evidence survives of its Anglo-Saxon origins, and the most dramatic single feature is the west wall of the nave, which is 9th to 10th century. This is a sheer stucco surface pierced by a door into the west porch with the masonry arch protruding through the stucco and magnificent decorative stone carvings of a formulaic wild animal's head at the base of each end of the arch. At first-floor level is a blocked door, which led from a gallery above the nave into the tower, and to the left of it is a triangular opening as keen as an arrowhead, probably an aperture, or squint, to use the evocative technical term, for someone in the tower to look into the church without being seen. In the middle of the wall above that again is a double window, with triangular heads borne on square fluted pilasters. And above that is a flat stone panel that may once have been decorated. There are more squints and openings on the nave walls above the pointed arcade, but it is the west wall that counts, with its asymmetrical outbreaks of great blocks of masonry and dark spaces in the immaculate white.

Dodford

Arts and Crafts at the Church of Holy Trinity and St Mary

Dodford is an astonishing relic, a Chartist village at heart if no longer quite in fact. Chartism, with its inflammatory demands for annual parliaments, the abolition of property qualifications for Members of Parliament, the payment of MPs, secret ballots, equal electoral districts and universal suffrage (universal, that is, except for the half of the human race that was female), was a movement of labouring men and artisans, the 'blistered hands, fustian jackets, and unshorn chins', in the phrase of its charismatic leader Feargus O'Connor. It sprang up in 1837 and died out quite fast when the heady excitement of the continental revolutions of 1848 was followed by an economic upturn. But meanwhile, O'Connor led it into a new promised land of the peaceful settlement of allotments for the needy. He laid out the roads at Dodford that same year and 'location day', when families moved in, followed in 1849 and was greeted with abuse from the national press. It was the fifth of these settlements that promised 4 acres a family and the most successful, with market gardening well into the 20th century, when strawberries were going to Cadbury's for jam-making and garlic to Lee & Perrins for Worcestershire Sauce. Finally, Dodford men were going to Longbridge to work at Austin motors, and the Birmingham bourgeoisie were settling in Dodford Chartist bungalows as commuters. Conservation and listed building orders preserve the husk of the old idealism.

The village hall stands today where Dodford built its first chapel. Holy Trinity and St Mary succeeded in 1907–8 on another plot. Despite the Chartist song for Dodford

A charming plaster decoration carved by a craftsman of the Bromsgrove guild of the Arts and Crafts movement for Holy Trinity and Saint Mary, the simple church that replaced the original chapel in the village of Dodford

that promised 'less parsons and more pigs', the parson duly arrived with the new church. It was an enterprise of the Bromsgrove guild of the Arts and Crafts movement – modest, informal and hand-built and crafted – and so quite in line with the year when the Chartist tigers turned into pussy cats.

The architect, Arthur Bartlett, built it with some wit. There is a south transept ending in a tower (with a rose window) and that L-shape turns into a square for open air preaching with the enclosure of the space between nave and transept with an answering L-shaped wooden passage. Inside the carving, the plaster panels of the fruits of Dodford on the massive concrete arches and stained glass, more Peter Pan than St Peter, and delicately decorated clear glass quarries are pretty individually and amount to a successful

scheme lifted into the extraordinary by the big and decidedly immodest rood cross on the beam across the chancel arch. The metalworker Amy Walford made this in beaten copper set with silver and glittering, jewel-like enamels. It is an interpretation of the line from Revelation 22.2: 'the tree of life, which bare twelve manner of fruits, and yielded her fruit every month: and the leaves of the tree were for the healing of the nations.' But the ostensible symbolism is subsumed in a wonderful affirmation of beauty.

Dorchester
OXFORDSHIRE

*Carved and stained glass Jesse window,
Dorchester Abbey*

What remains of a town that was important
enough to have had a bishop in the early 7th
century is a fine High Street at the point in
the broad plain where the waters of the Isis
and the Thame meet and become the
Thames. It has a couple of famous old pubs,
the White Hart and the George. The original
abbey has left no traces except foundations.
The present abbey, a lopsided accretion of
various periods from 1140 to 1601 and later
renovations, is, however, a treasure house.
The greatest of these is the chancel, with, in
the north wall, the tree of Jesse, a stupendous
collaboration of carving and glass illustrating
the same theme and, since the east window
lost its original glass, unique. From the figure
of Christ's progenitor, Jesse, lying on the sill,
springs the tree with Christ's ancestors
carved on the branches with just enough
space between so that they are not treading
on one another's heads. King David stands
on the sill to the right playing a harp. The
ensemble is a fine conception, wonderfully
realised, and the blissfully slumbering figure
of Jesse himself is a great work of lyricism, its
shallow relief not far from the drawing
board, nor from the linear style of missal
illustration of the period, but far enough for
the sharply defined folds of drapery and the
broad, flat masses between to set up a lovely
harmony of light and shadow. The great
chancel ensemble has an east window entirely
of tracery carved with scenes of the Passion,
and the window in the south wall has a
horizontal (transom) bar on which carved
figures walk, carrying the bier of St Birinius.
Beneath this are the priest's seats, the sedilia,
with canopies rising in tall pinnacles
decorated with crockets and figures of saints,
and, very unusually, above the seats within
the canopy are small windows set with
stained glass.

Dyrham
GLOUCESTERSHIRE

*Paintings that Samuel Pepys saw at
Dyrham Park*

Whether Samuel Hoogstraeten (1627–78)
painted the pair of seductive Netherlandish
views in London or in his home town of
Dordrecht, he sold them in London to
Thomas Povey. Povey, who was highly placed
in the king's service, hung the paintings in his
house in Lincoln's Inn Fields. After dinner
one evening in January 1663 he showed one
of them, a small corridor view, to his
colleague Samuel Pepys and again a few
weeks later. Again, in September the
following year Pepys was at Povey's for
dinner, and again Pepys reacted with almost
childlike pleasure, this time to both paintings
(or maybe more): 'Here I was afresh
delighted with Mr Povys house and pictures
of perspective; being strange things, to think
how they do delude one's eye, that methinks
it would make a man doubtful of swearing
that he ever saw anything.'

   In due course Povey passed the paintings
on to his nephew William Blathwayt of
Dyrham Park. Blathwayt hung the second
view, of a courtyard, on the walnut staircase
but instead of hiding the view down a
corridor in a closet he placed it in a room
where it could be seen through the library (as
it now is) at the end of a vista of open doors
where it appeared to be a continuation of the
vista. It remains in the same position today
and has the same effect on visitors to
Dyrham as it had on Pepys in Lincoln's Inn
Fields.

   Like his uncle and Pepys, Blathwayt was a
civil servant, but in service to William III

rather than his predecessors Charles II and James II. England and Holland were rivals in trade and opponents in war, but such things rarely spilled over into cultural or even personal relationships, and the accession of William of Orange to the English throne in 1688 blew away the smoke of battle. Blathwayt built Dyrham on the site of an old manor house on a hillside a few miles east of Bristol and furnished it in the Dutch manner, a taste acquired in the service of the British ambassador to The Hague, hung his own collection of Dutch paintings as well as Povey's and added Delft china. His successors were men of limited means and ambitions, and the house and park eventually passed to the National Trust, its appearance still basically as the first William Blathwayt had planned it, still filled with Dutch artefacts.

Hoogstraeten was a pupil of Rembrandt's and published an appreciative analysis of his teacher's painting, but he himself turned to painting popular genre works, no doubt in response to the taste of a rising middle class. The National Gallery has his *A Peepshow with Views of the Interior of a Dutch House*, which is a box painted with views inside and supplied with peepholes. It appealed to exactly the same kind of Dutch public for whom in England Pepys stands as the open-hearted champion.

Hoogstraeten didn't regard this kind of work as merely crowd pleasing. 'A perfect picture is like a mirror of nature,' he wrote, 'in which non existing things appear to exist and deceive in an acceptable, pleasing, and commendable fashion.' Not too much theory there, no philosophising about the relationship of the flat surface to the three-dimensional representation, neither to art in the service of society nor in reaction against it, but next time I am near Dyrham I shall head straight for the view through three doors, across the library and a corridor, to Hoogstraeten's eye-twisting deception.

Eardisley
HEREFORDSHIRE

A Romanesque font, in the Church of St Mary Magdalene

As a village, Eardisley may not be as pretty as its near namesake and close neighbour Eardisland, nor is its church (of mixed periods from the 12th century) particularly inspiring, but the font that stands in St Mary Magdalene and that dates from around 1150 is one of the finest works of art of England.

The challenge for Romanesque sculptors was to follow the moulding of an arch or the shape of a keystone or a corbel or the bowl of a font. The constrictions of the format produced carving whose power resides in every inch within the allotted space becoming part of the design, and each separate design is linked in flat relief so that it is not simply embellishment but an intrinsic part of the architecture.

Emphatic bands of linked knot patterns at the rim of the bowl and the base contain the broader band of relief figure carving. To modern eyes the most dramatic subject shows a knight lunging with his spear below the shield of his adversary and running him through the thigh. Local historians think this is a re-creation of the mortal fight between Sir Roger Baskerville and his father-in-law, Lord Clifford, over disputed land. It's anyone's guess why it should merit such prominence on a font – perhaps the pope's pardon to Baskerville for killing his wife's father was related to another panel representing the harrowing of hell, a largely apocryphal but favourite medieval theme in which the crucified Christ liberates hell's prisoners. On the Eardisley font Christ grasps a poor sinner by the wrist and hauls him free of the sinuously intertwining creeper forms that symbolise eternal servitude. Further around, there is another figure with a halo

For the drawing room at Eastnor Castle, A.W.N. Pugin called on Minton for its tiles, Brussels for its tapestries, his lifelong collaborator John Hardman for his expertise with ecclesiastical hardware, and his own early experience as a stage designer to invent a Gothic domestic interior without precedent

whose identity and role are not clear, and a splendid lion, simultaneously heraldic and ferocious. The harrowing of hell is as remote to the modern world as the Easter Island statues, but Eardisley is another proof that formal magnificence retains for us the aura of art even though cultural meaning has drained away into the sands of time.

Eastnor
HEREFORDSHIRE

The best of fake Gothic, Pugin's drawing room at Eastnor Castle

The 1st Earl Somers built Eastnor Castle when the quaint medievalism of Sir Walter Scott's Waverley novels was captivating the nation. In 1812 he hired Robert Smirke (1780–1867) to build him a fake Norman castle big enough to impress his neighbours. It is big

but inert, a great grey mass of stone painfully hewn from the Forest of Dean and shipped by sea and river to his 13,000 acre estate in Herefordshire. The fakery extends to the rooms within, but this is where the fun starts, and there's a story to it.

The family abandoned this forbidding pile in 1939 but couldn't attract even wartime institutional squatters. They moved back in 1945, and the current Somers descendants, James and George Hervey-Bathurst, were brought up here, playing in the landscaped park in fine weather and pedalling their bikes through echoing empty halls when it rained. As the heir, James moved in with his wife Sarah in 1989, and she fell for Eastnor too. She painstakingly redecorated the state rooms, shifted some of the Renaissance armour out of the great hall to make it less forbidding, rehung the fake Titians, Holbeins and Van Dycks – "'follower of'", we say here,' one of the room attendants corrected me without a hint of frost – put the smaller family rooms lovingly into liveable shape, brought in English Heritage for the sake of the loot (£400,000 and ongoing) and opened to the public. At the end of all that, the best room is still the most faked of all, the drawing room, originally designed as the dining room, by A.W.N. Pugin (1812–52) for the 2nd earl.

Pugin grew up when the Gothic revival was at first no more than a fashion, a few pointy windows, cusped arches and light-hearted Gothic motifs on plastered ceilings. And then it became a requirement of the church commissioners appointed to build great brick barns from which Christianity would be dispensed to the new labouring poor in the fast-spreading city slums. These too fulfilled a pattern-book minimum of basic Gothic. Pugin brought religious passion and archaeological correctness to his work, but when he received domestic commissions there was no true archaeological precedent. So he made it up. And it works.

It may be that he drew on his early experience as a stage designer (among other things, he had created a set for a ballet of Scott's *Kenilworth*) as well as on his personal collection of medieval artefacts and applied them to his deep well of knowledge of Gothic architecture. At any rate, at Eastnor he devised a room of slender pilasters rising to a gorgeous fan vault, a chamber built around a gorgeously decorated fireplace inlaid with Minton tiles beneath a low pointed arch and an overmantel of richly decorated low relief with a central panel of lions supporting the Somers coat of arms flanked by two panels of harts lying in fields of scrolly decoration, a motif repeated in the wall space between the splayed fan vaulting. The lovely Brussels tapestries of mythological scenes around the walls were a wedding present from the 2nd earl's wife. John Hardman of Birmingham manufactured the extraordinary chandelier to the design of Pugin, his lifetime collaborator. It was shown in the Great Exhibition of 1851, and its twin sister is in the Pugin–Barry Houses of Parliament. Here it hangs from the centre of the ceiling, spikily Gothic, more thorn than rose.

Eton

BERKSHIRE

Unique 15th-century mural scheme by 'sundry painters', in Eton College chapel

The Eton wall game is more famous than the Eton wall paintings, but there is nothing within England like this scheme of medieval murals and nothing like it for its extent or fine condition. Whoever the artists were, they worked on the panels between 1479 to 1487 – that is, relatively soon after Henry VI founded the college in 1440 in Buckinghamshire, where it belongs historically, but though it is now in Berkshire, we are retaining its historic identity north of the Thames. The date signifies that the college chapel is Perpendicular. It is 190 feet long, although it consists only of chancel and ante-chapel. A nave had originally been intended, as at Merton College, Oxford, which would have made it a huge church. One name is known from documents about the mural commission, William Baker, and half of another one, Gilbert, but nothing else is known of either, and some writers assume Flemish authorship.

Judging by the names and initials, generations of ruffians have hacked into the stone walls and balustrade of the stairs ascending to the chapel. Eton could only be a school or a prison, and prisoners could scarcely have dealt with the murals more barbarically than successive authorities did at Eton. The new militant Protestantism during the reign of Elizabeth was the first cause of the murals being whitewashed over as superstitious images (the college barber did the deed). Eton uncovered them in 1847, but the provost took much the same line as Elizabeth's commissioners, declared them unfit for a religious community, had the top row of murals destroyed (one survives) and hid the rest behind new choir stall canopies. In 1927 the college removed the canopies and once again revealed the surviving rows on the north and south walls of eight large square panels divided by painted canopies above niches with statues.

The painting is assured and elegant with a linearity close to the best sculpture and illustration of the period, and there is a sophisticated organisation of interiors and exteriors and of incident: a man manoeuvring a small boat through rough waters, men and women on horseback, or praying, fighting or lying abed in sickness. It is a rich tapestry, metaphorically, though in fact they are all in oils painted in grisaille (monotone) directly on to the wall – the large blocks of dressed stone show through.

Each panel on the north side shows a miracle performed by the Virgin Mary: events such as the woman who fails to attend a Candlemas service and that night dreams of the Virgin and awakes with a holy candle in her hand, and the woman in bed who has died unshriven but who is brought back to life, confesses and dies again, which no doubt passed for a happy ending in church circles. The eight panels on the south wall are a continuous narrative of an empress, falsely accused of immorality by the emperor's brother and proved innocent by intercession of the Virgin. In the last panel she renounces her crown before a discomfited emperor as she kneels before an abbess to take the veil, an inspiration no doubt, but not a frequent career move by Old Etonians.

Fairford
GLOUCESTERSHIRE

A full set of medieval stained glass, Church of St Mary's

The demonic vision of blood-dark flames engulfing the souls of the damned in the Last Judgement in the big west window of St Mary's is surrealism 400 years before the event. But pre-Reformation surreal was the real thing. It was the stuff of sweaty nightmares and dealt in eternal damnation, the threatened fate of all mankind. Even so, the healthily agnostic Alec Clifton-Taylor is sniffy about the Fairford glass in his book *Parish Churches as Works of Art*, and with some reason. To stay with the Last Judgement, there is no point in pretending that the craft of its makers comes anywhere near the mastery of their contemporary creator of nightmares, Hieronymus Bosch, even allowing for the difference in his case of oil on canvas or panel.

But in the context of English church art the comparison is almost beside the point. The architecture of St Mary's is contemporary with the stained glass windows – that is, Perpendicular Gothic, that wonderfully rational and exclusively English taming of the florid Decorated Gothic that had gone before. Fairford is among the most handsome of Cotswold wool towns, and its church was built from the bottom up at the turn of the 16th century by one of its wealthy burghers, the clothier John Tame, so it is Perpendicular through and through, with a grandly proportioned central tower. In the great churches of this period we are usually most conscious of the beneficent rhythm,

This Doom window in St Mary's, Fairford, is the most spectacular of the only complete scheme of medieval stained glass in an English parish church. The Netherlander Barnard Flowers, glazier to Henry VII of England, was in charge of the workshop that produced it

ordered intervals and light, but in Fairford this order and intellectual restraint contrast strikingly with a window narrative bursting with horror of the hereafter and cruelty and bloodshed on earth.

Nobody knows how or why, but neither Henry VIII's commissioners nor Cromwell's licensed Puritan hooligans smashed any of the windows, so Fairford remains the only parish church in the country with a full set of pre-Reformation glass, giving a unique insight into the dark depths of the mind of Merrie England. As a matter of fact, the head of the stained glass workshop was not English but, like Bosch, Netherlandish. His name was Barnard Flowers, and he was Henry VII's master glazier, but using his name as the artist is shorthand. Fairford's narrative of the twenty-eight windows is a joint production of designer and glazier and their assistants in harness, the medieval faith factory at full blast, running from the temptation of Eve to the crucifixion, resurrection and ascension, balancing Old Testament against New, the Last Judgement flanked by the judgement of Solomon on one hand, and on the other the verdict of David on the messenger who brought the news of Saul's death and admitted to having helped his suicide: 'And David said unto him, thy blood be upon thy head.' Flowers, at his best with terror, shows the executioner with a samurai-like sneer and the headless corpse of the transgressor at his feet. This mood persists into the chancel window of the Deposition where, instead of the normal convention of a gracefully expired Christ being tenderly lowered from the cross, the artist has used the confined space of the narrow window light to show the bloodless corpse doubled at the waist like a hairpin, the head dangling at the level of the feet – a case of architectural circumstance imposing, or inspiring, a passage of startling realism.

There is finer stained glass in England, but nowhere else is it possible to sense what a church must have meant in a local community, with the confidence of its architecture, the wonderful naturalism of the carvings on the string course and, inside, the great narrative sequence, at once community Bible, work of art and cinema.

Fownhope
HEREFORDSHIRE

Along the road from Holme Lacy, the 18th-century house, now a holiday hotel, where Pope inscribed his lines to the Man of Ross (see Ross-on-Wye, below), is Fownhope, a relaxed and unspoilt composition of houses and cottages, pubs and a couple of shops strung out along the B4224 south of Hereford on the wooded eastern bank of the River Wye. It would be worth stopping here anyway for a stroll along the street and down to the river, as well as to find the cider press monument to Fownhope's under-celebrated bare-knuckle champion, Tom Spring. But the main sight is a fine church, mostly 14th century but substantially Norman, with a Romanesque central tower and part of the nave, with, above all, an exceptionally fine carved tympanum.

A Virgin and Child beside the Wye, Church of St Mary

In the profound depths of the Wye valley, on the B4224 between Hereford and Ross, in a 14th-century church retaining a central Norman tower, is another monumental tympanum of the mid-12th century from the hand of one of the great Herefordshire school of Romanesque sculptors. It has been removed from the outside door and fixed to the inside wall beneath the west window, and it shows the Virgin and child, deeply carved and well preserved. The mother and child raise their right hands in blessing, hands massively over sized like the hand of God that appears at the top of certain sculptures (the Romsey rood, for one; see Romsey, South), prodding apocalyptically through a cloud. In fact, the suggestion has been made that the Fownhope tympanum might represent not the mother and child but the holy trinity. However, that means interpreting the bird of prey at the left as a dove and ignoring the winged lion in the equivalent right-hand position. So the Virgin and child let it be, a group of immense stability in deeply pleated garments dropping from the Virgin's knees to her widely spread feet, an inwardly contained rhythmic movement that is released by the two blessing hands into the loosely looping powerful rhythms of the three-strand vegetation entwining the bird and lion. Nothing could be further from the classical ideal of form, nor more gloriously articulated.

An English sport celebrated, the Tom Spring memorial

When I asked the way at the Green Man in Fownhope to the Tom Spring memorial, the lad behind the bar had never heard of it. His predecessor 150 years ago would certainly have known, for Tom Spring was, in his time, the bare-fist champion of all England. He was born Tom Winter, the son of the Fownhope butcher, but once he had beaten everyone in sight locally and turned pro, he skittishly changed his name to Spring. Bare-fist pugilism, like cricket, cheese rolling, horse racing and two kinds of football, was a sport born in England and spread around the world – only cheese rolling, inexplicably, went no further than the counties of its birth. Spring was one of the first to turn it into something like the athletic art to which Muhammad Ali succeeded. In 1821 Tom Cribb abdicated as champion of England and handed his title to

his protégé Spring. Twice in 1824 Spring fought epic contests against the Irish champion, Jack Langan. The first match, at Worcester, went seventy-seven rounds; the second, at Chichester, seventy-six. Each time Langan fought until he dropped, and Spring, his fists ruined by drumming on Langan's skull, retired unbeaten.

Hadn't the barman of the Green Man heard of Jack Johnson, Joe Louis, Sugar Ray Robinson and Rocky Marciano? In 1992 the International Boxing Hall of Fame posthumously inducted Spring as a member alongside these 20th-century successors. The locals of the Green Man and the New Inn were quicker off the mark and joined a campaign in 1954 to create a local monument by the side of a rivulet in a field eight-tenths of a mile on the road to Woolhope (I received my directions from the New Inn). It's close to the road but out of sight. A fingerpost points the way along the firm, grassy edge of the field. A badly eroded inscription says that the memorial was erected 'by his countrymen in the land of cider', and the monument is a cider press reassembled: a large stone well and a millstone with an engraved stump of limestone thicker than a pugilist's thigh quarried from Capler Hill nearby. It is a sculpture of found objects before the term was current in English art, and a mightily well-judged countrymen's tribute to a champion who died in 1851 aged fifty-six in the pub where he was guvnor, the Castle tavern in High Holborn, London.

Geddington
NORTHAMPTONSHIRE

A king's token of love for his dead queen, in the marketplace

Until Shah Jehan built the Taj in memory of his wife Mumtaz Mahal, there cannot have existed in the world a lovelier tribute from a

man to his beloved than Edward I's to Eleanor when he erected twelve crosses in her name. Geddington is the most northerly of the three surviving at the overnight resting points as her body was brought back from Lincolnshire, where she died in 1290, to London. This cross is clearly not as grand as either of the other two, the Waltham and Hardingstone crosses. It is a slenderer, triangular structure, and the three niches containing statues of the queen are shallower, so she does not have the fluid movement of the queen in the other Northamptonshire cross a day's journey away on horseback at Hardingstone (see below), although the broader masses of drapery and the queen's pose, as calm as a Madonna, has its own grave assurance. It tends to get less attention from art historians, but whether Edward thought it one of the lesser crosses or not (he spent the most on the Charing and Cheapside crosses, both destroyed by Oliver Cromwell's licensed vandals), it sits in a tiny square that must have had some part in the decision not to make the cross too opulent.

At Waltham Cross and Hardingstone the architecture of the crosses is highly decorative, a rich sequence of fretwork and elaborate arches and crocketed pinnacles. At Geddington the queen's images stand in simple trefoil-arched canopies with half a dozen pinnacles above and a few more at the summit. To compensate, the surface has few plain areas but is covered in low relief diaper-work decorations, as though a goldsmith had engraved it. Against the weight of the evidence I choose this cross as my favourite of the three for its setting in a marketplace with post office, pub, thatched house and the church spire behind.

The simplest, most complete and loveliest of the three surviving Eleanor crosses, in the little square at Geddington. Edward I erected twelve to mark the stopping places of Queen Eleanor's cortège between Lincolnshire and Charing Cross (chère reine cross)

Great Malvern
WORCESTERSHIRE

Stained glass given by Henry VII, in Malvern Priory

Malvern became popular in the 18th and 19th centuries as a spa with health-giving waters, and it remains popular as an upmarket commuter town. Princess Victoria was keen on holidaying here, and it is said that the late Queen Mother took its water in her health-giving scotch. It clings vertiginously to the eastern slopes of the Malvern Hills, but somehow 11th-century Benedictine monks found a flat bit high up and built a priory. After the Reformation the priory church – late Gothic, with a surviving Norman nave – became the parish church, and it is one of our finest Perpendicular churches, a cruciform building with a noble crossing tower. What truly marks it out, though, is its 15th-century stained glass, which managed to survive the Reformation and then escape destruction at the hands of Cromwell's men when the parishioners of Malvern bought it for £20 in 1639. Best of all is actually 16th century, just – the window in the north transept was given to the priory in 1501 by Henry VII as part of his policy of peace and consolidation after he had overturned the Yorkist victory in the War of the Roses with his own defeat of Richard III at Bosworth.

Its intrinsic historical interest is that the image of Henry VII himself appears in the window bottom right, and, two lights to the king's left, is his elder son, Prince Arthur, whose youthful marriage to Catherine of Aragon and death in nearby Ludlow Castle within a year of the Malvern window being installed would lead to the succession of Henry VIII, his marriage to Prince Arthur's widow and much trouble. History apart, it is the most coherent of the windows. The other medieval glass in the church has assumed an almost abstract beauty, after weathering and other damage, with pockets of narrative still recognisable among rearranged glass in the east window, the chancel south aisle, the west window, the nave north aisle and high up around the clerestory. The Henry VII window, however, is in astonishingly good condition, even though, apart from the customary state-sponsored vandalism, it suffered from boys using it for target practice, the great gale of 1703 that damaged churches across the west of England and a vicar who nonchalantly removed some glass to allow his homing pigeons access to their loft above the transept.

It is otherwise known as the Magnificat window because some of the words of Mary's song of praise to God for making her the mother of Jesus are on scrolls in the glass ('My soul doth magnify the Lord …' from Luke 1:46–55). She appears with the holy trinity in a blue halo against a gold background, spreading across three lights beneath the tracery, and there are scenes from her life interspersed with saints and angels. Throughout the church the glass is mostly in blues and yellows with browns, reds, purples and greens, not the deep blues and reds of the 12th century throwing dark colours into the church, but brighter, with a lot of white letting in the daylight to this magnificent basilica with a clear view from end to end unencumbered by screens.

Great Tew
OXFORDSHIRE

Mary Ann Boulton, in death's waiting room, in the Church of St Michael

The pub in the village, the Falkland Arms, commemorates the 17th-century owners of the Great Tew estate, the Carys, viscounts Falkland. It stands with the church on a hill above the centre of the village, one of the most benign landscapes in England. St Michael has a Norman south doorway, but the church is a late 14th-century rebuilding around it (that is, late Decorated) with a good tower.

Great Tew was an unlikely home for Mary Ann Wilkinson. She was born in 1795, the daughter of a Cumbrian ironmaster, and grew up in a circle of free-thinkers. She married Matthew Robinson Boulton, heir to a hard-headed Birmingham industrialist who had been part of a circle of friends including the engineer James Watt and the physician poet Erasmus Darwin. Matthew Robinson Boulton was his father's son, and although when he bought Great Tew he cultivated the land with experimental farm machinery built at his Soho works in Birmingham, he also cultivated softer manners, installed his wife as lady of the manor and employed the fashionable artists of his day. He had his own portrait painted by Thomas Lawrence, and, when Mary Ann died young in 1829, he commissioned a monument to her from the most acclaimed English sculptor of the day, Francis Chantrey (1781–1841).

Chantrey's huge success enabled him to leave a fortune to be used to create a national collection of British art, but he also left the administration of the bequest to the Royal Academy. He himself was an academician, and he thought he knew that it knew best. Perhaps it did in his time, but when the Tate Gallery opened in 1897 it found itself with an inheritance chosen by an institution it didn't rate and with an annual accretion of more art it despised, now mostly stacked in cellars in dark seclusion. Chantrey himself is still regarded in art historical circles as the finest English sculptor of his time. There wasn't much competition in the floodtide of Victorian pomposity, sentimentality and sheer bathos, but though occasionally submerged, Chantrey mostly managed to come bob, bob, bobbing along. He was self-taught and well taught. He was one of the first artists to hone his skills by examining the Parthenon marbles, which Lord Elgin had sold to the government in 1816. His busts were the product of hard observation. He developed a Reynolds-like ability to create tender studies of women, and the Great Tew monument is one of them.

Chantrey shows Mrs Boulton on a tomb chest marked out with polite Gothic decoration (the Boultons had built Gothic extensions to Great Tew), but she sits as though on a chaise longue, her back supported by a pillow, her hair up in a bun showing her long, exquisite neck to advantage, her simple, elegant contemporary dress reaching to her ankles but exposing bare arms with a simple bangle on her wrist. Her feet are crossed, and they, too, are bare. She could be reading a copy of *Northanger Abbey*, but step close and we see that under her lovely, elegantly folded hands the opened pages are not Jane Austen's Gothic novel, though naturally she would have read that, but instead the exposed text reads: 'Thy will be done.' She is not dead, she is in death's waiting room. Her eyes are dreamy, her face has an expression of mild acceptance. It is a fine, measured piece of work, extolling the eternal benefits of middle-class virtue, wealth and leisured comfort.

Great Witley
WORCESTERSHIRE

Venetian rococo interior, in St Michael's Church

The 1st Lord Foley had St Michael's designed adjacent to his Jacobean house, Witley Court, maybe by James Gibbs (1662–1754), architect of the Radcliffe Camera in Oxford and St Martin-in-the-Fields in London, and his widow had it finished after he died in 1732. Their son shunted the village off down the

road, and in the 19th century the Earl of Dudley rebuilt Witley Court to incorporate the church. In 1937 the house burned down, the church was saved, and chance, that friend to all artists, had created a dramatic composition of baroque splendour, ruined picturesque and nature. The villagers have returned to keep the church alive.

What is certain about Gibbs's part is that he fixed the interior, but the reason this late baroque building looks rococo inside is the overriding impression given by the windows, which were designed by Francesco Sleter (1685–1775), and by nearly two dozen ceiling paintings by Antonio Bellucci (1654–1727), both of them part of the wonderful late 17th- and early 18th-century period of Venetian decoration of palaces in Venice itself and in Germany and Austria. Neither of them could match the sublime Giovanni Battista Tiepolo's swift sureness of touch nor his ability to suffuse his decorations with Venetian light – who could? – but between them Sleter and Bellucci have created England's only interior that might, on a sunny day, be taken to be a church looking out over the Zattere. There is nothing in England's foggy ecclesiastical history like these three big paintings (the ascension in the centre flanked by the nativity and the Deposition) interspersed with twenty riffs on putti disporting themselves in the clouds. The glass, executed for Sleter by Joshua Price – one of a York family of glaziers, who emphatically appends his signature – is not stained but enamelled and has its own quite different opalescent beauty. Sleter, incidentally, liked the work so much that he stayed for life, did his last paint job aged ninety at Mereworth Castle in Kent and was buried as Slater in Mereworth churchyard, in another village rebuilt out of sight of the lord of the manor.

As it happens, none of this decor was done for Great Witley, but at the command of the Duke of Chandos for Canons, his new house

A little bit of 18th-century Venice transposed to Great Witley. James Gibbs designed the church, but the overwhelming impression is left by the stained glass and ceiling decorations by the Venetian-trained Francesco Sleter and Antonio Bellucci

near Edgware, completed in 1725 and, following a little local financial difficulty, demolished in 1747. Foley bought the paintings and glass and had them shipped by sea, river and wagon to Great Witley, where Gibbs installed them and where they look for all the world as though this is what they had been intended for. The stucco work on the ceilings and walls by Pietro Martire Bagutti (1719–1805) is also said to have been imported from Canons, though the dates of the stuccadore seem to preclude that. The work is very lovely but not, in fact, stucco: he used papier mâché, a recent (English) invention, for the advantages of its lightness and, as it turns out, its durability.

Hanbury

WORCESTERSHIRE

An English painter takes on the Italians, in Hanbury Hall

Most of the big English mural commissions that came in the wake of the Restoration of the monarchy in 1660 went to an Italian, Verrio, and a Frenchman, Laguerre, until in 1707, the year that Verrio died, James Thornhill (1675/6–1734), a struggling young English artist, won the commission to decorate the great hall at the Royal Naval Hospital, Greenwich (see Greater London, London). This huge task took until 1726 to complete and remains the greatest and most complete scheme of murals in Britain. In his spare time, as the saying is, he undertook smaller schemes for the houses of the aristocracy and the emergent gentry, one of whom, the lawyer Thomas Vernon, had

recently built Hanbury Hall near Droitwich in the fashionable baroque of the time (1701), brick dressed with stone, a five-bay central block containing a handsome three-bay pediment with a little oval ox-eye window, two three-bay wings projecting forwards and a little octagonal cupola with clock and weathervane.

To this perfect English classic Thornhill came in 1710, and in the well of the grand staircase he painted his own version of the Homeric myths. We know the year because of the one contemporary reference in the scheme – Thornhill included an imitation popular print bearing a portrait of the preacher the Rev. Henry Sacheverell, whom the Whig administration of 1710, in a rush of blood to the head, impeached for sedition in delivering a Tory sermon in St Paul's Cathedral. The trial turned sour on the Whigs, and Sacheverell was freed to popular acclaim. Thomas Vernon, of course, was a Whig. Thornhill's main subjects include Achilles, disguised as a girl, giving himself away by choosing a spear from a pile of jewellery; Hephaestus and the Cyclops making armour for Achilles; and Ajax and Ulysses contending for the armour after the death of Achilles. On the ceiling is Zeus surrounded by the gods, including, prominently and inevitably, Minerva the goddess of war – the background to Sacheverell's impeachment was that the Whigs were prosecuting a war against France to which the Tories were opposed.

Thornhill handles the baroque bag of animated tricks adroitly, the surface agitation so unlike Renaissance orderliness as gods hurtle through the sky, the eye-deceiving painted architectural orders holding the chaos in classical check, and, in a device invented by Michelangelo for the Sistine Chapel, Mercury gliding between paintings, head and shoulders on the ceiling, torso and legs on the west wall. He is a better painter than Verrio and Laguerre and incomparably better than the artist who replaced him in national favour, William Kent (everyone was), but the National Trust guide booklet reproduces a lovely pen and wash study for the ceiling and a wall, and if only Thornhill could have translated the vigour and freedom of that into paint he might have ranked among the greatest masters of his time. As it is, the murals suffer from his usual inanimate handling of paint (some of this possibly because of restoration) and a confined space, which turns them into posh wallpaper (but better than his ceiling paintings in three of the rooms, which suffer death by formula).

Hardingstone
NORTHAMPTONSHIRE

Feats of naturalism on an Eleanor cross, off the A45 at the edge of the village

Eleanor of Castile was a child bride when she married the future Edward I in 1254, and he was only fifteen. She joined him a year later and rarely left his side. When he went on crusade, she went too; she was with him when he campaigned in Gascony and Wales; and when his battles north of the border won him the sobriquet Hammer of the Scots, Eleanor was there. Historians discount the story that she sucked the poison from his wound when he was stabbed at Acre in the Holy Land because, it seems, it was first told a hundred years later, but it says something about how their marriage was popularly perceived.

She bore him at least fourteen children, and in 1290, when she died of a fever at Harby in Lincolnshire, there would be nothing now to tell of King Edward's grief if stones did not speak. But they do. Between 1291 and 1294 the king erected twelve monuments, the Eleanor crosses, to mark the resting places as the queen's cortège moved

towards Westminster Abbey, from Lincoln to Charing (*chère reine*), a point now just in Trafalgar Square at the top of Whitehall where Le Sueur's equestrian bronze of Charles I stands (see West End, London). The cross outside Charing Cross railway station is a replica; the others have all, but three, been destroyed. The three surviving are at Geddington (see above) and Hardingstone, both in Northamptonshire, and at Waltham Cross.

All of these are remarkable, though Waltham Cross is in Hertfordshire at the border with Essex, where London has stretched out a finger across the M25 and clawed the country town into its maw. The cross is set in a crassly planned shopping precinct in unlovely subtopia. It was thoroughly restored in the 19th century, and the statues are replicas; the eroded originals are on loan to the Victoria & Albert Museum.

Geddington's cross remains closest to its original state, Hardingstone's is the biggest and most elaborate. The spot for the monument chose itself: it was by the road adjacent to Delapré Abbey (now a records office), where the queen's body rested overnight, though now it is an incident off a roundabout on the A45 skirting Northampton. John of Battle built the cross, and John of Ireland was the sculptor of the four statues of Eleanor – the king's exchequer paid him £3 6s 8d for each figure, money well spent. He was one of the select group of craftsmen known in documents of the time as 'imaginator', which meant that he was both the artist and designer of the total project. Hardingstone is the earliest surviving work in England on which the ogee arch, made up of S curves, makes a substantial appearance, and it would become greatly characteristic of the sinuous Decorated Gothic. On the lowest level of three are the handsomely chiselled coats of arms of England and of Eleanor's family connections, Castile, Leon and

Ponthieu. The crowning level, from which the
top has snapped off, is discreetly less ornate
than the second level, where four figures of
the queen stand under canopies with gables
and pinnacles ornately decorated with foliage,
and the folds of her long gown suggest that a
light breeze is playing about her. On one
figure her hand delicately grasps the material
at her hip as though to hold the hem clear of
the ground. Regardless of period, these figures
are lovely feats of naturalism.

Hatfield

*A political giant commemorated at the
Church of St Etheldreda*

Old Hatfield, as it is called to distinguish it
from the post-war new town, clusters prettily
at the foot of a short sharp climb to the big
flint-built parish Church of St Etheldreda.
Immediately to the north of the church is the
Old Palace, of red brick and tile, built in the
1480s, its mellow beauty yielding nothing of
its history as childhood home of the Tudor
royal children, Edward and Elizabeth, and
Elizabeth's virtual jail during the reign of her
sister Mary. Here on her accession in 1558 she
held her first council of state, attended by her
first minister, William Cecil. Cecil's son
Robert, 1st Earl of Salisbury, succeeded him
in office, knocked down some of the Old
Palace and built Hatfield House hard by. A
long line of Cecils to the present day have
remained in the service of the crown, one of
them as Tory party kingmaker as late as
Harold Macmillan's accession – in 1957
Robert Cecil, 5th Marquess of Salisbury,
joined Lord Kilmuir in interviewing R.A.
Butler ('Rab') and Macmillan for the
premiership and asked, 'Well, which is it to
be, Wab or Hawold?' They are also patrons of
St Etheldreda, where they have customarily
buried their dead. Here in the Salisbury

Chapel is the tomb of the 1st earl, who died
in 1612 but who took the precaution of
commissioning his own monument, from
Maximilian Colt (active 1595–1641), one of
the many Protestant artists who sought
refuge in England during the religious wars
in the Netherlands.

This monument is one of the most
remarkable in England, brilliantly designed,
brilliantly carved and unlike anything else in
the land of the period. Colt worked as sculptor
to James I and had previously carved the fine
monument to Elizabeth I in Westminster
Abbey, but that is in strictly traditional form,
an effigy lying stiffly on a tomb chest.
Nevertheless, the portrait of the queen gives
an indication that he was capable of the
sensitive work in Hatfield. Lord Salisbury lies
on a platform borne as though on a catafalque
on the shoulders of four kneeling allegorical
female figures representing the cardinal
virtues: Fortitude, holding a broken column;
Temperance, pouring a jug of water into wine;
Justice, with sword and scales; and Prudence,
gazing into a mirror, a serpent wrapped
around one arm, and bare breasted, itself a
step forward from the Gothic Tudor norm.
Between them, at the base of the tomb
beneath the earl in full dress pomp, lies his
skeleton. Colt has carved coils of hair falling to
shoulder and back and the swing of the skirts,
the broad brows and downward cast eyes in
lovely oval faces with wonderful judgement.
The figures are all white marble, the platform
and base black marble, a fine, dignified
architectural ensemble.

It is doubly remarkable that the chapel also
contains alongside Robert Cecil's tomb a
highly original memorial by Nicholas Stone
(*c.*1585–1647) to Sir William Curle, a priest or
a retainer at Hatfield House. Like Colt, Stone
or his workshop was capable of routine work,
but his sculpture of John Donne in his
shroud in St Paul's Cathedral, his
Michelangelo-esque monument in

Westminster Abbey to Francis Holles and this piece showing Curle as though he had just collapsed are spectacularly original. Holles lies on a low slab on the floor, his legs bent at the knees, arms lifeless beside him, his head turned to the left and already scrawnily assuming the proportions of a skull, even his robe flattened and lifeless. This is a remarkable performance, unblinking in its portrayal of death as oblivion.

Iffley
OXFORDSHIRE

The Romanesque decor of a great Norman church, St Mary

By good fortune, each of the three best Norman parish churches in England, Barfreston, Kilpeck and Iffley, survives in an unspoiled setting. St Mary, Iffley, so close to 20th-century mass spec building in the eastern suburbs of Oxford, has been buffered by a Cotswold village full of character and amenity, and it stands in a good churchyard watched over by a massive yew. All the best things about Iffley church are Romanesque, and none of them is overtly religious. The west doorway is decorated with rich zigzag and beakhead decoration, and though the rose window and gable show necessary 19th-century restoration after 17th-century butchery, they are in keeping. The powerful and beautifully proportioned central tower between chancel and aisle-less nave features round-arched blind arcades. As for the sculpture, there are, apart from the head of a king (possibly Henry II), a small battle scene that could be a celebration of the Norman Conquest, centaurs, undoubtedly from classical mythology, a horse with a wyvern's head biting its own rear leg, animals and abstract flowers. Some historians argue that all this has a religious connotation.

John Piper picked up the wildlife theme in his tree of life window near the 12th-century font from the text: 'Let man and beast appear before Him and magnify His name together.' He designed it in 1982 in his late relaxed style in which the animals have speech balloons containing Latin tags approximating to the sounds all children credit them with making: 'quando, quando,' says the duck, 'ubi ubi' says the owl. There is no dog Latin.

Quite the best beast in this holy menagerie is the small carved bird behind a chancel column, like all the other sculpture contemporary with the structure of the 1170s. Since it is within the church it undoubtedly has religious significance. The church guidebook suggests that the reference is to Psalm 84:3: 'The sparrow hath found her an house, and the swallow a nest where she may lay her young; even thy altars O Lord of hosts.' It stands athwart its basketweave nest, every tense line spelling fear and aggression, its head raised, beak like a talon, its wings and tail feathers weapons of war, its eye glaring.

Kilpeck
HEREFORDSHIRE

A profusion of Romanesque carving, in the Church of St Mary and St David

The sculptures beneath the eaves of tiny Kilpeck church, about eighty of them packed into 60 feet of nave, chancel and rounded apse, are the most enjoyable, the most sheer fun, of any carvings anywhere. They portray farmyard animals, grinning grotesques, devils, a boar and a bear, a delicately trotting horse contriving somehow to balance a cross on one raised forehoof, an ibex, a pop-eyed pairing of hare and hound, which look as though they are straight out of the studio that brought you Wallace and Gromit, though they have had around 850 birthdays more.

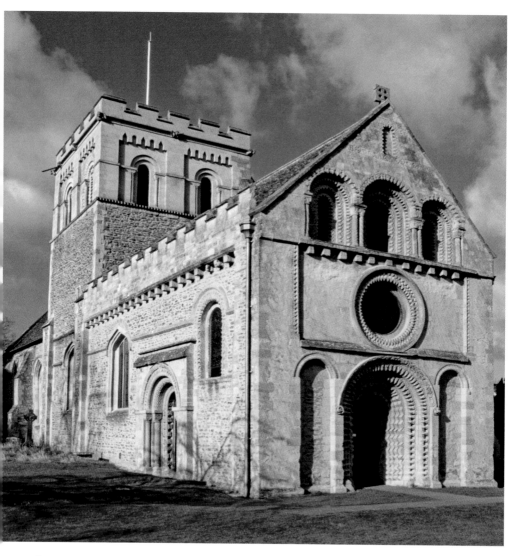

The Norman church of St Mary, Iffley, is a showcase for powerfully realised 12th-century abstract and figurative sculpture

These are the work of a master mason working in the 1140s, but the south doorway has sculpture on a yet more impressive level, with a carved chain on the outer order of the arch in which each link contains a fantastic formalised bird, conceived and executed like the finest imaginable coin design with curved neck, scimitar wings and fanlike tail following the circle of the medallion. If not a bird, then there is a dragon or fish, and on the inner order an angel flanked by more

monsters, dragons and beakheads from the bestiaries so popular in the Middle Ages in symbolising the perils of life and the afterlife, but exposing the nightlife of the medieval mind as well. The columns supporting the arch are each carved with two elongated figures, one above the other, caught up in a pattern of tendrils, and inside, on the chancel arch, each column again has two figures, solemn and less fantastical.

Kilpeck is one of a series of churches

decorated by a group of Romanesque sculptors known as the Hereford school, masons who may have learned the building skills but then focused on carving. The master who did the south door also worked on the fonts of Eardisley (see above) and Castle Frome (see above). The landed oligarchs of Herefordshire, like the baron who ruled from the now ruined castle of Kilpeck, are known to have walked the pilgrim routes to Santiago de Compostela and visited churches like Poitiers and Conques; and as I write and crop close into the snap I took of the Kilpeck doorway I see that the angel in the arch, Cubist in the boldly inventive disposition of its wings and limbs to fit the available pictorial space, is conceptually very similar to the angel on the west door at Conques, shown on the postcard I bought on my own pilgrimage to the Aveyron. Maybe the evidence is too scant and two and two don't actually add up to four, but there's no doubt that these mighty men and their Norman overlords travelled and looked and thought and left the marks of their chisels on our history.

Kinnersley
HEREFORDSHIRE

Flemish panels as a mirror of history, in the Church of St James

If pressed by roadworks Hereford these days can put on a decent traffic gridlock, but the rest of Herefordshire seems almost as remote as it ever was. When William I's commissioners compiled the Domesday Book (1086–7), Hereford's population was all of 103, counting those both inside and outside the walls. Eardisley was waste, returning no taxes. Kinnersley had been waste in the time of Edward the Confessor, 'and is now worth 30s'. If Kinnersley partook of the later Norman splendour of its near

neighbour Eardisley it has vanished in the rebuilding from the 14th to the 19th centuries of St James, tucked in the lee of a tremendously tall house, once a castle, and by not much else.

Its own curiously out-of-step little bit of history is the pulpit, a modern piece of no particular interest, but set with four beautiful and flauntingly erotic 16th-century allegorical Flemish carved wooden panels. The most beautiful figure is a woman seen from behind. She is in motion, one foot on the floor, the other almost palpably moving a few inches above the floor, almost destabilised, a statue about to step off her plinth, her movement multiplied by the swinging folds of the drapery that covers her legs from the ankle but leaves her naked from voluptuously rounded bottom to a head apparently crowned with laurel. Her pointing right arm extends diagonally to the top right corner of the panel, her left arm is bent at the elbow tucked into her side and she is holding what seems to be a scroll. She stands within a classical arch wilfully foreshortened to emphasise the flatness of the pictorial space. Antwerp carvers made it in about 1530 soon after Emperor Charles V's troops, looting and raping in the approved fashion, devastated Rome, turned St Peter's into a stable, and drove the new capitalist markets of Germany into turmoil. The Kinnersley panels are little masterpieces in the style that emerged from the chaos, which is known, hopelessly inadequately in the historical circumstances, as Mannerism, its elongated, often tortured forms in shocking contrast, as it seemed at the time, to the calm grace of Raphael.

There are no records and next to no literature about these pieces, nothing to explain why they were carved, how they came to Kinnersley or what they mean. The only art I can think of in which women are so well muscled is Michelangelo's, especially the

William Tierney Clark designed this suspension bridge across the Thames at Marlow in 1829; twenty years later he built the famous Széchenyi chain bridge over the Danube at Budapest. Both bridges are still fully functioning. The plaque fixed to the pier on the right commemorates this dual achievement

The chapel was a creation of the rebuilding of 1865, the redecoration a late wedding present to the 7th earl from his wife carried out by the Birmingham Group, an offshoot of the Arts and Crafts movement, which tackled the reredos, the sanctuary lamp, the stained glass and the painted ceiling. Henry Payne's murals are about as feeble as a Pre-Raphaelite offshoot can be, a kind of religious family romp in jolly colour showing Christ in glory flanked by angels, while the earl in his Edward VII coronation ermine and his wife in her wedding dress kneel below in adoration. On a flanking wall the child Viscount Elmley, the Beauchamp heir, reaches out tentatively to touch an angel's harp, while his younger brother, Hugh Lygon, swipes the heads off daisies. Payne had student helpers, one of them only fifteen, and it shows, but it seems pitched just right for a family with small children, albeit one with a house of more than a hundred rooms, and its charm is undeniable. As Charles Ryder remarks on seeing the chapel, 'Golly.'

Marlow
BUCKINGHAMSHIRE

A bridge that links the Thames with the Danube

When the old wooden bridge across the Thames between Marlow and Bisham collapsed in 1828 the local authorities commissioned a new one from William Tierney Clark (1783–1852). Clark designed an elegant suspension bridge and supervised its construction between 1829 and 1832. It has a 235 feet span with the cables securing the bridge in the middle anchored in triumphal arches on each bank. After the Second World War the cast iron began to show signs of stress, and a hastily formed

Marlow support group fought to save it, so instead of commissioning a new design Buckinghamshire county council reconstructed it exactly to Clark's design, but in steel, and, triumphal arches apart, it still looks modern.

Tierney Clark worked successively for two of the great 19th-century civil engineers, Thomas Telford and John Rennie. He devoted himself mainly to bridge building, including three other suspension bridges. Two, the last Hammersmith Bridge and another at Newhaven, have been replaced. The fourth is the impressive Széchenyi chain bridge of 1849 across the Danube, linking Buda and Pest. They were so pleased with it in Budapest that they named a street after Tierney Clark, and when the rebuilt Marlow Bridge opened in 1965 the mayor of Budapest flew over to perform the ceremony.

Middle Claydon
BUCKINGHAMSHIRE

Rococo going for broke, Claydon House

Some plasterwork here, a roomful of Chippendale furniture there, an elaborate pier mirror, a little of the mock oriental style known as chinoiserie, a touch of light-hearted Gothick all adds up to rococo, the frivolous style of the court of Louis XVI and Catholic Germany, the last twitch of the exuberant but heavier breathing baroque, all frills and furbelows. England saw little of this except in a few interiors, and of these, Claydon House is the most spectacular.

Down among the Claydons in north Buckinghamshire, Claydon House is rococo run riot. In 1757 Lord Verney felt he needed to entertain in style, so he rebuilt his old house as a palace to rival Stowe. He licensed a woodcarver and stonemason called Luke Lightfoot (c.1722–89) to take charge both of the building, possibly as master mason, and

of the interior decorations. There were two wings linked by a gigantic ballroom. The surviving block remains grand enough with its state rooms on the ground floor and a staircase of sheer fantasy ascending in slow, grand stages to the neoclassical coffered ceiling and glass dome at the top of the house. The balustrade is of black iron scrollwork throwing out golden ears of corn, and the stairs are built of mahogany inlaid with ebony and boxwood so that the components of the tread shift and rub against each other with, it is said, a seductive whispering, but it is all too fragile for visitors to be permitted to test the truth of this with their own stiletto heels and size tens.

Lightfoot turned out to be something of a barking genius. He promised 'such a Work as the World never saw', words that turned against him when Verney fired him in 1770. It was already too late. Verney was bankrupted, and after his death in exile in 1791 his successor pulled most of the building down. Although many of the surviving rooms were finely decorated by Joseph Rose, who was recommended to Lord Verney by Sir Thomas Robinson of Rokeby as 'the first man in the kingdom as a plaisterer', what remains of Lightfoot's interiors is a monument of etiolated extravagance.

The nine-bay north front and the seven-bay west front with a heavily emphasised Venetian window beneath a three-bay pediment are standard and grave Palladian practice with nothing to lead a visitor to suspect what lies within. Lightfoot's most astonishing coup is the Chinese room on the first floor, an extravagant confection of chinoiserie, but the absolute monument to his exquisite talents is the north hall, a double cube with broken pediments giving the doors a hint of pagoda shapes, fruit and foliage half-hiding human heads, monsters and strange birds here and on the extravagantly convoluted decoration of the marble fireplace, with its caryatids and the mirrors on either side and with garlands of flowers of unqualified beauty at the top of the overmantel. In the ceiling are the head of Minerva, goddess of war, on an oval plaque, sprouting cannon and sword, and rifle and pike and a plumed helmet surrounded by plaster cartouches with the Verney monogram. Lightfoot is known to have worked in his Southwark premises from pattern books of rococo decoration, and the sense is of a man liberated by his ignorance of how the patterns were actually deployed in great houses across the Channel.

In the 19th century the house passed to the Calvert family, who adopted the Verney name. Sir Harry Verney turned Claydon into a house fit for his sister-in-law, Florence Nightingale, to visit. On the principle, no doubt, of fighting fire with fire, he hung the north hall with trophies of the hunt, regimental flags and military hardware. The National Trust has stripped all this out and left Lightfoot's work to speak for itself, such a work as the world never saw.

Nettlebed
OXFORDSHIRE

Piper memorial window for Peter Fleming, in the Church of St Bartholomew

Peter Fleming was the elder and some would say more talented brother of Ian. He wrote a fine history of Hitler's plans for the invasion of England, worked as a freebooting *Times* correspondent, turned down the editorship of the *Observer* and wrote brilliant columns for the *Spectator* in a vintage period for the magazine in the 1950s. He lived and, in 1971 at the age of sixty-four, died in Nettlebed, where he is buried in the churchyard. John Piper (1903–92) lived a few miles away near Henley. He experienced a bumpy career ride as a painter and created instead a reputation

as a stained glass artist and author and photographer and, finally, editor of John Betjeman's Shell guides. Not surprisingly, the Fleming family turned to him to create a memorial window.

Piper and his constant craftsman in stained glass, Patrick Reyntiens, had already made the east window in 1970 in memory of a much-loved local doctor, Robin Williamson. It's an undistinguished little mid-19th century church in a Chilterns village that straddles the A4130 between Henley and Oxford, and the three basic Decorated lights and the tracery of the Williamson window are as muffled as though they had been carved out of lava, so Piper's glass gives the church a charge of energy. The Fleming window, tucked beside the south door, is quite small and even sweeter, with its predominant nocturnal blue, than the east window's fish (out of water on a brilliant red ground), fruit tree and butterflies. The south, Fleming, window has two little lights with what might pass as a quatrefoil above. Piper devised a plan by which the central mullion becomes the tree of life, with birds in the boughs and foliage reaching into the quatrefoil where it is outlined against the satellite view of the white disc of the earth, with the moon and sun behind. It picks up the best of the daylight and is gorgeous.

North Cerney
GLOUCESTERSHIRE

An outstanding restorer at the Church of All Saints

The vicar of North Cerney in 1908, the Rev. E.O. de la Hey, was on a antique hunting trip to northern Italy with the church's architect for restorations, F.C. Eden, and its principal benefactor, William Croome, when he stumbled in an antique shop and dislodged the lid of a packing case. Eden and Croome

*In the little wayside Church of St Bartholomew,
Nettlebed, John Piper charmed the birds in the tree.
His design utilises the central mullion as the
tree of life*

found inside a beautiful and expressive
carved wooden figure of Christ in agony on
the cross. It was made around 1600 and was
worth the lire equivalent of £10 to the dealer,
but it is of inestimable value to North Cerney
since Eden installed it more than twenty
years later at the centre of his new rood loft,
where it gives a new meaning to the modern
sense of found art.

Eden (1864–1944) wasn't part of the Arts
and Crafts movement, but his mind worked
along similar lines given that he held to no
particular dogma. He could do Gothic revival
or Renaissance on demand, which sounds
flash but is nothing of the sort. His lovely high
altar reredos of Christ granting crowns to the
saints looks like a miniaturised take on the big
carved limewood screens of the Northern
Renaissance in Germany, but Eden's paradise
has wall hangings of tasteful red and gold
stripes. Like the Arts and Crafts workers, Eden
would not have regarded himself as an artist
innovator, but as a craftsman, recognisably
20th century, but working within a long
church craft tradition. North Cerney is a
deeply satisfying achievement.

It combines his designs with the skills of
local craftsmen and several more strokes of
serendipity. In 1912 workmen repairing the
floor of the lady chapel found beneath it the
medieval altar that had been hidden from
Henry VIII's commissioners in the 1530s. It
was made of Cotswold stone with a table top
a single piece weighing one and a quarter
tons, and it seems almost a pity now that it is
usually hidden under a richly woven frontal
left over from a length commissioned in 1914
for Chartres Cathedral. Someone else with
North Cerney in mind discovered the lectern,
a golden (well, brass), 15th-century Flemish

eagle on a 15th-century Spanish pedestal of
steel, lying unclaimed and with no known
destination in marine stores at Gloucester
docks.

When Eden first saw North Cerney on its
green hillside above the Churn valley there
were stone steps leading to a rood screen,
which had been destroyed in the
Reformation. What could be more natural
than to make a new one? He had it made
from oak felled locally and carved on site. It
might not make much sense in an
architectural age of steel, concrete and glass,
but it fits. He designed a chancel screen and
another for the lady chapel and decorated the
front of the gallery with an antique marbled
effect. In the lady chapel are three 15th-
century wood carvings, two German figures
of bishops flanking a French carved Virgin
with a wonderfully naturalistic child – she
holds him a little like Abraham offering Isaac
for sacrifice, which, in fact, was an
iconographic alignment often made between
Old and New Testaments. It's a matter of
opinion whether the Virgin or the rood
screen Christ is finer, but it is Eden's eye and
touch that pull the whole thing together.

Northampton
NORTHAMPTONSHIRE

Daniel Defoe visited Northampton, 'the
handsomest and best built town in all this
part of England', on his big project, *A Tour
through the Whole Island of Great Britain*
(1724–6). Yet despite his keen interest in
industrial matters, he failed to mention the
shoe industry, although it was already tooled
up sufficiently for Cromwell's army to have
marched into battle shod in Northampton
leather. Today the industry is hugely
diminished, and Northampton, like most of
England, relies for employment mostly on
service industries and a new home-grown

university. The nickname of the town's Football League team, the Cobblers, derives from the shoe industry and apparently has nothing to do with them being rubbish. The town itself retains some of its character and many good individual buildings. This is despite the borough council's unenviable post-war record of destroying the 17th- and 18th-century fabric of Northampton created after a devastating fire in 1675 in favour of ugly office blocks and shopping centres.

At the centre is the Church of All Saints, rebuilt after the fire with a west portico that has a balustrade supported on Ionic columns. On top of the west tower is another balustrade around a pretty cupola. All Saints is on George Row, and further along is another fine post-fire building, the Sessions House of 1676–8. Close by is the big marketplace, a space dating from the weekly markets and occasional fairs of the 13th century, and north of that is Sheep Street, with a name commemorating an older trade than shoemaking. In it is the Church of the Holy Sepulchre with a Norman round nave, like the Templars' Church in London and the Round Church in Cambridge. Simon de Senlis, Earl of Northampton, built it in 1110 as a homage to the Holy Sepulchre in Jerusalem, which he may have seen when he took part in the First Crusade.

The site of the gaol that Defoe singled out as one of the fine buildings of Northampton is now occupied by the museum and art gallery (see below). Beyond the old city centre Northampton has more than doubled in size over the past century to a population of about 200,000. In one of the eastern suburbs, among the several 19th- and 20th-century churches, is the striking St Matthew (see below) on the Kettering Road, built by adherents of the Tractarians (the Oxford Movement of high Anglicans). It owes its fame today to Walter Hussey, then the vicar, who commissioned its *Madonna and Child* from Henry Moore and a painting of the crucifixion by Graham Sutherland.

Minor Italian masterpieces at the Northampton Museum and Art Gallery

The town's museum and art gallery has the biggest collection of footwear anyone is likely to see outside an Imelda Marcos museum. The art collection limps behind, a small collection of 16th-century Venetian paintings, mostly by relatively minor figures, put together during a purple patch in the 1950s and 1960s with help from the Victoria & Albert Museum and the National Art Collections Fund. Maybe I'm a philistine, but I wouldn't bother walking upstairs to see them, except that there is one eye-catcher: a glass-topped cabinet containing three small paintings, one by the Renaissance master Cima da Conegliano (c.1459/60–1517/18), one by Canaletto's contemporary and rival, Francesco Guardi (1712–93), and the third by Giovanni Antonio Pellegrini (1675–1741), a peripatetic mural painter whose work included decorating the grand staircase and state rooms of Kimbolton Castle, now a public school but open to the public.

In his little view of the Piazza San Marco, Guardi, as always, looks at Venice with the eye of a resident and shows it as a working city compared to canny Canaletto's tourist resort. Pellegrini's oil, *Jason Rejecting Medea*, illustrates the leader of the Argonauts dismissing his wife in favour of a new bride (her terrible revenge is the subject of the play by Euripides). It is probably a sketch for a ceiling decoration. The Cima Saul and Samuel is a tondo (circular canvas), solemn and jewel like despite a lot of lost pigment.

A Madonna of the Underground, in the Church of St Matthew

The real story of the *Madonna and Child* by Henry Moore in Northampton is the story of Canon Walter Hussey, vicar, like his father before him, of St Matthew. He went on to become dean of Chichester Cathedral and to forge a parallel career as a connoisseur and courageous patron of the arts. It began in 1943 when he commissioned Benjamin Britten to write the cantata *Rejoice in the Lamb* for the anniversary of the church built fifty years before for a new parish. Soon afterwards he saw some of the drawings made by Henry Moore (1898–1986) in the London Underground when the stations were being used as air raid shelters, and he commissioned Moore to do a sculpture for St Matthew's. He followed up with a commission to Graham Sutherland to paint a crucifixion.

The press attacked both works for their supposed ultra modernism. Both works now look very 1940s, Sutherland's because the style was altogether too personal for an artist without much spark of real originality, Moore's because it is a little tired, as though the effort of making everything he did express a great universal truth had taken something out of him. Yet if the fire in his belly was dying, this *Madonna and Child*, carved in Hornton stone and recognisable kin of those anonymous shrouded figures in the Underground, still looks monumentally reassuring in the north aisle of the church, its hands and knees rubbed shiny by devotees.

Northill
BEDFORDSHIRE

Heraldic glass at the Church of St Mary

John Oliver (1616/7–1701) was an all-round master. He worked as both surveyor and architect on the rebuilding after the Great Fire of London, he was one of the enforcers of the rebuilding act, and he was a cartographer and printmaker. Some of his work survives, but not much – the deanery in St Paul's Yard, where he may have collaborated with Wren, Skinners' Hall, Mercers' Hall – but his first trade was glass painting.

By the later 17th century religious glass had ceased to be popular, but after the Restoration of Charles II in 1660 there was a huge demand for heraldic glass. As with so much of Oliver's work, not much of his glass survives – so much was destroyed like his workshop near Mansion House in the Great Fire. What remains, dated 1664, are these three large, flamboyant heraldic panels, two covering three lights in one window, the third covering two lights in another window, fitting none too well but totally enjoyable and encapsulating a small, vivid and continuous strand of English history.

Northill is a handsome village with a handsome, basically 14th-century church on a large green, and though the church has been restored beyond the point of interest and modern building for prosperous commuters swamps the indigenous art of the builder and thatcher, the ancient configuration shows through. About the time of the Restoration of the monarchy a local grandee, Dame Margaret Slaney, gave the Grocers' Company of the City of London the cash to buy the rectory and the right to appoint the priest to the living. Perhaps her husband had been a member, perhaps it was simply that the Grocers were expanding their charitable activities beyond the City.

The stand-alone window shows the royal coat of arms of Charles II beneath a tent-like canopy in cloth of gold, all frills and furbelows, marvellously swash and swank with a swaggering lion and unicorn. The other window contains, on the left, the arms of the Grocers with the motto 'God graunt grace' and, on the right, the Slaney arms with passages of orange and green introducing new notes to the prevailing yellow, red and blue. It's a consummate design, intricate but eye-catchingly lucid, and incorporating the churchwardens, each of whom has a coat of arms as well, and the artist's decisive signature with the J splicing the O. As for the historical relevance today, a plaque beneath the royal arms reads like a legal document, and if so, it is one the Grocers wouldn't escape without embarrassment supposing they wished to: 'This window was thus Glazed and y Chancell Ceeled & Beautifyed by the Right Worshipfull Company of Grocers,' it reads, 'patrons of this Church and Rectory, being an Impropriation purchafed by that Company Setled for the Sole Benefit of the Church according to the trust and appointment of that Memorable Lady Dame Margaret Slany Deceased.' The memorable lady is long gone, but her notion that the Grocers might be the right patrons is alive: the company still owns the living. And the rectory still owns the two glass timepieces that Oliver made and presented to the rector of his time.

Oxford
OXFORDSHIRE

Better than a helicopter trip above the city, and cheaper, is to climb the 124 steps to the top of St Mary the Virgin, the university church that was home to Charles I's parliament during the Civil War and also, to begin with, the 14th-century university library of chained books that grew into the Bodleian. Laid out below the balustrade at the top of the tower is a perfect medieval and Renaissance city: a cobbled square immediately below the tower to the north of the church, the Radcliffe Camera at the centre, beyond that the Perpendicular Divinity Schools and Wren's Sheldonian Theatre (a stage for matriculation and degree ceremonies rather more than theatre). And next door to the Sheldonian is the building that first housed Elias Ashmole's museum, before it grew and grew and migrated to its grand new building on the west of St Giles's. The Old Ashmolean is now the Museum for the History of Science. The Gothic Divinity Schools and Brasenose College lie below St Mary's tower to the west, All Souls (graduates only, if you please) to the east. Down at the east end of the High, opposite Magdalen, lies the oldest botanical gardens in the world, with an elaborate gate by the Renaissance sculptor Nicholas Stone. Magdalen's long wall up Longwall Street helps to enclose the deer park. Every May day at dawn the college choristers climb Magdalen tower to sing the *Hymnus Eucharisticus*, composed by a 17th-century fellow of Magdalen. The tower stands above the River Cherwell, which effectively separates town from gown.

Town and gown was a dispute that ran almost from the foundation of the university, when the king granted rights to the colleges that impinged on townspeople's livings. It was fought out in the streets and, in the last half century, when town had a plan to run a ring road through Christ Church meadows, the battle resumed in council chambers and the media. Backing on to the meadows is Merton, one of the three oldest colleges (13th century; University and Balliol were the others), still with the best group of early buildings, around Mob Quad, and a splendid chapel, which I pick out for its historic glass. Christ Church itself is founded around the church of St Frideswide, college chapel and Oxford Cathedral. Christ Church was born with a silver spoon in its mouth and has never spat it out. St Frideswide (dedicated to a local saint) contains some very good art, and Christ Church picture gallery some great art.

Glass by Abraham van Linge, Balliol chapel

The story of William Butterfield's chapel for Balliol is a comedy of fellows in a college academically distinguished but architecturally undistinguished. Barely had the college fellows knocked down the 16th-century chapel and started building the new one to Butterfield's plans than they had second thoughts and commissioned a rebuilding as close as possible to the original. Third thoughts prevailed and they completed the new building, detested for its aggressive polychromy and minaret-like tower by Benjamin Jowett, the formidable master of Balliol ('My name is Benjamin Jowett,/There is no knowledge but I know it …'). Internally the chapel looks as though the college is hiding something. It is. In 1937 it hired Walter Tapper to plaster over Butterfield's gaudy north and south walls, install handsome 17th-century walnut panelling on the east wall and lay down a black and white marble floor quite out of tune with Butterfield's medievalism. This political and architectural charade fairly reflected attitudes to old buildings through the ages ('this is but old,' the 17th-century traveller Celia Fiennes would remark dismissively of anything built more than a century before). Balliol had been a poor and undistinguished college until the 19th century, when it gained academic reputation and riches and immediately began knocking down most of the medieval college. The success of Victorian Britain gave many of its inhabitants the quality usually attributed to Balliol men of effortless superiority, which spilled over in their attitude to the past. At one point Merton contemplated destroying Mob Quad, but fortunately, being equivocating dons, desisted.

Luckily, in Balliol's cellars was a quantity of the old chapel's former embellishments, including the exceptional 17th-century brass-crowned eagle lectern, together with 16th-century glass which had been intended for Cardinal Wolsey's new Cardinal College but which came to Balliol when Wolsey fell out with Henry VIII. It was probably by the king's glazier John Nicholson, who based it on Dürer engravings. Of this glass the scenes of the agony in the garden, the scourging, the crowning with thorns and the Ecce Homo were now reinserted in Balliol's east window. But the best of the glass, in the north of the chapel and the ante-chapel, is by the Fleming Abraham van Linge: two windows of 1637 given to the college by Peter Wentworth, a fellow, and Richard Atkins at a time when the biblical drought of ecclesiastical art after the Reformation had turned to a deluge as Oxford colleges hastened to fall in with the wishes of King Charles I's powerful favourite (and chancellor of the university), Archbishop Laud, by embellishing their chapels. The college reinstated the two windows to the north, in the east of the chapel and in the antechapel, but split each into two. The two windows nearest the east contain the tale of Philip and the eunuch (Acts 8:38: 'And he commanded the chariot to stand still: and they went down both into the water, both Philip and the eunuch; and he baptised him'). The ante-chapel has *The Sickness and Recovery of King Hezekiah* (2 Kings 20:5: 'Thus saith the Lord, the God of David thy father, I have heard the prayer, I have seen the tears, I will heal thee').

Pot lead was practically unobtainable at this time, but in any case medieval glass was regarded as coarse; Van Linge worked with enamel and worked well with lovely drawing and rich colours, a range of blues from turquoise to sapphire, lemon yellow, ruby, purple, sapphire green. The shallow perspective doesn't destroy the passages of broad colour that glass gives, deploying brilliantly, in the scene from Acts, mountain scenery with a falling cascade behind Philip as he baptises the eunuch, the pair dramatically contrasted. The old man Philip is white skinned, the eunuch with a glowing dark red gown stripped from the upper half of his body exposes a well-muscled black torso. It looks wonderful now. To Oxford scholars of the early 17th century it must have seemed like the word become manifest in colour.

Pre-Morris Burne-Jones window, Christ Church Cathedral

Christ Church Cathedral was the college chapel before it was a cathedral (and remains so), and it was St Frideswide's nunnery before it was a college chapel. Frideswide was feasibly said to be the daughter of an 8th-century king of Oxford, and she performed several miracles in Binsey, a village in the Oxford suburbs, including the utilitarian act of producing a health-giving well in Binsey churchyard. (It is still there and still a place of pilgrimage for the credulous.) Cardinal Wolsey was earlier than his master, Henry VIII, in suppressing monasteries, and one of them, in 1524, was St Frideswide's, which he promptly began demolishing so that he could replace it with Cardinal College. When the king suppressed Wolsey himself in 1529, the college became Christ Church, work stopped on the new chapel to the north of Tom Quad, and the condemned church of St Frideswide was saved to become the college chapel and, in 1546, cathedral of the diocese of Oxford.

History and myth are stitched together in the appearance of the cathedral today. The 8th-century building had been destroyed by Danish invaders, but there is work from 12th-century Romanesque to 16th-century fan vaulting by the Oxford mason William Orchard. There is 14th-century glass depicting St Frideswide, and although King Henry's men dismantled her shrine of 1289 and threw it down a well, it has been recovered and restored. And in 2002 it was rebuilt in the Latin chapel beneath one of Edward Burne-Jones's earliest windows and one of his finest in quite an unexpected way. Instead of his later norm of gracious single figures filling each of the window's four lights, here he has crammed four panels into each light to display the action-packed life of the saint: her education, her entry to a nunnery and her evil suitor's attempt to abduct her, her flight, the evil suitor struck blind on entering Oxford and Frideswide on her deathbed. Above the four lights is a roundel showing the ship of souls bearing Frideswide to heaven, the ship's hammock shape prettily rhyming with the moon and the billowing sail.

Burne-Jones had met William Morris as an Oxford undergraduate and on matters of art and design their hearts throbbed as one, but in 1859 they had not yet founded the first Morris manufacturing firm, so Burne-Jones produced this window for James Powell & Sons, who made the best stained glass available – the closest, that is, to the richness of the 12th and 13th centuries. Even though Morris later bought his glass from Powell, never again would Burne-Jones make a window with such a range of colour, from chocolate brown to pale brown speckled with a white flower pattern, reds, greys, orange, mauve, yellow, greens and saturated blues. Nor would he make a window so crowded with incident. His mature art gives the impression of a man lost in wan dreams of fair damsels, perhaps as sexually innocent and deprived as Ruskin, but in fact Ned, as he was known, had a robust humour, managed a happy marriage and a passionate love affair, spun off amusing caricatures of his circle of friends and worked a little joke into this lovely Frideswide window. In an alcove in a corner of the room he has placed a flushing lavatory bowl.

A painting rescued from the kitchen, in Christ Church Picture Gallery

Other colleges and universities have art collections and even great paintings, and the public may be admitted to some of them from time to time. But the only British college I know of with a great collection that is effectively run as a public art gallery is Christ Church. And what a collection. It resides now in tiny Canterbury Quad, the college's backyard off Oriel Square, in an understated but beautifully planned 1960s building by Powell and Moya. Originally it hung between book stacks in the college library, except for *The Butcher's Shop* by Annibale Carracci (1560–1609), which was consigned until the 1950s to hang above the great fireplace in the Tudor kitchens. This may have entertained the chefs but can hardly have helped its condition.

Christ Church is toffs' territory, and its historical toffs have been donating their personal holdings of art over the last 300 years. The collection is based on an initial bequest of 1760 from a graduate of the college, the gallant General John Guise, who had fought with Marlborough in the French wars and developed from his continental travels a fine taste in Renaissance art. He put together a stupendous collection of old master drawings, Italian paintings from the dawning of the Renaissance to Veronese, and the demonstration piece with which Van Dyck blew Gheeraerts and other associated Flemish artists then working for the English court out of the water. *The Butcher's Shop* is the most extraordinary of his bequest of 255 works. Many connoisseurs believe that Carracci's masterpiece is not the great decorated ceiling of the Palazzo Farnese in Rome but a small surpassingly translucent easel painting of *The Flight into Egypt* in the Palazzo Doria Pamphili. Yet although this big canvas in Oxford comes from the same

brush, it is closer to the everyday realism of a pub sign than to the dark drama of Caravaggio, Carracci's only real 16th-century rival.

Here we are with Carracci on a butcher's premises in Bologna in 1582 in full-frontal daylight. On the right of the canvas an aproned assistant hoicks a carcass off the floor to hang it on a hook suspended from a rail above. Another butcher weighs a joint of meat. A live ram passively submits to its fate as a slaughterer pins it to the floor. Behind a block another butcher trims cuts of meat.

In the following century Rembrandt painted a famous picture of an ox's carcass. The Belgian realist Soutine did something similar in the 20th century. These are magnificent canvases, each making a point about brute mortality. Carracci does nothing of the sort. He came from a family of butchers, so he may have painted this documentary picture as a trade sign. It's just about possible to see that it is based on one of Michelangelo's panels on the Sistine ceiling, *The Sacrifice of Noah*. Despite this noble precedent, Carracci's painting stands for nothing but itself, an unembellished scene of daily trade.

Medieval stained glass dedicated to a Merton fellow, Merton College chapel

With Balliol and University, Walter de Merton's college is the oldest in Oxford, and his chapel is the oldest. It was built in the years 1289–97 but was never finished and consists of a very big choir, the transepts and crossing under a handsome 15th century-tower. The T-shape this makes became an archetype for Oxford college chapels; Cambridge caught up in the 19th century. Twelve of the fourteen windows in the north and south walls of the choir have the original glass made over the same period and dedicated, very obviously by himself, to a fellow of Merton. He appears twice in each of the twelve windows of three lights, in the outside lights facing inwards to a saint occupying the central light. In some panels a scroll looping around the kneeling donor is inscribed with the message, 'Magis Henricus de Mamesfeld me fecit' ('Master Henry Mansfield made me'), and those that do not have a scroll have instead an inscribed plaque beneath the figure. Clearly yet another medieval power broker fixing his future with the Almighty.

At first glance the programme of the glass looks repetitive and dull. Closer examination shows it to be repetitive and exquisite. The coloured panels of saints and donor run as a band through the windows, with white grisaille glass above and below. The praying figure of the donor hardly varies except for the colour of his mantle. The colour gives variety. In one panel the saint is wearing amber against a lapis lazuli background, embellished with slightly paler blue leaves; in another he wears green; in a third, a brilliant red. In another window, the saint and the flanking figures of the donor all wear white against lapis lazuli. All the figures appear under canopies, scalloped or ogee shaped, with a hint of buildings behind, a church or perhaps the Holy City. The clear glass has either vine leaves or oak leaves and acorns inscribed on it, and it is set with little blue roundels circled with amber containing crowned heads, a king in one, a queen in another, perhaps Edward I, during whose reign the arts flourished, and his first consort, Eleanor of Castile.

A new chapter for Jacob Epstein, New College chapel

The janitor of the chapel at New College (which is 700 years new) confessed to me that when he had started work there forty years earlier he had not much cared for the carving of *Lazarus* by Jacob Epstein (1880–1959) in the ante-chapel. Every day now he comes in with his mop and bucket and greets it with a cheery good morning. It has that effect on people. It had it on the college warden in 1951, Alec Smith, who was sitting to Epstein for his portrait in bronze and remarked on his admiration for the *Lazarus*. Epstein let him have it for a knockdown price and Smith raised the cash and placed Lazarus in the college ante-chapel. It was, said Epstein, 'one of the happiest issues of my working life'.

He had carved it in 1947–48 and showed it in Battersea Park as part of the great post-war celebration, the 1951 Festival of Britain. For Britain in 1951 the symbolism of Lazarus rising from the dead was not easily missed. But symbolism in sculpture was already becoming old hat, and a quarter of a century later, when Nikolaus Pevsner, a great champion of his own generation, wrote of Epstein's Lazarus, 'It is impressive in its intense emotion', he knew that he would be perceived as ranging himself with the dinosaurs and added tartly, 'though no doubt hopelessly corny to the devotees of Anthony Caro'. Now the pendulum, as is the way with pendulums, has swung back again, and Epstein looks like one of the major sculptors of the century. He was certainly the British sculptor (American, naturalised in 1907) who drew most of the anti-modern fire in the first four decades of the century, some of it foully anti-semitic. The sculptures he did for the British Medical Association headquarters in the Strand (now Zimbabwe House) were vandalised by the owners. His powerful *Night* and *Day* on London Transport headquarters in St James's were ridiculed (see West End, London). His Oscar Wilde memorial in Paris was bowdlerised by the French, of all people. The Fleet Street gutter ran with sewage about him.

Lazarus opened a new chapter for him. He

Jacob Epstein let New College have his sculpture of Lazarus cheap, but the deal was, he said, 'one of the happiest issues of my working life'. As this detail shows, Lazarus is imagined still wrapped in his winding cloth as he rises from the dead

had absorbed influences from the art of ancient Egypt, Africa and pre-Columbian America and added his own bent for an emotional but controlled expressionism to arrive at an archetype without repetitiveness. It was a touch of creative genius to show Lazarus upright but wrapped tight in the winding sheet of the grave, his head lolling on to his shoulder, eyes still closed as though he cannot yet quite gather the energy to shake off the sleep of death, and in this great chapel it has found a perfect home.

The janitor, by the way, pointed out the El Greco *Apostle* to me, which he also likes. In case he's on a tea break, it hangs above the north stalls in the chancel.

Carvings by Grinling Gibbons, Trinity College chapel

Celia Fiennes, the 17th-century Puritan turned travel writer, saw Trinity's chapel when it was new as its fresh paint, and she was impressed. In her journal, *Through England on a Side Saddle in the time of William and Mary*, she remarked that when she visited Oxford previously the chapel was not finished but that 'now [it] is a beautifull magnificent structure'. Building started in 1691, and Wren saw the plans a year later – 'now' was 1694, the year the chapel was consecrated. Strangely for such a great interior of that period, no one can name either architect or designers, though many have tried. All experts assume that the woodcarving of the reredos is so good that it must be the work of Grinling Gibbons (1648–1721). Other evidence is purely anecdotal, but Fiennes asserts in her casual way that the carving is 'just like that at Windsor, it being the same hand'. At Windsor Castle the hand is Gibbons's.

The chapel forms the south range of Durham Quad. Like Balliol next door, Trinity was a County Durham foundation, set up by the Durham Cathedral priory in about 1286, and it was at first called Durham College. From the outside the chapel is handsome enough, with an apparent west tower, which turns out to be a gatehouse, though well set back from the decorative iron gates on Broad Street.

Inside, it really is beautifull magnificent. The richness of carved wood and moulded plaster is set against plain panels of plaster between the windows, north and south, and below window level are set plain veneered panels of wood and understated carved stalls lining the walls. The floor is black and white marble. The supposed Gibbons carving on the reredos of tumbling festoons of fruit and foliage is in lime, the supplest of woods for sculpture, pale against the veneered juniper, and angels recline on the pediment carried by two slender Corinthian columns, a motif repeated with variations at the west of the chapel, where the carved screen shuts off a small ante-chapel in which the organ on a gallery covers the top half of the wall. But this is not all, because the moulding above the reredos and the windows and the circlets of golden flowers against white foliage on the ceiling, all as opulent as the limewood carving, creates a deeply satisfying ensemble not spoilt by the painted ceiling panel of the ascension because, although this is by a little known French artist, Pierre Berchet, his style, easing into rococo, sits easily with the surrounding luxury of craftsmanship.

A fantastical gateway at Oxford Botanic Garden

In 1622 Sir Henry Danvers gave to the university £5,000 and 5 acres of land, which had formerly been a Jewish burial ground. This largesse was for the university to set up a botanic garden 'for the glorification of God and for the furtherance of learning'. Most of

To an England bathing in the introduction of classical architecture in Inigo Jones's Queen's House at Greenwich, Nicholas Stone's heavily embellished monumental gate of 1632–4 for the Oxford Botanic Garden would have seemed heresy

the money was used up building the grand walls and paying Nicholas Stone (1586–1647) for the three monumental gateways, one grand arch facing Magdalen and two minor arches. Stone was the leading sculptor and builder of his day and did a lot of work in Oxfordshire, including, a few years later, the barley column porch to the university church, probably prompted by one of the easily accessible Raphael cartoons owned by Charles II (now in the Victoria & Albert Museum).

The fantastical main gate, built 1632–4 and most probably inspired by the extravagant designs for gates published by the influential 16th-century Italian Sebastiano Serlio and available in England, where the public was just about coming to terms with the pure classicism of Inigo Jones's Queen's House at Greenwich. This was a crystallisation of ancient Roman classicism that must have

seemed to Jacobeans as extreme in its modernity as the sheer glass skyscrapers of Mies van der Rohe did in the early 20th century. In these terms, the unbridled decorative post-modernism of Stone's gateway, like the entrance to some dark grotto, would have looked at first like architectural heresy. The arch has two flanking bays with their own pediments, which overlap the main pediment over the arch. Two columns support each supplementary pediment, and between them on each bay is a niche with statues of Charles I and Charles II (later additions). The central pediment contains another niche with a bust of the donor, Danvers. All this is complex enough, but the columns and archway are heavily rusticated as well, and the projecting blocks of stone have a vermiculated (wormy) surface, so the onlooking eye is never at rest. It's splendid, but curiously disturbing as well.

Walter Sickert's wartime pierrots, in the Ashmolean Museum

The Ashmolean Museum is a masterpiece of C.R. Cockerell, a mid-19th-century classic revival built when everybody else in Oxford was dreaming Gothic. It moved from an even finer building, the 17th-century neighbour of Wren's Sheldonian Theatre on Broad Street, when its collections grew too big for the site.

The architect Rick Mather has designed thirty new galleries to double the Ashmolean's exhibition space, though no doubt it will still be looking for more to house collections of Western art and Eastern art, ancient art from the Near East and Cyprus to the Cyclades and Crete, ancient Rome, European archaeology, a fabulous collection of Renaissance drawings, including Michelangelo and Leonardo, and a fine gathering of British art from the celebrated Albert Jewel to the Christopher Sands Trust gift of works by Walter Richard Sickert (1860–1942).

Sickert is surely the best British painter of the early years of the 20th century, full-blooded where his Bloomsbury and Post-Impressionist English contemporaries were anaemic. He was a student at the Slade School of Art in London when the celebrated James McNeill Whistler told him he was so good that he was wasting his money and his time there and whisked him off to study instead as his apprentice. With Whistler, Sickert learned etching, drawing, how to knock in the broad plan of a large painting and the gentle art of making enemies. But the best service sorcerer did for apprentice was to send him on an errand to deliver a painting for exhibition at the annual Paris Salon. Sickert carried with him a letter of introduction to Edgar Degas. The two became friends, and Sickert realised that what he had taken for the genius of Whistler was a pale shadow of Degas.

Sickert's growing knowledge of contemporary French art gave him the confidence to follow his own genius in England. 'The plastic arts are gross arts, dealing joyously with gross material facts,' he wrote. He came into his own in townscapes of Dieppe and London and in excursions into smokily dusky music-halls like the New Bedford in Camden Town. They are mostly rendered with a brown tonality, but *The Brighton Pierrots* is a turning point, high keyed and brilliantly lit. Sickert stayed with a friend in Brighton in August and September 1915 and by his own account visited the pierrot show on the seafront every evening for five weeks. He painted *The Brighton Pierrots* on his return to London. He might almost have called it *Oh! What a Lovely War*. Some critics see in it a melancholy metaphor of England engaged in an empire-sapping struggle. The western sky is lurid with the sinking of the sun. There are empty deckchairs on the beach, and the dim electric lamps onstage throw splashes of light like hastily slathered make-up on the pierrots' brick-red costumes and white boaters. The columns supporting the canopy over the stage are striped sugary pink and grey like sticks of rock, and beneath the canopy, where the light gleams in yellow pools, a pierrot in green with pointed hat sits slumped with a drum at his feet, while a pierrette in a flounced pink frock with a big yellow ruff tinkles an old joanna.

Whether or not the sense of a passing era was intended, this painting is a prime example of the artist 'dealing joyously with gross material facts'. When Morton Sands, a collector and the brother of Sickert's friend Ethel Sands, saw the painting in Sickert's Fitzroy Street studio in Camden Town he immediately bought it. The eminent advocate Sir William Jowitt saw it soon after and asked for a replica, which, almost similar (the pierrot with a cane goes without in the later version), is now in Tate Britain.

A forgotten controversy, the Martyr's Memorial, at the south of St Giles's Street

Between the front quad of Balliol College and the garden quad is a doorway blackened by fire. It is said to be the door that once hung in the Broad Street gateway adjacent to the spot where Catholic Queen Mary had the Protestant martyrs Thomas Cranmer, Hugh Latimer and Nicholas Ridley burned at the stake. Cranmer, Archbishop of Canterbury, watched from his cell in the Bocardo prison at the northern end of Cornmarket as Latimer and Ridley burned in October 1555. On 21 March 1556, having recanted his Protestantism under duress and then revoked the recantation, Cranmer himself went to the stake at the place where his co-religionists had died and thrust the hand that had signed the recantation into the flames, calling out, 'This hath offended! Oh this unworthy hand!' A cross in Broad Street marks the spot where the three men died.

Fast forward three centuries to the 1830s, when a group at Oxford University, which became known as the Oxford Movement or the Tractarians, argued in a series of tracts that the Anglican Church was in direct apostolic succession from Christ. Other Anglicans opposed them on the basis that they were drawing too close to Catholicism and sullying the sacrifice of the Oxford martyrs (indeed, in due course some of the movement became Catholics, of whom the cardinals Manning and Newman were only the most famous). In 1838 the opponents of the Oxford Movement determined to set up a memorial to the martyrs. They invited the twenty-eight-year-old George Gilbert Scott to design it. Scott (1811–78) modelled it on the Eleanor Cross at Waltham, but, being Victorian, his cross was bigger, more elaborate and agitated. Conceived in the fire of politics, which is cold ashes now, the Martyrs' Memorial lives as the first work of the new Gothic revival, one based not on aestheticism but on research. Scott had, independently of Augustus Pugin (see Cheadle, North Midlands) but encouraged by his pronouncements, reached the conclusion that the 13th- and 14th-century Decorated was the best style. 'Every aspiration of my heart had become medieval,' he said, and he based his career on faithful re-creations, more or less imaginative (more frequently less), of the trefoil forms, the blank arcades, the fretted entablature, the diaper patterning, the coats of arms of donors. All of these feature in the Martyrs' Memorial, starting as a hexagonal structure with crocketed canopies, then a second stage for the three martyrs, carved by Henry Weekes (1807–77), a competent Royal Academician. Above that, a fantastic spire bearing a cross. For years, the crockets and pinnacles gave purchase to undergraduate climbers whose activities contributed to the decay of the memorial, but a restoration in 2003 has made it as good as new.

Perry Green
HERTFORDSHIRE

Henry Moore's ivory tower, Hoaglands

Hoaglands was Henry Moore's sculpture studio, home, office and ivory tower, away from the glare that the post-war success of his work focused on him. He bought the old farm when he became rich and famous, and though he needed it as a quiet rural retreat, he basked in the glory as well. The Paris-domiciled British sculptor Raymond Mason tells of how Moore was in Paris for a Courbet show and decided to take in a solo exhibition by Mason. He arrived at the gallery and announced that he had come to see the work of his friend Raymond. 'It was at this point,' as Mason tells it, 'that the staff of the gallery, who had known me for fifteen years, started calling me "maître".

This is a typically waspish Mason tale, and it stings. The (British) press always referred to Henry Moore (1898–1986) as the greatest living English artist, and towards the end it dropped the qualifier, English. His work was disseminated throughout the world, and as he grew rich he added more land to Hoaglands, more farm buildings to use as studios (now exhibition halls), more assistants. Here in a showcase is a photograph of the Grand Old Man and the architect of the Louvre pyramid, I.M. Pei, wreathed in smiles and applauding each other at some great opening; here with Sophia Loren; here receiving the Grand Cross of the Order of Merit from Chancellor Helmut Schmidt. If there was any faltering of enthusiasm for Moore abroad, the British Council took care of it, working tirelessly at propaganda on the sculptor's behalf. But the best ambassador for Moore's sculpture was always his own photographs of them. He was a great photographer of his sculpture. Was he a great sculptor?

Sometimes: all through his life he made underpowered pieces as well, and these grew more common the more famous he became and the bigger the sculpture. His best pieces are those in which there are no special connotations. either of human beings or of landscape. Sculptures like *Sheep Piece* (1971–2), which isn't about sheep, it just happens to have been placed in a field of sheep. They, unlike the human visitors to Hoglands, are allowed to rub up against it freely and seem to enjoy it, though their expressions are hard to read. It is 18 feet high, but, unlike, for instance, the late, huge and vacuous *Double Oval* elsewhere in the park, it punches its weight. *Sheep Piece*, though a bronze, has the unforced feel of a rugged rock outcrop. He studied the work of rivals in the field and acknowledged a debt to Henri Gaudier-Brzeska, who died in the war that Moore survived, but he looked long and hard

at the work of Barbara Hepworth too, yet refused to pay tribute to her when asked to by the BBC on her death.

Another word from Mason. He was at a glitzy reception for Moore at the Plaza Athenée hotel in Paris. Mason noticed among all the beautifully shod feet on the lovely carpet a row of white footprints. At the end of them was the great Swiss sculptor Alberto Giacometti. He had left his plaster-filled studio in his working clothes, jumped into a taxi and come straight to the hotel. There's a moral there somewhere.

Pershore
WORCESTERSHIRE

13th-century figure of a knight, Pershore Abbey

From the west the inside of the abbey unfolds to the gaze like a butterfly, as delicate and as seemingly perfect. No screen blocks the view of the tall, single lancet in the apse at the east, allowing a steady flow of light into the sacristy and pointing upwards. In the roof of the chancel is one of the finest Decorated lierne 'star' vaults in England with forty-one exquisitely carved foliate bosses. In a sense, all this was extemporised, even more than in most church buildings. Two fires in the 13th century occasioned a lot of rebuilding, including that wonderful vault, which soars from capitals that were undamaged by fire. The nave has gone, and the west end starts with what once was the central tower and the two main transepts. The Early English lancet in the apse is by Sir George Gilbert Scott in his restorations of the 1860s (one of those Victorian intrusions that works beautifully). So, in fact, is the curved apse. The tower was rebuilt after the fire of 1288, and Scott took out the bell ringers' floor to open up the fine tracery panelling of the windows. Since so much was design on the wing, it becomes less surprising to discover evidence of Norman building all over the church and on the exterior, and in a clapped-out font. Nor is it surprising that during restoration Saxon foundations were found beneath the floor.

At this time as well the tomb of the knight who had died between the two fires was removed from the churchyard and placed in the southwest transept. On the tomb chest is a warlike effigy of the knight, one of several in the country with his legs crossed, not as splendid as the very best, like the wonderfully vigorous knight in Dorchester Abbey evidently about to draw his sword, but famous anyway among, admittedly, that small band of devoted scholars who study the armour of the period, because he has been sculpted with great attention to getting the realistic detail of his equipment right.

This was the long reign of Edward I, when gentry owing fealty to their lords (that is, performing military service when called upon), began to have their own effigies installed in churches where before these had been only of the higher nobility. So in the 13th century we see the introduction of the cheaper but also more malleable freestone for monuments instead of Purbeck marble, and so, in Pershore, the detailed carving possible produced an effigy of a knight who, beneath a surcoat, wears chain mail from head to chopped-off feet, and between the coat and the mail he has reinforcements of plate armour, one piece at the front and one on his back, with the straps and buckles fastening back and front plates showing beneath the right armhole of the surcoat. His mail includes the mittens, one of which he has shaken off so that it hangs free at the wrist. With that same hand he grasps a hunting horn (the only known example). The other arm is bent to support a long shield before his body, and this hand is covered by the second mitten and lightly rests on top of the scabbarded hilt of his sword.

Ross-on-Wye
HEREFORDSHIRE

'The Man of Ross' makes his mark at the Kyrle Gate

Do not, as I did, ask for directions to John Kyrle's gate. His house still stands in the marketplace at Ross, there's a Kyrle Street and a Kyrle school, and beside the church there's a Prospect garden planned and financed by John Kyrle. He tended the sick and succoured the poor, he repaired the St Mary's Church spire and added pinnacles and arranged to have water pumped uphill from the River Wye as a water supply to this town on a bluff high above the river. But no one knew where Kyrle's gate was until I went to the heritage centre in the ancient market hall, and then they didn't know whether the gate was, as it were, open or shut to the public. Outside Ross, Kyrle's name probably never was on the lips of many people, and it would have been none at all except that Alexander Pope immortalised him in his third *Moral Epistle* as 'the Man of Ross', as an example to show up the vanity of most of English high society:

> But all our praises why should lords
>   engross?
> Rise, honest muse! And sing the Man of
>   Ross …
> Whose causeway parts the vale with shady
>   rows?
> Whose seats the weary traveller repose?
> Who taught that heaven-directed spire to
>   rise?
> 'The Man of Ross,' each lisping babe
>   replies …

and so on.

John Kyrle was born in 1637 nearby in Gloucestershire and after completing his education at Balliol College and studying law at Middle Temple, he lived in Ross for the rest of his life. When he died in 1724 he was buried in St Mary. He had held no great position in the town and, according to Pope, was worth £500 a year, a tidy sum but not a fortune. But he lived simply and took out a 500-year lease from Lord Weymouth on a field by the churchyard, then known as the Clevefield, which, hands on, he transformed into a public garden now called the Prospect (the prospect is a view to the Wye). He walled it in and built three beautiful stone gates, almost overwhelmingly grand for such a small garden. Two survive, one perilously. The earth bank on which it stands above the churchyard crumbled ominously in the heavy rains of 2007, and the gate leans at a dangerous angle. Both remaining gates are handsome. The east gate is splendid with big curving S-shaped volutes supporting piers either side of the gate and a large urn on each pier. The falling-down south gate is grandly classical with Corinthian pilasters, the date (1700) carved with a flourish on the lintel, and above that a pediment with a coat of arms, three fleur-de-lis and a chevron. Herefordshire county council has so far met the south gate problem with the traditional solution of coning it off. We must hope that this measure keeps the gate erect for the almost 200 years of the lease remaining.

Steeple Aston
OXFORDSHIRE

A hanging judge commemorated at the Church of St Peter

In our own times Lord Goddard, lord chief justice from 1946 to 1958, was a hanging judge with a nice line in gallows humour. In a speech at one Royal Academy dinner he speculated wittily on the nice distinction between hanging a picture and hanging a man. *Plus ça change.* In the 18th century the ferocious Sir Francis Page had similar tastes. A prisoner could, according to Pope, expect 'hard words or hanging if your judge be Page', and Fielding didn't bother to change the judge's name in introducing him as the savage-humoured Lord Justice Page in *Tom Jones.* He remained on the bench until his death in 1741 at the age of eighty, and near the end replied to a question about his health: 'My dear sir, you see, I keep hanging on, hanging on.' In an age of hanging judges, Page was the first among equals. Nor can it be said that Henry Scheemakers's memorial image of him shows him as a benign old buffer.

The judge was the son of a country parson, born in Bloxham, and as his legal practice received preferment and flourished under a Whig administration, he bought the manor of Middle Aston, a hamlet without a parish church just north of Steeple Aston. He commissioned the monument on the death of his second wife in 1730 and doubtless considered it expedient to include his own likeness and, to counter the gross slander of his literary critics, an encomium on the 'Judgement Honour & Justice' he dispensed in his courts. Sir Francis reclines on one elbow, corpulent and self-satisfied in full-bottomed wig and judicial robes, attired to take his place at the right hand of God. His wife, comfortably padded too, takes her ease on a lower ledge so that together they form a pyramid composition in front of the black marble pyramid behind them, all contained beneath a classical archway. At the apex of the pediment stand the judge's newly acquired arms.

This is one of only three works signed by Henry Scheemakers alone, brother (younger, probably) of the better known Peter, and it is considered his masterpiece. Mostly he worked in partnership with his neighbour in Westminster, Henry Cheere. Whatever else might be said about Sir Francis, he chose his sculptor well. Scheemakers's date of birth isn't known. He came to England in the early 1720s, moved to Paris in 1733 and died in Antwerp in 1750. None of his work on the continent is known, but the Steeple Aston monument is top-drawer baroque, beautifully composed and vividly carved.

Swinbrook
OXFORDSHIRE

Racks of Fettiplace family tombs in the Church of St Mary

The church itself is unprepossessing: it has a mean tower, small nave, smaller chancel and a single aisle stacked up against the south wall of the nave like a lean-to shed. The onrush of history slows to a crawl on the banks of the sleepy River Windrush. Every few hundred years or so the inhabitants wake to a small convulsion. In 1649 in Burford church a mile or so to the west, in a defining moment of English history, the parliamentary army summarily executed a group of its Levellers, a species of ultra democrat that had formed within the New Model Army. On 26 September 1940 a stray Luftwaffe plane dropped a bomb in Swinbrook, blowing out the church's east window (the vicar reset the fragments in the aisle in thanksgiving for their escape). On Sundays between the world wars the Mitford clan repaired to church here from their house at Asthall on the hill south of the valley, and after the war four of the six celebrated sisters were buried successively in the churchyard: Nancy, bright young thing, novelist, biographer; Hitler's poisonous little pals Unity and Diana (Lady Mosley); and Pamela, the quiet one of the clan.

Their resting place is becomingly modest, but not so the chancel tombs of the Fettiplace dynasty that dominated the parish from the reign of Henry VII until George III, when the last of the Swinbrook

line died and the house was razed without leaving a trace above ground. The latest, in the south wall, is a resplendent marble memorial to Sir Edmund Fettiplace, who died in 1743 and is commemorated in a bust by a little known London statuary called James Annis, who in this work could keep company with the celebrated foreigners Scheemakers and Rysbrack. But the most notable ones are earlier, filling the north wall of the chancel, six Fettiplace baronets in alcoves ranged one above the other three by three. As one historian put it, they look like nothing so much as seamen in ship's bunks. The first three, carved in the early 17th century, show an identical trio, each figure in armour, each with a ruff showing above the cuirass, the same long swept moustachio and beard sculpted into abstract wave patterns, not individual men but symbols of distinction precariously balanced, to our eyes, between dignity and comedy. The late 17th-century trio rest in the same pose as the first three, reclining with one knee raised, clad in gold-trimmed armour, but with each hand resting on a gauntlet. The sculptor was William Bird of Oxford, an artist of local distinction who had worked with Christopher Wren on his first project, the Sheldonian Theatre, though his statues are confined to the basement. His Fettiplace heads are portraits, clean shaven but with long ringlets and fleshier faces in the manner of the time, individuals and altogether worldlier, more relaxed, apparently not yet aware that they are dead.

Tackley
OXFORDSHIRE

Monument to a chief justice of Chester, in the Church of St Nicholas

John Morton died in 1780. He had been Member of Parliament for Abingdon for

This eccentric arrangement of effigies in the little country church at Swinbrook, to our eyes finely balanced between dignity and comedy, commemorate six 17th-century baronets of the Fettiplace family

many years and was a landowner in these parts, and Tackley was his place of retirement away from the world of affairs. The appointment as chief justice in Chester had given him real power. Until the 19th century Cheshire was a county palatine, and his remit as chief justice was equivalent to the authority of the court of common pleas and the king's bench in England. So for John Bacon (1740–99) the commission to carve a monument to Morton was a plum. All sculptors have assistants; Bacon was practically a factory. He had invented a new tool for cutting marble that worked fast and that enabled him to take on many assistants to fulfil commissions all over the country. Often they were stereotyped, but for the Morton memorial in Tackley he hit his best form.

Presumably no portrait of the chief justice existed, so Bacon, working fourteen years after Morton's death, simply devised a tall plaque shaped as a pointed arch with the figure of Justice on a plinth, ostensibly beneath a classical arch in low relief, and upon it a large draped urn. It is beautifully carried off, Justice commanding but relaxed, leaning her left elbow on a pile of books placed on a half column and holding the scales in her left hand while her right hand rests on the hilt of a sword with its point pressed against the ground. She throws her weight firmly on to her left leg, and her right leg is bent at the knee so that her toes are on the ground but her heel clear of it. The folds of her drapery help to animate the figure.

Bacon was coming to the end of his life, but it was the dawning of neoclassicism, a retro-Roman revival partly sparked by critics who were frankly fed up with the frivolity of rococo. But Bacon's noble figure of Justice has on her Roman shoulders a head of lilting rococo prettiness. The sculptor had no doubts about this piece, for he has signed it

prominently in characters as large as the name of the chief justice.

Tewkesbury
GLOUCESTERSHIRE

Avaricious, oppressive, ambitious, but memorialised in stained glass in Tewkesbury Abbey

Shakespeare's Avon meets the Severn at Tewkesbury, where the banks of the merged rivers are flanked by meadows – 'the finest meadows that ever were seen,' wrote William Cobbett in 1830. They still edge up to the abbey's precincts in the 'good, substantial town' as Cobbett thought it, and as it remains today, though the river increasingly tends to edge into the town as well. Still, it remains prosperous and relatively unspoilt. The abbey, Norman in origin, retains the noble Romanesque west arch that practically constitutes the great western façade. Within, the nave has multiple bays with Norman piers 30 feet high and well over 6 feet in

diameter, but in the 14th century those piers that continued into the choir had their height sliced in half to allow a three-sided clerestory above with windows full of stained glass installed in 1340–4, and the glass is the loveliest and most enlivening of that troubled century, when to the range of colours already available by mixing metal oxides with molten glass was added the discovery of a new range of silvery whites, greens and a yellow stain made more brilliant by flashing it with specks of silver. The clerestory is low enough above the floor and the windows big enough to make the stained glass some of the most accessible and easiest to read in the Gothic world.

The principle Tewkesbury window, in the east of the clerestory, is a Last Judgement in which Christ on a throne is flanked by the Virgin and the Archangel Michael, all of them under decorated Gothic canopies, a remarkably composed view compared to the fearful scenes depicted in the Last Judgement a few miles away at Fairford, no doubt because Tewkesbury's were installed not to intimidate the populace but as a memorial to Hugh Despenser, lord of the Welsh marches and patron of Tewkesbury, commissioned by his widow Eleanor. So the historical and local interest is in the figures in the westernmost clerestory, four in the north opposite four in the south, all eight knights clad, as this is the age of chivalry, in armour designed for the tilting yard, each one swankily emblazoned with the heraldic device of his family, a medieval precedent for the brilliant colours of modern sports teams – and for similar reasons. Hugh Despenser is second from the right in the northern window, and La Zouche, Eleanor's second husband, is on the right in the southern window. For all the immortality Hugh gains by the insertion of his image in the abbey, he and his father were avaricious, oppressive, ambitious and hated. They were Yorkists and backed Edward II and his despised companion Gaveston, and they paid the penalty when the king's widow invaded from France in 1326 and defeated them.

Eleanor herself, it is thought, appears in a small panel at the foot of the Last Judgement window, naked to display that she has cast off her worldly possessions in readiness to enter heaven, but her nakedness is coloured in the new silvery white, and she wears it like a suit of armour.

Upton House
WARWICKSHIRE

An oil baron's collection

The 2nd Viscount Bearstead inherited Mote House, Maidstone, as the family home when his father, the founder of Shell Oil, died in 1927, but by then he had already bought Sunrising House on the Banbury–Stratford road. When the chance came for him to acquire a neighbouring property, Upton

House, he took it, and sold Mote House – the hunting in Warwickshire was better than in Kent. On such quirks of social preference lies the destination of great collections of art, for in the 1920s and 1930s, when private collections were frequently coming to the saleroom, Lord Bearstead built up a collection of paintings at Upton House, and Kent remained in a state of old master deprivation. And what a collection. There are portraits by two great Bruges masters of the declining years of Middle Ages, Rogier van der Weyden and Hans Memlinc, and one by the great genius of the Northern Renaissance, Hans Holbein the Younger; *The Disrobing of Christ* (*El Espolio*), an El Greco that was once in the possession of the French 19th-century romantic Eugène Delacroix; and three down-to-earth country scenes by George Stubbs, the 18th-century master painter of the English hunt.

And then there is *The Death of the Virgin* by Pieter Bruegel the Elder (*c.*1525–69). We think of Bruegel as the Bruegel of the seasons, the peasant weddings, the *Hunters in the Snow*. Even the Prado's grisly *Triumph of Death* is full of colour and movement. But this scene is in grisaille, tones of grey, presumably as more suitable to the mournful occasion. It's not immediately attractive to our Impressionist-influenced eyes, but the more you look the more you see the humdrum paraphernalia of human life and death, the stock in trade of Pieter the great. The Virgin dies surrounded by peasants, men and women, already mourning her in a Flemish room lit by the holy emanation surrounding her and by candles and a scant fire in a grate, tended, presumably, by the blanket-wrapped woman who slumbers, slack jawed, beside it.

Waddesdon Manor

BUCKINGHAMSHIRE

A great English painter amid a lavish collection

It was mildly disingenuous of Wellington to remark that the Battle of Waterloo was won on the playing fields of Eton. It was won in the Rothschild counting house. The London Rothschild, Nathan, took a punt on Wellington against Napoleon and with his four brothers bankrolled him through the Peninsular War and at Waterloo. Wellington acquired a dukedom and the estate of Stratfield Saye out of it. The Rothschilds made a fortune and bought an estate in darkest Buckinghamshire. There are many pubs named for Wellington, one for the Rothschilds – the Five Arrows at the entrance gates of Waddesdon Manor. Each arrow symbolises a son of the founding father, Mayer Amschel, one son in each of London, Paris, Vienna, Naples and Frankfurt, each running a Rothschild bank.

It was a Viennese Rothschild, Ferdinand, who bought the Waddesdon estate above the vale of Aylesbury from the Duke of Marlborough in 1885. Like a 19th-century William Randolph Hearst, he sliced the top off the tallest hill and built a huge French Renaissance château there. Everything was of the best, the huge collection of Sèvres porcelain, some of it painted from designs by Boucher, the chest of drawers with ormolu decoration by Charles Cressent, the tapestries from Beauvais and the Gobelins factory, the secretaire made for Marie Antoinette. The keynote throughout is rococo, with several paintings by Nicholas Lancret and Jean-Bapiste Pater, but the principal genius of the collection of paintings is Gainsborough.

On his deathbed in 1788 Gainsborough wrote and asked his great rival Joshua Reynolds to visit him. Reynolds went, and in this last conversation Gainsborough told him that his main regret in dying was that he had only just begun to realise the deficiencies in his painting and begun to conquer them. Yet for many years since his death his later portraits were regarded as a sell-out to economic necessity. The truth is that it was the detested 'face painting' that was his bread and butter. The jam is ours. Waddesdon has three full-length portraits in his late manner: Mrs John Douglas, Lady Sheffield, and, in the pink, Francis Nicholls, thus mawkishly also known as *The Pink Boy*.

You can see the portrait of Mrs Robinson close up, and as it has recently been cleaned, this is very much to the purpose. Reynolds, in a moving passage in the discourse delivered in the year of Gainsborough's death (in which he told his students of the deathbed scene), realises that Gainsborough's work doesn't fit his own careful scheme of things, that all his categorising of the orders of importance of subject matter and treatment somehow don't meet the case. And yet he recognises Gainsborough's genius. His puzzlement is almost palpable in this great tribute:

However, it is certain, that all those odd scratches and marks, which, on a close exami-nation, are so observable in Gainsborough's pictures, and which even to experienced painters appear rather the effect of accident than design; this chaos, this uncouth and shapeless appearance, by a kind of magick, at a certain distance assumes form, and all the parts seem to drop into their proper places, so that we can hardly refuse acknowledging the full effect of diligence, under the appearance of chance and hasty negligence.

That is purposefully, honestly and perceptively put by a master of the sober. Look at the play of the brush across Mrs Robinson's shoes and on her silvery blue dress, and the way it creates the effect of evanescent light, look as close up as Gainsborough would have wished, and you are seeing, in effect, a surface as abstract as Monet's lily ponds and painted, as a matter of fact, more swiftly, more impressionist-ically, than the late work of the great Impressionist himself 120 years later.

Walsall

WEST MIDLANDS

A controversial artist celebrated at the New Art Gallery, Gallery Square

Kathleen Garman married the pioneering sculptor Jacob Epstein (1880–1959), and his knighthood, in 1955 after thirty-four years of being his mistress and running a parallel house and family to the household of Epstein's first wife, Margaret Dunlop, who died in 1949. When Epstein himself died, Kathleen, Lady Epstein, inherited his 'intimate, adventurous and eclectic' collection, as the New Art Gallery director Peter Jenkinson describes it, to add to the one she herself had made on joyous shopping expeditions around Europe with Sally Ryan, an American sculptor, sometime pupil of Epstein and mutual friend to Jacob and Kathleen. Then, when Sally died, the two collections became one, the Garman Ryan collection. Kathleen, Lady Epstein, decided to leave it to the town of her birth.

Walsall, across one motorway from Wolverhampton, another from Birmingham, is one of those ancient settlements that was chewed up and spat out by the Industrial Revolution. Some £23 million later, cash raised by council funding and the national lottery, the architects Caruso St John built among smokeless factory chimneys, across the road from a shopping centre, featureless apart from its tattiness, and on the wharf of a litter-harbouring canal an outwardly austere art gallery that internally is a poem in light and space, intimate and spacious, logical and easy to move around in, perfect for the art it now houses.

The collection is all about Jacob Epstein, his family, his artist friends who gave him paintings, his mistresses, his children and his grandchildren. It is about Epstein's daughter Kitty, who modelled for both Epstein and her first husband Lucian Freud ('that spiv Freud,' Epstein called him when he heard how he was abusing his daughter's trust); his other daughter Esther, who killed herself soon after her brother Theo Garman, another artist, died in unexplained circumstances; and his granddaughters Ann and Annabel Freud, of whom he made bronzes when they were babies. The rest of the cast, more or less peripherally, are Meum Lindsell-Stewart, mistress, model and mother in 1918 of Epstein's first child, Peggy Jean (of a famous portrait bust); and Isobel Nicholas, another long-term mistress, who had a son, Jackie (another bust), by Epstein in 1934.

This briefly described tangle is at the heart of the Garman Ryan collection, which has no outstanding pieces and nothing except sketches by Epstein from his early pioneering years, the years of the Oscar Wilde memorial in the Père Lachaise cemetery in Paris and the *Rock Drill*, that beetle-like robotic figure now in the Tate. Instead there are the kind of bronze portraits from which he made his fortune and that don't often seem to engage him deeply. The hirsute Indian seer Rabindranath Tagore is the subject of one; another is of Epstein's equally hairy pet dog Frisky. But as an entity the collection is a marvellous visual diary of one man's life, work and involvements.

There are paintings by Constable, Monet and Degas, artefacts from ancient Rome, the Ivory Coast and Oceania. In Lucian Freud's intense early manner there's a portrait of Kitty. Epstein himself bought the star of the show, a plaster head of Nefertiti of around 3500 to 3000 BC. It is only a little over 6 inches high, but Epstein's sleep in the days when he was suffering the whips and scorns of the yellow press must have been filled with dreams of its purity and colossal and eternal modernity.

Warkton

NORTHAMPTONSHIRE

Monuments to the Montagus of Boughton House in the Church of St Edmund

John, 2nd Duke of Montagu, the family that later morphed into Buccleuch, presided over the creation of the great landscape at Boughton House, with its canals and lake and miles of rides created by planting avenues of elm and lime, now being restored after the wipe-out of Dutch elm disease. The 2nd duke John and his wife, Mary Churchill (yes, those Churchills), were grand tourists as well, and among the things they brought back was a taste for the latest developments in art, which led them to commission Roubiliac to design their monuments in the nearby church of Warkton.

Louis-François Roubiliac (1695–1762), younger than the other two of the brilliant group of foreign sculptors working in England, Rysbrack and Scheemakers, had also a more vivid talent if not the classical poise of Rysbrack. The older pair were Flemish and baroque. Roubiliac was French and perfectly placed to have taken in rococo with his mother's milk. Rococo was the 18th-century reaction against the otiose grandeur of Versailles baroque in the previous century, all those miles of ceiling paintings proclaiming the power and majesty of the Bourbons. It was more playful, more bourgeois even, and in the hands of a master like Roubiliac the brilliant, broken, light-catching surfaces of Boucher's rococo

canvases became a tool for creating sculptural naturalism. The reason he came to England is not known, but he quickly became celebrated for his brilliant portrait busts, which, if not the greatest ever produced in any medium in England, are certainly among the greatest of the period, with Reynolds, Gainsborough and the best of Hogarth. He had been in England around twenty years when, in about 1749, the duke commissioned monuments for himself and the duchess in the chancel of the nearby Warkton church. The duke died that year, the duchess two years later, and the monuments were erected in 1752 and 1753. They quite match the best of Roubiliac's great sculpted groups at Westminster Abbey and St Paul's.

They are the first two of four Montagu memorials at Warkton (the others were to be designed by Robert Adam with sculpture by Peter van Gelder and by the Scot Thomas Campbell), and they face each other across the entry to the chancel. The monument to the duke has a tomb-like structure of grey marble. One naked putto lies on a ledge hanging a portrait medallion of the duke from the front of the structure. To his right the female figure of Charity carries another child on one arm and with her free arm helps the first putto. Beside her, another child holds an expired torch upside down, and the duchess stands on a step at the foot of the monument, leaning forward to gaze at the portrait. Poking out from behind the monument, a flag, a trumpet, cannon balls and cannon refer to the duke's military prowess (nothing special). It's almost what we would call an installation, but with brilliantly carved figures liberated from the convention of being placed before a constricting pyramid shape and moving easily in the dynamic space of Roubiliac's composition.

The monument to the duchess is even better. This time there is an apse-like space

above a handsome three-stage plinth. Two
putti cavort in the apse as they deck a large
urn with generous garlands of flowers.
Beneath them are three beautiful young
women, the Fates. Clotho, sitting on the left
of the ledge of the apse, spins the thread of
life from her distaff, as Lachesis, sitting facing
Clotho, feeds out the thread, in balletic mime
since there is no actual thread, and Atropos,
who determines the moment of death by
cutting off the thread, stands at the foot of
the monument with her hand on a skull.
Another child transforms the composition
into theatre in the round by stepping off the
monument into our space.

Warwick

WARWICKSHIRE

Joan of Arc's nemesis commemorated, the
Beauchamp Chapel, Church of St Mary

Richard Beauchamp, Earl of Warwick, was
one of the richest men in England and one of
the bravest. He fought side by side with
Prince Hal, he was captain of Calais, he took
on a queue of French challengers in
tournament on three consecutive days, he
undertook to care for Henry V's son and heir,
and when the boy was nine months old he
personally presented him for coronation in
Westminster Abbey. He grew up in the age of
chivalry though he extended no chivalry at
all to his prisoner in Rouen, Joan of Arc, a
woman who had dared to fight as a man. But
English history treated Joan as a trick of the
light and when Beauchamp died at Poitiers in
1439 in the embers of the Hundred Years War
his reputation and fortune suffered no
diminishment in England, and his chantry
chapel in St Mary, Warwick, went ahead as he
had specified in his will. Whatever history
finally says about the man, the chapel he left
and the tomb at its centre are the finest in
English art of the 15th century.

It was built on to the noble Church of St
Mary on a hill at the centre of Warwick as a
lady chapel, but in its disposition there isn't
much doubt that the glory here is the earl's,
with a little reflected glory for the Virgin and
the later incumbents, the Dudleys from
nearby Kenilworth Castle, including Queen
Elizabeth's favourite Robert, Earl of Leicester.
Everything was of the best. The king's glazier,
John Prudde, made the glass in the east
window (fragmented since the Civil War).
The quality suggests that John Manningham,
the greatest English sculptor of the time,
made the carvings of the nine orders of
angels in the mullions of the window, though
the contracts are vague about who did what.
But Richard Beauchamp lies plumb centre in
a tomb of Purbeck marble beneath a ceiling
boss of the Virgin. His effigy is of gilded
bronze. His head lies on a great tournament
helm encircled by a coronet, and he is clad in
a perfect representation of the very latest
thing in Milan fashion, a suit of Italian
armour fit for a king. At his feet is the
muzzled bear of Warwick. The masons
completed the chapel ten years after the earl's
death, but his head may have been modelled
from a death mask as it is intended as a
portrait. He lies with his hands held above
him as in prayer, but the face says he is giving
orders, from the furrowed brow to the long,
blunted nose, the thin mouth, tight skin and
tense expression. There is no letting go here –
he is a general in command.

What he cannot have predicted was that
his fine effigy would be surpassed by the
family mourners on the sides of the tomb,
also gilded bronze. The finest sculptors in
northern Europe in the first half of the 14th

The Beauchamp tomb (foreground) in the magnificent
Beauchamp chapel in the parish church of St Mary,
Warwick, holds the remains of Richard Beauchamp,
15th-century Earl of Warwick, captain of Calais, and
scourge of Joan of Arc

century worked in Dijon at the Burgundian court of Philip the Good (who also employed Jan van Eyck). These Warwick figures are in that class, transitional from Gothic, though they stand in Gothic niches, and intensely realistic. Their stillness and the heavy folds of their long gowns make them look faintly sinister, like death's golden emissaries, the women if anything more than the men, with their headdresses pulled down over their eyes. In this turbulent reign, with war abroad and at home, art of this stature seems a miracle.

Wing
BUCKINGHAMSHIRE

The Master of the Golden Light, Ascott House

Marie Antoinette had her *petit hameau*, a pretend village where she and her female intimates could play at being simple milkmaids. Baron Meyer de Rothschild had Ascott, his vast 19th-century pretend Jacobean cottage, where he could take a break from the arduous business of being high sheriff of Buckinghamshire by being master of the foxhounds. But not for long – he died a year later, and Leopold, one of the Rothschild cousins who colonised Buckinghamshire with their beautiful houses (Tring, Mentmore, Waddesdon, Aston Clinton), inherited Ascott House. The half-timbered palace as it appears today is based on the core of a small Jacobean farmhouse, and it avoids absurdity by being organised to look containable and homely.

Leopold brought in the first part of the wonderful collection of art. On the death of his widow in 1937, their son Anthony de Rothschild inherited. He had visited China as a young man in 1911 and was hooked, and the world-class collection of English art and

Chinese porcelain at Ascott was his. Between them the Rothschilds introduced *ancien régime* furniture from France and, from England, Chippendale.

As with all the Rothschild collections, it is hard to know where to begin. They never collected one kind of thing, and most of what they acquired was the sort of thing lesser mortals would place in bank vaults. Among the paintings there is one of Gainsborough's fine, late, full-length portraits in the library, once thought to have been of the Duchess of Richmond, but since cleaning revealed red hair instead of black, she is classed now as an unknown beauty. There is a lovely Stubbs canvas, one of his best, *Five Brood Mares*, no more realistic than those 17th-century family portraits in which the sitters have obviously posed at different times and different places and been transplanted into a classical setting. But for me the covetable painting is the *View of Dordrecht* by Aelbert Cuyp (1620–91), a wide panoramic take on a low skyline punctuated by a spit of land with the Grote Kerk, another smaller church, houses, a windmill and shipping before and behind on a mirror-like Maas. If Cuyp's name had been lost he would have been known as the Master of the Golden Light. He was a supreme painter of evening scenes. I think this is the best I have seen.

Woburn
BEDFORDSHIRE

Moses Trampling the Pharaoh's Crown, at Woburn Abbey

Woburn Abbey, a great house in place of the Cistercian foundation looted by Henry VIII and then granted to the Russells, was one of the first of the stately homes to open to the public after the last war and one of the finest, though finances were in a parlous state. To help things along, Ian Russell, the 13th Duke of Bedford, equipped the park with a herd of bison, but the house did its own talking, a palace of many periods, each of them as stately as the last: a delicate red and white Chinese dairy, a great collection of art, and a room built around a suite of Canaletto views of Venice. Tucked away among the other paintings is *Moses Trampling the Pharaoh's Crown* by Nicholas Poussin (1593/4–1665).

To the nation's immeasurable gain Poussin was popular with British collectors. He didn't work on much else while he was executing his absolute masterpiece, the second sequence of Sacraments (the seven canvases in Edinburgh; the first group is on loan from Belvoir Castle to the National Gallery), but the Moses of about 1645 was an exception. The story is that the pharaoh has placed a royal coronet on the head of the foundling Moses, who takes it off and tramples on it. A sacred scribe sees this as a warning that the infant will grow up an enemy of Egypt and draws a dagger to slay him. A nurse snatches Moses away from the scribe. The pharaoh's daughter Thermutis pleads for Moses's life, and the pharaoh accedes. Poussin's painting compresses the whole sequence into one tableau, as utterly artificial as a pre-Christian frieze, frozen music set against a background he has adapted from the Temple of Fortuna Virilis in Rome, a distancing accentuated by the cold colours, inimitably Poussin's, of vermilion, acid yellow, icy blue and the white of alpine snows. This very great painting hangs in a roped-off area of the blue drawing room several feet from passing visitors, one of the penalties to set against the benefit of seeing art in great domestic settings instead of public galleries.

Wolverhampton
WEST MIDLANDS

Gainsborough among the tradesmen in the town art gallery

David Rodgers, the curator in the 1970s, fought hard against municipal indifference and built what the gallery claims is the biggest gathering of Pop Art in Britain outside the Tate. I didn't see it because Wolverhampton, now proud of its work by Richard Hamilton, Peter Blake, Joe Tilson and Patrick Caulfield, plus the Americans Andy Warhol, Roy Lichtenstein, Jim Dine, Larry Rivers and others, was in the throes of building a new gallery. Thomas Gainsborough (1727–88) in a room of 18th-century British art isn't a bad substitute, especially as his full-length portrait of James Donnithorne shows quite another aspect of his work, dictated by the nature of the client.

Donnithorne was a businessman and, by the look of him, one who didn't stand on ceremony, even if he knew what ceremony was. On the table beside him are his account books inscribed with his name, occupation (tin merchant) and address (Lincoln's Inn, London), as well as sheets of paper on a spike and a quill pen standing in an inkwell. It's easy to sense that Gainsborough was fully engaged by this robust-looking man of affairs. The painting dates from 1760, the year Gainsborough moved to Bath, but possibly he painted Thomas Donnithorne in his peripatetic few months between leaving Ipswich, where commissions were drying up, and settling in Bath, where he encountered elegant society in its pomp.

The North Midlands

DERBYSHIRE * LEICESTERSHIRE
LINCOLNSHIRE * NOTTINGHAMSHIRE
RUTLAND * SHROPSHIRE
STAFFORDSHIRE

CHESHIRE

Eyam

❖ Buxton

Bakewell

Haddon Hall

DERBYS

Cromford ❖

Wirkswo

Stoke-on-Trent

Ashbourne

Cheadle

Kedle

❖ Ashley

Der

STAFFORDSHIRE

❖ Ingestre

Shrewsbury

SHROPSHIRE

❖ Weston under Lizard

Lichfield

Twyc

❖ Ironbridge Gorge

❖ Acton Burnell

WEST

MIDLANDS

❖ Holdgate

❖ Stottesdon

❖ Kinlet

❖ Ludlow

WORCESTERSHIRE

WARWIC

NORTH
SHIRE

❖ Mattersey

❖ Lincoln

LINCOLNSHIRE

❖ Ossington

NOTTINGHAMSHIRE

❖ Hawton

❖ Carlton
Scroop

❖ Nottingham

❖ Bottesford

❖ Belton

❖ Stapleford

❖ Whatton

❖ Grantham

❖ Bourne

❖ Pickworth

❖ Crowland

❖ Exton

LEICESTERSHIRE

RUTLAND

❖ Stamford

❖ Leicester

CAMBS.

NORTHANTS.

| 0 | 5 | 10 | 15 mi |

| 0 | 5 | 10 | 15 | 20 | 25 km |

Acton Burnell
SHROPSHIRE

The lord of the manor commemorated,
Church of St Mary

Once just Acton (meaning 'place of oaks'), the village took the suffix Burnell after a 13th-century lord of the manor who rose to be a powerful and innovative chancellor to Edward I and bishop of Bath and Wells. The king visited Acton for seven weeks in 1284 and summoned a parliament to the great barn whose stone gables still stand a hundred yards to the east of the church, where it promulgated the statute of Acton Burnell, which was intended to recover mercantile debts. Soon after Burnell received a licence to crenellate his manor house, so this Englishman's home became his castle in about 1285. It is now a ruin, but the cruciform church (1275–82) is an exquisite example of the mature Early English style, rich in detail and similar in quality to the lovely chapel Burnell built in the bishop's palace at Wells. The connection might be that he used Westminster masons on both.

The monuments are in the north transept, entered through an arch supported on foliate capitals, which themselves each stand on a short Purbeck marble shaft supported by a small carved head. There is a brass commemorating one of Burnell's 14th-century descendants, but the bishop is buried at Wells, and the best monument in Acton Burnell is by Nicholas Stone (c.1587–1647) of the lord of the manor, Sir Humphrey Lee, and his wife. Stone was one of the best English sculptors of his generation, and here he has carved an entirely classical monument in line with the belated English lurch into the Renaissance that was prompted by Inigo Jones and Van Dyck. As a young man Stone had been taken by the pre-eminent Dutch sculptor Hendrik de Keyser (1565–1621) to

work as a journeyman in his Amsterdam workshop, and there he saw the genesis of de Keyser's greatest work, the monument to William the Silent, the assassinated hero of the Dutch struggle against Spain's suzerainty. Stone later outstripped de Keyser, and when Stone set up his own workshop in London he had mastered architecture as well as portraiture. The Lee monument is well done, and the figures are outstanding, the heads unflattering, robustly shaped with old, blunt, plain yeoman faces above the strongly carved costume of the gentry, Sir Humphrey in doublet and hose, his wife in a matronly gown with a long mantle falling from her shoulders and wrapped around her legs. This has a strong sense of how they must have been in life, neither to be trifled with nor befriended.

Ashbourne
DERBYSHIRE

A touching memorial to a dead child,
Church of St Oswald

There had been nothing quite like it in a church before, anywhere. In the Boothby chapel of St Oswald where Penelope Boothby lies entombed, the shining white marble image of her figure, apparently sleeping, is surrounded by sombre alabaster tombs bearing the sepulchral figures of the unequivocally dead adults of powerful families, the Cockaynes and the Bradbournes of the 15th and 16th centuries, the Taylors of the 18th century and the Boothbys of the 17th and 18th centuries. Penelope, who died in 1791 at the age of six, wears a classical long, simple, pleated dress with a sash circling her body high up in the waist, just like those in George Romney's paintings of children at the time or of fashionable women by Elisabeth Vigée-Lebrun. Her hands are lightly clenched beside her face, her bare feet poke out from

Penelope Boothby was six years old when she died in 1791. Her effigy in the Church of St Oswald, Ashbourne, is the finest work of the sculptor Thomas Banks, and the maquette for it is said to have reduced Princess Charlotte and her children to tears when it was exhibited in the Royal Academy

beneath the hem of the dress, and her eyes are closed almost as though she is pretending sleep.

The sculptor, Thomas Banks (1735–1805), would carve nothing better or better known than this monument. Princess Charlotte and her children saw the plaster maquette for it in the Royal Academy (now in the Soane Museum) and are said to have wept. It is a prelude to a century of increasing sentimentality in the portrayal of children, which has tipped over in our own post-Freudian times into a climate where the portrayal of children has to be approached with extreme caution and under the eye of the law.

Penelope's father, Sir Brooke Boothby, was a friend, translator and first publisher in England of Jean-Jacques Rousseau, and he had his own portrait in oils taken by Joseph Wright of Derby (see Derby, below) in which he reclines on the ground in parkland holding a volume of Rousseau. He would certainly have been familiar with *Emile*, the text in which his friend put the case that children, far from being miniature adults as they almost always seem to have been regarded, certainly in art, were a force of nature and should be treated naturally, sent to play in the fresh air and dressed in loose, easy clothes.

Boothby commissioned Joshua Reynolds to portray Penelope at the age of three. The painting, now in the Ashmolean in Oxford, shows the child sitting in a sylvan scene wearing a commodious wrap-around dress and a big beribboned mob cap. She is at the age of innocence, a phrase, in fact, which Sir Joshua used for another child portrait that same year, 1788.

One side of Penelope's tomb chest carries lines from a Petrarch sonnet about young beauty turning to dust; the other has something straight from the hearts of her mother and father: 'The unfortunate parents ventured their all on this frail bark and the wreck was total.' Academics studying childhood in that period of high infant mortality still argue over whether parents could possibly have mourned deeply for the children they lost. Their answer lies here in Ashbourne.

Ashley
STAFFORDSHIRE

An outbreak of art and industry, in the Church of St John the Baptist

Josiah Wedgwood found pottery a hand craft; he left it a mass industry. Soon after Wedgwood had opened his first London showrooms, Debora Chetwynd, the daughter of his friend Viscount Chetwynd of Brockley Hall in Staffordshire and lady-in-waiting to Queen Charlotte, recommended Wedgwood's tea sets to the queen. She bought a line in cream, ordered more, Wedgwood was launched, and the line is known as queen's ware. The viscount died in 1770, and Debora asked Wedgwood to design a monument to him in St John the Baptist. He did the job personally, and it is there above the chancel arch. It is faultless: a black basalt funeral urn standing on a ledge before a small arch. Unfortunately, it is too high up – it was built for the old church, which was torn down and replaced in 1860–2, so it stands among clumsy imitation tudorbethan black rafters, which obliterate it. Hamlet's words on his father form the inscription (I have it on good authority because it can't be seen without binoculars): 'He was a man, take him for all in all, I shall not look upon his like again.' Which is a good deal more fulsome than the inscription on Wedgwood's tomb in the parish church of Stoke-on-Trent: 'He converted a rude and inconsiderable Manufactory into an elegant Art and An important part of the National Commerce.'

Bakewell
DERBYSHIRE

Medieval grandees commemorated, Church of All Saints

Sir Godfrey Foljambe was a great magnate of medieval Derbyshire. With their customary imaginative freedom, genealogists have traced his descent from Ragner Lodbrok, an 8th- or 9th-century king of Denmark, hero of the Viking sagas and Hollywood hero impersonated by Ernest Borgnine in *The Vikings* (1958). Ragner himself claimed descent from the god Odin. More to the mundane point, many generations later Godfrey de Foleschamp came to England with the Conqueror. His descendant, Sir Godfrey, served in all the parliaments of Edward III, died aged sixty in the same year as the monarch, 1377, and lies buried in All Saints, an old church largely of the 13th century and with fragments of Saxon and Norman ornamentation in the church and churchyard.

The richly glowing alabaster wall monument commemorates Foljambe and his second wife, Avena, née Ireland, who seems to have died on 'the Saturday next after the Nativity of the Blessed Virgin' in September 1382. It is an odd object, quite small, the half-length figures only about 12 inches high, and covered by a flattened ogee arch, itself surmounted by a battlemented rim. Above each figure are the Foljambe and Ireland arms. He is clad in armour, helmeted and chain-mailed to the eyeballs. She wears a high-necked, long-sleeved gown, with her hair in a net headdress. It would be as though they were looking out from a shallow oriel window except that their hands are clasped before their chests in prayer and their heads rest on pillows. In other words, it's like a tiny tomb sculpture raised vertically. Nothing like it had ever been seen before, and despite its incongruity it is a beautiful object, the coats of arms still brightly coloured. His shield is blue with gold scallop shells ('sable, a bend between six escallops or,' as the College of Arms puts it), hers is red with gilded fleur-de-lis ('Gules, 6 fleurs de lis argent'); sable is black and argent silver, so perhaps the colours were freely interpreted in restoration.

The armour was not a fashion gesture. Edward III's was a reign of great battles, from Crécy to Neville's Cross, and the nation's elite were duty-bound to serve. Foljambe may have served under the command of John of Gaunt, younger brother of the Black Prince, but since he came from the gentry and not the aristocracy, he was one of the members of the Commons who, during the so-called Good Parliament of 1376, voted military supplies to the king only in exchange for measures that were the foundation of many of today's liberties.

Belton

LINCOLNSHIRE

The Brownlow earls took a paternalist and beneficial interest in the villagers of Belton. Now their seat, Belton House, is owned by the National Trust there is a vestigial remnant of the old ties: visitors have to gain admission to the parish Church of St Peter and St Paul through the gardens of the house. After all, the church, too, was part of the fiefdom of the related Brownlow and Cust families whose monuments occupy most of the space available for tombs in the church, which is most of the space. The pretty village itself is largely 19th century, but imaginatively built by the architects Jeffry Wyatville (1766–1840), whose work here and in the house and church made him practically a Brownlow

family retainer, and Anthony Salvin (1799–1881), a busy architect mostly of domestic buildings. Between them they erected a pub, cottages, almshouses, a school and a village pump.

A lady in a Napoleonic pose, in the Church of St Peter and St Paul

Antonio Canova (1757–1822) was regarded as the foremost sculptor of the period. He caught the flood tide of neoclassicism and of post-Revolutionary France: he was lionised by the Bonaparte family and even made an erotic sculpture of Napoleon's sister Pauline, half-naked and reclining on a divan. But Canova was born in the Veneto and his heart was Roman. The year after Sophia Hume's death Napoleon fell, and Wellington and Castlereagh helped Canova to recover for Italy the art Napoleon had looted. If Canova felt an urge to visit the country of his new heroes he now had a reason: his recently completed heroic statue of Napoleon as a naked Greek god had become suddenly obsolete, so Canova travelled to England to set it up as a trophy of war in the victor's house at Apsley House, Piccadilly. While he was in London Lord Brownlow stepped in and commissioned a monument to his wife Sophia. She had died in 1814, and he had been casting about for someone good enough to carve a memorial. St Peter and Paul was not big and bulged with monuments, so while Canova worked in Rome on the assignment, the earl engaged Jeffrey Wyattville to remodel the north chapel to receive it. In 1818 the white marble statue was erected behind an iron screen and gates, one of only two monuments by Canova in an English parish church; the other is at Speen in Berkshire (see South).

The Belton monument is an allegorical female figure dressed in the flowing costume of a Greek goddess. Her right hand, apparently, once held a cross, and her left hand holds steady a large medallion bearing the head of the departed Sophia, which rests on a half-column; cross and column were two of the attributes of the Passion. The piece is said to be loosely based on Canova's monument to Pope Clement XIII in St Peter's, but the curious thing is that this Lincolnshire neoclassical statue strangely recalls the redundant figure of Napoleon. She has the same pose but in reverse: her right arm is held out sideways from the shoulder and bent at the elbow so that she is pointing upwards, and her left arm is lowered as her forearm and hand support the medallion. Napoleon's left arm is bent upwards to grasp a mighty sceptre, and his right hand holds an orb at waist level. Each figure has its weight thrown on to the forward foot, her left, his right. Well, all artists occasionally repeat themselves, and artists with full order books do it more than any. All the same, it's hard to avoid feeling that Speen has the better of it with its modestly magnificent Canova tablet to the Margrave of Anspach.

A surfeit of Dutch fruit and vegetables at Belton House

After Charles II's Restoration to the throne, Sir John Brownlow, builder of Belton, asked the fine amateur architect Sir Roger Pratt (1620–85) for advice on employing an architect to design his country house near Grantham. 'Get some ingenious gentleman who has seen much of that kind of thing abroad,' Pratt said. So he employed William Winde (c.1640–1722), who built him a house that was for a long time taken for the work of Christopher Wren. It is, indeed, one of the very best English country 17th-century post-Reformation houses, set in beautiful formal gardens within a deer park. It could have had one of the finest private art collections as well, but over a period in the 20th century

the best of the Brownlow paintings were scattered to the corners of the earth, including the late Titian *The Death of Actaeon*, which the National Gallery bought in 1972. The Brownlows followed this in 1984 by handing the house over to the National Trust. What's left is mostly portraits by the usual suspects, the late 17th- and 18th-century artists who flourished on country house and royal commissions – Kneller, Riley, Dahl, Hoppner, Hudson, Reynolds – plus the American John Singer Sargent, a favourite among wealthy Victorians and Edwardians, and a theatrical Lord Leighton portrait of Adelaide, Countess Brownlow, in 1879 (the family is still in residence), wearing a white silk gown that won the praise of Gladstone, though perhaps the gown was his code for what was wrapped in it. But the most extraordinary ensemble is the three very big still lifes by the Utrecht artist Melchior d'Hondecoeter (1636–95) set into the wood panelling in a room specially designed to take them.

For modern taste Dutch still life is just too much: too much game, too much fruit, too many flowers. And Hondecoeter's art is too, too much, but with a creative edge that makes it unique in the genre. He takes it into a different dimension, almost literally, with still life dominating deep perspective views of fantasy parkland and wildly inventive baroque architecture. At Belton three canvases pretty well fill the wall space in their room. Nobody knows who owned the paintings originally, but the 3rd Earl Brownlow brought them to Belton in 1873. One of them shows swans and ducks in the foreground of a view of a man and a woman strolling together up an avenue of trees and ornamental stone urns, but the pièce de résistance is the big canvas with a pageboy descending steps from a terrace bearing a tray laden with fruit to a stone pavement where a tumble of dead game lies with a

Surreal and spectacular, the Hondecoeter room at Belton House, specially designed to take three spectacular canvases by the 17th-century Dutch still life painter, Melchior d'Hondecoeter

hunting gun and fishing net. A spaniel stares out of the picture expectantly, his tail poised to wag, while a couple of unscathed ducks wander unconcernedly by. Behind is a mock triumphal arch in a wall with statues in niches (you infer this, only one shows), a further arch in deep perspective behind and a park in which appear tall cypresses butressed by the sheer wall of a mansion. It's all a little surreal and majestically spectacular.

Bottesford
LEICESTERSHIRE

Wren's master carver at the Church of St Mary

Grinling Gibbons (1648–1721) was, wrote the politician and all-round connoisseur Horace Walpole, 'an original genius, a citizen of

nature … There is no instance of a man before Gibbons who gave to wood the loose and airy lightness of flowers … with a free disorder natural to each species.' In his day the name of Gibbons was nonpareil, and it remains synonymous with wood carving. His fortune, however, was built on carving monumental figures in marble, and at this he was a dunce. Fortunately for him, the 16th- and 17th-century struggle in the Netherlands for independence from Spain produced a wave of immigrant craftsmen to the shores of England who were, initially anyway, grateful to Gibbons for employing them and then stealing the credit for their work.

The word got around, and Gibbons was constantly engaged in quarrels with clients, who thought he charged too much, and with Flemish assistants, who thought he paid too little. But he had the luck to be working a generation before the great immigrant sculptors Roubiliac, Rysbrack and Scheemakers brought their superior talents to these shores. At Bottesford he carried out two prime commissions, for this lovely village on the River Devon was close enough to Belvoir Castle, and the large but plain church with an elegant spire had a chancel big enough for the Earls of Rutland to settle on it as the mausoleum until they built their own at Belvoir in the 19th century. Eight earls lie in the chancel of St Mary under elaborate heaps of stone, and the 7th and 8th are by Gibbons.

The interesting one is the 8th earl's. Although the 7th earl died in 1641, both monuments were commissioned after the death of the 8th in 1679. His monument contains the figures of both earl and countess; they are adequate but inert, as uneasy in their Roman togas as a couple in fancy dress at a Buckingham Palace tea party. On the other hand, the monument as a whole is both innovatory and handsome. The couple stand either side of a big, shapely urn on a plinth. Behind them is a slab of black Tournai marble, at their feet is a skull, and above them two carefree putti use a broken pediment as a slide. From the pediment is suspended a cartouche with the Rutland arms and a garland of fruit and flowers, which gives the lie to the tale that Gibbons couldn't carve in marble – it was the human figure that stretched him. A few years later he made a more elaborate version of the 8th earl's monument for Viscount Campden at Exton.

Bourne

LINCOLNSHIRE

A playwright-architect's great Roman hall, Grimsthorpe Castle

Castle here means stately home, not fortress, though this one has the massiveness of a barbican, with heavy pillars, two flanking towers that thrust forward, baroque groups of sculpture writhing against the sky – Hercules wrestling with Antaeus, Pluto's rape of Proserpine – and, reaching from the outer sides of the tower, walls with large niches along their length ending in pavilions joined by wrought iron railings and an elaborately scrolled gate. This was the final masterpiece by John Vanbrugh (1664–1776). He died while he was working on it, and his collaborator on Castle Howard and Blenheim, Nicholas Hawksmoor (1661–1736), finished it, but only the north range of his plans for a complete rebuilding of the Tudor house was completed.

The estate in the undulating countryside of Lincolnshire a few miles before it flattens into the fens has belonged to the Willoughby de Eresby family since Henry VIII gave it to them (with a special dispensation for the baronetcy to descend through the female line). When the king visited to pacify the country after the rebellious Pilgrimage of Grace of 1536–7, Katherine Willoughby de Eresby's husband, Charles Brandon, Duke of Suffolk, is reported to have hastily torn down the adjoining abbey and used the stone to build a house grand enough to entertain a monarch on his progress. This is the house that a 17th-century visitor described as 'an extempore structure, set up of a sudden', which still exists in the wings behind Vanbrugh's north front.

Vanbrugh's hall stands tall, the full two storeys, between the north front towers. Behind the open arcade on each side it is flanked by a double staircase rising above a doorcase based on Michelangelo's for the Capitoline Palace. The round arched arcades around the four sides of the hall pick up the theme of the windows on the outside. In the hall's south wall the matching arcade of the top storey is blind, and the niches are filled with imaginary grisaille portraits by James

John Vanbrugh's great hall (centre) between the north front towers of Grimsthorpe Castle, his culminating work, massive in totality and in detail, the interior Roman in its stern gravity

Thornhill of those monarchs perceived to have returned favour to the family for their services, from left to right, William I, Edward III, Henry V, George I, William III, Henry VIII and Henry VII. In the arches of the upper storey east and west arcades are antique busts brought from Italy and superimposed in the effective 18th-century manner on coloured marble togas by expert jobbing statuaries. Nancy Willoughby de Eresby, granddaughter of the first woman MP, Nancy Astor, and herself the 27th or 28th baroness (they've lost count in the mists of times since 1313), has introduced a capacious settee and armchairs to try to make it the kind of room where you might curl up before the fire with a Jeffrey Archer novel, but it defies the feminine touch. The fireplace itself is the size of a small kitchen, and it is a room massive in its totality and in detail, a Roman

stage-set utterly different in spirit from Vanbrugh's own restoration comedies, the sort of hall in which Brutus would have stoically watched his sons, dead in battle, borne in on their shields.

Buxton
DERBYSHIRE

Flamboyance at the Buxton Opera House

Frank Matcham's masterpiece is held to be London Coliseum, these days the home of English National Opera. It's good, but for sheer faery flights of fancy, eclectic exoticism and operatic opulence Buxton takes the palm, handed out, no doubt, by one of the flying urchins or garlanded sibyls gracing the ceilings of the Opera House foyer and auditorium. This gem by Matcham

(1854–1920) is encased in an exterior that promises excitement but withholds delivery for later: a stone portico with round arch and balustrade above, flanked by two domed round towers and with an iron and glass canopy with dress circle, grand circle, stalls and Opera House spelled out on coloured glass in the playful pre-jazz, experimentally exuberant typography that sprang up like tendrils of art nouveau in the new 20th century. There are tours of the Opera House, but short of that, when the box office is open anybody can pop into the white and gold foyer with its wall decorations of gilded lyres to catch a sense of the place.

The dizzying drive up from Macclesfield past the Cat and Fiddle puts Buxton's boast that it is the highest spa town in Britain beyond ready argument. Although the town is much smaller than Bath, William Cavendish, 5th Duke of Devonshire, decided in the 1780s to build the Crescent, and John Carr gave him something more finely drawn than Bath's braggadocio Royal crescendo. The Square followed, and terraces of houses and the Cavendish Hospital. A hundred years later the town created the 23 acre Pavilion Gardens behind the Crescent and the glass pavilion and conservatory into which Matcham's 1903 Opera House nestles slightly uncomfortably. Maybe one day Buxton will pull a trick like the Royal Opera House's happy marriage of convenience with the Floral Hall. Meanwhile, it will do fine staying single. In 1980, when the Buxton Festival was young, I saw a production of the Ambrose Thomas opera *Hamlet* at the Opera House. *Hamlet – The Musical*, as it is sometimes derisively known, seemed somehow appropriate for the theatre created by a master of the absurd. (See also Blackpool, Northwest, and Leeds, Northeast.)

Carlton Scroop
LINCOLNSHIRE

Medieval window commemorating the presentation of a new priest, at the Church of St Nicholas

With the exception of a shortage of sokemen and villeins to occupy the executive housing edging the main road at Carlton Scroop between Grantham and Lincoln, the village cannot have changed much since the Domesday Book in 1086. Apart from a demesne farm and wider acres beyond, William the Conqueror's commissioners made note only of a church, and that remains all there is to detain the traveller now. What survives of the Normans is a font, but in the tracery of the east window we have the intriguing sight of two quatrefoils of stained glass showing a figure in each kneeling and facing the other, a knight and a priest. The knight is clad in chain mail and a red surcoat, he has knee guards (known as poleyns) and spurs, and a sword in its scabbard swings from his belt. The priest wears a blue robe.

The yellow passages, principally the plinth on which the knight kneels, are pot metal yellow, a basic technique in which the glass blower takes molten glass from the pot and blows it to produce thick glass that is an opaque yellow right through. The art of creating a delicate transparent yellow with silver nitrate, which can be painted on to the surface of the glass, was invented late in the 14th century, so the pot yellow and the knight's armour of this window place it as early 14th century. The knight holds a shield bearing the arms of the Newmarch family, and a shield in the priest's quatrefoil identifies his name as Briddeshall. That much has long been known. Then in 1987 the organisers of the Royal Academy exhibition of the art of the Plantaganets, the Age of Chivalry, came across an entry in the Lincoln archives recording that in 1307 John de Newmarch, lord of the manor, presented William de Briddeshall to the living of Carlton Scroop. The window records that event. It was, of course, another case like the famous sequence of windows at Merton College, Oxford (see West and East Midlands), recording one donor's largesse, of a member of the ruling class leaping aboard the bandwagon to heaven, or, as William Langland wrote in *Piers Plowman*:

> Would'st thou glaze the gable, and grave
> therein thy name,
> Secure should thy soul be for to dwell in
> Heaven.

Cheadle

STAFFORDSHIRE

Pugin's best church, St Giles

Augustus Welby Northmore Pugin (1812–52) invented the Gothic revival in its truest sense. He despised the light-hearted furbelows and curlicues of earlier revival buildings, like Horace Walpole's house, Strawberry Hill, at Richmond in Surrey. He excoriated the imitation of Perpendicular in the new 'commissioners' Gothic' churches, pattern-book architecture built in anything cheap enough for the Church of England to afford, even at a pinch brick and cast iron. He went so far as to reject not just the imitation but the original 15th- to 16th-century Perpendicular and turned in his own practice to, as he saw it, the only architecture fit to herald the kingdom of God, the early Decorated of the 13th century. In short, Pugin was a rigorous proselytiser for the true way, and his writings became a beacon for successors like John Ruskin and even, at a socialist remove, William Morris. Yet in his own actual buildings he fell far short of his ideal, except in one: St Giles.

The God for whom he built was the pope's. Pugin converted from Anglicanism to savour the heady incense of Romanism, the faith, he pointed out, that had covered the land with houses of worship in the time of King Edward I. His financial backer was the last of one of the great recusant families, the Earl of Shrewsbury, who put up with a church projected to cost £5,000 but running up a tab for £45,000 by the time it was consecrated in 1846. What the good lord got for his money was a church with a slender spire so tall (200 feet) that it dominates the town even though it stands lower than the Anglican church, which is only slightly older and is also dedicated to St Giles. But Pugin's ultimate masterpiece is the interior.

He covered every square inch (no cliché this) with colour. He picked out the arches of the nave arcades in green, red and gold, and he had gilded corbels carved as angels or as lions' heads. He carpeted the floor with Minton tiles. Painted chevrons decorate the piers, and portraits of saints appear in roundels above the arches. The choir screen with its rood is alive with pierced decoration, and a horizontal band of gilded foliage in carved relief.

Well, other architects have performed these reawakened rituals, but Pugin's power comes from the sense that one Pugin is fighting another. He thought, like the very first builder of Gothic, Abbot Suger of St Denis, that luxurious ornament was an aid to worship and pleasant in the eyes of God. But he nursed a chip of Puritan ice close to his heart, his belief in the absolute authenticity and primacy of Decorated Gothic, and this prevented him from breaking out, from doing anything truly original. Niggardly budgets had constrained his previous church projects, and his own imitative historicism deadened them. Now nothing held him back but this sense that the great builders of 13th-century England must not be gainsaid, and the tension between luxury and dogma produced Pugin's masterpiece.

He died in September 1852, and Lord Shrewsbury died that November. Without them this little cotton and silk industrial town would be an unremarkable outpost on the Staffordshire moors. The earl's son died childless, and the Catholic family line ceded all to its Protestant cadet branch. The family home was Alton Towers, and that has gone into altogether another line of business.

Cromford

DERBYSHIRE

The first-born factory, on the Derwent by the A6

Richard Arkwright's mill at Cromford must always have looked grim. The oldest and biggest prison-like building in the complex, of 1771, is four rows of small windows in a big rectangular brick box with no windows at all on the ground floor and the entrance end rounded and blank walled as a bastion. This is where the world's factory system was born. Here the millhands, mostly children, worked shifts all day and all night. Yet it had a dark beauty, especially by moonlight, as Joseph Wright of Derby, friend and portraitist of Arkwright (1732–92), shows in a landscape view of 1782 from, at a guess, the road up to Wirksworth, bright under a full moon with its windows illuminated by its hundred lights between the dark trees of the dale. The diarist and traveller John Byng, Lord Torrington, described the mill at night as 'like a first-rate man of war' (his uncle was Admiral John Byng, who was court martialled in 1757 and executed after a lost sea battle against the French, but other visitors, too, saw the mill as a great ship).

Arkwright built Cromford mill before he had perfected the roller spinning machinery for cotton yarn, an invention he ripped off

from an engineer from Leigh in Lancashire and patented. Confronted by the inventor, Arkwright faced him down. 'Suppose if any man has found out a thing, and begun a thing, and does not go forwards, he lays it aside … another man has a right to take it up,' he said. Very soon the mill was in production. Arkwright went on to build the village of Cromford, church, school and all, for the workforce, and to build Masson mills, a little upstream just south of Matlock, with a main factory building that nods to polite civilisation with its central hall and staircase with Venetian windows and a cupola. Cromford mill ceased production in the mid-19th century, but Masson mills kept going until 1991. Both receive visitors and Masson still has working machinery. The whole stretch of the industrial Derwent from Matlock to Derby is a Unesco World Heritage Site.

Crowland

LINCOLNSHIRE

14th-century sculptured west front, Crowland Abbey

Crowland still feels like a place that time passed by. Once it was a group of islands in the fens, and its streets were waterways. The British Museum has a 12th-century scroll showing St Guthlac sailing in choppy water to the island of Crowland to found the abbey. The extraordinary, not to say unique, 14th-century three-way stone bridge, known as the Triangular Bridge, stands over dry, paved land at the head of the main street, but it once crossed three streams at the meeting of the Rivers Nene and Welland. At the foot of one of the three arches that meet in the

This sweet, mouldering, 13th-century statue of an angel is one in a gallery of sculpture on the great ruined west wall of Croyland Abbey in Crowland

centre is a crowned figure. The ravages of time have left it undateable but massively archaic. Henry Moore's lean, ascetic *King and Queen* look like a near modern equivalent. The figure on the bridge seems most likely to have come from the collapsed gable of the ruined west front of Crowland Abbey.

This remnant of glory – 'bare ruined choirs, where late the sweet birds sang' (Shakespeare, sonnet 73) – is a monumental survival of the abbey that replaced Guthlac's 8th-century foundation. What was once the north aisle survives complete as the parish church, but after the dissolution during Henry VIII's reign and the ravages of Cromwellian troops camping there, all the rest of the monastic buildings vanished. Nothing shows through the great, empty window of the west wall but sky, but what remains to each side of the window and above it is a majestic show of four tiers of sculpted saints, kings and a queen (Matilda), lords and churchmen – nineteen figures and three missing. The bottom two rows are 13th century, the top two 15th century, added when the Early English window was converted into a taller Perpendicular window. Above this was the vanished gable with the figure of Christ the King inserted flat against the wall, which would explain the shape of the figure of the bridge and the position of the head, bent towards passers-by.

Sweetest and best of all, to the right of the entrance to the old nave, also from the earlier period, is an angel as beautiful as anything in the angel choir at Lincoln, possibly because the same craftsmen were involved, and, even though damaged, it is as fine as the famous musical angel in the vault of Gloucester Cathedral. Crowland's angel sits upon a corbel supported by the straining shoulders of a defaced figure and partly beneath the remains of what must once have been a canopy supporting another full-length figure (corresponding to the ruined sculpture to the left of the portal). Everything about this angel speaks of a master sculptor: the slightly inclined head, gaze directed into the churchyard, the little smile, the clearly articulated folded wings, the natural easefulness of the pose, the drapery falling loosely from the shoulders to the waist and over the knees, with one calf showing, the other covered, feet comfortably apart.

Derby
DERBYSHIRE

Worlds within worlds in the painting of Joseph Wright, Derby Art Gallery

Opposite Joseph Wright's painting of an orrery is a working model (operated by clockwork in Wright's day, but in this new model by electricity). Contained within the confines of a concentric series of elliptical rings, little spheres representing the planets and their moons turn at speeds relative to the rotation of the real heavenly bodies. In Wright's painting, *A Philosopher Giving that Lecture on the Orrery, in which a Lamp is put in place of the Sun*, to give it its full, generous title, the philosopher of the age of enlightenment – in other words, a scientist – holds forth to a rapt circle of listeners. One man avidly makes notes, another shades his eyes with his hand as though against the real sun, while eager, bright-eyed children lean as close as they can to this simulacrum of their universe. The heads of this group tilt and their faces catch the light from the lamp like so many planets of the sun, they form a hemisphere echoing the orrery's, and their clothes are thrown into the outer darkness with the white hair and red gown of the scientist picking him out from the group. It's a quiet drama of dawning knowledge and intellectual excitement and, for the painter, a consummate answer to the challenge of defining spatial depth on a flat surface.

Before they named the high road into Derby from the M1 Brian Clough Way, after the manager who took Derby County from nowhere to be the European champions, before Rolls Royce or even the railways, Derby had been a force in the emerging industrial world, and the artist Joseph Wright (1734–97) had been a part of it. To distinguish him from another Wright during his peripatetic years trying to make a living as a portrait painter, he was called Joseph Wright of Derby, and he settled on Joseph Wright of Derby both as his own claim to uniqueness as a painter of industry and of his native town's fame as a cradle of new industry. Derby has repaid him by displaying the biggest collection in the world of his paintings.

In Wright's time the city was a centre of the heavy industries of iron smelting, china manufacture and textiles, and even of precision instrument making. He was the son of a Derby lawyer and, like Reynolds, studied painting in London under Thomas Hudson, but he failed to make his way as a portrait painter in the elegant social circles of Bath and returned to his home base. His friends and clients were not, like Reynolds's, aristocrats and London intelligentsia, but industrialists, scientists, cartographers, men of business, Josiah Wedgwood, the pottery king of Stoke, and Erasmus Darwin, the botanist. He sold paintings to Wedgwood and painted portraits, now in Derby Art Gallery, of Darwin and Richard Arkwright (see Cromford, above), the ruthless capitalist visionary who patented cotton spinning machinery, not necessarily his own, and transformed an industry and the landscape of Derbyshire and Lancashire.

Wright's portraits were carefully worked, close to with fine brushes, technically and mimetically admirable, smoothly finished, but with none of the warmth of a Reynolds portrait or the swift, life-enhancing certainty of Gainsborough. His empirical approach came into its own in his paintings of scientific explorations and working life.

Exton
RUTLAND

Carvings by Grinling Gibbons in the Church of St Peter and St Paul, at the edge of Exton Park, Rutland

The 18th-century arts patron and letter writer Horace Walpole wrote that the skill of Grinling Gibbons 'did not reach to human figures, unless the brazen statue of James II, in the Privy Garden [now in Trafalgar Square] be, as I have reason to believe it, of his hand'. Yet he continued in the same passage: 'Gibbons made a magnificent tomb for Baptist Noel Viscount Camden, in the church of Exton, in Rutlandshire; it cost £1,000; is 22 feet high, and 14 wide. There are two figures, of him and his lady, and bas reliefs of their children.'

There are two things here. One is that even during Gibbons's life (1648–1721) the belief was that the only successful large figures carved in his name were actually done by his Flemish partner Arnold Quellin or one of the many assistants he employed to work in his growing statuary practice, and particularly the figures of Charles II (one at the Royal Exchange, destroyed, and another at the Royal Hospital, Chelsea) and James II (see also Bottesford, above). The other is that Walpole's purely factual description of the Exton monument, from a man so vivid in his turn of phrase, suggests he was writing at second-hand. It is certainly big and £1,000 was a lot of money, but the figures of Camden and his fourth wife are not successful. In fact, they are conventional and inert, pointedly so in the same church as two fine Nollekens memorials.

The viscount and his wife stand either side

of an urn on a pedestal bearing the date 1686. On the plinth beneath them are two friezes carved with reliefs of two of his wives and their children, and the other two wives appear with their children in medallions on large obelisks supporting the central part of the memorial: four wives and nineteen children, including several babies, who are the conventional representation of children who died in infancy. The friezes are a delight, delicately carved as though a light breeze had deposited them here. The top frieze has a border of oak leaves and acorns, but the carver has dispensed with this on the lower frieze, which somehow lets the air in. The gloomy, marmoreal splendour of the monument here becomes a lyrical dance to the music of time, a pastoral celebration of young lives, the youths in Roman dress, the girls in loose, diaphanous-seeming gowns, low cut in the fashion of Gibbons's day – a light-hearted moment frozen in time and tinged with the grief and pomp of the deaths marked here and the ruined ancestral house close by.

Eyam
DERBYSHIRE

9th-century cross outside the plague church, St Lawrence

I asked Mrs Furness, the duty parishioner on the church bookstall, how Eyam should be pronounced: Eeyam? Iyam? 'Eeem,' she said severely, 'as in redeem.' Apocalyptic thoughts seem never far from the surface in this Peaks moorland village, famous for its heroic calmness in 1665 when it placed itself in quarantine after a bale of cloth from plague-hit London arrived at the local tailor's and brought bubonic bacteria with it. When its virulence was spent the following year, eighty-three villagers had survived from a population of 350.

The survival of the stone cross in the churchyard is only slightly less remarkable than the survival of the village itself. It has withstood the erosion of driving wind and rain 800 feet above sea level with its carved interlace not just intact but deeply incised. One panel depicts the Virgin and her child, and the cross-head is carved with angels on each of its facets. The carving of the figures is cruder and the vine scrolls and interlace are less fluent than the great works of art at Bewcastle (see Northwest) and Ruthwell in the northwest of what was then Northumbria, but it remains clearly legible.

The disease took its first terrible toll in the row of cottages alongside the churchyard, which now carry plaques listing the names of the mothers, fathers and children who died, eight or nine to a family. Several of the families that left survivors still have descendants in the village, Mrs Furness's among them. But outsiders are moving in, property prices are rising, and the bonds that have kept the community so close since the days of quarantine seem destined to dissolve. What will remain is the cross, which stood in Eyam 800 years before the plague, 500 years before the church.

Grantham
LINCOLNSHIRE

Royalty at the Angel and Royal Hotel, High Street

Grantham has adapted with the times. Prosperity founded on wool funded the fine church of St Wulfram with one of the most glorious spires in England. Agriculture stepped up to the mark with the late medieval decline in the wool trade, and a canal supplemented the Great North Road and then the mainline railway between King's Cross and Edinburgh. It remains a prosperous industrial town with a largely

18th-century centre around St Wulfram. The stone-faced Angel and Royal Hotel is much older though. The locals insist on calling it the Angel, which is what it was before the management added 'Royal' after a visit in the 19th century from the Prince of Wales, later King Edward VII. Theoretically, the addition to the name could have been made in the 13th century since, seen through a beer glass mistily, legend claims a visit by King John, though that would not just have been under different management but in a different building, probably a Knights Templars' guest house on the same site. Edward III and Queen Philippa are also said to have visited the inn, as did Charles I before Civil War broke out in 1642, and his nemesis Oliver Cromwell. The building we see today is late 15th century, and a letter from Richard III of November 1483 to his chancellor ordering the execution of the Duke of Buckingham for treachery was written at this time and in this inn.

If the gilded angel apparently supporting the oriel window above the archway has any particular significance it may well lie in the royal crown he holds. The building is oddly off centre, with two projecting bays at either end, two bays inside each of those, and the wide central bay with the arch and oriel. All of this is yoked together by a parapet with a band of decoration that has been lopped off short at one side. Other features, possibly corbels, have been half-effaced, but the effect is a rich addition to the texture of the High Street.

Haddon Hall
DERBYSHIRE

Medieval alabaster carving in an
undisturbed medieval setting

Like Sleeping Beauty's castle, Haddon Hall lay wrapped in slumbers for 200 years from 1703, when its owners, the Manners family, became Dukes of Rutland and rode off to lord it over the estates of Belvoir Castle. It was restored to life by a kiss from the returning 9th duke at the beginning of the 20th century and emerged from the cobwebs as the most perfect fortified manor house in all England, unobtrusively modernised but its effect overwhelmingly achieved by its medieval builders and furnishers from 1195 until the 16th century. It sits high above the River Wye, its rose gardens carved into terraces in the hillside, its long gallery, great chamber, parlour, state bedroom, bakehouse, banqueting hall, chapel, towers and turrets and two gatehouses all built around two ancient stone courtyards. The superlatives in the literature dealing with this hall pile up like banks of summer flowers.

Throughout, the decoration is achieved by wood panelling, moulded plastering, carved chimney pieces and fine Mortlake tapestries. The most remarkable single building in this ensemble is the chapel, a small, complex space embracing styles from Norman to 15th-century Perpendicular, with pre-Reformation frescos top to bottom of the west wall like a curtain covered with a glorious leaf pattern. Behind the altar is the finest item at Haddon Hall, a 15th-century polychrome alabaster reredos showing nine scenes from the last days on earth of Christ. It made its appearance here as late as 1933, when the 9th duke bought it. If there is nothing remarkably original about it, it is remarkable nonetheless as a wonderful remnant of the great period of alabaster from Derbyshire quarries manufactured in Nottingham and London and exported all over Europe (see Westminster Cathedral, West End, London). It coincided happily with a sweet vein of earthy Nordic realism typical of Germany, Flanders and England. The Haddon reredos was originally eleven panels, but two are missing, including the central scene of the

crucifixion. The rest – from Christ's entry into Jerusalem on a donkey to the trial before Pontius Pilate, the mocking of Christ, the flagellation, the Deposition from the cross, the resurrection – are as crowded with figures and incident as an Arab souk, with the imperturbable figure of Christ, reviled and spat upon, moving serenely through the thugs and the bullies, the soldiers and the mourners in this great drama of the Passion.

Hawton

NOTTINGHAMSHIRE

Magnificent Easter sepulchre, sedilia and piscina, in the Church of All Saints

In detail and as an ensemble the sculpture in the tiny chancel of Hawton is some of the finest in England: doubtless the finest for its period, about 1330. That it survived the Reformation so complete is one thing; to have survived the Civil War with parliamentary troops laying siege to Newark in 1645 and camped very close to All Saints is incredible.

The early 14th century was when English Gothic was in full flower. The disciplines of architecture and sculpture had begun to be practised as separate arts, with a consequent loss of integration that has never been recovered, but at this stage the sumptuousness of sculptural decoration became richer than ever before or after. In Lincolnshire and Nottinghamshire and as far south as Ely there developed a school of sculptors who miniaturised their work. In Hawton every arch is covered with minutely

The 14th-century sculptor of these two Roman soldiers slumbering at the foot of Christ's tomb clearly modelled them on English soldiers who had imbibed too well before guard duty. It is a detail of the unparalleled Easter sepulchre in the Church of All Saints, Hawton

and deeply carved vegetation, small figures inhabit the cornices and niches, diaper patterning covers the surfaces. It seems probable that the craftsmen who provided Southwell Cathedral with its glorious screen also did the work in Hawton.

The chancel was built by the local magnate Sir Robert de Compton, who died in 1330, and the quid pro quo was that his tomb should be immediately adjacent to the Easter sepulchre, with its figure of Christ rising on the third day while the soldiers guarding it slumber below. Never has 'nearer my lord to thee' meant more. Often Easter sepulchres were temporary wooden affairs, since the celebration of Christ rising happened only once a year when the host would be buried in the breast of the dead Christ and watched over through the night before being removed in triumph and displayed to the congregation on Easter Sunday. But in the northeast Midlands stone sepulchres built into the chancel were especially popular. Sir Robert's chancel has a lovely three-seat sedilia opposite the sepulchre, and a piscina only comparatively restrained. But the Easter sepulchre is wonderful by any standards.

The main section of the sepulchre is divided into three, a central aumbry containing the figure of Christ, a smaller niche on the left for the host, and another on the right with the figures of the two Marys, the Magdalene and the mother of James, and the angel. One of the women draws back and the other falls to her knees as the angel says: 'Fear not ye: for I know that ye come to seek Jesus, which was crucified. He is not here, for he is risen.' Despite the mutilation of all these figures, they are dramatically expressive. From Christ's spear wound three rivulets of blood flow in parallel waves. His garment falls in stately folds, and he stands with one foot firmly planted, the other raised ready to move out of the sepulchre. These formal elements give the scene a sense of classical stasis, but the garments of the women are in agitated movement as they react with shock. Above the sumptuously decorated arches of these three niches a frieze shows the twelve Apostles gazing as Christ disappears into heaven among a sky full of angels. At the foot of the sepulchre are the guards. St Matthew says they 'became as dead men' at the appearance of the angel, but here they are clad in the armour of the licentious soldiery of the day and sunk in swinish slumber, no doubt drawn from the sculptor's memory of a recent carousal. Even these caricatures are beautifully handled, settled neatly and believably into their constricted spaces, part of a very English, wholly magnificent portrayal of the Easter drama.

Holdgate
SHROPSHIRE

12th-century font in the Church of the Holy Trinity

Helgot founded the church here in the 11th century, and it may be that the village's modern name is a corruption of his. This is still ancient England. The church is on a small hillock, which lifts it clear of the yard of Hall Farm, but only just. On the farmland there is the mound of a vanished castle. Both doors of the church seem to be chicken wire mesh on light wooden frames, and the one into the chancel is off its hinges, so it has to be gently moved to one side. Within, proper doors stand ajar – there's nothing portable inside worth making off with. There are medieval and 17th-century pews, limewashed walls, bare electric light bulbs, ancient carved stones on the chancel arch and a Norman font.

The font may be by the same Herefordshire school of Romanesque carvers responsible for the great Herefordshire fonts, who

operated in Gloucestershire as well and, in fact, in Shropshire at Chaddesley Corbett. Holdgate's is not as good as any of those, but well worth seeing, especially in the bare setting with light streaming through the open door and lapping over the font. The mason has given it a rope pattern around the rim, a massive zigzag on the pedestal and interlace and animal and floral designs on the bowl.

Ingestre
STAFFORDSHIRE

Wren in the country, St Mary's Church

Christopher Wren only built churches in London, except for one, at Ingestre (rhymes with industry), and even in the neighbouring village of Great Haywood they seem not to have heard of the church, just the hall. The truth is that Ingestre Hall – and its stables and its orangery – dwarf St Mary's, though their ebullience does not subdue it. The whole complex, plus Capability Brown's park, were built by Wren's friend from Oxford and the Royal Society, Walter Chetwynd. While there's no direct evidence that Wren did build the church, there is a lot of circumstantial evidence: a drawing of the west tower annotated by Wren, the friendship between Chetwynd and Wren and their mutual interest in mathematics, and, finally, there is the style of the church itself: the classical balustrade crowning the tower with urns at each corner, the five circular windows at clerestory level and the overall calm lucidity and visual wit all seem to shout Wren's name.

The interior is the pearl. The entrance porch under the square tower is circular, the ceilings – tunnel vaulted in the chancel, flat in the nave – have boldly baroque but delicately defined pure white stucco of fronds and roses and coats of arms. They are,

J.C. Bourne's lithograph shows Irish navvies completing work on the main line north from King's Cross through tunnels under Hampstead. It is part of the Elton collection at the Ironbridge Gorge Museum

however, merely a setting for the three-arched screen with, where the rood would have been in less vainglorious times, a big, elaborate and emphatically carved royal coat of arms, brazen as a trumpet call, with lion and unicorn supporters and on top of the lot a crown with another tiny lion standing pugnacious as a chihuahua. The congregation like to think that the woodwork is by Grinling Gibbons, not just for the screen but on the pulpit carved with fruit, putti and flowers. It's just possible, but there were other carvers of this period who rose to the challenge of Wren and the rising generation of glorious architects.

Ironbridge Gorge
SHROPSHIRE

Art and the industrial revolution at the Ironbridge Gorge Museum

When Sir Arthur Elton was looking around Manchester City Art Gallery with his wife Margaret in 1968 at the exhibition Art and the Industrial Revolution, based on the theme of the book of that title by Francis Klingender, she studied one picture especially closely and remarked: 'It would be really something if you owned that one, Arthur.'

'I do,' he said.

He told me this story at Clevedon Court, his ancestral home on the coast of north Somerset, when I interviewed him in December 1972 for a feature. The occasion was the publication of the paperback edition of Elton's much expanded version of Klingender's work, for which most of the illustrations had been drawn from the collection Elton had been forming from at least the age of eleven, a selection of which hung up the Queen Anne staircase and the stairs to Sir Arthur's study. On New Year's day 1973 Elton died, and in 1979 the state accepted his collection in lieu of death duties and allocated it to Ironbridge. At this Unesco World Heritage Site the Elton collection is one of the few things, apart from the iron bridge of 1779 itself, that can be viewed free, presumably because Coalbrookdale's popular appeal is its industrial archaeology, not its art.

Elton's interest was engaged when his nursemaid daily wheeled him in his pram through the streets of Bradford-on-Avon to her assignations with her boyfriend, a railway signalman, a detail Elton remembered because simultaneously he fixed his attention on the railway engines steaming over the level crossing. From that moment his future interests were set. The prints, drawings and paintings he accumulated after his initial enthusiasm for collecting engine numbers focus on the Great Exhibition of 1851 and on the canals and railways of the Industrial Revolution, especially the railways. Here are the lithographs of J.C. Bourne (1814–96) showing Irish navvies cutting the railway out of King's Cross and through tunnels under Hampstead; here is the back of the envelope bearing William Powell Frith's first sketch for his *Railway Station* (Paddington, in fact; see Egham, Southeast); here the watercolour competition entry by Owen Jones for St Pancras station hotel, a design he made to slot in seamlessly with the train shed and that would have served the purpose a good deal more handsomely than the extravaganza by G.G. Scott that actually was built.

Bourne was Elton's great rediscovery, a master recorder of the railway age. There are big prints of Queen Victoria opening the Great Exhibition, and a sectional view of the brick access shaft of the tunnel under the Thames from Rotherhithe to Wapping by Marc Brunel, Isambard's father (the tunnel has become part of the London Underground). Elton said he was sick of masterpieces and read the pictures in his collection like historical texts, but at least one of his works, a wash drawing by Alfred William Hunt of ironworks in Middlesbrough in the 1860s (a study for an oil now in Tate Britain), is a small masterpiece, poised between the influence of late Turner and the raw, visual impact of furnaces being tapped for the molten iron that runs off into pig beds.

Like so many visitors to Coalbrookdale, the Science Museum spurned the exhibition of Art and the Industrial Revolution because it was too artistic. Across Exhibition Road, the Victoria & Albert Museum rejected it because it was too much about applied science. Manchester and the Iron Gorge Museum itself recognised its value as an irreplaceable artistic record of an era that reshaped the nation.

Kedleston
DERBYSHIRE

Lord Curzon's cloned home, Kedleston Hall

The last time I saw Kedleston it was in Calcutta. It must have given Lord Curzon of Kedleston a bit of a turn as well when he arrived as viceroy in 1898 and found it there behind a big banyan tree. Curzon's great-great-grandfather completed the real (Derbyshire) Kedleston in 1765; Lord Wellesley, later the Iron Duke, ripped off the plans and started building Government House in 1799. Did Curzon find it home from home, sitting on the throne of one of Wellesley's defeated enemies, Tippoo Sahib? Perhaps not, but then, Kedleston doesn't look altogether a comfortable family home either.

It is a Roman masterpiece by Robert Adam with a glorious marble entrance hall to rival Vanbrugh's Castle Howard and Kent's Holkham Hall. Maybe it was here that the future viceroy learned to love beautiful buildings, because he set in hand a campaign in India that, among other successes, saved the Taj Mahal from falling down. But one of Curzon's 18th-century ancestors ran out of money building Kedleston, with its Robert Adam south façade and 40 foot high great hall with detached pink marble columns around the walls and a grand stucco ceiling, Adam furniture in the drawing room and great marble fireplaces throughout. All of which may partly account for the scarcity of great paintings. There is fine sculpture in the big state rooms, but they are plaster casts and copies of Roman pieces (not a point against them in the 18th century). The paintings, similarly, seem sparse, though there are charming portraits by the provincial artists Nathaniel Hone and Arthur Devis, *Daniel Before Nebuchadnezzar*, which was bought as a Rembrandt because Koninck specialised in Rembrandt imitations, and a lovely twilight landscape by the great 17th-century Dutch artist Aelbert Cuyp (see Wing, West and East Midlands).

Kinlet
SHROPSHIRE

The work of the alabaster man, in the Church of St John the Baptist

Outside the hundred acre park of Kinlet Hall and the church there are vestiges of a village, but then, to the world outside, Kinlet seems always to have been Kinlet Hall. As the 16th-century antiquary William Camden wrote, 'hard by standeth Kinlet, where the Blunts flourished. Their name in this tract is very great, so surnamed at first of their yellow

haire, the family noble and ancient, and the branches thereof farre spread.' The Blounts claimed to have come over with William the Conqueror and were certainly in Kinlet by the 15th century. The hall stands near the top of a hill high over the Severn valley. Different Georgian owners rebuilt the old hall, but now it is a private school, and visitors must call for the key to the church, which lies a little below the house.

John the Baptist, a 14th-century church on its own hill, is the resting place for the Blounts. Sir John Blount and his wife, Katherine Peshall, lie in stiff Gothic effigy on a tomb chest in the chancel. Katherine's father fought with Henry Bolingbroke at Bosworth, the battle that made Bolingbroke King Henry VII. She herself became a lady-in-waiting to the first of Henry VIII's wives, Catherine of Aragon, and John Blount accompanied Henry to France in his war against Louis XII. The king returned the favour by seducing the Blounts' daughter Elizabeth and fathering a son on her. As a parting shot he created Elizabeth Blount's son Duke of Richmond. That is the extent of the family glory.

Sir John died in 1531, Katherine around 1540. Clients at this time did not expect portraits: their tombs were status symbols, and the family position was expressed in the accoutrements of the effigies. After the vivid experiments with naturalism in the earlier years of Gothic, sculpture had become frozen in convention, entrusted to workshop production and sometimes carved from designs supplied by the client. That is why so many Tudor tombs in particular score high in historic interest and luxury, but low in artistic interest. The Blount effigies, carved in alabaster, are bog-standard splendid, Sir John in the plate armour of the period, Katherine in a long dress, with detailed headdress and jewellery. But the mason here felt free to use his gifts in rendering the small figures of mourners on the exposed side of the tomb chest. When these effigies were made, Burton upon Trent had become a centre for sculpting in Derbyshire alabaster. Its most skilled practitioner was a man named Richard Parker, about whom little is known apart from a mention of him in a contract at Belvoir Castle, Leicestershire, where he is called 'the alabaster man'. Judging from the quality on show here, he may well have been responsible for these effigies. Even in the central panel of three, the two lions supporting the coat of arms prance like household dogs with a gaiety not normally encouraged in sober heraldry, and the mourners, all male, presumably five sons of Katherine's eleven children, all grown to manhood and armed, stand in relaxed postures, gesticulating as though in conversation but peering outwards, engagingly like bench substitutes in a big rugby match, about to take their turn on the pitch.

Leicester
LEICESTERSHIRE

Red muse among the horses at the New Walk Museum and Art Gallery

In the catalogue of the Edinburgh Festival exhibition of 1960, the only British show of the German Blaue Reiter group (Blue Rider) I can remember in a lifetime, is a range of the subjects of the paintings of Franz Marc (1880–1916). There are foxes, deer in the snow and deer in the wood, a little monkey, two sheep, a tiger, but above all there are horses: *Grazing Horses*, *Red and Blue Horses*, *Little Blue Horse*, *Birth of the Horses*. Animals were his subject, because no religion or philosophy could be imputed to them, no political stance. They were pure being, but also untrammelled grace. They made shapes that he could combine with bold and expressive

colouring to make paintings close to abstraction, harmonies of colour. But Marc loved horses for themselves as well. In 1916 he wrote to his wife Maria from the blood-boltered Battle of Verdun, where 6,000 horses were killed: 'Oh, the poor horses!' A few days later, on 4 March, he himself was killed by a French shell.

There are Marc horses here in Leicester, a bay horse behind a blue donkey in an interlocking surface of pyramid shapes: the beasts' heads, the horse's tail, the broad-leafed foliage at the bottom edge. Marc had looked closely at the Cubists, partly in a conscious rejection of Wagner's edict that German artists must reject the trivial influence of French art. There is a woodcut of 1912, *Wild Horses*, from which he printed his own postcards, this one stamped and dated '14.III.1913' and sent by Maria Marc to Lily Klee, whose husband Paul had exhibited with the Blue Rider. The name and image of the Blue Rider was supplied by Kandinsky for the cover of the almanac with which he and Marc launched the group. The almanac contained their own work and the work of other artists they admired – lots of French art.

So what of this *Rote Frau* (Red Woman) by Franz Marc among all the animals? Marc painted her in 1912, and she is, like his horses, pure essence. That may be why he positions her with her back towards the viewer so that her shoulder hides her face below the cheekbone, and all we see are the accents of an eye and an eyebrow. She is naked but seen objectively, not, in the jargon of sexual politics, objectified, because she is not a sexual woman but a painted woman, almost certainly not painted from a model, an unerotic but beautiful muse, inspiring forms on a painted canvas, guava red and ice blue with a deep blue and green cascade of hair down her back and the primeval green of an imagined tropical forest and blood red rocks

Franz Marc's Rote Frau *('Red Woman') of 1912 is part of a rare and precious collection in the New Walk Museum, Leicester, of an art movement called Blue Rider. Marc died in the battle for Verdun in 1916*

around her. This is not Gauguin, not the celebration of an exotic culture, but a painting first and foremost.

Lichfield
STAFFORDSHIRE

A fine metal screen in Lichfield Cathedral

Cromwell's New Model Army knocked Lichfield Cathedral about more than a bit. Its soldiery, drunk only on hatred of idolatry, smashed a quantity of decoration that the soldiers of Henry VIII could only have dreamed about. Glass, statues, woodwork, even the central tower of 1300 came crashing down into the pulpit (in fact, it has been rebuilt twice since). So the medieval serenity of the views from inside town and out of the cathedral's three glorious spires, unique in England, is to some degree an illusion. The central spire has been twice rebuilt, the west front is entirely by George Gilbert Scott (1811–78), and the anodyne statues pasted on to the front without niches like dolls in a shooting gallery are to his prescription too. Victorian harshness is the price Lichfield paid to keep the cathedral upright and a setting for the riches inside.

In the decoration of the interior Scott came into his own, as resilient as the buildings he worked in. George Evans, an uncle of the novelist George Eliot, carved the exotic bishop's throne to Scott's design, beside the choir stalls (also Scott and Evans), but the best of Scott's work was the choir screen made with his frequent collaborator, the Coventry craftsman Francis Skidmore (1816–96), a prince among metalworkers (many of whose smaller ecclesiastical commissions are in the Herbert Art Gallery in Coventry). Together they had made the glorious cross now in Dunham-on-the-Hill (see Northwest) and screens at Salisbury and Hereford that were dismantled at the height of the indiscriminate anti-Victorianism in the 1960s. Lichfield not only hung on to its screen but, in 1973, had it finely restored.

Scott believed that Gothic churches needed to separate choir and sanctuary from nave, but by employing a metalworker he could provide a screen that not only did this job but also opened up the view from west to east. The grill-like screen has small, golden gates beneath a tall, pointed arch and gable with three flanking arches either side supported on slender, barely sugar columns and musician angels in roundels above. Painted in subdued orange and gold, studded with white enamelled flowers and semi-precious stones, this is High Victorian Gothic at its most ebullient. The sober archaeologising Scott had a little moan, as he had over the cross at Dunham-on-the-Hill, about the way Skidmore made free with his design, but in his heart he must have realised that this was something called inspiration.

Lincoln
LINCOLNSHIRE

For sheer power, the view of Lincoln Cathedral on entering the city from the south is second only to Durham's. The 14th-century central tower, soaring to 271 feet, the tallest building in Europe at the time, bisects chancel and nave, of equal length. The wide screen of the west front seen from Lincoln Castle is a panorama in itself. Yet L.S. Lowry, when he painted Lincoln from the south, managed to omit the cathedral and show only the factory chimneys that existed then on the still scruffy southern approaches. Maybe he was trying it on; at any rate, he finally brushed in the cathedral, and the painting now hangs in the Usher Gallery (see below).

The city's name is said to derive from the Roman *Lindum Colonia* spatchcocked together. Lindum survives in street names. It means 'the place by a pool', and there remains a natural widening of the River Witham known as the Brayford Pool, though the river itself, giving access to the sea, was always more to the point (the Romans used the pool as a port). The direct road to the cathedral is called, straightforwardly, Steep Hill, and naturally the Romans picked the summit as a fortification when they arrived in AD 47. All around are remnants of their activities: parts of the town walls, including a 25 foot high stretch of the Mint Wall, a part of the forum, public baths, roads, sewers, a wall tower and parts of gates embedded in more recent buildings, but especially the Newport Arch straddling the traffic from the north passing into Ballgate.

The castle was William the Conqueror's, built in 1068, and there remains at No. 15 The Strait a domestic building of the following century (c.1170) known as the Jew's House (now a restaurant) and the Norman House of not much later in Steep Hill hard by. Medieval Lincoln is still present everywhere in the old city, notably a chamber in the Guildhall, the Greyfriars building, now a museum of local life, and in Grantham Street the Cardinal's Hat, once a pub built around a courtyard, now offices. Curiously enough, very little survives of the many medieval churches, but Lincoln remains, in the centre, a city of great fascination.

In Memoriam Alfred Lord Tennyson, Lincoln Cathedral precincts

Isolated from the famous ranks of medieval sculpture on the walls of Lincoln Cathedral, on the grass beyond the café, stands Alfred Lawn Tennyson (in James Joyce's pun), pedestrian poet laureate but lyric genius, cast in bronze by England's Michelangelo, as Lord Leighton dubbed George Frederick Watts (1817–1904), in that tightly knit circle of mutual back-scratchers. Tennyson and Watts

were, besides, great friends, so although Tennyson was eighty-four when he died in 1892, Watts was stricken into illness by the news. When he recovered he responded to Lord Brownlow's proposal that a statue of the poet should be placed in the cathedral city of his native county by offering to do it free except for the costs of casting.

Tennyson might not have been best pleased: he thought public acclaim was the enemy of the good. But for Watts it was a last chance to live up to Leighton's tag. Although old and frail himself, he laboured from morning to nightfall pressing gesso to the armature, building up the larger than life-size figure of the poet with his wolfhound Karenina sitting at his feet half-sheltering under the big cape thrown over the poet's greatcoat. The hound looks up waiting for his master to do something, anything, other than gaze with furrowed brow at the plant in the palm of his hand.

As with Watts's painting, so with his sculpture. He put his best work as a painter into his dour portraiture. His sonorously titled paintings – Hope, Life's Illusions, Destiny – look vacuous today, and Physical Energy, the overwrought equestrian sculpture for Kensington Gardens that he was working on when he volunteered for the Tennyson memorial, is plain silly. But the monumental Tennyson, if too literal, a touch plodding, remains a sympathetic portrait of the man. It catches something of the lyric impulse, something of 'the dirty monk' (Rasputin) that Tennyson saw in the famous photograph of him by Julia Margaret Cameron, something too of Hardy's affectionate description of 'a beard and hair straggling like briars'.

OVERLEAF G.F. Watts's memorial to his great friend Alfred Lord Tennyson with his wolfhound Karenina in the precincts of Lincoln Cathedral. Watts saw in Tennyson something of the Russian monk Rasputin and tried to capture it in this statue

TENNYSON

De Wint, one-touch master of speed, at the Usher Gallery

Peter De Wint (1784–1849), later one of the famous 19th-century East Anglian School of watercolourists, met William Hilton in 1802 when they were both apprenticed to a London engraver called John Raphael Smith. De Wint was from Stone in Staffordshire, Hilton from Lincoln. Hilton took De Wint home with him for a short holiday in 1806, and De Wint fell in love with Hilton's sixteen-year-old sister Harriet and married her in 1810. The three of them, plus Hilton's new wife, lived happily ever after. De Wint's growing success overshadowed Hilton's career, but they remained friends for life.

In 1937, when the Usher Gallery had been open for ten years, it had one De Wint watercolour. Today it has the biggest public collection of his oils, watercolours, drawings and engravings in the country, sensitively placed in context. The gallery display starts with self-portraits by Hilton, and then follows a tender portrait by Hilton of his sister Harriet in the year of her marriage to De Wint. It shows Hilton to have been a born painter with such a lovely touch that it raises the question of why he didn't become one of the foremost artists of the age. Some of De Wint's own work is pedestrian, but the best, a few of the oils and more of the watercolours, rival the great watercolourist John Cotman. There is an oil sketch of about 1824 called *Lincoln Cathedral from the South at Little Bargate* with a monumental articulation of receding pictorial planes, and a *Drover at the Edge of a Wood* of about 1830 with a burst of setting sun in thick, creamy pigment behind the dark silhouettes of trees. It's not surprising that the *à la prima* (one-touch) speed of execution lent itself to watercolour. The discovery for me was a set of frames hinged on the wall containing tiny vignettes and multiple, instinctively brilliant pen and ink sketches of barges on a river and studies of the Lincolnshire wolds, each no bigger than an iPod.

Ludlow
SHROPSHIRE

The best prospect of Ludlow is from the heights to the west, with mighty castle, tall church tower and town spread on the hilltop below, but the best entry to the town is the southern crossing of the River Teme by the Ludford bridge and up the steep climb of Lower Broad Street, through Broad Gate, the last surviving of the seven medieval town gates, and along Broad Street flanked by medieval half-timbered houses. This is one of the handsomest streets in England – the most handsome, the people of Ludlow insist. The gate acts like a great church screen, opening from nave into choir and culminating with the reredos – the Butter Cross, which closes the view at the top of the hill with its confident if slightly agley mid-18th-century architecture (square sash windows looking oddly squashed, a surfeit of ball finials), with entrance pediment supported on Doric columns, well-accented balustrade and a clock set in a stone surround with cupola and wind vane above. This is the heart of town built on a quite geometric grid plan of streets running parallel to Broad Street on the hill, with other streets at right angles culminating at the Butter Cross, where High Street runs towards the castle and King Street towards the Bullring, with its magnificent rows of half-timbered buildings, among which the Feathers Inn is only the most swaggeringly handsome among many.

The church, St Laurence, is at the heart of the town, tucked into a close behind the Butter Cross. High Street widens into a marketplace at the west before the castle, which is a fortress that Walter de Lacy built and built big soon after the Conquest to stand against Welsh incursions. The castle has an outer bailey the size of a football stadium and a formidably fortified inner bailey where a Shakespeare play is the centrepiece of the Ludlow Festival every summer. Walter's 12th-century descendant, Gilbert de Lacy, went crusading and on his return built the circular nave of the inner bailey chapel based on the Church of the Holy Sepulchre in Jerusalem, one of only three such chapels in England (the other two are at Cambridge and Northampton).

Opulent 17th-century domestic interior at the Feathers Hotel

Rees Jones arrived in town from Pembrokeshire, an ambitious youngster seeking an apprenticeship with a lawyer, for Ludlow was a sessions town dealing with Marches matters, and when the court was sitting the streets and inns were full of lawyers. By 1619 Rees was a rich attorney himself, so he bought himself a house in the Bullring and rebuilt it to do justice to his magnificence. He lived there until he died in 1655, and in the late 1660s another lawyer, Timothy Littleton, one of the 'fire judges' who had sorted out the complex of claims after the Great Fire of London, leased the house until in 1670 it found its lasting vocation as an inn.

The Feathers, they called it, after the fleur-de-lis decorating the triple gables of the half-timbered façade in honour of the investiture in 1616 of a new Prince of Wales, the future Charles I. This corner of England, Herefordshire and Shropshire, is a region of timber-framed houses, black and white and unvarnished oak, first floors jettied, diagonal braces making a diamond pattern, timbers shaped into lozenges and arcades, arches and carved heads. These buildings age the way people age. A few miles down the A49, at Leominster, is a house whose gable stoops forward at a forty-five degree angle from the vertical, like a very old woman hobbling to market. And the Feathers itself stands out from a street of half-timbering. Its façade splendidly bedecked like cross-gartered Malvolio in *Twelfth Night*, it totters out of true as though it had imbibed a glass too much of the liquor dispensed from its bars for more than 300 years.

Step inside, through the heavily studded front door with its lockplate embossed with the initials of Rees Jones and his wife Isabel, past the Housman restaurant with its blandly comfortable late-20th-century refurbishment, and up one floor to the writing room and particularly its neighbour, the big, low-ceilinged James I room, and you walk back in history to the unaltered and richly decorated comfort Jones created, for visitors, perhaps, as much as for the family, since there is so much public display, particularly the heavily ornate overmantel with an arch either side flanked by terms (heads and torsos on a plinth) and at the centre the royal coat of arms proclaiming allegiance to James I. The whole room is oak panelled, floor to ceiling, with mullion and transom windows front and back in deep recesses and the ceiling – even the beams – plastered with vine patterns and indigenous roses and thistles.

Ludlow pilgrims' window, in the Church of St Laurence

As it stands now St Laurence is mostly the flower of a major 15th-century rebuilding, with a great new central tower 135 feet high and stained glass of the same period. The great east window is a rich narrative of the life and death of St Laurence, but arguably the most attractive glass is in the chapel of St John the Evangelist at the east of the north aisle, most attractive not just in Shropshire but in England.

This recounts episodes from the time of Edward the Confessor when the Ludlow Palmers Guild set sail on a pilgrimage to the Holy Land. Since the guild didn't exist until the 13th century the story seems a mite unlikely, but it is one the palmers deeply wanted to believe, and no wonder. It seems that King Edward gave a ring to a beggar he encountered in a wood. The beggar was St John in disguise. When the palmers went to Palestine St John manifested himself before them and gave them the ring with instructions to return it to Edward along with the message that they would soon meet again, in paradise. Well, palmers existed in twos and threes before the guild formed, so who knows? At any rate, they were a body of merchants, craftsmen, a few clergymen, a few nobles and, at one point, a Cambridge don. They collected subscriptions, subsidised prayers for the living as well as the dead, helped with the rebuilding and upkeep of their glorious church and paid for the windows telling their favourite story.

The eight lights of the window, four above, four below, with the arms of Edward the Confessor and of Ludlow in the tracery, depict the tale in scenes reminiscent of contemporary Flemish paintings and reliquaries. First the embarkation, the journey and its events, and the return to the royal court, each incident, even when it takes place in a wood, under an elaborate Gothic canopy – a convention, but one that perhaps suggests a city in paradise.

The elegant draughtsmanship and lucid passages of colour – blue, red, gold, white, grass green and olive – emerged well from restoration in 1878 by a solidly professional firm of ecclesiastical craftsmen founded by a pioneer of the Gothic revival, John Hardman of Birmingham. It involved rescuing glass that had been scattered through various other windows throughout the building, and this, presumably, brought some loss of absolute authenticity. But only the palmers would care, and they aren't much in evidence any more.

Mattersey
NOTTINGHAMSHIRE

14th-century reliefs by a master carver, in the Church of All Saints

An unremarkable church in an unremarkable village contains two remarkable carved panels, which seem, on grounds of style, to be by the sculptors who produced the chancel carvings of Hawton (see above). Hawton's Easter sepulchre and sedilia are worth travelling a long way to see; the two little carvings of Mattersey are certainly worth getting off the A1 to look at.

St Martin was the rich man who gave his cloak to a beggar, and here he is, mounted on a prancing steed, handing over the garment. St Helena, or Helen, the wife of the Emperor Constantine, is shown discovering the true cross on a visit to Jerusalem in 326. The ruined priory that was Mattersey's sole distinction was dedicated to her. The usual culprits have had a go at the St Martin, but have failed to destroy the beauty and economy of the little scene, which is contained in a squarish space beneath a cusped arch and triumphantly suggests with easy naturalism that, as Martin of Tours turns in the saddle to give the beggar the garment, the horse is rearing, even though its body is parallel to the ground. Above the arch are carved leaves, heavily undercut, just like the leaves of Southwell Cathedral.

The more beautiful if more conventional of the two is the St Helena and her companion, the saint captured in the swaying motion that the 14th-century masons of England and France were so good at. Two small symbolic crosses lie at her feet (the crosses of the thieves crucified alongside Christ?), and perhaps she held the third in her hand; we can't know because the hand is missing. Above her ogee arch the foliage is clotted thick as whipped cream.

Nottingham
NOTTINGHAMSHIRE

Nottingham Castle stands on a rock as riddled with caves as an Emmental cheese. The Trip to Jerusalem inn is built out from one of the caves and has its cellars in caves, and on that basis it claims to be the oldest pub in England, but so do three others in the city (for at least one older pub try the George Inn, Norton St Philip, Somerset). But from the caves the Nottingham underclass erupted in 1831 to burn down the castle in protest against the opposition of the Duke of Newcastle, its owner, to parliamentary reform. In the middle of the century a parliamentary act forbade the renting of caves to the poor of a city with one of the most impoverished populations in Europe. Today the caves attract as many tourists as the castle. The castle itself, of course, has Robin Hood, or at least a bronze statue of the saintly Saxon robber.

The duke's 17th-century ancestor had already rebuilt the castle as an Italian palazzo, and when the townspeople destroyed the rooms within, they inadvertently created the ideal halls in which to open a museum and art gallery. It opened in 1878 and was the first municipal gallery in England.

The castle and its rock are part of Nottingham's ancient centre. By great misfortune after the war the corporation held a referendum on a proposed dual carriageway through the centre of the city. The townspeople turned their thumbs down, but the corporation built it anyway, and it became by popular acclaim one of the direst urban roads in Britain. The castle was sundered from the rest of the old centre, everything contained between Upper Parliament Street and Lower Parliament Street, which marked the old town walls to the north and east, and the canal to the south: its immediate neighbour the lace market around the fine medieval church of St Mary; the lively shopping areas with one lovely Victorian baroque building in the High Street given an art nouveau shop front by Boots the Chemists in its early days (Zara fashions are there now); the older churches and eating places; and the great paved public space of the Old Market, newly redesigned with fountains and not enough benches. The bleakly uninviting dual carriageway, incidentally, is called with misplaced marketing chutzpah Maid Marian Way.

Today the council is trying to prompt people to play in the traffic of Maid Marian Way by encouraging shopper-friendly building and installing more and better road crossings between the east of the city centre and the 19th-century Park estate in the west, where two of the great attractions, the architect Peter Moro's Playhouse and the sculptor Anish Kapoor's mirror sculpture (see below), stand in Wellington Circus close by the Ropewalk, with its long and lovely flight of steps descending to Park Valley, where the barons who built the castle went hunting.

For every movie buff who thinks of Nottingham as the home of Errol Flynn and Basil Rathbone, there is a pill popper who knows that it is the home of Boots the Chemist. Certainly, it's a modern city unimaginable now as the battlefield of the real sheriff of Nottingham and the real Robin Hood, whoever they may have been.

Sky Mirror, a living theatre of possibilities, Playhouse

India's streets and bazaars are full of brilliant colours, on the stalls of the sweet wallahs, in the shops selling statuettes of the gods and their avatars, in the trays of bangles and necklaces. Seen from the entrance a Hindu temple can seem like a gaudy emporium, but as the visitor moves inside it becomes warmly womblike. Nobody would seem less likely than the elegantly middle-class Anish Kapoor (b.1954) to be affected by these qualities, and nobody is more middle class than a middle-class Indian. He was born in Bombay, the son of a rear admiral, and was educated with India's elite at the Doon School, but he came to live and study in England at the age of eighteen. Later, he set up shop as a sculptor and stayed to become central in the British art scene. But India draws him back regularly to renew his experience of the culture and breathe the evocative heat and smell of dung and spice that envelopes a traveller as soon as the aircraft door slides open.

His early work is simple, often little pyramids of brilliant powdered pigment in primary reds, blues and yellows, unmistakably Indian, or maybe a 4 foot pillar of sandstone apparently pierced with a hole that turns out to be a patch of dark pigment. The rough-hewn pillar itself evokes a primal shape, the menhirs of Europe and in India the stone pillars bearing the carved edicts of the 3rd century BC Emperor Ashoka. The ideas remain simple, but as Kapoor's fame grew so did the ambition of the projects and the size of the budgets. In 1995 Nottingham Playhouse commissioned a piece from him. Six years and £900,000 of lottery cash later it installed *Sky Mirror*, a 35 foot diameter stainless steel bowl like a satellite dish, on the terrace outside the theatre in Wellington Circus on the edge of a little water channel. *Sky Mirror* echoes the shape of this intimate urban space and picks up reflections of the trees in the small circular park, but it is tilted, of course, to reflect the sky and the neighbouring buildings, most closely the very fine theatre itself, a work of the 1960s by the German expatriate architect Peter Moro.

So the narrative is all to do with the changes of light and weather, from the darkness of a new moon to the intensity of a summer sun, which seems to burn the top edge of the dish away like etching acid. Kapoor's central project is to transform the properties of materials, blurring the distinction between the tangible and the intangible, light and dark, mass and space. Kapoor made the point when he placed a faintly ovoid globe of stainless steel, called *Turning the World Inside Out*, in the centre of the 5,000-year-old stone circle, the Rollright Stones in Oxfordshire, and it sat there for a few months as inscrutable as the stones. Like that piece, *Sky Mirror* is a living theatre of possibilities.

Masterly French painting by a young English genius, Nottingham Castle Art Gallery

This is definitely not the castle where Erroll Flynn ran rings around the sheriff of Nottingham, but it is the hilltop. Cromwell slighted the medieval castle after the Civil War, and William Cavendish rebuilt it as a baroque palace in 1679. Arsonists gutted Cavendish's house during riots over parliamentary reform in 1831, and it was not restored until 1878, when it opened as England's first municipal museum of art with a selection of the region's main art of the Middle Ages and early Renaissance, alabaster carving and some of the art of a painter who, in his brief life, sailed close to greatness, Richard Parkes Bonington (1802–28).

He was a native of Arnold, near Nottingham, but in the post-war economic depression after the fall of Napoleon his

Anish Kapoor's budgets grew along with his fame: the 35 foot diameter stainless steel Sky Mirror, a piece sited outside Nottingham Playhouse, cost £900,000, and is a hugely successful addition to Wellington Circus

parents took him to Calais at the age of fifteen, and he spent most of the rest of his short life in France. Bonington became a close friend of the great Eugène Delacroix, who was impressed by the Englishman's fluent technique, though after Bonington's death of tuberculosis Delacroix, embittered by a sense of his own failure, judged Bonington harshly. *Le Château de la Duchesse de Berry* is typical of the vivid approach to watercolour by Bonington that influenced not just Delacroix but the other Romantics too. Bonington painted it in 1824, the so-called English year at the Salon in Paris, when Bonington, Constable and Copley Fielding (another friend of Delacroix) all won gold medals. By a river in the foreground a fisherman in a brilliant red jacket and white shirt leans on a wall watching his rod for a nibble. In the background is a very French château set in a very English garden. The sky is streaked with wide bands of light from small patches of blue in the cloud cover, and the stream picks up the reflected colours of the sky. Only a master of the art could hold down the red and white of the fisherman so that it doesn't jump out from the cooler tones of nature, and this is a masterly performance. To this day Bonington is more admired in France than in England.

Ossington
NOTTINGHAMSHIRE

A sculpture of a jack-the-lad and his brother, in the Church of Holy Rood

Holy Rood feels as though it is in the depths of Sherwood Forest, which it probably once was, but the trees and shrubs crowding in on the pitted road to the church now are the ruins of the park of the demolished mansion. The lord of the manor, Colonel Max Denison, lives on in the old rectory – indeed, he is lay rector as his ancestors have been since William and Robert Denison, successful wool merchants from Leeds, bought the church and estate of Ossington in 1749. According to the lively pamphlet about Holy Rood by the vicar (who happens to double up as suffragan bishop of Southwell), William's big break came when one of his ships arrived in Lisbon harbour with supplies after the earthquake of 1755 killed 100,000 people. And there it is, depicted on the plinth of Denison's monument in the church: a ship arriving in Lisbon harbour (or so the vicar says).

The monument is one of a pair by Joseph Nollekens (1737–1823), and this one shows William as a slightly pompous character, flush with success, leaning on a tree stump with the manuscript of a poem scrolling out from beneath his elbow, but he has more the manner of a surveyor than a poet. His brother Robert commissioned the monuments on the death of William in 1782 and also rebuilt the church. It is said to be by John Carr, and that's likely if only because Carr was the architect of the vanished mansion. Robert seems a bit of a jack-the-lad, confident and well turned out with a long coat breezily thrown open, a stock at his throat. He leans casually on a conveniently vacant plinth looking as though the future lay spread out before him. He died three years after his brother.

The pieces are fine performances by Nollekens, combining his niceness of judgement and virtuoso carving with his greatest strength, his capacity to create vivid portraiture.

Pickworth

LINCOLNSHIRE

*Exquisite 14th-century figure of female
saint, in the Church of St Andrew*

Nothing much can ever have happened in
Pickworth until some spec builder came
along with government blessing and put up a
mess of executive houses, hugely out of scale
with the church opposite, raw, irredeemably
ugly, with a feeble attempt to add character
by pasting on pagoda-shaped porches. You
have to laugh, as they say, or you'd cry.

Maybe these particular executives are
today's equivalent of the medieval lords of
the manor, men who might spend money for
a quick fix for the future of their eternal
souls. The church needs it. It looks as though
it has been falling apart ever since it was built
around 700 years ago and the interior is
covered in bat droppings. The stairs to the
rood loft step out into space, which makes
the remnants of the doom painting on the
chancel arch singularly appropriate. And the
one treasure, a female saint carved from quite
soft sandstone in the early 14th century, has
been decapitated, has lost a hand at the wrist
and has lost a chunk from its skirt. The saint
survived because she was hidden by using her
as stone to block a north window, just as so
many other devotional sculptures were
hidden from the wrath of extremists by being
cemented, face down, to act as chancel steps
or paving stones. She was released from her
community service when she was
rediscovered during the war and stands now
on a corbel, her mantle still blue with the
pigment of the 14th century, her dress still
red, the drapery falling in those natural folds
that tell us that her wonderfully skilled
mason saw in the beauty of this world the
promise of the next.

Shrewsbury

SHROPSHIRE

The Anglo-Saxons founded Shrewsbury,
pillaging the old Roman city of Wroxeter
(Viroconium) for stone and carting it 5 miles
to the northeast. The site probably explains
the motive. It is on a hill within a loop of the
River Severn, more easily defensible than the
flat terrain of Wroxeter after the collapse of
the Roman imperium in Britain in the 5th
century. Shrewsbury proclaims itself from a
distance with the two church spires, St Mary
(see below) and St Alkmund, piercing the sky
from the highest points in the town. It is
entered from the east over English Bridge,
and from the west, Welsh Bridge:

> *High the vanes of Shrewsbury gleam*
> *Islanded in Severn stream;*
> *The bridges from the steepled crest*
> *Cross the water east and west,*

as A.E. Housman succinctly versified in *A
Shropshire Lad* (1896).

Up in town in Barker Street Rowley's
House Museum has a good collection of
Roman artefacts from Wroxeter. The
museum has been boringly renamed
Shrewsbury Museum and Art Gallery, but the
Salopian in the street will give directions by
its old name. Wroxeter has a better one, but
this will do. Shrewsbury's hill is clad in the
Middle Ages. Holy Cross, formerly the abbey
church (see below), is beyond the river in an
unpromising setting, but once the climb to St
Mary begins the town is richly textured with
half-timbered houses.

*The Church of St Mary the Virgin, Shrewsbury, is
filled with fine stained glass from the continent, but
the finest of all is this 14th-century English tree of Jesse
in the big east window illustrating the ancestors of
Christ and culminating with the crucifixion high in
the tracery*

The street layout retains the medieval plan and repays a leisurely exploration, not least to collect some colourful street names: Dogpole, Grope Lane, Gullet Passage, Shoplatch. The old market house of 1595–6 has an antique statue of the Black Prince (of Wales) under a canopy on the façade. In Fish Street, off Wyle Cop, is a nice, plain 15th-century house where John Wesley preached before the first Wesleyan chapel was built in the town. Everywhere the half-timbering, dormered, single and double overhung, timbers carved or arranged in decorative patterns, tops of buildings in narrow lanes leaning forward to bestow a neighbourly kiss on the houses opposite. On the edge of town, at the end of Abbey Foregate, is a monumental column to Lieutenant General Lord Hill, commander in eighteen battles in the Peninsular campaign and with Wellington at Waterloo. At 151 feet it is the tallest monument to any Napoleonic War commander, saving only Nelson's column in Trafalgar Square (185 feet).

14th-century Jesse window, in the Church of St Mary the Virgin

William Rowland was a young Shrewsbury curate when St Chad's Church fell down in 1792. He was very keen on stained glass and St Mary had none, so he turned on his persuasive charm and walked off with Chad's big Jesse window recording the supposed genealogy of Jesus to replace the plain glass in the east window of St Mary. It was his first coup, and the 14th-century glass remained the oldest in the church and the most beautiful.

In 1828 he became vicar. Shrewsbury is on a hill, and on the approach the spires of St Mary and nearby St Alkmund against the sky look like a 16th-century print (though Alkmund's spire is actually a late addition). Rowland wanted to make the body of his church match the beauty of its spire, and as monastic churches on the continent went through their own version of the dissolution, under the twin impact of the enlightenment and Napoleon, he disbursed £200 here, £400 there, and by the time he died in 1851 he had filled the place with coloured glass from Liège, from Herkenrode (also in Belgium), from two churches in Cologne and from the Netherlands. Yet the first and oldest glass, the 14th-century Jesse window, is English, initially from Shrewsbury.

The tree of Jesse remains the real spectacle. It was restored in 1858 by the Evans brothers of Shrewsbury, David and Charles, and all the glass in the tracery is theirs, as the bland drawing of the saints' faces shows. It is reckoned that in the eight lights below around 60 per cent of the glass is original; the rest matches well. It is suffused with brilliant lemon yellow, blue, purple, red, touches of pink and green. Blue-bearded and amber-robed Jesse, father of King David, the great propagator, slumbers in Byzantine splendour at the foot of the tree, and from him climbs a great yellow vine, twisting upwards through the eight lights like the life-giving DNA double helix, forming separate mandorlas, in each one of which is an ancestor of Christ, all kings or seers. The figure of Christ appears only in a shallow strip of figures beneath Jesse, partly hidden by the reredos, as the holy child on the crowned Virgin's knee, flanked by King Edward III and the donor, Sir John Charleton, and his wife, Hawis, two sons and two daughters. It might have been an anticlimax. Instead it is vibrant, with the father and sons charmingly made up from the same template, distinguished only by little variations in the decoration of the over-tunics. Sir John died in 1353, and the window was made before that; around 1340 is generally accepted.

Marooned in a public car park in Shrewsbury, this 14th-century pulpit is all that remains of the abbey refectory that once stood here. The abbey, now a parish church, stands on the other side of a main road

Refectory pulpit stranded in a car park at Holy Cross, once Shrewsbury Abbey

The great engineer Thomas Telford showed the way to the road builders of the 20th century when Shrewsbury town council took his pragmatic advice and built the main road from the north between the former abbey and the park where the monastic buildings had stood. After Henry VIII's dissolution the nave of the abbey church remained for the parishioners (the Victorian ecclesiastical artist J.L. Pearson added a new chancel). The park has become a municipal car park, and on its edge the 14th-century pulpit of the former refectory, an extraordinary survival against the odds, stands in a tiny patch of shrubs, witness to the brutality of succeeding ages. It's an octagon built and roofed with Shropshire's finest, the reddish sandstone from Grinshill, pierced with lancets under hood moulds, and at the bottom of the lancets there are little screens each divided into two ogee-topped niches containing damaged but fluidly carved figures of saints. A flight of ten steps leads to a little doorway, but this is an outdoor pulpit where preaching is strictly for the birds.

The local master sculptor of the Lion pub, Wyle Cop

John Nelson (no dates) never gained a reputation beyond Shrewsbury, where he practised in the 18th century as a skilled woodworker and statuary. The objects he made were for everyday and have become part of the fabric of the town, but at least one, the golden lion of 1777 on the door lintel of the early 17th-century Lion hotel, shows in the fluidity of its handsome proportions, tapering narrowly from a powerful maned head to the lithe body to the muscular hindquarters, a mastery of form quite exceptional, if not unique, for a pub sign. The beast is painted gold and rests a forepaw on a bunch of purple grapes, maybe a generic indicator of available booze, maybe a hint that something more la-di-da than Englishman's ale was available. Above the wide gateway to the coach yard (now car parking) is a head of Bacchus crowned with grapes. There is no attribution for this, but it is carved spaciously, and it seems likely that Nelson would have made this too.

Stamford

LINCOLNSHIRE

The road from Collyweston crests a hill and reveals a panoramic view of Stamford spread just below the brow of the next hill, the horizon pierced by church spires and towers. It seems a perfect medieval to Georgian Midlands town, and though this is partly illusory, because Stamford has grown from its 10,000 inhabitants a century ago to about 16,000 now, the harmony of its buildings preserves the unity. Stamford is clad in the stone of Barnack and Ketton and roofed in those famous tiles from Collyweston, all of these places within 3 or 4 miles of the town. Its good looks have been saved too by the

coincidence that the 19th-century builders of the main east coast rail route from London to Scotland bypassed Stamford, and in 1961 the Great North Road, which until then ran through the town, was diverted.

All the principal streets in Stamford run from Red Lion Square: Broad Street, with the 15th-century Browne's Hospital, built to house ten poor men and two poor women, St Mary's Street, St Peter's Street and the High Street, all gables and dormers, mullioned windows, sash windows and elaborate cornices. There is so much stonework left over from medieval religious establishments that later architects have used whole windows and arches to decorate courtyards of private houses. As for those steeples, already in 1085 the Domesday Book listed four churches in Stamford. (The only named one, St Peter, fell out of use and distintegrated some time after the 16th century. The site on St Peter's Hill remains empty.) Now 13th-century All Saints stands on Red Lion Square, with a crocketed 15th-century spire. St George, dating from at least the 12th century but with a 17th-century tower, stands in its own quiet square. St Michael in the High Street, has been converted into shops, and St John is behind the High Street. The loveliest of all, 13th-century St Mary (see below), in St Mary's Street, has a 13th-century tower running seamlessly into a 14th-century stone broach spire. And there is St Martin (see below), on the High Street of Stamford Baron, the parish on the 'wrong' side of the River Welland in what used to be Northamptonshire. This has served as the mausoleum to the Cecils, starting with the greatest of the line, Lord Burghley, Elizabeth I's lord treasurer, and continuing with his descendants, the Earls and Marquesses of Exeter, lords of Burghley House within the park wall standing just aloof of Stamford, one of the greatest of the great magnates' houses of Elizabeth's reign.

Cecil monument, Church of St Martin

Stamford, like Burghley House itself, is built of stone from the Barnack area and Collyweston tile. St Martin is close to the corner of Barnack Road, which runs east from Stamford beside the long northern wall of Burghley's park. It was the obvious church for the sepulchres of the Cecils of Burghley, and they made good use of it, starting with a tremendous six-poster Tudor affair for William Cecil, 1st Baron Burghley (d.1598), famous for being chief secretary of state and close adviser to Elizabeth I.

Like all aristocrats, the Cecils were not confined by the walls of their park, least of all when the grand tour became a desirable adjunct to nobility. The tour was a highly productive institution. Noblemen undertook it in the 17th and 18th centuries for the sake of their education, and from it found not just objects to embellish their houses and gardens but the style in which to build their houses: baroque or Palladian before the discovery of Herculaneum (in 1738) and Pompeii (1748), Roman afterwards. Architects went along to measure the ancient buildings and look at the gardens, and painters joined the entourages of the lords and made illustrations for their patrons' written accounts of the tours, and although Burghley, of course, was built as a tribute to Elizabeth and remained the greatest Elizabethan house, John Cecil, 5th Earl of Exeter, was as much at home in Paris as at Burghley and as much at home in Rome as in Paris.

Pierre-Etienne Monnot (1657–1733) was one of a group of French sculptors working in the Rome of Bernini and Algardi. Cecil engaged him to make busts of his family and a fine madonna and child, which still embellish Burghley. So when Cecil died the countess commissioned his tomb from Monnot. The sculptor had carved it by 1704 and shipped it to England, where William Palmer, a local mason who may have been to Rome as assistant to Monnot on the monument, set it up in St Martin. Monnot was good and this highly professional figure group is better than his tomb for the pope. It shows the reclining figures of the earl and countess with supporting figures of the helmeted Victory on one side and on the other Art, leaning her mourning head on her right hand with her elbow resting on a gold-painted book, in her left hand a sculptor's mallet and painter's brushes. Gold, too, the cushion on which the earl leans and the spear in Victory's right hand. The figures are all white marble, and the tall obelisk behind bearing the Cecil arms is brown.

14th-century statue of the Virgin Mary, Church of St Mary

The Stamford statue of the Virgin Mary is a lucky and beautiful survival of the excesses of the Reformation, when the Archbishop of York advised that statues should be 'deposed and sequestered from the sight of man'. The Stamford St Mary (1320–30) was hidden behind panelling until she was discovered there in 1853, the nose slightly damaged, the right hand broken off (later replaced in restoration) and the book in her left hand smashed. The statue stands now on a corbel in the north chapel, a sublime work from years of political unrest, war and regicide but the height of a great period for English art and architecture under the first three Edwards, and more or less contemporary with the chapel itself, though this handsome town church was largely rebuilt in 15th-century Perpendicular.

She stands in the swaying posture so marked in the 14th century, in images in glass as well as stone, her right hip thrust out, her weight on the right foot, her torso and head a counterbalance establishing the line of gravity through the centre of her body, a pose known to art historians as dehancement. A cloth covers her hair, and her dress, tightly ribbed in the bodice, falls to her feet in heavy, vertical folds crumpling at her feet, and the mantle loosely draped around her shoulders and looped around her hips falls in deep Vs to an orderly cascade of folding drapery at the hem. It looks simple but isn't conventional mannerism: the quality is packed into the realisation of the image, the articulation of form, the crisp technique bringing together vividly disparate elements into calm image of composure, sensuous and graceful in contrast to the tension of Gothic sculptural forms before and after this period.

Stapleford
NOTTINGHAMSHIRE

Golden age sculpture in the Church of St Mary Magdalene

Under the more or less rapacious early owners of Stapleford Hall, well-rewarded servants to a succession of monarchs, the village of Stapleford seems to have got mislaid. At any rate, the parish church and the remains of the market cross ended up in their park, now, along with the hall, a country house hotel. There is a miniature railway too, which is a miniature tribute to adaptability since the last Earl of Harborough used his influence during the railway boom of the mid-19th century to have the grown-up Midland Railway diverted around the park. But so few people today answer to the parish roll-call that St Mary Magdalene is maintained by the Churches Conservation Trust.

George Richardson, a little-known assistant in the London office of the Adam brothers, rebuilt the church for the 4th earl as Georgian Gothic. In the following century Pugin would have excoriated it as a typically 18th-century lightweight pastiche, but it is impeccably restrained in the dappled light shining through the big trees and has a very pretty pink plaster ribbed ceiling. It retains its importance for the fine monuments surviving from the old church, chief among them the memorial by Michael Rysbrack (1694–1770) to the 1st earl who died in 1732, one of his finest, carved with that high technical skill that was one of the marks of this golden period in English art.

Lord Harborough reclines on a tomb chest, his wife and child beside him, like a Roman at a banquet, leaning on a tasselled cushion with a toga thrown across a shoulder over his tunic, one foot straying off the surface of the chest to rest on the little ledge below (which the sculptor has signed M. Rysbrack Fecit). His wife sits upright beside him nursing their baby son; mother and son together form a group as poignant as a madonna and child, even if we hadn't known from the church guidebook that the boy died in infancy. The earl and countess appear on this monument not once but twice, the second time in medallions suspended on mock hooks from the grey marble obelisk. Above that hangs the quartered family coat of arms, a heraldic splash of red and black. The essential artificiality of this conventional composition is a kind of well-mannered restraint on the magnificent baroque realism of the carved figures, the dignity of their predecessors, the portrait busts of ancient Rome, enhanced by the dynamic countervailing movements of the folds of heavy drapery.

Stoke-on-Trent
STAFFORDSHIRE

North from Stoke the Waterloo Road to Burslem lies, the spine of the Potteries, bypassing Hanley, the city's shopping centre, past mean streets and razed buildings, ruined kiln chimneys, litter and rows of houses with

St Mary Magdalene, Stapleford, is unused but looked after and kept open by the Churches Conservation Trust. Inside is a monument to Lord Harborough, one of the best works of the 18th-century Antwerp sculptor Michael Rysbrack, who worked in England for most of his career

identical doorcases moulded like tombstones in a valley of desolation. This, roughly, is the geographical centre of the six towns joined in unholy matrimony in 1910 as a single county borough, the very year in which Arnold Bennett described the urban scene under a light disguise:

Edwin Clayhanger stood on the steep-sloping, red-bricked canal bridge, in the valley between Bursley and its suburb Hillport. In that neighbourhood the Knype and Mersey canal formed the western boundary of the industrialism of the Five Towns. To the east rose pitheads, chimneys, and kilns, tier above tier, dim in their own mists.

Most of that is mapped out on the bleak slope rising to Burslem, Josiah Wedgwood's native town. Stoke itself is at the south of the group, Longton and Fenton, with its Wedgwood seconds warehouse, off to the east, Hanley, Burslem and Tunstall strung out northwards. There is no real centre at all, and officially Barlaston has no official place in this, but in 1936 the managing director of Wedgwood, Josiah Wedgwood, the great-great-great grandson of the original Josiah, followed in the footsteps of the garden city pioneers and simultaneously abandoned the dereliction that the Wedgwood firm itself had unwittingly brought about by decamping to Barlaston with the firm, its

It could be a building-site tea mug, except that it was manufactured by Wedgwood with decoration by the post-war avant garde artist Eduardo Paolozzi – a summation of his form of machine-age Pop. It is exhibited in the Wedgwood Museum at Barlaston

factory, offices and showroom. Facts on the ground, as Israel describes its annexed territories.

The crowning glory of a Paolozzi tea mug, at the Wedgwood Centre, Barlaston

The great-great-grandfather of Josiah Wedgwood (1730–1795) had a pottery in Burslem, one of the six towns that amalgamated into the city of Stoke-on-Trent as late as 1925. Josiah's grandfather and father were Burslem potters. So too was his elder brother, Thomas. Josiah, the youngest (of thirteen children), was indentured to Thomas in 1744. In 1759 he set up business for himself at Ivy House Works, employing his cousin Thomas Wedgwood as a

journeyman. Ten years later Wedgwood opened his Etruria works, effectively a village combining houses, factory and the Trent and Mersey Canal, which Wedgwood had promoted. Here he turned the craft of pottery into a mass-production industry or, as the inscription under John Flaxman's memorial tablet to Wedgwood in St Peter ad Vincula, Stoke, puts it, he 'converted a rude and inconsiderable Manufactory into an elegant Art and An important part of the National Commerce'. People still visit the Potteries but the Wedgwood museum is at Barlaston.

Employing Flaxman, the author of the celebrated illustrations to Pope's Homer, set Wedgwood up for the accolades that were to follow. The fame never diminished. The work in agate, porphyry, black basalt, blue jasper, creamware and redware poured off the production lines, and samples of them all are to be seen in the new museum. Flaxman's white relief figures on Wedgwood blue are the signature pieces. Post-Flaxman it was downhill artistically until the 1930s and 1940s, when Wedgwood broke the mould with ceramics by such leading figures as Eric Ravilious, Arnold Machin, Robert Minkin and Keith Murray – pretty and desirable objects. But the real adventure was to commission a mug, just like any tea-break, building-site mug, except that this was decorated by a major avant-garde artist, Eduardo Paolozzi, who made a hugely personal contribution to post-war British art, including sculptures at the British Library and on Butler's Wharf on the Thames (see Greater London, London), and the mosaic decoration at Tottenham Court Road. He had already produced a limited edition of plates for Wedgwood, but the mug is a wonderful summation of the best of Paolozzi. All the junk he ever collected in his London and Edinburgh studios – electric circuitry boards, a toy saxophone, jelly moulds, a toy seaplane, a wooden aero propeller, plaster casts of giant hands – passed through the factory of Paolozzi's mind, and they are reproduced as a joyous abstraction as neat as precision engineering and much more colourful, a post-industrial tribute to the great age of invention.

Kipling's tribute to Wedgwood, Burslem

Burslem was where Josiah Wedgwood was born, and here at the heart of Burslem, the nearest thing to a successful sketch for a town centre in the Potteries, a combined initiative from the town and South Kensington Museum (now the Victoria & Albert), produced the Wedgwood Institute in Queen Street. It's an exotic Italianate Gothic building of 1871, constructed in red brick, fitting for the site of the Brick House works that was Wedgwood's second factory. And it's worth at least a third glance, because of its extraordinary terracotta façade, designed by Robert Edgar and John Lockwood Kipling, whose last work this was before embarking, with Mrs Kipling, for India where they would produce their greatest work, the infant Rudyard.

The tympanum of the pointed entrance is patterned with narrow green, white and red tiles laid diagonally, a testament to the over-confidence of the Victorians. The door is surmounted by a statue of Josiah Wedgwood, and he is flanked by twelve pointed arches supported on hybrid classical columns. In the arches are the labours of the month in good designs fitting the panels beautifully, though April is a young woman labouring at nothing much more than keeping her clothes on in a strong breeze. Beneath that is a strip-cartoon sequence broken into ten scenes of life in the pottery industry, beginning with troglodytes digging out the clay and hauling it away and finishing with, I take it, the muse of pottery drifting among craftsmen turning and finishing their pots. The façade is a fine performance in a setting that constitutes the price Stoke-on-Trent paid to be at the forefront of the Industrial Revolution: its birth and its death.

The man who made the Potteries, Stoke

Stoke begins with Wedgwood. Royal Doulton, Royal Albert and Minton might have argued about that, but they have been swallowed by Wedgwood. Even since it moved out to the village of Barlaston in 1936 it has dominated the Stoke scene. Such as that scene is, the best of it is Winton Square, with the railway station on one side and the North Stafford Hotel on the other, in a Jacobean style of red brick with blue brick

John Lockwood Kipling was involved in the design of this façade for the Wedgwood Institute in Burslem, Stoke-on-Trent, before leaving for India where his next tasks included designing the little Gothic garrison church in Simla and fathering Rudyard

diapering, and between them the statue of Wedgwood's founder, Josiah Wedgwood, by the Camarthen-born sculptor Edward Davis (1813–78). Most of Davis's chief endeavours had a bad press, but the Wedgwood statue is appealingly informal. The great man is shown holding the most famous of the firm's ceramics, the Portland vase (a copy from an ancient glass vase) in deep blue jasper with white relief figures reclining in an Arcadian scene (though the bronze shows it only as a perfectly ordinary bronze pot without the reliefs). Josiah is in a wig, stock at his throat, frock coat, waistcoat, knee breeches and stockings, and buckled shoes – formal dress, but the man himself is informally relaxed, pleased with the vase and pleased with the reception he seems sure it will receive.

Stottesdon

SHROPSHIRE

Romanesque font in St Mary

St Mary is basically a Saxon and Norman church with the best font in Shropshire, beautifully carved and surviving in crisp detail, and since the 12th-century masons who carved it were in the Herefordshire team that worked at Shobdon and Kilpeck, that means it is one of the best Romanesque sculptures in England. The proof of the authorship is circumstantial: a lion and a griffin and birds and the figure of a man on the Stottesdon font are very similar to carvings from the destroyed Shobdon church, surviving now in a park in an almost illegible condition.

The accepted theory about the Herefordshire school is that one master was in charge, though different hands can be detected in the carvings. The principal immediate influences come from the western Loire and along the coast to the Poitiers region, either as a by-product of the wine trade or simply because one powerful patron travelled to France (we know that the pilgrim route to Santiago de Compostella was popular) and brought back drawings, or he took a master carver with him. In any case, the 1140s produced the most sophisticated carving in England that had yet been seen.

The font is carved from top to base. Three-strand loose interlace make a series of connected loops beneath the rim; the base and stem have continuous tendril decorations; and the figures on the bowl are contained in large medallions, including the familiar delicately stylised agnus dei symbol, the lamb and flag as it has become on pub signs.

Twycross
LEICESTERSHIRE

The loveliest glass in an English parish, Church of St James

It is a heart-stopping moment to step through the south door into St James and turn right to face the east window, for set into the simple Decorated three-light window with tracery above is the loveliest medieval glass in England, all of it put together with a primal pleasure in pure colour that would hardly be manifested again until the last quarter of the 19th century. England, but not English. Pretty well all English stained glass came from France to be made up in England, but in this case the designs were French too. For what Henry VIII and Oliver Cromwell were to religious art in England, Robespierre and Danton were in France. Forewarned of the Revolution's anti-clericalism, French churchmen removed and hid many of their greater works of art,

and some of it found its way abroad.

To the unlikely destination of the small parish of Twycross on the broad Leicestershire plain where Richard III lost a horse and a crown, came some of the glass from the very first Gothic church, Saint-Denis, from Sainte-Chapelle, the chapel of St Louis, king of France, from the famous Burgundian church of St-Julien-du-Sault and from Beauvais. William IV acquired it, gave it to his friend Lord Howe of Gopsall Hall (now demolished), and it came in the 1830s to his parish church. The scarlet pimpernel had nothing on this rescue.

It is glass on a par with Canterbury's, and though small enough in quantity it has the parochial advantage that it can be viewed almost at eye level. The 12th and 13th centuries produced the purest form of stained glass made of single pieces of glowing colour clamped by the framework of lead strips, which also act as drawing, thick black lines describing the outline of a halo or a pointing hand, a sleeve, a foot, a head.

The oldest glass comes from the very birthplace of Gothic, the cathedral of Saint-Denis, where Abbot Suger began work on the nave started in 1136 and introduced glass in 1145. The Twycross fraction is a presentation in the temple. The scene is contained within a hemisphere against a field of heavenly blue. Mary and Joseph flank Jesus, Mary clasping the child's legs as he spreads his arms like a small bird about to fly from the nest. The shapes are simple, the colours red, lawn green, brown, white and yellow; yellow the altar, Christ's mantle red and his red halo interspersed with little white quarries so that it looks like the wheelhead of a standing cross. The scene is vivid, almost barbaric, with a Byzantine sureness in the handling of figures in lateral space and Byzantine hieratic splendour touched with Gothic tenderness. Suger luxuriated in fine art. For him, a church's richness was a hymn to divine glory.

This couple – an unknown saint and a female companion – were imported from France and installed in the Church of St James at Twycross in the wake of a revolution that had turned its anger against clericalism. The rich colours and calligraphic freedom of the painted details make this the loveliest medieval window in any English parish church

If this is one of the finest artworks in England there are others only a little less fine in this window. They are of the following century: from Sainte-Chapelle a Deposition from the cross and the two spies for Moses disguised as vineyard workers and searching out the lie of the promised land, Moses himself and a seated king; and from Saint-Julien-le-Sault two figures, an unidentified saint and his female companion, utterly simple, compellingly beautiful.

Weston under Lizard
STAFFORDSHIRE

Van Dyck masterpieces, at Weston Park

Almost nothing is known about Lady Elizabeth Wilbraham except that her heavily annotated copy of the Venetian architect Palladio's treatise on classical architecture suggests that she designed her large Restoration house of 1671, Weston Park, herself. The south front, with big pediments either side and a more sober central doorway, shows the house's pedigree most clearly. And of all the luscious rooms in all the lovely houses in England, the tapestry room at Weston Park vies with the best. Louis XIV style inlaid furniture known as boulle, Louis XV and XVI and George III furniture, and Yung Cheng dynasty porcelain (18th century). And the tapestries. These were made to measure by Gobelins with sexy rococo designs by François Boucher set against a red background or, more precisely, since Gobelins have literally hundreds of shades, *rose damas cramoisy*. It's unique, but not unparalleled, since Newby Hall, Moor

Sir Thomas Killigrew, in one of Antony van Dyck's best portraits – uncomplicated, vividly textured, the sitter alert with just a hint of depravity in his face. The portrait hangs at Weston Park. Killigrew was a Royalist who left for Venice as honorary consul for the future Charles II during the Civil War

Park, and Osterley all have similar rooms, with made-to-measure Gobelins–Boucher tapestries, but with different scenes and different colours.

But the greatest art at Weston Park is actually the portraits collected by the Bridgemans, Earls of Bradford, who bought the house in the 18th century: two portraits by Anthony Van Dyck (1599–1641), in particular of Sir Thomas Hanmer and Thomas Killigrew (both about 1638). Both men were courtiers, both survived the Civil war, Hanmer to become a famous horticulturalist, and Killigrew a theatre manager in Lincoln's Inn Fields, playwright and master of revels to Charles II. Gainsborough liked the portrait of Hanmer well enough to make a copy of it. In fact, it was Van Dyck whose work seduced Gainsborough from the innocent charm of his early Suffolk paintings. No wonder. Van Dyck's paintings brought to England the worlds of Titian and Rubens, in which the English king and queen and their courtiers had the inner fire of Renaissance princes instead of looking like warmed-up tomb sculpture. He glides from the stuff of Hanmer's black suit to the high white collar and shirt and from the swiftly touched-in white silk gloves to the texture of the one exposed hand and the sense of bone beneath. Above all this is Hanmer's fine head, not handsome but quick with warm intelligence.

The portrait of Killigrew, equally fine, shows him with a tawny shawl, a deeper accent of his hair colour, thrown over a breastplate. Under his arm he holds a copper-gleaming helmet, more likely to be a stage prop than the real thing. When the Civil War erupted Killigrew made off to the fleshpots of Venice as the exiled Prince Charles's honorary consul, where the authorities complained about his depravity. Nobody has painted better portraits in England since Van Dyck and before, only Hans Holbein.

Whatton

NOTTINGHAMSHIRE

King David and angel corbels of about 1300, Church of St John of Beverley

Until the age of fourteen, when he departed to Jesus College, Cambridge, Thomas Cranmer worshipped in the small chapel at the east of the north aisle of St John. Or so they say, and it is most probable because when the future Archbishop of Canterbury and Protestant martyr was twelve, in 1501, his father was buried here where a memorial slab engraved with a picture of him is set into the floor. Cranmer was born a mile away in Aslockton, but Whatton was the mother church. Neither Aslockton's of the 19th century nor Whatton's 19th-century restoration amounts to much apart from this atmospheric chapel.

The best things are two corbels, totally detached from any purpose they might have served before the restorers moved in. The angel playing a harp on one corbel has his legs drawn up beneath him and wings flattened out against the corbel ledge to support it. His head rests on the viol he plays with a sweet expression on his face. King David fingering his harp on the second corbel is even better, partly because the erosion has muffled the definition of the angel, partly because the David is more adventurous. The carver has completely undercut both the hand holding the head of the harp to steady it and the large flowers on the side of the corbel so that they exist in three dimensions.

The early history of the church is obscure, but it's clear that these light and joyful little objects were carved by craftsmen from one of the great centres like Southwell or Lincoln.

An Anglo-Saxon coffin lid, now set into a wall of the parish church at Wirksworth, includes in the top row the crucifixion treated symbolically with a cross surmounted by the Lamb of God. To the left of that Mary Magdalene washes Christ's feet and the row below includes the Ascension (left) and the Annunciation (right)

Wirksworth

DERBYSHIRE

Saxon 9th-century carving, in the Church of St Mary

Trucks loaded with blocks of rock, each the size of half a house, hurtle through the bends of narrow roads, reminding car drivers not just of their mortality but that the spectacular tourist area of the Peak District National Park is also industrial in a way that the Lake District, for instance, is not. In Derbyshire quarrying in the limestone and millstone grit seams goes on as it always has, though now to the exclusion of lead mining, an activity celebrated in a small Saxon sculpture set into the church wall in Wirksworth and which was prospering centuries before that. St Mary's is studded with bits of Anglo Saxon sculpture, which must be from an earlier building because the present church is a very big 13th- and 14th-century edifice with an impressive central tower and spire, transepts and a big nave and chancel.

In the chancel is the carving that really matters, the former lid of a coffin well over 6 feet long set into the south wall and dating from around the year 800. It is crammed with a vigorous series of biblical narratives in two rows. The top tier includes Mary Magdalene washing Christ's feet and the crucifixion of the lamb of God, and the row below includes the ascension, the Annunciation and, possibly, the presentation of Mary in the temple. The carving is crudely schematic, but the pictorial organisation is tight and rhythmic, like Vikings in a longboat, with a fine swirling sequence of drapery and angels' wings. Even allowing that realism was not the object, it seems clearly the work of local masons, yet the noble dignity of its figures connects, like so much else from the peoples of that remote but well-travelled age, through a western European style of concentrated piety in the court of Charlemagne to those great hieratic figures in the early Christian mosaics of Venice and Ravenna.

The Northwest

CHESHIRE ✳ CUMBRIA ✳ GREATER MANCHESTER
LANCASHIRE ✳ MERSEYSIDE

ORKSHIRE

EAST
YORKSHIRE

TH

IIRE

LINCOLNSHIRE

RE

NOTTS.

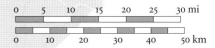

Acton, near Nantwich

CHESHIRE

17th-century monument to Sir Richard Wilbraham and his wife, Church of St Mary

Acton lies beyond the River Weaver and the Shropshire Union Canal in the shadow of Nantwich. Its great moment in history was 1644, when the royalist 1st Lord Byron (his descendant, the poet, was the 6th) set up his Civil War headquarters for the siege of Nantwich at Acton church. The Cromwellian General Fairfax defeated Byron and lifted the siege in a defining battle of the Civil War. Acton settled back into its rural slumbers as a retreat for gentry like Sir Richard and Lady Wilbraham, the couple commemorated in the church with white marble effigies on a grey and black tomb chest. We do not know what part, if any, they played in the war, although he appears here in armour. In fact, we have nothing but the barest genealogical details of them, though we do know that Sir Richard earned this place of honour in the chancel by building the fine chancel parapet. The two of them lie recumbent in contented amplitude, she looking as though dressed for church, her head covered, a bodice over a gown so long it covers her feet; she has bracelets on both wrists, and while she rests one hand delicately on her bosom, the other holds a book, presumably the Good Book. He has the aspect of a cavalier, complete with moustache and beard. They are not a handsome couple – the sculptor has aimed at a realistic likeness, not flattery.

It is a good enough piece to demand an attribution, but nobody has made one. It looks as though it could be by the king's mason Nicholas Stone, but royal patronage ceased, Stone's career ended with the outbreak of the Civil War (1640), and Sir Richard died in 1643, his wife not until 1660.

Pevsner's tentative suggestion of the London sculptor Edward Marshall (1597/8–1675) is attractive because the work is similar, he was ten years younger than Stone, and though nothing he designed reached Stone's heights, he was as good as the average, which means good. The two lean and hungry hounds on which the Wilbrahams' feet rest are more than good. The spinal cords stand out of the flesh right through to the tails of these twin curs. They have bodies tensed ready to spring at any incitement, glaring eyes, ears flattened back to the head, teeth menacingly bared, snouts like sawn-off shotguns. With curs like these to watch for them, no wonder the Wilbrahams look contented.

Ambleside

CUMBRIA

A Cumbrian exile from the Nazis at the Armitt Gallery, Museum and Library

Mary Burkett, deputy director of Abbot Hall Art Gallery in Kendal, discovered at the Brussels Expo of 1958 that Kurt Schwitters (1887–1948), son of a property owner and rentier, but one of the revolutionary innovators of 20th-century art, had died after the war in Ambleside. While living in Hanover he had invented a version of Dada called Merz, after a torn handbill in a little collage he'd made leaving just the last part of the word *Commerz*. Goebbels listed him as a degenerate artist, so he fled to Norway before the outbreak of war and then fled again as the Nazis invaded Norway. Burkett asked everybody she knew in the Lake District and some she didn't about Schwitters. Nobody remembered him until she mentioned him to the old newspaper seller at Ambleside bus station. Yes, he said, there was an old German, 'very strange man, he used to go up Langdale to Mr Pierce'.

Harry Pierce was a landscape gardener in

Elterwater at the foot of the Langdale Pikes. He told Mary Birkett the story of Schwitters arriving in Ambleside via an internment camp on the Isle of Man and knocking out portraits and landscapes for a living, and he showed her the huge collage Schwitters had built on a barn wall, the third of his Merz constructions, the unknown one and the sole survivor (see Hatton Gallery, Newcastle upon Tyne, Northeast). She set out to hunt down the work he'd done around Ambleside and found it, usually discarded in attics. She finished putting together a show of his bread-and-butter work together with some small abstract pieces, and before the art dealers of Bond Street got a whiff, Abbot Hall had added a body of his work to the permanent collection. The Armitt, which is really a tiny gallery appended to a library and museum, followed suit with a Schwitters collections bigger than any outside Germany.

In his landscapes there are sudden, beautifully realised details – as though he was suddenly taken by a particular feature. It's apparent here, in a 1946 canvas of the house of his companion Edith Tyson in Ambleside, where the passage of deep intensity is the sun low over a hill behind. He was also fully engaged in the portraits – there is one here of Harry Pierce and another of Schwitters's doctor, Ainslie Johnston, who had saved his life following a brain haemorrhage in 1946. The doctor was an impatient sitter, so Schwitters kept him still by putting a chess set in front of him.

With death hovering in the wings, Schwitters reconstructed a sculpture he had made in 1926–8 called *Autumn Crocus*, a gently spiralling white form to be placed on his grave in Ambleside. The vicar refused permission. So the monument to this 'genius in a frock coat', as his Dada colleague Richard Huelsenbeck spoke of him, is in Tate Modern instead.

Bewcastle
CUMBRIA

8th-century cross, Church of St Cuthbert

Bewcastle lies over a clatter of sheep grids in no-man's-land about 6 miles north of Hadrian's Wall. The Romans built a castle on the wall at Birdoswald, but they added an outpost fortress at Bewcastle. What remains is the remnants of the medieval rebuilding, and the Church of St Cuthbert was built at least in part with stone cannibalised from the castle. And that is all there is – church, demesne farm, rectory, castle motte, ruins and slender poles to act as markers when snow obscures the narrow metalled road. Further back on the road from Birdoswald and incorporated into a farm, there is a defensive pele tower, the remnant of incursions from north of whatever passed for a border by plundering Scottish reivers, the Bells, the Armstrongs, the Irvines, the Beatties, some of whom lie now in the accommodating churchyard of Bewcastle. The churchyard is also home to the Bewcastle Cross, the finest in England, and some of the best carving of its period in Europe (see also Eyam, North Midlands).

It probably stood in for a church, a marker and a meeting point for Christians to meet in this lonely spot. It has been ascribed to about AD 680 on stylistic grounds and on the basis of a runic inscription that appears to commemorate the northern 7th-century king, Alcfrith. But the view is growing that Alcfrith is a misreading of the now almost impenetrable runes and that the cross is actually 8th century. In any case, there is no disputing that it followed the Synod of Whitby of 664, which decided in favour of Rome in the dispute between the Roman church and the Irish church, which was by now practically indigenous to the north of England, over the timing of Easter. Like the

IN LOVING MEMORY OF
WILLIAM NIXON
who died at Fieldhead
10. April 1908, aged 64 years,
and SARAH, his wife
who died at Fieldhead
9 May 1934 aged 74 years
also their daughter
ANNIE MARY
in infancy

This 8th-century cross in the bleak northern no-man's-land at Bewcastle is one of the greatest works of art of its period in Europe and shows the cross-influences of Celtic decoration with motifs from Syria and the Coptic monasteries of Egypt

unparalleled Lindisfarne Gospels of the late 7th or early 8th century, the carving of Bewcastle Cross shows the influence, not just of Celtic patterning, but of Syria and the Coptic monasteries of Egypt that continued to influence English art right through the Romanesque period with those orderly folds of drapery between the knees and falling from the shoulders of saints and Apostles. It is an exotic glimpse of the art seeded in a civilisation far from the imagining of the west, now maybe more than then.

The cross-head is missing, but the whole east face of the shaft is carved with birds and squirrels and possibly a dog all entwined in a vine scroll. The tautly designed south and north faces have the Celtic interlace patterning known as knotwork, chequerboard patterning, runic inscriptions, foliage and a sundial. The west face has the misinterpreted runic inscription but also the figure of Christ beneath St John the Baptist and above, most likely, St John the Evangelist. These stately figures are some of the earliest and, along with the Ruthwell cross a few miles over the border in Dumfries, absolutely the finest of all the many Anglo-Saxon crosses surviving in the north.

Birkenhead

MERSEYSIDE

Philip Wilson Steer, the Impressionist of Merseyside, at Williamson Art Gallery

It took the first steam ferry 'cross the Mersey to coax 19th-century Liverpudlians to settle on the tip of the Wirral peninsula. Then, shortly afterwards, the shipbuilder William

Laing founded the first of the town's big shipyards. After Laing came the civilising philanthropists, one to found the central library, another to give the borough its first painting by its native son, Philip Wilson Steer (1860–1942), another, Alderman John Williamson, to build an art gallery in the second decade of the 20th century. There remain, just, 14th-century priory ruins, and so, just, the shipyard basins. But the art gallery survives entire, and though Steer's family left town when he was only four, it is the painstakingly built collection of his work that gives the gallery its heart.

Steer was a close friend of his biographer, the Scottish painter and critic, sometime keeper (director) of the Tate, D.S. MacColl. Birkenhead has two portraits by Steer of Mrs MacColl, one painted in 1903, the other in 1904, the first a muddy sketch, the other fussily over finished. Maybe MacColl was too close to Steer to tell him the paintings were failures. Steer himself called it a fluke if one of his paintings turned out well. This was hard on himself but probably indicates the lack of confidence that may have caused him to move out of his early high-keyed Impressionist manner after a few student years in France in the face of implacable opposition from the art press. It took the purchase of several key paintings from Steer's Impressionist phase by a later director of the Tate, John Rothenstein, to create his reputation. But by 1888, when Steer went all *à la français*, the French Impressionists were moving on, and Steer's better work is his low-keyed later paintings. In Birkenhead there is a fine full-length study called *Schoolgirl Standing by a Door*, which is a racy and accomplished take on Degas's snapshot compositions.

Best of all is his painting of a nude on a sofa. Steer was a good painter of women, clothed and unclothed. The model for this one sits awkwardly upright avoiding the

The auditorium of the Grand Theatre, Blackpool, is one of the most exuberant works of easily the most prolific theatre designer of the Victorian and Edwardian era, Frank Matcham

comfort the sofa offers, her legs thrust stiffly out before her, one foot resting on a pile of books, her gaze directed downwards, the expression on her face saying, 'I don't normally do this sort of thing'. The volumes of her body are fully realised against vigorously brushed-in stripy cushions and dark walls and floor. This is Steer on top form; no fluke here.

Blackpool
LANCASHIRE

Grand Theatre interior, Church Street

Frank Matcham's Grand Theatre opened in the same year, 1894, as two other Matcham creations, the Tower Circus and Tower Ballroom, but though the Grand is modestly tucked away in narrow streets behind the Promenade, it is a prime example of Matcham (1854–1920) stepping out in top hat and tails and twirling a cane. Just as

Chippendale's furniture was English rococo at its most refined, Victorian and Edwardian music-hall was rococo as burlesque. It's the kind of thing that Walter Sickert (1860–1942) committed to legend with his paintings of the Old Bedford music-hall in Camden Town.

Matcham's architectural career spanned the reigns of both Victoria and Edward VII. He built between 150 and 200 theatres, for music-hall or opera or cinema, or, in the case of the Hippodrome in London, for aquatic performances. He pulled in classical, baroque and French rococo, Tudor, Moorish and Hindu styles, sometimes a kaleidoscope of several in a single interior. Blackpool's Grand is his own brand of opulent rococo, predominantly gold, rich with borders and friezes, the attenuated S-curves cavorting like sea horses on the proscenium arch, scrolled plaster work and plaster busts of Handel and Mozart, more composers in garlanded frames borne by cherubs, arabesques on the arches, grotesques on the ceiling, oval panels painted with maidens in bucolic landscapes, and clusters of lights forming miniature universes spreading their light across the spectacle of the moulded and painted ceiling.

Matcham came to the fore as music-halls moved away from their origins as boozers, and although the Blackpool Grand was picked as the National Theatre of Variety in 2006 and has been home to acts from Marie Lloyd to Max Miller, Dan Leno, Arthur Askey, Gracie Fields, both George Formbys and a survivor of the species, Professor Chucklebutty, aka Ken Dodd, it also stages without a blush opera and ballet, musicals, straight drama and classical concerts. (See also Buxton, North Midlands, and Leeds, Northeast.)

Blackstone Edge
GREATER MANCHESTER

Lancashire's Via Appia Antica

Anyone who has walked the old Appian Way in Rome will be familiar with the feel and look of a genuine Roman road: slabs of (in this case) lava rock laid with gaps between them of something like an inch. This may not be the most scientific way to argue that the remarkable half-mile stretch of paved road climbing to Blackstone Edge in the Pennines off the A58 above Littleborough is also Roman and not, as some doubters feel, a route laid down at some later date, but it certainly has all the appearance of the genuine article. Moreover, there is no evidence that anyone bothered to build roads of this sort after the Romans until the coming of the turnpikes in the 18th century. Quite the contrary, in fact: the appalling state of the roads is why rivers and, later, canals were so important for transport.

The Blackstone Edge road has one other particularly Roman characteristic: it goes straight up the hill the direct way. It was part of the route from the fort at Manchester to Ilkley, and it is in excellent condition. One explanation for the wide groove that runs down the middle is that it was made to help braking, but since the road has no camber, my own guess is that it was put there simply to allow water to run off.

Bolton
GREATER MANCHESTER

Roland Penrose, British surrealist, at Bolton Art Gallery

English surrealism generally was a cottage garden adjunct to the international movement. There's a lot of it here in a building of 1939 in an already handsome town centre that embraced 19th-century classicism instead of Gothic. The surrealism is embedded in a collection of modern English art built up with the championship of a watercolour-fancying railway trade unionist town councillor. Roland Penrose's *Surrealist Composition* is a rogue strand of tough old bindweed in the flowery border of the Post-Impressionism of Harold Gilman and Charles Ginner, Duncan Grant and Vanessa Bell, a gutsy painting of Toledo by David Bomberg (the best of that great city on a rock since El Greco), Mark Gertler, late Hepworth and a group of Epstein bronzes.

A friend and biographer of Picasso, Penrose (1900–84) was also one of the organisers of the surrealist movement in England. In 1936 he set up the huge International Surrealist Exhibition in London, and in 1947 he founded the Institute of Contemporary Arts. In 1947, too, he married the American photographer and surrealist muse Lee Miller. He began painting *Surrealist Composition* in the same year, a double portrait of Miller and himself, a modern Arnolfini couple. Penrose worked hard at the painting, and it came out like most of his work, dogged. All the same, it's fun and a historical document. In the 1930s Miller had modelled for her lover, the surrealist photographer Man Ray, and he repaid her by teaching her photography. She was more than a good pupil, and from art photographs moved on to become a brave photojournalist. She conned her way on to the American troop convoy entering Paris in 1944 and, as she liked to tell it, personally liberated Picasso. Seeing her arrive at his studio in combat gear, he exclaimed, 'This is the first Allied soldier I have seen, and it's you!'

Penrose's painting does scant justice to her remarkable beauty, but neatly shows her head as a magnified Cyclops eye surrounded by an incandescent tungsten halo, which may also double as a frothy little wedding hat, since he himself is dressed in a three-part suit, pinstripe shirt and bow tie and stands with his arm around her shoulders. Her modest number has a small V-cut to show a discreet touch of cleavage. His own eye is an elongated probe, and his concave face, reflected in the pupil of her eye, is based on one of the heads in Picasso's *Les Demoiselles d'Avignon*. So the painting constitutes a page from the Penrose diary, a homage to his great wife and greater friend, and a leaf from the art history of these islands in the 20th century.

Brampton
CUMBRIA

The Morris team get together near Hadrian's Wall, at the Church of St Martin

Brampton is a good border town, a mile or so south of Hadrian's wall. Unexpectedly, its church of 1878, St Martin, is by William Morris's friend Philip Webb (1831–1915), which explains why all the glass is of the same period by Morris and Co., the best of it designed by Edward Burne-Jones. Burne-Jones was a self-taught artist, and it showed. In fact no less a person than the author of *The Stones of Venice*, John Ruskin, said so, in a letter to Burne-Jones from Venice in May 1869, a visit during which he had for the first time responded to the paintings of Carpaccio, forewarned by his friend's enthusiasm. 'My dearest Ned,' he wrote, '… this Carpaccio is a new world to me; only you have a right to be so fond of him, for he is merely what you would have been if you had been born here, and rightly trained from the beginning.' A charmingly double-edged compliment.

In Tullie House Art Gallery in Carlisle,

Burne-Jones's show-stealer at St Martin, Brampton: consummate use of an awkward-shaped window

near enough to make comparisons, there is a series of full-scale Burne-Jones drawings of the Good Shepherd and angels for the east window of St Martin, and they are dry, meticulous and colourless beyond the colourlessness of the medium. Of course, they are only maquettes, carefully done for the glass craftsmen to follow. All the same, the comparison perfectly demonstrates how much his work gains by being translated into another medium. All his work in stained glass or tapestry is better than the best of his paintings. His drawing of the human figure was not strong, and his figures were 'pale, sickly, and wan, like all his young people,' as Henry James put it. How sick of writers Burne-Jones must have become.

It's clear from the drapery of his figures that he has learned more from the art of the past than from the life class, so it was especially suited to the context of public art. Put his work into Morris's glass workshop and it is transformed into some of the finest

and most necessary British art of the century: necessary because the swift growth of industrial towns brought a huge increase in church building, a lot of it more or less done from pattern books with glass and fixtures to match. Morris set new standards, and Burne-Jones became his principal designer. Ned was a witty caricaturist, who drew waspish cartoons of Morris at work in the craft shop, but he must have known that it was the making of his own career as well.

In some respects, Morris's own glass is more enjoyable than Burne-Jones's. The designs are tight but eloquent, the figures unshowy, the decorative patterning adds to the broader drawing, and his figures totally lack the sentimentality that mars so much Victorian art. The sequence of Morris's own three windows in the south aisle at Brampton showing Faith, Hope and Charity are beautifully designed, put together with very fine glass and surrounded by lovely plant decorations drawn on to quartzes of plain glass. All the same, the show-stealers are Burne-Jones's for his consummate use of an awkward, heart-shaped small window with two angels lifting two souls to heaven, and for the church's masterpiece, the five-light east window, full of angels with the Good Shepherd at the top of the central light and a fantastic pelican, foliage and flower design at the bottom.

Bridekirk

CUMBRIA

A 12th-century font with the mason's self-portrait, at the Church of St Bridget

In every sense the biggest thing happening in the north in the 12th century was Durham Cathedral. The best part of the cathedral was finished with the completion of the nave in 1133, and that doubtless released craftsmen to other work. Richard the carver is supposed to have been one of these, and he found his way to Bridekirk in a remote spot close to the west coast of Cumbria. The font he carved here is an extreme rarity, signed and, in an early case of an artist putting himself into his own work, with a little carved image of himself chipping away with a large hammer and chisel at a stone tendril on his own font. Above, an unfurled pennant reads: 'Rikarth he me iwrokt and this gernr merthr me brokt' (Richard has me wrought and to me this glory has brought). The characters are runic, even though runes had been largely replaced in England by Latin script around 1100; the language is Anglo-Saxon. It was a multi-cultural community.

The font is shaped like a chalice, four sided and slightly tapering from top to bottom. The surface is divided into two bands of decoration, though the east side with Richard's signature motif effectively becomes three because of the scroll between the figure

of him and what he is carving and above him another little man eating fruit from the branch of a stylised tree and what looks like a dog bounding away through the foliage. The top half of this side has two dragons facing each other. On the south and west are grapevines in fruit, a cross, fabulous creatures, birds and a man and woman kneeling by a tree. On the north side an eagle-sized dove hurtles out of heaven as St John baptises Christ in a rural glade, beautifully created with abstract foliage on either side.

The church that contains this little work is carefully planned 19th-century Norman, but the living force of the carved font survives the erosion of time and by contrast demonstrates rule one: careful copying never makes a masterpiece.

Bruera

CHESHIRE

Virtuoso sculpture by Joseph Nollekens, at the Church of St Mary

Nollekens was a virtuoso in an age of virtuosity. The English-born son of a Flemish artist living in London who apprenticed him to his countryman, Peter Scheemakers (also London based), young Nollekens (1737–1823) swiftly built his own reputation for brilliant sculpted portraiture with a line in Whig grandees and for church memorials. Bruera's is a fine example. St Mary, opposite a possible iron age earthwork built perhaps to corral cattle safe from Welsh rustlers, serves a tiny and shrinking community. It is much rebuilt Norman with intriguing ancient carvings in the chancel arch that wouldn't conceivably have interested Nollekens. He went in more for curly haired putti. These are duly deployed here in a small monument commissioned by the local squirearchy, the Cunliffes.

The Bruera relief carving follows the convention of the age. A putto sits on a ledge with a cloth-draped urn bearing a medallion portrait of Sir Robert (d.1778). Behind is an obelisk with the family crest, beneath an inscribed plinth. So much for convention. The putto has his back three-quarters turned inwards, but his head turns in profile, and one leg is folded and tucked under the other in a beautifully observed natural movement resolving into relaxed posture. The wings won't ever sustain a flight, but folded they describe the arc continued by the raised left arm lifting the draped cloth clear of the portrait and rhyming with the shape of the urn. To see just how good this is, compare it with the neighbouring monument to Sir Ellis Cunliffe (d.1768). It follows the same convention, but is thoroughly conventional. The putto is stiffly posed, the portrait sits unsatisfactorily in the oval frame: a journeyman's work beside a master's.

Carlisle
CUMBRIA

Early Pop Art by Peter Blake, at Tullie House Art Gallery

The penny dropped in the 1930s that Tullie House wasn't making any advance on the foundation collection (1893) of Pre-Raphaelite pictures, so the gallery committee asked William Rothenstein (1872–1945), a painter and principal of the Royal College of Art, to advise them. He did a stint of this and was succeeded by more academicians, Edward le Bas, Carel Weight and Roger de Grey. Gradually Tullie House emerged blinking into the 20th century. It was Roger de Grey who recommended the Peter Blake painting. As it turns out, it is one of Blake's finest and most emblematic.

Blake (b.1932) was first up, really; the first to cross the barrier between art and the popular media. Richard Hamilton was the brains, the authority on Duchamp, the artist who'd not only read Joyce but illustrated Ulysses, who had laid down a manifesto for Pop consisting of one collage, *Just What is it that Makes Today's Homes so Beautiful, so Desirable?* (see Chichester, Southeast). Eduardo Paolozzi was there, growling, 'I coulda been a contender.' He'd pasted up cuttings from junk magazines lying around in his studio, making junk images of his own. The kid, Hockney, not yet out of Bradford, hadn't even reached for the peroxide bottle yet. But Pete was the one, painting all those strippers and wrestlers, a tattooed lady, pop stars and heroes of the silver screen, Babe Rainbow, Bo Diddeley, Little Lady Luck, Selina Silver, Masked Zebra Kid and Tarzan, Jane, Boy and Cheeta. He painted the Beatles, too, and the cover for *Sergeant Pepper's Lonely Hearts Club Band*.

First of the first was *Children Reading Comics*. Blake was still at the Royal College of Art when he painted this in 1954. He probably got the idea from the family photograph album, and, in fact, there exists a studio shot of Blake aged ten standing stiffly beside his sister Shirley who is posing in an upright chair. In 1952–3 he had done a self-portrait in front of a wall of peeling posters, but he treated the head traditionally, in the round. With the comics picture he has found what he wants: it reads flat across the surface of the hardboard it's painted on, like a child's painting. The children stare over the top of two comics, two children but only three eyes because the yellow-haired girl has a patch over one eye, an unexplained childhood accident that adds a disconcertingly alienating edge to the picture. Blake has brushed the pigment on fluently and scraped it back workmanlike to the texture of the canvas. The kids hold the *Eagle* comics vertically in front of their bodies, their surfaces scuffed and only semi-legible to

Seven hundred feet above sea level, Castlerigg's Neolithic stone circle is a ring of boulders marrying the site to the surrounding ring of mountains

bring the faces above into clearer focus. A tiny hint of a sketched landscape over the boy's shoulder tells you that this is a picture as much about painting itself as about children reading comics.

Pop Art was a wave that swept through England and America and then abated, but it left behind fewer elitist assumptions about the nature and sources of fine art.

Castlerigg
CUMBRIA

Neolithic stone circle

Castlerigg stone circle, although similar to hundreds more from Cornwall to Orkney, including a dozen more in Cumbria alone, is uniquely beautiful. It has a mightily resonant unity, a ring of unhewn boulders none more than about 8 feet high, set on a plateau at 700 feet above sea level as smooth as a cricket pitch within a ring of mountains, Wanthwaite Crags, High Rigg and Low Rigg, Castlerigg, Latrigg, Lonscale Fell, Blease Fell and massive Blencathra with Skiddaw looming to the northwest. It is around 5,000 years old, about the same age as Stonehenge and several hundred years older than Avebury. There are thirty-eight stones in the circle and another ten arranged in a rectangle like an enclosure at one edge, for what purpose no one knows.

A dig has yielded a couple of Neolithic stone axes and some charcoal, and that says just about all that is known. So multiple experts feel free to give their versions of why the circle was constructed, and oddly enough those who know the least pronounce with the most certainty. So Castlerigg was a meeting place of kings, or it was a centre of the axe industry, a great emporium, an astronomical observatory (of course; some stones align with one heavenly phenomenon or other, most don't), and from time to time mysterious lights have been observed hovering above the stones, so undoubtedly it is the focus of alien activity from outer space.

Strangely, poets have missed the point. Wordsworth chose ineffectual Little Meg at Little Salkeld as second only to Stonehenge. And Keats cast a gloomy eye on Castlerigg and recalled it as 'like a dismal cirque/Of Druid stones, upon a forlorn Moor'. Well, it was a November evening, and raining.

Coniston
CUMBRIA

John Ruskin's little weakness, at Brantwood, signposted from Coniston

John Ruskin (1819–1900), art critic, seer and keeper of the nation's conscience, would row from the village of Coniston to Brantwood on the northern slopes of the lake. By water on the Brantwood Trust's steam yacht *Gondola* from Coniston pier is still the safest way, so narrow is the road above the shore. In the last ten years of his life, after a final incapacitating bout of madness grounded him, Ruskin settled into this house with its grounds running down to Coniston Water and handed over the management of his affairs to his cousin Joan Severn and her husband Arthur. When Ruskin died aged eighty-one the Severns began to sell the contents of Brantwood, until by the 1920s it was stripped bare. The Brantwood Trust bought the house in 1951 and gradually reassembled many of the items that had added up to Ruskin's daily domestic surroundings. The study especially, which had been the heart of Ruskin's life, has returned to something close to its appearance in 1900. House and contents are a strange but human commentary on Ruskin's life.

By the time Ruskin had finished adding to

the house he had bought with the money his father had earned in a lifetime at the sherry merchant Domecq he had almost doubled its size. One of the new rooms was the bedroom, with the turret he added to it from which he could survey the scene when he rose in the mornings. It is a practical but deeply unaesthetic construction. Beneath is the dining room with a window of seven lights, one would think a reference to his influential book *The Seven Lamps of Architecture* (1849), since the window cushion is embroidered with the names of the book's sections, Memory, Truth, Sacrifice, Life, Obedience, Power and Beauty. Espousing these qualities brought fame to him in the 19th century but derision in the unhappily sceptical 20th. Among many paintings in the dining room are two portraits by James Northcote (1746–1831), who was old enough when he painted them in 1823 to have been a studio assistant to Joshua Reynolds and young enough to see in the railway age. One portrait is of Ruskin's mother Margaret, the other of Ruskin aged three-and-a-half. He wears a white dress with a bright blue girdle and sweet little blue shoes and waves a bright blue ribbon, all of which, since he adopted a cravat of the same blue after an adult life dependent on his parents until they died, may suggest something about his failure to consummate his marriage.

There's a good gallery of paintings and drawings, mostly by Ruskin, and over the study fireplace is a glazed and coloured terracotta Virgin and Child by the 15th-century Florentine Andrea della Robbia (1435–1525). The technique was perfected by his much greater uncle, Luca della Robbia, and proved so popular that Andrea and his five sons turned their moulds to mass production (see Nynehead, Southwest). Andrea's Virgin and Child over the fireplace isn't the one Ruskin bought, which is now in Washington, D.C., but is more or less a replica except for the unfortunate addition of

God the Father looking like Ruskin in his decline. But what's truly interesting is that Ruskin owned a piece by Andrea at all. Among his contradictions, the man whose art criticism embraced the whole of man's social endeavour also held the view that anything less than genius wasn't worth the candle. Not for Ruskin the parable of the talents. He describes Michelangelo's master, Ghirlandaio, as a painter who could do almost anything as it should be done, but the bit that he couldn't do meant that he was worth precisely nothing. And yet here is Ruskin behaving like the rest of us, failing in his own life to live up to the principles he professes in public. He strolls on his tourist's clay feet to the Florence flea market and spends a little more of his rich inheritance on acquiring this highly desirable piece of terracotta to hang above his fireplace just as we would on a dodgy repro of Michelangelo's *David*.

Dunham-on-the-Hill

CHESHIRE

Exiled from Chester, the cross at the Church of St Luke

Dunham-on-the-Hill's hill is the last one before the Mersey. The church is below the hill on the busy A56 that shadows the M56, the ship canal and the River Mersey to Manchester. It is practically an adjunct to the car park of a big roadhouse. For good reasons it is kept locked, but Clare Lyon, the daughter of the key-holding family, was with me five minutes after I rang. I told her I wanted to look at the big cross above the screen. She told me of the day in 1921 when James Richard Blackburn, her great-grandfather, drove his farm horse and cart the 4 miles from Chester with the cross on board down a traffic-free country road to Dunham. She didn't know why Chester Cathedral had

dispensed with the cross, but later her mother told me. It had been commissioned by the Brown family, of the 19th-century department store Browns of Chester (now inevitably a Debenhams). Francis Skidmore (1817–96), the Coventry art metalworker who was much in demand for ecclesiastical work, made it to the design of George Gilbert Scott (1811–78). It was suspended beneath the chancel arch. But after the First World War the dean and chapter decided that they would sooner pay tribute to the crew of a battleship by hanging the ship's flag under the arch and putting the cross in storage. The Browns relieved them of the cross and found it a new home at Dunham.

It is a glorious piece of art from an architect who said that he became a new man after experiencing 'the thunder of Pugin's writings' but who in his own architectural practice was too often pedantic to the point of dullness. Maybe Skidmore's exuberance was catching. Scott and he worked together often, usually in making open-work iron chancel screens, intended to serve the liturgy without obstructing the view, but it has been the fate of both men to have their works ditched by 20th-century church elders, as at Chester, Salisbury and Hereford. Nor can it have helped that Scott fell so seriously out of fashion, particularly after the hatchet job done on his Albert Memorial by Lytton Strachey in *Eminent Victorians*. Yet the 4 foot cross here illuminates Dunham's sub-Scott Victorian church with its wild, knobbly, gilded surface edged by feathery curls and its big semi-spherical bosses. The overall impression is not so much Gothic as blazing Byzantine.

Fleetwood

LANCASHIRE

The boom and bust lighthouses on Morecambe Bay

During the railway boom of the 1830s Peter Hesketh, owner of the rich Rossall estate in northwest Lancashire, spotted what we would now call a gap in the market. The main line from Euston to the northwest got no nearer to Scotland than Preston, and he felt that if he founded a town on the empty southern tip of Morecambe Bay and persuaded the railway to push a branch line through from Preston, he could set up a ferry service to Ardrossan on the Ayrshire coast. He named the town Fleetwood after his mother's maiden name and hired Decimus Burton (1800–81) to be his architect. Burton knew about this kind of thing. He was both architect and landscape gardener and had laid out the Calverley estate at Tunbridge Wells, built the Athenaeum Club in St James's, the elegant Holme house in Regent's Park and a swath of St Leonard's-on-Sea in Sussex.

Nowhere, though, had Burton been required to design a lighthouse, but at the as yet unborn Fleetwood he built two. He laid out the town, with a railway station and a large hotel, the North Euston, for overnighters alighting from the trains from London and catching the boat to Ardrossan on the Ayrshire coast the following morning. Visitors may still stay in the North Euston in comfort and with a sea view, once again without a railway to get them there. All went well from the completion of the railway in 1840 until 1847, the year Queen Victoria travelled from Ardrossan to Fleetwood, disembarked and caught the royal train to London. The town might have expected to celebrate, but this same year the London & North-West Railway extended its main line to Glasgow. Hesketh went bankrupt, retired

hurt to New Brighton, and his seat at Rossall Hall became Rossall School.

Fleetwood today, without its fishing fleet after cuts in the quotas of allowable catches, has higher than the national average of unemployment and lower than average earnings, but it keeps up appearances. Burton's splendid lighthouses were engineered by a Captain H.M. Denham, who also placed a third, openwork, lighthouse of iron on a sandbank 2 miles out where the Wyre joins the Irish Sea. They all still function. The Pharos lighthouse is in the middle of town in Pharos Street beside the tramline that still links Fleetwood with Blackpool, a tall sandstone column on a square plinth with a little circular gallery beneath the lamp more than 100 feet above ground. The very pretty Beach lighthouse, as it is known though it stands opposite the hotel on the Esplanade, is half as high as the Pharos and stands on a square, open arcade supported by Doric columns and with an elegant balustrade; above that a tall rectangle that looks like the tower of a Florentine palazzo, but with round-headed sash windows and little circular portholes; a gallery, and above that, the octagonal light-housing with a conical roof and weathervane. It could be a highly desirable address, though without room to swing a cat.

Furness Abbey

CUMBRIA

Knights and ladies of stone

It's easy to miss the turning on the road into Barrow-in-Furness and finish up driving past rows of dismal post-war utility housing, scattered warehouses, petrol stations and eateries in this sombre old ship- and submarine-building town. But it's worth persisting, and you will be rewarded by the sight of a red sandstone arch by the side of

Human torpedo, somewhat damaged: this effigy at Furness Abbey of a 13th-century knight shows him encased crown of head to sole of foot in steel plate armour

the road, a narrow winding lane descending to another arch and then the abbey itself, set in a seductive sward by a stream, a site selected by the 12th-century Cistercian monks sent here to establish a monastery in the name of King Stephen.

This is one of the loveliest of monastic ruins, not just for its huge, empty windows and soaring chancel arch, nor for its flight of steps leading from midair at about chest height to a leap into another space in another ruined chamber. Nor for the wonderful survival in a roofless chancel of a five-seat sedilia with delicately carved canopies, one seat more capacious than the others, presumably for the abbot. What gives the ruin its touch of distinction are the fine effigies and grave covers excavated from within the ruin and displayed in English Heritage's elegantly designed entrance and museum. The best of them are a knight and a lady of the 14th century and two impregnable-looking knights of the 13th. The 13th-century pair carved in marble look like human torpedoes. Each wears a pot helmet encasing the whole head with only a slit to see through, and the body is covered with a streamlining crusader's curved shield. The bottom of the surcoat shows beneath; below that would have been plate armour, and the legs, too, are totally encased in steel. The colour has vanished and with it the heraldic display on the shields that would have identified the knights. Portraiture was clearly not an issue: what mattered was the nobility and long tenure of the family.

The 14th-century knight and lady are in freestone, the same red sandstone of the abbey building, with more detail and naturalism in the carving. It is still likely that the heads were idealisations, and the knight is covered head-to-toe in chain mail. He wears a surcoat too, with a loosely fastened sword belt, his shield held to one side of his torso, his gauntleted hand on the hilt of his sword, his legs nonchalantly crossed in the sculptural fashion of the time. Though damaged, the lady's face is still lovely. She wears a wimple and a long pleated gown.

Gosforth
CUMBRIA

A Viking cross, at the Church of St Mary

Gosforth lies just off the road that runs along the west coast of Cumbria between the industrial outposts of Barrow-in-Furness and Whitehaven, and under the shadow of England's highest mountain, Scafell. Its latest settlers are the scientists and technicians working at Sellafield nuclear power station; the earliest settlers to have left a sign of their passing were the Vikings a millennium before. Among the hunks of carved stone at St Mary's are a couple of typical Viking hogback tombs, and on one wall is something known locally as the fishing stone, which historians say is a carving of the Viking god Thor in a boat with impressively large fish swimming beneath. Presumably the church now reinterprets it as Christ on Galilee. But what gives Gosforth its real distinction is the cross in the churchyard.

It is 15 feet high, tall, slender and elegant as a young tree, growing from a circular base squared off about a third of the way up, and culminating in a wheel cross. It is covered with intricate abstract patterning and some scenes of figures, hopelessly carved but fascinating because they are a mixture of Christian and pagan themes. Christ is shown crucified on one side of the shaft, though with his feet apparently firmly on the ground and arms outstretched like a football manager modestly accepting the crowd's applause. Beneath is Longinus, the soldier who pierced Christ's side with a lance, and one other figure. All the other scenes, however, are from the Norse myth of the fall of the gods, which,

like the fishing stone, can easily be elided with Christian belief to suggest, in this case, the coming of doomsday.

Since their first savage attack on Lindisfarne in 793, the Vikings had continued to raid the north, but late in the following century they came not primarily for plunder but to settle the land, and as they did so they adopted the local religion, Christianity. Clearly in doing this they maintained their own traditions and myths. The Gosforth Cross is 10th century, at least 200 years younger than the great Christian crosses of Bewcastle (see above) and Ruthwell. The settlement with King Alfred in 878, which fixed a boundary for the so-called Danelaw, didn't include Gosforth, so the newcomers must have been anglicised enough by then to be accepted. One story suggests (without a shred of evidence) that they came from the Viking settlement of Dublin. But why not? It's as feasible a guess as any about a period when, if Alfred wasn't writing the history himself, nobody was.

Hawkshead
CUMBRIA

A sundial where Wordsworth became a poet, at Hawkshead grammar school

When he left school for Cambridge William Wordsworth (1770–1850) composed a few valedictory lines:

> … *wheresoe'er my course shall end,*
> *If in that hour a single tie*
> *Survive of local sympathy,*
> *My soul will cast the backward view,*
> *The longing look alone on you.*

If he read these piously poetic platitudes, his teacher at Hawkshead grammar school must have hoped that young William would forget about verse at St John's and stick to the maths

The sundial above the lintel at the humble village grammar school of Hawkshead was there a century before the schoolboy William Wordsworth arrived in 1779 and showed promise as a mathematician and classicist

and classics at which he had been so successful at school. But, as Wordsworth tells us in *The Prelude*, it was at Hawkshead where, as an orphan, he lodged with a woman who became a much-loved mother surrogate, that he awoke to the grandeur of nature and committed himself to a future as a poet.

The school is at the southern end of the village, the bit visitors bypass to reach the pretty marketplace, a slate-roofed, stuccoed red sandstone building of three bays of windows on two floors interrupted by the entrance. The doorway extends almost to the eaves. First, there is a lintel dated 1585, the year when Edwin Sandys, Archbishop of York, founded the school, then a slate panel, and above that a sundial. It's a jolly ensemble in exposed sandstone. The slate panel, within a scrolly frame, bears the founder's coat of arms and an inscription to him, and at the top the sundial has lettering picked out in blue, the Roman numerals of the hours in gold. It was installed a hundred years before Wordsworth arrived in 1779, and walking through this splendid portal with its standing reminder to the passing of time must have helped to shape the pantheism that, in the poet's prime, produced his lines:

No motion has she now, nor force;
She neither hears nor sees
Rolled round in earth's diurnal course
With rocks, and stones and trees.

Isel

CUMBRIA

A bastion and a Tudor house joined

North of Bassenthwaite Lake and Skiddaw, mountains and water give way to the hinterland of the Solway Firth, but for the first few miles a network of narrow lanes link tiny communities, none smaller than Isel, where the only visible buildings are a little Norman church and Isel Hall, poised above a garden that drops steeply to a bend in the River Derwent. At strategic points the garden walls have integral pairs of arms holding up a friendly looking sun. These were installed by the family who once lived here and were lawyers called Lawson. As a play on the surname, the family arms display a shaft of wit as blunt as a jokey rear-window car sticker, but with the evident advantage of having been carved by craftsmen.

Isel Hall began with the massive 15th-century pele tower, now amalgamated with the Tudor house. The tourist booklet claims that a tower stood here in the 12th century and was razed in passing by Earl Douglas in the 14th century during a raid on Cockermouth. The first building after the tower was a separate great hall, which during the reign of Henry VIII was extended into a long, narrow house and joined to the tower. There is a 15th-century oak door at the top of the staircase into the tower, with the hefty doorposts and lintel too heavily grooved to

be described as fluting. The great hall has an oak screen wall with linenfold panelling; the downstairs oak room has Tudor panels covered with painted armorial bearings glowing like gold dust; and the oak bedroom has panels painted with Tudor figures. I discovered from experience, having slept in both the pele tower and the Tudor house as a guest of the present owner, that the Tudors knew more about human comfort than their reiver-beset predecessors. The fetching pink the owner has painted the tower seems to have deterred marauding reivers.

Kendal

CUMBRIA

Romney's masterpiece on his own patch, Abbot Hall Art Gallery

The painter George Romney (1734–1802) was born in Dalton-in-Furness and from childhood worked in his father's cabinet-making business. When he had reached the advanced age of twenty his father realised that he had a strong bent for art and apprenticed him in March 1755 to an itinerant painter called Christopher Steele, who happened to have dropped anchor in Kendal among a flotilla of local portrait painters – Kendal was a prosperous wool town and had its own newssheet, coffee house and theatre, indispensable to the civilised 18th-century life. You feel that on the walls of a scatter of the farmhouses and town houses of Cumbria there must be an unrecognised Romney or two. But what Abbot Hall has among a group of Romney portraits is his masterpiece, *The Leveson-Gower Children*.

Although Abbot Hall earned its reputation with its modern art, it was fated to become synonymous with George Romney. Soon after Romney's arrival in the town, George Wilson, a colonel of the foot guards, built

George Romney, a native of Kendal who made his living by portraiture but hated it, felt liberated by the Leveson-Gower children and painted this, his masterpiece, now in Abbot Hall Art Gallery

Abbot Hall. When it showed signs of falling down after the Second World War a group of local and national sympathisers rescued it and restored it as an art gallery. Abbot Hall had its first Romney by 1963 and steadily acquired more over the 1970s and beyond, both for the local connection and the period fitness – the downstairs rooms have been restored and furnished as Georgian.

Judging purely by his order books, Romney was London's portraitist of choice in the 1780s and 1790s, if only because he kept his prices lower than Reynolds and Gainsborough. After his death the realisation crept in that not only was his output uneven, but at his best he didn't match either of his immediate rivals, nor the Scots Allan Ramsay and Sir Henry Raeburn. Like Reynolds and like Hogarth, Romney wasn't good at imaginative figure compositions, the 'history pictures', which Reynolds had proclaimed as the only genre of painting through which true greatness could be attained. This was agony for Romney, who already hated face painting. But the four daughters and one tiny son of the Leveson-Gowers liberated him, precisely because they were children.

Of course it is as intensely artificial as all Georgian portrait compositions were to various degrees, very much a Work of Art. Romney had visited Rome and looked at classical friezes. His own description of a

May Day dance he had seen in Nice is at least as pertinent: 'Hand in hand … they were perfectly in time with each other … I thought myself removed a thousand years back and a spectator of the scenes at Arcadia.'

Lady Anne, at about fifteen and the oldest child, taps a tambourine held above her shoulder. She is dressed in an ivory-coloured gown, and the other children's gowns vary from plum to a deep olive green, treading a subtle measure across the picture surface, lit up by the eagerness of the children's eyes and the freshness of their complexions.

Lancaster
LANCASHIRE

The city of Lancaster has two town halls for its population of 45,000, but one castle is deemed sufficient. The castle, however, contains the shire hall, the crown court and the jail, and fills in as a tourist attraction too. Roger de Poitou built the massive keep at the end of the 11th century on a tremendous site on a hill above the city centre and the River Lune. 'Old John of Gaunt, time-honoured Lancaster,' as Shakespeare's Richard II addresses him, added to the defences, and there is a statue of him in a niche above the much-restored entrance arch. He was the third son of Edward III and the Duke of the Duchy of Lancaster. Oddly, the queen is the duke today, thanks to her predecessor Victoria, who decreed that anybody who held a dukedom must be a duke. The duchy modestly describes the current duke's holdings of something over 46,200 acres as 'a unique portfolio of land, property and assets'. A glance at the map shows that it stretches from Cumbria to Merseyside and into North Wales. Some duke, some majesty.

Downhill from the castle, in Castle Hill and Castle Park, the houses are Georgian, and that, rather than medieval, is the keynote of Lancaster. Where buildings aren't actually Georgian they often pretend to be, usually quite successfully. The old town hall, now a museum, is genuinely late 18th century with a big classical portico and pediment, an octagon above that with a clock and above that again a tall cupola with slender Ionic columns. The new town hall in Dalton Square is much bigger, and although it, too, has a giant portico, pediment and tall cupola, it can't help looking what it is, slightly clumsy, late 19th-century municipal. Opposite the town hall is the Victoria Monument with a statue of the old queen and relief bronzes of eminent Victorians. Town hall and Victoria Monument were both gifts of the munificent Lord Ashton (see Ashton Memorial, below).

The Lune is wide and navigable, and Lancaster's port was once its main economic asset, but that business has long passed to Heysham on the west coast. Instead, Lancaster is the major market and shopping centre of north Lancashire and centre of an administrative district that includes Heysham and Morecambe.

A folly dressed as a monument, in Williamson Park

On a clear day you can see the Isle of Man and the Lake District hills across Morecambe Bay from the viewing gallery of the Ashton Memorial; and there to the south is Blackpool Tower. On any old day the memorial is impossible to miss from the M6. On its hill above Lancaster it looks like an elongated Sacré Coeur, though the Montmartre basilica is reticent compared to the exuberant, not to say wild, baroque of the Ashton Memorial. A Lancaster lino millionaire called Lord Ashton, when he was plain James Williamson, donated Williamson Park to the town in 1880, and in 1906 began building this in memory of his wife. The popular architect John Belcher (1841–1913) designed it in the florid style that suited the mood of the Edwardian era. It took three years and is 150 feet high. A grand staircase leads up to the main portico with a balustrade above, and above that is the huge drum that supports the central dome and four domelets. The drum on which the central dome stands rises in tiers, the lowest surrounded by paired columns and with high windows and pediments breaking through in three places, then a balustrade and above the balustrade bull's-eye windows and at last the dome itself surmounted by a tall lantern. Inside the main door there is a huge, empty chamber, nothing, not even a tomb like the world's most famous memorial to a wife, the Taj Mahal. It's the folly to cap all follies.

John Rennie's Lune aqueduct

It is not the best known of John Rennie's structures: that was the London Bridge that was dismantled in the 1960s and sold to a rich American who set it up as a tourist attraction in Arizona. The finest was old Waterloo Bridge, which so elegantly framed the City of London in the view from upriver, and which John Constable portrayed in 1829 as it looked ten years earlier on its opening day of carnival gaiety. But the Lune aqueduct runs it close for dignity if not glory. Rennie (1761–1821) was a civil engineer, but in the way of those multi-disciplinary times he acquired the skills of an architect. He combined both on the Lancaster canal, which he engineered as well as designing the bridges and aqueducts. The Lune aqueduct has five round arches, each spanning 70 feet, which carry the canal 664 feet across the river at a height of 61 feet. Those are the bare statistics. Aesthetically, it is very much a Georgian building, monumental, nicely proportioned, unshowy but calmly impressive.

A pity then that the cost of £48,320 18s 10d

Like the Moghul emperor Jehangir (though not quite), who built the Taj in tribute to his dead wife Mumtaz Mahal, the Victorian lino millionaire Lord Ashton built the Ashton Memorial in memory of his wife in the park he donated to Lancaster

brought the canal company close to bankruptcy and that Rennie was denied the chance to build the Ribble aqueduct. So the canal remained marooned from the network, meandering across the Fylde plain between Lancaster and Preston following the lie of the land to avoid the necessity for locks. Later the company extended the northern branch to Kendal, but when the M6 was built nearly two centuries later the canal was unceremoniously fed into a culvert and Kendal became inaccessible.

Lanercost
CUMBRIA

13th-century sculpture of St Mary Magdalen, Lanercost Priory

The sculptured figure of Mary Magdalen, patron saint of remote Lanercost, was hoisted into the niche built for her high in the west gable between 1250 and 1275, not too long after the Augustinian priory was completed, though dates are uncertain. She has stayed there ever since, viewed by Edward I on the several times he visited on his way north and unmolested by the marauding Scottish bands who repeatedly sacked the monastic buildings in the soft countryside on the little River Irthing a few hundred yards from Hadrian's Wall. She survived the dissolution of the monasteries under Henry VIII, after which the church was allowed to fall to pieces, and the Civil War, when Cromwellians did their best to smash all idolatrous images. True, at some point she lost both hands, but otherwise she remains as crisply carved and as calm and

composed as from the beginning, a glorious red sandstone figure in a serene red sandstone Early English façade of pointed portal, blind arcade stretching between north and south buttresses, and above that three very tall lancets set into another arcade. The saint presides over what remains of the priory – the big nave (adapted as the parish church), the picturesquely ruined choir, transepts and monastic buildings. The arms of Sir Thomas Dacre, of the family to whom Henry VIII granted the lands at the dissolution, are inset mildly intrusively either side of the saint's niche.

Edward I bestowed blessings on the abbey, from silk cloth to (it is said) the sculptor who had worked on the figures in the judgement portal at Lincoln Cathedral, as well the king might, since in one of his frequent visits he fell ill and spent the winter here at Lanercost's expense with a mighty retinue. As it happens, the Magdalen wears a large brooch to pin her mantle between her shoulders, and it is a brooch of the style that was found in Edward's tomb when it was opened and his remains examined in the 18th century. It was the fashion among the wealthy of both sexes in the 13th century. Mary Magdalen stands quite upright, her bodice in neat vertical folds, her mantle thrown over the left arm so that it falls in widening ripples to a point just above her ankle. Beneath that her skirt picks up the rhythm of her bodice, falling in neat and fluid vertical folds to her feet.

Liverpool

Liverpool from the boat deck of the Cunard liner *Mauretania*, converted for use as a troopship during the war and shipping British military families back from pre-independence India. It is drizzling, and the sky is an undifferentiated grey. But there, across from the Cunarder in its red and black livery, is the Cunard Building sandwiched between the Liverpool and Mersey Docks Board headquarters and the Liver Building – the three graces. Behind them on a hilltop high above the city stands the unfinished hulk of Liverpool Cathedral by Giles Gilbert Scott, the last and grandest flourish of the Gothic revival. The cathedral, built from east to west like the Gothic cathedrals of the Middle Ages, would be completed in 1978, eighteen years after Scott's death. The Catholic cathedral was still only a crypt by Lutyens to be finished in a quite different modernist style by Frederick Gibberd. Sixty years later into the 21st century there are no great liners, but Liverpool looks and feels much the same, despite the later poverty and dereliction, dominated by the seafront and the great Anglican cathedral on the hill, the Catholic cathedral nearby and the university built around Abercromby Square.

Liverpool had grown from the ground up in the 18th and 19th centuries. Even Manchester had medieval buildings, one of them fit for purpose as a cathedral. Liverpool had nothing. It built St George's Square with the magnificent hall, the museum and the Walker Art Gallery founded on the collection of William Roscoe, a publican's son who lived to write a biography of Lorenzo the Magnificent and to endow Liverpool if not as grandly, then in similar style to the Medici enrichment of Florence. Now from mercantile and industrial riches, followed by a plunge into poverty, it has sprung into renewed life as a post-modern city. The Albert Dock, with its Tate and its shops and galleries and offices and cafés, is as living and vivid an assertion of Liverpool pride and identity as the great Greek revival city centre, and it comes not just from local pride but from a national flair and spirit of optimism. The Mersey Sound asserted a world identity in a setting that is Scouse through and through, though adulation of the Beatles has generated some of the poorest of a poor crop of recent sculpture, watering down the quality of the rest, new and old: Tony Cragg, on the quay near the Tate; Barbara Hepworth at the university; Richard Westmacott's equestrian George III a short step from Lime Street railway station and his father's weather-worn statues on the façade of the 18th-century town hall. When I last looked, Liverpool had become a vast building site and it was impossible to park close to the Tate. A bit late in the day, it seemed, since these were preparations for its year as European city of culture, and this was already 2008.

The Lennon and McCartney boyhood homes, in Woolton and Allerton

The National Trust minibus was in for a service, and the hired replacement had no CD player for the recorded commentary, so the driver busked it. He said something like let me take you down, 'cos I'm going to Strawberry Fields. And he drove to the middle of Woolton, out on the edge of Liverpool and still recognisably a village, shops clustered around a centre, a pub, the church, the church hall and Church Fields, where John Lennon's schoolboy skiffle group the Quarrymen (Quarry Bank is where he went to school) were playing a gig at the 1957 summer fete when Paul McCartney cycled over to listen and met Lennon. And, yes, there is Strawberry Fields, with walls and gateposts of red sandstone like Liverpool Cathedral because they were both built with rock from Woolton quarry. Finally Menlove Avenue.

Here, at No. 251, is the posh 1933 semi where John Lennon grew up with his childless Aunt Mimi and Uncle George from 1945 until 1963, with its mass-produced art nouveau stained glass in the front door and porch and the lounge bay window, its biscuit-coloured art deco tiled gas fire in Mimi's and George's bedroom, the lodger in the back room, the wood-cased Obell wireless set and the Singer sewing machine in the morning room, and – the final sales pitch – the bellboard to summon non-existent servants to the front door or a room where the lady of the house might be reclining. It was a house like thousands of others in Britain, but here the builders bestowed names on their semis to give a bit more class, so No. 251 became Mendips. It was nicer than most anyway, because the avenue outside had trees and grass down the middle where the trams had once run. Lennon's dad, Fred, a steward on Cunard White Star, sailed out of his family's life altogether when his son was five. John's mum, Julia, found a lover, and that's when her sister Mimi persuaded her to let John come to her at Mendips.

A few minutes' walk away Mather Avenue runs into Liverpool, converging with Menlove Avenue just before Penny Lane. Each morning Paul McCartney would leave home, a council house in Allerton, number-20-with-no-name Forthlin Road, to catch the bus in Mather Avenue to Liverpool Institute, the big grammar. On the bus one day he met George Harrison on the way to the Inny too, from Speke. Paul took him to John's, but Mimi banned him from Mendips because he wore a teddy boy suit to impress. 'That's when I knew George was right for the Quarrymen,' Lennon said.

Westmacott's statue of George III, Monument Place

In 1809 the mayor of Liverpool confidently laid a foundation stone at the spot selected for a glorious equestrian statue of George III to celebrate his golden jubilee the following year. The spot was selected carefully, on the London road, and Liverpool corporation committed £500 to the project and proposed raising the rest, something over £2,000, by public subscription. At the end of 1810 popular Farmer George had declined into Mad King George, the Prince Regent had taken over the reign, and the enthusiasm of a loyal populace for the statue had waned to vanishing point. In 1815 the town council decided to plug ahead and held a competition between three sculptors. They chose the design by Richard Westmacott ahead of those by John Bacon and F.C. Wyatt, but public enthusiasm had been drained by the monument to Nelson at the Exchange building (designed by Wyatt but executed by Westmacott, perhaps because he could offer the economic advantage of his own foundry), so the council voted the rest of the £3,000 that was Westmacott's price. It was erected on a Westmorland stone plinth carved in Kendal in 1822.

At the busy point a few hundred yards from St George's Square where the London road splits into two, the statue is just an urban blur to passing traffic, though it is one of Westmacott's finest pieces. He cribbed wholesale from the ancient Roman equestrian statue of Marcus Aurelius, on the familiar basis that there was no point in reinventing the wheel. Within the same lineaments, Westmacott's statue displays a grand, classical repose. Westmacott's king does not carry a marshal's baton. He is not a warrior king, like William, but a wise ruler. He stretches out his arm in a relaxed salute to his people, a people who didn't give much of a damn, for Mad King George had died in 1820.

A stone pond beside Paddy's wigwam, at the Metropolitan Cathedral of Christ the King

Site-specific art is, as one would expect, art designed for a particular place. When Richard Serra had a 72 ton curved spar of steel around 7 feet high and 120 feet long and laid diagonally across Federal Plaza in New York, commuters went to court to have it removed. Serra argued before the judge that it was site-specific because it was nuanced with all sorts of apparently anti-establishment political sub-texts, but the court ruled in effect that it was anti-commuter and men came by night to remove it.

Susanna Heron's *Still Point* is site-specific less speciously than Serra's piece was because, though it would look good anywhere, its full visual meaning is in the context of the Catholic cathedral of Liverpool. The architect, Frederick Gibberd, designed a church according to the new liturgical demand that the altar should be visible to the whole congregation. So the cathedral is circular, rising tent-like, inviting its Scouse nickname, Paddy's wigwam. The high altar is in the centre of the cathedral within a circular sanctuary. *Still Point*, Heron's ground-hugging sculpture, is the same diameter as the sanctuary, a circular platform of hammered grey Indian granite and black Indian granite honed smooth, just under 20 yards across and arranged as a wide slightly irregular central disc of grey surrounded by a circle of black, and an outer circle of grey. For the viewer looking down from the wide steps into the cathedral and catching sight of the sculpture at the bottom of the garden the black granite, especially in the rain, looks like a still water channel.

Heron was an innovative jeweller who switched to sculpture and her experience of jewellery and sculpture come together in the lucid harmony and simplicity of *Still Place*, like a pond at the bottom of the little garden beside the cathedral.

This former gin palace, now dignified as the Philharmonic Dining Rooms, is still one of the best pubs in Liverpool.

The Philharmonic Dining Rooms, Hope Street

It is written in the book of John Lennon that the price of fame is not being able to have a pint at the Phil. There are plenty of other good boozers in Liverpool, but this is by general consent the best. It's probably the best in England, among city pubs at least. The posh name for this former gin palace comes of an ambition to be associated with the institution opposite, the Philharmonic Hall, which burned down in 1933, was rebuilt and, like the dining rooms, survived the bombing but, though smoother, is nothing like as grand.

Walter W. Thomas, an architect employed by the Liverpool brewer Robert Cain, built the Phil in 1898–1900, so almost by default it is flamboyant art nouveau with its gables, one stepped, one languorously curved, its oriel windows, copper domes and curving, balustraded balcony above exotic gates of iron and beaten copper. There is loads of beaten copper inside as well, and crystal chandeliers and coloured glass skylights. The central bar is rich with mahogany and inlaid with ornate green, crimson and gold patterns repeated in the floor. Even the men's lavatories are so posh they do tours of them, for women as well.

Manchester and Salford

The *Manchester Guardian*, founded in the wake of the Peterloo massacre of 1819; Owens College, which grew into the first redbrick university in England and is still one of the best; Market Street, transformed from a filthy lane into a great shopping area; Piccadilly Gardens; Mosley Street; Waterhouse's Town Hall and its city history murals by Ford Madox Brown (see below); the Hallé Orchestra and the Free Trade Hall where it performed (now a hotel); the fantasy of the Barton Arcade (see below); the City Art Gallery built by the young Charles Barry and the Whitworth Art Gallery, as the original institute became when the university took it over: these were among the great middle-class contributions to the explosive growth of 18th- and 19th-century Manchester. There were the churches too, among them St Mary, Mulberry Street, a Catholic church for the city's Irish population (see below). The other face of the city was the stinking congeries, graphically described by a mid-19th-century observer:

foul courts, lanes, and back alleys, reeking of coal smoke, and especially dingy from the originally bright red brick, turned black with time, which is here the universal building material … nothing but narrow, filthy nooks and alleys … Everywhere heaps of debris, refuse and offal; standing pools for gutters, and a stench which alone would make it impossible for a human being in any degree civilised to live in such a district.

Thus Friedrich Engels, working in the offices off Deansgate of his father's cotton factory, gracing soirées in the mansions of the business class and riding with the Cheshire Hunt, but also secretly prowling among the working men's hovels, noting it all down as vividly as Mrs Gaskell, and gradually building up a head of steam that would be released in his collaboration with Karl Marx.

With admiration, Engels mentions the Barton aqueduct on the Bridgewater Canal as one of the heights of civilised accomplishment, and if this canal (1765) brought the first great surge of prosperity to the area, the Manchester Ship Canal (1894) funded the surge in public amenities, the hospitals, theatres and one of the first cinemas (the former Picture House of 1911 on Oxford Street, its name carved in art nouveau characters), the libraries and slum clearance. In the 1970s public authority vandalism ruined or destroyed many fine buildings and ripped the heart out of the city to build the abysmal Arndale Centre, which the IRA blew up in 1996. Overlapping the IRA's fit of architectural criticism came new law courts, new night clubs, a new and burgeoning music industry and high prosperity with, in this former 'city of dreadful night', a boom in centrally located loft conversions as habitations for the new youthful rich. The revivalist tram network, Manchester Metro, arrived too, linking far-flung areas to the centre, not least the newly flourishing Salford Quays, the basin for large ships at the Manchester end of the ship canal, home now to Manchester United's Old Trafford stadium, the northern Imperial War Museum and the cultural centre at the end of pier 22 by Michael Wilford & Partners, known as the Lowry: it's anyone's guess what L.S. Lowry would have made of all this shiny steel glitz, but he certainly has a starrier showing here than in the more authentic grottiness of the old brick and terracotta Salford Art Gallery above one of his favourite subjects, Peel Park.

Samuel Palmer, an English visionary in Manchester City Art Gallery

In the last decade of the 20th century Michael Hopkins & Partners, high-tech authors of the Mound Stand at Lords cricket ground, linked two separate 19th-century classical buildings by Charles Barry, Manchester city art gallery and the Athenaeum. It has proved popular with the public but controversial for what it lost as a home for, in the words of the guidebook, 'our world-famous collection of Pre-Raphaelite paintings'. Among the rest and best of the 19th-century collection (there's a good 20th-century collection too) are a wonderful, small Constable cornfield, a knockout David Cox oil of Rhyl beach and *The Bright Cloud* by the visionary Samuel Palmer (1805–81).

As it happens, when his own art had stultified in old age Palmer grew to admire the Pre-Raphaelites, but what he had lost they lacked entirely: in a phrase, the poetry of Palmer. W.B. Yeats encapsulated this quality in a couple of lines of his own poetry as:

The lonely light that Samuel Palmer engraved,
An image of mysterious wisdom won by toil.

Truly mysterious, for in the years of recession after 1815 the Kent countryside was alive with rick-burning and machine-breaking, but Palmer's sainted peasants are as ignorant of this as he was. He painted *The Bright Cloud* in the last year or two of his magical period, 1827–35, when he was living in the Darent valley at Shoreham. Palmer called this secret fold in the land through which the River Darenth flows to the Thames at Dartford, his valley of vision. He lived there from 1825 or 1826 until about 1835, and its remoteness spoke to him deeply.

Palmer was a Londoner, and his dreams were the dreams of every commuter who ever moved out among the apple orchards and hop gardens. When he stepped out of doors from his house by the river in Shoreham, instead of disaffected workmen he saw a paradise on earth, a valley of deep plenty, and he made it manifest in his paintings, in scenes of orchards laden with golden fruit, cornfields of dream-like abundance and country folk who drift through the fields like ghosts.

His friendliest environment was a moonlit valley. The moon appears sometimes like a blazing comet, sometimes sitting in the branches of a tree like a friendly owl. *The Bright Cloud* is set in the evening, as the sun sinks behind a hill, throwing light on to one side of an enormous cloud and clothing the hills in deepening red shadow and the deep fissures of the valley in dark blue and green. A rider on a donkey leads three other figures dressed like no real agricultural labourer since biblical times along a track with a herd of cattle following. Palmer built up the depth of colour and warm texture with a combination of oils and the water-based medium tempera painted on to mahogany. It is one of his most accomplished works, and with the poignancy of being one of the last before the rick burning invaded his parish paradise within sight of his own house.

In 1832 he had bought a house in north London and begun slowly to withdraw from Kent. Already it is clear that the drawings for *The Bright Cloud* carry a stronger charge than the painting itself. By 1835 he had moved to London and was contemplating marriage (which was not a success). Domesticity and daylight dumbed his art down.

Ford Madox Brown's history murals cycle, Town Hall

Alfred Waterhouse's Gothic town hall in Manchester was completed in 1877. In the same year Ford Madox Brown (1821–93) began painting his first and last major public commission, the scheme of twelve murals on the history of Manchester to decorate the great hall, baronial in concept, each painting measuring 10 feet 6 inches wide by 4 feet 9 inches. He completed the last painting in 1892, six months before his death. It might be argued that episodes like *The Expulsion of the Danes in AD 910* need some imaginative licence to pin to Manchester, but it was obviously more politically acceptable to the city's elders than Brown's vetoed suggestion of the massacre of Peterloo in 1819, when cavalry were brought to bear on a crowd demonstrating for parliamentary reform. Peterloo happened quite near this spot. Now health and safety have moved in, and you can't get into the hall with the murals even if someone's only pushing a Hoover around. Phone first.

Brown, in fact, was politically radical though artistically conservative, whatever the growing band of revisionists say about the Pre-Raphaelites. He was older than his Pre-Raphaelite friends, and although he never joined their brotherhood he agreed with their espousal of utter fidelity to observable fact and even anticipated the French Impressionists, if only by painting out of doors. It's a pity about the title of his best-known painting of this period, *The Pretty Little Baa Lambs*, which is actually a portrait of his wife Emma and their daughter with sheep imported daily to model for him on Clapham Common.

Perhaps because he was older than Rossetti and Burne-Jones, perhaps because he had trained in Antwerp instead of the Royal Academy Schools, Brown was never drawn into the sentimental anecdotage of so much Victorian painting for the polite drawing room, and in the town hall series he treated his characters as brothers under the skin, so the 17th-century children in Chetham's School are kin to the kids accompanying Brown's older contemporary John Dalton in his quest for marsh gas, fishing for it with stick and jamjar in the local pond. And in the scene of the opening day of the Bridgewater Canal in 1761, a seminal event in the Industrial Revolution and the prosperity of Manchester, the woman handling a coal barge would have recognised across a century the tousled proletarian woman with a babe in arms in Brown's work as a sister.

The most successful of the sequence is the

final scene of John Dalton, exactly because it was near enough contemporary for Brown to understand it instinctively. It touched his own circumstances too. Emma was the illiterate daughter of a bricklayer, and Brown taught her to read and write and dream of a burgeoning family instead of his single surviving child. In imagination, the happy family on Dalton's expedition (not Dalton's own; he was unmarried) is the one Brown wished for himself. So this scene of scientific research becomes a rural idyll, scientist and older boy in collusion clearing a space in the pond's algae to explore, one of the smaller children on the bank with his own stick and jar. Dalton kneels in front of a crab apple bush, or perhaps a may rose, and a path swings round behind a stunted willow in a slower rhythm than the curve of the pond. A background cow peers dolefully over a fence. In everything except the dry handling and the Kate Greenaway children, this is closer to Constable than to Pre-Raphaelitism, but it suggests the future in its almost Expressionist foreshortening and the understated sweeping curves of the composition that in a few years, fully blown, would become art nouveau.

A modern stations of the cross in Manchester's 'hidden gem', Church of St Mary, Mulberry Street

St Mary, the hidden gem, as Manchester knows it in parentheses, is actually paste, a sham, a small Roman Catholic church tucked away in an alley opposite the town hall. It's made to seem even smaller by a dominating array of large, feeble religious statues in niches at the east of the basilica. It is hidden indeed among bars and boutiques, sandwich takeaways and quick food outlets, but it is a refuge in a time of need for hundreds of Catholics who crowd in daily.

In 1994 Father Denis Clinch had the notion of commissioning Norman Adams to paint the fourteen Stations of the Cross for the walls inside the mock Italian arcade with its columns painted to look like marble. It was an inspired idea – at any rate, so said Sister Wendy Beckett, the consecrated virgin and art-fancying nun who drew up the shortlist for Father Clinch on which Adams was one of the names.

Adams (1927–2005) was head of painting at Manchester College of Art in the 1960s, when I also worked in the city. 'All art is religious,' he told me one day, not brooking an argument. I looked at the work of some of his brilliant staff (these were high days in art colleges) and thought, well, if you stretch a point. There was no stretching a point for Adams; his own work was religious, even when he was doing a five-finger exercise with watercolour in front of a landscape. The commission for St Mary was clearly some kind of culmination for Adams, a huge creative enterprise that he completed in time for it to be installed in November 1995.

Once Adams had decided to narrate the story in cinematic close-ups of Christ's head, the big decisions had, of course, already been taken for him by Gauguin, by Picasso, by Epstein: the use of 'primitive' forms from alien cultures or distant times, African masks, Iberian carvings, Aztec ritual sculpture. Adams's invention was to add to the crude mask of Christ's pain in the first canvas, *Ecce Homo*, indigo flowers for eyes and blood for tears, to extend the line of his eyes and the bridge of his nose into a cross piercing his head, not the heavy cross that would be Christ's next burden but something like the palm crosses priests distribute to children on Palm Sunday. After *Ecce Homo* some of the paintings break up into almost abstract expressions of agony, the crown of thorns like shards of metal, the head laid horizontally across the canvas. When Veronica wipes the sweat from Christ's face she holds the cloth before her body and the impression of his large round eyes fall just where her breasts would otherwise be, a visual merging of suffering and sympathy, and her flowers/eyes weep petals that turn to drops of blood. At the Deposition flowers cluster in an arc above his head, and finally at the entombment the lurid, furnace colours of the sequence turn at last to a kind of paradise garden, a Resurrection already taking place. All this is quite unlike any other art, the only modern English religious painting I have seen that doesn't seem to be going by rote through formulaic motions.

Barton Swing aqueduct, Stretford

'From this foul drain the greatest stream of human industry flows out to fertilize the world,' wrote the French observer Alexis de Tocqueville on his English and Irish travels in 1833. He could have meant the Irwell, but the foul drain was a metaphor for Manchester itself, and the man who claims first prize for setting this all in motion is the 3rd Duke of Bridgewater, who opened the Bridgewater Canal in 1761 to carry the coal from his Worsley estate to Castlefield basin in the Manchester city centre, which cut the price of coal in Manchester by three-quarters within a year. Later he extended the canal to the Mersey at Runcorn. His engineer was James Brindley, and his greatest fame rested upon his famous, beautiful but undoubtedly old-fashioned aqueduct to carry the canal across the river at Barton-upon-Irwell.

By 1882 the canal wasn't big enough, and, aristocratic wealth having been overtaken by corporate capitalism, a group of businessmen planned the Manchester Ship Canal, which usurped the Irwell and rendered the aqueduct obsolete because what was now needed was a new crossing that could be moved out of the way when big ships came through. The engineer this time was Edward Leader Williams. The ship canal itself was

reckoned to be an achievement of the order of flights to the moon today, and the Barton aqueduct, which swept away Brindley's, was a wonder in its own right. It's a swing bridge with its axis on an island in the ship canal, which when it is closed allows Bridgewater Canal boats to pass over the Manchester Ship Canal and ship canal boats to pass under the bridge simultaneously. When a major cargo ship on the ship canal needs to go through, gates at either side of the bridge close to contain the water and barges in the Bridgewater Canal like fish in a tank, and the aqueduct, still full of water, pivots through 90 degrees to align itself lengthways to the canal. The control tower on the island, four storeys high and a bit like a prison watchtower, simultaneously operates the road swing bridge that carries the B5521 across the ship canal a little to the west. The beauty of this wrought iron aqueduct is purely functional, a problem elegantly dealt with and producing a result that remains thrilling to watch in operation, even if the craft passing above the ship canal today are only pleasure boats.

The Packet House, Worsley, Greater Manchester

Worsley village, with its green and big trees and the timber-framed Packet House on the Bridgewater Canal, is a picture postcard of suburban bliss in a village caught up in the outer suburbs of Manchester. A big golf course on the far side of the M60 completes the setting. Ironbridge it isn't, yet historically it is even more fundamental. If the beginning of the Industrial Revolution could be assigned to any one place, this is it. The two archways on the canal just beyond this point at Worsley Delph are where the boats disappeared underground and into a 40 mile network of canals in the Duke of Bridgewater's coal mines. Boats fetching coal were raised and lowered on an incline by a

L.S. Lowry's mother died in this faded, tidy room in 1939 and the artist painted it soon afterwards. The picture now hangs in The Lowry, Salford Quays, and is a meticulous examination that makes loneliness palpable

pulley system. The operation transformed the business and brought the duke riches beyond compare. He extended the canal as far as Runcorn and mapped out the future a century hence when the Manchester Ship Canal would make Manchester, 40 miles inland, Britain's third busiest port.

The buildings that serviced the Worsley canal basin survive: the nailmaker's house, the granary, the boatyard and dry docks, the iron footbridge, the duke's wharf, the sluice gates. Most are put to other uses, most of them listed, along with a telephone box of a later vintage. The green was a huge industrial yard, principally for boatbuilding. The oldest looking part of the Packet House, the very attractive black and white magpie timbering with an overhanging first floor that looks so medieval, is actually the newest, put up in 1850 at the end of a group of brick buildings of the mid-18th century. After the canal

began operations in 1761 packet-boats moored at the jetty below the wide flight of stone steps from the house, where passengers bought day-return tickets for the trip to Manchester. It is a very pretty scene, and the ducks will be even happier when the work going ahead to stop old iron ore workings from discolouring the canal water are complete.

A house where Lowry's mother isn't at home, The Lowry, Salford Quays

The stickmen are what we know best, the red-eyed unemployables, the industrial chimneys and the workers, like ants, off to the factory or the football match. It's easy to love this work or, for southerners, to patronise it. But look at this painting, *The Bedroom, Pendlebury* by L.S. Lowry (1887–1976). It is 1940, and the bedroom is where

his mother died the previous year. There's a big iron bed with a white bedcover and a dingy olive green and prussian blue quilt, a cylinder heater, a locker, a chair, a stool, the door with white handle and fingerplates, some pictures on the wall – by Mrs Lowry's son? Impossible to tell. Anyway, that's the inventory. There's nobody in, only the artist outside the picture looking in, painting. The painting is loneliness made palpable, but without self-pity, just a meticulous examination of the room. Faded, but neat and tidy. Put your nose as close to the picture as the attendant will allow: the texture of the dun-coloured wallpaper is actually the close weave of the thinly painted canvas. It pulls the room together; a masterly touch, a kind of alternative version of the bits of actual wallpaper Braque would stick on to his Cubist canvases to jostle against the illusionist painting. It is similar, as well, to the way Constable deployed the grain of the wood he used as occasional surfaces for oil sketches to accentuate the movement of clouds and treetops on a windy day. Who says Lowry was naive?

His friend, the artist Harold Riley, told me once that Lowry used to paint his canvases white – not just prime them, but paint them – then leave them stacked against the wall for months to dry, then use that milky white as ambient atmosphere in his factoryscapes or as barely distinguishable ocean and sky in one of those empty seascapes. That explains why Lowry's north looks as though it will always exist in a drizzly industrial haze. He wasn't trapped in a mannerism though. Near the bedroom painting is another mildly untypical piece, because all the scurrying folk are at the seaside, and the edges of the figures are slightly eaten away by the white haze as

though everybody is running through a slight sea fret, and their colours, instead of being unarguable blacks and primary yellows and reds, are sun-washed pinks and beiges – and there are frisky dogs getting into the spirit of things and trying to vanish too. Lowry knew his stuff; and he was a one-off.

Barton Arcade

The Barton Arcade, tucked between Deansgate and St Ann's Square, is Manchester's little piece of Milan, though its model, Giuseppe Mengoni's grand Galleria Vittorio Emanuele designed ten years earlier, in 1861, is really a grand baroque stone-arcaded street beneath a glass tunnel roof, whereas the Barton Arcade's glass and iron is gossamer. Architects called Corbett, Raby & Sawyer take the credit, though the splendid scrolly ironwork was off the peg, straight out of the pattern books of the Saracen iron foundry of Macfarlanes in Glasgow, which specialised in an eclectic range from bandstands to urinals. The arcade looked good even when it was a backwater of deteriorating gentility in the 1960s. Spruced up today it is practically new minted. From either Deansgate or St Ann's Square it appears quite unannounced, but from the square the splendid approach is towards a wide entrance beneath rows of tall window lights held in a slender iron grid in four sections, one above another, of alternating columns and arches. Inside, the galleries of shops rise in three tiers to the glass roof with its climax of two large octagonal domes.

An unforced abstract by John McLean, Whitworth Art Gallery

When the Whitworth acquired John McLean's acrylic abstract *Sweet Briar* in 2003 nobody much paid attention. The Whitworth had already built up a representative

Gossamer-like domes above scrolly ironwork from Glasgow in this creation of the 1870s, the Barton Arcade in Manchester

selection of British abstract painting in the 1960s, mostly by St Ives artists like Ben Nicholson (1894–1982), Patrick Heron (1920–99, Roger Hilton (1911–75) and Peter Lanyon (1918–64). McLean is a Scot, born in Liverpool in 1939 but brought up in Scotland, and by the time he had matured, the circus had moved on. Artists behaving badly or making a lot of loot or being bought by the millionaire advertising man Charles Saatchi made better copy for a press bored with the general acceptance of abstraction. Meanwhile, at least one of the best colour abstractionists of the McLean generation was struggling to afford the basics of pigments and a surface to paint on. And then, by the time *Sweet Briar* arrived in Manchester the Whitworth had gone back to its own roots. As a university adjunct it began to focus on educational displays of the original core collection of textiles – displays that can't just be enjoyed for their own sake: you have to tap at interactive computers to get much out of them.

Manchester University took over the Whitworth Institute as late as 1958, renamed it the Whitworth Art Gallery, and installed its professor of art history, the eminent and energetic John White, as director. It was he who added to the Whitworth's existing collections of textiles and watercolours – especially strong in Turner – the collection of British modern art with a sideline in international surrealism. He initiated the transformation that continued beyond his directorship of the Whitworth's sombre chambers into gleaming white spaces, a mezzanine floor, lecture hall and a glass curtain wall looking out on the park.

But Joseph Whitworth had founded the collection on a different basis. His was the classic story of a poor boy who moved from rags to riches in the 19th century as he became a celebrated engineer rewarded with a baronetcy for his skill in making artillery a more efficient killing machine by its ability to penetrate 4 inch armour plate. He died full of years and honour in 1887, and a portion of his bequest went to fulfilling the happy notion of setting up the Whitworth Institute devoted to the peaceful arts. The money built a grandiose Victorian gallery and set it in an expansive park on what had been a piece of wasteland called Potters' Field. That is the heritage that the Whitworth is now re-emphasising.

So let us blow a trumpet for the late-flowering *Sweet Briar*. It is a painting of 1980 from an artist who found colour abstraction a given, no longer a gladiatorial arena as it had been until the end of the 1950s, with eminent critics declaring that abstraction was an alien art with no validity in England. McLean doesn't seem to do much with the colour, he just brushes on thinned-out acrylic in broad, atmospheric strokes ranging from a dark, carbonated brown, a couple of streaks of reddish brown and a beige almost as pale as the raw canvas, to mauve, blue and a blue-tinged green that was a particular Matisse favourite. Some of the colours run as though they had been applied with a soaked sponge, some applied unmixed, some with a touch of white added. That's it. Is colour then enough? Evidently. The reference to Matisse is relevant only in the sense that *Sweet Briar* is a lineal descendant of Fauvism (which had introduced strong colours for their own sake, not for their description of appearances) but English, or Scottish even, because colour looks mistier in our island light, and abstract, because it became obvious in the 1950s and 1960s that colour abstraction without any reference to any natural phenomenon except light was a logical extension of the vocabulary. In its intimate scale, its amplitude and completeness, *Sweet Briar* looks more up to the minute than almost any of the work of the new young darlings of fame.

Nantwich

CHESHIRE

Wood carvings in the chancel, Church of St Mary

According to the Domesday commissioners with their keen interest in how the pre-Conquest taxation system worked, Nantwich was the centre of the salt industry when Edward the Confessor ruled. It had a brine pit for making salt and eight salt-pans. Anyone here or in Middlewich who so overloaded his cart that either the axle or the horse's back broke had to pay a fine of two shillings. This was serious stuff, so serious that in a very long entry covering every way the king and Earl Edwin, whose lease it was, could skim off the top, there is no mention of a church.

Since the earliest and major part of St Mary is 14th-century building, maybe there wasn't one earlier. Perhaps the salt-workers went to the neighbouring village of Acton, where there were two priests. But while the Nantwich salt industry declined and died in the 19th century, leaving Middlewich and Northwich to take care of salt panning while Nantwich adapted itself to being a pleasant market town, the cruciform church remains on a hill in the centre behind a green park, dominating the town and surrounding country with its noble octagonal tower of mild red sandstone. The tower is over the crossing, and the spectacular part of the church is to the east of that, the chancel, filled with wonderful carving from the scatological to the angelic, stone corbels supporting arches, bosses recounting the story of Christ and his mother in the stone ceiling, robustly rural misericords and 14 foot high choir stalls carved into tall canopies with floriate and crocketed pinnacles and little unfurling vaults supporting nothing but tiny bowls for angels to peer out from like spectators at a procession.

Many churches have amusing misericords, but there are few where high art rubs along with folk art quite so amicably. The rude carvers were given licence to decorate underneath the stall seats on the basis that monks' behinds would be capacious enough to reveal only a suggestion of carved surfaces to the monks opposite, and if they had seen more, monks were worldly wise and incorruptible. So here the misericords vary from crude craftsmanship to highly skilled. There is a down-at-beak duck with a man's face peering out from her backside, presumably the parson's nose. There is a fox carrying a longbow with a quiver of arrows over its shoulder, and facing it another poaching fox carrying a plump dead bird, maybe a pheasant, in one hand and the other holding a staff on its shoulder with a couple of rabbits strung from it. There's a mermaid, a woman beating a man with a ladle, and a couple of wrestlers grappling for a fall, the sort of stuff Shakespeare saw and put into *As You Like It*, countryside stuff all of it, myth and sport and everyday verities that Langland and Chaucer knew too and wrote about but that finds expression in visual art only under the posteriors of worshipers.

Port Sunlight

MERSEYSIDE

The king of rose painters at the Lady Lever Art Gallery

Lord Lever of Sunlight Soap (Viscount Leverhulme, to give him his proper title) founded Port Sunlight in 1889 for the workers at his adjacent factory on the Wirral peninsula, south of the Mersey off the road to Birkenhead. It's an idealistic village with lots of green, Flemish-gabled houses and terraces of tudorbethan cottages, a big mock-Tudor pub that opened as a temperance hotel but acquired a licence when the villagers let it be known that they fancied the occasional pint, and in the centre of all this the domed Lady Lever Art Gallery with a grand Ionic portico designed by William Owen, now in the care of the National Museums and Galleries on Merseyside. There are portraits by Reynolds, Gainsborough and Hoppner, there's a late Constable, a Turner and some Turner drawings, but overwhelmingly this is the home of Lord Leighton and Millais, Burne-Jones and Rossetti, paintings of history and myth, of chivalry and imagination – and William Holman Hunt's famous and absurdly literal painting *The Scapegoat*, actually painted in Palestine and showing an actual goat actually dying in colours that suggest Holman Hunt had an actual touch of sunstroke.

Among these popular 19th-century favourites is the still small voice of a little flowerpiece by Henri Fantin-Latour (1836–1904), *Roses in a Vase*. Fantin-Latour was a friend of Manet, Degas, Courbet, Whistler and some of the Impressionists, but as a student he spent more time in the Louvre perfecting his technique by copying old masters (and selling the copies) than in the *plein air* of his friends – the Impressionist Pissarro, indeed, advocated burning the Louvre down. In 1870, when the Impressionists were not yet exhibiting as a group, Fantin-Latour immortalised them with a group portrait called *A Studio in the Batignolles Quarter*, which effectively is a homage to Manet, shown painting at an easel surrounded by writers and artists, including Zola, Renoir and the brilliant young Montpellier painter Fréderic Bazille (who in the same year was killed fighting in the Franco-Prussian war).

Like the Impressionists at this time of schism between the admirers of the neoclassicist Ingres and the romantic Delacroix, Fantin-Latour was in the Delacroix camp, and despite the sobriety of his own work he did, in fact, model in colour rather than, like Ingres, draw and then fill in with colour. But he remained a loner, impressed by the gritty realism of the older artist, Courbet, and never tempted by the light palette and attack of the Impressionists. He was a fine portrait painter, but principally he painted flower pieces. When Whistler brought him on a visit to England he found a new and ready market for his work and returned frequently; it might be said that flower pieces became his bread and butter, except that the phrase implies staleness. He never did grow stale.

He painted the Port Sunlight roses in 1876. They are white and meaty, fully open or tightly budded, one of them edged by pink shadow, rising from thick stalks immersed in a glass vase, as central on the canvas as a painted icon, but intensely realistic, standing for nothing but themselves. The table is suggested by a dark area, a wall behind the roses by a thinly brushed pale green: the flowers dominate. Fantin-Latour's flowers show little of the sheer joy of execution that a tumble of flowers by Renoir possesses or a jug of Manet's magnificent peonies. Instead, they draw you in by the their exquisite perfection, the intense expression of Fantin-Latour's visual experience before these flowers. He never flagged in his portrayals: flower piece after flower piece, still life after still life, sometimes just of a simple household item like a coffee cup, painted with utter objectivity, existing in complete volume, totally believable.

Preston

LANCASHIRE

Devis's Preston manikins at the Harris Art Gallery

The Harris, as it is always known locally, was already on the drawing board in 1883 when a Preston millowner left his art collection to the town. The municipality responded by expanding the original concept. It is one of the grandest buildings in the north, with a line in grand municipal buildings and, not surprisingly, has the biggest collection of its native artist, Arthur Devis (1712–87). Devis is not a name on everyone's lips, even though on his travels he left portraits all over the country, from Oxfordshire and Suffolk to Uppark in Sussex and Pencarrow in Cornwall (see Southwest), where the house staff told me they love it more than their fine Reynolds portraits.

One of the new acquisitions is *The Du Cane Family Triptych*. Peter du Cane was a landowner, an investor in the markets and a director of the Bank of England and of the East India Company. Arthur Devis specialised in conversation pieces – that is, family groups standing around informally, though the last thing they do is converse with each other, any more than the Madonna and saints do in the *sacra conversazione* altarpieces of Italian Renaissance art. Devis and Du Cane were made for each other. Du Cane hired Devis in 1747 as people today who want something better than a family snapshot hire studio photographers. And the Du Cane family, like all the other families who commissioned Devis, posed as though for a long exposure – actually, they didn't pose. Devis presumably painted or made studies of the faces, but he drew the bodies from lay figures 2 feet 6 inches tall with costumes made to measure. Just as with the early portraits of Gainsborough, the sitters look like dolls

because they were dolls. The only Devis portrait I can think of where the sitter looks relatively natural is also in the Harris, and that is not a conversation piece but a portrait of his own wife, Elizabeth, leaning slightly on a table before her and even smiling with obvious familiarity. Du Cane originally wanted only the portrait of his children playing in a landscape in a red four-wheeled cart, the older boy pulling the two younger children. He and his wife must have been impressed, because a couple of years later they commissioned Devis to make separate portraits of the couple to hang, presumably, as we see them now, on either side of the landscape-shaped painting of the children.

Towards the end of his life Devis fell out of fashion and was swiftly forgotten until a revival of his fortunes in the 1930s, when historians discovered that he illustrated perfectly the aspirations and manners of the rising 18th-century middle class, people precisely like the Du Canes.

Southport

MERSEYSIDE

Gerald Kelly, fuddy-duddy with a forgotten talent, Atkinson Art Gallery

I went down to the front to see the sea, and it wasn't there. It never is in Southport. Across the bay, beyond St Anne's, there's Blackpool Tower, in the lit-up town where the sea is always in. Apart from donkey rides on the endless sands, Southport's counter-attraction is Lord Street, one of the handsomest high streets in England, newly reburnished and looking much as it did when Fortunino Matania, who had come from Italy as a star illustrator for the magazine *Sphere*, used it as the backdrop for an oil in 1936, designed to serve as a printed poster for Southport corporation and the London, Midland & Scottish Railway. 'Come to Southport in the

Winter,' it says, and it shows Lord Street in the rain at night with top-hatted, long-gowned and fur-stoled glitterati spilling on to the pavement under a well-lit canopy outside an art deco theatre, where an alert and smiling chauffeur waits for his employers beside a Rolls-Royce. It is a world innocent of war, hunger marches, economic decline or yobbery. The painting sparkles with the detail of night life, and it hangs now as a welcome to the gallery stairwell: period commercial art with attitude.

The Southport he invented was just the place for a painting by Gerald Kelly (1879–1972), portrait painter to the establishment, president of the unreformed Royal Academy, bluff, eccentric and by definition a fuddy-duddy. As a matter of fact, *Spanish Girl* shows that he had an unflashy, thoroughly well-grounded gift for painting technically consummate portraits. Being guided like most people by prejudice, I've never really looked at his portraits of the rich and powerful, but this Spanish girl, turning her head against the direction of her body, is based on a triangle like Whistler's famous portrait of his mother, more fully embodied by Kelly and less dreamily atmospheric than Whistler. Though he lived to be our contemporary, Sir Gerald had been a young Irishman about Paris when the great Impressionists and Post-Impressionists were still going strong, and he had met many of them, including Whistler's master, Degas. I suppose the vital missing sparks in Kelly are creative imagination and the gutsy pleasure in shoving pigment around the canvas. But take a look at this lovely painting: it's a corrective to casual prejudice.

Tatton Park
CHESHIRE

Chardin, out of the kitchen

Not as much fun as Blackpool, not as big as Chatsworth, Tatton Park is close enough to Manchester to pull in the crowds. In fact, the Earls of Egerton, who lived here, could travel to Manchester without leaving their own land, bought and cultivated around an early 19th-century mansion by James Wyatt on the fortune made from industrial Trafford Park and the Manchester and Salford docks.

Painters are always opening doors and windows for the flood of light in an interior, and for the further prospect into another room or a glimpse of the world outside. From Vermeer to Matisse they do it. Jean-Baptiste-Siméon Chardin (1699–1779) did it too once he had lifted his eyes from the copper pot and eggs on the table or the dead rabbit with a game bag and powder flask and turned to human subjects. Behind the young boy being gently scolded by his governess for getting his tricorn hat dirty is a door half-open into the next room, where the wall covering, a subtle blue, echoes the colour of the woman's blue dress beneath her enveloping white apron and crucially floods the brown walls and parquet floor with daylight.

'One stops in front of a Chardin as if by instinct,' wrote Chardin's contemporary Denis Diderot, 'just as a traveller exhausted by his trip tends to sit down, almost without noticing it, in a place that's green, quiet, well watered, shady, and cool.' That's precisely how I came to be looking at this small painting after I glimpsed it in an ante-room to the saloon, and that, the attendant told me, is a common reaction to this picture. It must be something to do with the stillness of the painting and its absolute fidelity to the eternal in the everyday. Diderot saw in

The 18th-century French critic Denis Diderot wrote, 'One stops in front of a Chardin as if by instinct', and visitors to Tatton Park prove it by homing in from the saloon to the little anteroom to savour Chardin's The Governess

Chardin a forerunner of a return to classicism, which was to arrive with Jacques-Louis David. With Chardin, it is the classicism of the humble. Low-keyed, slightly enigmatic among the paraphernalia of domestic life, the workbox, the clothes brush,

the shuttlecock, the boy in his neat frock coat and stockings, eyes cast down in mild shame, this Chardin has more in common with one of Vermeer's timeless domestic interiors than with the revolutionary Paris of David.

The sculptor Thomas Woolner has been almost forgotten except as the model for Ford Madox Brown's painting The Last of England, *but Wigton market square harbours a fountain mounted with his bronze reliefs of the* Four Mercies: *this one,* Teaching the Ignorant, *is typical of the quartet's beautifully restrained neo-classicism*

Wigton

CUMBRIA

Bronze reliefs on a town fountain, marketplace

Wigton is a small town inland from the Solway Firth that is famous for one export, the novelist Melvyn Bragg. Its small triangular marketplace has a dispiritingly elaborate Victorian fountain in marble the colour of boiled pressed pig's head (once a northern delicacy) and I would frankly not

have looked at it twice had I not been carrying Pevsner around as my gazetteer. But on the sides of the fountain are bronze reliefs by Thomas Woolner (1825–92). Woolner's fame today rests more on his role as the inspiration for Ford Madox Brown's best painting, *The Last of England*, than for any work of his own, but he was one of the original Pre-Raphaelite Brotherhood. His PRB dedication to truth and passionate expression buttered no parsnips in London, so he decided to take his wife and try his luck as a gold prospector in Australia. *The Last of*

England shows a couple huddled together in a boat on choppy waters off the white cliffs of Dover. Brown must have been on to something with the choppy waters metaphor: before long the Woolners were back without gold, and Thomas was trying his luck again as a sculptor.

By this time the Pre-Raphaelites were successful, and soon Woolner was busy with portrait busts and church monuments. His patron at Wigton, George Moore, was lord lieutenant of Cumbria and a local benefactor who set up the fountain as a memorial to his wife, a curious intrusion of private mourning into public life to which the new rich are prone (Moore had grown up from childhood poverty). Woolner's subject was four acts of mercy; again, not cheery, but despite a leavening of Pre-Raphaelite solemnity, the figures are a neoclassical carry-over from the beginning of the century and very finely wrought. The panels show one or two women of classical mien (that is, Greek profiles and flowing robes) in each episode, succouring the starving, teaching the ignorant, comforting the bereaved and clothing the naked (who avert their faces for very shame). The noblest of the panels is on the south face, showing a woman like a Sistine Chapel sibyl holding a tome like the tablets of Moses on her knee and pointing to it gently as two boys with a discarded hoop listen raptly, their mother with a babe in arms stands beside them, and three little girls hover respectfully in the background, presumably apprentice muses in no need of education.

Windermere
CUMBRIA

Arts and Crafts at Blackwell House

Mackay Hugh Baillie Scott (1865–1945) had scarcely finished building his Arts and Crafts holiday retreat, Blackwell House, in 1900 on the brow of a hill in private grounds sloping down to a boathouse on Windermere, than the movement slipped into decline in the face of indifference from the public and opposition to its unconventionality from the architectural establishment. It then took root in Germany following the publication in 1904 of a glowing assessment of Blackwell and Arts and Crafts in general in the influential magnum opus of Hermann Muthesius, *Das Englische Haus*. In it he wrote these two telling sentences: 'Baillie Scott's concept of the house is already that of an organic whole to be designed consistently inside and out. Architect and interior designer merge, so that one is unthinkable without the other.'

Baillie Scott designed Blackwell House for Sir Edward Holt, a brewer and former lord mayor of Manchester. It has tall gables, steeply pitched roofs and small windows – designed for the weather and to fit in with the vernacular architecture of the region. The innovations are inside. The big central hall, two storeys high with a rich and elegant peacock frieze around the walls and a mock minstrel's gallery, has an ample corridor that yields a tantalising glimpse of the white drawing room, so that the eye is drawn first to its oriel window and then the view beyond: Windermere and the Coniston Fells. It's almost a prototype for open-plan design. The Holts filled it with Victorian furniture and ornaments. The Lakeland Trust has reopened it with Arts and Crafts pieces: an oak bed by Peter de Waal, a washstand by Ernest Gimson, chairs and tables by the famous and fashionable Simpsons of Kendal. But all the Trust had to do with the white drawing room was to commission a reproduction rug of the period in palest greens, blues and faded red. This room is a dream of how a house should be. The oriel looks west. Facing south for the sun is a big bay window, then a kind of arrow slit and a

The saloon of Blackwell, the Arts and Crafts architect M.H. Baillie Scott's house above Windermere: a dream of how a house should be

small window in the fireplace recess filled, like many other subsidiary windows, with ornamental art nouveau stained glass. The fireplace itself is a raw stone arch with an open grate against a backing of bright blue tiles, all in a room of chaste white panelling. Two tall, sapling-like firedogs terminate in sprays of leaves, half a dozen white daisy-like flowers and red berries, picking up a similar motif in the corbels of the poles supporting the wide mantelshelf that runs around the room. There's a small recessed bookcase and an illuminated shelf with a display of plates enclosed in a grid above the fire. This is where visitors tend to pause, and sit, and read, and gaze. 'With Baillie Scott,' Muthesius also wrote, 'we are among the purely northern poets among British architects.'

Wrenbury

CHESHIRE

Shropshire Union Canal lifting bridge by Telford

The first phase of the Industrial Revolution, transport by canal, left a prettier footprint on the landscape of England than the later one, the railways, nowhere more so than just outside Wrenbury, where the unclassified minor road that runs through the little village crosses the Llangollen branch of the Shropshire Union Canal just outside the village over a lifting bridge devised by the young Thomas Telford (1757–1834). It is one of his earliest works, of about 1790, and looks very similar to the painting Van Gogh made almost a century later of the lifting bridge over a canal at Arles, but French canals are

The prettier footprint of the Industrial Revolution (in need of a lick of paint): a bridge over the Shropshire Union Canal at Wrenbury, one of the early works of the great engineer Thomas Telford

wider and Van Gogh's bridge was a double drawbridge. This is single, with a wooden platform hinged at one end so that it can be lifted by a system of counterweights attached by chains. Van Gogh's is pristine white; so would this be with a lick of paint. In the few minutes I was there the bridge carried a major truck crossing to the village followed by a 4×4 towing a caravan. Not surprisingly, the other two Telford bridges on this short Wrenbury stretch are in better nick, but they simply link towpaths. On one side of the road bridge, there's a large brick and tin storage building, now a centre for renting out longboats, and the canal itself is bright with a fleet of gaily painted craft roped together.

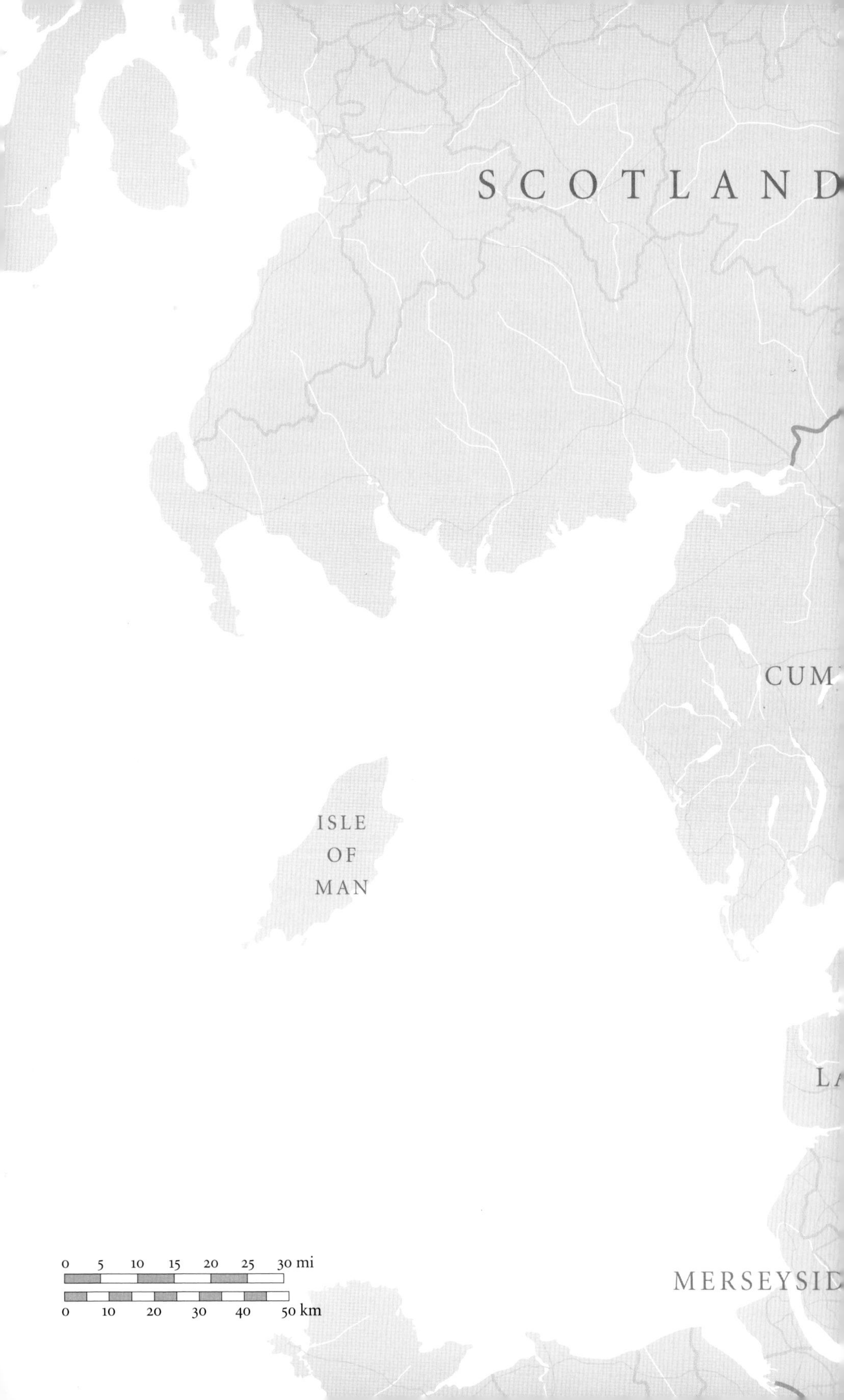
SCOTLAND
CUM
ISLE
OF
MAN
LA
MERSEYSID
0 5 10 15 20 25 30 mi
0 10 20 30 40 50 km

The Northeast

COUNTY DURHAM
NORTHUMBERLAND
TYNE & WEAR
YORKSHIRE

Berwick-upon-Tweed

Holy Island

Alnwick

Otterburn   Elsdon Tower

NORTHUMBERLAND

Wallington Hall

Newcastle   Jarrow
Chesters   upon Tyne   TYNE &
Corbridge   South Shields
Hexham   WEAR
Cherryburn   Gateshead   Sunderland
Consett   Penshaw

Ireshopeburn   COUNTY   Durham

Bishop Auckland   Hartlepool

DURHAM

Barnard Castle   Middlesborough
Egglestone Abbey   Darlington
Greta Bridge   Rokeby Park   Whitby
Richmond

NORTH YORKSHIRE

Ripon

Knaresborough   Bridlington

EAST

York   Nunburnholme
YORKSHIRE
Saltaire   Escrick   Beverley

ASHIRE   Welton   Hull
Bradford   Leeds

WEST YORKSHIRE   Patringtor
Wakefield   Nostell
Huddersfield
West Bretton

GREATER   SOUTH

MANCHESTER   YORKSHIRE

Sheffield   LINCOLNSHIRE

Thorpe Salvin

Alnwick

NORTHUMBERLAND

The Percy lion, tail outstretched, is all over town, most noticeably on the arms of the castle's barbican gate, on the Lion Bridge in the Berwick road and 83 feet up on the tenantry column. The column stands by the old great north road, the spine of a town entered from the south through the medieval Hotspur Gate, built as part of the vanished town walls and named, of course, after another Percy, Henry Hotspur of historical fact and Shakespeare's *King Henry IV*. There is a 19th-century Percy Street and a Percy Terrace, and in Percy Street the Church of St Paul was built by Anthony Salvin, the architect who did the 19th-century Italian Renaissance style interiors to Alnwick Castle (the first of the Percys, William de Percy, arrived with William the Conqueror in 1066, but it took until 1307 for his descendants to buy the castle).

The only other lion to come to town was King William, the Lion of Scotland, who was taken captive in 1174 when he attacked Alnwick, and there is a monument to him at the entrance to Hulne Park. There's a stone cross near St Leonard's Hospital too, marking, it is said, the spot where another Scottish king, Malcolm, was killed laying siege to Alnwick Castle in 1093. The castle now is a major restoration, much bigger than it was in the days of its military glory, and very impressive, despite the unscary gesticulating statues scattered on the skyline among the battlements since the 18th century. And, of course, it is further softened by the gardens.

This, then, is Percy town, once Earls of Northumberland and, since 1766, Dukes of Northumberland. The Assembly Rooms, a grand early 19th-century building above an open arcade on the market square, is

normally known as Northumberland Hall, because the 3rd duke funded it. And there is a Duke School and a Duchess School. Enough. Despite new industry on the outskirts, Alnwick remains one of the finest towns of the north.

A great Royalist portrait painter in a hard time, Alnwick Castle

It's no wonder that Henry Percy, 11th Duke of Northumberland, mislaid one tiny Raphael hanging in a corridor, until Nicholas Penny of the National Gallery identified it for him and the National Gallery bought it. The Percy castle is stuffed with paintings. There are works by Sebastiano del Piombo and Palma Veccio, colleagues of Titian in 16th-century Venice, one portrait by Titian that is not among his best and several would-be Titians, including, sadly, a triple portrait that Byron rhapsodised as a true original:

> 'Tis but a portrait of his son, and wife,
> And Self; but such a woman I love in life!

There are Van Dycks and four Canalettos, one of Alnwick Castle itself, another of the Percy palace on the Thames, Syon House.

But the memory I take away from Alnwick is another triple portrait, by the short-lived Caroline court painter William Dobson (1611–46). This is a mildly perverse preference since there are also several good portraits by Dobson's superior, Van Dyck, but for the four years he was at the top of the tree Dobson was the best native English artist of the 17th century; the only one of real note at any time before Hogarth except for the miniaturist Nicholas Hilliard, and this is one of his most accomplished paintings. Dobson had been recommended to King Charles I by Van Dyck, but his career took off only when Van Dyck died in 1641 and it was cut short by his own sudden death in 1646. He moved to

Oxford to work for the royalist camp and set up studio in the High Street, filling in when the king's painter, the younger John de Critz, was killed in the fighting in Oxford in 1642. He returned to London when Oxford was lost to Cromwell in 1646, was imprisoned for debt and died a pauper at his house in St Martin's Lane.

The three men in this group portrait are the painter himself, his friend and patron, Cotterell, on the right of the group, who seems to be restraining Dobson in some sort of argument with the third man, on the left of the canvas, possibly the master of the king's musick, Nicholas Lanier. Lanier was one of the many lovers of the Neapolitan painter Artemesia Gentileschi (see Buckingham Palace, West End, London).

Despite what Dobson learned from looking at Van Dyck and Italian paintings in the king's collection, he was very much his own man, very variable, but at his best, as with the Alnwick triple portrait, very good indeed. He probably painted it when the king's cause was lost and the painter out of employment. The lived-in faces of the men in the triple portrait are telling, and the general dishevelment of Dobson in particular hauntingly suggests something of the illness that probably killed him. But the consummate technique shows that the acute eye and steady hand were still functioning.

The tenantry column

Eighty-three feet tall on a hillock at the entry to Alnwick and overtopping the street monument to the 20th-century war dead, the Alnwick tenantry column may just be the biggest symbol of a tugged forelock in history. The tenants organised a whip-round in 1816 to thank Hugh Percy, 2nd Duke of Northumberland, for dropping their rents by a quarter when agricultural prices plunged after the Napoleonic Wars. The duke died

before the column was finished, and the 3rd duke, local legend has it, decided that if his tenants could afford to fawn at a price of £2,600 they could afford higher rents. So he raised them, and many of his tenants went bankrupt. The townspeople renamed the column Farmers' Folly. In 1822 William Davison, an Alnwick bookseller, printer and historian, perfected the tenantry cringe with his comment that the column induced 'the idea of an approach to a place flourishing under the protection and auspices of a family whose wealth and power are only exceeded by their virtue and benevolence'.

The Northumbrian architect David Stephenson designed it as a Doric column on a square plinth crowned by the growling Percy lion on a drum, his tail outstretched like an arrow. There are four more crouching lions on the plinth of the monument, which Landseer may have seen before carving Nelson's lions for Trafalgar Square. The original tribute to the duke was sandblasted away, so a plaque on the base has been re-inscribed: 'To Hugh, Duke of Northumberland, K.G., this column is erected, dedicated, and inscribed by a grateful and united tenantry. Anno Domini MDCCCXVI.' Above that is the ducal motto, *Esperance en Dieu*, though one might think that since the Percys hold a large chunk of Northumberland in fiefdom they hardly need hope in God as well.

Railway station turned bookshop, Barter Books

The railway came to Alnwick in 1887 and was axed in 1961, leaving a railway station building built wide and handsome enough to impress royalty visiting the seat of the Duke of Northumberland. There are 33,000 square feet of it, and the stone façade is embellished with a glass canopy supported on scrolly ironwork. In 1991 Mary Manley wandered

This 83-foot-high column of 1816 with the Percy lion on top, which dominates the entry to Alnwick, was a thank you from his tenants to Hugh Percy, Duke of Northumberland, for dropping their rents in hard times. The duke's successor is said to have acted on the thought that if the tenants could afford the column, they could afford raised rents

through the abandoned building and envisaged it as a gigantic bookshop to be called Barter Books, because bartering is what it would do (though it sells them as well). And so in the main hall, where the engines hit the buffers, are antiquarian and rare books; in the ladies' first-class waiting room, outsize books; history and topography in the gentlemen's first-class waiting room; and the general (third class) waiting room is still a waiting room, with coal-burning fires, armchairs, coffee and, since Mary Manley is American, cookies. Mrs Manley supplies the literary intelligence, her husband Stuart Manley the business management, and the model railway tracks suspended above customers' heads has two trains running night and day as the pre-Beeching British Rail trains never did. And there on the wall above the doorway into departures is the fruit of Mary Manley's best idea, a mural almost 40 feet wide by 16 deep portraying a gathering of life-size figures of English-language literary eminences in a railed-off gallery swapping gossip, Salman Rushdie with Angela Carter, Jane Austen with George Eliot and Virginia Woolf, uniformed Wilfred Owen in conversation with Keats in a green frock coat; showing off (Hemingway); gazing dreamily into space (Ted Hughes); declaiming (Dickens); keeping an eye on Toad and Ratty (Alan Bennett). T.S Eliot caresses a cat, doubtless Old Deuteronomy; James Joyce is there on a higher mezzanine gallery, slightly remote, close to Oscar Wilde and Tom Stoppard, who are about to crown a bust of Shakespeare with laurel. And so on,

nearly forty of them and a list of the names of others who couldn't make it to the party painted along the railings.

Peter Dodd, the painter, is a friend of the Manleys. He was born in Alnwick and trained as a film animator. The mural took him two years and was conceived as a monumental conversation piece – fresh, fun and spot on for the site.

Barnard Castle
COUNTY DURHAM

El Greco in Teesdale's French château, the Bowes Museum

Set in formal gardens on the Rokeby road from Barnard Castle is the most unexpected and bizarre sight in England: the Bowes Museum. It is a huge French château – a sudden apparition, Pevsner calls it: 'big, bold, and incongruous, looking exactly like the town hall of a major provincial town in France.'

In fact, a Frenchman, Jules Pellechet (1829–1903), designed the museum to a commission from John and Josephine Bowes. The Bowes family came to County Durham with the Conqueror. To the land they took then they added more over the centuries, their wealth reinforced by the coal seams the land contained. John Bowes was the son of the 10th Earl of Strathmore (the father of Queen Elizabeth the Queen Mother was the 14th earl). In short, he was rich and well connected. Born in 1811, he became Josephine's lover in 1847 when they met in France. She was a twenty-two-year-old actress, but also a painter of literally rendered landscapes and a collector. They married and together put together a French-accented collection of paintings, furniture and art objects, from 15th-century altarpieces to Boudin and Fantin-Latour, with Luca Giordano, Canaletto and Boucher along the

Peter Dodd, a local artist, took two years over this huge homage to literature in the former Alnwick railway station, now Barter Books. The authors are, in the lower gallery left to right: Charlotte Brontë, Toni Morrison, Salman Rushdie, Angela Carter, Jane Austen, George Eliot, Virginia Woolf, W.B.Yeats, William Faulkner, Samuel Beckett, Dorothy Parker, Ernest Hemingway, George Orwell, Mark Twain, T.S.Eliot with, possibly, Old Deuteronomy the cat, R.L.Stevenson, F.Scott Fitzgerald, Emily Dickinson, Ted Hughes, John Keats, Wilfred Owen, Alan Bennett. Upper gallery: G.B.Shaw, Langston Hughes, Walt Whitman, Oscar Wilde, Shakespeare, Tom Stoppard, James Joyce, Doris Lessing with her two cats, Charles Dickens, Edward Lear.

way. Bowes came across *St Peter in Penitence* by El Greco in Paris and reluctantly parted with about £8 to add it to the collection.

El Greco was a Cretan (Domenikos Theotokopoulos, 1541–1614) who had started life making Byzantine icons, then retrained, as it were, in the Venice of Tintoretto and settled finally in Toledo, the heart of Catholic Spain. His paintings are at the heart of the Catholic Counter-Reformation. The Bowes canvas embodies the moment when Peter realises he has denied his Lord in the hour of his trial and thus fulfilled Christ's prophecy; he falls upon his knees appalled at his act of betrayal. It is religious theatre, in which Peter

seems to have returned to the garden of Gethsemane, a rocky terrain lit by an unnaturally brilliant night sky blasted by a strange fiery light. El Greco is at his best in the big canvases, like *The Burial of Count Orgaz* at Toledo, and in his portraits. The Bowes painting is small, about 3 feet 8 inches high by 3 feet wide, and the emphasis is all on Peter's face – huge eyes upturned to heaven and streaked with tears, an almost languid expression of submission on his face – lacking the realism of the portraits and succumbing to sugary religiosity. But for all that, it shows exactly how El Greco used every inch of canvas, every nervous flicker of

the brush, to animate the picture surface and express the ardour of his passion. Narrow your eyes and suspend disbelief, and you could be sucked into one of those black holes in the sky.

Berwick-upon-Tweed
NORTHUMBERLAND

Monet's master Eugène Boudin at the Borough Art Gallery

Vanbrugh either designed the barracks above Berwick town centre personally or supervised it. Thus we are obliged to admire it, but like barracks anywhere, this formidable building around a square has a lowering effect. In the constant struggles between medieval England and Scotland, Berwick changed hands thirteen times, but the Scots have shown no recent sign of fighting to get it back, so the barracks have now no need to serve a military use and are currently home to

several museum collections, including the King's Own Scottish Borderers. Another corner is kept for the celebrated collection that Sir William Burrell decided in 1949 to keep separate from the rest of his collection, housed in the Glasgow museum.

The cream of a beautiful collection may be the Degas study of dancers (it wasn't on show when I visited), but Eugène Boudin's landscape *River Touques above Trouville* has a strong claim, too. Boudin (1824–98), born in Honfleur, the son of a sailor, ran a picture-framing shop in Le Havre where he showed his own work and where a youngster contributing cartoons to the local newspaper, Claude Monet, chanced upon it. Monet initially disliked the older man's work but bumped into him one day and was converted. Boudin followed his own precept: 'Everything that is painted directly and on the spot has a force, a power, a vivacity of touch that is not to be found in studio work.' He persuaded Monet to try. The rest is art history.

But art history casts shadows, and Boudin deserves to be in full sunlight. He specialised in beach scenes usually set in Trouville, harbour scenes in Honfleur and Le Havre, Seine estuary scenes and study after study of skies, like a French Constable. His friendship with Monet brought him to Paris to show in the first Impressionist exhibition in 1874. Between 1880 and 1896 he began to paint inland around the little River Toques that flows through the Calvados to the sea between Deauville and Trouville, pictures like this one, with a heavily loaded brush and broad wedges and swirls of pigment on canvas, showing the river eating into the low, green, marshy bank beneath a wind-driven cloudy sky. His touch, as always, is sure and quick and his eye sharp to catch the essentials of the scene. Boudin was a prototype Impressionist with a shrewd peasant mentality, happy to tackle the same scenes day after day, registering the changes of light on river and meadow through the days and the seasons, just as his young follower would do later.

Beverley
YORKSHIRE

Any town with a church as beautiful as St Mary, Beverley, would be proud. Beverley is doubly blessed, for barely half a mile away is the even better minster, taken all in all, the finest parish church in England. And all this in a town on the edge of England, well off the main north–south routes. Yet it has always had access to the sea by the navigable Beck to the nearby River Hull upstream of the Humber, and it once had a shipbuilding industry, a tanning industry and a cloth-making industry associated with its wool merchants. Exports were principally to the Netherlands, and Flemingate, linking the minster to medieval Beckside, marks the presence in the Middle Ages of Flemish cloth merchants.

Saturday Market and Wednesday Market drew traders from all over England. Both still flourish. In Saturday Market, a long, very wide street surrounded by good shops, is a very pretty market cross of 1714, an open octagon with a cupola roof supported on eight Doric columns in pairs and crowned by a lantern with a weathervane on a finial. The cloth trade dwindled in the 16th century and the wool trade vanished, but by the 18th century Beverley was established as the administrative hub of the East Riding, and the big Georgian houses are the legacy. Until the 1960s the town was still building trawlers, but as that industry succumbed to foreign competition, it once again flourished as a centre of local government administration.

The Percy Tomb, Beverley Minster

Lovely Beverley Minster, standing proud to the south of this prosperous market town, is surely the noblest of all parish churches. It was founded in the 9th century, but the present building was started in about 1230 when the old church tower collapsed, taking most of the existing building with it, and work then continued into the 15th century. Beverley was a rich port when Hull was a fishing village, and the new church was suitably grand. Built as a monastery, it is cathedral-sized at 365 feet long and was fortunate at the time of the dissolution of the monasteries under Henry VIII only to lose its chapter house before passing to the town as the parish church. Perhaps the king was persuaded to spare it because of the belief of his royal predecessors in the 13th century that the banner of St John of Beverley ensured success in the Scottish wars.

Despite its scale, few churches have such an air of calm purity. It has a wonderful series of misericords, an exotic 18th-century font cover and a gothick west door designed by Nicholas Hawksmoor. Best of all is the 14th-century sculpture: seventy stone carvings of musicians with bagpipes, flutes, fiddles and drums; a magnificent stone screen designed initially to carry the shrine of St John; and, the climax, the Percy Tomb, standing between the north aisle and the choir.

Who the structure commemorates isn't certain. One view is that it isn't a tomb at all (there is no effigy) but an Easter sepulchre. The more generally held view is that it is the tomb of Lady Eleanor Percy (d.1328), though one knight leaning a trifle uncomfortably against the side of a spandrel carries a shield embossed with the lion rampant, and the shield of another is quartered with the arms of England and France, a device not adopted by Edward III until 1340. Never mind. Beverley had its own stone carvers' shop responsible for all the sculpture in the cathedral, and the mason in charge grew in skill and confidence to the point where he created in the Percy Tomb a work of sheer fantasy. It is contained beneath a tall ogee arch covered with profuse carving of fruit and flowers and with multiple cusps holding little angelic figures at the tips. Christ sits in glory at the pinnacle of the arch on the richest throne ever devised by man, holding in his hands the soul of the departed, supported by angels on corbels borne by willing he-men. Given that Beverley's stained glass suffered at the hands of Henry VIII's men, it is miraculous that the tomb, including the figure of Christ, escaped desecration.

A minstrel's pier, Church of St Mary

It seems unfair that Beverley should hog not just one of the most beautiful churches in England, but two, though the local authority has gone some way towards righting this

wrong by building a high-rise block in the vicinity to spoil the mostly Georgian urban scene. In 1520 the tower at St Mary fell, and, as at the minster, destroyed the nave. It also took some of the congregation with it, though most were enjoying an illicit away-day to watch bear-baiting. God works in a mysterious way.

The minster was the churchman's church since effectively it was the East Riding's cathedral; St Mary's was the town church. It stands in North Bar Within, a broad street where the horse market was held and that leads to the only surviving medieval gate, the North Bar of 1410. So this church was popular with the lawyers, merchants and craftsmen who moved in numbers to Beverley from all over England because of the renown of its markets, and the merchants and guilds combined in the rebuilding and redecorating, embellishing it with fine misericords and a unique timber ceiling painted with forty English kings, from Brutus of legend to Henry VI (and, since a restoration of 1939, with George VI, too).

The northern minstrels guild had adopted Beverley as its headquarters and met there every Ascension Day (usually in May) to elect its officers. After the tower collapsed they contributed money to the rebuilding, and among the new carvings they donated was a little group of five minstrels sculpted as a hood mould stop – that is, the figures gathered informally at the bottom of a moulded arch, in this case in the nave arcade. These chubby-faced, doll-like figures benefit from the addition of bright colour, black, shoulder-length hair, brown tunics and pleated skirts, blue coats (one worn, one thrown lightly over a minstrel's shoulder), black stockings, chains of office around their necks. It's not great art, perhaps, but it is great showbiz.

Bishop Auckland

COUNTY DURHAM

From the north over the River Wear, from the south over the Gaunless, the roads lead into the marketplace, for long before Bishop Auckland became a centre of the Durham coal industry it was home to a market and a prince bishop's palace. In 1832 the bishop gave Durham Castle to the new university and ever since, Auckland Castle, behind a wall to the east of the marketplace, has been their only country residence. The marketplace has character without beauty: in the middle of the square are the parish church, St Anne, of 1847, and the mansard-roofed town hall of 1860–2, both curiously French looking, though the church is supposed to be 12th century (Early English). There are almshouses, and a big Georgian house, banks and a pub. Football is important here, as in all of Durham's former pit villages and towns, and there is a Bob Hardisty Street, named after a celebrated amateur international who made Bishop Auckland the finest amateur team of the post-war years. They have nothing to compare, though, with West Auckland down the road (different village, same conurbation) whose amateur team of coalminers beat the best professionals Europe could put up in 1909 to win the Sir Thomas Lipton trophy (put up by the Lipton's tea millionaire) and then repeated the feat two years later to keep the trophy. It was stolen in the 1990s, so anyone knocking on the door of West Auckland Working Men's Club to see it will be looking at a replica.

A dozen Zubaráns at the palace

Auckland Palace is the last country seat of the prince bishops of County Durham, who, once, wielded princely power in the northeast, losing the final medieval vestiges of the palatinate in 1836. But the palace beyond an archway at the end of Bishop Auckland's marketplace has lost none of its splendour and still guards its improbable treasure: a sequence of paintings of *Jacob and his Twelve Sons* by Francisco de Zurbarán (1598–1664). At the sale in 1756, when the then bishop, Richard Trevor, bought twelve of the set of full-length portraits, one got away. Lord Ancaster, who believed he was descended from the tribe of Benjamin, had already bought it, and it still hangs in Lincolnshire at Grimsthorpe Castle. The bishop completed the set of thirteen, including Jacob, by commissioning a jobbing painter called Arthur Pond to copy Benjamin for him. It shows. Pond misses Zurbarán's intensity.

Zurbarán was born in the remote farming region of Extremadura, and his commissions came mostly for monasteries that wanted single figures of monks or saints contemplating the divine, so he rarely painted big figure compositions. But his single figures rank him alongside Velázquez, El Greco and Goya. *Jacob and his Twelve Sons* was intended for one of the Spanish American colonies, but the canvases were seized by pirates in mid-voyage and sold to James Mendez, a Portuguese Jewish merchant in London who sold them to Bishop Trevor for £124, and instead they hang in the bishop's dining room. Each of the thirteen figures appears in full daylight, standing tall against the sky with a landscape hugging the bottom of each canvas. Zurbarán takes his characterisation of the sons from Jacob's blessing to each of them (Genesis 39). Reuben, the firstborn, stands abashed because he slept with his father's concubine,

so though he is 'the excellency of power …
[he] shalt not excel'. Judah, 'the lion's whelp',
the ancestor of King David and of Jesus's
earthly father Joseph, is glorious in brown
and gold with a maroon underskirt and
sandals and a gold circlet crowning his head.
Gad is a fierce moustachioed soldier, for 'a
troop shall overcome him, but he shall
overcome at the last'. Each of the twelve is
characterised as simply as this but powerfully
envisaged, no displays of technical virtuosity,
the detail as readable as Genesis itself, the
ensemble a triumph of concentration.

Gateway on to the marketplace, Auckland Palace

Richard Trevor, the bishop who brought the
Zurbarán paintings to Auckland Palace (see
above), also spent £8,000 on improving the
palace – that is, in making it more Gothic
externally than it already was. Some of that
money went to erecting a gateway at the end
of a very short street leading from the
marketplace in the castle park. The man he
chose to design it was Sir Thomas Robinson,
an amateur in the architectural lists who had
redesigned Rokeby Park (see below), his seat
in County Durham. Although he had done
the house as an exercise in Palladian
classicism, Robinson was quite happy to
design for the bishop in Gothic, or rather
gothick, the 18th-century light-hearted
version: 1760 in this case.

The walls flanking the gateway each have
wicket gates, but the centrepiece is a
triumphal arch with abstract shapes like
angels' wings in the spandrels and clustered
shafts either side, emerging above the
battlements as obelisks. Above the arch is a
square tower with a big, round clock,
pinnacles and a lead-covered cupola. It has
the clarity of classicism, the decorativeness of
totally unscholarly and eclectic Gothicism
and nothing at all of a bishop's solemnity.

Bradford
YORKSHIRE

Pre-Raphaelite stained glass, Bradford City art gallery

The industrial Midlands and north were
fertile ground for Pre-Raphaelite artists.
Municipal art galleries are stuffed with
paintings that came to them from mill
owners and merchants who built themselves
big houses above the valleys. One of them,
Walter Dunlop, had the bright idea of
commissioning William Morris's firm to
make stained glass for his house, Harden
Grange near Bingley. It was 1862, and the
firm had been set up by several friends.
There was Morris himself, Edward Burne-
Jones, D.G. Rossetti, Ford Madox Brown
and Philip Webb, who had just built the Red
House at Bexleyheath for Morris, plus P.P.
Marshall, an amateur painter and friend of
Brown, and Charles Faulkner, an academic
who had become a friend of Morris and
Burne-Jones when they were Oxford
undergraduates. Each of the seven took out
a £20 share, and they hoped to get by on
making and selling painted furniture.
They existed on a wing and several prayers
through the first year of the company's
existence before Dunlop's commission came
as a godsend.

Dunlop wanted thirteen windows
illustrating the part of the ancient tale of
Morte d'Arthur in the Malory version. This
tells the story of King Mark of Cornwall
sending his nephew Tristram to Ireland to
persuade Isoude's royal father to give Mark
her hand in marriage. On the voyage back
Tristram and Isoude accidentally drink the
love potion intended for Mark and Isoude.
Isoude marries Mark, Tristram marries
another Isoude in Brittany, the love affair
continues, and Mark slays Tristram.

Morris, Brown, Burne-Jones and Rossetti

Enough to have brought a sparkle to Bridlington again: part of the nautical mile of Bridlington seafront brought to life by the partnership of the artist Bruce McLean and the architect Irena Bauman of Bauman Lyons

each designed panels, and Morris called in two other Pre-Raphaelites, Val Prinsep and Arthur Hughes, to do the others. It is not among the firm's best glass, but it works well as a dramatic sequence. In 1906, after Dunlop's death, the glass was removed from Harden Grange, and Bradford bought the lot for £100.

Bridlington
YORKSHIRE

The English seaside revived in the South Promenade

There was a royal age of the seaside, when the Prince Regent raised an oriental pavilion in Brighton, Bognor became Regis, and resorts decked themselves out in gay plumage. Then the hoi polloi started taking annual holidays. Scrolly iron piers reached out into the waves, dance-halls and theatres opened, there were sedate promenades for the old, while the young cavorted on the beaches. In time there were ice cream parlours and fish and chip shops, Donald McGill's saucy picture postcards and Billy Butlin's holiday camps. People thronged in their millions to Blackpool and Margate, Torquay, Weston-super-Mare, Southport, Scarborough and Redcar. Come to Sunny Skegness, the posters cajoled railway passengers. And they did. But after the Second World War a brighter sun than Skegness ever saw drew the new holidaymakers abroad, and even the older versions of those laughing sepia shadows in family photograph albums flew off to the Costas as well.

Bridlington suffered with the rest of the seaside: crowds dwindled, paint peeled off hotel façades, and even the flowers in the neat beds looked like pensionable Butlin redcoats on parade. In 1992 the town council had to close the North Promenade because the structure was crumbling dangerously. They took advice and hired one of an uninvitingly named new breed, a site-specific artist, in this case Chris Tipping. He produced a strikingly successful redesign of the North Promenade. From that point Bridlington minds were focused on creating a new look for the rest of the seafront that would be more than skin-deep. Working against a background hum of Civic Trust and English Tourist Board reports on the failing seaside industry, Bridlington planned a way forward; Irena Bauman and Bruce McLean (b.1944) brought genius to the mix.

McLean is the Scarlet Pimpernel of art; you see him here, you see him there, and each time he wears a different coat, drawing on art of the past but never following a rigid scheme. Bauman is the public face of an architecture practice that believes in diversity. The Bauman–McLean solution for Bridlington was to remake the promenade a nautical mile long (1,852 metres), with cafés and beach huts, paddling pool, showers and water channel, and the surface of the promenade itself an indissoluble combination of architecture and art, sculpture and building and wandering line. They brought in McLean's friend the art critic Mel Gooding to create a verbal link, a text that in point of fact forms an edging strip along the nautical mile sandblasted into red terrazzo – a material in which marble chippings are mixed into concrete and colour pigment – but in effect strolls down the promenade mixing nuggets of fact about Bridlington history, Brid heroes, and arcane Brid facts with a vaguely poetic daydreaming ramble.

Elsewhere a formerly ghastly water pumping station is transformed into a happily nautical-looking pavilion: flowing white lines on the wall indicate open-air showers for big kids and others for little kids, while a water wall is covered in big scribbled faces that resemble Picasso-esque graffiti. There's a café where the sunlight throws the legend 'explain that' on the glass wall as a shadow on to the floor inside, and at night the electric light throws the legend back on to the promenade outside. And a curved corner of the paddling pool has another McLean face drawn and raised stone lips vaguely reminiscent of a blow-up mattress for floating on to the water. It's enough to have brought a sparkle again to the faces of those 1920s and 1930s villas on South Marine Parade above the dreaming promenade.

Cherryburn
NORTHUMBERLAND

Thomas Bewick's birthplace

The engraver Thomas Bewick was born in the cottage at Cherryburn where the south bank of the Tyne slopes sharply down to the river. It's not a couple of miles from Wylam on the north bank, where George Stephenson was born, but although there were nearly thirty years between them (Bewick was born in 1753; Stephenson in 1781), and the paths they took were very different, they lived in the same world. The pits of Durham and Northumberland were already producing millions of tons of coal by the 18th century, and the area around Newcastle upon Tyne was crisscrossed with wooden railway lines for wagons conveying coal. Stephenson seized the moment, went to work at Killingworth colliery north of Newcastle, and his story is written in iron across the railway networks of the world. Bewick looked about him as he walked over the narrow Tyne

The nightjar and the golden-crested wren from Thomas Bewick's A History of British Birds, *displayed at Cherryburn on the banks of the Tyne, the birthplace of the 'father of wood engraving'*

bridge to school in Ovingham and, although his father owned one of the small mines in the area, saw only fields and hedgerows, birds and beasts. He sat and sketched the things he saw, and his life's work and history is contained in a couple of rooms of this cottage birthplace. It's easy enough to see how Bewick could have made this choice, because only 12 miles west of Newcastle city centre, it remains just about believable that the Industrial Revolution never happened.

Bewick was apprenticed to the engraver Ralph Beilby in Newcastle, and Cherryburn, which opened as a museum in 1988, contains some of the commercial work he did in his early days, work like an engraved metal dog collar and an engraved copper plate for the £1 banknote issued by the Northumberland Bank. It was jobbing work, but in his training Bewick learned wood engraving and found that with hard boxwood he could engrave almost as finely as on copper or silver, but with the strength of line and boldness of black and white that is the preserve of woodcuts. By 1790 Bewick and Beilby were partners in the engraving business and cooperated on publishing of *A General History of Quadrupeds*, with 700 woodcuts by Bewick and text by Beilby. Bewick became, in Geordie folklore, the 'father of wood engraving', though up in the artists' Valhalla Albrecht Dürer might have something to say about that. The most beautiful of his illustrations aren't simply of the subject but have an idyllic landscape background as well. He followed up in 1797 and 1804 with his two-volume masterpiece, *A History of British Birds*, containing woodcuts of such exotic but homely birds as the greater spotted woodpecker, the golden crested wren, the nightjar and the crested grebe.

Chesters

NORTHUMBERLAND

Statue of the goddess Juno, Roman fort

The fort lies athwart Hadrian's Wall, a third to the north, the rest to the south in a quiet glade on the North Tyne River. It was built to support an *ala*, a single cavalry unit of 512 men employed to defend this border point and to make swift punitive raids against the turbulent enemy to the north. Behind 5 foot thick walls its compact rectangular layout has barrack blocks, stables, granaries, a commandant's house and bath-house, headquarters block, hospital, guardroom, aqueduct and reservoir; and outside the fort on the west bank of the river is a large and once magnificently equipped bath-house for the men. To the Romans, Chesters was a strategic position because this was where the wall crossed the North Tyne on a bridge. What strikes us is the contrast of its setting in a lovely wooded valley with the harsh, high, craggy and treeless ground through which so much of the wall runs.

Close by is the 18th-century house, Chesters, finely embellished in 1897 by the architect Richard Norman Shaw (1831–1912)

with curving wings and a grand Ionic colonnade. From 1854 until his death in 1890 the lawyer and classicist John Clayton owned the house and estate and bought up land from Chesters to Housesteads, a large part of the central part of Hadrian's Wall, to protect it from pilfering. When he died a Clayton trust opened Chesters museum in 1903. It still owns it, and even though English Heritage administers it, there remains the fusty overstuffed feel of an antiquarian enterprise. But the collection of objects from Carrawburgh, Chesters and Housesteads (which, of course, has its own museum as well), if not as fine as Corbridge museum's (see below), has spectacularly the single finest item, the stone figure of Juno.

Juno was sister and wife of Jupiter, mother of Hebe, Vulcan and Mars, a distinguished family even by the standards of divinity. Whereas the snarling lion at Corbridge is most likely to have been the work of a gifted craftsman travelling with the legions, Juno, also made of the local sandstone, may have been carved by a Syrian from the great centre of sculpture, Palmyra, trained in the classical tradition and brought to one of the sculpture workshops of South Shields or Carlisle. The Celtic arts of the British Isles were abstract, curvilinear, fantastic; Roman classicism was typically realistic, even pragmatic, but the Syrians brought with them a powerful element of stylised dignity. Juno's head and arms from above the elbow are missing, but her monumentality is asserted by the dignified pleating of the tunic that covers her from neckline to pelvis, with a band of a continuous wave motif decorating the hem and again the hem of the apron beneath, which reaches to her knees. Below that a gown drops to her ankles, with shallow V-shaped folds marking her legs but pleats between and to the sides. At the waist her garments are fastened with a knotted girdle ending in arrow points. The artist has aimed at Junoesque grandeur rather than realism. The columnar dignity of the statue is quite like the five 12th-century saints and prophets surviving from St Mary's Abbey, York (see below) and may have performed a similar symbolic and decorative function at Chesters. There was more to these rough men of war than bread and circuses.

Consett
DURHAM

Tony Cragg's new world sculpture, old steelworks site

More dramatic to anybody who was there in the 1950s and 1960s than even Sunderland stripped of its shipyards is Consett. It's a town with a population of under 30,000 in limestone country, and beneath it lie deposits of coal and iron ore, the basic necessities for iron and steel production. In the 1960s travellers passing through the beautiful uplands of central Durham dotted with occasional small pit villages would crest a hill and see with shock in the valley a town contained within one of the loveliest of northern landscapes, the Derwent valley, yet huddled under a satanic and constant pall of smoke. This was Consett, dotted with slag heaps, dominated by the rows of steelworks buildings, riven by quarries. Here even the earth left a man's hands black if he handled it. There was a puddling mill, a steel plate mill, a cogging mill, an angle mill, and there were blast furnaces. And there were 6,000 men. The steelworks closed in 1980, and in a huge demolition job the heart was ripped out of the town. Today the new housing estates for commuters to Durham City creep into the gap left behind and circle like caravans around odd objects of industrial detritus – a huge vat that once contained molten metal, a pit pony of a works railway engine – sited like found sculptures.

And then there is a huge sculpture commissioned from Tony Cragg, born in 1949 and one of the two or three most gifted sculptors of a gifted generation. He calls the Consett work *Terris Novalis* ('In New Lands'). Naturally, it is made of steel and consists of two gigantic, gleaming models of surveyors' instruments: a theodolite standing some 20 feet high and a level – the sort of tools that would have been used to assess the lie of the land for the line the Great North Eastern Railway laid here across the edge of the steelworks. The instruments stand on a mixture of feet, a horse's hooves, a lion's paws and the huge feet of a lizard-like creature. *Terris Novalis* stands on and beside its little hillock on the reclaimed land surveying past and future, mutely suggesting nothing, but maybe constituting an optimistic gesture by the artist and by his commissioner, Sustrans, the civil engineering charity that has laid a cycle path from Consett to Sunderland over the old railway track.

Corbridge
NORTHUMBERLAND

The Corbridge lion, Roman town, fort, and museum

Most of the ruins of Cnaeus Julius Agricola's Corbridge lie under modern Corbridge, but some are still visible a few hundred yards to the west, and they give a haunting sense of the general who built Corbridge in AD 80 as a military fort on the north bank of the Tyne and who consolidated the Roman occupation of Britain. The fort stands at the junction of Dene Street, the high road to Scotland, and

Six thousand men once worked at the steelworks at Consett. Tony Cragg's steel sculpture on the site, Terra Novalis *('in new lands'), a gigantic simulation of surveyors' instruments, looks both backwards and forwards at Consett's history*

Whoever carved this piece in Corbridge fort during Hadrian's reign in about AD 120–30 had clearly seen a lion making a kill. Because excavations suggest the remains of an amphitheatre in Chester, where lions may have been part of the entertainment, the sculptor could have been native British

Stanegate, the road to Carlisle. In 117 the natives destroyed it, and five years later Hadrian visited Britain and set afoot the building of the wall from Tynemouth to Solway. A few years later Corbridge, 2½ miles behind the wall, began to grow again, not just as a military garrison for Hadrian's Wall but as a civilian settlement as well. That much we know, but there are still gaps in the story of the Roman occupation of this island, and every year brings new finds and expanding knowledge, not least in Corbridge.

In 1907, when archaeologists dug up the so-called lion of Corbridge down by the river, there was no available explanation about who on Tyneside in the 2nd or 3rd century might have carved a lion of such vivid naturalism.

The sculpture is in the local sandstone, but there was no evidence that the Roman legions brought with them flesh and blood lions either as mascots or to fight gladiators in the amphitheatres, and no evidence that in this benighted province of the empire public entertainment ever ran to anything starrier than cockfighting and bull baiting, so what local craftsman might have met a lion? Just another of the unsolved problems of Roman art in Britain. Then, in fresh excavations at Chester starting in 2004, archaeologists pieced together a jigsaw of a Roman amphitheatre built in AD 100 and later developed into a smaller provincial version of the Colosseum. Fragments of fractured human and animal bone and armour and a heavy stone with an iron ring embedded in it for tethering combatants to keep them fighting and dying in the middle of the arena under the popular gaze suggest that not only did Rome export its more savage amusements to Britain, but that Chester had one of the empire's most important amphitheatres.

The Corbridge lion crouches snarling at all the world, his four massive paws planted on his supper, a deer lying helplessly prone with its tongue lolling pathetically, even comically, from its mouth. It's not a sophisticated piece, but it is, so to speak, red in tooth and claw. It's well designed too: it seems to have been carved out of a block of sandstone a bit over 3 feet square, and the sculptor has maintained the stability of that shape to create in the muscular hindquarters, barrel-like body and heavy mane a sense of contained power. The excavation team found it in a water cistern. It was probably originally a gravestone but had been converted at some point into a fountainhead with water pouring from its mouth.

Darlington
COUNTY DURHAM

The hub of the town is the big marketplace, and south of it is St Cuthbert, one of the most complete Early English churches in England. North of the marketplace the Quaker architect Alfred Waterhouse (1830–1905) built the covered market as a single unit with the clock tower and old town hall, and beyond that he built the High Row bank (now Barclays) of the Quaker family, Backhouse, which helped to finance the Quaker Edward Pease for his Stockton & Darlington railway project. Below High Row, Prebend Row heads through the town centre and a couple of hundred yards further along becomes Northgate, which in turn morphs

into North Road. This is where all the action was for most of the 19th and 20th centuries: the railway works, the rolling mills, engineering works, the Cleveland Bridge company. But for a period this was a one-company town, and it began on the opening day of the Stockton & Darlington Railway, 27 September 1825, when George Stephenson's Locomotion No. 1 hauled a train from Shildon to Stockton via Darlington of thirty-four open wagons for coal and flour with workmen clinging on and a covered coach up front for company directors. At one point it travelled at full steam and attained the dizzying speed of 16 mph.

Everything followed from that opening day: the massive investment in the south Durham coalfields and the steelworks at Consett, the investment in the Tees Navigation Company and the foundation of Middlesbrough as a port and industrial centre, the destruction of the Tyneside monopoly, the transformation of Darlington from a market town with a wool industry to a railway and industrial centre. Locomotion survives as the prize exhibit in Darlington Railway Museum on the site of the Stockton & Darlington railway station at the end of McNay Street off North Road (I declare a vestigial interest here: the McNay in question, Thomas, company secretary of the Stockton & Darlington, was my great-great-grandfather). And on the bypass to Stockton, there is David Mach's life-size brick sculpture of one of the Mallard engines so familiar on the King's Cross to Edinburgh route in the late age of steam.

The market cross that never was, junction of Blackwellgate and Horsemarket

Most people who lived in Darlington in the past century are unlikely to have known its market cross. The market had been there from time immemorial: the first documented mention of it was in 1003, when Ethelred the Unready licensed it to the Bishop of Durham. Successive bishops did not take this lightly, and they were still collecting tolls at the entrance to the market square into the 19th century, by which time the town had acquired a market cross, presented in 1727 by Dame Dorothy Browne, the wife of the bishop's town bailiff.

What happened after that was the railway revolution. Darlington prospered mightily, and major new building works were embarked upon. What had to give, in 1862, was the little market cross. For a while it was shoved into a space between stalls in the new covered market, then it was taken down, dismantled and put into storage. But in the smokeless post-industrial age and with the approach of the new millennium, Dame Dorothy's market cross appeared at the junction of Blackwellgate and Horsemarket to reassert Darlington's ancient identity. It's a simple undressed limestone column; above is a handsome entablature, a well-tooled ball and drum inscribed in a relaxed serif letter face, 'This Cross Erected By Dame Dorothy Browne 1727'. The carver missed out the final e and inserted it above the n. It was worth it to get in the lovely freehand squiggly mark indicating an inserted correction.

Brick train, by the A66

The monumental engine by David Mach (b.1956) is going nowhere, but its viewers are drivers on the A66, one of those bypasses built to get cars around and out of town fast. He constructed it of 181,754 bricks beside the road at Darlington as a monument to the enterprise of the town's millowners, coal masters and bankers who made it the home of the world's first steam-operated public railway. It works bracingly, like music composed of dissonances, but if the location seemed a good idea at the time (it was

unveiled in 1998), it isn't working well. Drivers looking for it can pull over into a litter-strewn lay-by; if they drive past all unaware they will be gone scarcely knowing what they have glimpsed. Their alternative is to follow the A66 signs with the little brick-coloured railway engine motif into a car park at the back of a warehouse on the same site as Morrison's, one of those bleak areas hopefully known as business parks, and look at the train from close to. The experience suggests a wary engagement with post-modernist art that isn't worthy of Darlington's initial brave decision to go with Mach's wittily resonant sculpture.

Mach's model was the Mallard, a class A4 4–6–2 Pacific loco built in Doncaster in 1938 and holder of the world steam record speed of 126 mph. It stayed in service on the old London & North-Eastern Railway and then British Rail until 1963, travelling from King's Cross to Edinburgh Waverley, shaking the rust from the train shed roof of Bank Top, Darlington's mainline station, as its wheels spun on the slight uphill gradient beside platform 1 before it managed to engage the rails from a standing start. Now it is in honourable retirement at the National Railway Museum in York. The Mach 2 Mallard, made of the type of brick once commonly in use locally for railway buildings, is one of the sculptor's deadpan solutions to the challenge of a realistic full-scale representation of an engine – after all, brick implies monumentality not speed. Mallard could be emerging from a tunnel (the grassy mound behind), but the engine is actually transfixed in space and time on a grassy bank top of its own beside the bypass (en route to Stockton, as it happens), and the train exists only in the mind's eye. Incidentally, Mallard's precursor, George Stephenson's Locomotion No. 1, built for the opening day in September 1825 of the Stockton & Darlington Railway, today stands

David Mach's brick sculpture, Train, *on the A66 at Darlington, commemorates the town's entrepreneurs, bankers and industrialists who, with a little help from George Stephenson, introduced the world to travel by railway. Mach based the engine on a Mallard class A4 4–6–2 Canada locomotive built in 1938 and in service until 1963*

in Darlington North Road railway station, which doubles as station and railway museum on the site of the original line.

Gothic that never went away, Church of St Cuthbert

St Cuthbert sits as it has for the best part of a thousand years at the bottom of a gentle slope that stretches from marketplace to churchyard. It was built between 1192 and 1250, but until the 1980s its beauty had been hidden for many decades because it was under the shadow of three cooling towers visible for miles around. Now the waves of the Industrial Revolution have passed over Darlington and left it the central market

town of Teesdale as it was before the railway works, rolling mills, wire mills, power station and heavy engineering dominated, and St Cuthbert shows up as one of the most beautiful Early English edifices in the country. It has a central crossing tower and a 15th-century spire rising to more than 183 feet 8 inches, 40 feet taller than the church is long. Inside is a spectacularly tall oak spire font cover in the south transept that seems to echo the stone spire above and certainly seems medieval. Actually, it was made two centuries later, in 1672, for the early Gothic revivalist John Cosin, Bishop of Durham.

Cosin (1594–1672) was a follower of Charles I's Archbishop of Canterbury, William Laud, and, like the prelate, was a high churchman close enough to Rome to make him feared and hated. The English Civil War did for Laud and Charles, both of whom had their heads chopped off, but Cosin went to France, where he served exiled members of the royal family, and when Charles II was restored to the throne in 1660 Cosin was made Bishop of Durham, a position endowed with princely powers. Because of the power traditionally wielded by the Bishop of Durham the county had long escaped both fashionable influences and the decline in church decoration that followed Henry VIII's breach with Rome, and a group of craftsmen continued to work in the Decorated tradition. As rector of Brancepeth church in central Durham in the early 1640s and as Bishop of Durham later, Cosin seized on this, and he personally drew detailed plans for work carried out in churches across the county, entrusting the carpentry and, in a few cases the masonry, to local craftsmen. His masterpiece was Brancepeth, which he embellished with rood screen, pulpit, font cover, lectern and chancel stalls, but which was destroyed by fire at the end of the 20th century. Now, except for the palace at Bishop Auckland and a couple of churches where it is aggravatingly difficult to gain access, his work has mostly vanished. But the font cover at Darlington shows that Cosin's Gothic was deeply felt – as Pugin's was to be in the 19th century – and very far from the purely decorative Gothic styles of the next century, often adopted by those who found it theatrical or amusing.

The St Cuthbert's cover is of oak, 15 feet high, and carved in Decorated Gothic to match the existing font of 1375 of Frosterley marble and sandstone. It is an octagon and climbs in five diminishing stages of cusped arches, quite plain until the top stage of abstract spiky foliage carving culminating in a tall, embellished spike.

A Victorian shop braced with cast iron, Doric House, Tubwell Row

In the gung-ho days of the 1960s the demolition men obliterated all but a rear stone arch of the Nag's Head in Tubwell Row, a fine brick-built 17th-century pub and a rare survival, but the 18th-century Golden Cock survives in a lively cocktail of architectural styles along this stretch of road. The most festive building here, though, is a latecomer – Doric House, built in 1860, a shop (now offices) with its façade framed in cast iron constructed by the Glasgow firm of Walter Macfarlane & Co. From his beginnings as a blacksmith, Macfarlane built a hugely successful business of decorative ironwork. Most of his commissions were Scottish, but one of his best works is the Barton Arcade in Manchester (see Northwest), and his shop fronts, fountains, bandstands, gates, railings and lampposts graced streets and parks in Singapore, Cyprus, South Africa and Brazil. In Madras he built a great iron banking hall.

The Tubwell Row premises was an early work. The ground-floor windows and entrance are framed in iron with free-standing columns supporting a scrolly frieze that spreads across the width of the façade. Above this is a canopy, and above the canopy a two-storey oriel. Disconcertingly, beside this frontage a second, deeper oriel breaks out from the surface, supported on scrolly brackets beside a doorway, with a three-sided window on the first floor and on the second a two-sided window – that is, triangular. Classical it isn't; not even the columns are Doric. But it does add to the gaiety of the street scene.

Durham

COUNTY DURHAM

Nothing in all of England is more majestic than Durham Cathedral and Durham Castle side by side on a sandstone bluff above the deep loop of the Wear. The castle, it is true, is a visual adjunct to the cathedral, a spreading of the visual load. Historically, it was built where it is to defend the northern approach, where there is no river. Two successive bishops, William of Calais and Ranulph Flambard, built the cathedral. Building began in 1093 and was finished by 1133. After that there were just a few magnificent details to add: the magical Galilee Chapel, completed in 1189; the west towers in the early 13th century; the Chapel of Nine Altars finished in 1280s; and, in the 15th century, the central tower. The cloisters are to the south and the main entrance is the north door hung with the finest bronze sanctuary door knocker in Christendom, a savagely grinning face with the skin stretched in parallel curving creases across the ship's prow nose and the cheeks, brow like a helmet and spearhead ears, round eyes, which would once have been filled with coloured enamel, glaring out of a sunburst setting. What's there now is a convincing replica; the original is in the cathedral treasury. This was a great centre of power, with the prince bishops given almost royal authority over the county palatinate until this was abolished in 1835.

Visits should begin on Palace Green, the great grass square with the dominating cathedral bordering the south, the castle north (with its own fine Romanesque chapel) and precinct buildings mostly occupied by University College, the oldest of the Durham University colleges, founded, in fact, the same year as the university, 1832. East, below the cathedral, are North Bailey and South Bailey, leading from the marketplace, with Hatfield College, St Chad's, St John's and the little church of St Mary the Less, now the St John's College chapel, with its fine and little known 13th-century carving of Christ in Majesty. The Baileys and Saddler Street, teeming with student life, lead into the marketplace north of the cathedral–castle complex. Victorian Durham obliterated anything old in and around the ancient marketplace, though the 18th-century statue of Neptune, which originally marked the terminus of a piped water supply, has recently been restored and replaced. The other statue, of 1861, shows the 3rd Lord Londonderry on horseback. He is splendid in a hussar uniform, but his real occupation was colliery owner. The city has spread beyond the river, and on the high ground to the south in a happy mixture of suburban residential and university colleges and departments, is Millhill Lane with the oriental studies department in a 19th-century house linked by a glass screen wall to the excellent Gulbenkian Museum of Oriental Art.

St Cuthbert's coffin, Durham Cathedral treasury

St Cuthbert's body was reported uncorrupted when his coffin was opened eleven years after his death in 687. Indubitably, when Durham Cathedral canons reopened it in 1827 it contained the richly jewelled pectoral cross that had been buried with the saint together with the slight but significant remnants of a silver portable altar, and wonderfully preserved sumptuously embroidered vestments that the Northumbrian king, Athelstan, had placed there in 698.

Cuthbert travelled more in death than in life. He was exhumed from Lindisfarne (where he had been bishop), possibly in the face of Viking attacks, but since the priory's lands remained intact if not inviolate there is a suspicion that because he began to perform the usual posthumous miracles he became an early roadshow, attracting donations to the community of monks accompanying him. After several peripatetic years the Danish king Guthfrith endowed the monks and their holy cadaver with land at Chester-le-Street, which he donated to Cuthbert by name.

Finally, in 1104 the saint's remains were interred behind the high altar of the new Durham Cathedral. The north had rebelled against the Norman conquerors, and William had suppressed their insolence with sword and fire. When the new rulers rebuilt, they shaped the cathedral on its steep height above the Wear into the most awesome Romanesque monument in the world. Its aggressive grandeur represented the iron fist of the Norman enforcers. Cuthbert's tomb was the velvet glove.

When the cathedral canons had finished with the coffin in 1827 they reburied his skeletal remains in a new coffin, took the large fragments of the coffin that had probably been made in 698 and assembled them on a new casket for public display. With it went the treasures. All these things now form a sub-collection in the cathedral treasury off the south arcade of the cloisters opposite the restaurant. At a guess, the carver of the coffin's figures was a monk who had difficulty translating his skills with quill and brush to carpenter's tools. But these engravings are important as the only surviving Anglo-Saxon wood carvings whose figures, whatever their deficiencies, relate to the great contemporary manuscript art. The lid has a figure of Christ surrounded by the symbols of the evangelists; the sides have the twelve Apostles and five archangels; the Archangel Gabriel and the Archangel Michael are carved on one end and the Virgin and Child on the other.

Cuthbert's pectoral cross is gold with fifty garnets inset; a big mottled round red stone set in a white shell at the centre, small ones in the arms of the cross in little cells defined by thin ribbons of gold. Its splendour is almost barbaric, emphasised by a decorated border of raised dots, like tiny rivets, but then for all the Christian civilisation tenuously held against the marauders, Vikings and Anglo-Saxons were brothers under the skin.

Hiroshige's Scenes from One Hundred Favourite Views in Edo, Gulbenkian Museum of Oriental Art

Visit the Gulbenkian, in a lane well on the way out of Durham, and you're as likely as not to want to just sit and listen to a university group practising Thai music. But this is a wonderfully eclectic museum of Eastern arts with fine collections of Egyptian, Islamic and Buddhist art, Chinese ceramics and terracotta horses of the Tang dynasty (618–907). It also houses *ukiyo-e*, a genre of woodblock prints and paintings that was popular in the 18th and 19th centuries and that had a huge impact on the Post-Impressionists. It has to be said that if not precisely despised in Japan, it was looked down upon as an inferior mass-produced artform that appealed to uneducated popular taste – it dealt with such popular subjects as kabuki theatre, courtesans, sumo wrestlers, samurai, geishas, tea houses and brothels. It arrived by devious routes in the West, often as wrapping to more precious consignments, and its unassuming lyrical beauty had an immediate success among artists from Monet, Pissarro, Manet and Degas to the younger Van Gogh. So it is right that these little woodblock prints should hold their own in this very diverse museum.

Hiroshige (1797–1858), born Ando but in the Japanese fashion signing himself Utagawa Hiroshige after his master, came at the tail end of the tradition. By 1830 the great Hokusai had just introduced landscape as a subject for *ukiyo-e* ('pictures of the floating world'), and his younger contemporary Hiroshige finessed it. The Gulbenkian has a group of prints from his series *One Hundred Views of Famous Places in Edo*. Edo (Tokyo) was Hiroshige's birthplace, but the views concentrate on the rural landscapes beyond the city: a family of three and their possessions all on the back of a mule moving along a tree-lined footpath on the sedgy banks of a lake whose waters reflect Mount Fuji; a winter scene of travellers on foot hunched under parasols as they cross a bridge over a river in a snowstorm. They are a lyrical distillation of acute observation of the way people move, what they wear and how the weather affects them, and the landscapes themselves are sublimely unified by pale but strong colour suggesting the ambient atmosphere. Mass-produced these prints were, but they are the result of exquisite teamwork applying the sensibilities of artist, engraver and printer.

Kingsgate footbridge, Durham

The River Wear confines Durham City in a deep horseshoe loop, so bridges have been as central to the cityscape since the Middle Ages as castle and cathedral. There are Framwellgate Bridge and Elvet Bridge of the 12th century, Prebends Bridge of the 18th (the viewpoint of the cathedral for every great artist since Turner and every Sunday painter), and tucked away unobtrusively to the east of the cathedral Kingsgate Bridge of 1963, straight as a laser beam, which leaps the Wear gorge lying between the university colleges on North and South Bailey below the cathedral and the new campus on the far bank. It was the last entirely personal project of Ove Arup (1895–1988) and, it is said, his favourite.

This is a big claim for a man whose firm built a huge list of landmark buildings, including the Pompidou Centre, Sydney Opera House, Coventry Cathedral, the Hong Kong and Shanghai Bank in Hong Kong and Snape Maltings concert hall. But although Arup was the son of Danish parents and was educated in Germany and Denmark, and in Denmark qualified as an engineer, a blue plaque at Jesmond Vale Terrace in Newcastle records that he was born there (his father was a consul), and it was in Newcastle in 1938 that he set up his first private practice. It is a firm with a global reach and is still growing, but from his days working with the architect Ernst Lubetkin (the penguin pool at Regent's Park zoo is one of theirs) he retained a belief in what he termed 'total architecture', a concept of a seamless merging of architecture and engineering summed up by Kingsgate footbridge. It's built of concrete and spans 350 feet some 57 feet above the river. Arup built it in two sections aligned with the riverbank and on cylindrical piers so that he could swivel the two halves 90 degrees to join up at the middle. He supported the deck with concrete beams on each side formed as a cleft V. In its inspired simplicity and elegance this is one of the great structures of its time.

13th-century carving of Christ, St John's College chapel (St Mary the Less)

The tiny church of St Mary the Less lies hidden until you are there on South Bailey; this is part of the narrow lane that runs uphill from the marketplace to a point just below the cathedral and then drops sharply into the ravine. Here, Prebends Bridge crosses the River Wear near the old fulling mill that figures in every painting ever made from across the river, offering a vernacular counterpoint to the massive solemnity of the Norman cathedral. The whole of this natural bulwark of Durham is textured with cobbled streets, little churches and fine old houses, stucco covered or dressed, some with

Georgian hood mouldings, some with classical porticoes.

The 17th-century house that is now St John's College was built as the town house of the Eden family (the prime minister who triggered the abortive Suez invasion was one of the Durham Edens). St Mary the Less, almost opposite, has been the college chapel since 1919. It was rebuilt in the mid-19th century and practically nothing original survives. Even the magnificent carving of Christ in Glory was actually transferred to St Mary from St Giles in the 19th century. Its quality suggests that it was made by one of the cathedral masons at the dawning of the Gothic era. As pointed arches, slender piers, clustered columns of Purbeck marble and tall lancets replaced hefty Romanesque piers supporting massive round arches, so sculpture too became lighter, more naturalistic, less imposing but more sensually appealing. This carving is from the second decade of the 13th century and shows Christ contained within a mandorla, raising one hand in blessing, the other supporting a book balanced on his thigh. The mandorla is surrounded by the symbols of the evangelists, the eagle of St John, the angel of St Matthew, the winged lion of St Mark and the (badly damaged) winged ox of St Luke.

All this follows a Christian convention that stretches back to the magisterial figures of Christ in Byzantine art. But what is different about this one is Christ's relaxed pose. His dignity is asserted in his basically upright seated position, the trunk of his body rising vertically above feet centrally planted, and the haloed head erect above the body. But although the feet are close together and his left leg is more or less vertical to the knee, his right knee pushes out further to the right so that his legs are spread and the drapery of his mantle stretches in soft, round folds from one knee to the other, falling in liquid freedom to his ankles with the more delicate

cloth of his gown showing beneath dropping on to his feet in ripples. His features are effaced but what remains heralds the glorious naturalistic sculpture of the west fronts of Wells and Lincoln Cathedrals and Henry III's fantastic sculptural embellishment of his rebuilt Westminster Abbey.

Egglestone Abbey
COUNTY DURHAM

Tomb of an unknown abbot

The white canons chose Egglestone as the site for their new abbey in about 1195 with care. It was 1½ miles away from the nearest settlement, Barnard Castle; it was heavily wooded and a few yards south of the Tees with a stream convenient for drainage running into the river; and the fast-running Tees bounding over boulders ideal for turning a mill (there was still a mill here when Turner painted the scene in 1818). The canons, named for the colour of their robes, were Premonstratensians, a strict order founded earlier in the 12th century by St Norbert at Prémonstré in France. They remained poor and the abbey small, but in 1540 it met its inevitable fate at the hands of Henry VIII, and today even the house that the 16th-century secular owner built in the monastic range north of the cloisters is a ruin, recognisable only by one wall with hooded square-headed windows.

Today the land is open pasture where cattle from the farm on the abbey's western border graze among the ruins. The remains of the monastic buildings are so dislocated that it is not easy to decode the layout, though visitors enter through a nicely moulded pointed doorway into the south transept and face to their right the surviving three walls of the chancel. A wonderful view from the road high above the river on the northern bank pulls the plan together, 12th-, 13th- and

14th-century styles standing in the harmony imposed by rain and sunshine in an equality of ruination.

Despite the thunder of heavy trucks on the A66, time stands still in this enchanted part of north Yorkshire and south Durham that encompasses Greta Bridge, Rokeby and Egglestone. Within the ruins in the nave of the old church is a scattering of grave slabs. Some were planted here after the dissolution, like a Rokeby family grave. But there is one stone, the tomb of an unknown abbot, set flush with the turf around it, which, although not especially wonderful in itself, is made so by its surroundings and the fact of its survival here. No name survives, no inscription, but simply a stone spotted by lichen with raised carvings of large staff with a decorated head and a rudimentary arm reaching in from the edge of the stone with the hand clutching a crosier.

Elsdon Tower
NORTHUMBERLAND

A symbol of Anglo-Scottish rivalry

High up on the south wall of the massive pele tower of Elsdon in the wilds of Redesdale are carved the arms of the Umfravilles. They were, in the words of an ancient chronicle, 'of the old blode of that contre of Normandy' and had arrived with William the Conqueror. Possibly in the 11th century, certainly in the 12th, they settled in the dangerous border country between England and Scotland, with estates both in Northumberland and Stirlingshire. South of the border they were known by the Scottish title of Earls of Kyme, and in Scotland as Earls of Redesdale. They were earls of neither, in fact, though this hardly detracted from their distinction. One fought at the Battle of Otterburn in 1388, and Sir Gilbert Umfraville (1390–1421), famed for his prowess at jousting, fought at Harfleur

and Agincourt, and made the peace after the siege of Rouen, helping to negotiate the marriage between Henry V and Catherine of Valois. Elsdon Tower was one of their fortified houses, and it is the most spectacular of all the pele towers and fortified farmhouses known as bastles remaining in Northumberland.

It stands at the north of a triangular green on the road from Alnwick to Otterburn. On the other three sides are houses and in the middle the parish church of St Cuthbert, where a hundred cadavers unearthed in the churchyard last century were presumed to be some of the Scottish and English dead of the Battle of Otterburn. The tower is a stirring site from the stream below the village. It is huge and medieval in feel, though largely rebuilt in the 16th century, with 8 foot thick walls of rubble with long quoins and a shallow-pitched slate roof set back behind battlements. There are well-cropped lawns and pretty flowerbeds, but the red and yellow flag of Northumberland stiff in the breeze off the Cheviots says more about the valley history.

Escrick
YORKSHIRE

Memorial tablet to the rector by Eric Gill, Church of St Helen

Eric Gill (1882–1940) was twenty-one when he decided he did not enjoy being articled to an architect and joined classes run in Hammersmith by the renowned calligrapher Edward Johnston. In 1907, when Gill was twenty-six, Escrick church installed his memorial to Stephen Willoughby Lawley, who had been both the moving force behind the building of St Helen's on the road between York and Selby in 1856–57 and its rector. Gill was not a great sculptor, but his drawings and engravings had a wonderfully lissom line, not altogether surprisingly from a man who certainly was a great calligrapher. His Lawley tablet of Hornton stone is a thing of great felicity, with the feathered tops to capital Ys like a lovely hat at Ascot, the loop of the lower case letter f reaching across the space between words to embrace the vertical of the k of kindness, the wondrously long curling tendril of the bottom diagonal of a k at the end of a paragraph. Not much in creating an abstract work of art gets closer to the act of love than this. Functionally, it's an animated surface that simultaneously attains high legibility.

Gill went on to create two famous typefaces: Gill Sans, which, as the name reveals, has no serifs but which had a liveliness that sat well with the jazz age; and Perpetua, not far removed in its fluidity from his Escrick tablet and flourishing still. The tablet itself is both functional and a work of art.

Greta Bridge
COUNTY DURHAM

The Greta Bridge by John Carr of York

The bridges over the Swale, Greta, Tees, Derwent, Wear and Tyne, crowded together within about 30 miles from south to north Durham, are special in their mixture of venerable age and beauty and their functionality in standing against rapid flood waters. Among them, Greta Bridge, which John Carr (1723–1807) built over this tributary of the Tees in 1779, is both a work of art itself and the inspiration for paintings by Turner, Girtin and, especially, John Cotman, whose *Greta Bridge* of 1805 (now in the British Museum) is one of the finest English landscape paintings of the 19th century.

The River Greta rises on the Westmorland border and debouches into the Tees north of Rokeby Park. The bridge is on the Roman road between Scotch Corner and Penrith, less than half a mile from this meeting of the waters. During the Second World War the Royal Engineers threw a bailey bridge across the river closely adjacent to Carr's Bridge; I vaguely remember in post-war years that westwards traffic on the A66 gingerly crossed Carr's Bridge, eastwards it traversed the bailey bridge. Today the A66 is the most used east–west tourist and freight link for the Lake District and Scotland, and it traverses the river about a hundred yards from Carr's Bridge, which carries nothing more than cars bound for the Morritt Arms and farm tractors, screened from the main road by trees.

So much for the 20th-century story. From footpaths either side of the bridge today it looks much as Cotman showed it, better viewed before the mature trees are in full leaf. Carr's was at least the fourth bridge. The 16th-century antiquarian John Leland described the first-known structure as a bridge of three or four arches; a report in 1587 said that 'Gretay Bridge' was 'in very great decaie, for that both the pillars are undermined with water'. Its successor was swept away in 1771, and a temporary bridge filled in until John Morritt of the adjacent Rokeby Park handed the commission for a replacement to Carr, who forestalled the likelihood of a river in spate sweeping his bridge away too with the Georgian rationality of a balustraded single arch, a drawn longbow as beautiful as the Crescent he was simultaneously finishing for the Duke of Devonshire in Buxton.

Hartlepool
COUNTY DURHAM

Seaton high light, Seaton Carew

Seaton Carew grew up as a favourite seaside resort in the late 18th century. Darlington Quakers, railway promoters and wool merchants, rich beyond the bounds of their stripped-down Christian lives, financed the new building around three sides of the green; the fourth is open to the sea. The 20th century added trades union days out, kiss-me-quick hats, one-armed bandits, an art deco town clock and, in 1996, the discovery of the shipwreck of a 100 foot long late 18th- or early 19th-century collier brig. This was probably one in a sequence of wrecks that led to the Tees Navigation Company (also Quaker) building the Seaton high light on the seafront in 1838. It's a monumentally fine Tuscan column, moulded top and bottom and standing on a handsome rusticated pedestal with a door at the foot. Inside is a newel staircase leading nowhere because the lantern is long gone. The Seaton high light can't be allowed to slowly crumble. It could easily be turned into a monument to seamen lost off the Durham coast. The expense need not run to more than renovation and an engraved plate.

Hexham
NORTHUMBERLAND

St Wilfrid's throne, Hexham Abbey

Bishop Acca of Hexham died in 740, and the standing cross in the abbey of around 740 is generally taken to be a memorial to him. Anyway, it is known as Acca's cross. Even so, it is one of the newer things in the abbey. Acca was successor at Hexham to St Wilfrid, the founder of the abbey in about 674, and the town lies 3 miles west of Roman Corbridge and the same distance south of Hadrian's Wall. So the abbey, though it now faces east over the busy marketplace of a small country town, stands on a piece of ground considered holy before it was Christian. There are three reused Roman altars, one without inscription, the other two dedicated to a pagan god. There is a carved

relief monument to Flavinus, a standard-bearing cavalryman, and other Roman relics dug up during restoration a century ago. The only surviving parts of Wilfrid's church are the crypt, built with Roman stones and bare as a hermit's cell, and Wilfrid's throne, or cathedra (Hexham was a diocese until the Vikings sacked the abbey in 876).

The throne is carved from a single rectangular block of stone, its seat hollowed out so that back and arms of the same height describe a single broad curve. The abbey guidebook says it is the only Anglo-Saxon cathedra of this sort in England apart from Beverley Minster's. Beverley's, though, is undecorated, whereas the arms of Hexham's throne are carved on top with interlace culminating in three linked ovals. As with knives and forks, there isn't basically much a designer can do with a chair. Unlike a sculptor, he is stuck: form must follow function. The throne, a Chippendale piece and an Eames office chair serve basically the same purpose. But of course, the differences between the occasions of their use do make a difference, and the Hexham cathedra is like a piece of sculpture. Its monumentality was always impressive; add to that its history, and it moves us in the same way as Acca's cross does, a mute witness to an age of tenacious belief held in an untamed country.

Holy Island
NORTHUMBERLAND

This is where the Irish monk St Aidan came from Iona in 635 to introduce Christianity to godforsaken Northumbria. The monks of the priory he founded bestowed the name Holy Island to replace Lindisfarne; an early case of piety overcoming poetry. Old hands today remember having to cross the lagoon to this harp-shaped island at low tide across sands scattered with the carcases of cars sunk axle-deep and rusted by the incoming sea. Today, the passage is still only negotiable at low tide, but over a tarmac causeway, 3½ miles long, scattered only with picnickers among the dunes. The jumbly island village of about 160 souls still has a sense of life being eked out on the exiguous edge of civilisation. From the red ruin of the priory there are views of the castle on its vertiginous rock pinnacle, and from the castle are equally fine views of the priory and village and, to the south, faintly, Bamburgh Castle about 6 miles along the coast.

Viking grave markers of the 9th century, Lindisfarne Priory

St Cuthbert reluctantly left his hermit's cell on Farne Island off the coast of Bamburgh to become Bishop of Lindisfarne in 684. The Irish monk St Aidan had come from Iona earlier in the century and founded the priory. Not one stone remains set upon another of that original church, which was razed by the Vikings. All that exists today was portable: Cuthbert's pectoral cross, which is in the treasury of Durham Cathedral, and the greatest work of art in Europe of the period, the Lindisfarne Gospels, which are in the British Library.

Now instead there is the gloriously picturesque ruin of the succeeding Norman priory in red stone. On the promontory alongside the priory is the parish church of St Mary's and a little English Heritage museum with a big collection of bits and pieces of stones engraved and carved with Anglo-Saxon runic inscriptions that must have been part of the daily scene for both Aidan and Cuthbert. As is the way with history, the conqueror had the last word, not just the Norman but the marauding Viking: the best piece in the museum collection is a Norse grave-marker of the 9th century.

By that time the Vikings had come to

settle, not to raid, though the reliefs on the grave marker send out opposed messages. On one side is a cross; above the left bar of the cross is a disc representing the sun; the right bar, a new moon; the hands of God point towards the cross from each side, and beneath are two praying figures. Four holes on the cross suggest that the figure of Christ was once fixed there. The sun and moon may symbolise the day of judgement. But on the other side warriors in procession flourish axes and swords above their heads. This may be simply a friendly reference to the carver's pagan ancestors, or it may be that the scene represents the evil enemy of all that's holy that Christ will cast out.

Edwin Lutyens at Lindisfarne Castle

In 1902 Edward Hudson, the founder of *Country Life* magazine, bought Lindisfarne Castle, a Tudor fort set spectacularly on a tall rocky outcrop looking north across the harbour towards the village and priory and south across the North Sea to Bamburgh Castle. It was well on its way to ruin, but one of his close friends was Edwin Lutyens (1869–1944), who remained a friend in spite of being the parent of a disobliging little daughter who refused to allow Hudson, her godfather, to kiss her because she thought him ugly. Hudson commissioned Lutyens to convert the castle into a holiday house. It was, in effect, a dry run, if the term may be used of Holy Island, for his entirely new Castle Drogo, built on Dartmoor eight years later (see Drewsteignton, Southwest). At Lindisfarne there was no garden, but Lutyens drafted in his frequent collaborator, the inspirational garden designer Gertrude Jekyll, who converted an old kitchen garden a few hundred yards north of the castle to a walled garden (since restored by the National Trust).

Lindisfarne was a seriously intended

Vikings who had finally come to the northeast coast – and to Holy Island – no longer to pillage but to settle, carved this image of a savage raiding party, but on the other side is a cross and the hands of God

Tudor fortress, last modernised on the orders of Queen Elizabeth I. So the things Lutyens had to invent at Castle Drogo were already there for him at Lindisfarne, especially the dining room and ship room (a sitting room named after part of the decor, a ship in a bottle), which were vaulted to take the weight of cannon on the terrace above and converted from dynamite stores. Lutyens inserted little Gothic windows into the deep window recesses in both rooms and hinged the curtain rails so that instead of opening the curtains in the morning the servants, for of course there were servants, swung the curtains back and the window arches were displayed in their full glory. Everywhere corridors are like bomb-proof tunnels, stairwells are deep and dramatic

beyond mere necessity, floors are herringbone pattern brick or great stone slabs. He built a huge fireplace in the ship room, which poured smoke into the room, as anyone who has had an ingle nook could have told him was likely. The entrance hall is supported on big round arches and great circular piers. In the kitchen he designed the oak dresser and bought in the 19th-century elm settle with a cupboard in the back for hanging sides of bacon. In the scullery is the gear for operating the portcullis in the gateway below. It has to be remembered in all this that Lutyens was the man who built a dolls' house mansion for the infant Queen Mary. The Hudson house guests had to be prepared for fun more than comfort. Not all of them were up to it. Lytton Strachey recorded peevishly: 'nothing but stone under, over & round you, which produces a distressing effect – especially when one's hurrying downstairs late for dinner – to slip would be instant death.'

Huddersfield
YORKSHIRE

Early Francis Bacon, Huddersfield Art Gallery

Hitler postponed art in Huddersfield. His war caused the new gallery in the library building to be taken over instead as a hospital ward. What Hitler failed to do was flatten the town, but the decimation of the textile mills, the building of Soviet-era tower blocks and the traffic engineers have torn the shape out of a place that still has its grand Corinthian railway station and a great new sports stadium in the town where professional rugby league was launched in 1895. The 1930s stripped classicism of the (listed) library and art gallery isn't much to write home about, and inside it is distinctly tatty, but the contents form a collection of modern British art to rival any in a town this size.

The most astonishing of these to find in this kind of collection is a painting of 1945–6 by Francis Bacon, *Figure Study II*. Although Bacon's popular reputation is worldwide, no one splits the artist community as he does. The first time I published an anti-Bacon piece, a very good painter and friend of mine told me he tore the *Guardian* up in a rage when he read it; and, of course, Bacon's colleague and friend, Lucian Freud, who certainly can paint, is only the most eminent of artists who admired him. The St Ives painter and *New Statesman* critic Patrick Heron didn't, on the grounds that painting was about painting, not about grand guignol.

Bacon started life as a designer but created his first paintings in 1929 after being

impressed by some of the images Picasso was then making of mutated beings. In the late 1930s he had his first solo show and retired hurt for seven years after a disparaging *Times* review. In the 1940s he started again, and *Figure Study II* of 1945–6 is one of a sequence of similar images – the Scottish National Gallery has *Figure Study I*. It was an important series to Bacon personally because the Museum of Modern Art in New York bought the most famous of them, *Painting 1946*, and encouraged him to feel that he was on course.

His imagery resonated for post-Holocaust man. *Figure Study II* shows a harsh orange panelled room, a 'foyer to a private hell' as an American exhibition catalogue described it. In it is a figure bent double with a tweed coat draped over its rear half, an umbrella suspended somehow over the head with, of course, a darkly gaping mouth. The naked torso is white, softly slug-like, defenceless; the head is thrust down among palm fronds.

So far, so creepy. The problem is the execution. Bacon was often praised for his handling of paint, and there are passages where it does come off – the naked torso here is one. But too often precisely the opposite is true. A single line across the floor changes direction to suggest that the figure is on a platform, but this gesture towards defining the pictorial space is too cursory to mean much. All the same, this is among the most interesting of his paintings. Afterwards, he paid a high price for success. His rich fans continue to pay a high price for the canvases.

Hull
YORKSHIRE

Hull has all the airs and some of the graces of a major maritime city. Even the sheds housing mega-markets like Currys and B&Q lining the A63 by the Humber have a nautical feel for, in a post-modern style of leisured affluence, Hull lives cheek by jowl with the sea, the city centre penetrated by creeks and abandoned docks. The great open space at the heart of Hull, Victoria Square, and the city hall and Ferens Art Gallery stand beside the old Princes quay, now a glittering shopping mall with the old dock a marina. And, of course, Kingston upon Hull, to give it its full dress name, also lies on the River Hull, a navigable river that brings its tribute of spring water from the Yorkshire wolds to the salt Humber, which it joins just below a tidal barrier. It is also the cause of traffic jams as the many lifting bridges in the city effectively close the roads when barges are passing through.

The city's most glorious chapter was the day it locked its gates in the face of King Charles I. It then maintained its opposition to royal presumption until William of Orange ended the short Catholic reign of James II, a passage of history celebrated by the Scheemakers equestrian sculpture of William III in the marketplace. Its great parish church looking down on the marketplace is the biggest in England and is a fortunate survival in a city whose medieval quarter was almost obliterated in the Second World War, though the anti-slavery campaigner William Wilberforce was born in Hull, and his Georgian house in the old High Street survives as a museum. When Hull became a city in 1897 a burst of creativity produced a fine new Edwardian city centre focused on Victoria Square, with a florid new town hall and a new guildhall.

Frans Hals at the Ferens Art Gallery

The Ferens Gallery is not exactly narrow in the scope of its collection. There's everything from a fine English 15th-century resurrection carved from alabaster quarried at Chellaston in Derbyshire to an offbeat collection of English painting with some cityscapes of Hull in the days when it was a great port for merchant sailing ships. There are some French baroque works. There is also a fine Dutch collection – only to be expected, perhaps, of a rich city with direct trading links to The Hague and Amsterdam. And within the Dutch collection is a portrait by the frequently underrated but magnificent master Frans Hals (c.1582–1666).

Nothing is known of the sitter in this portrait, made some time in the 1650s, except that, as her costume indicates, she was the wife of a bourgeois, about the highest status afforded in the newly renascent Protestant Netherlands. Hals confronts the straightforward simplicity of her direct gaze, the slight tiredness around her eyes, the reserved smile, the broad brow and the big white kerchief tied neatly around her shoulders, the mild frivolity of dangling earrings, with a matching simplicity of pose: head on, direct, no drama, just a mild inclination of the head as she sits sizing up the nature of the man painting her. It's a portrait worthy of the history of the city that bought it, the community that stood up for Parliament against an overmighty Spanish Catholic king.

The key to Hals is that he is never diverted in his painting from what he sees before him. He pays court to no man and to no woman. He records status but equally dispassionately sets down the stigmata of genetic inheritance and the ineradicable traces of life's ravages. In this he is close to his contemporary Rembrandt. Both came from the Protestant northern Netherlands where the hallmarks of society were a booming market economy and a free-thinking individualism – very different from Catholic Flanders where Rubens and Van Dyck grew up. The flipside was that Hals and Rembrandt lacked Rubens' and Van Dyck's rich aristocratic patrons and so ran the risk of public indifference. Hals lived out his poverty-stricken old age in an almshouse. Here he painted two group portraits of the governors and the governesses. Age and illness and in one case a stroke have made these worthy old men and women into pathetic caricatures of what they once were, but in the Hals painting there is no satire, and the compassion we feel looking at it is what we ourselves bring to the feast. Hals is the recording angel.

He is often taken for an inferior Rembrandt, but the virtuosity of his swift brushwork was unequalled until Edouard Manet's two centuries later. Manet, too, was a genius occasionally accused of facility. Hals's portraits do not seem, like Rembrandt's, to be a window into the soul, but all of them are ripe with present circumstance, observed mortality and approaching death, *The Laughing Cavalier* as much as the young woman in the Ferens portrait.

Stained glass window by a children's illustrator, Church of the Holy Trinity

Holy Trinity is the biggest parish church in England, with an eight-bay nave that can seat a congregation of 2,000 and a five-bay chancel. It dates from the 14th century to the 16th when the last stage of the big central tower was added. It boasts a window in the south transept that is almost certainly unique, since it is assembled from fragments of glass from another window destroyed in a Zeppelin raid.

At first glance the left of the two windows by Walter Crane (1845–1915) in the south aisle could be mistaken for another unfortunate accident. It is the more exciting of the two (installed in 1897 and 1907), full of writhing forms composed of small elongated glass quarries with leading between them and rising in an ecstasy of colour, raised angels wings and clapping hands through the five lights of the window to more figures in the

tracery. The human figures across the bottom of the window are medieval peasantry and knights with, oddly, a single Sikh among them, and trumpeters in short, yellow Roman tunics. Beside the trumpeters another musician clashes cymbals. It seems to be a celebration in heaven and on earth, but of what? I asked one of the associate vicars, and he hadn't a clue either. The central figure of the drama is missing. A dove descends through a shower of apples, but if it is the Holy Spirit, it travels incognito.

Crane spent his life suffering under the general apprehension that his best work was in children's illustration. But he was a devoted follower of William Morris, and although he never worked for Morris's firm he followed Morris into socialism and designed banners and posters for the trade unions. He wanted to be recognised as a great painter, but his one painting in Tate Britain tells us why he wasn't. Instead, when Morris died Crane rose to the forefront as a designer, famous for his cartoons, general book illustration, his ceramics and wallpaper and his stained glass. It has to be said, though, that a conventional heart beats beneath all the vivacity to be found in this window. Everyone depicted, from human to angel, seems to be in fancy dress, having a ball. The children's illustrations really are better.

Statue of William III, marketplace

The plinth of Scheemakers's statue of William III declares that it was set up in 1734 'To the Memory of King William the Third, our Great Deliverer'. Not only did he deliver the city from James II, the Catholic monarch it opposed, but he saves it today from the ignominy of having utterly destroyed its fine marketplace with dreary post-war building and the open wound of the dual carriageway A63 severing the marketplace from the old docks. Scheemakers's king on his prancing horse commands the space like the true Roman he's togged out to be, though it is known with friendly familiarity as the King Billy Statue.

Peter Scheemakers (1691–1781) designed the statue for the competition proposed by Bristol's ruling Whigs in 1733 for the commission to erect a memorial to the king in Queen Square (see Bristol, Southwest). He lost to Michael Rysbrack, and Hull moved quickly. As it turned out, Rysbrack's winning statue wasn't in place in Bristol until three years after Hull set up the Scheemakers version. Rysbrack's William, and even more, his horse, are a livelier and more romantic conception, but Scheemakers's king has a sense of effortless authority, and here he is in his element. Hull, after all, grew from a fishing village on trade with the Hanse of Germany and with the Low Countries. What better than that William of Orange should fit himself for the throne of England by marrying the Protestant daughter of the Catholic James and sharing the monarchy with her? The Hull burghers gilded the statue in 1768, an exhilarating notion that comes into its own against the open sky over the Humber estuary beyond the wretched A63.

The biggest election bribe in history, the Humber Bridge

The 1964 general election had installed Harold Wilson's Labour government with a majority of four. In 1966 this fell to three with the death of the member for Hull North, Henry Solomons. It was vital for the survival of the government to hold this highly marginal seat at the by-election, but the maverick left-wing journalist Richard Gott put the wind up Labour by standing as an anti-Vietnam War candidate. Wilson sent in his elite corps. Among the smoothly smiling ministers who arrived at the hustings in droves was the secretary for transport,

Barbara Castle (nothing smooth about her), who promised that yellowing plans for the long-touted Humber Bridge would be taken out of the pending tray, dusted off and activated. Gott received 253 votes, and somewhere in the stratosphere of the real contest Labour trounced the Conservatives. Fifteen years and £151 million later (and rising with the accumulation of interest) the Queen snipped the tape to open the new bridge. In political mythology it has become known as the biggest election bribe in history.

The remaining question was whether or not the Humber Bridge would prove a white elephant. The engineer was Ralph Freeman (1911–98), so it was always going to be a good bridge. He had honed his skills with the Royal Engineers, throwing bailey bridges over the rivers of northern Europe as the Allied armies pushed into Germany, so working on the Forth Road Bridge, the beautiful Erskine Bridge over the Clyde west of Glasgow and the Severn Bridge (1966) must have been relatively blissful. The challenge of the Humber is that it is fast-flowing and the riverbed constantly shifts, so Freeman devised a single-span bridge with a steel deck suspended from concrete towers by steel cables 28 inches in diameter. It is 4,627 feet long, and at the time it was the longest single-span bridge in the world. Looking from the A63 into Hull, which passes under the bridge, it is a wonderful spectacle, and in misty weather poignantly beautiful. But as for the white elephant question, there is nothing at the southern end but an east–west motorway and a long haul to Lincoln on an old Roman road. 'Not very busy today,' I remarked tactlessly to the man on the tollbooth when I last drove through. 'Not yet,' he said darkly, 'but it will be.' For the trip to Scunthorpe or Grismby it's excellent, but they've been waiting for the crowds since 1981; and the debt stands at £333 million.

Ireshopeburn
COUNTY DURHAM

Wesley memorial, next to the Wesleyan chapel

When he died in 1791 John Wesley was still within the body of the Anglican church, though for many years he had taken upon himself the ordination of clergy, having concluded that the apostolic succession of bishops was a fiction. But whatever church he felt he belonged too, once he had taken to preaching in the fields and at the wayside because the Church of England had banned him from preaching in its churches, he was consciously consolidating disparate local groups of evangelicals, putting together a different and nationwide organisation, the Methodists. His travels covered an area between London and Bristol and up to Northumbria with excursions into Cornwall. Ireshopeburn (pronounced Eyesepburn) was one of his places, a tiny village on the rushing burn that grows into the Wear. Over the years he visited Weardale on thirteen occasions. At first Wesley came to Ireshopeburn to preach by the roadside, and there is a memorial in a little garden by a bridge over the burn to mark the place. Then beside this spot in 1760 the Wesleyans inaugurated High House chapel, which has become the oldest Methodist chapel to have held weekly services continuously ever since. The lead mines have gone, the young generation is shrinking, so it can't last much longer.

Architecturally it pays spartan tribute to the Gothic commandeered by the Anglicans – pointed windows, pointed gables – but it is the memorial that, once found, catches the attention. It is no bigger than a birdbath, so I missed it on my first couple of sweeps up and down the road. It's a simple round column with a couple of rings near the top and an entablature carrying a diagonally inclined face with a metal plaque bolted to it recording the bare facts: 'The Rev. John Wesley (1703–1791) renowned evangelist and founder of Methodism, preached in this vicinity on some of his many visits to Weardale.' It's as spare as the church, but this column carries in it the sense of proportion, unadorned handsomeness and plain dignity that the best art of the 18th century had rediscovered.

Jarrow
TYNE & WEAR

Bede's World, the Museum of Early Medieval Northumbria, Church Bank

Jarrow became known as Hunger City in the 1930s when the shipyards closed and the hunger marchers reached Whitehall. The war intervened, and afterwards dereliction gave way to the livid gashes of housing estates and shopping centres sundered by massive pylons stalking through to Northumberland and a road system converging on the Tyne tunnel. But alert drivers will find their way to the Bede museum and St Paul's Church and monastic ruin together in a little park at the confluence of the River Don and the Tyne. This monastery, conjoined with St Peter in Wearmouth, was Bede's life.

He is known for his *History of the English Church and People*, written in 731, which created an English culture before the fact of a unified England. And it contains its little autobiographical note:

I was born on the lands of this monastery, and on reaching seven years of age, I was entrusted by my family first to the most reverend Abbot Benedict and later to Abbot Ceolfrid for my education. I have spent all the remainder of my life in this monastery … And while I have observed the regular discipline and sung the choir offices daily in church, my chief delight

*has always been in study, teaching, and
writing.*

He died on Ascension day, 26 May 735, having
only minutes before penned the last line of
the last book of many.

His autoportrait suggests that at first he
was with Benedict Biscop, the abbot at
Wearmouth and founder of Jarrow, and this
must be so because work on St Paul's, Jarrow,
started only in 681, the year after Bede joined
the monastic community, and it was
dedicated in 685. So he moved into it when it
was brand new and he wasn't quite, and what
we see in the museum, the church and the
ruins could be the things and places he lived
among. Bets have to be hedged, because a lot
of scholarly ink, and blood, is being spilled
over dating Anglo-Saxon sculpture. But since
excavations in the 1960s and 1970s produced
several fine carved pieces from the site of St
Paul's, and as Viking depredations after the
death of Bede blighted the cultural soil, what
is now displayed in the Bede's World
Museum is likely to be the art that Bede lived
with, and the fragments of coloured glass are
the outstanding European proof that stained
glass windows existed already in Bede's time.
Ruins of the monastery apart, the chancel of
the church of St Paul survives entire from
Bede's time, despite Viking raids, a shrine
poignantly evocative of the struggles of early
Christianity in the north. The museum
building, incidentally, based on the kind of
Roman villa built and described by Pliny, is a
little masterpiece by Eldred Evans and David
Shalev, the husband and wife team who also
designed Tate St Ives. (Presumably no secular
Saxon building could have served the
purpose). Among many remarkable objects
inside, the most beautiful is the figure of a
hunter apparently forcing his way through a
thicket, intricately but lucidly designed. It's
what's known by architectural historians as
an inhabited plant scroll, and a plant scroll is

usually based, however remotely, on vine
scrolls in Mediterranean sculpture, which, in
turn, derived from Christ's words reported in
John 15:1, 'I am the true vine'. There's also a
horse's head – half-horse and half-solid rock
– which, had he seen it, Picasso must surely
have incorporated into his own art.

Knaresborough
YORKSHIRE

*Monument to Sir William Slingsby,
Church of St John*

The attribution of the monument to
Epiphanius Evesham (*c.*1570–*c.*1633) is a trifle
hesitant on the basis that Sir William de
Slingsby died in 1634, and Evesham's date of
death ranges from the 1620s to 1633 according
to which expert you read. Since there is no
documentary evidence, it can only be said
that in England only his younger
contemporary Nicholas Stone was working
in anything like a naturalistic mode (and he
too had trained on the continent), but his
style was grander, not the mode of relaxed
naturalism that marks Evesham out.

Most of Evesham's surviving work is in
London and the home counties, principally
Kent (see Lynsted, Southeast), but he did
work for families living further afield, no
doubt from his workshop in London. For the
rich and powerful, and the royalist Slingsby
family were both, England was a small place.
They were MPs and landowners: Sir William
owned property and land in Knaresborough
and the West Riding as well as in London. The
north aisle chapel holds four Slingsby
monuments, and two of the figures step
outside the convention of recumbent effigies:
Sir Henry, who also died in 1634, is shown
upright in a shroud, a format newly invented
by Nicholas Stone for John Donne's memorial
in St Paul's; William's shows him in cavalier's
dress with a broad-brimmed hat and wide

collar over a tunic, trousers meeting spurred, calf-length boots. He stands informally in a niche with one leg crossed over the other and holds a shield vividly painted with the Slingsby arms – gold, silver, red and black. He has thrust his sword into the ground at his feet, rests his left elbow on it and leans his head against his left hand as casually as a modern man of his class might perch on a shooting stick. It's a quite remarkably informal arrangement, beautifully realised.

Leeds

YORKSHIRE

The best J.B. Priestley could find to say about Leeds was: 'It is a large, dirty town that might almost be anywhere, and mostly built of sooty brick.' But that was in 1933, and Leeds has cleaned up its act since. Anyway, Priestley has the prejudice of a Bradford man. Although Leeds runs into Bradford with only the tiniest break, with Cleckheaton, Dewsbury and Batley similarly attached, all these places in this huge urban agglomeration fiercely defend their own individuality. In that sense, Leeds is different, grander, but lacking, as Priestley says, 'the authentic, queer, carved-out-of-the-Pennines look of Bradford and some of the other towns'.

On the wrong side of the tracks, in Hunslet, it could have rivalled anywhere in the West Riding for squalid slum housing, the notorious back-to-backs; but they have been swept away. The employers of these working people lived in the salubrious villas of Headingley and Roundhay within reach of the attractive towns and villages of Wharfedale. Yet Asa Briggs called his chapter on Leeds in his *Victorian Cities* 'A study in civic pride', and central Leeds bears him out. This, now, is contained between a loop of the M64 and A58 to the north and the River Ayre

to the south. Its spine is Westgate, broad and comely, running into Headrow. Visitors who aren't primarily coming to Opera North in the Grand Theatre or to take in Whitelock's pub or the fine art gallery will wander along Westgate and the Headrow to see what civic pride can do. To the north of Westgate is the huge, handsome town hall with a multi-columned dome built by the 19th-century Yorkshire architect Cuthbert Brodrick and one of the best four or five municipal art galleries in the country, with the Henry Moore Institute alongside. The Grand Theatre is worth seeing just for its luxurious auditorium, never mind the opera. South of the Headrow either side of Briggate are blocks of Victorian shopping arcades – early examples of private–public enterprise that actually worked, glass roofed and gloriously extrovert. Beyond those is the huge Edwardian iron girt Kirkgate Market, where Mr Marks and Mr Spencer started out in business trading from a stall. In the vicinity is Whitelocks, one of the best of pubs, with 1880s decor and a long white marble-topped faience tiled bar. Plenty of brass around Leeds, not much muck.

A neglected English painter, Leeds City Art Gallery

Leeds City Art Gallery was built largely on money raised for Queen Victoria's golden jubilee in 1887; it opened a year later. It has been lucky in its local benefactors and has enough European art from the Renaissance onwards to be able to put together a guide that convincingly walks visitors through the periods up to the 20th century. My pick of the lot would be the study for *Young Ladies of the Village* by Gustave Courbet (1819–1877), but if that seems too quirky, there is a brilliantly coloured oil of barges on the Thames by the Fauve André Derain, domestic interiors by Pierre Bonnard

(1867–1947) and his compatriot Edouard Vuillard, a Renoir girl, a glittering impression of the interior of the New Bedford music-hall by Walter Sickert (1860–1942), and a lot of good British 20th-century art. Out of all this I choose Norman Stevens (1937–88), not only because he was a great talent, but also because he was a friend who died too young. Stevens was acidly witty, phlegmatic, articulate, blunt, subtly sympathetic, limped heavily from the after-effects of polio and smoked heavily; a bit like a Yorkshire Hogarth in character.

He was also, more to the point, a friend of David Hockney from when they went together to Bradford Grammar School, Bradford art college and the Royal College of Art. As students on their first visit to the United States they hired a car and drove from New York to the west coast. Hockney's take on New York, in his series of etchings after Hogarth's *The Rake's Progress*, made him a star. Stevens's talent burned more slowly. He brought back studies for paintings of the ribbon of road in the far west disappearing over the low horizon with featureless desert stretching away on each side, effortlessly abstract. Later, he was with other artists in the generation who joined the Royal Academy when it loosened up following the long reactionary years. 'Bloody 'ell,' he said to me as he left the pub where we'd met one day, 'I'm an ARA and I can't afford a bloody taxi.' A few months later he was dead.

Until then he was still exploring perspective and illusion. The subjects had become simple, even pastoral, though only on the face of it: five-barred farm gates, topiary, dark openings in dense garden hedges and in the 5 foot square Leeds painting entitled *Collapsing Structure in the Art Historian's English Garden* (1975) , Maybe the mildly whimsical irony of the title refers to a real art historian's real garden. In any case, the painting is about form and dissolving form, the effect of light and shadow on the tangible world, the balance of straight line against curve. It consists of posts and beams holding up trellis walls and an open roof structure; diagonal shadows fall across uprights and beams; the floor is painted in pointillist dots, the 'sky' in flat jade green; the light shifts very subtly in intensity from one side of the structure to the other. Finally, there is a shower of sticks falling from the structure but held in complete stasis. It's a painting that obeys nothing but its own rules, referring to real things but laying them out as abstractly as a Mondrian grid.

A mosaic for the working class, Church of St Aidan, Roundhay Road, Harehills

The young Frank Brangwyn (1867–1956) attracted the attention of that late 19th-century proponent of 'art for arts' sake' James McNeill Whistler. He was sixteen when he first exhibited at the Royal Academy. In Paris he beat off the challenge of the brilliant Austrian, Victor Horta, to decorate Frank Byng's innovative art gallery, L'Art Nouveau, and in Austria he was associated with artists like Gustav Klimt and Oskar Kokoschka in the socially more than artistically rebellious avant-garde movement, the Vienna Secession, at its foundation in 1897. He was celebrated in Europe and in America. He designed posters and graphics; he worked in ceramics, metal, textiles and glass; he exhibited at the Paris Salon and was a gold medallist at the Venice Biennale. He produced in all something like 12,000 works of art. In 1926 he received the commission to decorate the House of Lords with murals. The Lords turned down his first effort: colours too low key. He repainted brilliant scenes of empire, and the peers threw him out altogether: colours too bright. The bubble had burst. Brangwyn, whose career had started in the studio of William Morris,

The bubble of fame burst suddenly for Frank Brangwyn, but in 1916 when he was still internationally renowned he designed this gigantic mosaic (detail) for the working-class Church of St Aidan in Leeds, celebrating the career of the saint who brought Christianity to the north of England

lived long enough to see his reputation dwindle until it was no longer even a footnote in art history. In 1952 another fading institution, the Royal Academy, gave him a huge retrospective, and in 1953 the failing magazine *Studio* carried a fawning piece in its diamond jubilee issue to which Brangwyn contributed a bitter little coda: 'Anyone can paint meaningless rubbish,' he wrote, 'it takes an artist to see beauty and express it.'

He was at the height of his fame in 1916 when St Aidan's unveiled his 1,000 square foot chancel mosaic on the life of its patron, the saint who came to Northumbria to convert the heathen. The Church of England had built this church as a beacon to the working class, so Aidan, champion of the downtrodden, must have seemed appropriate, and Brangwyn did them proud. He had the skills of a fine draughtsman, and if this were his only surviving work we would wonder what other prodigies he might have performed. He wanted to be a realist celebrating the working man, but this masterpiece succeeds because it has some of the splendour of Ravenna's mosaics, not just because of the medium but because he unified the huge curving wall by laying out a Cinerama-like blue sky streaked horizontally with reddish-tinged clouds and punctuated vertically by slender poplar-like trees. In these sylvan groves we see the saint feeding the poor, arriving by boat at Holy Island from Iona, preaching to the natives and on his deathbed. The low chancel screen has further figures moving forward to hear him preach.

Brangwyn never seems to have quite understood the thrust of William Morris's work, but though outside its immediate context as church decoration this Leeds mosaic must have seemed dated and backward-looking at the time of the artist's death, now it looks what it is, the product of the possibly misbegotten ideal of a group of writers, artists and craftsmen who proposed more for public art than a celebration of wealth and empire.

Theatrical shopping arcades in the Victoria Quarter between Briggate and Vicar Lane

The Regency arcades around Piccadilly in London were shopping for the elite, exclusive enclaves where the rich and titled could buy and promenade. Leeds, at the end of a century of increasing prosperity, introduced shopping as vaudeville, as fun, as retail therapy as we say today, only half-jokingly. The choice in 1898 of Frank Matcham (1854–1920) as architect signals the intention: he was the most productive and successful of theatre architects in an age when opera rubbed shoulders with music-hall (see Buxton, North Midlands, and Blackpool, Northwest), and his Leeds arcades were exotic blooms planted on the compost of the old meat market, the Shambles, amid the grandeur of the city's town hall and riverside warehouses.

George Smith had preceded Matcham in 1887–8 with Thornton's Arcade and Edward Clark with Queen's Arcade, but Matcham's County Arcade is easily the finest. After the Second World War it fell into dingy decline,

with Matcham's marble Ionic columns maladroitly recased and tawdry shop signs at all heights and angles and multiple styles or no style at all, some of them half-obscuring the mahogany-framed shop windows. But in 1988–90 the Derby architects Derek Latham & Co. sensitively restored Matcham's work, with its glass tunnel vault carried on openwork iron arches and first-floor balconies in cream and green. The walls, floors and pillars are in pink Siena marble, faience, terracotta, mosaic, and there are generous ball light globes suspended from elongated iron cages. The artist Brian Clark (b.1953) glassed over Queen Victoria Street as part of the Latham restoration to pull it into the Victoria Quarter arcades, and his high, light roof with irregular colour areas of blue, red, green and yellow squares invading each other like bright clouds drifting above is different but quite in sympathy with Matcham's work. A dome crowning Cross Arcade pulls the whole ensemble together: commerce as king.

Temple Newsam, Temple Newsam Road

The original Temple Newsam was Tudor. As we see it now it looks Jacobean but is wholly Carolean, mostly of the 1620s. It was built on three sides of a terrace in 900 acres of parkland overlooking once prosperous mill towns. The original Tudor house witnessed the birth of Lord Darnley, who later married Mary Queen of Scots and was murdered at the instigation of her new lover, but not before he had fathered James I and VI. The house today is magnificent but dominating and unlovable, partly because of the huge inscription set in open lettering against the sky that runs around all three wings and reads: 'All Glory and Praise be given to God the Father the Son and the Holy Ghost on High, Peace on Earth, Goodwill towards Men, Honour and True Allegiance to our Gracious King, Loving affection amongst his subjects, Health and Plenty be within this House.' The great Tudor magnate Bess of Hardwick was pithier, simply repeating her initials over and over against the sky.

Later, Temple Newsam came to the Woods family, whose descendant Lord Halifax, later Neville Chamberlain's foreign minister and leading appeaser, sold it to the city of Leeds but stripped it of most of its paintings, selling many. Leeds has been doggedly buying back some of this dispersed collection, and Halifax returned many, but not the best. The latest Lord Halifax has recently removed one of the paintings retained by the family, a Titian *Portrait of a Man*, from the walls of the National Gallery with a view to a sale, by the looks of it, abroad.

One of the finest paintings from the old collection hangs again in the place it once had in Temple Newsam's picture gallery. *Rocky Landscape with a Hermit and a Lay Brother* by Pier Francesco Mola (1612–66), a strange, romantic and beautiful evening-lit landscape, belongs to Denis Mahon, the collector and historian who was foremost in restoring the reputation of Italian 17th-century painting, and he has promised it to Leeds by bequest. It is typical of Mola's best work, and it might be described as dream-like if it weren't for the intense rendering of the scene, a white-cowled monk in the middle foreground against a sky that seems to threaten something supernatural and a landscape that could be a combination of the Roman campagna and North Africa, though Mola has probably simply borrowed the palm trees from Rome itself.

Middlesbrough
YORKSHIRE

Modern Middlesbrough began as a notion in the head of the Quaker Joseph Pease, a prime sponsor, with his father Edward, of the Stockton & Darlington Railway (see Darlington, above). He realised that the Tees at Stockton was too shallow for the heavy cargoes of coal coming down the line. At the time Middlesbrough was four cottages with twenty-one inhabitants among them, but Pease dreamed of it as his future Port Darlington. It stubbornly stayed as Middlesbrough, but by the middle of the 19th century Gladstone described it as an infant Hercules, and it grew into a fully grown Hercules, not just as a port but also as a huge producer of pig iron after ironstone deposits were discovered in the Cleveland Hills. It was twice as big as Darlington by the end of the 19th century and still has twice the social problems. The Quaker notion of a city growing in civility quickly became swamped as industrialists moved in, and such civic amenities as existed were quickly swamped in steel manufacture, shipbuilding, bridge-building and, later, petro-chemicals.

Today the town has started again. The Gradgrind mentality has vanished. The top-flight football club that allowed Wilf Mannion, the ironworks lad who became a shining light in English football history (late 1930s to early 1960s), to live and die in penury because he had defied maximum wage regulations (specifying £10 a week) has put a statue of him outside its new stadium, the Riverside, which may be a way of saying sorry. The gaunt, towering transporter bridge has become a famous and loved landmark, spotlit at night. The Peases created Central Square with a grid of streets around it. This decrepit site is now mooted as one of the biggest open spaces in Europe, and its renaissance has started with the hi-tech glass-walled Middlesbrough Institute of Modern Art, Mima, which started with a good collection and has lavish funds to keep abreast. There is a Claes Oldenberg sculpture nearby and more to come. Watch this space, as they say.

Bridget Riley at the Middlesbrough Institute of Modern Art

If ever an art gallery was a mirage, it is Mima, the new glass palace built by the Dutch architect Erick van Egeraat as part of his planned new city centre on the windswept vacancies of the old Centre Square in Middlesbrough. Van Egeraat won a competition to inject new life into this grim, blighted town, and he began work with the Rotterdam landscape architects West8 on replanning the square. Mima closes one side of the square, a screen wall of large blocks of limestone enclosed in a glass atrium and behind this five functionally handsome exhibition spaces. Mima comes on like the Pompidou Centre: even the diagonal groove on the limestone screen behind the glass mimics the Richard Rogers–Enzo Piano escalator, and in publicity mock-ups beautiful people disport themselves in the square.

Middlesbrough started with an advantage: it already had a good collection of 20th-century British art. And on this basis it became one of fifteen museums in Britain chosen by the Contemporary Arts Society to receive new work by the generation of Tracey Emin and Gavin Turk. Whatever other qualities these newer works have, they also throw into relief the enduring brilliance of Bridget Riley's work of 1965, seven prints on Plexiglass called *Fragments 1–7*, created only a year after she announced her arrival along with David Hockney, John Hoyland and others at the famous New Generation exhibition at the Whitechapel Gallery. She wanted to print the sequence of seven abstracts on to Plexiglass (similar to Perspex, but a different trade name), but it was an unfamiliar job to specialist fine art printers, so Riley (b.1931) was forced outside to a commercial art company. With each image on the back of thick, transparent plastic

blocks, it looks as though they are floating in space, especially as the prints need no framing. All seven *Fragments* are black and white, comprising dots of varying sizes, lines going from thick to thin and thin to thick in waves, zigzags, rows of dots apparently disappearing into a deep fold, a hallucinatory play of variations on a theme of minutely varied basic shapes. These fragments of art might seem distantly related to the painting of Seurat, where dots of pure colour mix on the eye's retina to create images. In fact, Riley's early painting based on appearances took off from Seurat's Neo-Impressionism, and the link has never broken. She speaks of looking closely at lichens, gazing at the blue of the sky in a sandy pool, watching the dark streaks of ruffled water or wind-blown grass like little silver pennants. Her astonishing, meticulous art remains rooted in the everyday world of appearances. Or so Riley believes, and it makes no difference to our response to these perfect, dazzling surfaces whether or not we believe it as well. Her repertoire has depended on the same sort of abstract elements throughout her career. The variations come in fine judgements of shape, space, colour, scale and medium.

The transporter bridge

The transporter bridge is to Middlesbrough what the Empire State Building is to New York, though Middlesbrough has never been on the tourist route. As far back as I remember it was wrapped in hellish smoke, but the bridge drew all eyes through the gloom even then. The Cleveland Bridge Company of Darlington built it in 1911. It stands 285 feet high and is 850 feet long, a gantry supported on pylons, spanning the Tees between Middlesbrough and Port Clarence, linking the docks and heavy industry of one to the chemical industries of the other. So few people use it that the

The transporter bridge links the Middlesbrough docks on the south bank of the Tees to Port Clarence on the north bank. Neither is central to the economy today and the bridge has been painted a festive blue, more in keeping with its heritage status than its hard-working past

nine-car capacity of the moving cage slung by cables from the gantry above is sufficient, not least because Port Clarence is a kind of hell hole itself now: high unemployment, high crime and a dismal street scene. The Middlesbrough approach to the bridge is through a post-industrial void along Durham Street. Now it's painted bright blue, which feels like King Kong got out in a Winnie-the-Pooh T-shirt. But English Heritage has listed it grade II, of architectural and historic interest. Once, nobody would have given a damn. Now, with Middlesbrough striving to clamber aboard the heritage bandwagon, it's something to boast about.

Newcastle upon Tyne and Gateshead

The Angel of the North looms through the mist enveloping the A1 approach to Tyneside. A couple of visitors on the grassy embankment stand a bit over instep height to the heavenly messenger, eyes bent upwards to look for the head in the sky. That's one way of viewing it, but Antony Gormley designed his steel angel to be seen the modern way, from a car passing by at 70 miles an hour; 90,000 people a day, they reckon, or 33 million a year see it this way, one person every second. It is the height of a five-storey building and has a wingspan as wide as a Boeing 747, it weighs 200 tonnes, and it punches its weight visually. It was made of Cor-ten steel from the United States Steel Corporation, because the British steel industry was defunct. If this heraldic angel could sing, it would sing a threnody of Consett and Jarrow. If it could speak, it would be in implacable Geordie. Can you tell me where the Shipley Art Gallery is please? Ay hinny, away doon the toon.

Doon the toon means along the A167 to Prince Consort Road, one of the pleasanter parts of Gateshead, where, close to the town hall where the idea for Antony Gormley's sculpture was generated, the Shipley gallery stands with its own treasure, the vast canvas of *Christ Washing the Disciples' Feet* by Tintoretto. Back on the A167 the road dips sharply to the most vivid approach to any English city. From the deck of the Tyne Bridge can be seen, to the left, Robert Stephenson's High Level Bridge with the train above, road below; further into the city the cathedral pushes the open crown of its tower into view above the waterfront buildings. Nearby, the keep of the new castle survives, obliterating the site of a fort on Hadrian's Wall, and the Black Gate Museum, which used to be living quarters within the castle but now contains mostly Roman artefacts. To the right of the Tyne Bridge are the glitzy Millennium Bridge, Norman Foster's Sage Music Centre and the Baltic Centre, a flour mill converted into a contemporary arts arena and looking like a Geordie cousin somewhat removed to an Aztec ziggurat, both of these on the Gateshead bank. Further west in Gateshead a riverside area of dereliction is now a sculpture park, part of the same initiative that brought the Juan Munoz *Conversation Piece* to South Shields (see below). Directly ahead of the bridge is the peopled rock face of the Northumberland riverbank, and from the Newcastle bank the A167 becomes a motorway that carves around the centre of Newcastle to rejoin the high road to Scotland.

Feeder roads lead from it to John Dobson Street (with the Laing Art Gallery), which

John Dobson didn't design, and Grey Street, which he did. The trio of Dobson (1787–1865) as architect, Richard Grainger (1797–1861) as builder and the visionary town clerk John Clayton, over a period of only ten years mostly in the 1830s replaced a brick and timber town centre with Grainger Town, the big stone buildings that now define the finest modern town centre in the north. There are 450 buildings, 250 of them listed, much of the area targeted in the 1960s by the leader of the city council, T. Dan Smith, for demolition to make way for a new centre. Dobson's fine Eldon Square fell to the hammers before Smith was jailed for corruption and Grainger Town was saved.

Grey Street is at the heart of it, sweeping down from the Grey Monument past the great pediment of the Theatre Royal to the Tyne (the monument is in memory of Earl Grey, the prime minister; another of his memorials is the name of the tea). England's finest railway station, perched high above the river and the great market, is Dobson's too. The Royal Shakespeare Company has its northern headquarters in the Theatre Royal and has been given the freedom of the city, right up there with the Newcastle football hero Alan Shearer. Beyond the monument is the Civic Centre, and behind that is Town Moor, 800 hectares of common land bigger than any park in London, though the usual sharks have nibbled away around the edges. Newcastle University edges in close with the Hatton Gallery, which, apart from the unique Kurt Schwitters work that I describe below, is a fine museum of modern art. You cannot park there, so either leg it or take a cab.

Tintoretto at the Shipley Art Gallery, Gateshead

Joseph Ainslie Davidson Shipley, a prosperous Victorian solicitor, offered his collection of undistinguished paintings to

Newcastle, and when the city elders there turned him down, he donated them to his native town together with £30,000 to build a gallery. The Newcastle architect Arthur Stockwell built it in municipal classicism with a Corinthian portico as dignified as a mayor in ermine and gold chain, and it opened in 1917. There were more than 500 paintings to hang, and today there is an interloper acquired in 1986 and hanging on the far end wall, unlabelled and in a setting of Victorian narrative pictures. Almost 18 feet wide by more than 7 feet high, it is *Christ Washing the Disciples' Feet* by Tintoretto (1518–94). It had been regarded as a copy of one in the Prado but has recently been convincingly designated the original, painted in 1547 for the church of San Marcuola in Canareggio, the district of Venice where Tintoretto lived all his life – the Madrid version is also an autograph Tintoretto, painted a few months later, and there's another, smaller one in the National Gallery.

Tintoretto worked in the shadow of Titian, friend of the mighty. Princes, popes and bankers were not Tintoretto's patrons. He worked mostly for churches and religious colleges in Venice, especially for his own parish church, Madonna del Orto, which is full of his paintings, and the Scuola san Rocco, where he laboured for twenty years. 'For more than half a century,' wrote Jean-Paul Sartre, 'Tintoretto the Mole burrows in a labyrinth whose walls are splattered with glory.' Mole or not, Tintoretto's method of working at speed produced that late style of wraith-like figures, realistic enough to exist on earth but with one foot already in the afterworld, a technical elision of necessity and inspiration.

Christ Washing the Disciples' Feet was a spectacular concept, because the subject of this very wide canvas is shoved off to the right-hand side and the lines of perspective converge along a heavily foreshortened table carrying scattered remnants of the Last Supper and down an avenue flanked by classical buildings to a focal point at a triumphal arch in the distance, well to the left of centre. Dead centre in the foreground, providing a point of balance in a space once reserved for Christ or the sainted, a dog lies with its head raised alertly, watching the scene between Christ and Peter in which, as John (13:8) recounts, Jesus explains to his disciple: 'If I wash thee not, thou hast no part with me.' Titian had pioneered this dislocation with his off-centre Pesaro Madonna; Tintoretto took it to his customary extreme.

Maybe for the usual reason (to raise cash for a capital project), within a hundred years of Tintoretto fulfilling his commission, San Marcuola sold the Gateshead canvas and had a copy made, which still hangs in the church, opposite a genuine Tintoretto of *The Last Supper*. In 1814 *Christ Washing the Disciples' Feet* turned up in Phillips's showroom in London, and in 1818 Sir Nicholas White Ridley, of a Northumberland merchant family, presented it to the cathedral of St Nicholas, Newcastle. It is a great painting with its muted blues and greens and tawny browns and yellows; too muted, perhaps: it looks in need of sensitive restoration and cleaning.

Gauguin at the Laing Art Gallery, Newcastle upon Tyne

Alexander Laing, a Scottish wine and spirits merchant, spent £30,000 building a gallery for the city where he had made his fortune. It isn't exactly as familiar to Geordies as St James's Park is, though it has been there since 1904 and lies on New Bridge Street just off the motorway that now bisects the city centre. The bricks and mortar were assured, but there was no art, so C. Bernard Stephenson was appointed director in 1900 to put together something to be ready for opening day four years later. He survived until 1953, built a big collection of British art with brilliant highlights, and when Paul Gauguin's little *The Breton Shepherdess* slipped into the collection via the National Art Collections Fund in 1945, it did so almost unnoticed among the grand opera of John ('Mad') Martin's *Destruction of Sodom and Gomorrah*, William Holman Hunt's famous *Isabella and the Pot of Basil* and *Laus Veneris* by Edward Burne-Jones.

All these painters were already famous when Gauguin (1848–1903) was a successful stockbroker with a wife, five children and a nice little collection of Impressionist paintings. In 1883 he began to paint, encouraged by Pissarro. In 1884 he gave up his job, in 1885 he left his Danish wife and their family in Copenhagen, and, after a miserable winter in Paris as a billposter, he moved in 1886 to Pont Aven in Brittany where there were cheap lodgings and long credit. One of the pictures he painted that year was *The Breton Shepherdess*. It was a turning point. He was still painting with soft, faintly misty touches of colour, still an Impressionist, but he was looking for something beyond. Though the Laing canvas retains elements of the Impressionist softly atmospheric, almost misty touches of colour, it edges towards a new clarity of design, an emblematic simplicity that Gauguin began to see in the roadside crucifixes of Brittany and in the simple peasant dress of the Bretons, and in the ceramics and wood carvings he began to make: a clarity of colour and design that became specific in his painting when he visited Martinique in 1887.

So *The Breton Shepherdess* is a milestone in Gauguin's rapid progress and a beautiful picture in its own right. He already possesses the palette of a master, ranging from soft apricot hues to the deep greens shadowed with blue of the tree before the pink thatched cottage and the pale greyish-blues lit with pink of the wooded horizon. The deep perspective signposted by the grazing sheep and goats leading into the mid-distance is an element Gauguin would dispense with in future: too sophisticated, too western. The future was Tahiti.

A Dadaist at the Hatton Gallery, Newcastle University

'Eternal lasts longest,' Kurt Schwitters (1887–1948) remarked. Life is long, art is short, he might have added. His two major works, collages on a monumental scale that he called Merzbau, were destroyed, one by Allied bombing on Hanover in 1943, the other by accidental fire in 1951. He began a third in an English Lake District barn donated to him in 1948 by a landscape gardener called Harry Pierce (see Ambleside, Northwest), building it up and across one dry-stone wall with found objects embedded in wet plaster, a wheel rim, the seating for a gutter, a sewerage pipe, the spout of a watering can. In 1965 Pierce offered the crumbling Merzbau free to any gallery that could take it. The Tate turned it down unseen, but with the Louvre waiting in the wings to take it to Paris if no British institution took it up, the artist Richard Hamilton, then teaching at Newcastle University, decided it must be taken to the Hatton Gallery.

Schwitters had made his first Dada collages in 1918. A fellow Dadaist said that for Schwitters art was as necessary as the forest was to the forester. His forest was the city street, his art was street art – bus tickets, newspaper cuttings, pamphlets, bits and pieces of lace and rag – as well as twigs found by the riverside and discarded machine parts from junkyards. He began his first Merzbau – same principle on a gigantic scale – in his flat in Hanover, and as the son of a rentier was able to eject the inhabitants of the apartment

This collaged wall is the only survivor of three started by the pioneer Dada artist Kurt Schwitters, a refugee from Hitler. The other two fell victim to the war and he was working on this wall of a damp barn near Ambleside until his death in 1948. It is now installed in the Hatton Gallery, Newcastle

above so that his gigantic, ever-changing sculptural collage could grow through the ceiling. In 1937 he fled from the SS to Norway, where he started the second Merzbau. In 1940 he fled again, this time to England, where he was interned as an enemy alien. Released, he lived first in Barnes and then the Lake District, where he scraped a living by painting portraits and landscapes. Harry Pierce commissioned a portrait, listened to Schwitters talk about his life and art and offered him the barn at Elterwater. Moma gave him a grant of $1,000 to enable him to concentrate on his work. Four months later, as he was completing the second half of his commission for Pierce – a portrait of Mrs Pierce – he fell ill and was taken to hospital in Kendal where he died. In 1965 at Elterwater a gang from the building contractors Laing backed the wall with concrete and a steel frame, and took an agonising day edging it down the track to a Pickford's trailer. Ten snail-paced days later, over by-roads, Schwitters's barn wall arrived on Tyneside.

Today, in a space cantilevered out beyond the main gallery, the Merzbau, restored with touches of sky blue, apricot, scarlet and lemon, might have been a beached whale, and perhaps there is a touch of the mortician's art about it. But forty years on it is moving, both as a work and for the pride that had gone into its rescue and presentation, flanked by texts and with a small skylight throwing daylight across the wall just as a gap under the eaves had at Elterwater. 'It needs a poet like Schwitters to show us that unobserved elements of beauty are strewn and spread all around us,' reads one of the texts, by another refugee, the Russian Naum Gabo, whose own machine age constructivist sculpture could hardly be more different.

Nostell
YORKSHIRE

Copy of a lost Holbein of the More family, Nostell Priory

The house, in the grounds of a dissolved priory, is early 18th century, but the best of the interiors are late 18th-century neoclassical by Robert Adam with painting by his associate Antonio Zucchi and furniture by Chippendale. So it's a lovely place to visit, even though the paintings are decidedly secondary. That applies to *The Family of Sir Thomas More* by Raymond Lockey (active 1593–1616), but it has the deep historical interest that it is the only extant copy of a destroyed original by Hans Holbein the Younger.

They say that when Holbein first came to England in 1526 he stayed in Chelsea with Thomas More. There is no proof of this, but it seems likely. With the Reformation in full swing in the Germanic north, Holbein ran out of work for churches in Switzerland and Germany, and Erasmus, whom Holbein had painted at least three times, recommended him to More. On his second visit, which lasted for life, Holbein became the painter to Henry VIII, but this time his energies were mostly absorbed by the big painting of the More family and all the associated studies, marvellous portrait drawings now in the royal collection at Windsor (see South). Lockey deviates a little from the small Holbein working drawing now in Basle; there are pet dogs and a monkey and a man in the doorway rather than further back in the next room, but that may come from the defunct painting.

The picture shows the extended family, More's father, his wife, his daughter and step-daughter and adopted daughter, his fool, kept to mock his worldly pretensions, his sons-in-law, some of them in jobs he had procured for them at court, which seems a worldly enough act but was common at the time. More himself wears the Tudor regalia. He was sent on missions to the French court, he was Chancellor of the Duchy of Lancaster, he would become Lord Chancellor following Wolsey. But he opposed the king's divorce and for this he was executed in 1535.

Lockey, a pupil of the great Elizabethan miniaturist Nicholas Hilliard, was evidently a good painter, though this copy has none of the sense of intense scrutiny typical of Holbein himself. However, one could hardly expect that: there is, after all, a book on a shelf behind Erasmus in the Holbein portrait at the National Gallery, and it is inscribed in Latin, possibly by Erasmus: 'I am Johannes Holbein, whom it is easier to denigrate than to emulate.'

Nunburnholme
YORKSHIRE

A Saxon cross found in a later wall, in the Church of St James

Thank God, in alliance with the vicar of Nunburnholme, for making sure that the younger George Gilbert Scott didn't touch the tower arch of St James in 1872–3 when he was embellishing the church with a new south porch and various other restorations. The vicar, incidentally, was the Rev. Francis Orpen Morris, author of *A Natural History of British Birds* and hurler of thunderbolts from his pulpit against the blasphemy of Darwin's *Origin of the Species*. You might have thought, though, that the frontally naked little hominoid in the tower arch would have given him pause: this tiny Romanesque relief sculpture clearly represents the missing link.

Not much has changed in this quiet village a few miles east of Pocklington with a population that has hovered at little more than 200 for as long as records exist, but the tower itself was built in 1903 in memory of the vicar, who died ten years earlier. The tower arch is Norman, set into a wall constructed of huge blocks of masonry. It must have been the inner arch of the porch before there was a tower. It rises from simple columns with barbaric capitals carved with heads spewing ribbons of decoration. The arch is wide and low and defined by two orders, one with two rows of Norman zigzag,

Standing in a copse on the reputed site of the battle of Otterburn, this stone, known as the Percy Cross, recalls the battle 'on that day, that day, that dredful day', as the battle of Otterburn of 1388 is celebrated in the ancient 'Ballad of Chevy Chase'. Here Henry Percy won his spurs in a losing fight against the Scots, and the winning Scottish earl, James Douglas, was slain

the other with carved animals and humans, including the hominoid.

This is merely the warm-up for the main act, a damaged but tremendous cross-shaft of the 9th or early 10th century, which Scott's builders discovered built into the walls in 1872 when they were dismantling the old south porch. It was in two pieces that have been wrongly assembled, with the top half back to front (but the useful little church guide has a diagram of how it should have been). It is a mixture of Nordic and Christian motifs, including a warrior in profile with his hand on a Scandinavian broad sword, maybe scabbarded, and on the opposite side the Virgin and Child. Then there is a cowled figure above a fairly chaotic mutilation in which one large figure looms above smaller ones – one authority has suggested that this is a crucifixion scene. The fourth side shows a saint above a turmoil of entwined animals. Above the main figures are angels and mythic animals. Scholars suggest that the warrior figure is the donor of the cross; but though their supposition is better than ours, it rests on educated guesswork. All that's certain is that this is a magnificent relic well displayed under the tower.

Otterburn
NORTHUMBERLAND

The Percy Cross marking the Battle of Chevy Chase

Half a mile north of the Percy Arms in Otterburn, almost hidden in a copse of conifer, stands the Percy cross, marking the presumed battlefield of Otterburn in 1388. Here the doughty Earl of Douglas fell but won a famous Scottish victory, and Harry Percy earned his spurs in a losing fight. The heroism and carnage were immortalised in the Northumbrian 'Ballad of Chevy [Cheviot] Chase' and the account by the French historian embedded in the English court – 'I, John Froissart,' as he announces himself – who later met several of the battle's veterans. Without Froissart and the ballad's variants the battle would have remained a footnote to the Hundred Years War, which ranged England against France and her partner in the auld alliance, Scotland.

In August 1388 James Douglas had plundered into the north of England as far as Durham and in passing had snatched the Percy pennant from Newcastle before retiring as far as Otterburn. Henry Percy, the Earl of Northumberland's eldest son, not for nothing known as Hotspur, rapidly gathered 9,000 men and rode in pursuit. He arrived at night but insisted on engaging the enemy immediately, thus losing not only his advantage of 2,000 men over the Scots, who had spent a day preparing their positions on the high ground above Otterburn, but negating the power of his archers armed with longbows, a weapon whose prowess had been proven at the Battle of Crécy in 1346. On 'that day, that day, that dredful day', in the mournful dirge of the ballad, a hundred Scots and 1,800 English were cut down.

The Percy cross is actually a simple 17th-century obelisk tapering towards the top and set on a six-step plinth. It is the Percy cross in the same way the village inn is the Percy Arms, the way most things in the uplands of Northumberland are Percy owned or Percy in tribute, for once the battle was over the Scots retreated beyond the border bearing their own dead to Melrose Abbey. There is no Douglas cross, but in the various ballads celebrating the deeds of 19 August 1388 his best memorial lies in the 'Ballad of Otterburn':

But I hae dream'd a dreary dream
Beyond the Isle of Skye,
I saw a dead man win a fight
And I think that man was I.

Patrington
YORKSHIRE

13th-century Madonna and Child
sculpture, St Patrick

The welcome sign at St Patrick adds unequivocally that we are entering England's most beautiful church. Few would argue. It is a cross-shaped building, a church with transepts, mostly built in under half a century between the end of the 13th and middle of the 14th century. The Black Death interrupted, and the inimitably beautiful spire circled by a coronet was added before the end of the century. This building is as near perfection as Gothic gets.

It is not a coincidence that four such great churches as Patrington on the Holderness peninsula north of the Humber, Beverley Minster, St Mary, Beverley, and Holy Trinity, Hull, should have been built so close together. The area was a great entrepôt for trade with the Netherlands and the Baltic, and even Patrington, with a population never bigger than 2,000, had a small port on the coast the way another parish might have a chapel at ease. So the church here is as fine as money and great artistry could make it. Nationally, Henry III's reign coincided with a loosening of the purse strings and mobility of labour. Lay craftsmen came to work for him on short contracts in refurbishing Westminster Abbey and his palaces, and they were paid in cash. The long-term effect of the movement of money and skills created a new middle class and a demand for artworks, just

as the lay influence in parish churches was increasing. The sweet naturalism of the Patrington Virgin and Child is part of this movement, a revolution in art comparable to the Renaissance and 19th- and 20th-century modernism. It is placed in the lady chapel under a lovely ribbed vault with floral bosses as part of a reredos on a slab base with canopies of aerial freshness. Once, however, the Virgin and Child stood outside the church and so became both eroded and defaced. The Christ child has lost his head, but the visual integrity shines through. The Virgin sits with the habitual ease of any mother through the ages balancing her child on her lap, her left hip pushed outwards but her head and feet aligned to establish stasis. The drapery falls in a sharp V from her knees, and then the folds follow the line of her legs to fall diagonally to the ground, a style familiar from the contemporary Westminster workshop sculptures, so many of which still grace the abbey. The Patrington Virgin is one of the first of a type that provided a template for Michelangelo's breathtaking adaptation of the theme in his Madonna and Child in Bruges.

Penshaw
TYNE & WEAR

A monument to Radical Jack, Penshaw
Hill

'Radical Jack' Lambton (1792–1840), self-styled man of the people, remarked to his fellow politician Thomas Creevey, who was broke, 'a man might jog along on £40,000 a year'. He himself jogged along on £80,000; he was a cricketer, horse racing enthusiast, heir to the intellectual legacy of the maverick Whig Charles James Fox, and ambassador to Russia, governor of Canada and 1st Baron Lambton. He lived in Lambton Castle, built on a hill above Chester-le-Street in 1828 by the

With the aid of an old-fashioned shoe horn, 214 theatregoers can squeeze into the Georgian Theatre Royal, Richmond, the least altered of Britain's four surviving pre-1830s playhouses

Durham architect Joseph Bonomi (1739–1808). Under his estate was coal, the source of his annual £80,000, and he was loved indeed by 'the people', whose lot he did his best to improve politically and through private munificence. They, in turn, subscribed to the mother of all whip-rounds to build the most staggering monument in the north – probably anywhere in England – a copy of the Theseion on the Acropolis in Athens, half-size but visible for miles around. The nearby upstart Angel of the North (see Newcastle and Gateshead, above) is a modern motorway monument, a jolt of adrenaline for drivers hurtling north. The Penshaw acropolis is a design from an age of elegance, though hemmed in on all sides, Sunderland to the east, Washington to the north, and at the foot of the hill the former mining villages of

Penshaw itself, Philadelphia, Fatfield and Shiney Row. It's been there since 1844, built by the father and son architectural team of John and Benjamin Green, four Doric columns on the short sides, seven on the long, entablature, frieze, no roof, no inscription and no one now, I'd bet, knows what it's about, except maybe a few old pitmen down there in Penshaw and Shiney Row.

Richmond
YORKSHIRE

18th-century theatre in miniature, the Georgian Theatre Royal

Richmond lies at the northern end of north Yorkshire but likes to think of itself as the centre of Richmondshire. They think big in

Richmond: there's a big church in a big marketplace with a big market cross, but then if they weren't big they would be swamped by the big castle keep on the highest point of this hilltop town commanding Swaledale.

That's why the Georgian Theatre Royal comes as a shock. On the outer ring of the town centre, which means thirty seconds' walk from the marketplace, the street façade of the Georgian Theatre is a building for the 21st century that slots nicely into a typical market town street scene of stone terraced houses and two or three pubs. Now step into the auditorium and it's a shoebox, and presumably with the aid of an old-fashioned shoehorn 214 people can squeeze in. It is an 18th-century theatre in miniature, the sort of thing you might buy an imaginative small child for Christmas. There are seven rows of bench seats in the rectangular sunken pit, flanked by four boxes on each lateral side and three at the back. Above is a tiny rectangular gallery. The boxes, gallery and pillars supporting the gallery are greenish-blue, the ceiling is white clouds floating in a blue sky. Hanging iron rings hold gas flares to light the auditorium, but the flares are only virtual – an electrical device is operated by something called random flicker technology and extinguished at the flick of a switch. The northern impresario Samuel Butler opened the theatre in 1788. It closed in 1848, the year of revolution, and the auditorium became an auction room and the vaults a wine cellar.

Despite that, or maybe because of it, when it reopened as an active theatre in 1963 it was the least altered of Britain's four surviving pre-1830s theatres, not quite as old as the Theatre Royal, Bristol, but much more complete. In 2003, with forty years more research on the building complete, plus evidence of the other Yorkshire playhouses run by Butler and £1.6 million in gifts and grants, the architect Robert Finch of the Leeds firm Allen Tod Architecture restored it fully with a team of theatre and period specialists. The playhouse already owned what it says is the oldest scenery in England, a woodland vista probably painted between 1818 and 1836. To this it has added a new front cloth (the curtain that greets the audience as they file in). There was no evidence of what the original front cloth was like, although it was usual in theatres of the time to decorate them with a local scene; and as there was evidence that the Richmond artist George Cuit had painted scenery for the theatre's inauguration, the restorers came up with a copy within an oval of Cuit's *Richmond Castle and the River Swale* (1810): what else but a *coup de théâtre*.

Ripon
YORKSHIRE

Ripon is small for a cathedral, but then the city was made a diocese only in 1836. The present building began in the 12th century as a collegiate parish church. The town crowds in on its wonderfully austere Early English west front, with towers either side of a portal and with three lancets arranged vertically in each tower and rows of five tall lancets above the portal. The lower row is regular, but in the row above the lancets are stepped, with the tallest in the centre. There are three smaller lancets in the gable and three portals under a triple arch flanked by a row of five blind arches in each lower range of the towers. It is worth describing in detail because this pellucid 13th-century west front is the finest of its period in England, understandable at first glance. Inside is an excellent Romanesque crypt and a fine set of varied 15th-century misericords of angels, men and beasts.

Ripon lies on the River Ure, and the medieval North Bridge was maintained from at least the first decade of the 17th century by a

Room by Robert Adam, tapestries by the Gobelins works, mildly erotic panels by Mme de Pompadour's favourite artist, François Boucher. What would Robespierre have said? He didn't get a look in because William Weddell ordered the tapestries before the French Revolution, made to measure for his seat at Newby Hall in Ripon

charge on both North and West Ridings. A document of 1641 demanded the high charge of £70 from the two ridings because 'His Majesty's subjects cannot passe that wayes without great danger'. The mazy streets of the town follow the medieval pattern, and although the houses are not ancient they form a fine close texture to the little city (population under 16,000). At the other end of Kirkgate from the cathedral is the big rectangular marketplace with town hall of 1801, designed with an Ionic portico by James Wyatt and inscribed, 'Except Ye Lord keep Ye Cittie, Ye Wakeman Waketh in Vain' – the wakeman was (and is, though now merely ritually) an alderman elected annually to be head of the constables. At the centre of the square is a 90 foot obelisk of 1781 commemorating the forty years as member of Parliament served by William Aislabie of Studley Royal, the great park embracing Fountains Abbey just beyond the town. Newby Hall, too, falls within Ripon's jurisdiction; it has fine interiors by Robert Adam, including a magisterial sculpture gallery.

Boucher's Gobelins tapestries at Newby Hall

It's nice, we are often told, when the aristos and the higher gentry can show their great works of art in the settings where they have been since time immemorial. And it is. Just as William Kent's statue gallery at Holkham Hall would hardly be the same without the fine Roman sculptures that Lord Leicester bought on his 18th-century grand tour, so Newby's statue gallery by Robert Adam, graced by its greatest treasure, the Newby Venus bought from the Palazzo Barberini in Rome 250 years ago, couldn't be without it. Or could it?

Newby's owner, Richard Compton (who through a genealogical maze that I can't follow is descended from a line of Weddels, one of whom brought the Barberini Venus to Newby from his grand tour), needed cash to refurbish and convert the stables into offices. So he sold the Venus for £8 million. Never mind, Mr Compton assures us in a Newby information sheet, we have delightful news of a freshly installed copy 'which is virtually indistinguishable from the original'. Virtually is the *mot juste*, because the copy was made from a 3D laser scan and polished up by 'one of Carrara's top craftsmen'. I for one can't tell the difference, except that the marble copy looks quarry fresh in a way that the genuine article hardly ever does. But once you know that it's a copy it dies. It's no more than a good reproduction. This isn't a quibble. As the French polymath André Malraux argued, any good craftsman or forger can copy; only a genius can create the original.

With the statue gone, it is now the tapestry room that harbours Newby's greatest treasure: tapestries designed by Boucher, ordered from the French Gobelins works in 1763 by William Weddell and placed in a room specially designed by Adam to receive them. Boucher's style was perfectly adapted to tapestries. In fact, from 1755 this favourite artist of Mme Pompadour was director of the Gobelins works, founded by Pompadour's lover Louis XVI. Boucher's work was the ultimate expression of a class and an era, the *ancien régime*. Combined with the cool chasteness of Robert Adam, Chippendale furniture, Axminster carpeting and Antonio Zucchi's painted cameos in wall and ceiling panels, Boucher has a setting better here, probably, than in France for his priapic gods and busty godesses.

A church paid for by blood money, Skelton on Ure

Lady Mary Vyner built the church of Christ the Consoler with the blood money of one million drachmas originally intended to ransom her son, Frederick Vyner, kidnapped by Greek bandits on a tourist trip to Marathon in 1870 but killed in a skirmish before the cash could be handed over. The murder jolted Lady Mary into deep mourning and shook her son-in-law, the Marquess of Ripon, future viceroy of India, out of his evangelical low churchiness into an enhanced appreciation of high church sacrament. So the marquess's wife joined her mother Lady Mary in spending the ransom money on the services of the most spectacular Gothicist around, William Burges (1827–81), to build his last two churches, Christ the Consoler at Skelton in the park of Newby Hall and St Mary's at Studley Royal in the same park as Fountains Abbey (see below). The original projections seem to have been £10,000 for Skelton and £15,000 for Studley, but it finished up costing a lot more.

The daughter got a better deal than the mother. It's not that Burges fell short on the Skelton job, it was just in the glum nature of the commission. Although Christ the Consoler was supposed to be the parish church for Skelton (until 1991, when the village turned again to its former parish church, St Helen's, and the Churches Conservation Trust took over Christ the Consoler), it is all too obvious that the impulse that created it was similar to the motivation for founding pre-Reformation chantry chapels. The church is within the park of Newby Hall. The very beeches surrounding the church were cultivated to weep for the dead Vyner son, lowering their sad boughs to the ground. Armorial shields on the buttresses speak of the Vyners and their ancestors, the tombs outside the east wall are family tombs, the font is in memory of a dead child of Lord Ripon's family.

Everything else that went into Burges's churches – and they were crammed with decoration – was subservient to the whole. He admired the Morris workshops, the Arts and Crafts movement, the Art-Workers' Guild, all of which abolished the distinction between art and craft, artist and craftsman, but Burges made damned sure everyone knew who was in charge on his projects. Nothing was too good for Christ the Consoler. Outside Burges used grey limestone from Catterick and Morcar, near Ripon, but inside he built as though he was designing a precious casket, not a piece of architecture. He chose a creamy white stone from Lord Ripon's own quarries. He heightened the colour with porphyry, alabaster, white marble and black marble, he had the stalls carved from walnut, he set the wall above the chancel arch with a forest of sculpture, Christ at the apex in a mandorla, angels in tondos, eleven disciples (Judas missing), in a pointed arch arcade. It's overwhelmingly morbid, sunk deep in mourning, as self-indulgent as Lady Mary could have hoped, a memorial to a rich woman's son and to hell with the parish.

Paradise Regained at St Mary's Church, Studley Royal

William Burges (1827–81) carried a team of artists and craftsmen from one project to another, like Orson Welles with his repertory company of film actors. So the talk is of Billy building a church, Billy filling it with his sculpture, with his stained glass, with his carved decoration, and all that is true, even though he worked with a raft of skilled craftsmen. But Billy was the boss. He threw big tantrums if things didn't go as he wanted, a little man celebrated in a limerick by his friend Dante Gabriel Rossetti:

There is a babyish party named Burges
Who from infancy hardly emerges.
If you had not been told
He's disgracefully old,
You would offer a bullseye to Burges.

But they all loved him.

Like his Christ the Consoler at Skelton (see above), St Mary is quite small. Unlike his Skelton, it doesn't hide behind a mournful screen of trees but is part of the glorious vista along the grand drive of the combined estates of Fountains Abbey and Studley Royal that culminates in a majestic view of Ripon Cathedral to the west. The theme of the church is Paradise Lost (in the nave) and Paradise Regained (in the chancel). It is carried through in similar materials to Skelton's – white limestone, marbles of many hues, porphyry and alabaster – but the emphasis is quite different. The glass admits more light, the sculpture of the splendidly maned Assyrian-looking Lion of Judah between slender green and pink shafts supporting the arches on a south windowsill of the chancel is balanced by a charming frieze carved beneath the north wall of gold-painted foliage with little birds perched between the fronds.

Rokeby Park

COUNTY DURHAM

Former home to Venus's backside

John Bacon Sawrey Morritt, the squire of Rokeby Park, bought Velázquez's painting of the toilet of Venus in 1813. 'My fine picture of Venus's backside,' as he described it, the *Rokeby Venus*, as it has been known ever since Morritt's descendant, the huntin' shootin' and fishin' Major H.E. Morritt, sold it to the National Gallery in 1906. The attraction of Rokeby to me was to see what other kind of paintings a house that had once owned a prime Velázquez might have. The answer is, a full-size copy of the Venus.

Morritt was a friend of Sir Walter Scott, and he installed a bust of the highly popular novelist in the first-floor saloon. Scott was a frequent guest and sang for his supper by choosing it as the location for his long narrative poem *Rokeby* and dedicating it to Morritt. The poem was a doubtful blessing, a pot-boiler designed to raise funds for improvements to Scott's own house, Abbotsford in the Scottish borders. The satirical poet Thomas Moore seized on this and lampooned Scott before all London in one of his series of satirical *Twopenny Post Bags* as a hack who

> *Having quitted the Borders to seek new*
> *   renown,*
> *Is coming by long quarto stages to town,*
> *And beginning with Rokeby (the job's sure*
> *   to pay),*
> *Means to do all the gentlemen's seats by the*
> *   way.*

Morritts still live at Rokeby and open the house for a couple of days a week in summer. It is a living example of the smaller kind of country house with a collection of art

displayed in rooms not much touched since John Morritt's death in 1843, consisting largely of copies, attributeds and maybes mostly by nobodies, not as much of it picked up on the grand tour as might have been expected, since J.B.S. Morritt did a very grand grand tour indeed, taking in not just Italy but Greece, Austria, Hungary and Turkey as well, where he visited the two likely sites of Troy (and picked the wrong one as the likeliest). The *Rokeby Venus* seems to have been a one-off; it had belonged to the prime minister of Spain, Don Manuel de Godoy, but when he went into exile in 1812 Morritt picked up the Velázquez at a sale the following year.

The squires of Rokeby Park earned a very local kind of fame. Sir Thomas Robinson, who built the house in the Palladian style, was a fine amateur of architecture and acquaintance of another great amateur and reviver of Palladianism, Lord Burlington. In 1769 Robinson sold the estate to John (Venus) Morritt's father, J.S. Morritt. J.S. worked hard at improving this already magical stretch of the River Tees from the Balliol Tower and bridge of Barnard Castle to the Rokeby estate. He built Greta Bridge (see above) outside the southern gate of the park in 1779 and a few years earlier the bridge over the Tees near the lovely ruin of Egglestone Abbey (see above), which he opened in a ceremony on which the *York Chronicle and Weekly Advertiser* reported in 1773: 'The rocks and trees were covered with people, and it is computed that upwards of a thousand spectators were present.' On departing at the end of the ceremony, it seems, the masons smartly 'faced round and gave three huzzas to the ladies'.

Saltaire

YORKSHIRE

David Hockney collection, 1853 Gallery, Salts Mill

In Bradford City Art Gallery at Cartwright Hall in a salubrious park above the city, I ask the attendant where the Hockneys are. In the basement, that's where, giving way to a temporary show of local talent. But, he says, try a mile down the road. A mile down the road is a steep descent from Shipley to Saltaire in the Aire valley: a long street and rows of mills and houses beside the river, the railway and the Leeds and Liverpool Canal. It's a living map of the age when the millowner was king, almost literally so in this valley, where Titus Salt came from smoky Bradford in 1853 and built his fiefdom: mills for his alpaca and mohair industry, a couple of churches, neat rows of sanitary houses, public baths and wash-houses, infirmary, school, institute, a park, no pub. And he saw that it was good and he called it Saltaire.

In 1987 a successful young man in the rag trade called Jonathan Silver bought the mill and saved it from demolition. As a fourteen-year-old boy at Bradford Grammar School he had seen the twenty-six-year-old former pupil David Hockney on a bus and with some chutzpah asked him to do a cover for the school magazine. Hockney obliged. The two became friends. Silver made his first million fast and contributed to Hockney's own first million by buying his work. Next he turned Salts Mill into a huge museum for his Hockneys and an emporium – you could order a made-to-measure suit on the way in and buy a postcard and eat a risotto on the way out. What are not for sale are the Hockneys, possibly the biggest collection anywhere, certainly in Britain. There's early work from the Bradford School of Art, a fine series of lithographs, especially of Celia

Birtwell through the years, pieces from the playful Picasso-esque phase, the Polaroid montages, a big showpiece for Jonathan Silver of Saltaire, a toy-town view in summer, colours as bright as Holman Hunt's *Hireling Shepherd*, and another canvas as a get well card; too late, for Silver died of cancer in 1997.

It's a wonderful collection hung a bit ad hoc like the art on the railings along Green Park in Piccadilly on a Sunday afternoon. The knock-out is the third floor. Walk through the Café Opera and you're into a display of Hockney's sets for the first three of many operas he has tackled, Stravinsky's *The Rake's Progress* (1975) and Mozart's *The Magic Flute* (1980) for Glyndebourne and, Stravinsky again, *Le Rossignol* (1981) at the New York Met. If it was permitted, you could almost walk into them, though at a guess they're about a quarter of the staged size, like gigantic pop-up books. Hockney made these models for an exhibition in Minneapolis, and because he reckoned that stage sets would be inert without actors, he decided to repaint the initial concepts as a cross between easel paintings and his own original cardboard models for the stage painters to work from, with cut-out figures taking the place of actors. So what Silver brought to Saltaire amounts to works of art as good as anything Hockney has done, cannibalising his own eclectic art for motifs from pre-Renaissance Italian frescos, Egyptian art, Hogarth (*The Rake's Progress* sets are crosshatched like Hogarth's prints). *The Rake* comes in black and white, the sands of the Nile for *The Magic Flute* are burning yellow with the funny-looking rocks you get in 13th-century Italian frescos and a lion and a couple of sphinx cut-outs with a cut-out dragon crossed with a croc. For the porcelain palace of the Chinese emperor in *Le Rossignol* Hockney painted a blue take on an early Renaissance town by Piero della Francesca, figures deconstructed and then reconstructed on flats like his own experiments in Polaroid montages, a cut-out Matissean tree, and a stream of water quoted from his own painting *A Bigger Splash*. I guess if Picasso could have seen these before he created his sets and costumes for the Diaghilev ballet *Parade*, he would have looked twice – and borrowed.

Sheffield

YORKSHIRE

Bonnard's Nude with Black Stockings, Graves Art Gallery

This good gallery has an exceptionally strong room with a gathering of paintings hung under the rubric Towards Modern Art: 1850–1950, which covers the period from Corot to Monet then Cézanne, Leger, Kandinsky, Braque and on to English post-war painting. Among the continental group is Pierre Bonnard (1867–1947), an artist who in the post-war years and after his death was often patronisingly written off as a comfortably innovative figure of the *belle époque*, the mainland European parallel to well-upholstered Edwardian. The Graves nude Bonnard evokes so erotically is of this period, and the nude is Maria Boursin, Bonnard's companion from 1893 until she died in 1942. They had been together thirty years when they married. (A year later, 1924, his other lover of about four years standing, Renée Monchaty, whom he had painted in a sunlit garden portrait, committed suicide.) Bonnard continued to use his wife as his model for the nudes bathing even when she grew old – presumably as a prompt to his memory and imagination.

He painted *Nude with Black Stockings* in 1900, and the palpable fleshiness of the model, of her belly and hips and thighs, her sheer sensuousness as she pulls a white chemise over her head, marks a full return to naturalistic painting. For more than ten years in *fin de siècle* Paris he had been painting under the influence of Japanese prints, Gauguin, and Toulouse Lautrec, but towards the end of the century he began looking again at the Impressionists and liked what he saw. He liked the broken touch, the soft volumes that threw out light, the subtlety of the spaces around objects, and what he retained from his decorative painting in flat colours was the sense of objects impinging randomly on his peripheral vision. In *Nude with Black Stockings* Maria sits on the edge of a bed beside a locker and a bedside lamp, both of which are cut off by the left-hand edge of the canvas. Later he would paint his wife in a bath, but the bath would be disappearing out of the bottom of the picture and the half that could be seen would just contain the bather's legs. Someone dining at table or a smoker in a living room might be manifested by only half a head or a hand holding a cigarette with the rest of the figure out of sight beyond the picture plane.

The subject of the painting, in other words, was not necessarily disclosed by its title. Bonnard's subject, increasingly, was the equality of everything in the field of vision. There was no primacy for the supposed subject: the floor of the bathroom and the edge of the bath are as important in Bonnard's world as the bather. Bonnard's paintings, unfailingly domestic, exist in a state of heightened informality. They bring closure to the great Renaissance tradition of perspective in which the viewer appears to be looking down a deep avenue towards a fixed point in the distance. (Hobbema's famous avenue of trees is the perfect illustration of this.)

Although Bonnard's nudes become less erotic after 1900, there is never any sense that he is painting to a programme. His people dress and undress, man and wife in their

Maria Boursin, Pierre Bonnard's companion and then wife from 1893 until her death in 1942 modelled for him throughout. This painting, Nude in Black Stockings, *now in the Graves Art Gallery, Sheffield, marks his return to naturalism after ten years of decorative painting*

By the shore in the former fishing and shipping town of South Shields, twenty-two bronze figures comprise Conversation Piece *by the short-lived Spanish artist Juan Munoz. 'I'm a storyteller,' Munoz said, but he left his figures to move the public to fill in the narrative details*

bedroom, with the casual intimacy of long acquaintance. Bonnard is painting from daily experience. There is a similarity to that other great painter of informal nudes, Degas, but Degas is a peeping Tom, he's looking from the outside in. Bonnard is inside the room, and the woman knows he is there even when he isn't actually in the painting. That is Bonnard's quality. His legacy was a new way of organising the picture surface, its objects and its spaces, without appearing to be intellectually engaged at all.

South Shields
TYNE & WEAR

Juan Munoz's story without a beginning, middle or end

Juan Munoz's *Conversation Piece* has stood uncelebrated on Littlehaven beach by the harbour of South Shields on the Durham side of Tynemouth since 1999, twenty-two

bronze figures with a mottled green patina inscrutably engaged with each other and disengaged from us. Why do they ignore us? What excludes us from their dialogue? Like all Munoz's figures, they seem blind, their eyes merely slight indentations in the skull. They are grouped but seem poised to move off in different directions. Some reach out but never touch. They wear tunics, which shade off into creased, sack-like bottoms, weighted like Subbuteo table footballers, though you wouldn't try to flick these about on their little terrace among the coarse grass and sand dunes – each one weighs a quarter of a tonne and stands at 5 feet 9 inches, maybe around medium height in Spain, which is where Munoz (1953–2001) was born and where he worked, though he trained in London and spent most of his time abroad before his early death.

Conversation Piece arrived at the end of a century during which the surprisingly narrow stretch of rivermouth between South

Shields and Tynemouth, with its ancient ruined priory on the opposite bank, had seen 10 million tons of shipping sailing out every year and had harboured a fishing fleet besides. 'I'm a storyteller,' Munoz said, but this story remains inscrutable. In the turbine hall of Tate Modern a few years ago Munoz's installation of figures standing peering down into the hall from different floors and lifts travelling up and down, ceaselessly travelling from basement to roof and back, introduced a powerful sense of the loneliness of city life. Maybe that's the clue to all his work.

Sunderland
TYNE & WEAR

Nissan is signposted from the A19 northeast coast road like a great city, as well it might be, since Nissan saved Sunderland from destitution in the 1980s. This was the dire decade when the shipbuilding industry sank with all hands after 600 years on Wearside. The old industry had survived the Second World War when the Luftwaffe flattened most of central Sunderland, but it died when the post-war tiger economies of the Far East began to deliver much cheaper shipping. And then, what was built in the aftermath of war was mostly nasty and brutish, a legacy Sunderland has found difficult to shake off, though to replace the bombed Winter Garden in Mowbray Park, Eric Carter of Napper Architects designed an exotic crystalline replacement with a water sculpture by William Pye, a hothouse display of exotic tropical plants, a museum and, tucked away at the top, an art gallery. Here the most unexpected cache is a group of paintings by L.S. Lowry. Lowry was exhibiting in Newcastle in the 1960s when he discovered Sunderland. He had fallen out of love with factory chimneys, and this was love on the rebound. He based himself at a small hotel in Seaburn, a faded, would-be genteel suburb on the seafront north of Roker. It was, the painter said, his second home, and many of the views he painted of the grey North Sea and his studies around Sunderland of the ruins of the Industrial Revolution have found their own home in the Winter Garden.

Some of Sunderland escaped the destruction. In Monkwearmouth St Peter with St Cuthbert, the small remainder of the monastery founded by Benedict Biscop on the north bank of the Wear in 674 on land granted by King Ecgfrith of Northumbria, still stands, with the original 7th-century tower (see below). On the monastic lands round about stands Sunderland University (the old poly elevated in 1992, named best new university in 2001). Roker too escaped the worst of the bombing, so thankfully St Andrew, Roker, E.S. Prior's fine Arts and Crafts church (see below) stands also; these two are Sunderland's best treasures.

The Adoration of the Magi, Church of St Andrew, Roker

St Andrew's Church professes Gothic values but expresses them in terms of the 20th century: massive masonry, windows with harsh stone grids separating the panes, clear light flooding the nave from the west. It is also almost an apotheosis of the Arts and Crafts ideal, almost but not quite. The movement's aim was for work to be carried out with local materials, but here in Roker, a new suburb growing northwards along the North Sea front on the basis of Sunderland's shipbuilding prosperity at the beginning of the 20th century, the architect, E.S. Prior (1852–1932), cheated a little. His building is of local grey limestone, the roof is supported by rafters of English oak, but the sturdy stone of the arches along the length of the nave is merely cladding – behind the stone is concrete.

From Eric Gill's exquisitely carved lettering of the welcoming stone tablet to the pews, the lovely candlesticks and crucifixes, the painted glass, the font and the pulpit, the artists and craftsmen are a roll-call of the Arts and Crafts movement: Prior himself, who was a founder of the Art-Workers' Guild, his assistant Randall Wells, Gimson, Waal, Morris and Co., Alfred Bucknall and Eric Gill's younger brother, MacDonald Gill, whose ceiling over the chancel is the most light-hearted, at a guess, in all Christendom: the hand of God over the east window benignly commanding the creation, paradisal trees stretching out towards an azure firmament dotted with golden stars and the curly golden rays of the sun, an electric bulb glowing behind an alabaster globe.

The focus of it all, the jewel, is the Burne-Jones reredos, a tapestry of *The Adoration of the Magi*. Or rather, the Burne-Jones–Morris tapestry, for as well as the skills of Morris's Merton Abbey workshop, the quality of the materials for both this and the fine Morris carpet on the floor of the chancel and sanctuary is so good that the colours are probably as fresh now as when the church was consecrated in 1907. The tapestry is one of a number of variations on this design. Burne-Jones and Morris made the first in 1898–90 for Exeter College, Oxford, where they had met as undergraduates, and there are variants in Eton College, Norwich, Manchester Metropolitan University, St Petersburg and Australia. But of the three I have seen, Roker's is the best. The others are composed in dusky greens, mauves and blues, like one of Burne-Jones's paintings, but in the Roker version two of the kings wear vermilion and crimson robes, one of watered silk, the other printed with a broad band of golden foliage, and the third king is in gleaming armour like a knight in a medieval romance. Mary and Joseph are more soberly clad, but not sombrely. At the centre is a willowy, feminine Pre-Raphaelite angel in a figured gown of burning gold with a small golden fire sparkling between cupped hands, angel and light together casting radiance over the night-time scene. The four men, three proud kings and Mary's humble husband, have lean, intelligent, semitic faces, and all stand in a flowery bower enclosed by a basketweave fence, while Mary sits with her child under a thatched roof supported by slender tree trunks. Burne-Jones's inspiration was medieval, but this stands as a glorious work of 19th-century England in a building intended for glory.

Inexplicable 7th-century carving of serpents, Church of St Peter, Wearmouth

All that exists of Benedict Biscop's original Wearmouth church is the inner wall of the west porch and the lower part of the tower above. But after the slum clearance in the late years of the 20th century the tower and west wall of the church stand ancient and serene in a green space surrounded by the strenuously modern Sunderland University, the National Glass Centre and Sunderland football club's arena, the Stadium of Light. The wall's distinction is that it contains two engraved stones that, because they are an integral part of the church construction of 674, are the only Anglo-Saxon carving in Britain that can be securely dated. They are so low down on the archway into the nave that they're easily missed, and then the disappointment is that they are so rudimentary that nothing much can be extrapolated. Yet they remain compelling as ancient art is, a witness to a remote time that still, no matter how faintly, speaks across the centuries to us.

Benedict founded the joint monastery of Wearmouth–Jarrow as a weapon of Roman Christianity. The Synod at Whitby Abbey in

664 had ruled in the most contentious issue of the time in favour of Roman liturgy and against the Northumbrian liturgy that had been introduced from Iona. But Northumbria had been slow to adapt. Nobody was better qualified for the task of making the synod's decision a working fact than Biscop. He knew many of the participants at Whitby. He had shuttled between Durham and Rome as frequently as a tourist on easyJet. He had escorted the newly appointed Archbishop of Canterbury, Theodore of Tarsus, from Rome to his new see and had his confidence. He was a native Northumbrian of a rich family and had the confidence of the king of Northumbria, Egfrid. He reached Wearmouth and founded St Peter in 674. St Paul's a few miles north, on Tyneside, followed in 682.

The engravings in the western porch of St Peter show within a rectangular space two serpentine creatures with fish tails and beaked heads, entwined at the tail and with jaws locked upon each other. In Christianity serpents usually denote evil. In Matthew 23:33 Christ attacks the scribes and pharisees: 'Ye serpents, ye generation of vipers, how can ye escape the damnation of hell?' Perhaps the serpents with locked jaws mean that evil goes no further than the door to the church. Who knows? Art history hasn't yet gone very far in tackling Anglo-Saxon iconography.

Thorpe Salvin
YORKSHIRE

Romanesque font carvings of the seasons, St Peter

The message on the door of St Peter reads: 'Key at farmhouse opposite.' Accordingly, I interrupt the farmer in his preoccupation with repairing a bicycle puncture to ask if I may borrow the key. 'You can,' he says,

retrieves it from the house and advises me, 'You put it in upside down and turn it the wrong way round.'

It is a village of around 400 people, famous for its gardens and with the great ruined wall of a 16th-century house dominating the scene. The church has additions of the 13th, 14th and 15th centuries, but the way in is through a powerfully articulated 12th-century door, and the 12th-century origin of the church is its best period. The west tower is decorated with bold zigzag but is pointed, so is probably late Norman. Beneath it is the font. It is less than ideally placed, shoved up against a wooden screen, though it's just possible to see that the back of the font is decorated with interlocking arches of a blind arcade of the sort that Norman churches sometimes have down the aisles. But what you can see clearly is delightful. Beneath round arches supported on circular piers are two relief carvings of a baptism and four of the seasons: an old man sits before a fire in winter; a horseman rides out hawking in spring; in summer a man cuts corn and binds it into sheaves; in autumn a husbandman spreads seed.

It is not as famous as the Romanesque fonts of Herefordshire (see, for example, Castle Frome, West and East Midlands), but here the mason has been trying for something quite different in spirit from those declarations from a thundercloud, something closer to naturalism. The Thorpe Salvin carvings are fairly crude, though the carver's observation of the worker in the field is quite acute, caught in the act of pulling the twine tight around a stook of corn. But it is the hunting scene that is especially worth travelling to see. The mason for this panel may have been a different craftsman because it is carved with skill and aplomb. It fills the niche and spills out so that the horse's head and hindquarters encroach over the piers defining the niche as it trots across a bridge over a stream. The rider wears a cloak that drops from his shoulders and is thrown casually over the bridle, forming a loop that mirrors the loop of the niche's arch. The scene is altogether well planned, well executed and carved with clear affection.

Wakefield
YORKSHIRE

Henry Moore and Barbara Hepworth at the Wakefield Art Gallery

Wakefield opened its art gallery in 1923. In 1927 it founded what is now the friends organisation to fund art purchases. In 1934 it moved into a warm and welcoming Victorian town house with the firmly stated intention of keeping 'in touch with modern art in its relations to modern life'. It has, with a few good old master paintings and a representative modern British collection. The cream of the collection celebrates the extraordinary coincidence that two of the most eminent British sculptors of the 20th century, Henry Moore (1898–1986) and Barbara Hepworth (1903–75), were born within half a dozen miles of each other in Castleford and Wakefield.

Moore made his piece *Head of a Woman* in concrete in 1926, and Hepworth carved her wooden *Kneeling Figure* in 1932. They are both clumsy pieces compared to their later work, but in a sense Moore's future is all there in this deeply felt sculpture, although Hepworth developed in many more directions. Moore derived his woman's head from the depersonalised grandeur of pre-Columbian Mexican sculpture. He remained always inward looking, drawing on his experience of the Yorkshire landscape and his desire to combine its aspects with the contours of the female human figure. Hepworth, too, aims for the monumental within direct representation of a woman's figure, but she hasn't quite finessed the two

aspects. She went on to learn from the extraordinarily coolly judged abstract paintings and reliefs of her second husband Ben Nicholson, to produce the finest purely abstract sculptures of her generation of British artists (see St Ives, Southwest).

Two later pieces in the same room as their sculptures tell the story: Hepworth's white marble *Pierced Hemisphere* of 1937, cool, beautifully poised, totally abstract, and Moore's *Reclining Figure*, carved in elmwood in 1936, which the Wakefield guidebook describes as 'one of the most significant works of modern art produced in the 20th century'. It's certainly fine and significant in his own canon; only the best of his post-war pieces equal it.

Wallington Hall
NORTHUMBERLAND

A paean to Robert Stephenson's railway works

Pauline, Lady Trevelyan, decided to take the advice of her friend John Ruskin to turn the open courtyard at her big, square, two-storeyed 18th-century classical house Wallington into a grand Renaissance Italian hall. She gave the job to the architect John Dobson (1787–1865), a man well used to roofing over large spaces. He had recently built the railway station at Newcastle upon Tyne with its quarter mile long platform. And for the decorations she summoned another friend, the head of Newcastle School of Design, William Bell Scott (1811–90). Around the upper arcade, Scott painted *The Ballad of Chevy Chase*, an account of the bloody 14th-century Battle of Otterburn nearby, from which

Of fifteen hundred Englishmen
Went home but fifty-three;
The rest were slain in Chevy Chase
Under the greenwood tree.

Whatsoeuer · thy · hand · findeth · to · do · do · it · with · thy · Might

When Lady Trevelyan turned Wallington Hall's open courtyard into a grand 19th-century hall she hired the head of Newcastle School of Design, William Bell Scott, to paint the history of Northumbria around the walls. Scott was at his best with this final panel, a scene of industry in a forge within view of Newcastle High Level Bridge

Within the new arcade on the ground floor he painted a history of Northumbria, which ends in 1861 with *Iron and Coal*, a dramatically realised scene of heavy labour in a forge in Robert Stephenson's Newcastle locomotive works overlooking Stephenson's new High Level Bridge over the Tyne.

The other seven scenes amount to not much more than entertaining illustration, but there's no doubt that Bell meant us to feel pride at the triumphant march of history. The first canvas has a Roman on the half-finished wall obviously outraged at the sight of the native builders' labourers taking an early tea break; the final scene shows the mighty rhythm of the swinging sledgehammers in the grip of three sturdy young men caught in broad shafts of sunlight and the glow of the forge's furnace. Outside is a scene of bustling activity on the quay and sail of all kinds jostling on the river as a train steams across High Level Bridge.

In one corner of the foreground, tucked safely out of range of the swinging sledgehammers and the glowing furnace, sits a little girl clutching a dish wrapped in a napkin that she has brought for her father. Her face shines with optimism, her eyes are as blue as the patch of blue in the sky between the smoke-tinged clouds; she is the glorious dawn. Heavy-handed symbolism, but Bell's bravura energy carries it off. In the other corner the dateline on a discarded newspaper reads 11 March 1861 (presumably the day the cycle of paintings was finished), and the front page carries an advertisement for an exhibition involving Scott himself and news of the victory at Caserta of the Italian nationalist Garibaldi, a popular figure among workers on Tyneside, which he had visited for a month in 1854. The paper is folded so that only half of the masthead shows, 'The Northern …'. The *Northern Star* of Leeds and the *Northern Liberator* of Newcastle were recently defunct, but each had been a Chartist newspaper popular with working men and liberal intellectuals. The Trevelyans were a liberal family, and one of the workmen on the canvas is a portrait of Wallington's young heir, Charles Edward Trevelyan, so maybe Scott's painting is both a homage and an optimistic clarion call for democratic freedom as well as progress and prosperity.

In any case, it is the only major account in painting of the Industrial Revolution. Scott was a follower of the Pre-Raphaelites, a movement that accidentally spawned a monstrous progeny of sentimental narrative painting, but if any painting could carry off the Pre-Raphaelite programme of naturalism in minutely observed detail it is this one. Scott may have seen Ford Madox Brown's study of road gang labour in Hampstead, *Work*, in progress, but for all that Brown's painting is more famous, *Iron and Coal* is a grander project, burning with the intensity of Scott's passion for the subject. The unexpected public success of the Wallington decorations after the comparative failure of a Palace of Westminster scheme probably gave Manchester the confidence to engage Brown to paint his mural cycle on the history of Manchester when Alfred Waterhouse's new town hall in Albert Square was complete at the end of the next decade (see Manchester, Northwest).

Welton
YORKSHIRE

Morris and Burne-Jones in harness as artists, Church of St Helen

Burne-Jones wrote to a friend, 'I mean by a picture a beautiful romantic dream of something that never was, never will be …'. Morris, of course, believed that 'nothing can be a work of art that is not useful'. Morris's practicality saved Burne-Jones from himself by providing a context, church buildings, in which his romantic medievalism could live convincingly.

At Welton (a commission stretching between 1872 and 1895) in the two-light window they made together in the south transept, Burne-Jones did St Ursula in the left-hand light, Morris did St Catherine in the right-hand light. Stylistically they work in tandem, but look carefully and it's clear who did which. Burne-Jones's St Ursula is one of his Victorian beauties. Her long brown hair falls to her shoulders and frames a swan-like throat and oval face, eyes downcast, nose long, lips full, hands elegantly long-fingered, her body slightly swaying as though, one is tempted to add, she is moving down the catwalk. Morris's St Catherine, by contrast, is slightly careworn, one bony hand clutching her sword's hilt, the other holding a book propped against her hip. She has roses in her hair like a village May queen, where Ursula's tresses are adorned only with a crimson halo. And Catherine's complexion is pale from study indoors, quite unlike the moon-struck marmoreal pallor of Ursula.

Morris & Co. bought in their glass from Powell & Sons, a stained glass manufacturer working with a chemist who had recovered the secrets of the richly hued glass to be found in medieval windows. It has to be said, though, that Powell & Sons were never able to use the glass as effectively as Morris. Here, each saint wears a garment rendered silken by the estuarial light shining through from outside, richly figured in floral patterns, falling in heavy folds. Catherine's gown is green, Ursula's mantle blue, and depending on how close the viewer gets, deep turquoise or pale silvery blue, with a brilliant yellow, almost tangerine, girdle, offset by a pale buff gown showing at the waist. It has to be remembered that in referring to Burne-Jones windows, the colour and the backgrounds of flower-decked lawns and emerald foliage were Morris's responsibility. Similarly the clear quarries of glass in the early days of Morris & Co., lightly drawn upon with patterned foliage outlines, were by Morris and his friend, the artist and architect Philip Webb.

This is one window, and the best, of six. Morris and his colleagues came to this pretty village, a dormitory to Hull as early as the 18th century and still surviving peacefully very close to the busy A63, to fulfil a commission for a memorial to a family related to Burne-Jones. Four of the other windows are by Burne-Jones alone. The first window, in the south aisle, was another team effort, though on this occasion Burne-Jones

did both main figures, the saints Cecilia and Agnes, while Morris did the musical angels above – from their expressions they are obviously professionally dedicated, socialists like Morris himself, and probably enrolled in the Musicians' Union.

West Bretton
YORKSHIRE

Eduardo Chillida reaching for the sky, Yorkshire Sculpture Park

As I write, Eduardo Chillida's abstract *Buscando la luz IV* ('Searching for the Light') doesn't so much greet visitors at the entrance to Yorkshire Sculpture Park as accost them, as it has for the past couple of years. He had been a goalkeeper for the San Sebastian football club Real Sociedad and, as a critic wrote on his death in 2002 at the age of seventy-eight, he had the goalkeeper's instinct for contesting and commanding territory. *Buscando* is 20 tonnes of solid rusted steel, and it stands implacably nearly 37 feet high.

Chillida was a Basque in a 20th-century Iberian tradition of iron sculpture, and, like Picasso, he made a memorial to the German bombing of Guernica during the civil war of the 1930s, but his is in a square in the town itself. In Chillida's sculpture politics, life and art are the same thing. *Buscando la luz* reaches imperiously for the sky.

Whitby
YORKSHIRE

Church of St Mary

The whole of Whitby is a single composition, the plan dictated by the deep gorge of the River Esk, which flows northwards into the North Sea and opens out into the harbour from which Captain Cook set out on his explorations of the southern seas. From the town there is a compelling view of the east cliff with its summit grouping of ruined abbey, founded by St Hilda of Hartlepool, and ground-hugging parish church of St Mary. There is a climb of 199 stone steps to the top, where the view below is of the pantile and slate roofs of the town clustered on either bank of the Esk; to the east, just sea and sky. The abbey ruin alone is finer in some respects than my favourite, Rievaulx, especially for the east wall, which retains its gable end and so has three soaring rows of Early English lancets compared to Rievaulx's gableless two rows. It was here that the correct dating of Easter was decided in 664 by the Synod of Whitby, to the continuing bewilderment of secular England today.

The church is unique. Round-headed windows and arches indicate its origins as Norman, but other windows with slender glazing bars show it to be Georgian gothick and Georgian domestic as well. That's the outside. Inside the wide, aisle-less building is a totally dotty ensemble of 17th- and 18th-century box pews and galleries, apparently added as need dictated. The Church of England being a module for class distinction in society at large, the lord of manor, as in so many churches, had his own pew. But here in the 17th century the powerful North Riding family, the Cholmleys, were lords of the manor who clearly thought of themselves as lords of creation too, and they built their pew on tall, twisting barley sugar columns right across the front of what might be a fine Romanesque chancel arch if it could be seen. It took more than a century for a vicar to cap this, and he did so in 1778 with a triple-story pulpit, ceremoniously capped by a hood like the howdah on an elephant. The sole lighting is by window, skylight and an 18th-century chandelier for services by candlelight. An antique cast iron coke stove in the body of the church, with a tall chimney climbing through the roof, takes care of creature comforts.

York
YORKSHIRE

The wool trade was declining in York from the 15th century and by the 16th religion was the basis of the city's economy. So when the Reformation destroyed the stained glass works, the image makers, the trade in rich clerical vestments and the chantry chapels, and stripped away the riches of the church itself, an act of parliament was passed in 1547 to allow York to close fifteen of its forty parish churches. And yet on any weekend today the air can be as full of the sound of bells as it was in the Middle Ages. Church building started again in the 19th century, and now, apart from the mighty minster itself, there are among others All Saints (with glass by John Thornton, who created the minster's east window) and All Saints Pavement; Holy Redeemer and three Holy Trinitys; twenty-eight churches named for saints, from Saint Aidan to St Wulstan, with a St Martin-cum-Gregory and St Martin-le-Grand; of course, there's a St Mary (Castlegate); and of two St Michaels, one is St Michael-le-Belfry.

Needless to say, York is a medieval city. No need to rehearse the streets that tell you that, just follow the crowds. But to demonstrate the healing properties of history, the tourist-happy Shambles was once the home of a butcher's wife, the sainted Margaret Clitheroe, a Catholic martyr who was executed in 1586 by being crushed between rocks (hence, no doubt, the saying about a rock and a hard place) for refusing to plead to a charge of harbouring Catholic priests. She was canonized by Pope Paul VI in 1970. History here began long before this, when the Romans founded it as Eboracum in AD 71, and here in 306 the legions proclaimed Constantine the Great emperor. There's a modern statue of him outside the minster, seated and looking mildly sceptically at the sword he balances on its point so that it assumes the shape of a cross. The Romans built the first city walls too, which, as so often, bequeathed foundations to the wall builders of the Middle Ages, of which lengthy stretches survive, along with several towers and fortified gateways: Micklegate Bar, Victoria Bar, Fishergate Bar, Walmgate Bar, Monks Bar and Bootham Bar, which is on the site of a principal Roman gateway to the city and beside the ruins of St Mary's abbey inside the grounds of the Yorkshire Museum.

The Vikings came later and called Eboracum Jórvíc, which we later Anglos sloppily elided to York. There are multiple signs of the Roman and Viking occupations, and, of course, the museum of Viking artefacts, the Jórvíc Centre. William the Conqueror brutally razed the city after the north rose against him. He rebuilt, and it is from then that the walls date and the building of the new minster began, though the finely articulated building we see today is mostly of the years from 1220 to 1470. Somehow, York managed to accommodate the railway revolution as well, and it has one of the great train sheds as well as the National Railway Museum.

The best glass outside the Minster, All Saints North Street

The Corporal Acts of Mercy window (*c.*1420) celebrates an obligation the Church laid on its members to succour the hungry and thirsty, to clothe the naked, to visit the sick, to shelter the homeless and to visit the imprisoned (the window dispenses with the seventh requirement, the burial of the dead, which perhaps in a church where the dead are very much with us beneath the floor slabs would have seemed superfluous). *The Pricke of Conscience* (*c.*1410–20) was a Middle English verse account of the fifteen days leading to Doomsday, days of flood, fire and brimstone, earthquakes and monsters from the deep, falling stars and the grand final conflagration. For stained glass artists, both subjects were perfect: dramatic, various, colourful.

These two windows in All Saints were originally in other parts of the church but have been brought together in the north choir aisle, and rightly, because they sit together so well in what nowadays appears as an English comedy of manners. The Corporal Acts of Mercy window is full of amusing social observation. Best of all is the imprisonment, interpreted as a row of men in the stocks with the gaoler looking disapproving but uncertain as a good Samaritan dispenses food and drink to the manacled rogues. The Samaritan is the same in each scene, Nicholas Blackburn, the donor of the window, who thus has two birds in hand: he contributes to the splendour of the church and he buys himself an advance billet in heaven.

The city's merchant adventurers grew fat on trade with the Netherlands and Germany through downriver Hull, so every one of its medieval churches – and there are still around two and a half dozen in the centre of town – had at least one patron. But this glorious sun of York spread its beneficence especially over All Saints North Street, where, experts concur, the best known of the 15th-century York stained glass artists, John Thornton, or his workshop, quite possibly created the *Pricke of Conscience* window. Thornton's only documented commission is for the huge and complex east window in the minster, but his style crops up in Yorkshire and further south (Thornton was born in Coventry) and is marked by bold definition and lucidity. The All Saints window has

The Gospel of St Luke translated into a medieval comedy of manners in this window of about 1420 in the Church of All Saints North Street, in which the Good Samaritan brings succour to wrong-doers imprisoned in the stocks. The Samaritan is the donor of the window, a York merchant called Nicholas Blackburn

landscapes with apple-dumpling trees, like Samuel Palmer's 19th-century visionary paintings of the Darenth valley, but here about to be consumed by hellish red flames, flood waters rising, monsters leaping from the deep and a grinning figure of death entering stage left.

Most beautiful of all is the so-called Joys of the Virgin window of 1340, almost a century older than the windows in the north choir aisle, with magnificently emphatic leading, wonderful greens, blues and reds with yellows added for the canopies and some of the linked lozenges framing the separate scenes of the Annunciation, the magi and the nativity, with a Virgin as fresh as the girl next door and a wise old donkey and a blood red ox peering at the scene from above.

Great west window, Church of All Saints Pavement

In 1086, according to the Domesday Book, All Saints Pavement was held through favour of the king by the Bishop of Durham, doubtless because York was one of the places where the body of St Cuthbert had rested during its posthumous travels before settling in Durham Cathedral. But All Saints' great beauty was an endowment of the early 15th century, an octagonal tower with open lattice work of delicate pinnacles at the top like a paper chain. Internally, it was beautifully embellished after 1957, when the minster glass workshop restored and reset the 14th-century scenes of Christ's Passion and the resurrection that had been stripped out of the deconsecrated St Saviour's. They fill the

middle three lights of the five-light east window. This can never have been one of the great windows and now the joins show, but the colour is strong, the outline clear, and the drama moves along like a graphic novel, Christ in his agony praying in the garden of Gethsemane, being nailed to the cross, the crucifixion, the soldiers gambling over his seamless garment, the Deposition, and a scene that I take to be Doubting Thomas pushing his fingers into the wound in Christ's side, which either because the glass has faded or by wonderful intent, is bathed in the strange pale light of the imagined afterlife.

Theophilus stained glass roundels, Church of St Denys Walmgate

St Denys is a Norman foundation in a northern town of great importance to the Norman kings, and it has a French dedication (to the saint executed by the Romans who tucked his head under his arm and walked to the place now known as St Denis before expiring). This may be the reason that two roundels in the church are some of the oldest glass in England and tell the French story of Theophilus, who sold his soul to the devil, repented and prayed to the Virgin Mary to intercede for him. The windows have lost some detail, but the colour is strong and the story still discernible. In one window Theophilus kneels before the Virgin; in the other she wrests back his bond from a couple of fiery devils.

St Denys is only the stub of the original, the big east end of what must have been a very big church (the chancel is now the nave). Whole York families whose names are recorded were involved in making stained glass windows, and St Denys has its share of fine glass, but it is most famous for the 14th-century east window in the north aisle, which has the loveliest, most fluid tracery in any parish church in the city, brilliantly enhanced by an ensemble of stained glass fragments reassembled into a pattern controlled by something like a DNA pattern running the depth of the five equal lights.

Portrait of a Man with a Book by Parmigianino, York Art Gallery

When York threw open the doors to its art gallery for the first time in 1892 above the Italian Renaissance round arch was a carved head of William Etty (1787–1849), marking an end to the city's unease with its most famous native painter. The difficulty in acknowledging his worth had been that his great speciality was painting the nude, and his nudes were as robust as Courbet's. As his sympathetic younger contemporaries the art chroniclers Richard and Samuel Redgrave delicately phrased it: 'Though himself a particularly pure-minded man, with a most chivalrous respect for women, it must be allowed that many of his pictures were of a very voluptuous character, and clashed with the somewhat prudish temper of the age.'

Things have moved on for the collection as well as for the moral outlook of York, and the addition in 1955 of the F.D. Lycett Green bequest of European old masters brought a painting by Parmigianino (Francesco Mazzuoli, 1503–40) that would effortlessly command any room in which it hung. It does so in York, quite outshining a portrait by Annibale Carracci and a particularly fine one by Joshua Reynolds, and even during its extended loan to the Frick Collection in New York in 2004–5 while old York was refurbishing the city gallery, it was a star of a world-class gallery that lacks a Parmigianino.

In his *Discourses* to the students in the Royal Academy, Joshua Reynolds described Parmigianino as a successor to Raphael. But Parmigianino's portraits have something else, something both easier and harder: the ability

of the artist to produce the quality Reynolds describes as 'plenitude of effect' achieved by 'the art and management of uniting light to light and shadow to shadow' (that's the easy bit), and to arrive at what we call psychological insight but is actually a dispassionate rendering of appearances coloured by the artist's passion before the subject (that's not just difficult, but inscrutable).

This was the first golden age of painted portraiture, and Parmigianino brought to it an unprecedented intensity, both in his paintings of men, like the York portrait, and in one of the greatest of all female portraits, his sublimely vital painting in Naples of Antea, the elegant woman with a marten stole, looking intently at the viewer but poised as though to move out of the canvas at any moment. I visited York only a few months after seeing Antea in the Capodimonte museum and recognised before I had seen the whites of his eyes that, though in repose, the man with the book is her brother-in-art: he has that same quality of coiled energy as he gazes into space beyond the blue-bound gilded volume he holds, his brow clenched in thought, his huge dark eyes framed by black hair, beard, hat and gown, his wealth proclaimed by the elegant flaring of his white cuff and brown satiny sleeve, his intelligence palpable.

Early Gothic sculpture at York Museum

The people in York who aren't tourists are probably archaeologists. So many civilisations have left traces of their art and architecture that the work of finding and categorising them will continue as long as there is a street left unturned. Every time someone digs in Coppergate or Mickelgate or Fishergate, Blossom Street, Barker Hill, Clifford Street or Newgate, they turn up something the Romans or the Vikings or the

Anglo-Saxons left behind, and these impressive relics find their way into the Yorkshire Museum. But the museum is set among the ruins of the once powerful St Mary's Abbey, and the most splendid of its exhibits are the five remaining sculptures of the original late 12th-century series of twelve Apostles and twelve prophets from the chapter house. Only two of them kept their heads and are identifiable, Moses and St John the Evangelist, both of them the finest work of the period in England.

These two dozen statues were designed to be incorporated into the pillars supporting the chapter house vault, rather along the lines of the caryatids on the Erecthyum of the Acropolis, and in fact St John was part of a classical revival that coincided with the development of early English Gothic architecture, much like the Renaissance four centuries later. Henry of Blois, Bishop of Winchester in the mid-12th century, who was so fond of the fine arts that the spartan Cistercian monk St Bernard described him as 'the old whore of Winchester', had imported cartloads of finds of classical sculpture from the ruins of ancient Rome, and it is highly likely that drawings were made of them and circulated around English workshops. St John's drapery is both stylised and naturalistic, adding to the beauty of the formal composition but following the positioning of each leg, one bearing his weight, the other lightly bent at the knee. And the head, beautifully modelled and weighted, youthful of aspect, has the freshness that betrays an artist waking to a new morning.

GLOSSARY

apse the semi-circular or polygonal east end of a church. Most English parish churches are square ended.

arras tapestry wall hanging, named from the French textile town of Arras where it was the principal industry from the 14th to the 16th centuries.

Arts and Crafts movement late 19th-century English movement of architects and artist-craftsmen seeking a rebirth of local building styles in hand-crafted local materials (*see* **vernacular**). Blackwell House in Windermere is an archetype.

baroque in England, a flamboyant late 17th-century style involving dramatic silhouettes, gigantic columns, deep cuts between blocks of masonry etc., such as in Vanbrugh's Grimsthorpe Castle. The style originated in Rome.

barrel vault *see* **vault**

basilica a hall with aisles and **clerestory**; in ancient Rome basilicas were secular buildings and **Early English** churches are based on that plan.

blind arcade a series of arcade-like arches, but against a wall and so without openings.

broach spire a spire rising as a tapering ocatagon from a square tower.

butter cross a market structure where butter was sold: anything from a simple medieval stone cross to a Georgian town hall above an open arcade.

chancel the space at the east end of the church for the officiating clergy, often separated from the **nave** by the chancel arch and, in rare cases, the **rood screen**.

classic, classicism style based on ancient Greek or Roman buildings.

clerestory the walls of the **nave** and **chancel** of a church above the aisle roof, pierced by windows. (The word is used of some secular buildings too.)

coffered, coffering sunken ornamental panels in a ceiling, an idea adopted from ruined buildings in the Roman forum.

corbel a projecting block or bracket, often decoratively carved, usually supporting a beam or an arch.

crocket a little decorative projection carved into a leaf shape and used in profusion on pinnacles, spires etc.

cross-beam *see* **tie-beam**

cusp a projecting point in the **tracery** of, usually, a Gothic window.

Decorated Gothic style of architecture of between, roughly, 1240–1360, characterised by much naturalistic carving and complex organic forms in the **tracery** of windows.

Early English the first Gothic, originated in St Denis near Paris. English architectural historians before the 19th century classified it as Pointed Gothic. A simple, pure style with characteristically tall narrow **lancet** windows, often grouped.

entablature a horizontal element borne on columns or walls.

fan vault *see* **vault**

Gothic the name, originally applied as a derisive term meaning 'barbaric', for the period of Christian architecture from about 1140 until, in England, the 16th century. Its main feature consists of pointed arches and vaults. It continued in England after the Reformation, but in Wren's buildings and in Georgian Gothic (sometimes Gothick) it was more decorative than structural. The resurgence in the 19th century is usually known as Gothic Revival.

groin vault *see* **vault**

hammerbeam an attenuated **tie-beam** which becomes, in effect, two brackets on facing walls, designed to take the thrust of vertical beams supporting the roof without cluttering the intervening roof space. Hammerbeams became a great decorative as well as structural feature of some churches, especially in East Anglia and the West Country.

hood mould moulding above a window or door arch, originally outside to deflect rain; the ends, or label stops, are often carved with heads.

lancet simple slender, pointed arch window associated with the **Early English** style.

lierne vault *see* **vault**

misericord the underside of a lifting bench seat, usually in a church **choir**, often carved with humans, animals, caricatures, fables, and sometimes used, one feels, to pay off old scores.

mullion a vertical upright dividing a window into two or more lights.

nave the western part of a church (originally ancient Roman secular **basilica**) where the congregation worships.

neoclassicism severely refined form of **classicism** of the late 18th and early 19th century in art, architecture and the decorative arts: Jacques-Louis David, house artist of the French revolution, is the obvious archetype; in sculpture, Canova.

English examples include the early architecture of John Soane and sculpture of Richard Westmacott.

ogee the S and reverse S-shape combined in **Decorated** arches and **tracery**, thought to originate in Islamic architecture.

Palladian, Palladianism a form of **classicism** based on the practice and writings of Andrea Palladio (1508–80) and introduced into England in the early 17th century by Inigo Jones. Colen Campbell and Lord Burlington revived it in the 18th century after a period when **baroque** was in favour.

Perpendicular late English Gothic style from the mid-14th century to around 1530, typically featuring elaborate fan vaulting (as in the Henry VII chapel in Westminster Abbey), quite severe vertical **tracery** in windows with flattened arches and, externally, battlements.

pier a massive form of weight-bearing column.

piloti (also pilotis) term adapted and made popular by Le Corbusier for the more or less slender columns lifting modern movement buildings above the open ground.

piscina stone basin near the altar for washing communion vessels; some are magnificently embellished with carved canopies or arches.

reredos a decorated screen behind an altar.

retable a decorated screen at the rear of an altar, or fixed to the back of it.

rib vault *see* **vault**

rococo the last fling of **baroque**, characterised by airiness and lightness of touch, sexiness and, as critics of the time alleged, flippancy.

Romanesque usually associated in England with Norman buildings from the 11th century, though it is arguable that Anglo-Saxon architecture had elements of Romanesque. It characteristically has round arches, massive **piers** and zigzag patterning.

rood/rood screen/rood loft the rood was the crucifix, of powerful symbolic importance and something to swear by ('No, by the rood, not so!' – *Hamlet* act III scene iv). It was usually set at the top of the rood loft, an open structure above the rood screen supporting images of saints as well as the crucifix. Where any of this has survived the Reformation, it is usually the rood screen, set across the crossing between **nave** and **chancel**.

rusticated, rustication masonry laid with accentuated channels between blocks to give an impression of masculinity, especially favoured in the **baroque**.

scagliola composite stone imitating marble but with a highly attractive quality of its own.

sedilia stone seats set into the wall of the chancel for attending priests, the surrounds often gorgeously embellished.

spandrel the roughly triangular space between two arches.

string course rim of stone running along the wall of a church, known when **corbels** are spaced along it as a corbel table.

tie-beam lateral roof beam between the top of one wall and another. May be used to prevent the walls bulging outwards.

tracery openwork patterning in stone or timber, usually in a window. When it is in the top of a church window, it is one of the surest guides to the church's period, assuming it isn't a Victorian replacement; if it is, it can often be spotted because of its machine finish.

triforium walled passage above the **nave** arcade.

transom horizontal bar across a window.

tympanum the wall space between a door lintel and the arch, in Romanesque architecture often magnificently carved.

tunnel vault *see* **vault**

vault arched ceiling of wood or stone. A barrel vault (also tunnel vault and wagon roof) is semi-circular in section (think Gypsy caravans). A groin vault is composed of the meeting at right angles of two tunnel vaults. Many Gothic vaults are ribbed, initially for structural reasons, later for decoration. Fan vaulting (which looks as the word suggests) is one of the latter and can be sublime. Lierne ribs cross other ribs. Star ribs form star shapes. Rib vault is generic.

vernacular loosely, as in speech, an architecture and culture rooted in locality.

volute the scroll on an Ionic column, also S-shaped buttress supporting, say, a gate pier.

wagon roof *see* **vault**

ILLUSTRATION ACKNOWLEDGEMENTS

page ii King John's Cup in Trinity Guild, King's Lynn. (By kind permission of Tales of the Old Gaol House and Regalia Rooms, King's Lynn)

THE WEST COUNTRY

p. 3 *The Circle of the Life of Man* by William Blake at Arlington Court, the Chichester Collection, National Trust. (© NTPL/John Hammond)
p. 6 Sibthorp Memorial at Bath Abbey. (© Alan Morley/by kind permission of Bath Abbey)
p. 9 Robert Adam's Pulteney Bridge in Bath. (© Yuri Hermoza/fotolibra)
p. 12 Romanesque font in the Church of St Petroc, Bodmin. (© Ian Smith/fotolibra)
p. 16 Arnolfini Gallery café-bar in Bristol. (© Carl Newland/Jamie Woodely/Kirsty Mackay – deps of photo/by kind permission of Bauman Lyons Architects)
p. 21 Quellin's angel in the Church of St Andrew, Burnham-on-Sea. (© Graham Witts/by kind permission of the Church of St Andrew)
p. 22 Hood monument in Butleigh. (© Ian Smith/fotolibra)
p. 25 *Memorial Figure* 1945–6 by Henry Moore at Dartington Hall. (The Dartington Hall Trust/reproduced by permission of the Henry Moore Foundation)
p. 26 Castle Drogo, Drewsteignton. (© NTPL/Dennis Gilbert)
p. 28 *Dartmoor* by Edward Burra in the Royal Albert Memorial Museum, Exeter. (The Royal Albert Memorial Museum, Exeter/The Bridgeman Art Library/Courtesy of the Edward Burra Estate, c/o Lefevre Fine Art, London)
p. 31 First World War memorial in Mells. (© Wayil Rahmatalla/fotolibra)
p. 36 *Portrait of Rev. Samuel Reynolds* by Sir Joshua Reynolds in Plymouth City Museum and Art Gallery. (© Plymouth City Museum and Art Gallery: Cottonian Collection)
p. 38 *Epidauros* by Barbara Hepworth in St Ives. (© Barry Hitch/fotolibra/© Bowness, Hepworth Estate)
p. 40 Stained glass in the Church of St Neot. (© Sonia Halliday Photographs)
p. 44 Mary Rand plaque in Wells. (© Christopher Nicholson/Alamy)

THE SOUTH

p. 52 Christ carving in the Church of the Holy Rood, Buckland Newton. (© Richard Bonnie/by kind permission of the Church of the Holy Rood)
p. 54 Stained glass by William Morris in Christchurch Priory, Cattistock. (© Sonia Halliday Photographs)
p. 57 *Christ Preaching at Cookham Regatta* (detail) by Stanley Spencer in the Stanley Spencer Gallery, Cookham. (Stanley Spencer

Gallery/© The Estate of Stanley Spencer 2008. All rights reserved DACS)

p. 61 Highcliffe Castle. (© dbphots/Alamy)

p. 62 *The Judgement of Solomon* attr to Sebastiano del Piombo in Kingston Lacy, the Bankes Collection, the National Trust. (© NTPL/Derrick E. Witty)

p. 67 Malmesbury Abbey porch. (© Shaun Martin/by kind permission of the Vicar and Churchwardens of Malmesbury Abbey)

p. 68 Effigies of Lord and Lady Milton by Agostino Carlini in Milton Abbey. (© Sydney Cross/fotolibra)

p. 70 Stained glass by Laurence Whistler in the Church of St Nicholas, Morton. (© Peter Vallance/fotolibra)

p. 74 Lady Ailesbury monument by Alfred Gilbert in the Church of St Katharine in Savernake Forest. (By kind permission of the Church of St Katharine)

p. 76 *The Patriot* by George Fullard in Southampton City Art Gallery. (© Southampton City Art Gallery/The Bridgeman Art Library)

p. 80 George III sculpture by James Hamilton on the Esplanade in Weymouth. (© Peter Vallance/fotolibra)

p. 83 *Mary Zouch* (?) by Hans Holbein the Younger in the Royal Collection at Windsor Castle. (© 2008 Her Majesty Queen Elizabeth II)

THE SOUTHEAST

p. 90 Annunciation mural by Vanessa Bell in the Church of St Michael and All Angels, Berwick. (© Peter Vallance/fotolibra)

p. 91 De La Warr Pavilion in Bexhill. (© Tim Anderson/fotolibra)

p. 94 *Mae West's Lips* sofa by Salvador Dali in the Brighton Museum and Art Gallery. (Royal Pavilion & Museums, Brighton & Hove © Salvador Dali, Gala-Salvador Dali Foundation, DACS, London)

p. 103 *Francesca* by G.F.Watts in the Watts Gallery, Compton. (© Watts Gallery, Compton)

p. 105 Walmer Castle. (© Skyscan.co.uk

p. 107 Lighthouse in Dungeness by Ward & Co. (© Mr A. Robins/fotolibra)

p. 109 *Submarine Series: Commander looking through a periscope* by Eric Ravilious in the Towner Art Gallery, Eastbourne. (By kind permission of the Towner Art Gallery)

p. 119 The Tudor chapel at Ightham Mote. (© NTPL/Nadia Mackenzie)

p. 122 Roman mosaic of Europa and the Bull in Lullingstone Roman Villa. (© English Heritage Photo Library)

p. 124 *Self Portrait* by William Hazlitt in the Maidstone Museum and Art Gallery. (© Maidstone Museum and Art Gallery/The Bridgeman Art Library)

p. 126–7 *Brighton from the Sea* by J.M.W. Turner in Petworth House. (Petworth House/ The Bridgeman Art Library)

p. 131 Rochester Cathedral. (© Manu/Alamy)

p. 133 Penfold pillar box on Rochester High Street. (© World Pictures/Alamy)

p. 136 Stained glass by Marc Chagall in the Church of All Saints, Tudeley. (© Sonia Halliday Photographs/ADAGP, Paris and DACS, London)

p. 138 Interior of the Church of King Charles the Martyr, Tunbridge Wells. (© Emma Hepburn/by kind permission of the Church of King Charles the Martyr)

p. 142 Iron gravestone in the Church of St Peter and St Paul, Wadhurst. (© Ruth Dunnett/by kind permission of the Church of St Peter and St Paul)

p. 145 East window in St Andrew's Church, Wickhambreaux. (© Brian Maxted)

p. 147 Shah Jehan Mosque, Woking. (© Malcolm Forrow/fotolibra)

LONDON

p. 152 Façade of 219 Oxford Street. (© Nigel Wilcockson)

p. 154 Devonshire Gates on Piccadilly. (© Nigel Wilcockson)

p. 157 *Self portrait* by Artemesia Gentileschi in The Royal Collection at Buckingham Palace. (© 2008 Her Majesty Queen Elizabeth II)

p. 159 Doorcase of 28 Queen Anne's Gate. (© Nigel Wilcockson)

p. 162 Tombs of Henry VII and Elizabeth by Pietro Torrigiano in Westminster Abbey. (© Dean and Chapter of Westminster)

p. 164 King Charles I sculpture by Hubert le Sueur in Trafalgar Square. (© Nick Francis/fotolibra)

p. 168 *Portrait of Captain Coram* by William Hogarth in the Foundling Museum. (© Coram in the care of the Foundling Museum, London/The Bridgeman Art Library)

p. 171 Interior of the Sir John Soane Museum. (By courtesy of the Trustees of Sir John Soane's Museum/ Photo: Martin Charles)

p. 176 Temple Bar. (© Justin Kase zonez/Alamy)

p. 179 Interior of the Church of St Stephen Walbrook. (© Arcaid/Alamy)

p. 181 Leadenhall Market. (© David Stuckey/fotolibra)

p. 183 Interior of Bevis Marks synagogue. (© Angelo Hornak Photograph Library, London)

p. 188 Blackwall Tunnel ventilation shafts designed by Terry Farrell. (© Peter Cook/VIEW)

p. 192 Ben Pimlott Building at Goldsmiths designed by Will Alsop. (© Andy Stagg/VIEW)

p. 194 Entrance hall at Eltham Palace. (© English Heritage Photo Library)

p. 197 *Invention* by Eduardo Paolozzi at Butler's Wharf. (© David Stuckey/fotolibra/© Trustees of the Paolozzi Foundation, licensed by DACS 2008)

p. 199 Rose window in the Bishop of Winchester's Palace. (© John Joannides/Alamy)

p. 201 *The Triumphs of Caesar: Caesar on his Chariot* by Andrea Mantegna in the Royal Collection at Hampton Court. (© 2008 Her Majesty Queen Elizabeth II)

p. 205 Sudbury Town underground station designed by Charles Holden. (© Clive Collie/fotolibra)

p. 206 Kensal Green Cemetery. (© Dan Bachmann/fotolibra)

p. 209 Erno Goldfinger's house, 2 Willow Road. (© NTPL/Andreas von Einsiedel)

p. 210 *The Guitar Player* by Johannes Vermeer in Kenwood House. (© English Heritage Photo Library)

EAST ANGLIA

p. 215 Carving of Christ in Majesty in the Church of St John the Baptist, Barnack. (© David Carter/fotolibra)

p. 217 Angel roof in the Church of Holy Trinity, Blythburgh. (© Sid Frisby/fotolibra)

p. 220 Three-way signpost in Brampton. (© Ian Stacey/fotolibra)

p. 224 Gate of Honour in Gonville and Caius College, Cambridge. (© Susan Davie/fotolibra)

p. 227 *The Red Stone Dancer* by Henri Gaudier-Brzeska in Kettle's Yard, Cambridge. (Courtesy Kettle's Yard, University of Cambridge)

p. 231 Monument to Marcus Favonius Facilis in Colchester Castle Museum. (Reproduced with the kind permission of Colchester and Ipswich Museum Service)

p. 233 Effigy of Henry Howard in the Church of St Michael, Framlingham. (© David Harding/fotolibra)

p. 234 Interior of the Church of St Mary the

Virgin, Great Warley. (© English Heritage)
p. 237 *Golding Constable's Flower Garden* by John Constable in Christchurch Mansion and Art Gallery. (© Ipswich Borough Council Museums and Galleries/The Bridgeman Art Library)
p. 238 King John's Cup in Trinity Guild, King's Lynn. (By kind permission of Tales of the Old Gaol House and Regalia Rooms, King's Lynn)
p. 240 Angel lectern in the Church of All Saints, Landbeach. (© Ian Stacey/fotolibra)
p. 243 The Church of St John, Little Gidding. (© Alan Spain)
p. 248 *The Marl Pit* by John Sell Cotman in the Norwich Castle Museum and Art Gallery. (© Norwich Castle Museum and Art Gallery/The Bridgeman Art Library)
p. 252 The chapel and bridge in St Ives, Cambridgeshire. (© Ian Stacey/fotolibra)
p. 254 Saxtead Green windmill. (© Skyscan.co.uk)
p. 257 Retable in the Church of St Mary, Thornham Parva. (© Sid Frisby/fotolibra)
p. 260 Monument to John Yorke by Richard Westmacott in the Church of St Andrew, Wimpole. (© Michael McNay)
p. 264 Interior of Wymondham Abbey. (© Sid Frisby/fotolibra)

THE WEST AND EAST
MIDLANDS

p. 268–9 *First Movement in Pink* by Alan Davie in the Cecil Higgins Art Gallery, Bedford. (© Alan Davie/by kind permission of the Trustees of Cecil Higgins Art Gallery, Bedford and Alan Davie)
p. 278 Arras at Chasteleton House. (© NTPL/Ian Shaw)
p. 282 Panelling in the Church of St John the Baptist, Cockayne Hatley. (© David Stuckey/fotolibra)
p. 284 *A Female Saint* by Tilman

Riemenschneider at Compton Verney. (© Compton Verney)
p. 287 Plaster decoration in the Church of Holy Trinity and St Mary, Dodford. (© Ruth Seadon/fotolibra)
p. 290 Drawing room in Eastnor Castle. (© Martin Avery/by kind permission of Eastnor Castle)
p. 293 Doom window in the Church of St Mary's, Fairford. (© Sonia Halliday Photographs)
p. 296 Eleanor cross in Geddington. (© Bob Caddick/Alamy)
p. 300 Interior of St Michael's Church, Great Witley. (© R.J.L. Smith of Much Wenlock)
p. 305 Church of St Mary, Iffley. (Ben Ramos/Alamy)
p. 309 Suspension bridge in Marlow, designed by William Terney Clark. (© Greg Balfour Evans/Alamy)
p. 312 Memorial window for Peter Fleming by John Piper in the Church of St Bartholomew, Nettlebed. (© Sonia Halliday Photographs)
p. 321 *Lazarus* (detail) by Jacob Epstein. (© Courtesy of the Warden and Scholars of New College, Oxford/The Bridgeman Art Library © The Estate of Sir Jacob Epstein)
p. 323 Gate to the Oxford Botanic Garden by Nicholas Stone. (© Jon Bower Oxford/Alamy)
p. 330–1 Fettiplace family tombs in the Church of St Mary, Swinbrook. (© Cotswolds Photo Library/Alamy)
p. 337 Interior of the Beauchamp chapel in the Church of St Mary, Warwick. (© Sonia Halliday Photographs)

THE NORTH MIDLANDS

p. 343 Penelope Boothy monument by Thomas Banks in the Church of St Oswald, Ashbourne. (© Rev. Derek Tinsley)
p. 347 Hondecoeter room in Belton House. (© NTPL/Andrewas von Einsiedel)

p. 349 North front of Grimsthorpe Castle in Bourne, designed by Sir John Vanbrugh. (Ray Biggs/by kind permission of the Grimsthorpe and Drummond Castle Trust Ltd)

p. 353 Angel statue on the west wall of Croyland Abbey, Crowland. (© David Carter/fotolibra)

p. 358 Easter sepulchre (detail) in the Church of All Saints, Hawton. (© Michael McNay)

p. 361 *Irish Navvies Completing Work on the Mainline North* by J.C. Bourne in the Ironbridge Gorge Museum, Ironbridge Gorge. (Image by courtesy of the Ironbridge Gorge Museum Trust)

p. 365 *Rote Frau* – 'The Red Woman' by Franz Marc in the New Walk Museum, Leicester. (© New Walk Museum, Leicester City Museum Service /The Bridgeman Art Library)

p. 368 Tennyson Memorial by G.F. Watts in Lincoln Cathedral precincts, Lincoln. (© Stuart Lord/fotolibra)

p. 374 *Sky Mirror* by Anish Kapoor next to the Nottingham Playhouse, Nottingham (© Martine Hamilton Knight/Builtvision/reproduced by kind permission of Anish Kapoor)

p. 377 Jesse window in the Church of St Mary the Virgin, Shrewsbury. (© Sonia Halliday Photographs)

p. 379 Rectory pulpit (remains of Shrewsbury Abbey) at Holy Cross, Shrewsbury. (© Barry Hitchcox/fotolibra)

p. 383 The Church of St Mary Magdalene, Stapleford. (By kind permission of Stapleford Park)

p. 384 Wedgwood tea mug by Eduardo Paolozzi in the Wedgwood Museum, Barlaston. (By courtesy of the Wedgwood Museum Trust/ © Trustees of the Paolozzi Foundation, licensed by DACS 2008)

p. 386 Façade of the Wedgwood Institute in Burslem, Stoke-on-Trent. (© Steve Birks of www.thepotteries.org)

p. 388 Stained glass (detail) in the Church of St James, Twycross. (© Michael McNay)

p. 389 *Sir Thomas Killigrew* by Sir Anthony van Dyck at Weston Park. (© The Trustees of the Weston Park Foundation/The Bridgeman Art Library)

p. 391 Anglo-Saxon coffin lid (detail) in the Church of St Mary, Wirksworth. (© Edward Higgins/by kind permission of the Church of St Mary)

THE NORTHWEST

p. 396 Cross, by the Church of St Cuthbert, Bewcastle. (© Andy Norris)

p. 398 Auditorium of the Grand Theatre in Blackpool, designed by Frank Matcham. (© Sean Conboye/by kind permission of the Grand Theatre)

p. 401 Stained glass by Edward Burne-Jones in the Church of St Martin, Brampton. (© Sonia Halliday Photographs)

p. 404 Stone circle at Castlerigg. (© Egil Saeboe/fotolibra)

p. 408 Effigy of a knight in Furness Abbey. (© English Heritage Photo Library)

p. 410 Hawkshead grammar school. (© Mike Reed, Arps./fotolibra)

p. 412 *The Gower Family* by George Romney in Abbot Hall Art Gallery, Kendal. (© Abbot Hall Art Gallery/The Bridgeman Art Library)

p. 415 Ashton Memorial in Lancaster. (© Jonathan Bean/fotolibra)

p. 419 Interior of the Philharmonic Dining Rooms in Liverpool. (© David Lyons/Alamy)

p. 425 *The Bedroom, Pendlebury* by L.S. Lowry in The Lowry, Salford Quays. (© The Estate of L.S. Lowry 2008)

p. 426 Barton Arcade, Manchester. (© Jeanette Dawson/fotolibra)

p. 433 *The Governess* by Jean-Baptiste-Siméon Chardin in Tatton Park. (© Tatton Park/Cheshire County Council/The National Trust)

p. 434 *Teaching the Ignorant* by Thomas

Woolner on a fountain in Wigton market square. (© Stuart Walker/fotolibra)

p. 436 Saloon in Blackwell House, Windermere. (Courtesy of the Lakeland Arts Trust)

p. 437 Shropshire Union Canal bridge in Wrenbury, designed by Thomas Telford. (© Phil King/fotolibra)

THE NORTHEAST

p. 442 Tenantry column in Alnwick. (© Gwyn Headley/fotolibra)

p. 444–5 Mural by Peter Dodd in Barter Books, Alnwick. (By kind permission of Barter Books and Peter Dodd)

p. 450 Bridlington promenade designed by Bruce McLean and Irena Bauman. (By kind permission of Bauman Architects Ltd.)

p. 452 Nightjar and golden-crested wren from *A History of British Birds* by Thomas Bewick.

p. 455 *Terra Novalis* by Tony Cragg in Consett. (© Christopher Ridley/fotolibra/by kind permission of Tony Cragg)

p. 456 The Corbridge lion. (© English Heritage Photo Library)

p. 459 *Train* by David Mach, in Darlington. (© Michael McNay/by kind permission of Lesley Mach, David Mach Limited)

p. 469 Viking grave marker on Holy Island. (© English Heritage Photo Library)

p. 478 Mosaic by Frank Brangwyn in the Church of St Aidan, Leeds. (© Alan Spain)

p. 482 Transporter bridge in Middlesbrough. (© Julian Stelling/fotolibra)

p. 486 *Merzbarn* wall relief by Kurt Schwitters in the Hatton Gallery. (The Hatton Gallery, University of Newcastle Upon Tyne/The Bridgeman Art Library/ © DACS 2008)

p. 488 Percy Cross in Otterburn. (© JPV/fotolibra)

p. 491 Interior of the Georgian Theatre Royal, Richmond. (© Sean Conboy of photo-genics.com/by kind permission of the Georgian Theatre Royal, Richmond North Yorkshire)

p. 493 Room by Robert Adam in Newby Hall, Ripon. (© Jerry Hardman-Jones/by kind permission of The Newby Hall Estate)

p. 499 *Nude Woman with Black Stockings* by Pierre Bonnard in Graves Art Gallery, Sheffield. (© Sheffield Galleries and Museums Trust/The Bridgeman Art Library/ADAGP, Paris and DACS, London 2008)

p. 500 *Conversation Piece* by Juan Munoz in South Shields. (By kind permission of South Tyneside Council)

p. 505 *Industry of the Tyne: Iron and Coal* by William Bell Scott in Wallington Hall. (Wallington Hall/National Trust Photographic Library/Derrick E. Witty/The Bridgeman Art Library)

p. 510 Stained glass in the Church of All Saints North Street, York. (© Sonia Halliday Photographs)

All maps © Darren Bennett

INDEX